PEARSON ALWAYS LEARNING

Lester Faigley • Harvey S. Wiener

Backpack Writing with Readings

ENC 1101 College Composition

Custom Edition for Daytona State College

Taken from:
Backpack Writing, Second Edition
by Lester Faigley

Major Themes for Modern Writers
by Harvey S. Wiener

Cover Art: Courtesty of Photodisc/Getty Images.

Taken from:

Backpack Writing, Second Edition
by Lester Faigley

Published by Longman
New York, New York 10036

Major Themes for Modern Writers
by Harvey S. Wiener

Published by Longman

Pearson Learning Solutions, 501 Boylston Street, Suite 900, Boston, MA 02116
A Pearson Education Company
www.pearsoned.com

Printed in the United States of America

1 2 3 4 5 6 7 8 9 10 V357 16 15 14 13 12 11

000200010270763799

MP/AM

PEARSON

ISBN 10: 1-256-27986-2
ISBN 13: 978-1-256-27986-0

CONTENTS

PART 1
The Writer as Explorer

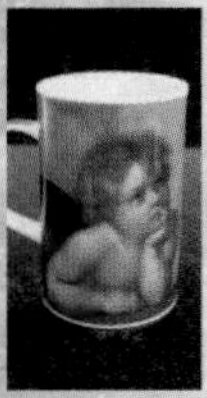

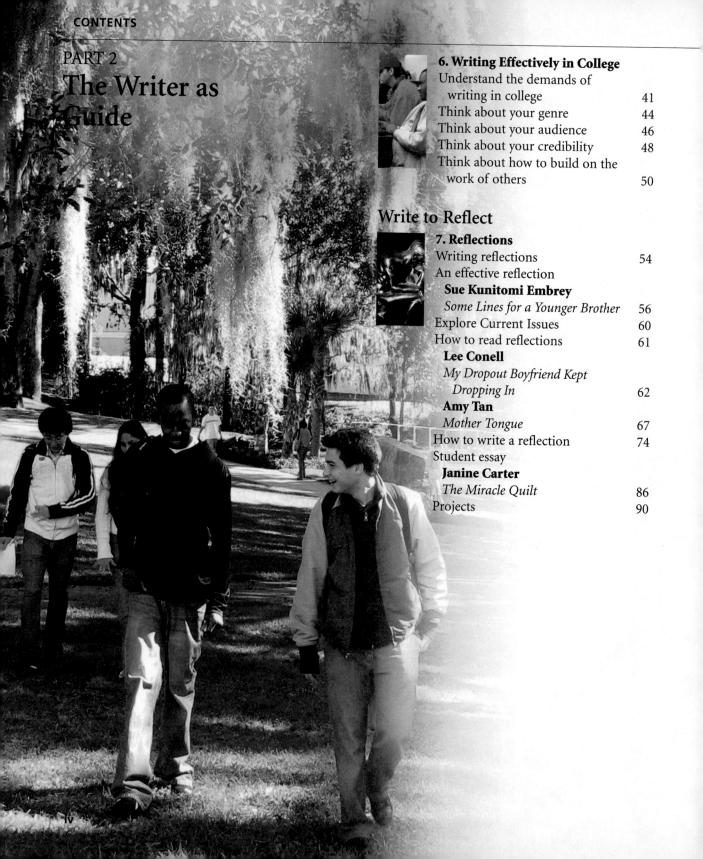

PART 2

The Writer as Guide

Write to Reflect

Write to Inform

Write to Analyze

Write Arguments

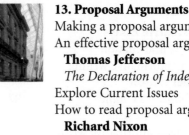

PART 3
The Writer as Researcher

Preface

Backpack Writing starts from the often overlooked fact that writing courses make students better writers not just for other college courses, but for writing situations throughout their lives. Perhaps more than anything else I have learned about writing in my decades of teaching and practicing writing is that all meaningful acts of writing involve complex negotiations of particular subject matters, audiences, purposes, and genres. Students who learn how to adapt these processes of negotiating for particular contexts go on to achieve success in their educational, professional, and public lives.

I am pleased and grateful for the enthusiastic response of many instructors and students to the first edition. *Backpack Writing* began with the question: How do students learn best? I continue to ask that question in the second edition. These principles underlie the second edition.

Students learn best when a guide to writing is student oriented	It should start from the student's point of view, not the teacher's.
Students learn best when a guide to writing is easy to use	No matter where you open the book, the content on a particular page and the place of that content in the overall organization should be evident.
Students learn best when a guide to writing shows what readers and writers actually do	Students learn best from examples of what readers and writers do, not by reading discussions of what they do.
Students learn best when they can see examples of what works and what doesn't work	Seeing effective and ineffective examples side-by-side demonstrates strategies to employ and pitfalls to avoid.
Students learn faster and remember longer when a book is well designed	Textbooks don't have to be dull.

The second edition also maintains that the broad goals for a first-year college writing course are those identified in the Outcomes Statement from the Council of Writing Program Administrators.

1. Rhetorical knowledge	Students should respond to different situations and the needs of different audiences, understand how genres shape reading and writing, and write in several genres.
2. Critical thinking, reading, and writing	Students should find, evaluate, analyze, and synthesize sources and integrate their ideas with those of others.
3. Processes	Students should develop flexible strategies for generating, revising, editing, and proofreading, and should understand how to collaborate effectively with others.
4. Knowledge of conventions	Students should learn the common formats for different kinds of texts, practice appropriate documentation, and control surface features of grammar, mechanics, and spelling.

What's new in this edition of *Backpack Writing*

New process maps and other visual guides

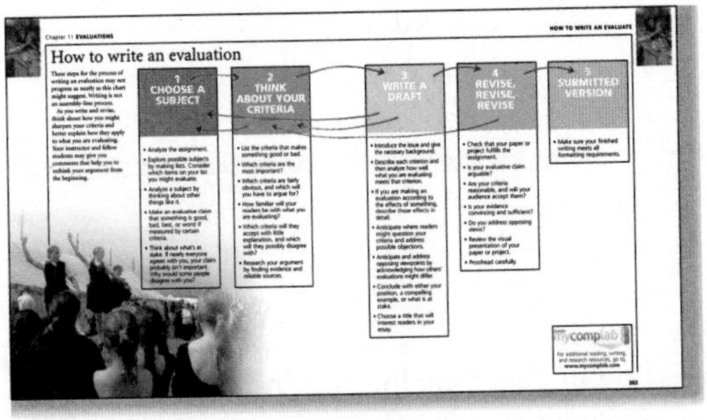

Redesigned two-page process maps lay out the process for different kinds of writing in Part 2. The process maps give students an overview of the sometimes messy process of writing and help them to stay oriented as they come up with ideas, draft, and revise.

More attention to argument

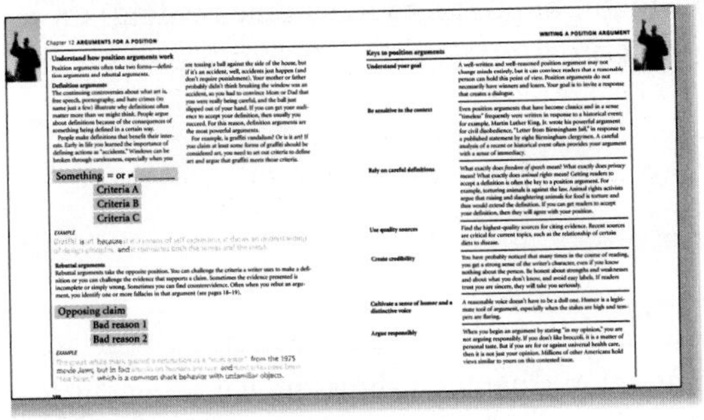

Three chapters treat in detail evaluation, position, and proposal arguments. New visual models demonstrate how each kind of argument works.

Explore Current Issues

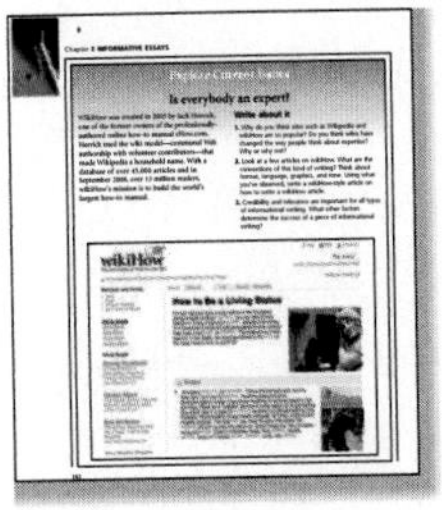

Explore Current Issues, a new full-page writing assignment in Part 2 chapters encourages students to find ideas and write about current issues. In Chapters 7 through 13 you'll find this feature on topics such as reality television, fast-food marketing to children, smart video games, and the responsibility of government for disaster victims.

New engaging readings

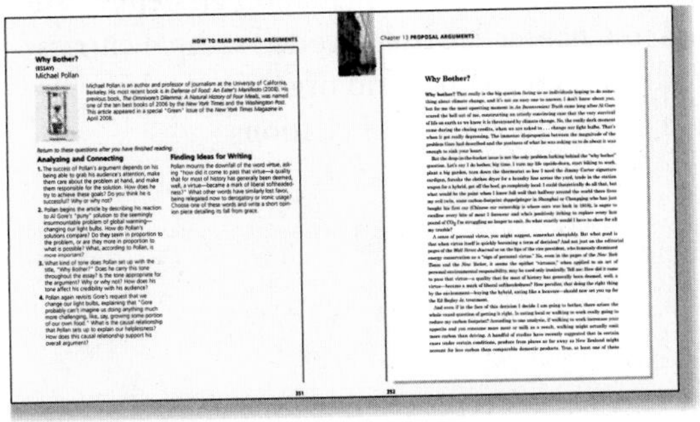

In response to advice from teachers and students, half of the readings in the second edition are new. There are more longer readings and more essays of the kind written in college in this edition, including Chip Walter's investigation as to why humans kiss, Stephanie Coontz's exploration of the future of marriage, and Michael Pollan's proposal for how we can eat healthier and consume fewer resources.

Updated instruction on research

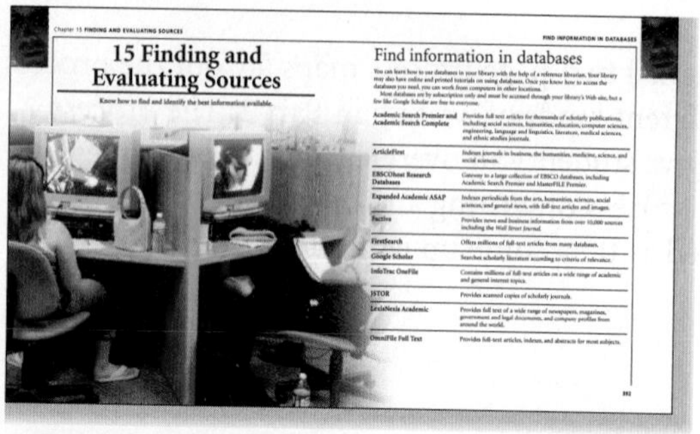

New material has been added on how to use library databases effectively and to sort the wheat from the chaff with Web sources in Chapter 15.

More ideas for writing

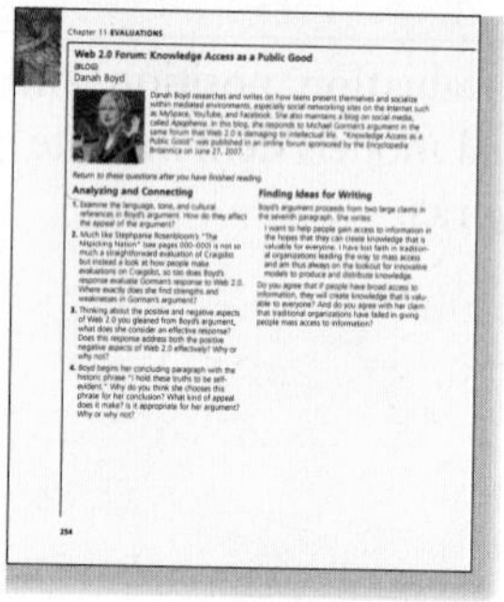

Every reading in Part 2 includes "Finding Ideas for Writing," new additional writing assignments specific to each reading. These assignments suggest how students might build from ideas in the readings in their own writing.

More on building from sources

New material in Chapter 6 shows how writing engages in a conversation with what has been written before on a subject and how to build on the ideas of others.

New MLA documentation guidelines

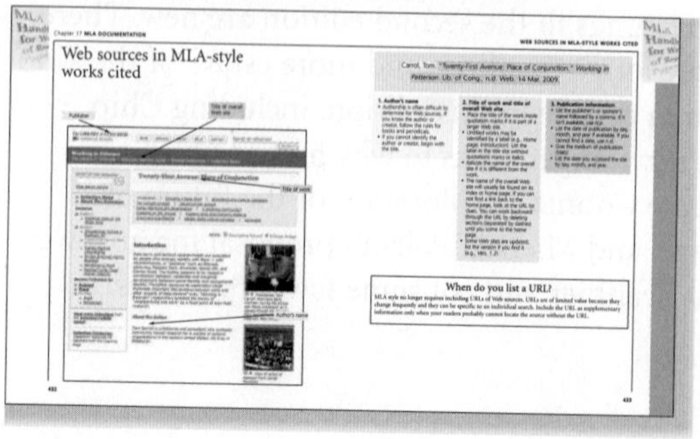

The most recent MLA documentation guidelines are included in Chapter 17. Color-coded sample entries help students to recognize and organize the key elements of different kinds of citations.

Resources for teachers and students

Instructor's Resource Manual	The *Instructor's Resource Manual*, prepared by Susan Schorn of the University of Texas at Austin, offers detailed chapter-by-chapter suggestions to help both new and experienced instructors. For every chapter in the student text, this manual includes chapter goals and chapter challenges, suggestions for different ways to use the assignments and boxed tips in the chapter, additional activities and resources, and more. It also features an overall discussion of teaching a writing class, including discussion of the Writing Program Administrators Outcomes for first-year composition. Finally, the manual offers suggested syllabi and ideas for teaching students with different learning styles.
MyCompLab	The new MyCompLab integrates the market-leading instruction, multimedia tutorials, and exercises for writing, grammar, and research that users have come to identify with the program with a new online composing space and new assessment tools. The result is a revolutionary application that offers a seamless and flexible teaching and learning environment built specifically for writers. Created after years of extensive research and in partnership with composition faculty and students across the country, the new MyCompLab provides help for writers in the context of their writing, with instructor and peer commenting functionality, proven tutorials and exercises for writing, grammar and research, an e-portfolio, an assignment-builder, a bibliography tool, tutoring services, and a gradebook and course management organization created specifically for writing classes. Visit www.mycomplab.com for more information.

In July 2007, seven friends and I traveled in a float plane to the headwaters of the Nigu River in northern Alaska. The Nigu originates on the north slope of the Brooks Range, which stretches east to west across northern Alaska and separates rivers that flow north to the Arctic Ocean from those that flow south and west to the Pacific. The circle of stones in the foreground is the prehistoric remains of a lookout used by the ancestors of modern Iñupiaq people to observe caribou migrating through the valley.

The Nigu River flows through the National Petroleum Reserve in Alaska (NPR-A), created in 1923 but remaining a wilderness and one of the least visited areas of the United States. The NPR-A has the largest caribou herd in Alaska with over 500,000 animals along with the highest concentration of grizzly bears in the state, the nesting grounds of several rare migratory birds, and significant archaeological sites of native peoples. The NPR-A also sits on top of major resources of oil and coal. The future of northern Alaska will be determined through policies shaped by written arguments. The ability to write well can give you a voice in the future of our planet.

Acknowledgments

I am quite fortunate to work with the same team of co-creators in London, New York, New Jersey, Massachusetts, Maine, and Texas that contributed to the success of the first edition. Executive editor Lynn Huddon and I have collaborated on sixteen previous books and editions, and I much appreciate the vision she has brought to each project along with her talents as an editor and manager. She has well earned her reputation as one of the best in her profession. My development editor, Katharine Glynn, has also brought a wealth of knowledge to the book. Even more appreciated is the calmness she inspires in the often stressful process of publishing a book. Joseph Opiela, editorial director, and Mary Ellen Curley, director of development for English, have also been close to the project and have made many insightful suggestions.

Others at Longman who contributed their wisdom and experience include Roth Wilkofsky, president; Tim Stookesberry, vice president of marketing; Megan Galvin-Fak, executive marketing manager; Sandra McGuire, senior marketing manager; Laura Coaty, market research director; Donna Campion, senior supplements editor; Wendy Ann Fredericks, cover design manager; Rona Tuccillo, visual researcher; Bob Ginsberg, production manager; and Rebecca Gilpin, assistant editor. At Pre-Press, two other excellent people whom I have enjoyed working with in the past guided the book into print: Lindsay Bethoney, production manager, and proofreader Elsa van Bergen.

The experience of working across the Atlantic with Stuart Jackman, design director of DK Education in London, again has been a great pleasure. Stuart continues to teach me a great deal about using effective design for learning. I thank Oona Curley for contributing three of her excellent photographs.

I also thank collaborators in Austin, especially Susan "George" Schorn, who assisted in assembling the work of student writers and who wrote the instructor's manual. Victoria Davis helped me find readings and develop the headnotes and questions that accompany them. I cannot say enough about how much I have learned over the years from colleagues and students at the University of Texas, a few of whom are represented by their writing here.

I have benefited enormously from the advice of colleagues across the country who contributed many splendid ideas in reviews. I am especially grateful to these colleagues: Shana Bartram, *Fresno City College;* Bennis Blue, *Virginia State University;* Michael G. Boyd, *Illinois Central College;* Jennifer Brezina, *College of the Canyons;* Michael Dubson, *Bunker Hill Community College;* Jo Gibson, *Cleveland State University;* Richard Iadonisi, *Grand Valley State University;* Bradley Joseph Lint, *Indiana University of Pennsylvania;* Maureen Murphy, *Dakota State University;* Michael Pennell, *University of Rhode Island;* Eric G. Waggoner, *West Virginia Wesleyan College;* and Sara Webb-Sunderhaus, *Indiana University-Purdue University, Fort Wayne.*

Finally, without my wife Linda's deep reserves of patience in putting up with a husband who becomes distracted and grumpy when he is writing, the book would never have been written.

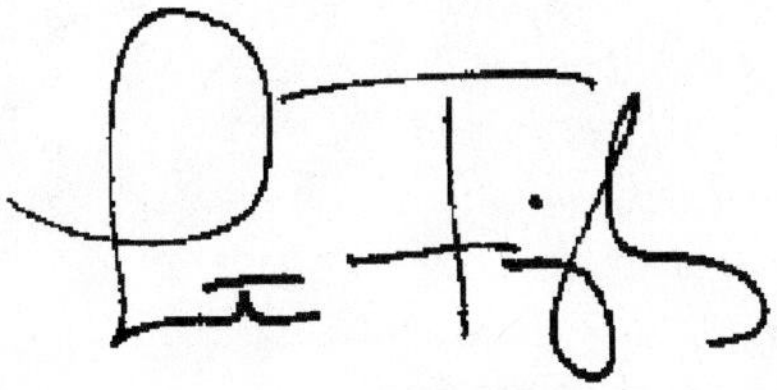

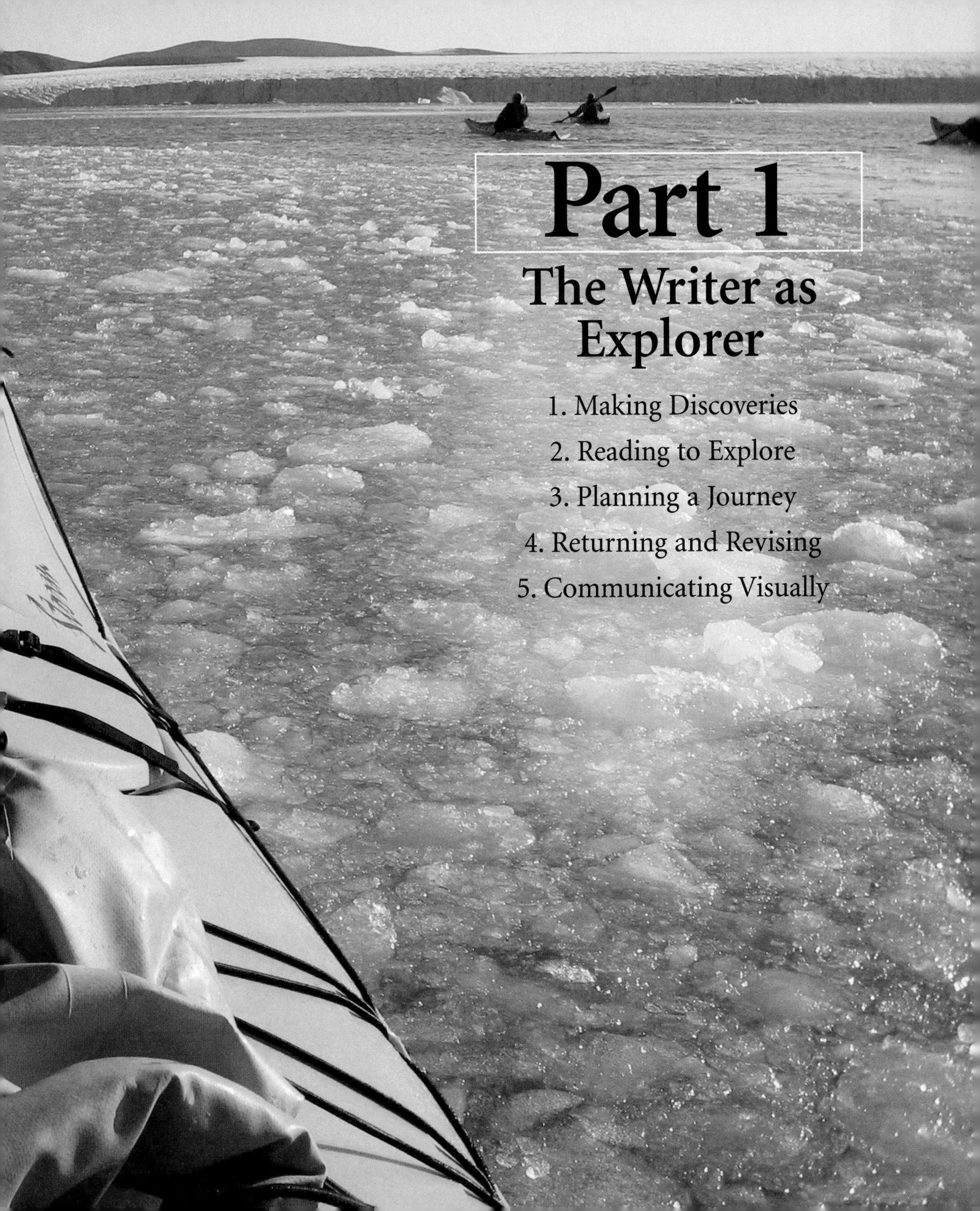

Part 1

The Writer as Explorer

1 Making Discoveries

Go outside. Don't plan where to go. Walk slowly. Look up. Look down. No matter how familiar you are with the place, you'll see something that you have never seen before.

Look with new eyes

Walk long enough so you forget about what is most pressing at the moment. Look for secrets that no one else sees. The dance of light in the canopy of a tree. A second-story cornice on a building. The clarity of reflections in dark puddles. The faint outline of a chalk drawing on the sidewalk. The date stamped on a fire hydrant. The dark blue of a distant slope dotted with blue-green trees.

Take in the sounds. What can you hear besides human-made noises? Even in the middle of a city you may hear birds claiming territories. Listen to the sounds wind makes. Take in the smells. Close your eyes and focus. You can distinguish different smells. Feel the leaves on different plants. Touch the trunks of trees. The world is full of distinct textures.

A city's pride can be expressed on its water meter covers. A water meter cover is also a historical document of American industry. Over the decades the manufacturers of water meters moved from New England to the Midwest, and more recently to India and Taiwan.

An aging door reveals the secrets of its construction and the rates of deterioration of its materials.

Find a territory

Writers begin by exploring. When they start writing, exploration doesn't stop. Once they start, writers find things they could not have imagined. Where writers end up is often far away from where they thought they were going.

Most writing in college concerns exploration because academic disciplines seek to create new knowledge and to rethink what is known. Colleges and universities bring together people who ask interesting questions: How does recent archaeological evidence change our understanding of Homer's *Iliad* and *Odyssey*? Why does eyesight deteriorate with age? How do volcanoes affect the world climate? How do chameleons regenerate lost body parts? How do Rousseau's ideas about nature continue to shape notions about wilderness? How do electric eels generate voltage and not get shocked in the process? How can a poll of a thousand people represent 295 million Americans with only a 3 percent margin of error?

Writers in colleges and universities respond to these questions and many others. They challenge old answers and contribute new answers. Readers of college writing expect to learn something when they read—new knowledge, a fresh interpretation, another point of view that they had not considered.

At first glance the expectations of college writing seem impossible. How can you as an undergraduate student expect to contribute new knowledge? But just as there is a great deal that maps do not show, you can find many uncertainties, controversies, and unresolved problems in any field of study. You just have to ask the right questions.

Ask interesting questions

Good questions can take you to places that will interest you and your readers alike.

- Focus on an area you don't know and want to know more about.
- Find out where experts disagree. What exactly is the source of the disagreement? Why do they come to different conclusions using the same evidence?
- Analyze explanations of current trends and events. What possible causes might be left out?
- Examine proposals to solve problems. Does the solution fix the problem? Will people support the solution if it costs them effort or money?
- Compare what people claim and the reality. Often people (especially politicians) represent things and their role in making them as much better than they actually are.

Local questions are often more interesting than broad, general questions. For example, should historic neighborhoods be preserved, or should they give way to urban renewal and gentrification, as has happened to Chinatown in Washington, DC?

Use strategies for finding a topic

Sometimes your instructor will assign a topic, but more often you will have to come up with your own topic. Look first at material from your course. You might find a topic to explore in the readings or from class discussion.

Start with what interests you. It's hard to write about topics that you care little about. If your assignment gives you a range of options, make more than one list.

PERSONAL	1. History of Anime in Japan 2. Cave exploration and conservation 3. Learning to windsurf
CAMPUS	1. Pros and cons of computer fees 2. Excessive litter on campus 3. Fellowships for study-abroad programs
COMMUNITY	1. Safe bicycle commuting 2. Bilingual education programs 3. Better public transportation
NATION/WORLD	1. Advertising aimed at preschool children 2. Censorship of the Internet 3. Genetically altered crops

Write Now

Mapping your campus

Your campus likely has an information desk for students and visitors. Information centers typically will have several brochures with maps. Visit the information desk and collect everything that includes a map. Then compare the maps. Make a checklist for what the maps show and don't show (building names, streets, shuttle bus routes, bicycle routes, parking, landmarks, hotels, and more).

Create a map for new students on your campus that contains insider knowledge that would not appear on the maps your school produces. For example, where can you find the best burger on or close to campus? The best cup of coffee or cookies? A quiet place to study? A great place to meet friends? Make a list of places that need to be included on your map. Then draw the map.

Use guides

Writers can take advantage of guides developed by libraries. Your library's online subject catalog often divides big subjects into smaller and more manageable ones. For example, if you type "nanotechnology" into the subject search window in your online catalog, you likely will get results similar to those below.

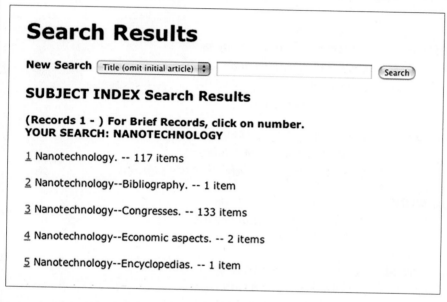

Search Results

New Search Title (omit initial article) [Search]

SUBJECT INDEX Search Results

(Records 1 -) For Brief Records, click on number.
YOUR SEARCH: NANOTECHNOLOGY

1 Nanotechnology. -- 117 items

2 Nanotechnology--Bibliography. -- 1 item

3 Nanotechnology--Congresses. -- 133 items

4 Nanotechnology--Economic aspects. -- 2 items

5 Nanotechnology--Encyclopedias. -- 1 item

A subject search for "nanotechnology" in a library's online catalog generates a list of subtopics that may point to a manageable, specific topic.

Online subject directories including Yahoo's Search Directory provide lists of links on particular subjects.

YAHOO! SEARCH Directory — Search: the Web | the Directory | this category [Search]

Science > Nanotechnology — Email this page

Directory > Science > **Nanotechnology**

CATEGORIES

- Companies@
- Nanotubes (10)
- Organizations (7)
- Research (31)

SITE LISTINGS **By Popularity** | Alphabetical (What's This?)

Sites 1 - 22 of 22

- Zyvex.com: Nanotechnology - provides a brief introduction to the core concepts of molecular nanotechnology, followed by links to further reading.
- U.S. National Nanotechnology Initiative - committed to long-term nano science and engineering research; synthesis, processing, and application of nano materials; and the exploration of nanodevice concepts.
- Engines of Creation: The Coming Era of Nanotechnology - complete text of the book by K. Eric Drexler.
- Nanotechnology Now - offers a resource portal for nano science and nano tech news with event information, interviews, directories, glossary, and a tutorial on the basics.
- NanotechNews.com - news for nanotechnologists.
- NanoComputer Dream Team - desires to directly influence the design and development of a nanometer scale computer.
- Nanomedicine - analyzes developments in molecular machine systems to address medical problems.
- Scientific American: Nanotechnology - features current coverage, highlights, and article archives.
- A to Z of Nanotechnology - offering nanotechnology information, news, new products, suppliers, and expert directory.

Yahoo's subject directory provides links to online sources for "nanotechnology."

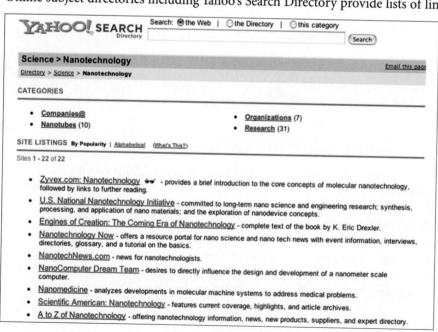

Write Now

Make an idea map

Start with the general subject you plan to write about. State it in a few words. Draw a box around it.

Next think about what can be said about this topic. At this point you don't want specifics but general categories.

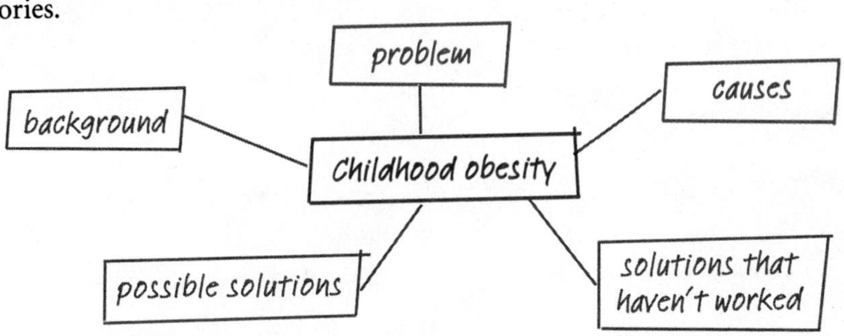

The third stage is to generate topics about each category.

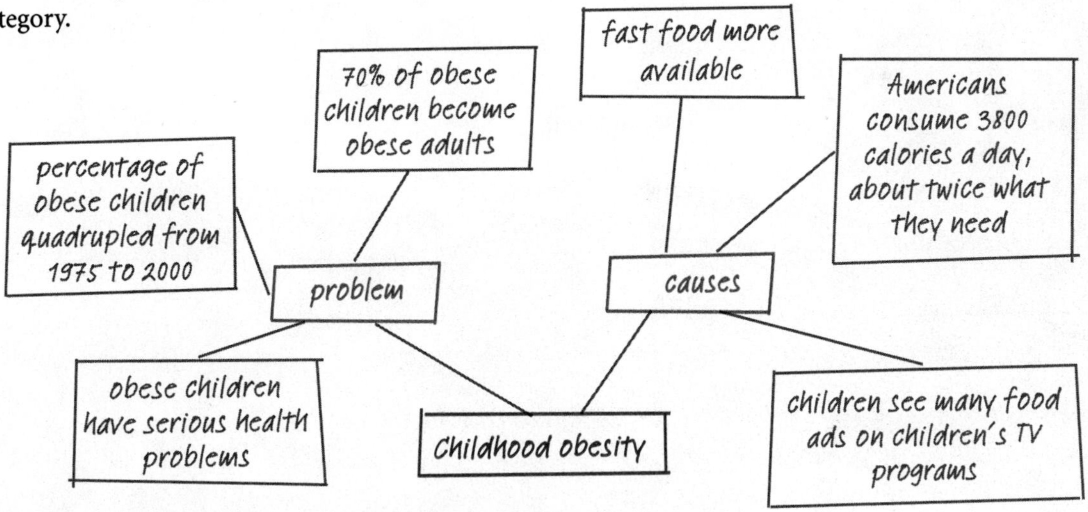

The process continues until the topics become specific.

When you finish the map, look at how it might be translated into writing. Probably you don't want to include everything that is in the map. Get a colored marker and put a line around those parts you intend to write about.

2 Reading to Explore

Along with learning to write well, learning to think critically is the most important skill you will gain in college.

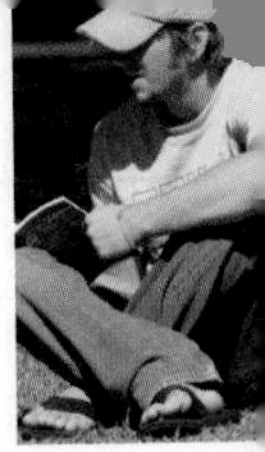

Become a critical reader

Critical thinking begins with critical reading. For most of what you read, one time through is enough. When you start asking questions about what you are reading, you are engaging in critical reading. Critical reading is a four-part process. First, begin by asking where a piece of writing came from and why it was written. Second, read the text carefully to find the author's central claim or thesis and the major points. Third, decide if you can trust the author. Fourth, read the text again to understand how it works.

1. Where did it come from?

- Who wrote this material?
- Where did it first appear? In a book, newspaper, magazine, or online?
- What else has been written about the topic or issue?
- What do you expect after reading the title?

2. What does it say?

- What is the topic or issue?
- What is the writer's thesis or central idea?
- What reasons or evidence does the writer offer?
- Who are the intended readers? What does the writer assume the readers know and believe?

3. Can you trust the writer?

- Does the writer have the necessary knowledge and experience to write on this subject?
- Do you detect a bias in the writer's position?
- Are the facts relevant to the writer's claims?
- Can you trust the writer's facts? Where did the facts come from?
- Does the writer acknowledge opposing views and unfavorable evidence? Does the writer deal fairly with opposing views?

4. How does it work?

- How is the piece of writing organized? How are the major points arranged?
- How does the writer conclude? Does the conclusion follow from the evidence the writer offers? What impression does the writer take away?
- How would you characterize the style? Describe the language that the writer uses.
- How does the writer represent herself or himself?

Write Now

Analyze information for students on your campus

No doubt your school mailed you a great deal of information when you were admitted. Schools continue to distribute information to students when they get to campus. You can find informative brochures and flyers at your school's student services building and in the health center.

Pick one of the brochures or flyers to analyze. Remember that you are the intended audience.

Write a one-page evaluation about why the brochure or flyer is effective or ineffective for an audience of college students. If it is ineffective, what changes need to be made to make it effective? If it works, what does it do well?

Look with a critical eye

Critical viewing, like critical reading, requires thinking about where the image or visual came from. Begin by asking the following.

- What kind of an image or visual is it?
- Who created this image (movie, advertisement, television program, and so on)?
- What is it about? What is portrayed in the image?
- Where did it first appear? Where do you usually find images like this one?
- When did it appear?

The Pharaoh Menkaure (Mycerinus) and his queen, Giza, Old Kingdom, 2548–2530 BCE. One of the finest statues from ancient Egypt depicts a royal couple. Compare the statue to formal portraits of couples today. Why does the queen have one arm around his waist and the other touching the king's arm? Do you think it depicts how they looked in real life? Or how they might have wanted to look in the afterlife? How do you think people in ancient Egypt might have viewed this statue?

The following questions are primarily for still images. For animations, movies, and television, you also have to ask questions about how the story is being told.

- What attracts your eye first? If there is an attention-grabbing element, how does it connect with the rest of the image?
- What impression of the subject does the image create?
- How does the image appeal to the values of the audience? (For example, politicians love to be photographed with children.)
- How does the image relate to what surrounds it?
- Was it intended to serve purposes besides art and entertainment?

Arthur Rothstein made this photograph of black clouds of dust rising over the Texas Panhandle in March 1936. Look closely at the photo. What attracts your eye first? Snapshots usually put the horizon line in the center. Why did Rothstein put the horizon at the bottom? What impression does this photo convey to you?

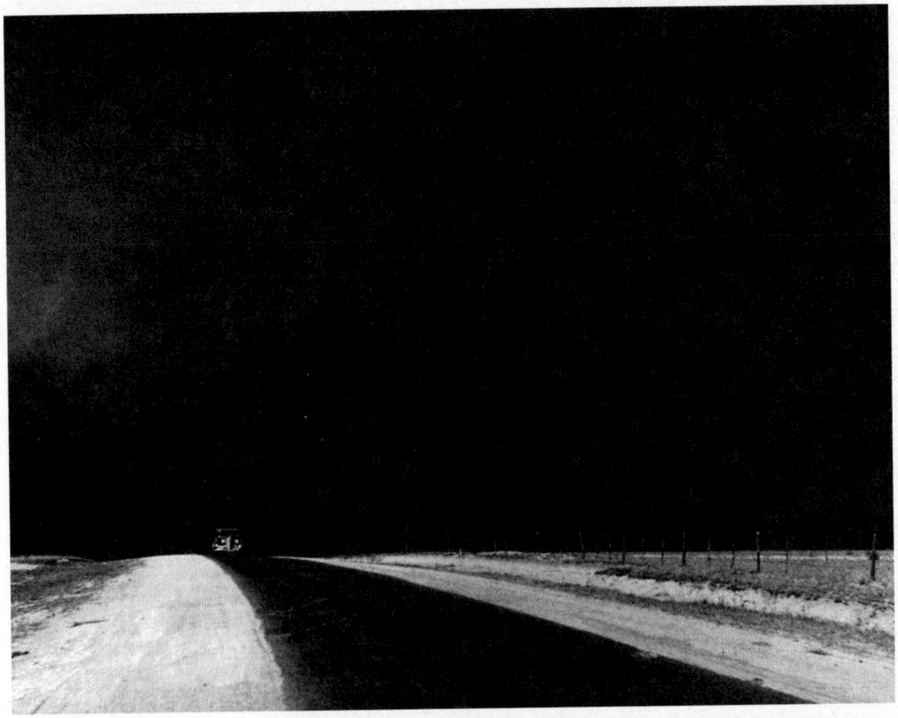

Working Together

Analyze political cartoons

Political cartoons make comments on politics in drawings combined with words. Bring a political cartoon to class. You can find many political cartoons on the Web in addition to ones in newspapers and magazines.

Answer these questions.

1. What is the point of the cartoon?
2. What do you need to know to understand the cartoon? Political cartoons usually make reference to current events, television shows, and popular culture.
3. Political cartoons often exaggerate physical attributes. Is anything exaggerated?
4. Political cartoons are often ironic—pointing to the difference between the way things really are and what they are expected to be. Is the cartoon ironic?
5. Why is the cartoon funny or not funny?

Organize in groups of three or four students. Exchange your cartoons and answer the same questions for your classmates' cartoons.

When all finish, compare your answers for each cartoon. Where there is disagreement, stop to discuss why you came up with different answers.

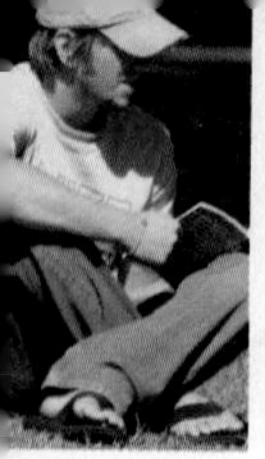

Read actively

If you own what you are reading (or are able to make yourself a photocopy of borrowed materials), read with a pencil in hand. Pens and highlighters don't erase, and often you don't remember why you highlighted a particular sentence.

Annotate what you read

Using annotating strategies will make your effort more rewarding.

Mark major points and key concepts	Sometimes major points are indicated by headings, but often you will need to locate them.
Connect passages	Notice how ideas connect to each other. Draw lines and arrows. If an idea connects to something a few pages before, write a note in the margin with the page number.
Ask questions	Note anything that puzzles you, including words to look up.

Annotate difficult readings

Much of what you read in college will deal with unfamiliar concepts, which are often defined by other concepts. Annotating a difficult reading will help you understand the relationship of concepts, and the annotations will be valuable in remembering key points when you come back to the reading later. In this passage from John Heskett's *Toothpicks and Logos, Design in Everyday Life*, the author defines function in terms of two other concepts.

A more inclusive definition of function is needed, which can be opened up by breaking the concept of function into a twofold division: the key concepts of utility and significance.

definition of function – utlity and significance

Utility can be defined as the quality of appropriateness in use. This means it is concerned with how things work, of the degree to which designs serve practical purposes and provide affordances or capabilities. A simple example is a professional kitchen knife used to prepare food: its primary utility value is as a cutting tool. In order for it to work effectively, the blade needs to possess material qualities enabling a sharp edge to be maintained and for it to remain stable in use.

definition of utlity

affordances? ? odd word – author is British

example – kitchen knife

Significance, as a concept in design, explains how forms assume meaning in the ways they are used, or the roles and meaning assigned them, often becoming powerful symbols or icons in patterns of habit and ritual. In contrast to the emphasis on efficiency, significance has more to do with expression and meaning.

definition of significance

It is possible to find designs of many kinds defined solely in terms of utility or significance. Many examples of the former are products related to the performance of professional services, tools with highly specific purposes, such as a hand saw or a lathe, or medical equipment, such as an ultrasound machine. Where information has to perform a highly specific task, as in a railway timetable, the layout and type forms should be clean, simple, and directed wholly to imparting essential facts. A primary condition of utilitarian design is that it must effectively execute or support certain tasks. In contrast, a piece of jewelry, a porcelain figurine, or a frame for a family photograph has no such specific purpose—instead their purpose can be described in terms of contemplative pleasure or adornment.

examples of designs for utility

other examples: computer keyboard, pencil, traffic light

examples of designs for significance

Map what you read

Drawing a map of a text can help you to identify key points and understand the relationships of concepts.

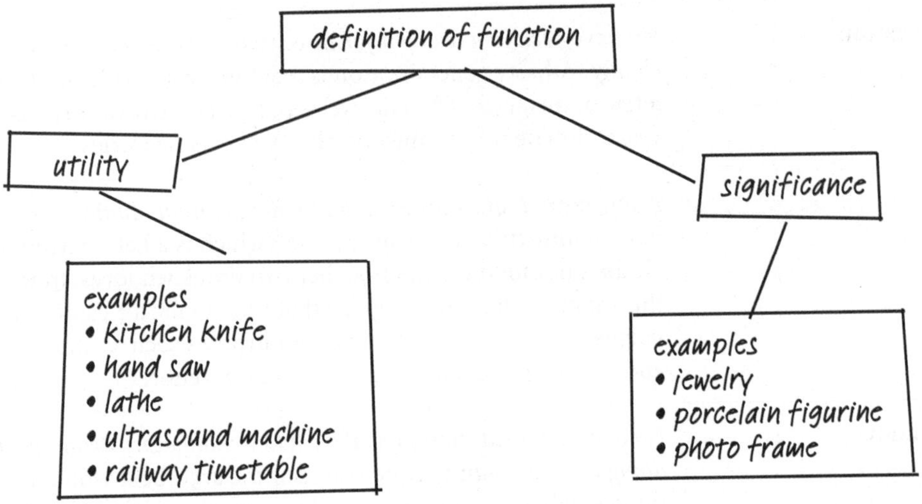

Make notes

Write down your thoughts as you read. Often you will find that something you read reminds you of something else. Jot that down. It might give you ideas for writing. Think about which ideas impress you as you read. And think about what else you might read if you want to write about this subject.

Recognize fallacies

Reasoning depends less on proving a claim than it does on finding evidence for that claim that readers will accept as valid. The kinds of faulty reasoning called logical fallacies reflect a failure to provide sufficient evidence for a claim that is being made.

Fallacies of logic

Begging the question	*Politicians are inherently dishonest because no honest person would run for public office.* The fallacy of begging the question occurs when the claim is restated and passed off as evidence.
Either-or	*Either we eliminate the regulation of businesses or else profits will suffer.* The either-or fallacy suggests that there are only two choices in a complex situation. Rarely, if ever, is this the case. (In this example, the writer ignores the fact that Enron was unregulated and went bankrupt.)
False analogies	*Japan quit fighting in 1945 when we dropped nuclear bombs on them. We should use nuclear weapons against other countries.* Analogies always depend on the degree of resemblance of one situation to another. In this case, the analogy fails to recognize that circumstances today are very different from those in 1945; many countries now possess nuclear weapons, and we know their use could harm the entire world.
Hasty generalization	*We have been in a drought for three years; that's a sure sign of climate change.* A hasty generalization is a broad claim made on the basis of a few occurrences. Climate cycles occur regularly over spans of a few years; climate trends must be observed over centuries.
Non sequitur	*A university that can raise a billion dollars from alumni should not have to raise tuition.* A *non sequitur* (which is a Latin term meaning "it does not follow") ties together two unrelated ideas. In this case, the argument fails to recognize that the money for capital campaigns is often donated for special purposes such as athletic facilities and is not part of a university's general revenue.
Oversimplification	*No one would run stop signs if we had a mandatory death penalty for doing it.* This claim may be true, but the argument would be unacceptable to most citizens. More complex, if less definitive, solutions are called for.
Post hoc fallacy	*The stock market goes down when the AFC wins the Super Bowl in even years.* The *post hoc* fallacy (from the Latin *post hoc ergo hoc,*

	which means "after this, therefore this") assumes that things that follow in time have a causal relationship.
Rationalization	*I could have finished my paper on time if my printer was working.* People frequently come up with excuses and weak explanations for their own and others' behavior that often avoid actual causes.
Slippery slope	*We shouldn't grant citizenship to illegal immigrants now living in the United States because no one will want to obey our laws.* The slippery slope fallacy maintains that one thing inevitably will cause something else to happen.

Fallacies of emotion and language

Bandwagon appeals	*It doesn't matter if I copy a paper off the Web because everyone else does.* This argument suggests that everyone is doing it, so why shouldn't you? But on close examination, it may be that everyone really isn't doing it—and in any case, it may not be the right thing to do.
Name calling	Name calling is frequent in politics and among competing groups *(radical, tax-and-spend liberal, racist, fascist, right-wing ideologue).* Unless these terms are carefully defined, they are meaningless.
Polarization	*Feminists are all man-haters.* Polarization, like name-calling, exaggerates positions and groups by representing them as extreme and divisive.
Straw man	*Environmentalists won't be satisfied until not a single human being is allowed to enter a national park.* A straw man argument is a diversionary tactic that sets up another's position in a way that can be easily rejected. In fact, only a small percentage of environmentalists would make an argument even close to this one.

Write Now

Analyze opinion writing

Examine writing that expresses opinions: blogs, discussion boards, editorials, advocacy Web sites, the letters to the editor on the editorial pages of your campus or local newspaper. Read with a pencil in hand, and mark where you think there may be fallacies.

Select the example that has the clearest fallacy. Explain in a paragraph the cause of the fallacy.

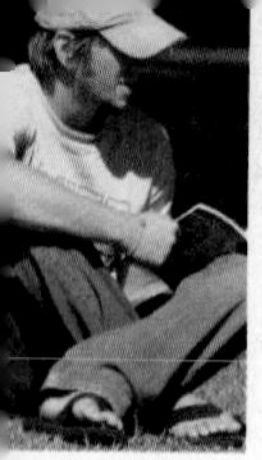

Respond as a reader

Engage in a dialogue with what you read. Talk back to the author. If you are having trouble understanding a difficult section, read it aloud and listen to the author's voice. Hearing something read will sometimes help you to imagine being in a conversation with the author.

Make notes

As you read, write down your thoughts. Something you read may remind you of something else. Jot that down.

- Imagine that the author is with you. What points does the writer make that you would respond to in person?
- What questions would you have of the author? These indicate what you might need to look up.
- What ideas do you find that you might develop or interpret differently?

Write summaries

When you summarize, you state the major ideas of an entire source or part of a source in your own words. Most summaries are much shorter than the original because they include just the main points, not most of the examples and supporting material.

The keys to writing a good summary are identifying the main points and then putting those points into your own words. If you use words from the source, you have to put those words in quotation marks.

John Heskett argues that the concept of function in design should be understood in terms of "utility" and "significance." He defines utility as the degree a design accomplishes its purpose, such as how well a knife cuts. Significance is defined as the degree to which an object is designed to give pleasure or create meaning. A piece of art is an example of something designed exclusively for significance.

Build on what you read

Keeping a reading journal is a good practice for a writer. You'll have a record of your thinking as you read that you can return to later. Record your first impressions, note any ideas you find stimulating or useful, explore relationships, and write down questions. Often you can connect different ideas from different readings. A reading journal is a great place to test ideas that you can later develop for a writing assignment.

Heskett says, "It is possible to find designs of many kinds defined solely in terms of utility and significance." I'll grant the distinction, but his examples suggest that most things have elements of both.

He uses tools as objects designed strictly for utility, but look at a tool catalog and you'll see lots of bright colors and handsome cases. He uses a photograph frame as an example of significance. True enough that frames are often decorative, but a frame also has to fit the picture. The frame should use non-glare glass to reduce reflected light. A frame has to do more than just look good.

But a bigger point is that anything can have significance for a particular person. I have my grandfather's hammer. It is nearly worthless because the handle is so old and worn that it would snap if you swung it hard against a nail. I took the hammer to work one day to hang a picture, and it shortly disappeared. I searched and couldn't find it. I forgot about it, but then I noticed it in a storeroom months later and recovered it.

Write Now

Respond to what you read

Select a reading in one of the chapters in Part 2 that interests you. Write a one-paragraph summary of either the entire reading or of a part that contains a stimulating idea.

Write a second paragraph that develops one or more of the ideas in the reading. Think of some way of expanding or extending one of the author's ideas, either by relating it to your own experience or to something else you have read.

3 Planning a Journey

In some buildings, you feel comfortable and at ease right away. But in others you always feel disoriented. The problem is the layout or plan of the building.

A disorienting building lacks central spaces and signs. Directions are missing at intersections. All the hallways look alike.

Strong central spaces, like the Piazza Navona in Rome, organize neighborhoods and attract people.

Determine your direction

Poorly organized writing is like a poorly designed building. It takes too much effort to get to where you want to go. Effective writing keeps readers oriented. Writing that succeeds is organized around a central idea, much as successful buildings and even thriving neighborhoods are.

Identify your center

Often the challenge in writing is finding the center that connects your sentences and paragraphs. Probably you have had the experience of driving around looking for a store or a house without having the address. Unless you were lucky, it was probably frustrating. Knowing your center is like having an address. It makes the journey far easier.

Having a big topic like privacy is like knowing only the general area of where something is located.

BROAD TOPIC:
privacy and surveillance

SPECIFIC TOPIC:
Which public spaces should be under constant surveillance with micro-devices invisible to the human eye?

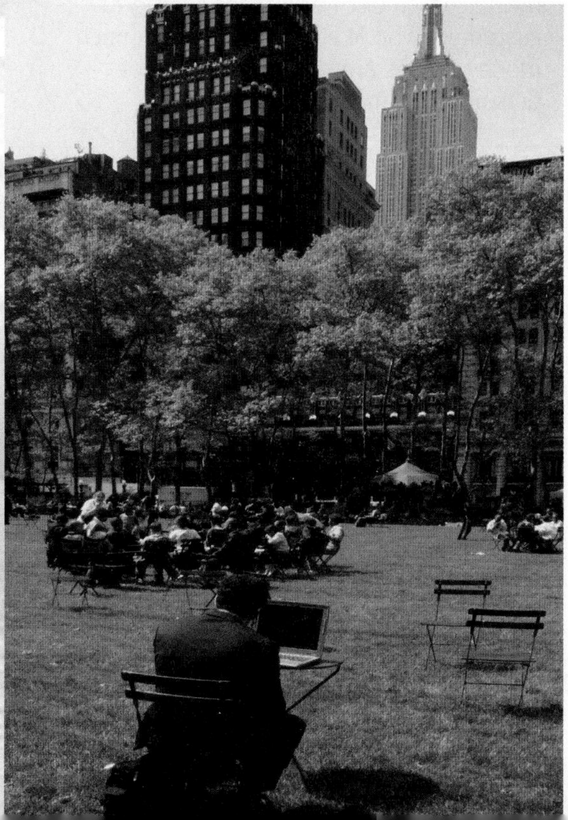

Think about where you are headed

Writing is a dynamic activity that goes back and forth between your mind and the page. Nevertheless, it helps to have an overall strategy that enables your thinking to evolve into writing that communicates with your readers.

Read your assignment again. Often the assignment will tell you which direction to go.

Reflect

You will need to think about an idea or concept in terms of your own history and life experience (see Chapter 7).

Inform

You will need to report information or explain a concept or idea (see Chapter 8).

Analyze

You will need to interpret a text or a set of data to find connections and reach conclusions (see Chapter 9).

Analyze causes

You will need to identify probable causes of a trend or phenomenon and give evidence for your analysis (see Chapter 10).

Evaluate

You will need to determine whether something is good or bad based on criteria that you identify (see Chapter 11).

Argue

You will need to take a position on an issue or propose a course of action (see Chapters 12 and 13).

Write a thesis

Central ideas in writing are often expressed in a thesis statement. Just as many urban neighborhoods grow up around strong central spaces, most writing you will do in college and later in your career will have an explicit thesis, usually stated near the beginning. The thesis announces your topic and indicates what points you want to make about that topic.

Write a working thesis

Your thesis should follow the direction your assignment calls for. These examples show how the broad subject of databases and privacy can be approached from different directions, depending on your purpose.

Describe

THESIS: My Amazon.com account has a list of every book I have purchased from them dating back ten years, plus Amazon records every item I browse but don't buy. No wonder Amazon's recommendations of what I might like are so uncannily accurate!

Analyze

THESIS: Understanding how the concept of privacy is legally defined is critical for strengthening privacy laws.

Inform

THESIS: Imagine a government that compels its citizens to reveal vast amounts of personal data, including your physical description, your phone number, your political party, your parents' and spouse's names, where you work, where you live, what property you own, what it is worth, and every legal transaction in your life, and then making that data available to anyone on the Web—which is exactly what federal, state, and local governments are doing today in the United States.

Argue

THESIS: Unlike the government, companies have almost no restrictions on what information they collect or what they do with that information. Laws should be passed that make companies responsible for the misuse of personal information and allow people to have greater participation in how that information is used.

Evaluate

THESIS: Using personal consumer data to refuse service or offer inferior service to customers who likely will not spend much money is an example of the misuse of personal information.

Reflect

THESIS: I had never thought about the consequences of data profiling until I read about Netflix's policy of "throttling" frequent users, which explained why deliveries of movies I had requested from Netflix grew slower and slower.

Analyze causes

THESIS: Many laws to protect privacy are on the books, but these laws are ineffective for the digital era because they were written to protect people from government spying and intrusion rather than from the collection and selling of personal information by companies.

Evaluate your working thesis

Ask yourself these questions about your working thesis.

1. Is it specific?
2. Is it manageable in terms of the assigned length and the amount of time you have?
3. Is it interesting to your intended readers?

Example 1

THESIS: Steroids are a problem in Major League Baseball.

- **Specific?** The thesis is too broad. What exactly is the problem? Is the problem the same now as it was a few years ago?
- **Manageable?** Because the thesis is not limited, it cannot be discussed adequately.
- **Interesting?** The topic is potentially interesting, but many people are aware that baseball players used steroids. How can you lead readers to think about the topic in a new way?

Example 1 revised

THESIS: Home run records from 1993 through 2004 should be placed in a special category because of the high use of steroids in Major League Baseball before testing began in 2004.

Example 2

THESIS: "Nanotechnology" refers to any technology that deals with particles measured in units of a nanometer, which is one billionth (10^{-9}) of a meter.

- **Specific?** The thesis is specific, but it is too narrow. It offers only a definition of nanotechnology.
- **Manageable?** The thesis states a fact.
- **Interesting?** Nanotechnology could be interesting if some of its potential effects are included.

Example 2 revised

THESIS: Nanotechnology may soon change concepts of social identity by making it possible for individuals to alter their physical appearances either through cosmetic surgery performed by nanorobots or changes in genetic sequences on chromosomes.

Write Now

Write a bold thesis

Too much of what we read says what we've all heard before. Instead of serving up what readers likely know, try challenging readers. For example, in *Everything Bad Is Good for You*, Steven Johnson argues that video games are not a total waste of time but teach children valuable problem-solving skills.

Think of something that many people accept as common sense or general wisdom—that junk food is bad for you, reality television is garbage, or graffiti is vandalism—and argue the opposite. Or that something thought of as boring might be really interesting: bird watching, classical Indian music, or ancient Greek drama. Write a thesis that stands that common wisdom on its head.

Then write a paragraph about how you might argue for your controversial thesis. What evidence might you supply?

Plan your route

Experienced travelers have multiple strategies for getting to their destinations. Sometimes they have the route planned in advance and follow it exactly. In other cases, they know they have to be flexible, just as when you find traffic stopped and you take an alternate route. Experienced writers work in much the same way, using different strategies for different writing tasks.

Determine a plan

Get out your notes and all the information you have collected. You may find it helpful to write major points on sticky notes so you can move them around. If your topic is the effects of nanotechnology on the body, you might produce an organization plan similar to this one.

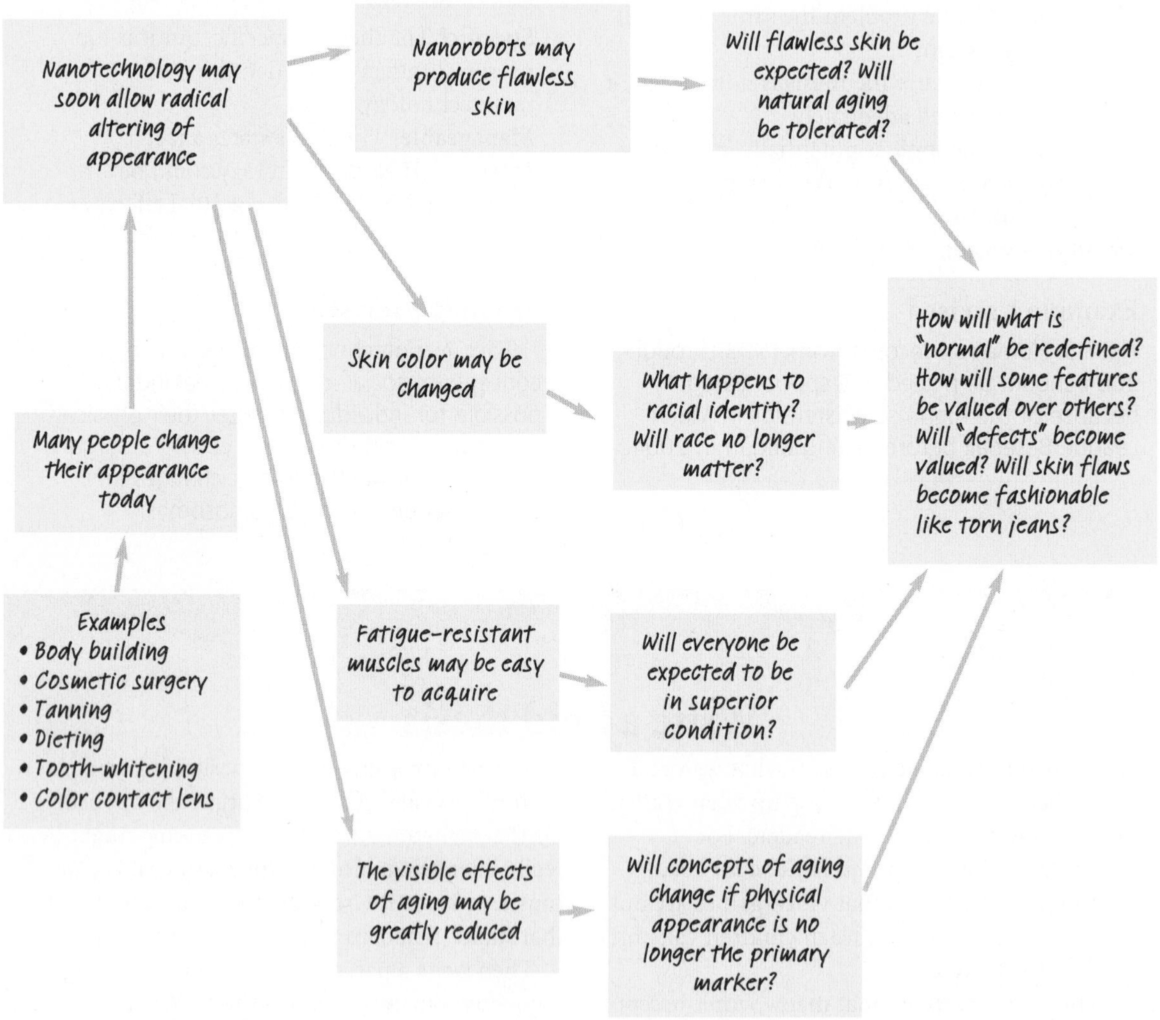

Make a writing plan

Writing plans often take the form of outlines, either formal outlines or working outlines.

A formal outline typically begins with the thesis statement, which anchors the entire outline.

THESIS: Nanotechnology may soon allow radical altering of the human body, which will have major social consequences.

I. Altering the appearance of the body has become common.
   A. Cosmetic surgery is now routine.
   B. Body building is popular.
   C. Most people are aware of diet and many attempt to control their weight.
   D. Tanning, changing eye color, and tooth-whitening are frequent.

II. Nanotechnology may soon radically accelerate these trends.
   A. Nanorobots may produce flawless skin.
   B. Skin color may be changed.
   C. Wrinkles and other signs of aging may be eliminated or reduced.
   D. Muscle tissue may be enhanced.

A working outline is a sketch of how you will arrange the major sections.

Effects of nanotechnology on the body

SECTION 1: *Begin with how people change the appearance of their bodies today.*

SECTION 2: *Discuss how nanotechnology will accelerate these trends, giving people the potential for perfect skin, changing their skin color, and reducing aging.*

SECTION 3: *Move to the questions these technologies raise, such as how aging will be perceived and how race will be understood.*

SECTION 4: *Raise the issue of how "normal" will be defined if people can choose how they look.*

SECTION 5: *Expand the idea of "normal" to who will control what is desirable and how social hierarchies might be changed or reinforced.*

SECTION 6: *End by connecting body issues to larger issues such as who gets to live for how long.*

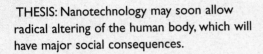

Write Now

Make a plan

First, write a working thesis. Ask the questions on page 21.

- Is the thesis specific?
- Is it manageable?
- Is it interesting?

Revise your thesis if necessary.

Then use two of the three methods—a visual organization plan, a formal outline, or a working outline—to develop a plan for writing a paper based on the thesis. When you finish, compare the plans. Which will be easier to use for writing your paper?

4 Returning and Revising

In order to revise effectively, you must "re-see," which, after all, is what revision means.

Evaluate your draft

Use these questions to evaluate your draft. Note any places where you might make improvements.

Does your paper or project meet the assignment?

- Look again at your assignment and especially at the key words such as *analyze, define, evaluate*, and *propose*. Does your paper or project do what the assignment asks for? If not, how can you change it?
- Look again at the assignment for specific guidelines including length, format, and amount of research. Does your work meet these guidelines? If not, how can you change it?

Do you have a clear focus?

- Underline your thesis. Think how you might make your thesis more precise.
- Underline the main idea of each paragraph. Check how each paragraph connects to your thesis. Think about how you can strengthen the connections.

Are your main points adequately developed?

- Put brackets around the reasons and evidence that support your main points.
- Can you find places to add more examples and details that would help to explain your main points?

Is your organization effective?

- Make a quick outline of your draft if you have not done so already.
- Mark the places where you find abrupt shifts or gaps.
- Think about how you might rearrange sections or paragraphs to make your draft more effective.

Do you consider your potential readers' knowledge and points of view?

- Where do you give background if your readers are unfamiliar with your subject?
- Where do you acknowledge any opposing views your readers might have?

Do you represent yourself effectively?

- To the extent you can, forget for a moment that you wrote what you are reading. What impression do you have of you, the writer?
- Does the writer have an appropriate tone?
- Is the writer visually effective? Is the type easy to read? Does the writer use headings and illustrations where they are helpful?

When you finish, make a list of your goals in the revision. You may have to scrap the draft and start over, but you will have a better sense of your subject and your goals.

Learn strategies for rewriting

Now it's time to go through your draft in detail. You should work on the goals you identify in your review. Also, look for other opportunities using this checklist.

1. Keep your audience in mind.	Reread each of your paragraphs' opening sentences and ask yourself whether they are engaging enough to keep your readers interested.
2. Sharpen your focus wherever possible.	You may have started out with a large topic but most of what you wrote concerns only one aspect. You may need to revise your thesis and supporting paragraphs.
3. Check if key terms are adequately defined.	What are your key terms? Are they defined precisely enough to be meaningful?
4. Develop where necessary.	Key points and claims may need more explanation and supporting evidence. Look for opportunities to add support without becoming redundant.
5. Check links between paragraphs.	Look for any places where you make abrupt shifts and make the transitions better. Check if you signal the relationship from one paragraph to the next.
6. Consider your title.	Many writers don't think much about titles, but they are very important. A good title makes the reader want to see what you have to say. Be as specific as you can in your title, and if possible, suggest your stance.
7. Consider your introduction.	In the introduction you want to get off to a fast start and convince your reader to keep reading. Cut to the chase.
8. Consider your conclusion.	Restating your thesis usually isn't the best way to finish; conclusions that offer only summary bore readers. The worst endings say something like "in my paper I've said this." Effective conclusions are interesting and provocative, leaving readers with something to think about.
9. Improve the visual aspects of your text.	Does the font you selected look attractive using your printer? Would headings and subheadings help to identify key sections? If you include statistical data, would charts be effective? Would illustrations help to establish key points?

Respond to others

Your instructor may ask you to respond to the drafts of your classmates. Responding to other people's writing requires the same careful attention you give to your own draft. To write a helpful response, you should go through the draft more than once.

First reading:
Read at your normal rate the first time through without stopping. When you finish you should have a clear sense of what the writer is trying to accomplish.

- Main idea: Write a sentence that summarizes what you think is the writer's main idea in the draft.
- Purpose: Write a sentence that summarizes what you think the writer was trying to accomplish in the draft.

Second reading:
In your second reading, you should be most concerned with the content, organization, and completeness of the draft. Make notes as you read.

- Introduction: Does the writer's first paragraph effectively introduce the topic and engage your interest?
- Thesis: Where exactly is the writer's thesis? Note in the margin where you think the thesis is located.
- Focus: Does the writer maintain focus on the thesis? Note any places where the writer seems to wander off to another topic.
- Organization: Are the sections and paragraphs ordered effectively? Do any paragraphs seem to be out of place? Do you note any abrupt shifts? Can you suggest a better order for the paragraphs?
- Completeness: Are there sections and paragraphs that lack key information or adequate development? Where do you want to know more?
- Sources: If the draft uses outside sources, are they cited accurately? If there are quotations, are they used correctly and worked into the fabric of the draft?

Third reading:
In your third reading, turn your attention to matters of audience, style, and tone.

- Audience: Who is the writer's intended audience? What does the writer assume the audience knows and believes?
- Style: Is the writer's style engaging? How would you describe the writer's voice?
- Tone: Is the tone appropriate for the writer's purpose and audience? Is the tone consistent throughout the draft? Are there places where another word or phrase might work better?

When you have finished the third reading, write a short paragraph on each bulleted item above, referring to specific paragraphs in the draft by number. Then end by answering these two questions:

1. **What does the writer do especially well in the draft?**
2. **What one or two things would most improve the draft in a revision?**

Pay attention to details last

When you finish revising, you are ready for one final careful reading, keeping the goals of improving your style and eliminating errors in mind.

Edit for particular goals

1. Check the connections between sentences.

Notice how your sentences are connected. If you need to signal the relationship from one sentence to the next, use a transition word or phrase.

2. Check your sentences.

If you notice that a sentence doesn't sound right, think about how you might rephrase it. Often you will pick up problems by reading aloud. If a sentence seems too long, then you might break it into two or more sentences. If you notice a string of short sentences that sound choppy, then you might combine them.

3. Eliminate wordiness.

Writers tend to introduce wordiness in drafts. Look for long expressions that can easily be shortened ("at this point in time" –> "now") and for unnecessary repetition. Remove unnecessary words like *very*, *really*, and *totally*. See how many words you can take out without losing the meaning.

4. Use active verbs.

Anytime you can use a verb besides a form of *be* (*is*, *are*, *was*, *were*) or a verb ending in *–ing*, take advantage of the opportunity to make your style more lively. Sentences that begin with "There is (are)" and "It is" often have better alternatives.

Proofread carefully

In your final pass through your text, eliminate as many errors as you can. To become an effective proofreader, you have to learn to slow down. Some writers find that moving from word to word with a pencil slows them down enough to find errors. Others read backwards to force concentration on each word.

1. Know what your spelling checker can and can't do.

Spelling checkers are the greatest invention since peanut butter. They turn up many typos and misspellings that are hard to catch. But spelling checkers do not catch wrong words (e.g., "to much" should be "too much"), where you leave off endings ("three dog"), and other similar errors.

2. Check for grammar and punctuation.

Nothing hurts your credibility more than leaving many errors in what you write. Many job application letters get tossed in the reject pile because an applicant made a single, glaring error. Readers probably shouldn't make such harsh judgments when they find errors, but in real life they do.

Write Now

Write a helpful response

Read the following first draft and use the guidelines on page 27 to write a response that will help the writer to revise the paper. Resist the urge to edit sentences and correct mechanical errors. The assignment asked the student to analyze an ad.

Analysis of an Ad

In our modern world of today, Americans see thousands of advertisements every year, we buy many products because of ads. One of the products advertised a lot is milk. I chose an Andy Roddick ad for this assignment because he is my very favorite tennis player. There was another totally awesome milk ad with Stone Cold Steve Austin, but I couldn't find it.

I found the picture of Andy in Seventeen magazine. I don't read Seventeen any more, but my younger sister does, and I needed to find an ad. Andy looks totally cool in this photo. He was on the court with his tennis racquet. His milk mustache is visible to the eye.

I suppose the milk people wanted him because he is popular and good looking. The milk ads all have celebrities and sports stars. I read that the milk people were worried that younger people aren't drinking milk and they wanted young stars to pitch milk and praise it's benefits. I guess its working because the ad campaign has been around as long as I can remember. I've even heard copycats use slogans like "Got cookies?" "Got fish?" "Got fish?" "Got sports?" and even "Got Jesus?"

The Roddick ad probably works because Roddick is good looking. As I said before, the milk people like good looking stars. He has kind of a sexy pose too. He looks like a movie star.

In conclusion, the Andy Roddick ad is a good ad because young people like Andy Roddick. If they see Andy Roddick drinking milk, they want to drink milk to.

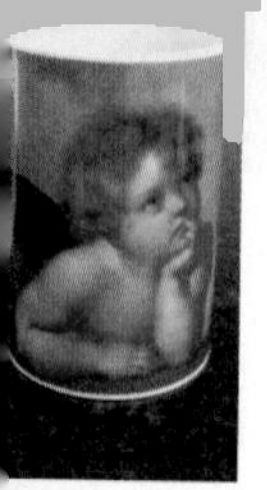

5 Communicating Visually

The principles of good design, like those of good writing, begin with your audience and what you are trying to accomplish.

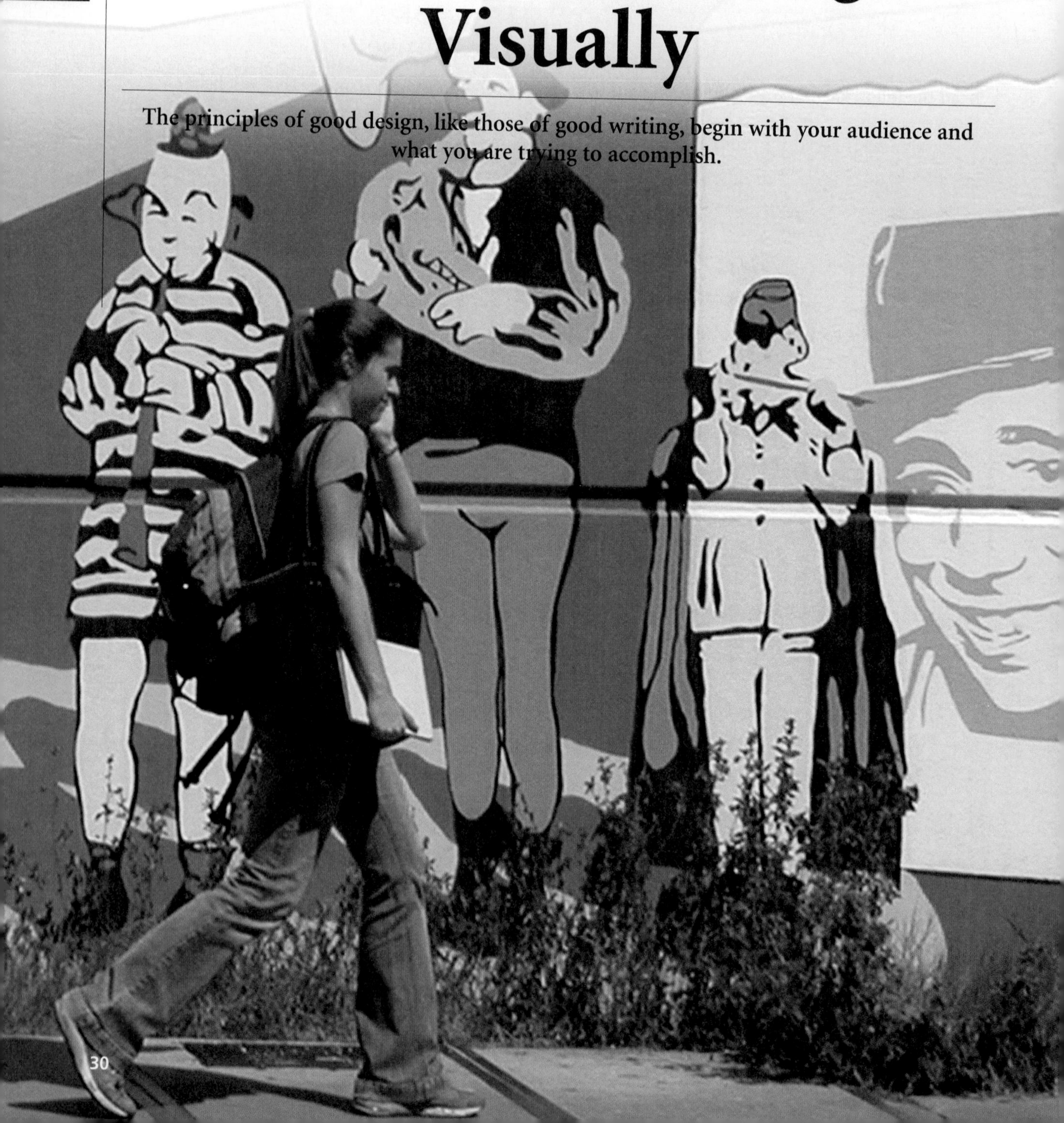

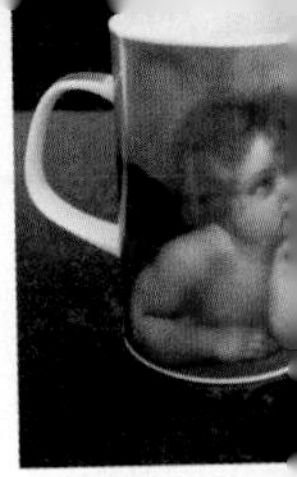

Communicate with visuals and words

The word *writing* makes us think of words, yet in our daily experience reading newspapers, magazines, advertisements, posters, and signs, we find words combined with images and graphics. Similarly, the dominant visual medium of our time, television, uses words extensively; think of the words you see on commercials when you have the sound off and the running text across the bottom of the screen on news, sports, and financial programs. Understanding the relationships of words and visuals will make you a better writer.

What do visuals do best?

We've become accustomed to deciding whether we'll need to wear a sweater outside tomorrow by looking at the colors on a weather map. But even then, we depend on words to tell us whether the forecast is for today or tomorrow, and what each color signifies. Visuals work well when they

- Deliver spatial information, especially through maps, floor plans, and other graphic representations of space
- Represent statistical relationships
- Produce a strong immediate impact, even shock value
- Emphasize a point made in words

What do words do best?

Words can do many things that images cannot. Written words work best when they

- Communicate abstract ideas
- Report information
- Persuade using elaborated reasoning
- Communicate online using minimal bandwidth

What can words and visuals do together?

Combining words and visuals allow writers to present very complex ideas: how the quick thinking of Union generals to rush soldiers to high ground at the battle of Gettysburg led to a decisive victory; how atomic structure influences ionic bonding; how the warming of oceans in the Arctic and Antarctic affects weather worldwide.

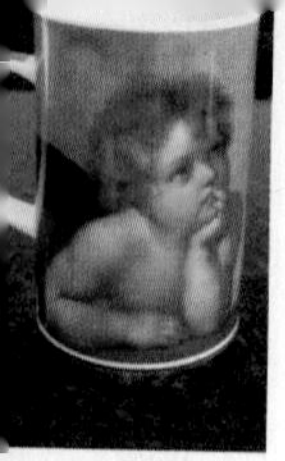

Know when to use images and graphics

Personal computers, digital cameras, scanners, printers, and the Web have made it easy to include images and graphics in what we write. But these technologies don't tell us when or how to use images and graphics.

Think about what an image or graphic communicates

- Think about your readers' expectations for the medium you are using. Most essays don't use images. Most Web sites and brochures do use images.
- Think about the purpose for an image or graphic. Does it illustrate a concept? highlight an important point? show something that is hard to explain in words alone? If you don't know the purpose, you may not need the image.
- Think about the placement of an image or graphic in your text. It should be as close as possible to a relevant point in your text.
- Think about the focus of an image. Will readers see the part that matters? If not, you may need to crop the image.
- Provide informative captions for the images and graphics you use and refer to them in your text.

Format images for the medium you are using

Images that you want to print need to be of higher quality than those intended for the Web or the screen. Pay attention to the settings on your camera or scanner.

Digital cameras frequently make images with 72 dpi (dots per inch), which is the maximum you can display on the screen. Most printers use a resolution from 300 to 600 dpi. Use the high-quality setting on your camera for images you intend to print.

Scanners typically offer a range of resolution from 72 to 1600 dpi. The higher the number, the finer the image, but the file size becomes larger. Images on the Web or a screen display at 72 dpi, so higher resolutions do not improve the quality but do make the image slow to load.

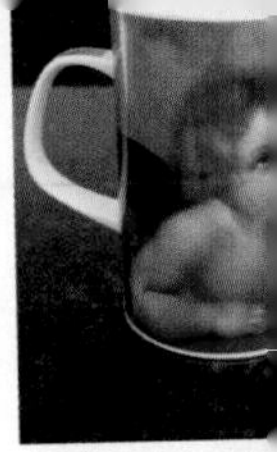

Create tables, charts, and graphs

Software makes it easy to create tables, charts, and graphs, which are often effective in conveying statistical information at a glance. Select the type of visual that best suits your purpose.

Table 25.1
Population Change for the Ten Largest U.S. Cities, 1990 to 2000

	Population		*Change, 1990 to 2000*	
City and State	*April 1, 2000*	*April 1, 1990*	*Number*	*Percentage*
New York, NY	8,008,278	7,322,564	685,714	9.4
Los Angeles, CA	3,694,820	3,485,398	209,422	6.0
Chicago, IL	2,896,016	2,783,726	112,290	4.0
Houston, TX	1,953,631	1,630,553	323,078	19.8
Philadelphia, PA	1,517,550	1,585,577	-68,027	-4.3
Phoenix, AZ	1,321,045	983,403	337,642	34.3
San Diego, CA	1,223,400	1,110,549	112,851	10.2
Dallas, TX	1,188,580	1,006,877	181,703	18.0
San Antonio, TX	1,144,646	935,933	208,713	22.3
Detroit, MI	951,270	1,027,974	-76,704	-7.5

Source: U.S. Cencus Bureau, Census 2000; 1990 Census, Population and Housing Unit Counts, United States (1990 CPH-2-1).

Tables

A table is used to display numerical data and similar types of information. It usually includes several items as well as variables for each item.

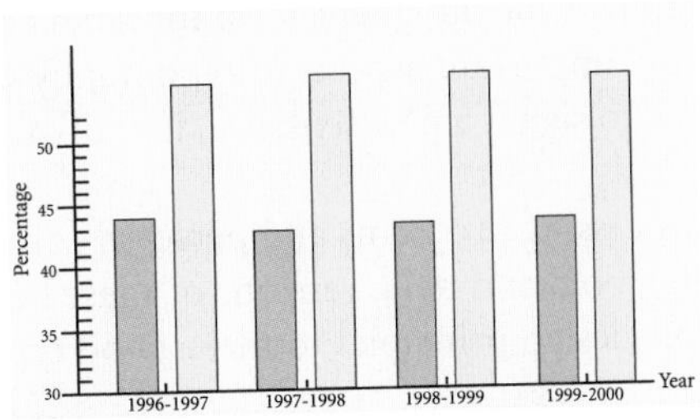

Bar Graphs

A bar graph compares the values of two or more items.

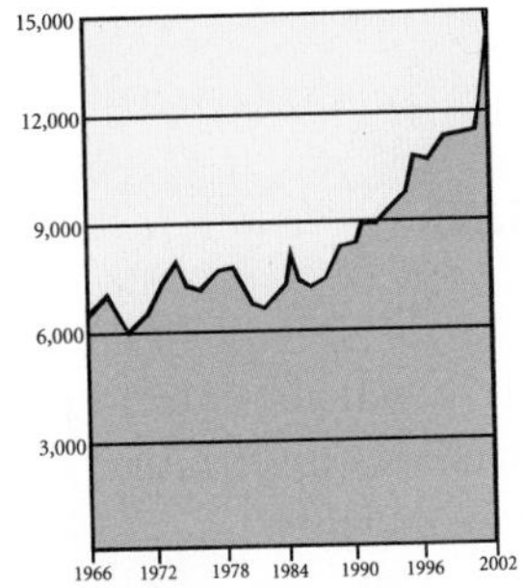

Line Graphs

A line graph shows change over time.

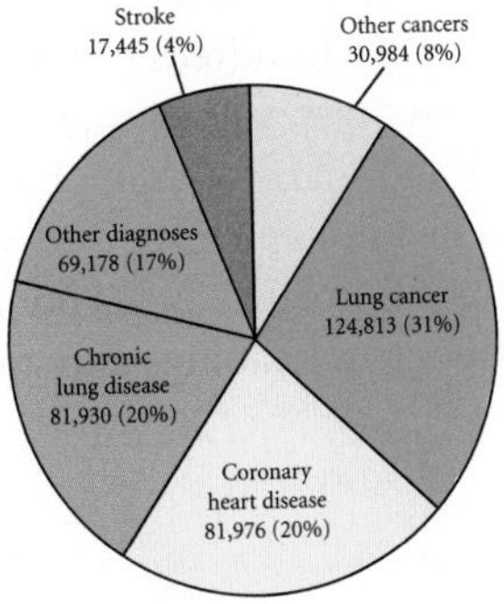

Pie Charts

A pie chart shows the parts making up a whole.

Working Together

Communicate with images and graphics

In a group of three or four students

Look at your textbooks for your other courses. Find one example where an image or graphic helps you to understand the material. Write briefly what exactly the image or graphic does that words alone could not. Find a second example where you think an image or graphic could be added. Write why an image or graphic would help.

Bring your examples to class and compare them with other group members. When do words work best? When is it more appropriate to communicate information through graphics and other visual media?

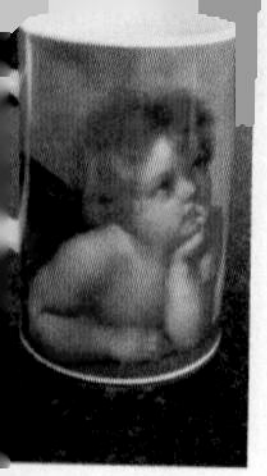

Understand typography

Just as people communicate with body language, texts have a look and feel created by the layout, typefaces, type size, color, density, and other elements.

Typography is the designer's term for letters and symbols that make up the print on the page. You are already using important aspects of typography when you use capital letters, italics, boldface, or different sizes of type to signal a new sentence, identify the title of a book, or distinguish a heading from the body text.

Word processing programs and personal computers now enable you to use dozens of different typefaces (fonts), bold and italic versions of these fonts, and a range of font sizes. Fortunately, you can rely on some simple design principles to make good typographic choices for your documents.

Choosing a font

A font family consists of the font in different sizes as well as in its boldface and italic forms. Although computers now make hundreds of font styles and sizes available to writers, you should avoid confusing readers with too many typographical features. Limit the fonts in a document to one or two font families. A common practice is to choose one font family for all titles and headings and another for the body text.

A Font Family

Arial Narrow
Arial Narrow Italic
Arial Regular
Arial Italic
Arial Bold
Arial Bold Italic
Arial Black

The font family Arial, shown above in 14 point, is composed of style variations on the Arial design that include a variety of weights.

Serif and sans serif typefaces

Typefaces are normally divided into two groups—serif and sans serif. Serif typefaces include horizontal lines—or serifs—added to the major strokes of a letter or character such as a number. Sans serif typefaces, by contrast, do not have serifs. Notice the difference opposite.

The typical use and stylistic impact of the typefaces vary considerably. Serif typefaces are more traditional, conservative, and formal in appearance. By contrast, sans serif typefaces offer a more contemporary, progressive, and informal look. Serif is often used for longer pieces of writing, such as novels and textbooks. It is also the best bet for college papers.

The difference between serif and sans serif fonts

The horizontal lines make serif easier to read because they guide the eye from left to right across the page.

This **SERIF** font is called Garamond

This **SANS SERIF** font is called Helvetica

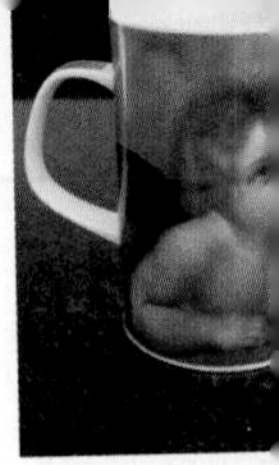

Think about font style

Not all fonts are suitable for extended pieces of writing. Sentences and paragraphs printed in fonts that imitate calligraphy or handwriting are difficult to read in long stretches. For most academic and business writing, you will probably want to choose a traditional font, such as Times Roman, that is easy to read and does not call attention to itself. This book is set in 10.5 point Minion.

Choosing the best font for the job

This piece of text is in a caligraphic font and may be right for some special situations, but there is no doubt that every single reader will be aware of the struggle to decipher it.

This font is **28 point Palace Script**

This piece of text is in a handwriting font, and although easier to read than the above is still very difficult in large amounts.

This font is **17 point Feltpen**

This is about as normal a font as you can find. It is called Times Roman, for the simple reason that it was designed for use in the *London Times* newspaper, and so had to be as readable as possible.

This font is **14 point Times Roman**

This font is also very readable and is very common as it is the default font on most computer software. It does, however, require much more space than other faces.

This font is **14 point Courier**

Think about font size

It's easy to change the size of a font when you write on a computer. For most types of writing in college, a 12-point font is the standard size for the main (body) text, with headings in a larger font.

Type sizes

8 point

12 point

18 point

36 point

48 point

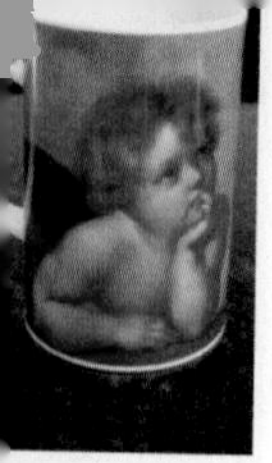

Height can make a difference

To ensure that what you write can be read easily, you need to choose an appropriate size. Fonts differ by height, called the x-height, as well as point size. Fonts of the same point size can look different because of height. Effective size depends on the appearance of a font, not merely its point size.

To ensure that what you write can be read easily, you need to choose an appropriate size. Fonts differ by height, called the x-height, as well as point size. Fonts of the same point size can look different because of height. Effective size depends on the appearance of a font, not merely its point size.

Both texts are set the same "size" (12 point) but they appear different because of the x-heights. Bembo, left, looks much smaller and takes much less space than Glypha, right.

Type sizes for computer monitors

For Web pages, you should consider using a larger font to compensate for the added difficulty of reading from a computer monitor. For overhead transparencies and computer-projected displays, you should use an even larger size (such as 32 point) to ensure that the text can be read from a distance.

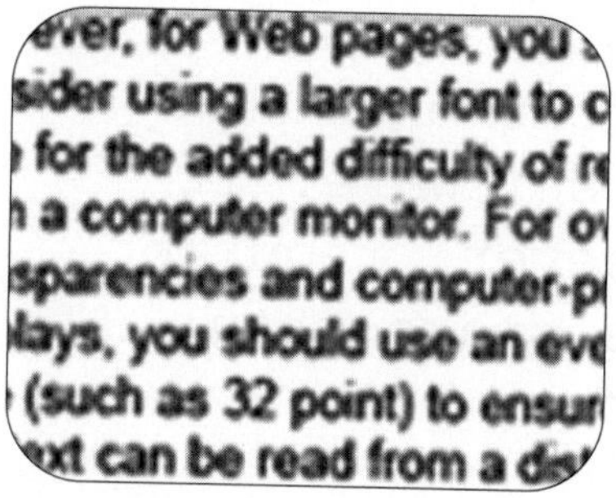

Pixilation on the computer screen breaks up the font; thus the 12-point type in this example is too small.

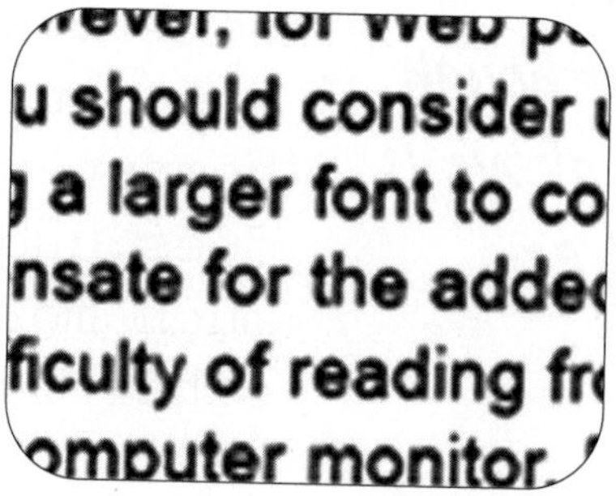

You should consider enlarging to 18-point type as in this example.

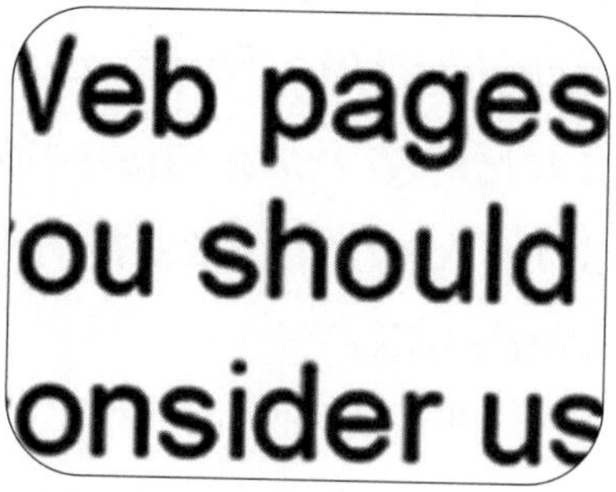

Or even 32 point if using an overhead projector or a computer-projected display.

Checklist for evaluating document design

1. Audience	Who is the intended audience? Will the design be appealing to them? How does the design serve their needs?
2. Genre	What is the genre? Does the design meet the requirements of the genre? For example, a brochure should fit in your pocket.
3. Organization	Is the organization clear to readers? If headings are used, are they in the right places? If headings are used for more than one level, are these levels indicated consistently?
4. Readability	Is the typeface attractive and readable? Are the margins sufficient? Is any contrasting text, such as boldface, italics, or all caps, brief enough to be legible? If color is used, does it direct emphasis to the right places?
5. Layout	Can the basic layout be made more effective? Is there adequate white space around headings, images, and graphics?

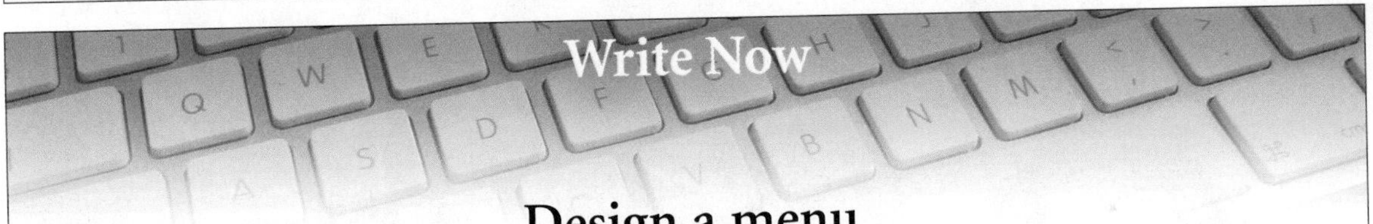

Write Now

Design a menu

Collect menus from a few restaurants, either in print or on the Web. Study the design of each menu.

Design a menu of your own. First, you have to decide what kind of food you will serve: burgers, Italian, Thai, seafood, and so on. Second, think about the clientele you want to attract: college students, families, office lunch crowd, or another demographic. Third, list a few food items for your menu. Fourth, name your restaurant and give it a theme.

Make a sketch of your menu. Decide what graphics, clip art, and backgrounds you want to use. Then create your menu using word processing software.

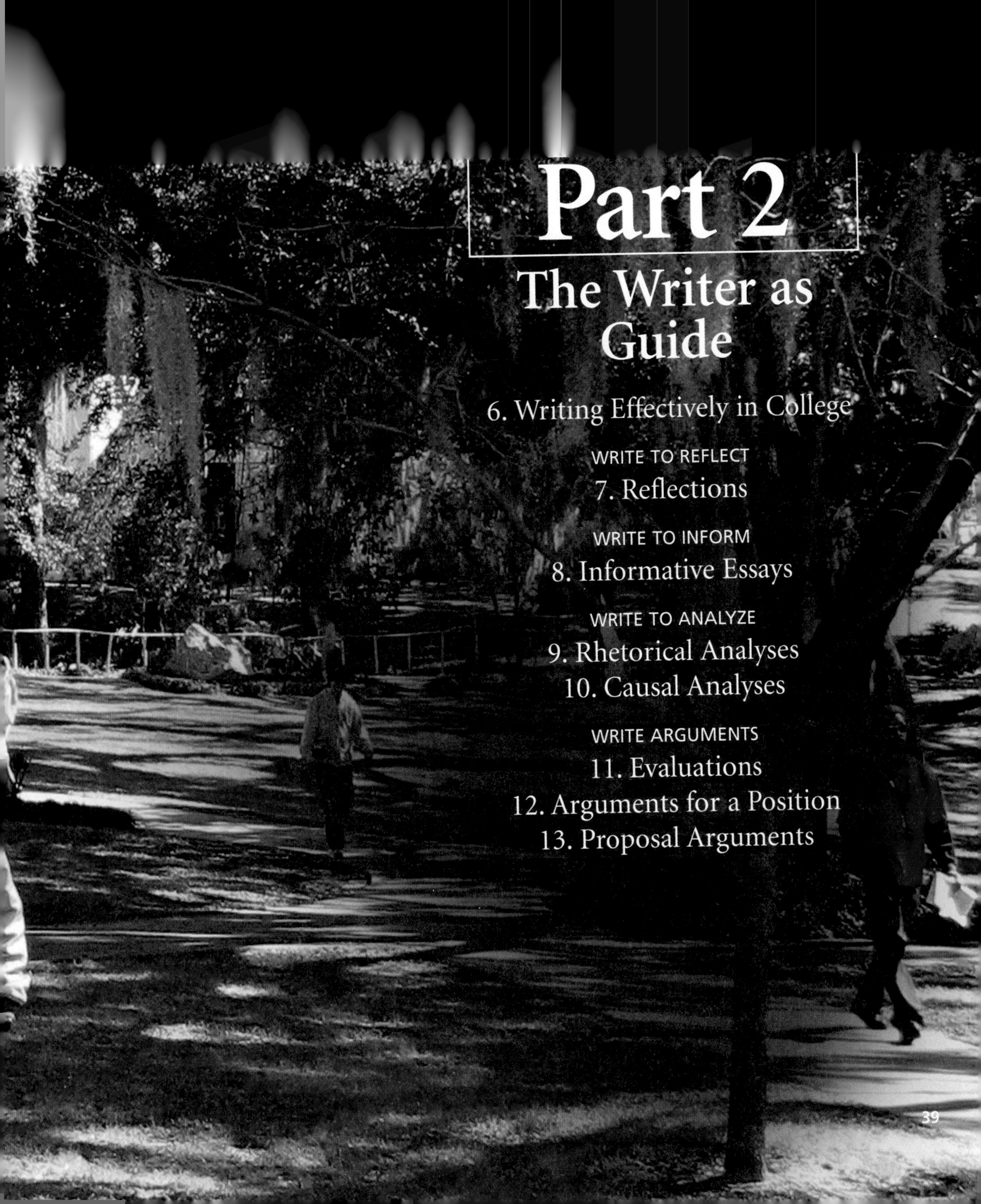

Part 2

The Writer as Guide

6 Writing Effectively in College

Writers today do many different kinds of writing for multiple purposes.

Understand the demands of writing in college

Writing in college changes from course to course depending on the requirements of the course's discipline. What is expected in a philosophy course differs from what is expected in a biology course.

Nevertheless, there are some common expectations about writing in college that extend across disciplines.

Writing in college . . .	Writers are expected to . . .
States explicit claims	Make a claim that isn't obvious. The claim is often called a thesis statement.
Develops an argument	Support their claims with facts, evidence, reasons, and testimony from experts.
Analyzes with insight	Analyze in depth what they read and view.
Investigates complexity	Explore the complexity of a subject, challenging their readers by asking "Have you thought about this?" or "What if you discard the usual way of thinking about a subject and take the opposite point of view?"
Organizes with a hierarchical structure	Make the major parts evident to readers and indicate which parts are subordinate to others.
Signals with transitions	Indicate logical relationships clearly so readers can follow a pathway without getting lost.
Documents sources carefully	Provide the sources of information so readers can consult the same sources the writer used.

Aim	Focus	Example genres
Writing to reflect	**Reflections:** Narrating personal experience and personal insights for a public audience (Chapter 7) 54	Journals, personal letters, blogs, memoirs, essays
Writing to inform	**Informative essays:** Communicating information clearly (Chapter 8) 94	Newspaper and magazine articles, academic articles, reports, profiles, essays
Writing to analyze	**Rhetorical analyses:** Analyzing what makes a text successful and why the author made particular choices (Chapter 9) 152	Rhetorical analysis, literary analysis, visual analysis, essays
	Causal analyses: Exploring why an event, phenomenon, or trend happened (Chapter 10) 194	History, accident analysis, financial analysis, essays
Writing arguments	**Evaluations:** Assessing whether something is good or bad according to particular criteria (Chapter 11) 244	Reviews, essays, performance evaluations, product evaluations
	Arguments for a position: Convincing others through reasoned argument to accept or reject a position (Chapter 12) 286	Speeches, letters to the editor, op-ed columns, editorials, essays
	Proposal arguments: Convincing others through reasoned argument to take action (Chapter 13) 336	Speeches, business proposals, grant proposals, essays, advocacy Web sites

Use your aim as a guide

In many cases, if you know your aim in advance, you have a good start toward how to structure your paper or project.

For example, you might want to evaluate a Shetland Sheepdog (sheltie) as a breed. For an evaluation, you know that your thesis will take the form of ______ is a good/bad, better/best/worst _______ according to these criteria: ______, _______, _______. With this guide, you come up with the following: *The sheltie is one of the best breeds because shelties are highly intelligent, extremely loyal, responsive, and easy to train.*

Chapters 7 through 13 show you how to use your aim to guide the development of your paper or project.

Working Together

Use aims to create thesis statements

In a group of three or four students

Come up with a list of subjects that your group has some interest in and knows something about. They could be big subjects like global warming or more limited subjects like your school's shuttle bus system.

As a group, brainstorm thesis statements for at least three aims. For example, on the subject of eating disorders, you might come up with something like the following.

Writing to reflect
My younger sister overcame her bulemia disorder during her last two years of high school when successes in school and in music improved her self-esteem.

Writing to inform
Anorexia nervosa is diagnosed when patients weigh 15% under the normal body weight for their height and is characterized by starvation, excessive exercise, and sometimes forced vomiting.

Writing to analyze
The causes of eating disorders are not a failure of will but are medical illnesses that take on a life of their own.

Writing arguments
Less money and effort should be spent to find drugs to treat eating disorders, and more effort should go toward teaching adolescents to deal with negative thoughts about their bodies and to develop a positive body image.

Think about your genre

Be aware of genre

Genre is a term for a kind of writing or form of communication. When you walk into your video store, you find movies classified by genre: action, animation, comedy, documentary, drama, family, horror, sci-fi, and so on. The music industry classifies music by genre: alternative, blues, classical, country, electronic, folk, gospel, jazz, rap, reggae, rock, world, and so on.

Most of the time we recognize genre in writing immediately—junk mail, a letter of application, a novel, a lease for an apartment, an informative brochure. We know a great deal more than just the form. We know, for example, that junk mail is trying to sell something, and we know to be suspicious of any offers of free products. Likewise, we know that the person writing a letter of application wants to get a job or enter a selective program.

Be aware of how genre influences style

The genre you select has a strong influence on the style you use. Compare the first paragraphs of a research report, a news article, and a blog on beach erosion.

Research report

Coastal management as a distinct practice emerged just a few decades ago, when ideas and information were exchanged through mostly conventional means. Scientists and coastal planners gave talks and presented posters at conferences and workshops, as they still do. Field trips and tours organized as part of these events highlighted problems and success stories. Agency experts prepared and distributed reports and guidelines. Academics researched problems and systematically evaluated methods to address them, reporting their results in new periodicals like the *Coastal Zone Management Journal.* Face-to-face meetings, telephone conversations, the U.S. Postal Service, and later the fax machine played key roles in the development of ideas and movement of information to address coastal problems. Working with these communication tools, professionals and concerned citizens alike drew from their personal experience, new state and federal legislative mandates, and a palpable sense of urgency to create a new practice called coastal zone management. At the time, the demand was great for scientific data and information about coastal resources and use, for tools to interpret this information, and for strategies and processes to apply it for problem solving. And the information flowed freely, albeit by slower and less sophisticated means than today.

Innovation by Design: Improving Learning Networks in Coastal Management. Washington, D.C., The Heinz Center, 2004. Print.

News article

When scientists consider the possible effects of global warming, there is a lot they don't know. But they can say one thing for sure: sea levels will rise.

Dean, Cornelia. "New Victim of Global Warming: The Beaches." *New York Times*. New York Times. 20 June 2006. Web. 6 Oct. 2008.

Blog

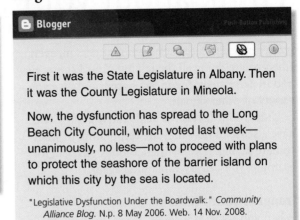

First it was the State Legislature in Albany. Then it was the County Legislature in Mineola.

Now, the dysfunction has spread to the Long Beach City Council, which voted last week—unanimously, no less—not to proceed with plans to protect the seashore of the barrier island on which this city by the sea is located.

"Legislative Dysfunction Under the Boardwalk." *Community Alliance Blog*. N.p. 8 May 2006. Web. 14 Nov. 2008.

Even though each writer is writing about the same subject, notice what is different.

Sentence length	• The report has much longer sentences than the newspaper article or the blog.
Paragraph length	• The report has long paragraphs compared to the short paragraphs of the newspaper article and the blog.
Word choice	• The report uses much more formal language than the blog. The newspaper language is neutral.
Relationship with the reader	• The report and newspaper writers are distant and objective. The blog writer is passionately involved with the issue.

Write Now

Compare styles across genres

Find a newspaper article on a current social, economic, political, or scientific issue. Then find a scholarly article on the same subject using scholar.google.com/ or one of the databases on your library's Web site. Next, search blogs for the same subject using blogsearch.google.com.

Compare the styles of the scholarly article, the newspaper article, and the blog using the following criteria: overall length, paragraph length, sentence length, word choice, relationship with the reader, and use of graphics and images. Write a summary of your analysis.

Think about your audience

When you talk with someone face-to-face, you receive constant feedback from that person, even when you're doing all the talking. Your listener may nod in agreement, frown, act bored, and give you a variety of other signals.

Unless your listener is deliberately acting, you have a sense of how they are responding to what you are saying. If your listener looks puzzled, for example, you can try explaining again.

Imagine your readers

When you write, you rarely receive immediate response from readers. Most of the time you don't know exactly how readers will react to what you write. You have to think consciously about your readers and anticipate how they might respond.

Write for college readers

Readers of college writing expect more than what they can find out from a Google search or an online encyclopedia. Facts are easy to obtain from databases and print sources. Readers want to know how these facts are connected.

Good college writing involves an element of surprise. If readers can predict exactly where a writer is going, even if they fully agree, they will either skim to the end or stop reading. Readers expect you to tell them something that they don't know already.

Analyze advertisements

Magazines sell advertising by targeting specific readers. Bring to class a magazine that you read regularly or one that you find interesting. Organize in groups of three or four students and exchange magazines with each other. Look at the articles and the advertising in the magazine.

Analyze your classmate's magazine for these criteria.

1. What is the target age group?
2. What percentages of men and women are likely to read the magazine?
3. What income level is targeted?
4. Is a particular ethnicity being targeted?
5. What else is being assumed about the audience? For magazines that cover a specific subject or activity (for example, backpacking, beauty, snowboarding, parenting, fitness, cats, and so on), what other products and services do you find being advertised?

Share your analysis with other members of your group. Ask the person who brought the magazine you analyzed if he or she agrees with your description of the target audience.

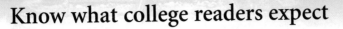

Staying on Track

Know what college readers expect

Readers expect to be challenged.
Simple answers that can be easily looked up are not adequate.

OFF TRACK
The United States entered World War II when the Japanese attacked Pearl Harbor on December 7, 1941. *(This fact is well known and not informative for college readers.)*

ON TRACK
The war with Japan actually began on July 25, 1941, when President Franklin Roosevelt froze Japanese assets and declared an oil embargo, leaving the Japanese with the choices of abandoning the war with China or neutralizing the United States Navy in order to secure oil resources in Indonesia.

Readers expect claims to be backed up with reasons and evidence.
Simple explanations without support are not adequate.

OFF TRACK
New York City is an exciting place to live, but I wouldn't want to move there because of the crime. *(Is crime really that much higher in New York City?)*

ON TRACK
Many people don't know that New York City is the safest large city in the United States according to FBI crime statistics. It even ranks in the top 20 safest cities among the 210 cities with populations over 100,000.

Readers expect complex answers for complex problems.
Simple solutions for complex problems are not adequate.

OFF TRACK
We need posters urging students not to litter so much on campus. *(Are posters alone likely to solve the problem?)*

ON TRACK
Most of the litter on our campus is paper, bottles, and cans—all recyclable—yet there are almost no recycle containers on campus. Putting recycle containers in high-litter locations along with a "don't litter" campaign could go a long way toward making our campus cleaner.

Readers expect writers to be engaged.
Readers expect writers to be curious and genuinely concerned about their subjects.

OFF TRACK
Older people have to deal with too much bureaucracy to obtain health care. *(The statement rings true but doesn't motivate readers.)*

ON TRACK
After spending a day with my 78-year-old aunt sorting through stacks of booklets and forms and waiting on a help line that never answered, I became convinced that the Medicare prescription drug program is an aging American's worst nightmare.

Think about your credibility

Some writers begin with credibility because of who they are. If you wonder what foods compose a balanced meal for your dog, you probably would listen carefully to the advice of a veterinarian. Most writers, however, have to convince their readers to keep reading by demonstrating knowledge of their subject and concern with their readers' needs.

Think about how you want your readers to see you

To get your readers to take you seriously, you must convince them that they can trust you. You need to get them to see you as

Concerned

Readers want you to be committed to what you are writing about. They also expect you to be concerned with them as readers. After all, if you don't care about them, why should they read what you write?

Well informed

Many people ramble on about any subject without knowing anything about it. If they are family members, you have to suffer their opinions, but it is not enjoyable. College writing requires that you do your homework on a subject.

Fair

Many writers look at only one side of an issue. Readers respect objectivity and an unbiased approach.

Ethical

Many writers use only the facts that support their positions and often distort facts and sources. Critical readers often notice what is being left out. Don't try to conceal what doesn't support your position.

Staying on Track

Build your credibility

Know what's at stake

What you are writing about should matter to your readers. If its importance is not evident, it's your job to explain why your readers should consider it important.

OFF TRACK

We should be concerned about two-thirds of Central and South America's 110 brightly colored harlequin frog species becoming extinct in the last twenty years. *(The loss of any species is unfortunate, but the writer gives us no other reason for concern.)*

ON TRACK

The rapid decline of amphibians worldwide due to global warming may be the advance warning of the loss of cold-weather species such as polar bears, penguins, and reindeer.

Staying on Track

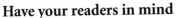

Have your readers in mind

If you are writing about a specialized subject that your readers don't know much about, take the time to explain key concepts.

OFF TRACK

Reduction in the value of a debt security, especially a bond, results from a rise in interest rates. Conversely, a decline in interest rates results in an increase in the value of a debt security, especially bonds. *(The basic idea is here, but it is not expressed clearly, especially if the reader is not familiar with investing.)*

ON TRACK

Bond prices move inversely to interest rates. When interest rates go up, bond prices go down, and when interest rates go down, bond prices go up.

Think about alternative solutions and points of view

Readers appreciate a writer's ability to see a subject from multiple perspectives.

OFF TRACK

We will reduce greenhouse gas and global warming only if we greatly increase wind-generated electricity. *(Wind power is an alternative energy source, but it is expensive and many people don't want windmills in scenic areas. The writer also doesn't mention using energy more efficiently.)*

ON TRACK

If the world is serious about limiting carbon emissions to reduce global warming, then along with increasing efficient energy use, all non-carbon-emitting energy sources must be considered, including nuclear power. Nuclear power now produces about 20% of U.S. electricity with no emissions—the equivalent of taking 58 million passenger cars off the road.

Write well

Nothing impresses readers more than graceful, fluent writing that is clear, direct, and forceful. Even if readers don't agree with you in the end, they still will appreciate your writing ability.

OFF TRACK

Nobody can live today without taking some risks, even very rich people. After all, we don't know what we're breathing in the air. A lot of food has chemicals and hormones in it. There's a big hole in the ozone, so more people will get skin cancer. And a lot of people have sexually transmitted diseases these days. *(The impact of the point is lost with unfocused writing.)*

ON TRACK

We live in a world of risks beyond our control to the extent that it is difficult to think of anything that is risk free down to the most basic human acts—sex in an era of AIDS, eating in an era of genetically altered food, walking outside in an ozone-depleted atmosphere, drinking water and breathing air laden with chemicals whose effects we do not understand.

Think about how to build on the work of others

All writing builds on the work of others. After all, we write in a language countless people have used before us, giving over time each word its individual meaning. Because ideas are expressed in language, each idea is in some sense recycled. Nevertheless, every time we write, we have the potential to build on existing ideas to create new meanings.

Read to find a question

If you have general interest in a topic, often reading about that topic can help you to find a question to investigate. For example, you may have traveled to Utah, Colorado, New Mexico, or Arizona and visited one of the ruins such as Mesa Verde built by ancient Pueblo peoples and abandoned in the thirteenth century.

Archaeologists know from tree-ring evidence that the area experienced extreme drought, but the reasons for the Pueblo peoples' departure remain controversial. Reading might lead you to a specific question.

> The discovery of twenty-four dismembered human skeletons from an ancient Pueblo site in Colorado dating around 1270–1300 AD suggests that warfare along with drought might have been a cause of abandonment of communities (LeBlanc 174).

Read to find diverse points of view

Readers of college writing on controversial issues expect writers to find and represent fairly different viewpoints on those issues. People often disagree on issues that at first glance might not seem controversial. For example, the conversion of wind energy into electricity is clean, renewable, and reduces carbon emissions by displacing fossil-fuel-generated electricity. Yet wind energy is controversial for a number of reasons. Some environmental groups oppose wind turbines because of danger to birds. If you advocate building more wind turbines, you need to take into account how significant is the potential threat birds.

> Although wind turbines do kill some birds, a article published in prestigious journal *Nature* in 2007 reports that the average yearly bird mortality rate per turbine is .03 or one bird killed for every 33 turbines (Marris and Fairless 126).

Read to find evidence

Readers of college writing expect any claims made by a writer to be supported with evidence. Furthermore, readers expect to be able to check the sources of facts, statistics, and other information; thus, readers expect that all sources will be carefully and accurately cited. For example, you might want to argue that the rapid rise of the price of gasoline during 2007–2008 was a major cause of a tumbling economy, but you will need statistics to argue just how big a bite out of consumer spending could be attributed to increased fuel costs.

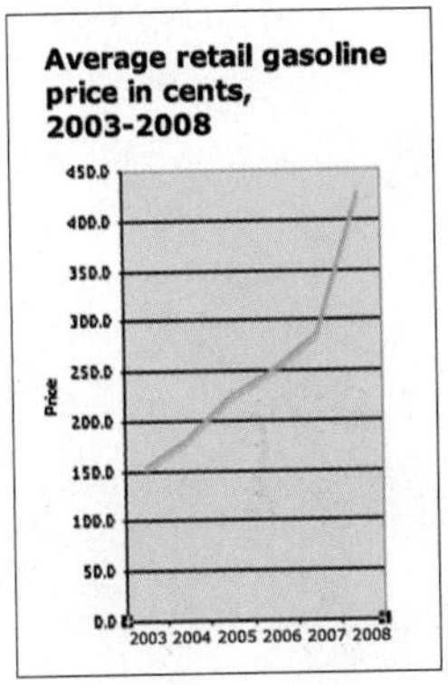

> During 2007 the rise in gasoline prices caused a 55% decline in consumer savings and less spending on cars and furniture (Weller).

Integrate sources into your writing

What you don't want to do with sources

- Let your sources speak for you.
- Fail to introduce a source.
- Fail to indicate the significance of a source for your writing.
- Fail to cite where a source came from.

What you want to do with sources

- Limit the use of long quotations.
- Check that each paraphrase and quotation of a source supports a point you make rather than make the point for you.
- Check that each paraphrase and quotation is introduced and attributed.
- Check that each quotation is accurate and properly formatted.
- Check that you cite the source of each fact that isn't well known and each quotation.

You can find more about integrating the work of others into your writing in Chapter 16.

7 Reflections

A successful reflection challenges readers to find out something about themselves.

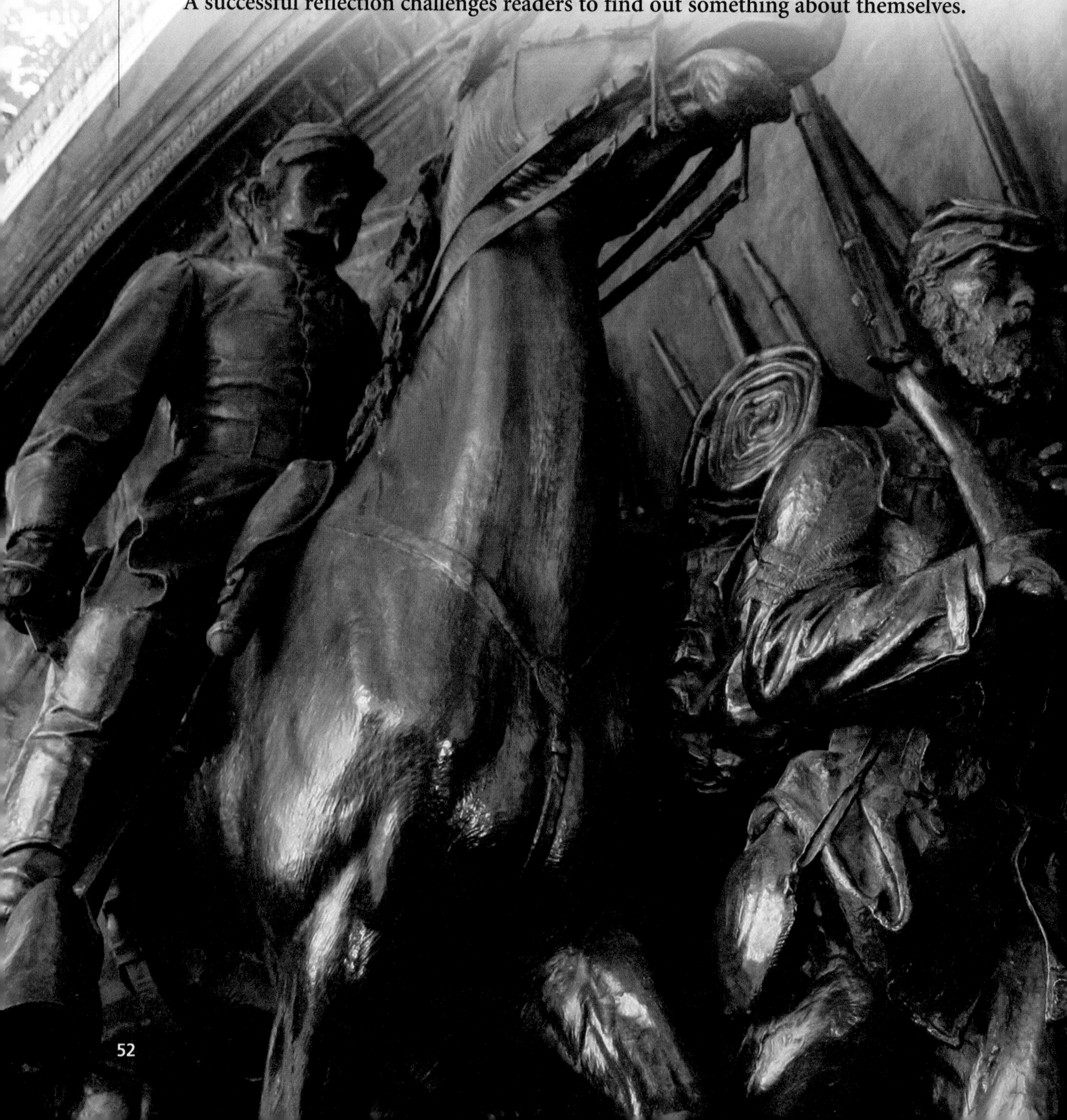

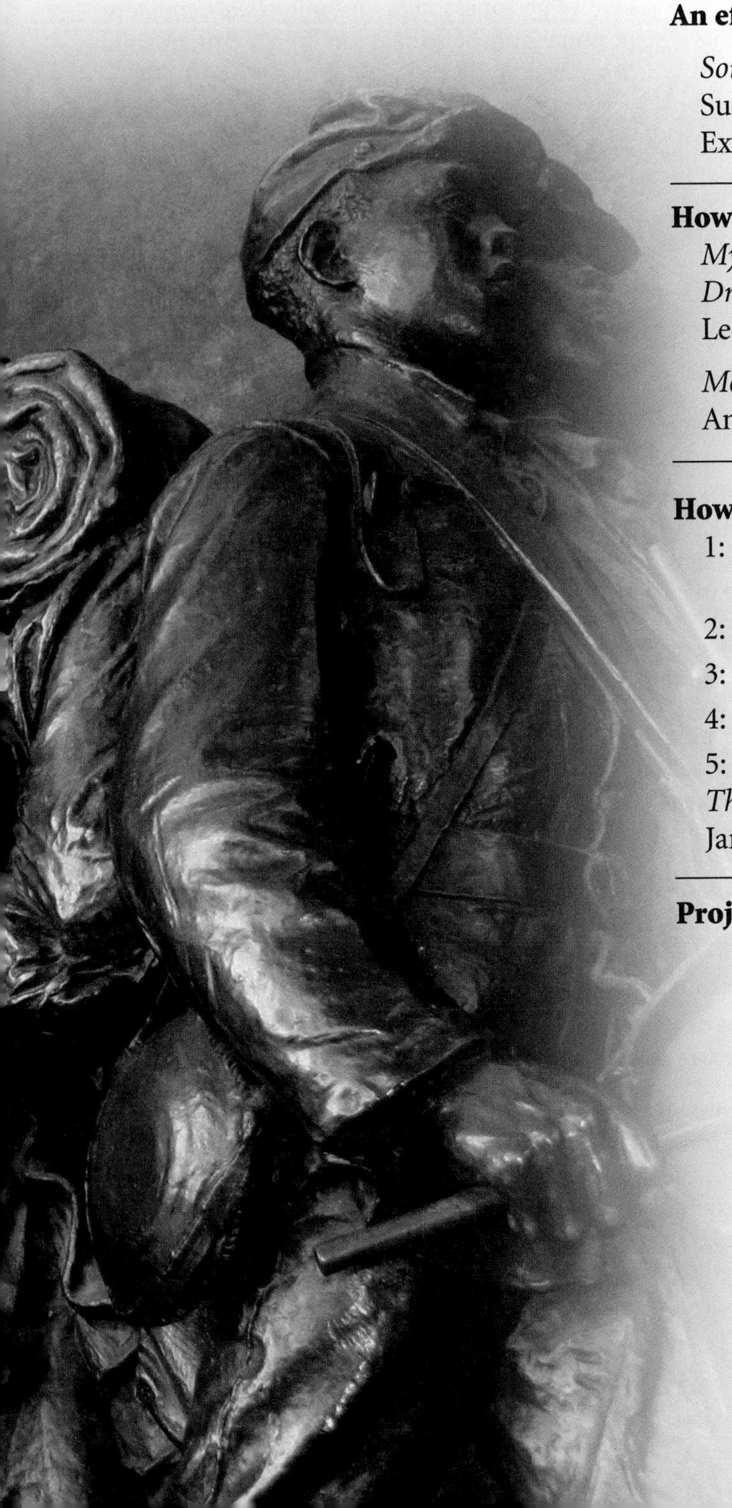

CHAPTER CONTENTS

Writing reflections

When we reflect, we consider an idea or experience in order to come to a greater understanding of its significance. Unless we are writing in a private diary or journal, we use reflective writing to share our experience and its significance with others. Reflecting is also a way of understanding ourselves. By connecting memories of the past to our knowledge in the present, we learn about who we were and who we have become.

Reflective essays can address deeply emotional issues like family relationships, personal failings, and dramatic crises. But reflection does not always involve personal topics. In some cases, being too personal or confessional can limit a writer's ability to connect to his or her audience.

The goal of reflection should not be simply to vent pent-up emotions or to expose secrets (although when done well, these techniques can be effective). Instead, it should allow the audience to share with the writer a discovery of significance. A reflection on an important event in the history of a family should do more than focus on the writer's feelings; it should explore how each family member changed as a result.

Components of reflections

What people, places, and events stand out in my memory?	**Find a reflective topic.** Listing is one way to identify possible topics for reflective writing. You might list people, events, or places that have been significant in your life, then look back over your list and check the items that seem especially vivid to you.
Will my readers be interested?	**Consider your readers.** How interesting will this topic be to your readers? Will they want to share in your experience?
What is my purpose?	**Identify a purpose.** A clear purpose makes the reflection coherent. Your purpose is not to teach a lesson about life but rather to convey the significance of the experience—why it is important or memorable and why it is worth writing and reading about.
What key details communicate the significance of my reflection?	**Provide concrete details.** Concrete details stimulate readers' imagination and make your reflection come alive. Use factual details such as dates to provide background information. Augment visual details with your other senses: smells, sounds, tastes, and feelings. **Use dialogue when possible.** Convey interaction between people with their words.
How do I organize my reflection?	**Think about your organization.** Telling what happened in a chronological order is the simplest organization for writers to use, but it is not the only one possible. Conceptual order explores different points and links them together. For example, you might reflect on a photograph, examining details one by one and discussing how they related to your family's past.

What is the most engaging way to begin?

Start fast. The beginning of a reflection must show the writer's involvement and gain the reader's interest.

Finish strong. Effective conclusions invite readers to reflect further. Ending with a question or an issue to think about is usually better than trying to sum up with a moral lesson.

Keys to reflections

Snapshots freeze important moments in people's lives.

Tell a good story. Readers have to be interested in your story to understand the significance. Often reflections gain and keep readers' interest by presenting a conflict or a difficult decision that must be resolved.

Let the details convey the significance. Select details carefully to communicate meaning. Identify people by more than how they look. Think about mannerisms, gestures, and habits to suggest their character.

Be honest. Telling the truth about your thoughts and actions can build a strong rapport with your audience, but beware of becoming sentimental. Too much emotion may turn readers off.

Focus on the little things in life. A reflection need not reveal earth-shattering secrets or teach crucial life lessons. It may be as simple as describing something that makes you happy. Remember that small moments of significance can be just as rewarding for readers as great events.

For a reflection on an image or object, let the reflection grow out of the details. Your close reading of details and your explanation of the significance of the experience is critical.

Working Together

Reflecting on photographs

In a group of three or four students

- Look at a selection of photographs from newspapers, magazines, or a photo Web log such as Flickr.
- Have each person work with two or three photos, making a list of the people each image reminds you of, the things the image makes you think about, and the places you associate with the image. Write a brief narrative for each image.
- Share your memories and narratives with the group. Which ones strike you as the most engaging and interesting? How would you develop or change the narratives of other students?

An effective reflection

Effective reflective writing can only come after honest examination of memories, perceptions, and meanings.

Some Lines for a Younger Brother . . .

Sue Kunitomi Embrey

Sue Kunitomi Embrey was born in Los Angeles and lived there until she and her family were forced to move to the Manzanar War Relocation Camp on May 9, 1942, where she stayed until the end of World War II. She has become a spokeswoman for the thousands of Japanese Americans who were incarcerated during the anti-Japanese hysteria of that time. In this essay, she recalls the life and death of her youngest brother Tets, who spent three years of his childhood in Manzanar.

Some Lines for a Younger Brother . . .

I still remember the day he was born. It was early April and Papa came into the kitchen with a smile on his face. He said we had a baby brother. In the months to follow, we were busy carrying and cuddling the brother who was many years younger than the rest of us. When he cried from hunger and Mama was busy, one of us would run into the bedroom and rock the bed or pick him up and quiet him.

Embrey begins with her earliest memory of her brother, making it clear that he will be the focus of her reflection.

We were a family of five sons and three daughters. Money was scarce. My father ran a moving and transfer business in L'il Tokyo, the Japanese community in the shadow of City Hall in Los Angeles, but people had little money to pay him. He came home with boxes of books bartered for his services, and we spent many hours curled up in a corner reading some popular fiction story.

Tets, as we called him, was eight years old when Papa was killed in an automobile accident a week before Christmas. Tets cried because he could not give his dad the present he had made at school. The bullies would beat him up now that he had no father, he said.

Pearl Harbor was attacked by the Japanese when Tets was in elementary school. Rumors of sabotage couldn't be separated from the facts. Soon there was a

Outside events are fitted into the family's personal chronology. Embrey shows vividly the impact of the decision to intern Japanese Americans.

clamor on the West Coast for wholesale evacuation of all Japanese into inland camps. The democratic process was lost in hysteria. The grocery store which we had purchased only a year before was sold at a loss. All the furniture we couldn't sell, the plants my mother had tenderly cared for, our small personal treasures went to a neighborhood junk dealer. Tears came when we saw the truck being loaded.

On the first Sunday in May, 1942, Manzanar Relocation Center became our war-time home. Before breakfast, we walked around the dry, dusty land, to get acquainted with the landscape. The sun sparkled against the Sierra Nevada mountains to the west. The brown Inyo hills were high-rising barriers, more formidable than the barbed wire which was soon to enclose us. As we wondered how the pioneers had crossed over the Sierras, someone asked, "How long do we have to stay here?" and someone quoted from the military instructions, "For the duration of the war, and six months thereafter." Six months are forever, and forever is a long, long time.

Details about the relocation camp reinforce the sense of isolation and hopelessness it evokes.

Some order became evident within a few months after the fear, confusion and shock of transplantation from the big city to the arid land of Manzanar. Catholic nuns, who had joined the evacuees, found empty barracks and started a school. The War Relocation Authority recruited teachers from the "outside." Many of them were Quakers with a real desire to serve their fellow man.

When I asked Tets what he was studying, he shrugged his shoulders. There were no chairs, no desks, no supplies, he said. "What's the use of studying American history when we're behind barbed wires?" he asked. I tried to tell him that it would matter some day, but I was not sure any more. "Someday," I said, "the government would realize it had made a mistake and would try to correct it." His eyes were narrow against the noon sun, his whole body positioned badly to the right as he looked at me and said, "You 'da kind'? I lose fight." The colloquial speech was everywhere among the second generation. "Da kind" categorically placed me among those who argued for and defended American democracy. The second expression was used

Embrey uses dialogue to recount a significant conversation she had with her brother, one that she has remembered for many years.

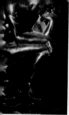

constantly, but it meant different things to different people.

"Try walking out that gate," he added. "See if they don't shoot you in the back." With that, he walked away.

The rest of us managed to get out of confinement—to Chicago, to Madison, Wisconsin. Three brothers entered the United States Army. Tets was left with his aging mother and he was to spend almost three years behind barbed wires.

By 1948 when the family was partially reunited and settled in Los Angeles, Tets was in high school, or we thought he was. One day a school counselor came to the door. He reported that Tets had not been in school for several weeks and that he had been missing school sporadically for several months. He saw the shock on our faces. We had been too busy working to be suspicious.

"I'm looking for a job," Tets said, when confronted.

"But you can't find a job without a high school diploma," I protested.

"So I found out," he answered. "Learning to say 'isn't' instead of 'ain't' doesn't get you a job. They want us to have experience to land a job, but how can we get experience if we can't get a job?"

I asked him what he was going to do.

"I'm going to join the Army," was his reply.

Day in and day out, this was his argument. "I'm going to join the Army when I'm eighteen. You won't have me around to bother you and I'll be doing some traveling. I'm tired of holding up the buildings in L'il Tokyo. There's nothing to do and no place to go where I can be with my friends."

He was sure that wars were over for a while and there would be no danger. He signed up one day and was gone the next. He came home on furlough, husky and tanned, a lot taller and more confident than when he had left. He had been in training camp in Louisiana and had seen much of the country. Before he left, he broke the news to us that he had signed up for another three years so he wouldn't have to serve in the reserves. He was transferred to the West Coast and we saw him often when he hitch-hiked home on

Again, Embrey uses dialogue to show viewers a turning point in her brother's life. As in the internment camp, this argument centers on whether he should go to school, but it is clear there are deeper issues at play for Embrey and for Tets.

weekends. One day he phoned collect from San Jose. He was being shipped out to Japan and it would probably be a year before he would be back.

His hitch was almost over when the Korean War broke out. Soon after his 22nd birthday, he wrote that he hoped to be home for Christmas. He explained that he had not been sleeping well lately since some veterans had been brought into his barracks. They had nightmares and they screamed in the night. The stories of war they told could not be shut out of his mind. There was a rumor going around that his company might be going over to replace the first groups. He hoped his timetable for discharge would not change. He was worried and that was why he had not written.

Embrey uses vivid detail to re-create her dead brother's funeral.

Tets came home before Christmas. He came home in a flag-draped coffin, with one of his buddies as a military escort. The funeral at the Koyasan Buddhist Church was impressive. There was a change of guards every few minutes. Their soft-spoken order mixed with the solemn chants. The curling incense smoke made hazy halos of the young faces who came mourning a dead friend.

On December 27, 1969, I joined several hundred young people who made a day-long pilgrimage to the Manzanar cemetery. While I helped clean out the sagebrush and manzanilla, pulled tumbleweeds out of my boots, I was interrupted many times to recall facts and figures for the NBC and CBS television crews who were there to record the event.

Mt. Williamson's peak crested somewhere in the grey clouds that drew menacingly closer as the hours passed. Soon there was no sun. No seven-mile shadow lay across Owens Valley.

Embrey ends with an almost wistful recollection of her brother.

Dedication services ended that freezing, windswept and emotional day. I looked beyond the crowd and the monument. Out of the painful memories my mind dusted out of the past, I saw again the blurred impressions of the barbed-wire fence, the sentry towers and the tar-papered barracks. For a moment I saw again the 12-year-old boy with his head cocked, his shoulders sagging, his eyes fighting to keep open in the sun, while the long and lonely desert stretched out behind him.

Explore Current Issues

Can a memory make an argument?

In her memoir, *The Hypocrisy of Disco: A Memoir*, Clane Hayward describes her childhood living in and out of communes in Northern California in the 1970s with her mother H'lane, her brother Haud, and her little sister Ki. In one chapter, Clane tells about her and her brother's sporadic schooling:

> At some point H'lane sent me and Haud to school. She did this in an offhand way, now and then in different places, in the middle of the school year or at the end, she didn't care. Schools are zoos run by the government to keep kids in cages, she said. Schools teach kids how to live in cages. Do you want to learn how to be straight, she would ask, with the I Ching laying open on the floor next to her, while she counted yarrow sticks in her lap. The skirts spread wide around her, incense burning, Ki chewing on one of the sticks and watching with her wide serious eyes. If being straight means wearing clothes that match and eating hot lunch, then yes, I want to be straight, I thought but didn't say.

Write about it

1. What does Hayward's description tell the reader about her mother H'lane? How do the details convey this information?
2. What does this passage tell you about Hayward? What does it tell you about her life at this time and her feelings about it? What does it tell you about her possible feelings about it now, as an adult looking back?
3. Hayward's book is a memoir, an account of her life during a specific period of time. Can a more general argument be made from her unique experiences? If so, what might that argument be?

How to read reflections

Make notes as you read, either in the margins or on paper or a computer file. Circle any words or references that you don't know and look them up.

What is it?	• What kind of a text is it? A memoir? a letter? a diary? an essay? a short story? a photographic essay? What are your expectations for this kind of text? • What media are used? (Web sites, for example, often combine images, words, and sounds.)
Where did it come from?	• Who wrote the reflection? • What do you know about the writer's background that might have influenced the reflection?
Who is the intended audience?	• What clues do you find about whom the writer had in mind as the readers? • What does the writer assume that the readers already know about the subject? • What new knowledge is the writer providing?
What is the significance of the reflection?	• Does the writer give precise, objective, concrete details? • Does the writer comment on the reflections? • What did you learn or come to understand differently by reading the reflection?
How is the reflection organized?	• Chronologically? In order of perceived importance? Or some other way?
How is it composed?	• How does the writer represent herself or himself? • How would you characterize the style? • How effective is the design? Is it easy to read? • If there are any photographs or other graphics, what information do they contribute?

My Dropout Boyfriend Kept Dropping In

(ESSAY)

Lee Conell

Lee Conell was in her junior year at the State University of New York at New Paltz when she wrote "My Dropout Boyfriend Kept Dropping In." She entered the essay in the Modern Love essay contest sponsored by the *New York Times* and was one of the five finalists out of the 1200 essays submitted. Conell's essay was published in the *New York Times* on June 1, 2008.

Return to these questions after you have finished reading.

Analyzing and Connecting

1. How does Conell describe Terry? What details does she use? How does her description of Terry affect the reflection as a whole?
2. In her reflection, Conell describes photographs she and Terry took during a visit to the Cloisters. Why did Conell choose to describe these photos? What do the photos tell about Terry? About the author? About their relationship?
3. The specter of real homelessness enters Conell's reflection a few times—for example, when she mentions how the economy can cause people to veer from their expected paths and when she mentions the campus "sleep out." How does Conell use these moments? How do they affect the reader's perception of Terry's experiment?
4. Conell admits that Terry's failure makes her feel "superior" about her own "safe choices." But she concludes by saying that this feeling "was hardly something to celebrate, and the dreamer in me knew it." What does she mean? Do you think it is an effective way to conclude the reflection? Why or why not?

Finding Ideas for Writing

Do you know someone like Terry? Or, are you the "Terry" of your family or group of friends? Choose a moment, similar to Conell's description of the visit to the Cloisters, and write a short reflection telling how this moment describes this person and your relationship to him or her. Or, if you are the adventurer, focus on how this moment represents the perceptions people have of you and your choices and your reaction to these perceptions.

In April of my freshman year, my boyfriend, Terry, decided he wanted to be homeless. Among the decisions I expected a college-age boyfriend to make (changing cellphone plans, or maybe going vegan), homelessness was not one of them.

Still, I took the situation calmly. I had known Terry since high school and had watched him pass through various phases: Goth, punk, anarchist, Marxist and Zen. When he explained that he was giving up his room to live on the farms and in the woods surrounding our Hudson Valley college town, I did not make a scene. I told myself this, too, would pass and politely asked him why he did not want to live in a house.

"I want to try to exist as free from material stuff as possible," he said.

I squinted at him. "But I like your apartment. It's in a great location."

Terry looked straight into my eyes. "This is just something I have to do for myself."

I didn't say anything. It's hard to argue with that personal power stuff.

Over dinner that evening, I told a girl who lived in my dorm about Terry's plan. "I'm really worried about it," I said.

A matter-of-fact business major from Brooklyn, she blurted, "He's crazy!" She plunged her fork into a pile of rice, and then offered a thinly veiled criticism of me: "I would never put up with that."

"He's not so crazy," I told her. "He's going to be saving a lot of money. And I can understand wanting to feel close to nature."

"No," she said. "He's definitely crazy."

My roommate was equally nonplused. Where would he keep his stuff or brush his teeth? Could a city kid like him really transition into the life of an ascetic?

I had no answers. How would I explain his decision to others? Shouldn't I have seen this coming? Several months earlier, Terry had given me the book *Into the Wild* for Valentine's Day (because nothing says "I love you" like the story of a young man starving to death in the Alaskan wilderness). That should have been a clue.

Luckily, Terry wouldn't have to worry about starvation in his own foray: he had a girlfriend with a college meal plan. I pictured myself sneaking cookies out of the dining hall and heading into the woods. People would think I was harboring an escaped convict.

An *Oprah*-esque voice in my head said: It doesn't matter what people think as long as he feels fulfilled. But another voice in my head, the one that avoided self-help books and talk shows, was less convinced. That voice told me times had changed, and we weren't in high school anymore.

Back then, before we started dating, Terry's acts of rebellion had impressed and attracted me. Just standing next to him, a boy who wore eyeliner and a safety pin through his eyebrow, was an easy and efficient way for me to act out. But I hadn't been Terry's friend only for rebellion's sake. At heart, I understood and agreed with many of his ideas. I just expressed my agreement quietly.

His Zen phase, for example, occurred at the same time as mine, in sophomore year of high school. But while I meditated alone in my bedroom, Terry would meditate publicly: in our high school hallway, on the subway and even, as a photograph I have demonstrates, under a fountain at the Cloisters in New York City (his lined eyelids shut serenely, legs crossed in lotus, bemused museum visitors stopping to stare).

In another photograph from the same day, I also sit under that fountain, but my eyes are wide open and I'm smiling sheepishly, aware of how I stick out, a teenager crouched on the ground, surrounded by medieval art.

We were attending separate colleges when Terry and I started dating in our freshman year, but after several months Terry, unhappy with school, dropped out.

This I defended to friends who gaped at the news by telling them that he was acting against the system, against the overplanned life of studying, choosing our majors, plotting out our meek life goals. What Terry was doing, I told them, was courageous, and I supported his decision even as I spent my nights in the library working wholly within the system to plot out my very own meek life goals.

When he rented a room in my college town and took a job as a taxi dispatcher, I was glad to have him nearby. Still, with the outdoors experiment beginning, I wasn't sure how his roof-free life would mesh with my own. I had thought the enormous buildup to college — APs, SATs, and other nefarious acronyms — was supposed to pave the way to middle-class normalcy, which didn't involve having to deal with decisions like Terry's.

Sure, you might get involved in the occasional good-natured protest, but over all once you attended college, you were on the straight-and-narrow path. Or at least, if the economy didn't sink, you were on the non-homeless path.

If Terry began to spend his free time lost in the woods finding himself, meditating next to a squirrel, in a state of perpetual nirvana, where would that leave me? Laboring away under fluorescent lighting? Of course, that was what I had chosen, just as I had chosen to smile for the camera under the fountain at the Cloisters while Terry sought the meaning of life in the same spot.

It was growing dark. I had an essay to start, a test coming up. Then there would be laundry to do, followed by several halfhearted attempts at matching socks and cleaning my side of the room. I took a deep breath and looked out my window. As I watched the light change, I thought of Terry underneath that sky.

Then I realized that I was jealous.

What sort of lessons would I learn if I fell asleep each night under the stars? What would happen if I left school and followed Terry's footsteps? I knew I wouldn't do it, being overly fond of my books, my room's four walls and the Internet. Still, I couldn't stop one image from transposing itself onto my textbooks: me, lying by a brook at night, listening to its babbling, knowing I was going down my own wide-open path.

But once the experiment was under way, I realized that even when you are fully committed to treading that unbeaten path, it's not so easy to lose yourself in the woods, particularly if you're from Queens and scared of the dark. On one of his first nights outdoors, around midnight, Terry called me at my dorm. In a small voice he asked, "Can I come over?"

He had been trying to sleep in an apple orchard. As darkness enveloped him, the apple trees began to look less like trees and more like zombies with skeleton hands. Terry was frightened by the scuttling sounds in the bushes, and just as frightened when the sounds stopped.

"It's really dark," he said in a hollow, frightened voice. "I'm worried the farmer might find me and shoot me."

So I told him to come by. And I made the same offer again and again over the following weeks, when around midnight my phone would ring, and Terry would ask me for shelter. He would say it was too cold for him to sleep outdoors, or that he thought he heard rabid dogs, or that the night seemed particularly dark.

Although he did manage to spend a bunch of full nights out there somewhere, he only became edgier as the experiment continued. Whenever I saw him early in the day, if he wasn't cranky from sleep deprivation, he would be twitchy with anxiety, watching the sky for the looming dark, for a sign that the time of terror approached. Conversation centered on where his sleeping spot for the night would be, and how cold Weather.Com said it would become.

I couldn't help but entertain the ways I would have done things differently if I were in his shoes, taking advantage of the peace in a way he seemed unable to do: sitting serenely in the wilderness, studying the movements of the stars, composing poetry about humanity's unbalanced relationship with the natural world and communing with the Disney-eyed wildlife around me. I would certainly not be scared of the dark and a few barking dogs.

Deep down, though, I knew I would be just as scared, or even more scared. And so I felt a little triumphant every time Terry's experiment went south, which happened often enough.

One night, bedded down by a river, he fell asleep with pepper spray in his grasp. Later he brushed his face with the back of his hand and immediately his eyes began to burn. Pepper spray had gotten onto his skin. Eyes smarting and sleep impossible, he walked out of the wooded area and into town, where he spent a few hours sleeping at a coin laundry before being awakened by the police. They threatened to arrest him, but let him go because they were impressed he had a legitimate day job.

That dispatcher job would prove handy during Terry's time outdoors, as it provided him with a bathroom for tooth brushing and face washing, two activities that became difficult in the wilderness. Dorms were useful for showering. The grungier Terry looked, the easier it was for him to pass as a college student, so it wasn't difficult for him to sneak into campus bathrooms.

Still, amid the run-in with the police, sleep deprivation and treks to showers, the ideology behind his experiment began to melt away. This became clear to me after I told him that the hunger and homelessness group on campus was doing a "sleep out." Students would spend one night sleeping outside a campus building to raise awareness about homelessness.

"Oh!" Terry exclaimed happily. "Maybe I'll do it with them. It'd be less scary if I could sleep near other people."

Not long after, he began spending most nights on the foldout couch outside my dorm room. In June he rented a room, at which point the experiment was declared over.

"Terry's living indoors now!" I bragged to friends.

Terry and I are still seeing each other, and he continues to live under a roof.

But my happiness at the experiment's failure had a darker side. In truth I had enjoyed watching his forays into the wilderness fail night after night because each retreat made me feel better, even superior, about my own safe choices: roof, college, stability. And Terry's final surrender only drove home the point.

This was hardly something to celebrate, and the dreamer in me knew it.

Mother Tongue

(ESSAY)

Amy Tan

Amy Tan is a world-renowned writer for her novels that concern the bonds between Chinese American mothers and daughters. She has introduced a rich world of Chinese myth and history to a global audience, but her themes of love and forgiveness are universal. Tan began writing fiction along with playing the piano to curb her workaholic tendencies, but with the publication of *The Joy Luck Club* in 1989, her talent as a writer became widely celebrated. She reflects on her career in this essay.

Return to these questions after you have finished reading.

Analyzing and Connecting

1. How did Tan's attitude toward her mother's language change over the years? Use evidence from the text to support your statements.

2. Tan writes about value judgments based on language. How does Tan account for these judgments?

3. Why was Tan's awareness of different Englishes important to her development as a writer?

4. Near the end, Tan says an insight she had as a beginning writer was to imagine a reader. Why was imagining a reader so important?

Finding Ideas for Writing

Tan says, "recently I was made aware of all of the different Englishes I do use." What different Englishes, or other languages, do you use? List each and explain the different contexts and relationships in which you use them.

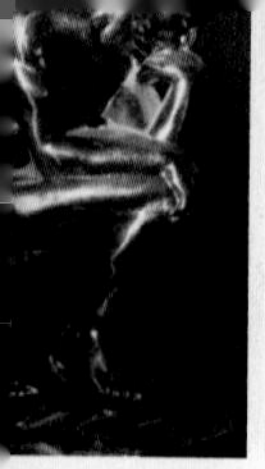

MOTHER TONGUE

I am not a scholar of English or literature. I cannot give you much more than personal opinions on the English language and its variations in this country or others. I am a writer. And by that definition, I am someone who has always loved language. I am fascinated by language in daily life. I spend a great deal of my time thinking about the power of language—the way it can evoke an emotion, a visual image, a complex idea, or a simple truth. Language is the tool of my trade. And I use them all—all the Englishes I grew up with.

Recently, I was made keenly aware of the different Englishes I do use. I was giving a talk to a large group of people, the same talk I had already given to half a dozen other groups. The nature of the talk was about my writing, my life, and my book, *The Joy Luck Club*. The talk was going along well enough, until I remembered one major difference that made the whole talk sound wrong. My mother was in the room. And it was perhaps the first time she had heard me give a lengthy speech, using the kind of English I have never used with her. I was saying things like, "The intersection of memory upon imagination" and "There is an aspect of my fiction that relates to thus-and-thus"—a speech filled with carefully wrought grammatical phrases, burdened, it suddenly seemed to me, with nominalized forms, past perfect tenses, conditional phrases, all the forms of standard English that I had learned in school and through books, the forms of English I did not use at home with my mother.

Just last week, I was walking down the street with my mother, and I again found myself conscious of the English I was using, the English I do use with her. We were talking about the price of new and used furniture and I heard myself saying this: "Not waste money that way." My husband was with us as well, and he didn't notice any switch in my English. And then I realized why. It's because over the twenty years we've been together I've often used that same kind of English with him, and sometimes he even

uses it with me. It has become our language of intimacy, a different sort of English that relates to family talk, the language I grew up with.

So you'll have some idea of what this family talk I heard sounds like, I'll quote what my mother said during a recent conversation which I videotaped and then transcribed. During this conversation, my mother was talking about a political gangster in Shanghai who had the same last name as her family's, Du, and how the gangster in his early years wanted to be adopted by her family, which was rich by comparison. Later, the gangster became more powerful, far richer than my mother's family, and one day showed up at my mother's wedding to pay his respects. Here's what she said in part:

Du-Yusong having business like fruit stand. Like off the street kind. He is Du like Du Zong—but not Tsung-ming Island people. The local people call putong, the river east side, he belong to that side local people. That man want to ask DuZong father take him in like become own family. Du Zong father wasn't look down on him, but didn't take seriously, until that man big like become a mafia. Now important person, very hard to inviting him. Chinese way, came only to show respect, don't stay for dinner. Respect for making big celebration, he shows up. Mean gives lots of respect. Chinese custom. Chinese social life that way. If too important won't have to stay too long. He come to my wedding. I didn't see, I heard it. I gone to boy's side, they have YMCA dinner. Chinese age I was nineteen.

You should know that my mother's expressive command of English belies how much she actually understands. She reads the *Forbes* report, listens to *Wall Street Week*, converses daily with her stockbroker, reads all of Shirley MacLaine's books with ease—all kinds of things I can't begin to understand. Yet some of my friends tell me they understand 50 percent of what my mother says. Some say they understand 80 to 90 percent. Some say they understand none of it, as if she were speaking pure Chinese. But to me, my mother's English is perfectly clear, perfectly natural. It's my mother tongue. Her language, as I hear it, is vivid, direct, full of observation and imagery. That was the language that helped shape the way I saw things, expressed things, made sense of the world.

Lately, I've been giving more thought to the kind of English my mother speaks. Like others, I have described it to people as "broken" or "fractured" English. But I wince when I say that. It has always bothered me that I can think of no way to describe it other than "broken," as if it were damaged and needed to be fixed, as if it lacked a certain wholeness and soundness. I've heard other terms used, "limited English," for example. But they seem just as bad, as if everything is limited, including people's perceptions of the limited English speaker.

I know this for a fact, because when I was growing up, my mother's "limited" English limited my perception of her. I was ashamed of her English. I believed that her English reflected the quality of what she had to say. That is, because she expressed them imperfectly her thoughts were imperfect. And I had plenty of empirical evidence to support me: the fact that people in department stores, at banks, and at restaurants did not take her seriously, did not give her good service, pretended not to understand her, or even acted as if they did not hear her.

My mother had long realized the limitations of her English as well. When I was fifteen, she used to have me call people on the phone to pretend I was she. In this guise, I was forced to ask for information or even to complain and yell at people who had been rude to her. One time it was a call to her stockbroker in New York. She had cashed out her small portfolio and it just so happened we were going to go to New York the next week, our very first trip outside California. I had to get on the phone and say in an adolescent voice that was not very convincing, "This is Mrs. Tan."

And my mother was standing in the back whispering loudly, "Why he don't send me check, already two weeks late. So mad he lie to me, losing me money."

And then I said in perfect English, "Yes, I'm getting rather concerned. You had agreed to send the check two weeks ago, but it hasn't arrived."

Then she began to talk more loudly. "What he want, I come to New York tell him front of his boss, you cheating me?" And I was trying to calm her down, make her be quiet, while telling the stockbroker, "I can't tolerate any more excuses. If I don't receive the check immediately, I am going to have to speak to your manager when I'm in New York next week." And sure enough, the

following week there we were in front of this astonished stockbroker, and I was sitting there red-faced and quiet, and my mother, the real Mrs. Tan, was shouting at his boss in her impeccable broken English.

We used a similar routine just five days ago, for a situation that was far less humorous. My mother had gone to the hospital for an appointment, to find out about a benign brain tumor a CAT scan had revealed a month ago. She said she had spoken very good English, her best English, no mistakes. Still, she said, the hospital did not apologize when they said they had lost the CAT scan and she had come for nothing. She said they did not seem to have any sympathy when she told them she was anxious to know the exact diagnosis, since her husband and son had both died of brain tumors. She said they would not give her any more information until the next time and she would have to make another appointment for that. So she said she would not leave until the doctor called her daughter. She wouldn't budge. And when the doctor finally called her daughter, me, who spoke in perfect English—lo and behold—we had assurances the CAT scan would be found, promises that a conference call on Monday would be held, and apologies for any suffering my mother had gone through for a most regrettable mistake.

I think my mother's English almost had an effect on limiting my possibilities in life as well. Sociologists and linguists probably will tell you that a person's developing language skills are more influenced by peers. But I do think that the language spoken in the family, especially in immigrant families which are more insular, plays a large role in shaping the language of the child. And I believe that it affected my results on achievement tests, IQ tests, and the SAT. While my English skills were never judged as poor, compared to math, English could not be considered my strong suit. In grade school I did moderately well, getting perhaps B's, sometimes B-pluses, in English and scoring perhaps in the sixtieth or seventieth percentile on achievement tests. But those scores were not good enough to override the opinion that my true abilities lay in math and science, because in those areas I achieved A's and scored in the ninetieth percentile or higher.

This was understandable. Math is precise; there is only one correct answer. Whereas, for me at least, the answers on English tests were always a judgment call, a matter of opinion and personal experience. Those tests were constructed around items like fill-in-the-blank sentence completion, such as, "Even though Tom was _____ , Mary thought he was _____." And the correct answer always seemed to be the most bland combinations of thoughts, for example, "Even though Tom was shy, Mary thought he was charming," with the grammatical structure "even though" limiting the correct answer to some sort of semantic opposites, so you wouldn't get answers like, "Even though Tom was foolish, Mary thought he was ridiculous." Well, according to my mother, there were very few limitations as to what Tom could have been and what Mary might have thought of him. So I never did well on tests like that.

The same was true with word analogies, pairs of words in which you were supposed to find some sort of logical, semantic relationship—for example, "*Sunset* is to *nightfall* as _____ is to _____." And here you would be presented with a list of four possible pairs, one of which showed the same kind of relationship: *red* is to *stoplight, bus* is to *arrival, chills* is to *fever, yawn* is to *boring*. Well, I could never think that way. I knew what the tests were asking, but I could not block out of my mind the images already created by the first pair, "*sunset* is to *nightfall*"—and I would see a burst of colors against a darkening sky, the moon rising, the lowering of a curtain of stars. And all the other pairs of words—red, bus, stoplight, boring—just threw up a mass of confusing images, making it impossible for me to sort out something as logical as saying: "A sunset precedes nightfall" is the same as "a chill precedes a fever." The only way I would have gotten that answer right would have been to imagine an associative situation, for example, my being disobedient and staying out past sunset, catching a chill at night, which turns into feverish pneumonia as punishment, which indeed did happen to me.

I have been thinking about all this lately, about my mother's English, about achievement tests. Because lately I've been asked, as a writer, why there are not more Asian Americans represented in American literature. Why are there few Asian Americans enrolled in creative writing programs? Why do so many Chinese students go into engineering? Well, these are broad sociological questions I can't begin to answer. But I have noticed in

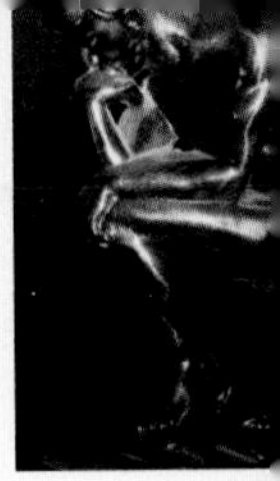

surveys—in fact, just last week—that Asian students, as a whole, always do significantly better on math achievement tests than in English. And this makes me think that there are other Asian-American students whose English spoken in the home might also be described as "broken" or "limited." And perhaps they also have teachers who are steering them away from writing and into math and science, which is what happened to me.

Fortunately, I happen to be rebellious in nature and enjoy the challenge of disproving assumptions made about me. I became an English major my first year in college, after being enrolled as pre-med. I started writing nonfiction as a freelancer the week after I was told by my former boss that writing was my worst skill and I should hone my talents toward account management.

But it wasn't until 1985 that I finally began to write fiction. And at first I wrote using what I thought to be wittily crafted sentences, sentences that would finally prove I had mastery over the English language. Here's an example from the first draft of a story that later made its way into *The Joy Luck Club*, but without this line: "That was my mental quandary in its nascent state." A terrible line, which I can barely pronounce.

Fortunately, for reasons I won't get into today, I later decided I should envision a reader for the stories I would write. And the reader I decided upon was my mother, because these were stories about mothers. So with this reader in mind—and in fact she did read my early drafts—I began to write stories using all the Englishes I grew up with: the English I spoke to my mother, which for lack of a better term might be described as "simple"; the English she used with me, which for lack of a better term might be described as "broken"; my translation of her Chinese, which could certainly be described as "watered down"; and what I imagined to be her translation of her Chinese if she could speak in perfect English, her internal language, and for that I sought to preserve the essence, but neither an English nor a Chinese structure. I wanted to capture what language ability tests can never reveal: her intent, her passion, her imagery, the rhythms of her speech and the nature of her thoughts.

Apart from what any critic had to say about my writing, I knew I had succeeded where it counted when my mother finished reading my book and gave me her verdict: "So easy to read."

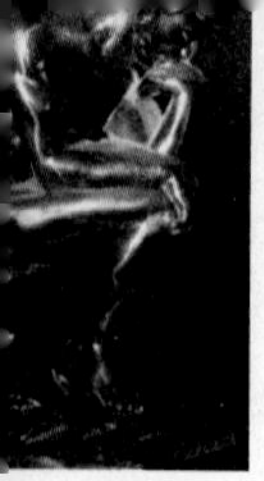

How to write a reflection

These steps for the process of writing a reflection may not progress as neatly as this chart might suggest. Writing is not an assembly-line process. Writing about a remembered event, place, or person is, in itself, a powerful way to reflect. Be open to uncovering insights and understanding more broadly the significance.

1 CHOOSE A SUBJECT

- Analyze the assignment.
- Explore possible topics. Make lists of memories connected with your family, work, school, friends, and travels.
- Examine your lists for what might interest readers.
- Consider why this person, place, event, or object is significant to you.

2 DEVELOP A RESPONSE

- Generate details. Remember sounds, smells, tastes, and tactile feeling in addition to visual details.
- Make people come alive. Recreate conversations that reveal character. Record gestures and other details that make people unique.
- Think about the context. What was happening at the time for you and the larger community?
- Relate your experience to the experiences of others.

3 WRITE A DRAFT

- Select vivid details and dialogue. Describe people's mannerisms, gestures, and voices.
- Decide on an organization.
- Craft a strong beginning. Engage the reader with an incident or place that establishes a focus.
- Conclude by inviting further reflection, possibly by what you discovered or how you changed.
- Consider your voice and tone. Decide if you want to sound more conversational or more formal. Your tone reflects your attitude toward the subject.
- Choose a title that will interest readers.

4 REVISE, REVISE, REVISE

- Check that your paper or project fulfills the assignment.
- Make sure that the subject is focused.
- Add details, description, or dialog.
- Make sure your voice and tone will engage readers.
- Examine your organization and think of possible better ways to organize.
- Review the visual presentation.
- Proofread carefully.

5 SUBMITTED VERSION

- Make sure your finished writing meets all formatting requirements.

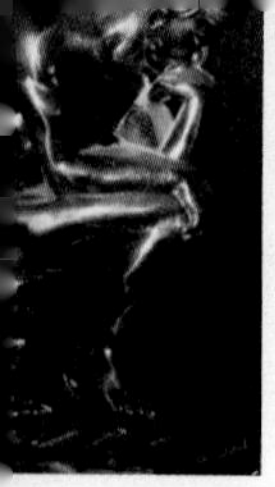

1: Find a reflective topic and a focus

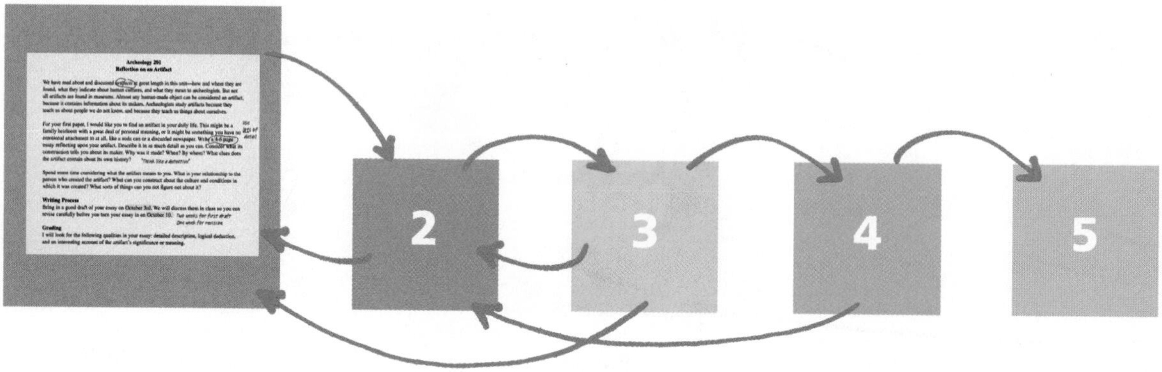

Analyze the assignment

- Read your assignment slowly and carefully. Look for key words like *reflect, reminisce,* or *contemplate.* These key words tell you that you are writing a reflective essay.
- Identify any information about the length specified, date due, formatting, and other requirements. You can attend to this information later. At this point you want to give your attention to your topic and the focus of your reflection.

Explore possible topics

- Think about your family. What memories stand out about your parents? your brothers and sisters? your own child or children? your grandparents and other close relatives? your pets? your shared family experiences including vacations and holidays? Make a list of events and situations associated with your family.
- Think about work experience. What was your first job? Did you ever have a great boss or a horrible boss? Do any other workers stand out? What important learning experiences did you have on the job? Make a list of events and situations associated with work.
- Think about your school experience. What school memories stand out? Did a teacher have a strong influence on you? Did a coach make a difference in your life? What were the social groups in your school? Make a list of events and situations associated with school.
- Think about friends and social relationships. What memories stand out about your friends? about people you've met? about people you've dated? Make a list of events and situations associated with friends and social relationships.
- Review all of your lists and put a check beside any items that look like interesting possibilities for writing.

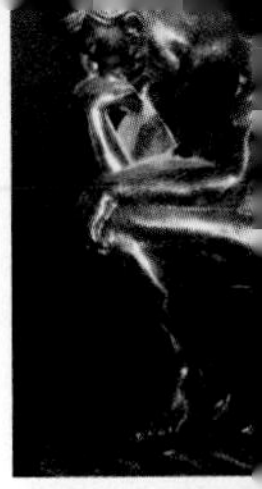

Remember places and objects

- Is a particular place important? Why is it critical? For example, how did you gain an understanding of your mother's attitudes when you visited the place where she grew up?
- Is a particular object important? For example, can you describe the locket that belonged to your great-grandmother and was passed down to you?

Consider the significance

- Ask yourself: Why is this person, event, place, or object significant to me?
- Think about why the person, place, event, or object seems more important now than in your initial experience. How did your view change?
- How did you change as a result of being around this person, event, place, or object?

Analyze your potential readers

- What do your readers likely know about the subject?
- What might you need to tell readers about your background?
- How can you engage readers?
- What will they gain from reading your reflection?

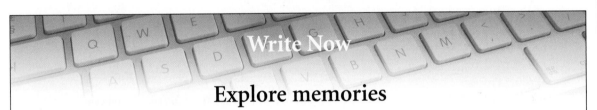

Write Now

Explore memories

- Select one of the items that you have checked on your lists.
- Write nonstop for five minutes to explore the event, situation, place, or object. What was your initial reaction? Who else was there? Did you share your reaction at the time?
- Write nonstop for five minutes to explore your current perspective. How did an experience change you? Why do you remember this person, event, place, or object so well? Looking back, what do you see now that you didn't recognize at the time?
- Stop and read what you have written. Do you see possibilities for writing at length about this person, event, or situation? If you do, then begin generating more content. If the idea seems limited, try writing nonstop about another person, event, place, or object.

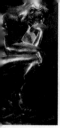

Writer at work

Janine Carter received the following assignment in her Introduction to Archeology class. She made notes on her assignment sheet as the class discussed the assignment.

Archeology 201
Reflection on an Artifact

We have read about and discussed *artifacts* at great length in this unit—how and where they are found, what they indicate about human cultures, and what they mean to archeologists. But not all artifacts are found in museums. Almost any human-made object can be considered an artifact, because it contains information about its makers. Archeologists study artifacts because they teach us about people we do not know, and because they teach us things about ourselves.

For your first paper, I would like you to find an artifact in your daily life. This might be a family heirloom with a great deal of personal meaning, or it might be something you have no emotional attachment to at all, like a soda can or a discarded newspaper. Write a 4-6 page essay reflecting upon your artifact. Describe it in as much detail as you can. Consider what its construction tells you about its maker. Why was it made? When? By whom? What clues does the artifact contain about its own history? "Think like a detective"

Use lots of detail

Spend some time considering what the artifact means to you. What is your relationship to the person who created the artifact? What can you construct about the culture and conditions in which it was created? What sorts of things can you not figure out about it?

Writing Process

Bring in a good draft of your essay on October 3rd. We will discuss them in class so you can revise carefully before you turn your essay in on October 10. Two weeks for first draft
One week for revision

Grading

I will look for the following qualities in your essay: detailed description, logical deduction, and an interesting account of the artifact's significance or meaning.

Then Janine made a list of possible objects to write about.

HEIRLOOMS/EMOTIONAL CONNECTION

- Aunt Marie's tulip quilt--shows my connection to a long line of quilters
- ~~Sea shells from Girl Scout camp~~-NOT MAN-MADE
- Bracelet from graduation
- Terry's photo
- Stuffed elephant–shows how much I have grown up. Where was it made?
- ✓ Garage sale quilt--don't know much about this; could guess a lot though.
- Diploma

LESS IMPORTANT OBJECTS

- Cereal box--ingredients show lack of nutrition. Pictures show how kids are bombarded with cartoons and colorful images. Expiration date and other clues to where it was made.
- Desk in dorm room--Must have been used by dozens of people like me (?)
- Old calendar
- Old cookbook
- A floppy disk--Could talk about how fast technology is changing. Do I have one?

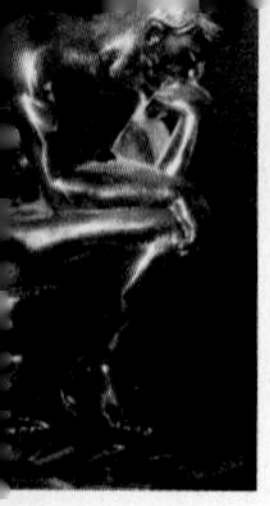

2: Develop a response

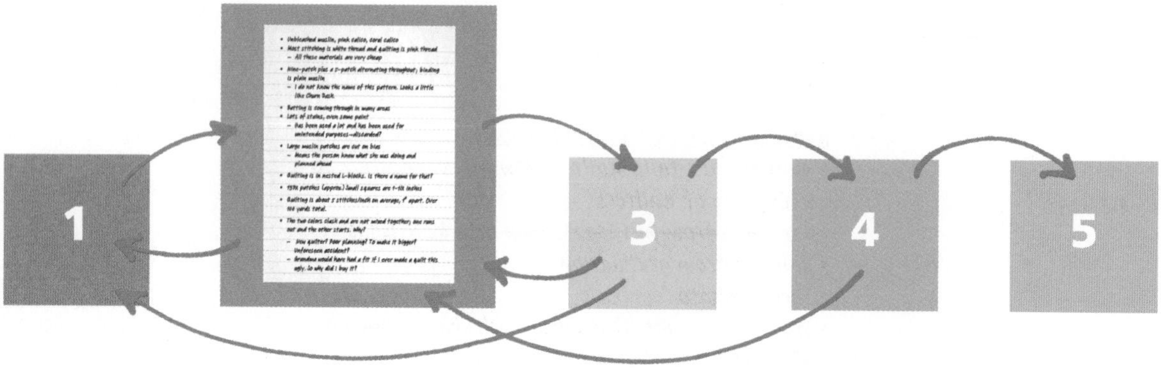

Generate details

- Write down all the sights, sounds, smells, tastes, and tactile sensations you associate with your topic.
- If you are using a photograph or other object, write a detailed description of it.
- If you are remembering a past event, write down everything that happened: what people said and did, how you felt as things happened, and anything else you remember or feel is significant.

Make people come alive

- Use dialog to let readers hear people talk, which reveals much about character.
- Record the little mannerisms, gestures, clothing, and personal habits that distinguish people.
- Don't forget to make yourself come alive. If you are reflecting on an incident from your childhood, how old were you? What do you remember about yourself at that age?

Think about the context

- How does your memory compare with similar experiences you have read or heard about from others?
- Does your memory connect to any larger trends or events going on at the time?

Relate your experience to the experiences of others

- The very fact that you find the topic memorable means there is something there you can share with others. Think about how to make it obvious to them.
- How is your subject particular to you? What do you notice, as you reflect, that other people might not notice? This is the "added value" that will make your reflection more than a mere description or memory.

Writer at work

Janine Carter sat down with her garage-sale quilt and a pen and paper. She observed it carefully and made a list of detailed observations about its physical appearance. Then, she added her conclusions and guesses about the quilt, its history, and its maker, based on these clues.

Janine thought about her relationship to the quilt. She jotted down, in no particular order, what she remembered about buying the quilt, conversations she had had with her grandmother about quilting, and ideas that occurred to her.

- Unbleached muslin, pink calico, coral calico
- Most stitching is white thread and quilting is pink thread
  - All these materials are very cheap
- Nine-patch plus a 5-patch alternating throughout; binding is plain muslin
  - I do not know the name of this pattern. Looks a little like Churn Dash.
- Batting is coming through in many areas
- Lots of stains, even some paint
  - Has been used a lot and has been used for unintended purposes—discarded?
- Large muslin patches are cut on bias
  - Means the person knew what she was doing and planned ahead
- Quilting is in nested L-blocks. Is there a name for that?
- 1372 patches (approx.) Small squares are 1-1/2 inches
- Quilting is about 5 stitches/inch on average, 1" apart. Over 100 yards total.
- The two colors clash and are not mixed together; one runs out and the other starts. Why?
  - New quilter? Poor planning? To make it bigger? Unforeseen accident?
  - Grandma would have had a fit if I ever made a quilt this ugly. So why did I buy it?

3: Write a draft

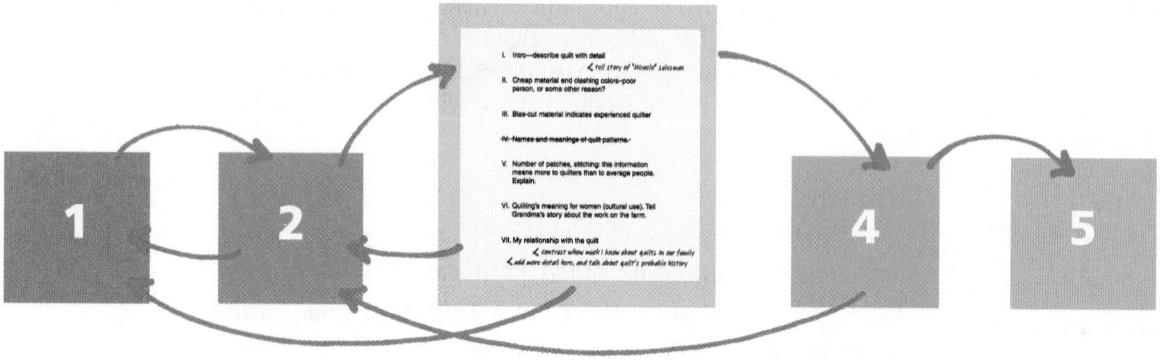

Select vivid details and dialog

- Don't rely solely on visual memory. Include sounds, smells, tastes, and tactile feelings.
- Describe people's mannerisms, gestures, and voices.
- Use dialog to reveal character.

Decide on an organization

- Use chronological order to help readers relive events with you.
- Use conceptual order to show connections and links between ideas.

Craft a strong beginning

- Start with an incident or a place that is the focus.

Conclude by inviting further reflection

- Have you discovered anything new in the process of writing the reflection to share in your conclusion?
- A conclusion can sometimes change the entire tone of a reflection. Do you want to surprise your readers?
- Above all, your conclusion should help readers make sense of your reflection.

Consider your voice and tone

- Do you want to sound informal and conversational? Or do you want to sound more distanced and objective?
- What is your attitude toward your subject? Serious or humorous? Positive or negative?

Choose a title that will interest readers in your essay

- Your title should suggest the direction or the significance of your reflection.

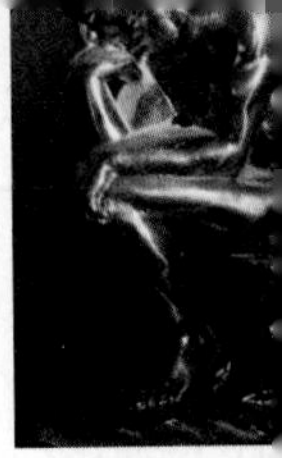

Writer at work

Janine Carter tried several organizational patterns for her essay. Because she knew so little about the quilt's history, she did not feel chronological organization would be a good strategy. However, as she worked through her draft she realized that readers would appreciate a firsthand account of her purchase of the quilt. She decided to include this story near the beginning of her essay, after describing the quilt. She organized the rest of her essay around the questions that occurred to her as she considered the quilt's appearance. As she worked, she referred back to her assignment frequently to make sure she was fulfilling all its terms. She decided to cut one section, about the names of various quilt patterns, because it was too general and distracted from the main focus of her essay. Here is the original outline Janine began working from, along with revisions she made.

I. Intro—describe quilt with detail

< *tell story of "Miracle" salesman*

II. Cheap material and clashing colors–poor person, or some other reason?

III. Bias-cut material indicates experienced quilter

~~IV. Names and meanings of quilt patterns.~~

V. Number of patches, stitching: this information means more to quilters than to average people. Explain.

VI. Quilting's meaning for women (cultural use). Tell Grandma's story about the work on the farm.

VII. My relationship with the quilt

< *contrast w/how much I know about quilts in our family*

< *add more detail here, and talk about quilt's probable history*

4: Revise, revise, revise

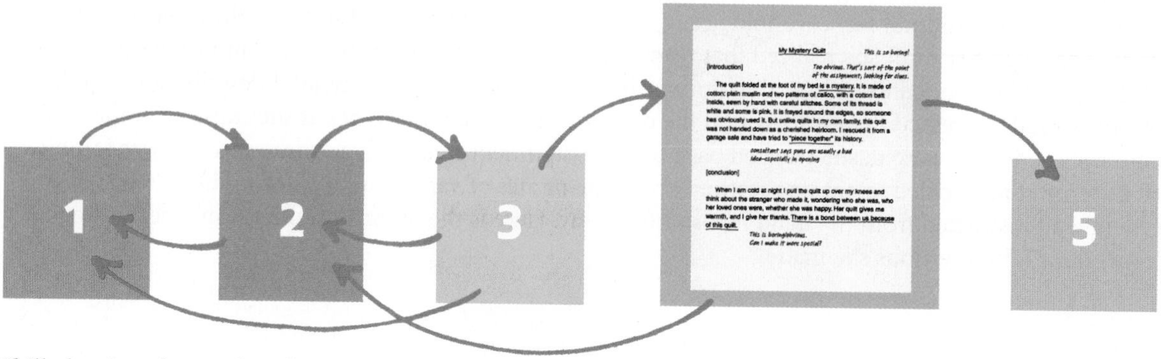

Skilled writers know that the secret to writing well is rewriting. Even the best writers often have to revise several times to get the result they want. You also must have effective strategies for revising if you're going to be successful. The biggest trap you can fall into is starting off with correcting errors. Leave the small stuff for last.

Does your paper or project meet the assignment?

- Look again at the assignment for specific guidelines, including length, format, and amount of research. Does your work meet these guidelines?

Is the subject focused?

- Will readers find your subject early on?
- Is the significance evident?

Can you add dialog, description, and other details?

- Can you make events and memories from the past more concrete?

Is your tone engaging?

- Will readers sympathize and identify with you, or will they find your tone too negative, angry, or intensely personal?
- Does your tone fit your topic? Some intensely personal topics may not be suited to humorous treatment.

Is your organization effective?

- Are links between concepts and ideas clear?
- Are there any places where you find abrupt shifts or gaps?
- Are there sections or paragraphs that could be rearranged to make your draft more effective?

Is the writing project visually effective?

- Is the font attractive and readable?
- Are the headings and visuals effective?
- If you have included an image associated with your reflection, where should it be placed for maximum impact?

Save the editing for last.

- When you have finished revising, edit and proofread carefully.

A peer review guide is on page 27.

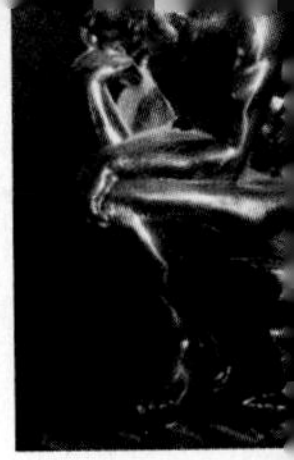

Writer at work

Janine Carter was not satisfied with her opening paragraph, or her title. After talking to a consultant at her campus writing center, she worked on ending her opening paragraph with a surprising twist that would engage readers. She also realized that she could draw out the concept of "miracles" from within her essay to tie together the beginning and end. Here are the first drafts of Janine's opening and concluding paragraphs, with her notes.

My Mystery Quilt

This is so boring!

[introduction]

Too obvious. That's sort of the point of the assignment, looking for clues.

The quilt folded at the foot of my bed is a mystery. It is made of cotton: plain muslin and two patterns of calico, with a cotton batt inside, sewn by hand with careful stitches. Some of its thread is white and some is pink. It is frayed around the edges, so someone has obviously used it. But unlike quilts in my own family, this quilt was not handed down as a cherished heirloom. I rescued it from a garage sale and have tried to "piece together" its history.

consultant says puns are usually a bad idea—especially in opening

[conclusion]

When I am cold at night I pull the quilt up over my knees and think about the stranger who made it, wondering who she was, who her loved ones were, whether she was happy. Her quilt gives me warmth, and I give her thanks. There is a bond between us because of this quilt.

This is boring/obvious.
Can I make it more special?

5: Submitted version

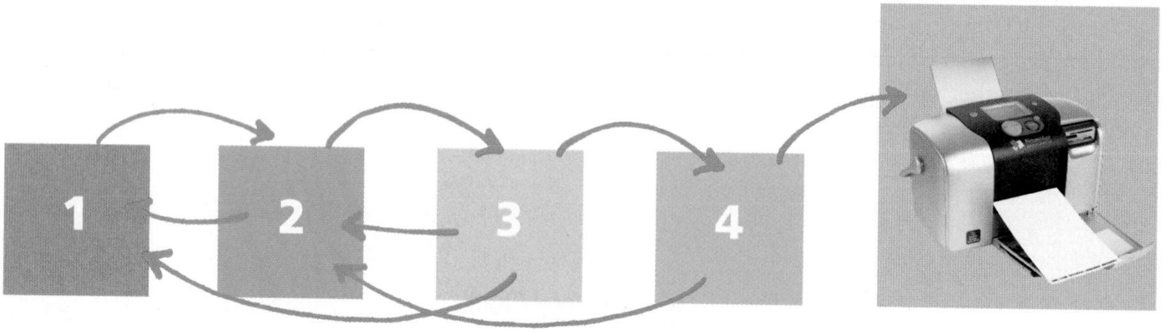

Carter 1

Janine Carter
Dr. Shapiro
Archeology 201
10 October 2008

The Miracle Quilt

The quilt folded at the foot of my bed has a long history. It is made of cotton: plain muslin and two patterns of calico, with a cotton batt inside, sewn by hand with careful stitches. Some of its thread is white and some is pink. It is frayed around the edges and has obviously lived a long, useful life. It is steeped in memories. Unfortunately, I don't know what any of them are.

I found the quilt at a city-wide garage sale. At the end of the auditorium, taking up half of the bleachers, was a vendor's booth called "Miracles by the Pound." The gentleman who ran the booth went around buying up vintage fabrics in bad condition. He would dump huge piles of them on the bleachers for people to pick through. When you had found what you wanted, he would weigh it on a scale and tell you how much it cost. Everything was five dollars per pound. As he weighed your purchase, he would call out the price so everyone at the garage sale could hear what a good deal you were getting. My quilt weighed three pounds. "Fifteen dollar miracle!" the vendor sang out as I opened my purse.

My quilt had already been dug out of the pile and discarded by another woman at the garage sale, who had two or three other vintage quilts in her

Carter 2

Fig. 1. Detail of the miracle quilt.

arms. She told me she bought old, damaged quilts and cut them up to make sofa pillows. My quilt didn't interest her because it wasn't in very good shape, and the blocks were the wrong size for the pillow forms she used. I come from a family of quilters, so when I saw the quilt I felt it needed a good home. I didn't like the idea of someone using it to wrap around furniture in a moving van, or even cutting it up for pillows. I took it home and washed it, and put it on my bed, and took a good look at it.

The quilt was probably made by someone poor, or at least very frugal, I decided. The muslin, which provides the background, is the cheapest unbleached kind. Even the binding around the edges, which in most quilts is a bright, contrasting color, is plain muslin. Whoever pieced the quilt—and it was almost certainly a woman, because quilting has always been women's work—started out using a coral-toned calico. But before she finished, she ran out and had to switch to a rose-colored calico. The effect is jarring, as the colors do not complement each other. The coral marches two-thirds of the way across the quilt, and then stumbles into rose. I do not know why the quiltmaker did not work the two colors evenly throughout the quilt; this is what my own grandmother taught me to do when I didn't have enough of

Carter 3

one color. Perhaps she was inexperienced; perhaps this was her first quilt, or perhaps she hadn't intended to make the quilt as large as it is. The coral would have been sufficient to cover a single bed; maybe, I think to myself, someone proposed to her while she was making it, and she ended up enlarging it to fit a double bed after she got married.

But there are other clues that suggest experience and planning. The octagon-shaped patches of muslin that center the five-patch blocks are cut so that the lines of quilting cross them on the bias—that is, diagonally across the up-and-down and side-to-side warp and woof threads of the fabric. Fabric is more flexible on the bias (this, my grandmother once explained to me, is why clothing cut on the bias fits and looks better, and is more expensive). A needle slips in and out between the threads more easily, so a quilter is wise to arrange pieces so as to maximize bias quilting. The quilting itself (that is the stitching through all the layers of the quilt) is respectable enough, about five stitches per inch. No fancy 12-stitch-per-inch quilting like you would see in a showpiece quilt, but quite firm and straight, in neat pink rows spaced an inch apart. The quilting pattern is in L-shaped blocks, which I have never seen before. There must be over one hundred yards of quilting all together; the length of a football field, taken one stitch at a time.

The quilt's pattern looks like a variation of wagon tracks, but it uses an octagonal block like a "churn-dash" pattern that sets it apart from a more straightforward Irish chain. Nine-patch and five-patch blocks alternate across it. By my count it contains 1,372 separate pieces, all cut, sewn, and quilted by hand. The nine-patch blocks use 1-1/2-inch patches. These may seem like insignificant details to most people, but to quilters they are important. They tell you how much work went into the quilt. The first nine-patch quilt I made with my grandmother contained a grand total of 675 patches, and I thought it would take forever to sew it (even using a sewing machine!). I remember asking my grandmother how she ever made her more complicated quilts: the flower garden with its thousands of tiny hexagons; the Dutchman's puzzle that was so mesmerizing you could hardly stop your eyes from running over it, trying to pick out the "real" pattern. "Doesn't quilting drive you crazy sometimes?" I asked her. She thought that was pretty funny. "Quilting was how we used to keep from going crazy," she told me.

When she first married my grandfather and moved to a farm in the Brazos River bottom over sixty years ago, there was no television and no

Carter 4

neighbors for miles. In the spring, rain would turn the roads to thick clay mud and no one could get off their property for days at a time. Quilting was the way women dealt with the isolation. "That is what the pioneer women did too," she told me. Stuck out alone on the prairies and in the mountains, they kept their sanity by cutting and arranging hundreds of pieces of cloth in different patterns, methodically assembling quilts to bring some order into their own bleak lives.

"It looks like hard work to you now," my grandmother explained, "but for us it was like a vacation. So much of women's work was never done, but you could sit down after dinner in the evening and finish a quilt block and feel like you had done something that would last. You might have spent the whole day dirtying and washing the same set of dishes three times, feeding the same chickens and milking the same cows twice, and you knew you'd have to get up in the morning and do the same things all over again, from top to bottom. But quilt blocks added up to something. Nobody was going to take your finished quilt block and sit down at the breakfast table and pick it apart, and expect you to sew it back together again before lunch. It was done, and it stayed done. There wasn't much else you could say that about, on a farm."

In my family, quilts are heirlooms and are handed down with stories about who made them, who owned them, what they were used for, and what events they had been part of. Some were wedding presents, others were made for relatives when they were first born. I don't know the stories that go with my miracle quilt. It has had a hard life; that is easy to see. Most of the binding has frayed off and there are some spots where the quilt has holes worn straight through it—top, batting, and backing. There are stains that suggest coffee or tea or perhaps medicines from a sickbed spilled on it. There are some spots of dried paint. Evidently at some point it was used as a drop-cloth. But at least, I tell myself, it has found a home with someone who appreciates the work that went into it, and can guess at some of its history.

When I am cold at night I pull the quilt up over my knees and think about the stranger who made it, wondering who she was, who her loved ones were, whether she was happy. Her quilt gives me warmth, and I give her thanks. Though we will never meet, or even know each other's identity, there is a bond between us because of this quilt. And so it seems that the man who sold me this quilt was right: it is a sort of miracle.

Projects

Reflections focus on people, places, events, and things—past and present—that have significance in the writer's life. Successful reflections engage readers in their subjects and convey the importance of the person, event, or place.

These projects are frequently written kinds of reflections.

Reflection on the past

List people, events, or places that have been significant in your life or in some way changed you. Many reflections focus on a conflict of some kind and how it was resolved. Look back over your list and check the items that seem especially vivid to you.

Take a few minutes to write first about the person, event, or place as you remember it, and then write about how you regard it today. What was your initial reaction? Did your initial reaction change over time? Why do you feel differently now?

Think about the significance of the person, event, or place in your life. What details best convey that significance? If conversations were involved, remember what was said and create dialog.

Organize your essay around the focus. Start fast to engage your readers. If there is a conflict in your reflection, get it up front.

Show the significance through describing, vivid details, and dialog. Make the characters and the places come to life.

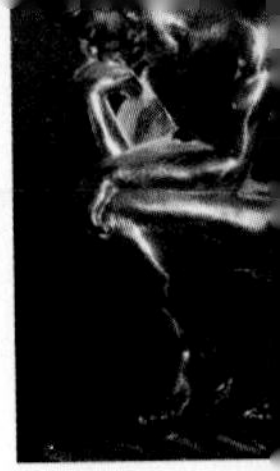

Family photograph

Family photographs and cherished objects can be subjects for reflection. Try carefully observing (or picturing in your mind) an object or photograph that has special meaning for you. Write down all the details you can. What memories does each observation evoke? Do you find that different aspects of the photograph make you feel different ways?

Choose as a topic something that is significant to you, and which you can recall with a reasonable amount of detail. But also consider how interesting this topic will be to others. Will an audience want to share in your experience?

Write a reflective essay about that photograph. What does the photograph convey that other similar snapshots do not? What does it hide or not show? What does it say about your family?

Literacy narrative

Think about a childhood memory of reading or writing that remains especially vivid. The memory may be of a particular book you read, of something you wrote, or a teacher who was important in teaching you to read or write. Or think of a more recent experience of reading and writing. What have you written lately that was especially difficult? Or especially rewarding? List as many possibilities as you can think of.

Look over the items on the list and pick one that remains significant to you. Begin writing by describing the experience in as much detail as you can remember. Describe who was involved and recall what was said. Describe the setting of the experience: where exactly were you and what difference did it make? Remember key passages from what you either read or wrote. How did you understand the experience at the time? How do you understand it now? What makes it special?

Review what you have written and consider how to shape your raw material into an engaging essay. You may want to narrate the experience in the order it happened; you may want to start in the middle of the experience and give the background later; or you may want to start in the present as you look back. Above all, start fast. Somewhere along the way, you will need to convey why the experience was significant for you, but avoid the temptation to end with a moral. Don't forget to include a title that makes your readers want to read your literacy narrative.

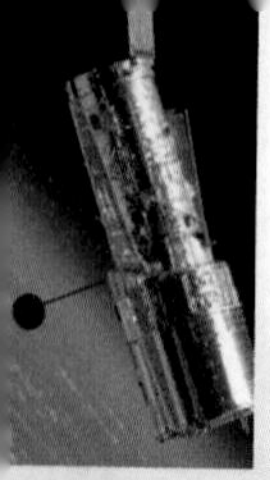

8 Informative Essays

Successful informative writing begins with what the reader needs to know.

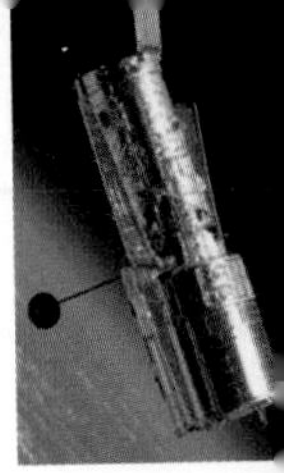

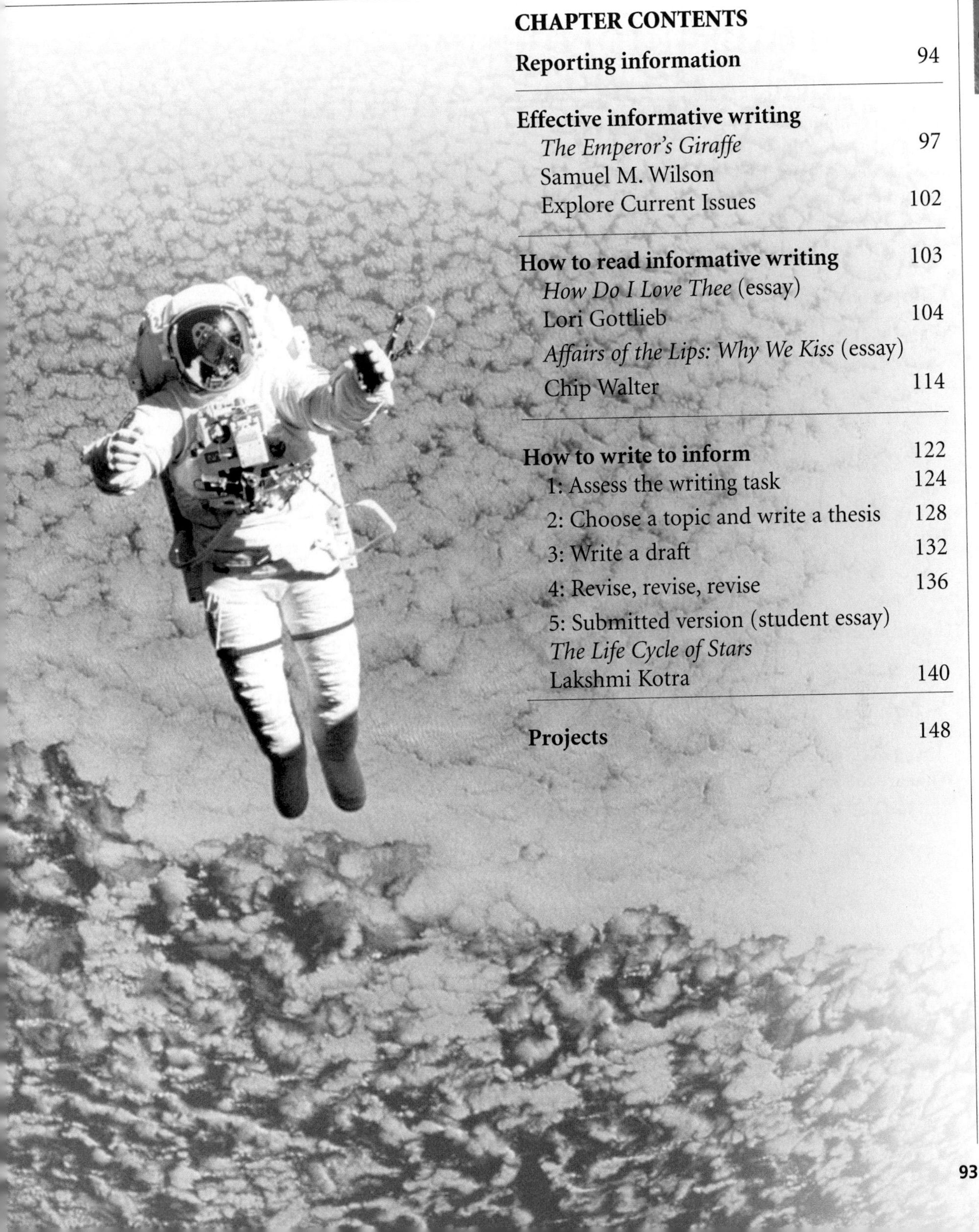

CHAPTER CONTENTS

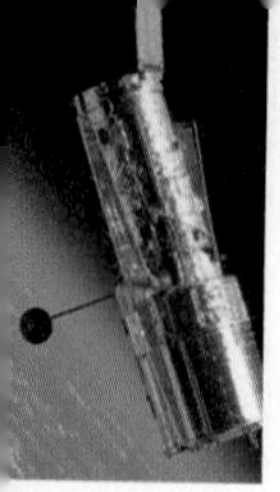

Reporting information

Whether reading the news, following a recipe, hooking up a new computer, deciding which course to take, or engaging in a multitude of other events in our daily lives, we depend on reliable and clear information. Reporting information takes many forms, ranging from newspaper articles and reports of experimental research to tables, charts, and simple lists of information.

In one sense, most kinds of writing, including writing to reflect and writing to persuade, also report information. The main difference is that the focus of a report and other informative kinds of writing is on the subject, not on the writer's reflections or on changing readers' minds or on getting them to take action.

Components of informative writing

Where do I find information?	**Find information.** Reports require research. Scientists make observations in the field and conduct experiments to create new knowledge. Journalists interview people for the information to include in articles. Accountants assemble financial information in order to write reports on the financial status of companies and organizations. Knowing where to find information and knowing how much you need is critical for writing reports.
What does it mean?	**Interpret information.** Writers not only report what they read and observe. They construct meaning through selecting what and what not to include and in organizing that information.
How can I explain it?	**Explain information.** Often what you know well is difficult to explain to others. In order to do so effectively, you will need to break down a process into steps that you can describe. Explaining a process sometimes requires you to think about something familiar in a new way.
What are the implications?	**Explore questions and problems.** Not all informative writing is about topics with which you are familiar or ones that you can bring to closure. Often college writing involves issues or problems that perplex us and for which we cannot come to a definitive conclusion. The goal in such writing is not the ending but the journey. Difficult issues often leave you conflicted; readers appreciate writers who deal honestly with those conflicts.

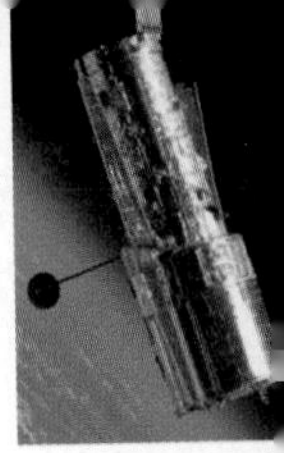

Keys to informative writing

Narrow the topic	A central difficulty in writing to inform is knowing where to stop. For any large subject, a lifetime may be insufficient. The key to success is limiting your topic to one you can cover adequately.
Start fast	The title and introduction should entice readers to want to read the rest. Dull generic titles and vague, general introductory paragraphs discourage further reading. Offer a new viewpoint that challenges the usual, commonplace viewpoint.
Keep readers interested	Readers become bored quickly if they have heard it all before. Once you have made your readers curious to know more about your subject, don't disappoint them.
Define key terms	Writers should define clearly any key terms and concepts that might be unfamiliar.
Provide relevant examples, illustrations, and details	The examples, illustrations, and details make or break informative writing, whether it is a news article, a profile, or even a set of instructions or a cookbook. Select them carefully.
Remain objective	Writers whose purpose is to inform usually stay in the background, taking the stance of an impartial, objective observer. An objective tone and the absence of bias help readers to believe the information is accurate and the writer is trustworthy.
Document the sources of information	If you use sources in a college assignment, you will be expected to document those sources. Lakshmi Kotra's essay at the end of this chapter (see pages 140–147) follows an academic format for citing sources.
Conclude with strength	Besides just stopping, a plain summary is the weakest possible conclusion. Leave your readers with something to think about—a memorable example, an anecdote that illustrates a key point, implications of the information you have provided, a quotation that expresses a main point vividly, or a projection into the future.
Explain with charts and graphs	Charts and graphs show facts and relationships that are often difficult to communicate using words alone. A good chart makes the significance of the data clear at a glance.

Explain with images

Pictures don't always tell a thousand words; indeed, we need words to understand what is represented in pictures. Nevertheless, photographs, drawings, maps, and other graphics can provide concrete evidence to support what is being explained in words.

Satellite photography helped the world to understand the damage caused by the tsunami that struck Indonesia on December 28, 2004.

Working Together

Explain a concept or activity

In a group of three or four students

First select a concept or activity that you know a great deal about (through your courses, your work experience, or your personal interests) but your classmates likely do not. Subjects might range from the second law of thermodynamics and postmodern architecture to competitive ballroom dancing and growing your own herbs. In your group give each person five minutes to explain the concept or activity.

Listen carefully to each classmate, and when each finishes, stop for a minute to note

- what you knew already
- what you found engaging
- what you wanted to know more about
- what you didn't understand

After the last person finishes, share your notes with the group. You'll have an immediate audience response to your explanation.

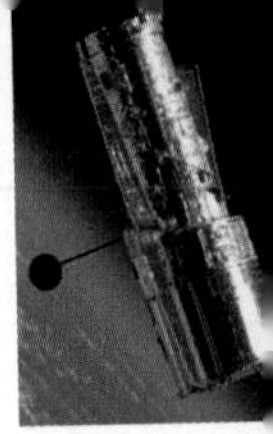

Effective informative writing

Informative writing succeeds when readers can connect new facts and concepts to what they know already.

The Emperor's Giraffe

Samuel M. Wilson

Samuel Wilson, a professor of anthropology, wrote "The Emperor's Giraffe" for the magazine *Natural History* in 1992. It was later collected with other essays and published in a book with the same title. Wilson had the challenge of writing about a subject unfamiliar to most of his readers, and moreover, he wanted to make a larger point. Notice how he leads his readers to his unexpected conclusion.

A HUGE FLEET LEFT PORT in 1414 and sailed westward on a voyage of trade and exploration. The undertaking far surpassed anything Columbus, Isabella, and Ferdinand could have envisioned. The fleet included at least sixty-two massive trading galleons, any of which could have held Columbus's three small ships on its decks. The largest galleons were more than 400 feet long and 150 feet wide (the *Santa Maria*, Columbus's largest vessel, was about 90 by 30 feet), and each could carry about 1,500 tons (Columbus's ships combined could carry about 400 tons). More than one hundred smaller vessels accompanied the galleons. All told, 30,000 people went on the voyage, compared with Columbus's crew of 90-some.

The 500th anniversary of Columbus's first trip to America was celebrated in 1992. Wilson uses the occasion to introduce his readers to a major Chinese voyage of discovery in 1414 that was massively larger in ships and personnel.

The commander's name was Zheng He (Cheng Ho), the Grand Eunuch of the Three Treasures and the most acclaimed admiral of the Ming dynasty. He was sailing from the South China Sea across the Indian Ocean, heading for the Persian Gulf and Africa. As the historian Philip Snow notes in his wonderful book *The Star Raft*, "Zheng He was the Chinese Columbus. He has become for China, as Columbus has for the West, the personification of maritime endeavour" (21). The flotilla was called the star raft after the luminous presence of the emperor's ambassadors on board.

Zheng He did not really set out to explore unknown lands—neither did Columbus, for that matter—for the Chinese were aware of most of the countries surrounding the Indian Ocean.

Wilson begins challenging commonly held views by pointing out that neither Zheng He nor Columbus was exploring unknown territory.

For centuries, China had been a principal producer and consumer of goods moving east and west from Mediterranean, African, and Middle Eastern trading centers. With this trade came cultural and ideological exchange.

Zheng He, like many Chinese of his time, was a Muslim, and his father and his father before him had made the pilgrimage to Mecca. But in Zheng He's day, the trade routes were controlled by Arabian, Persian, and Indian merchants. Private Chinese traders had been barred from traveling to the West for several centuries. China had been conquered by Ghengis Khan and his descendants in the 1200s, and the Mongol emperors of the subsequent Yuan dynasty were the first to impose these constraints. In 1368 the Chinese expelled the Mongol rulers and established the Ming dynasty, which was destined to rule for the next 300 years. (Thus, in 1492 Columbus was searching for a "Grand Khan" who had been put out of business 124 years earlier.)

A parenthetical aside—that Columbus was looking for the "Grand Khan" who had long ceased to exist—speaks to the lack of knowledge of China among Europeans.

After the period of Mongol rule, China became strongly isolationist, placing even more severe restrictions on Chinese traders. In 1402 an outward-looking emperor named Yong'le (Yung-lo) came to power. Seeking to reassert a Chinese presence on the Western seas and to enhance the prestige of his rule and dynasty, he began funding spectacular voyages by Zheng He. As sociologist Janet Abu-Lughod notes in *Before European Hegemony*, "The impressive show of force that paraded around the Indian Ocean during the first three decades of the fifteenth century was intended to signal the 'barbarian nations' that China had reassumed her rightful place in the firmament of nations—had once again become the 'Middle Kingdom' of the world" (343).

As Zheng He pressed westward in 1414, he sent part of his fleet north to Bengal, and there the Chinese travelers saw a wondrous creature. None like it had ever been seen in China, although it was not completely unheard of. In 1225 Zhao Rugua, a customs inspector at the city of Quanzhou, had recorded a secondhand description of such a beast in his

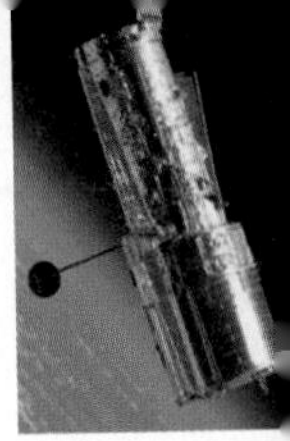

strange and wonderful *Gazetteer of Foreigners*. He said it had a leopard's hide, a cow's hoofs, a ten-foot-tall body, and a nine-foot neck towering above that. He called it a *zula*, possibly a corruption of zurafa, the Arabic word for giraffe.

The account of how a giraffe was described for those who had never seen one adds interest.

The giraffe the travelers saw in Bengal was already more than 5,000 miles from home. It had been brought there as a gift from the ruler of the prosperous African city-state of Malindi, one of the several trading centers lining the east coast of Africa (Malindi is midway along modern Kenya's coast, three degrees south of the equator). Zheng He's diplomats persuaded the Malindi ambassadors to offer the animal as a gift to the Chinese emperor. They also persuaded the Malindi ambassadors to send home for another giraffe. When Zheng He returned to Beijing, he was able to present the emperor with two of the exotic beasts.

A pair of giraffes in Beijing in 1415 was well worth the cost of the expedition. In China they thought the giraffe (despite its having one horn too many) was a unicorn (*ch'i-lin*), whose arrival, according to Confucian tradition, meant that a sage of the utmost wisdom and benevolence was in their presence. It was a great gift, therefore, to bring to the ambitious ruler of a young dynasty. The giraffes were presented to the emperor Yong'le by exotic envoys from the kingdom of Malindi, whom the Chinese treated royally. They and the marvelous gift so excited China's curiosity about Africa that Zheng He sent word to the kingdom of Mogadishu (then one of the most powerful trading states in East Africa and now the capital of modern Somalia) and to other African states, inviting them to send ambassadors to the Ming emperor.

Wilson explains why the giraffes took on great significance beyond their novelty.

The response of the African rulers was overwhelmingly generous, for China and Africa had been distant trading partners from the time of the Han dynasty (206 BC to AD 220). In the *Universal Christian Topography*, written about AD 525 by Kosmos, a Byzantine monk known as the Indian Traveler, Sri Lanka is described as a trading center frequented by both Chinese and Africans. Envoys from a place called

Wilson refutes another common view that sub-Saharan Africa was not engaged in international trade before Europeans arrived.

Zengdan—the name translates as "Land of Blacks"—visited China several times in the eleventh century. And a Chinese map compiled in the early fourteenth century shows Madagascar and the southern tip of Africa in remarkable detail, nearly two centuries before the Portuguese "discovered" the Cape of Good Hope. Archeologists find china (why the English word came to be synonymous with glazed pottery and porcelain, instead of silk or spices, is unclear) from the Han and later dynasties all along the east coast of Africa.

The African emissaries to the Ming throne came with fabulous gifts, including objects for which entrepreneurs had long before managed to create a market in the Far East: tortoise shell, elephant ivory, and rhinoceros-horn medicine. On their many visits they also brought zebras, ostriches, and other exotica. In return, the Ming court sent gold, spices, silk, and other presents. Zheng He was sent with his fleet of great ships on yet another voyage across the Indian Ocean to accompany some of the foreign emissaries home. This escort was the first of several imperially supported trips to Africa. According to official records, they went to Mogadishu, Brava, and perhaps Malindi; Snow (in *The Star Raft*) suggests that these Chinese expeditions may have gone farther—to Zanzibar, Madagascar, and southern Africa.

Meanwhile, as the Chinese were pushing down the east coast of Africa, Portuguese mariners were tentatively exploring the west coast. They had started the process in the early fifteenth century and were steadily working their way south. Bartolomeu Dias reached the Cape of Good Hope in 1488 and was the first of these mariners to see the Indian Ocean. Surely the Europeans and Chinese were poised to meet somewhere in southern Africa, where perhaps they would have set up trading depots for their mutual benefit.

That Chinese sailors might have met the Portuguese in Africa and established trade is a "what if?" that leads to Wilson's conclusion.

This did not happen, however. Emperor Yong'le died in 1424, and by 1433 the Ming dynasty discontinued its efforts to secure tributary states and trading partners around the Indian Ocean. In Beijing, those favoring an isolationist foreign policy won out, and the massive funding needed to support Zheng He's fleet—difficult to sustain during what was a period of economic decline in China—was canceled. As Edwin Reischauer and John Fairbank note in *East Asia: The Great Tradition:*

> The voyages must be regarded as a spectacular demonstration of the capacity of early Ming China for maritime expansion, made all the more dramatic by the fact that Chinese ideas of government and official policies were fundamentally indifferent, if not actually opposed, to such an expansion. This contrast between capacity and performance, as viewed in retrospect from the vantage point of our modern world of trade and overseas expansion, is truly striking. (478)

Wilson uses the conclusion of other scholars to set up the point he makes in the following paragraph.

The contrast also refutes the argument that as soon as a country possesses the technology of overseas trade and conquest it will use it. Zheng He's fleet was 250 times the size of Columbus's, and the Ming navy was many times larger and more powerful than the combined maritime strength of all of Europe. Yet China perceived her greatest challenges and opportunities to be internal ones, and Yong'le's overseas agenda was forgotten. Restrictions on private trade were reimposed, and commercial and military ventures in the Indian Ocean and South China Sea in subsequent centuries were dominated by the Portuguese, Arabs, Indians, Spaniards, Japanese, Dutch, British, and Americans. Zheng He's magnificent ships finally rotted at their moorings.

Wilson concludes his essay by making a significant point. He refutes the idea that those who have the best technology necessarily will use it to conquer others. Had he started with this point, readers might have been skeptical, but he gives the impression that his conclusion logically follows from the data.

Works Cited

Abu-Lughod, Janet L. *Before European Hegemony: The World System AD 1250-1350.* New York: Oxford UP, 1989. Print.

Reischauer, Edwin O., and John K. Fairbank. *East Asia: The Great Tradition.* Boston: Houghton, 1958. Print.

Snow, Philip. *The Star Raft: China's Encounter with Africa.* London: Weidenfeld, 1988. Print.

Explore Current Issues

Is everybody an expert?

WikiHow was created in 2005 by Jack Herrick, one of the former owners of the professionally-authored online how-to manual eHow.com. Herrick used the wiki model—communal Web authorship with volunteer contributors—that made Wikipedia a household name. With a database of over 45,000 articles and in September 2008, over 13 million readers, wikiHow's mission is to build the world's largest how-to manual.

Write about it

1. Why do you think sites such as Wikipedia and wikiHow are so popular? Do you think wikis have changed the way people think about expertise? Why or why not?
2. Look at a few articles on wikiHow. What are the conventions of this kind of writing? Think about format, language, graphics, and tone. Using what you've observed, write a wikiHow-style article on how to write a wikiHow article.
3. Credibility and relevance are important for all types of informational writing. What other factors determine the success of a piece of informational writing?

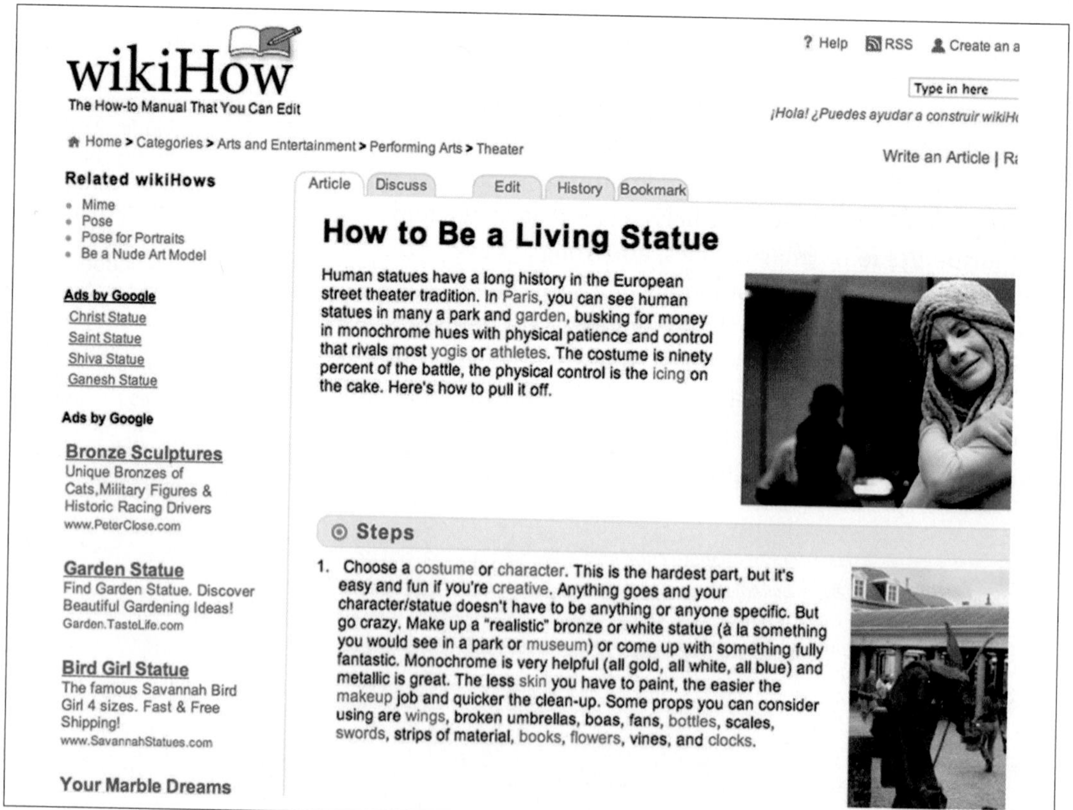
wikiHow
The How-to Manual That You Can Edit
? Help RSS Create an a
Type in here
¡Hola! ¿Puedes ayudar a construir wikiH
Home > Categories > Arts and Entertainment > Performing Arts > Theater
Write an Article | R

Related wikiHows
- Mime
- Pose
- Pose for Portraits
- Be a Nude Art Model

Ads by Google
Christ Statue
Saint Statue
Shiva Statue
Ganesh Statue

Ads by Google
Bronze Sculptures
Unique Bronzes of Cats,Military Figures & Historic Racing Drivers
www.PeterClose.com

Garden Statue
Find Garden Statue. Discover Beautiful Gardening Ideas!
Garden.TasteLife.com

Bird Girl Statue
The famous Savannah Bird Girl 4 sizes. Fast & Free Shipping!
www.SavannahStatues.com

Your Marble Dreams

Article | Discuss | Edit | History | Bookmark

How to Be a Living Statue

Human statues have a long history in the European street theater tradition. In Paris, you can see human statues in many a park and garden, busking for money in monochrome hues with physical patience and control that rivals most yogis or athletes. The costume is ninety percent of the battle, the physical control is the icing on the cake. Here's how to pull it off.

Steps

1. Choose a costume or character. This is the hardest part, but it's easy and fun if you're creative. Anything goes and your character/statue doesn't have to be anything or anyone specific. But go crazy. Make up a "realistic" bronze or white statue (à la something you would see in a park or museum) or come up with something fully fantastic. Monochrome is very helpful (all gold, all white, all blue) and metallic is great. The less skin you have to paint, the easier the makeup job and quicker the clean-up. Some props you can consider using are wings, broken umbrellas, boas, fans, bottles, scales, swords, strips of material, books, flowers, vines, and clocks.

How to read informative writing

Make notes as you read, either in the margins, if it is your copy, or on paper or a computer file. Circle any words or references that you don't know and look them up.

What is it?	• What kind of a text is it? An article? an essay? a profile? a set of instructions? a chart? a brochure? a Web site? an executive summary? What are your expectations for this kind of text? • What media are used? (Web sites, for example, often combine images, words, and sounds.)
Where did it come from?	• Who wrote this material? • Where did it first appear? In a book, newspaper, magazine, online, in a company, or in an organization?
What is the writer's thesis or main idea?	• Where is the thesis or main idea located? • If you cannot find a specific claim, what is the main focus? • What are the key ideas or concepts that the writer considers? • What are the key terms? Are they defined?
Who is the intended audience?	• What clues do you find about whom the writer had in mind as the readers? • What does the writer assume that the readers already know about the subject? • What new knowledge is the writer providing?
How is the piece of writing organized?	• Look for the main idea in each paragraph. It helps to write them down. Then examine how each paragraph connects to the others. • Where are the details and examples located? Do they support the main points?
What kinds of sources are cited?	• Are they from books, newspapers, periodicals, or the Web? • Are they completely documented?
How is it composed?	• How does the writer represent herself or himself? • How would you characterize the style? • How effective is the design? Is it easy to read? • If there are any photographs, charts, or other graphics, what information do they contribute?

How Do I Love Thee?

(ESSAY)

Lori Gottlieb

Lori Gottlieb is the author of *Stick Figure* (2000) and a coauthor of *I Love You, Nice to Meet You* (2006). She is a regular commentator on NPR's *All Things Considered* and has written for many newspapers and magazines. A longer version of this essay appeared in *The Atlantic Monthly* in March 2006.

Return to these questions after you have finished reading.

Analyzing and Connecting

1. Why does Gottlieb begin with the story of her visit to Dr. Neil Clark Warren's office rather than her central question: can cold, hard science be a facilitator of romance?

2. How does Gottlieb answer her central question?

3. Buckwalter's studies and Warren's observations conclude that happy couples have many similarities. Think about happy and unhappy couples you know. Is their degree of happiness a result of what they have in common?

4. Online dating and relationship Web sites have become some of the fastest-growing businesses on the Internet. Compare eHarmony.com with Perfectmatch.com, Chemistry.com, Match.com, and others. What does each promise on the first page? What does each claim to distinguish it from other similar online dating sites?

Finding Ideas for Writing

Who is Gottlieb's audience? How do you know? Choose a new audience for the piece—of a different age range, gender, social class, and level of education—and write a memo advising the author how to change the piece for this audience. How should she change the level of formality? the language? the tone? the references?

HOW DO I LOVE THEE?

LORI GOTTLIEB

I'd been sitting in Dr. Neil Clark Warren's office for less than fifteen minutes when he told me he had a guy for me. It wasn't surprising that the avuncular seventy-one-year-old founder of eHarmony.com, one of the nation's most popular online dating services, had match-making on his mind. The odd thing was that he was eager to hook me up without having seen my eHarmony personality profile.

I'd come to the eHarmony headquarters in Pasadena, California, in early October to learn more about the site's "scientifically proven" and patented Compatibility Matching System. Apparently, the science wasn't working for me. The day before, after I'd taken the company's exhaustive (and exhausting) 436-question personality survey, the computer informed me that of the approximately 9 million eHarmony members, more than 40 percent of whom are men, I had zero matches. Not just in my city, state, region, or country, but in the entire world. So Warren, who looks like Orville Redenbacher and speaks with the folksy cadence of Garrison Keillor, suggested setting me up with one of his company's advisory board members, whom he described as brilliant, Jewish, and thirty-eight years old. According to Warren, this board member, like me, might have trouble finding a match on eHarmony.

"Let me tell you why you're such a difficult match," Warren said, facing me on one of his bright floral sofas. He started running down the backbone of eHarmony's predictive model of broad-based compatibility, the so-called twenty-nine dimensions (things like curiosity, humor, passion, intellect), and explaining why I and my prospective match were such outliers.

"I could take the nine million people on our site and show you dimension by dimension how we'd lose people for you," he began. "Just on IQ alone—people with an IQ lower than 120, say. Okay, we've eliminated people who are not intellectually adequate. We could do the same for people who aren't creative enough, or don't have your brilliant sense of humor. See, when you get on the tails of these dimensions, it's really hard to match you. You're too bright. You're too thoughtful. The biggest thing you've got to do when you're gifted like you are is to be patient."

After the over-the-top flattery wore off—and I'll admit, it took an embarrassingly long time—I told Warren that most people I know don't join online dating sites to be patient. Impatience with real-world dating, in fact, is precisely what drives many singles to the fast-paced digital meat market. From the moment Match.com, the first such site, appeared in 1995, single people suddenly had twenty-four-hour access to thousands of other singles who met their criteria in terms of race, religion, height, weight, even eye color and drinking habits.

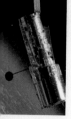

Nearly overnight, it seemed, dozens of similar sites emerged, and online dating became almost de rigueur for busy singles looking for love. According to a recent Pew survey, 31 percent of all American adults (63 million people) know someone who has used a dating Web site, while 26 percent (53 million people) know someone who has gone out with a person he or she met through a dating Web site. But was checking off boxes in columns of desired traits, like an à la carte Chinese take-out menu, the best way to find a soul mate?

Enter eHarmony and the new generation of dating sites, among them PerfectMatch.com and Chemistry.com. All have staked their success on the idea that long-term romantic compatibility can be predicted according to scientific principles—and that they can discover those principles and use them to help their members find lasting love. To that end they've hired high-powered academics, devised special algorithms for relationship-matching, developed sophisticated personality questionnaires, and put into place mechanisms for the long-term tracking of data. Collectively, their efforts mark the early days of a social experiment of unprecedented proportions, involving millions of couples and possibly extending over the course of generations. The question at the heart of this grand trial is simple: In the subjective realm of love, can cold, hard science help?

Although eHarmony was the first dating site to offer science-based matching, Neil Clark Warren seems like an unlikely pioneer in the field. Even though he earned a Ph.D. in clinical psychology from the University of Chicago, in 1967, he never had much of a passion for academic research—or an interest in couples. "I was scared to death of adults," he told me. "So I did child therapy for a while." With a master's degree in divinity from Princeton Theological Seminary, he went on to Fuller Theological Seminary's Graduate School of Psychology, in southern California, where he taught and practiced humanistic psychology (what he calls "client-centered stuff") in the vein of his University of Chicago mentor, Carl Rogers. "I hated doing research," he admitted, before adding with a smile, "In fact, I was called 'Dr. Warm.' "

Fittingly, it was Warren's family, not academia, that piqued his interest in romantic compatibility. "When my daughters came along, that was a big pivot in my life in thinking about how do two people get together," he told me. "I started reading in the literature and realizing what a big chance they had of not having a satisfying marriage. I started trying to look into it."

Soon he began a private practice of couples therapy—with a twist. "People have always thought, wrongly, that psychotherapy is a place to go deal with problems," he said. "So when a couple would come in, I'd say, 'Tell me how you fell in love. Tell me the funniest thing that's happened in your marriage.' If you want to make a relationship work, don't talk about what you find missing in it! Talk about what you really like about it."

Warren is a big proponent of what he likes to call "folksy wisdom." One look at the shelves in his office confirms this. "I've been reading this little book about the Muppets—you know, Jim Henson," he said. "And I've been reading another book about Mister Rogers. I mean, Mister Rogers was brilliant beyond belief! He got a hold of concepts so thoroughly that he could transmit them to six-year-old kids! Do you know how much you have to get a hold of a concept to transmit it simply? His idea of simple-but-profound has had a profound influence on me."

The basis of eHarmony's matching system also sounds simple but profound. In successful relationships, Warren says, "similarities are like money in the bank. Differences are like debts you owe. It's all right to have a few differences, as long as you have plenty of equity in your account."

He leaned in and lowered his voice to a whisper. "Mister Rogers and Jim Henson," Warren continued, "they got a hold of the deep things of life and were able to put them out there. So that's what we want to do with our products. We want to put them out there in a way that you'd say, 'This is common sense. This seems right, this seems like it would work.' Our idea of broad-based compatibility, I put it out there in front of you. Does that seem right?"

Whether or not it seems right on an intuitive level is almost beside the point. After all, eHarmony's selling point, its very brand identity, is its scientific compatibility system. That's where Galen Buckwalter comes in.

A vice president of research and development for the company, Buckwalter is in charge of recruiting what he hopes will be twenty to twenty-five top relationship researchers away from academia—just as he was lured away by Warren nine years ago. A former psychology graduate student at Fuller Theological Seminary (his dissertation was titled "Neuropsychological Factors Affecting Survival in Malignant Glioma Patients Treated with Autologous Stimulated Lymphocytes"), Buckwalter had become an assistant professor at the University of Southern California, where he was studying the effects of hormones on cognition, when he got the call from Warren.

"Neil knew I lived and breathed research, and he had this idea to try to develop some empirically based model to match people," Buckwalter said when I visited him at his office at eHarmony. He wore a black T-shirt and wire-rimmed glasses, and had a hairstyle reminiscent of Einstein's. "He wasn't necessarily thinking, over the Internet—maybe a storefront operation like Great Expectations." Relationships weren't Buckwalter's area, but he welcomed the challenge. "A problem is a problem, and relationships are a good problem," he said. "In the research context, it's certainly an endlessly fascinating question."

With the help of a graduate student, Buckwalter reviewed the psychological literature to identify the areas that might be relevant in predicting success in long-term relationships. "Once we identified all those areas, then we put together a questionnaire—just a massively long questionnaire," he said.

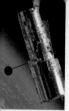

"It was probably close to a thousand questions. Because if you don't ask it, you're never gonna know. So we had tons of questions on ability, even more on interest. Just every type of personality aspect that was ever measured, we were measuring it all."

Because it wasn't practical to execute a thirty-year longitudinal study, he and Warren decided to measure existing relationships, surveying people who were already married. The idea was to look for patterns that produce satisfaction in marriages, then try to reproduce them in the matching of singles.

Buckwalter's studies soon yielded data that confirmed one of Warren's longtime observations: namely, that the members of a happy couple are far more similar to each other than are the members of an unhappy couple. Compatibility, in other words, rests on shared traits. "I can't tell you how delighted I was," Warren said, "when the factor-analytic studies started bringing back the same stuff I'd seen for years."

But could this be true across the board? I told Warren that my most successful relationships have been with men who are far less obsessive than I am. Warren assured me that's not a similarity their system matches for. "You don't want two obsessives," he explained. "They'll drive each other crazy. You don't find two control freaks in a great marriage. So we try to tweak the model for that. Fifty percent of the ball game is finding two people who are stable."

For Warren, a big question remained: What should be done with these findings? Originally, he had partnered with his son-in-law, Greg Forgatch, a former real-estate developer, to launch the business. Their first thought was to produce educational videotapes on relationship compatibility. After all, Warren had recently written his book, *Finding the Love of Your Life*.

"We tried so hard to make videotapes and audiotapes," Warren said. "I went into the studio and made lists. We came up with a hundred things singles need. But singles don't want education; they want flesh! They want a person. So that's when, in 1997, we said, 'We've gotta help people find somebody who would be good for them. Some body?' "

To connect singles and create a data pool for more research, the Internet seemed the best option. Based on a study of 5,000 married couples, Warren put together the compatibility model that became the basis for eHarmony. "We got encouraged by everybody, 'Get out there, get out there! The first person to market is going to be the most successful,' " Warren recalled. But he insisted on getting the matching system right before launching the site—and that didn't happen until August of 2000, during the dot-com bust. By 2001 he was contemplating declaring bankruptcy.

"And then," Warren recalled, "we found an error in our matching formula, so a whole segment of our people were not getting matched. It was an error with all the Christian people on the site."

This is a sensitive topic for Warren, who bristles at the widely held opinion that eHarmony is a Christian dating site. The company's chief operating officer, he offered by way of rebuttal, is Jewish, and

Buckwalter, who became a quadriplegic at age sixteen after jumping into a river and breaking his neck, is agnostic. And while Warren describes himself as "a passionate Christian" and proudly declares, "I love Jesus," he worried about narrowing the site with too many questions about spiritual beliefs. Which is where the error came in.

"We had seven questions on religion," he explained, "and we eliminated four of them. But we forgot to enter that into the matching formula! These were seven-point questions. You needed twenty-eight points to get matched with a Christian person, but there was no way you could get them! We only had three questions! So every Christian person who had come to us had zero matches."

Fortunately, a wave of positive publicity, featuring married couples who'd met through eHarmony and the naturally charismatic Warren, turned things around. Still, Warren said of the innocent mistake, "you kind of wonder how many relationships fall apart for reasons like this—how many businesses?"

Today, eHarmony's business isn't just about using science to match singles online. Calling itself a "relationship-enhancement service," the company has recently created a venture-capital-funded think tank for relationship and marital research, headed up by Dr. Gian Gonzaga, a scientist from the well-known marriage-and-family lab at the University of California at Los Angeles. The effort, as Gonzaga put it to me recently, is "sort of like a Bell Labs or Microsoft for love."

An energetic, attractive thirty-five-year-old, Gonzaga thought twice about leaving the prestige of academia. "It seemed cheesy at first," he said. "I mean, this was a dating service." But after interviewing with Warren, he realized that conducting his research under the auspices of eHarmony would offer certain advantages. He'd be unfettered by teaching and grant-writing, and there would be no sitting on committees or worrying about tenure. More important, since his research would now be funded by business, he'd have the luxury of doing studies with large groups of ready subjects over many years—but without the constraints of having to produce a specific product.

"We're using science in an area most people think of as inherently unscientific," Gonzaga said. So far, the data are promising: a recent Harris Interactive poll found that between September of 2004 and September of 2005, eHarmony facilitated the marriages of more than 33,000 members—an average of forty-six marriages a day. And a 2004 in-house study of nearly 300 married couples showed that people who met through eHarmony report more marital satisfaction than those who met by other means. The company is now replicating that study in a larger sample.

"We have massive amounts of data!" Warren said. "Twelve thousand new people a day taking a 436-item questionnaire! Ultimately, our dream is to have the biggest group of relationship psychologists in the country. It's so easy to get people excited about coming here. We've got more data than they could collect in a thousand years."

But how useful is this sort of data for single people like me? Despite Warren's disclaimer about what a tough eHarmony match I am, I did finally get some profiles in my inbox. They included a bald man with a handlebar moustache, who was fourteen inches taller than me; a five-foot-four-inch attorney with no photos; and a film editor whose photo shows him wearing a kilt—and not in an ironic way. Was this the best science could do?

When I asked Galen Buckwalter about this, he laughed, indicating that he'd heard the question before. "The thing you have to remember about our system is we're matching on these algorithms for long-term compatibility," he said. "Long-term satisfaction is not the same as short-term attraction. A lot of people, when they see their initial matches, it's like, 'This is crap!' "

In ads and on his Web site, Warren talks about matching people "from the inside out." Was eHarmony suggesting that I over-look something as basic as romantic chemistry? "When we started out," Buckwalter said, "we were almost that naive." But now, he added, eHarmony is conducting research on the nature of physical attraction.

"We're trying to find out if we can predict physical chemistry with the same degree of statistical certainty that we've used to predict long-term satisfaction through our compatibility matching. In general, people seem to be attracted to people who share their physical attributes," Buckwalter explained, noting that he has found some exceptions, like height preference. "There's a lot of variability on that dimension," he said. "A person's height, it turns out, is not a consistent predictor of short-term attraction." Meanwhile, Buckwalter's team is in the process of testing new hypotheses.

"We're still convinced that our compatibility-matching process is essential for long-term satisfaction, so we're not going to mess with that," he insisted. "But if we can fit a short-term attraction model on top of that, and it's also empirically driven, that's the Holy Grail."

Over at Chemistry.com, a new site launched by Match.com, short-term attraction is already built into the system. This competitor of eHarmony's was developed with help from Match.com's chief scientific adviser, Dr. Helen Fisher, an anthropologist at Rutgers University, whose research focuses on the brain physiology of romantic love and sexuality. Chemistry.com is currently assembling a multidisciplinary group of psychologists, relationship counselors, sociologists, neuroscientists, and sexologists to serve as consultants.

The company sought out Fisher precisely because its market research revealed that although a large segment of singles wanted a scientific approach, they didn't want it to come at the expense of romantic chemistry. "On most of the other sites, there's this notion of 'fitness matching,' " Fisher said from her office in New York City. "You may have the same goals, intelligence, good looks, political beliefs. But you can walk into a room, and every one of those boys might come from the same background, have the same level of intelligence, and so on, and maybe you'll talk to three but won't fall in love with any

of them. And with the fourth one, you do. What creates that chemistry?"

It's a constellation of factors, Fisher told me. Sex drive, for instance, is associated with the hormone testosterone in both men and women. Romantic love is associated with elevated activity of the neurotransmitter dopamine and probably also another one, norepinephrine. And attachment is associated with the hormones oxytocin and vasopressin. "It turns out," she said, "that seminal fluid has all of these chemicals in it. So I tell my students, 'Don't have sex if you don't want to fall in love.' "

Romantic love, Fisher maintains, is a basic mating drive—more powerful than the sex drive. "If you ask someone to go to bed with you, and they reject you," she says, "you don't kill yourself. But if you're rejected in love, you might kill yourself."

For Chemistry.com's matching system, Fisher translated her work with neurotransmitters and hormones into discrete personality types. "I've always been extremely impressed with Myers-Briggs," she said, referring to the personality assessment tool that classifies people according to four pairs of traits: Introversion versus Extroversion, Sensing versus Intuition, Thinking versus Feeling, and Judging versus Perceiving. "They had me pinned to the wall when I took the test, and my sister, too. So when Chemistry.com approached me, I said to myself, I'm an anthropologist who studies brain chemistry, what do I know about personality?' "

The 146-item compatibility questionnaire on Chemistry.com correlates users' responses with evidence of their levels of these various chemicals. One question, for instance, offers drawings of a hand, then asks:

Which one of the following images most closely resembles your left hand?

The relevance of this question might baffle the average online dater accustomed to responding to platitudes like, "How would you describe your perfect first date?" But Fisher explains that elevated fetal testosterone determines the ratio of the second and fourth finger in a particular way as it simultaneously builds the male and female brain. So you can actually look at someone's hand and get a fair idea of the extent to which they are likely to be a Director type (ring finger longer than the index finger) or a Negotiator type (index finger longer or the same size).

Another question goes like this:

How often do you vividly imagine extreme life situations, such as being stranded on a desert island or winning the lottery?

Almost never
Sometimes
Most of the time
All the time

"Someone who answers 'All the time' is a definite Negotiator," Fisher said. "High estrogen activity is associated with extreme imagination."

While other sites gather data based on often unreliable self-reports ("How romantic do you consider yourself to be?"), many of the Chemistry.com questions are designed to translate visual interpretation into personality assessment, thus eliminating some of the unreliability. In one, the user is presented with a book's jacket art. We see a woman in a sexy spaghetti-strapped dress gazing at a man several feet away in the background, where he leans on a stone railing. The sky is blue, and they're overlooking an open vista. "What is the best title for this book?" the questionnaire asks, and the choices are as follows:

A Spy in Rimini
Anatomy of Friendship:
A Smart Guide for Smart People
A Scoundrel's Story
Things Left Unsaid

According to Fisher, each response is correlated with one of the four personality types: Choice A corresponds to Explorer, B to Builder, C to Director, and D to Negotiator.

Even sense of humor can be broken down by type, with questions like "Do you sometimes make faces at yourself in the mirror?" (people with a sense of humor do) and "At the zoo, which do you generally prefer to watch?" (the reply "monkeys and apes" indicates more of a funny bone than "lions and tigers"). According to Fisher, a Director likes people to laugh at his or her jokes; a Negotiator likes to be around someone funny so he or she can laugh at that person's jokes; an Explorer is spontaneous and laughs at just about anything; and a Builder, she suspects, generally isn't as funny as the others.

But how to match people up according to Fisher's four personality types, and under what circumstances, isn't so straightforward. Another question, for instance, presents four smiling faces and asks:

Take a look at the faces below. Are their smiles sincere?

Fisher says that people with high levels of estrogen—usually women—have better social skills, and are better at reading other people. So users who choose the correct "real" smiles (pictures two and three) will be the Negotiators. This, Fisher says, is an area where "complementarity" might be important. The problem with sites like eHarmony, she believes, is that they place too much emphasis on similarity, whereas, in her view, falling in love depends on two elements: similarity and complementarity. "We also want someone who masks our flaws," she explained. "For example, people with poor social skills sometimes gravitate toward people with good social skills. I'm an Explorer, so I don't really need a partner who is socially skilled. That's not essential to me. But it may be essential to a Director, who's generally less socially skilled."

Chemistry.com's compatibility questionnaire also examines secondary personality traits. To illustrate, Fisher cited her own relationship. "I'm currently going out with a man," she said, "and of course I made him take the test instantly. We're both Explorers and older. I'm not sure two Explorers want to raise a baby together, because nobody will be home. But in addition, I'm a Negotiator and he's a Director type. Our dominant personality is similar, but underneath, we're complementary."

Determining which works best—similarity or complementarity—may change with the circumstances. A young woman who's an Explorer, Fisher said, might be attracted to a Builder, someone who's more of a homebody, loyal, dependable, and protective. But the pair will be more compatible if their secondary personalities match—maybe they're both Negotiators underneath.

"Nobody is directly locked into any one of these temperament types," Fisher said. "That's why we provide each person with both a major and a minor personality profile. Do Explorers go well together? Do likes attract likes? Sometimes they do and sometimes they don't."

If this sounds a bit, well, unscientific, Fisher is the first to admit it. "I have theories about what personality type a person would be most ideally suited with," she told me, "but I also trust people to tell me what they are looking for. All throughout the questionnaire are checks and balances to what are just Helen Fisher's theories."

This is why she decided to include an item on the Chemistry.com questionnaire that asks about the traits of a person's partner in his or her most successful former relationship: Was that person an Explorer, a Builder, a Director, a Negotiator? "Anybody can match somebody for values. But I'm hoping to create a system so that five years later they still fascinate each other."

At the same time, Fisher wants couples to be fascinated by each other early on. In other words, why waste time e-mailing back and forth to get to know a potential match over the course of several weeks, as eHarmony encourages its users to do, if there won't be any chemistry when they finally meet? Chemistry.com's guided 1-2-3-Meet system provides a step-by-step structure to get couples face to face as soon as possible for that all-important "vibe check." Then there's a post-meeting "chemistry check," where each person offers feedback about the date.

The goal is to incorporate this information into the algorithm to provide better matches, but it can also serve as an accuracy check of the data. Say, for instance, that Jack describes himself as a fashionable dresser, but Jill reports that he showed up for their date in flip-flops, cut-offs, and a do-rag. If the feedback from a number of Jack's first meetings indicates the same problem, Chemistry.com will send him an e-mail saying, "Jack, wear a pair of trousers."

Still, even a thoroughly researched biochemical model won't prevent glitches in the matching system. In Fisher's view, for example, no scientifically based site would pair her with the men she's dated, because, as she put it, "they're all better-looking than me."

"It would be preposterous for anyone to say they can create a formula that works perfectly," she said emphatically. "But I do believe that science can help us get close, and that there's a lot more to be learned."

Meanwhile, until these sites start sending me better dating prospects, I figured I'd take Neil Clark Warren up on his offer to introduce me to the thirty-eight-year-old single board member he thought would be such a good match for me. But when I asked a company spokesman about him, I was told that he had recently begun seeing someone. Did they meet through eHarmony? My potential soul mate declined to answer.

Affairs of the Lips: Why We Kiss

(ESSAY)

Chip Walter

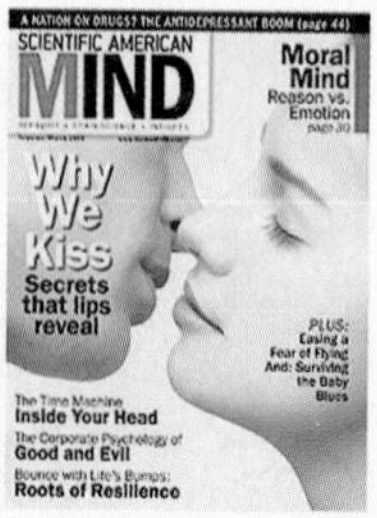

Chip Walter is a former CNN bureau chief, filmmaker, science journalist, and author. His science books, written for a mainstream audience, cover subjects as diverse as astrophysics, cognitive psychology, and evolution and are devoted to exploring why humans do what we do. "Affairs of the Lips: Why We Kiss" was the cover story of the February 2008 edition of *Scientific American Mind*. In this article, Walters explores why humans kiss and the wealth of information transmitted in this small act.

Return to these questions after you have finished reading.

Analyzing and Connecting

1. Walter cites a variety of sources on the subject of kissing, from scientists and psychologists to the poet e. e. cummings and a character from the movie *Hitch*. Why do you think he uses such a range of sources?
2. Informative writing assumes that its audience has a certain amount of information about the subject already and then provides new information on that subject. What information does Walter assume his audience has about his subject? What new information is he presenting?
3. Walter ends the essay with the sentence: "But romance gives up its mysteries grudgingly. And in some ways, we like it like that." Why does he end the essay in this way?
4. Most people think humans kiss just because it is pleasurable. With so many different opinions, why is it important to study behaviors such as kissing?

Finding Ideas for Writing

Philematologists, scientists who study the behavior of kissing, disagree on whether it is an instinctual or learned behavior. Those in the instinctual camp cite evidence of kissing in primates, like the Bonobos that Walter mentions. Those who lean toward it being a learned behavior point out, as Walter also does, that not all cultures kiss. Nonetheless, these scientists do believe kissing does have to do with choosing a mate. Walters does not seem to be championing either position. Write a concluding paragraph that could shift this essay to persuade the audience to believe one or the other.

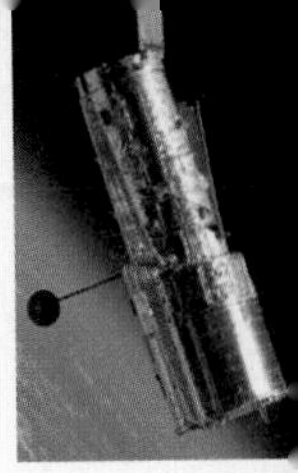

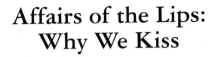

Affairs of the Lips: Why We Kiss

When passion takes a grip, a kiss locks two humans together in an exchange of scents, tastes, textures, secrets and emotions. We kiss furtively, lasciviously, gently, shyly, hungrily and exuberantly. We kiss in broad daylight and in the dead of night. We give ceremonial kisses, affectionate kisses, Hollywood air kisses, kisses of death and, at least in fairytales, pecks that revive princesses.

Lips may have evolved first for food and later applied themselves to speech, but in kissing they satisfy different kinds of hungers. In the body, a kiss triggers a cascade of neural messages and chemicals that transmit tactile sensations, sexual excitement, feelings of closeness, motivation and even euphoria.

Not all the messages are internal. After all, kissing is a communal affair. The fusion of two bodies dispatches communiqués to your partner as powerful as the data you stream to yourself. Kisses can convey important information about the status and future of a relationship. So much, in fact, that, according to recent research, if a first kiss goes bad, it can stop an otherwise promising relationship dead in its tracks.

Some scientists believe that the fusing of lips evolved because it facilitates mate selection. "Kissing," said evolutionary psychologist Gordon G. Gallup of the University at Albany, State University of New York, last September in an interview with the BBC, "involves a very complicated exchange of information—olfactory information, tactile information and postural types of adjustments that may tap into underlying evolved and unconscious mechanisms that enable people to make determinations . . . about the degree to which they are genetically incompatible." Kissing may even reveal the extent to which a partner is willing to commit to raising children, a central issue in long-term relationships and crucial to the survival of our species.

SATISFYING HUNGER

Whatever else is going on when we kiss, our evolutionary history is embedded within this tender, tempestuous act. In the 1960s British zoologist and author

Desmond Morris first proposed that kissing might have evolved from the practice in which primate mothers chewed food for their young and then fed them mouth-to-mouth, lips puckered. Chimpanzees feed in this manner, so our hominid ancestors probably did, too. Pressing outturned lips against lips may have then later developed as a way to comfort hungry children when food was scarce and, in time, to express love and affection in general. The human species might eventually have taken these proto-parental kisses down other roads until we came up with the more passionate varieties we have today.

Silent chemical messengers called pheromones could have sped the evolution of the intimate kiss. Many animals and plants use pheromones to communicate with other members of the same species. Insects, in particular, are known to emit pheromones to signal alarm, for example, the presence of a food trail, or sexual attraction.

Whether humans sense pheromones is controversial. Unlike rats and pigs, people are not known to have a specialized pheromone detector, or vomeronasal organ, between their nose and mouth [see "Sex and the Secret Nerve," by R. Douglas Fields; *Scientific American Mind*, February/March 2007]. Nevertheless, biologist Sarah Woodley of Duquesne University suggests that we might be able to sense pheromones with our nose. And chemical communication could explain such curious findings as a tendency of the menstrual cycles of female dormitory mates to synchronize or the attraction of women to the scents of T-shirts worn by men whose immune systems are genetically compatible with theirs. Human pheromones could include androstenol, a chemical component of male sweat that may boost sexual arousal in women, and female vaginal hormones called copulins that some researchers have found raise testosterone levels and increase sexual appetite in men.

If pheromones do play a role in human courtship and procreation, then kissing would be an extremely effective way to pass them from one person to another. The behavior may have evolved because it helps humans find a suitable mate—making love, or at least attraction, quite literally blind.

We might also have inherited the intimate kiss from our primate ancestors. Bonobos, which are genetically very similar to us (although we are not their direct descendants), are a particularly passionate bunch, for example. Emory University primatologist Frans B. M. de Waal recalls a zookeeper who accepted what he thought would be a friendly kiss from one of the bonobos, until he felt the ape's tongue in his mouth!

GOOD CHEMISTRY

Since kissing evolved, the act seems to have become addictive. Human lips enjoy the slimmest layer of skin on the human body, and the lips are among the most densely populated with sensory neurons of any body region. When we kiss, these neurons, along with those in the tongue and mouth, rocket messages to the brain and body, setting off delightful sensations, intense emotions and physical reactions.

Of the 12 or 13 cranial nerves that affect cerebral function, five are at work when we kiss, shuttling messages from our lips, tongue, cheeks and nose to a brain that snatches information about the temperature, taste, smell and movements of the entire affair. Some of that information arrives in the somatosensory cortex, a swath of tissue on the surface of the brain that represents tactile information in a map of the body. In that map, the lips loom large because the size of each represented body region is proportional to the density of its nerve endings.

Kissing unleashes a cocktail of chemicals that govern human stress, motivation, social bonding and sexual stimulation. In a new study, psychologist Wendy L. Hill and her student Carey A. Wilson of Lafayette College compared the levels of two key hormones in 15 college male-female couples before and after they kissed and before and after they talked to each other while holding hands. One hormone, oxytocin, is involved in social bonding, and the other, cortisol, plays a role in stress. Hill and Wilson predicted that kissing would boost levels of oxytocin, which also influences social recognition, male and female orgasm, and childbirth. They expected this effect to be particularly pronounced in the study's females, who reported higher levels of intimacy in their relationships. They also forecast a dip in cortisol, because kissing is presumably a stress reliever.

But the researchers were surprised to find that oxytocin levels rose only in the males, whereas it decreased in the females, after either kissing or talking while holding hands. They concluded that females must require more than a kiss to feel emotionally connected or sexually excited during physical contact. Females might, for example, need a more romantic atmosphere than the experimental setting provided, the authors speculate. The study, which Hill and Wilson reported in November 2007 at the annual meeting of the Society for Neuroscience, revealed that cortisol levels dropped for both sexes no matter the form of intimacy, a hint that kissing does in fact reduce stress.

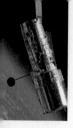

To the extent that kissing is linked to love, the act may similarly boost brain chemicals associated with pleasure, euphoria and a motivation to connect with a certain someone. In 2005 anthropologist Helen Fisher of Rutgers University and her colleagues reported scanning the brains of 17 individuals as they gazed at pictures of people with whom they were deeply in love. The researchers found an unusual flurry of activity in two brain regions that govern pleasure, motivation and reward: the right ventral tegmental area and the right caudate nucleus. Addictive drugs such as cocaine similarly stimulate these reward centers, through the release of the neurotransmitter dopamine. Love, it seems, is a kind of drug for us humans.

Kissing has other primal effects on us as well. Visceral marching orders boost pulse and blood pressure. The pupils dilate, breathing deepens and rational thought retreats, as desire suppresses both prudence and self-consciousness. For their part, the participants are probably too enthralled to care. As poet e. e. cummings once observed: "Kisses are a better fate / than wisdom."

LITMUS TEST

Although a kiss may not be wise, it can be pivotal to a relationship. "One dance," Alex "Hitch" Hitchens says to his client and friend in the 2005 movie *Hitch*, "one look, one kiss, that's all we get . . . one shot, to make the difference between 'happily ever after' and, 'Oh? He's just some guy I went to some thing with once.' "

Can a kiss be that powerful? Some research indicates it can be. In a recent survey Gallup and his colleagues found that 59 percent of 58 men and 66 percent of 122 women admitted there had been times when they were attracted to someone only to find that their interest evaporated after their first kiss. The "bad" kisses had no particular flaws; they simply did not feel right—and they ended the romantic relationship then and there—a kiss of death for that coupling.

The reason a kiss carries such weight, Gallup theorizes, is that it conveys subconscious information about the genetic compatibility of a prospective mate. His hypothesis is consistent with the idea that kissing evolved as a courtship strategy because it helps us rate potential partners.

From a Darwinian perspective, sexual selection is the key to passing on your genes. For us humans, mate choice often involves falling in love. Fisher wrote in her 2005 paper that this "attraction mechanism" in humans "evolved to enable individuals to focus their mating energy on specific others, thereby conserving energy and facilitating mate choice—a primary aspect of reproduction."

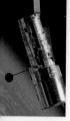

According to Gallup's new findings, kissing may play a crucial role in the progression of a partnership but one that differs between men and women. In a study published in September 2007 Gallup and his colleagues surveyed 1,041 college undergraduates of both sexes about kissing. For most of the men, a deep kiss was largely a way of advancing to the next level sexually. But women were generally looking to take the relationship to the next stage emotionally, assessing not simply whether the other person would make a first-rate source of DNA but also whether he would be a good long-term partner.

"Females use [kissing] . . . to provide information about the level of commitment if they happen to be in a continuing relationship," Gallup told the BBC in September. The locking of lips is thus a kind of emotional barometer: the more enthusiastic it is, the healthier the relationship.

Because women need to invest more energy in producing children and have a shorter biological window in which to reproduce, they need to be pickier about whom they choose for a partner—and they cannot afford to get it wrong. So, at least for women, a passionate kiss may help them choose a mate who is not only good at fathering children but also committed enough to stick around and raise them.

That said, kissing is probably not strictly necessary from an evolutionary point of view. Most other animals do not neck and still manage to produce plenty of offspring. Not even all humans kiss. At the turn of the 20th century Danish scientist Kristoffer Nyrop described Finnish tribes whose members bathed together but considered kissing indecent. In 1897 French anthropologist Paul d'Enjoy reported that the Chinese regard mouth-to-mouth kissing to be as horrifying as many people deem cannibalism to be. In Mongolia some fathers do not kiss their sons. (They smell their heads instead.)

In fact, up to 10 percent of humanity does not touch lips, according to human ethology pioneer Irenäus Eibl-Eibesfeldt, now head of the Max-Planck-Society Film Archive of Human Ethology in Andechs, Germany, writing in his 1970 book, *Love and Hate: The Natural History of Behavior Patterns*. Fisher published a similar figure in 1992. Their findings suggest that some 650 million members of the human species have not mastered the art of osculation, the scientific term for kissing; that is more than the population of any nation on earth except for China and India.

LOPSIDED LOVE

For those cultures that do kiss, however, osculation conveys additional hidden messages. Psychologist Onur Güntürkün of the Ruhr-University of Bochum in Germany recently surveyed 124 couples kissing in public places in the U.S., Germany and Turkey and found that they tilted their heads to the right twice as often as to the left before their lips touched. Right-handedness cannot explain this tendency, because being right-handed is four times more common than is the act of kissing on the right. Instead Güntürkün suspects that right-tilted kissing results from a general preference that develops at the end of gestation and in infancy. This "behavioral asymmetry" is related to the lateralization of brain functions such as speech and spatial awareness.

Nurture may also influence our tendency to tilt to the right. Studies show that as many as 80 percent of mothers, whether right-handed or left-handed, cradle their infants on their left side. Infants cradled, face up, on the left must turn to the right to nurse or nuzzle. As a result, most of us may have learned to associate warmth and security with turning to the right.

Some scientists have proposed that those who tilt their heads to the left when they kiss may be showing less warmth and love than those who tilt to the right. In one theory, tilting right exposes the left cheek, which is controlled by the right, more emotional half of the brain. But a 2006 study by naturalist Julian Greenwood and his colleagues at Stranmillis University College in Belfast, Northern Ireland, counters this notion. The researchers found that 77 percent of 240 undergraduate students leaned right when kissing a doll on the cheek or lips. Tilting to the right with the doll, an impassive act, was nearly as prevalent among subjects as it was among 125 couples observed osculating in Belfast; they tilted right 80 percent of the time. The conclusion: right-kissing probably results from a motor preference, as Güntürkün hypothesized, rather than an emotional one.

Despite all these observations, a kiss continues to resist complete scientific dissection. Close scrutiny of couples has illuminated new complexities woven throughout this simplest and most natural of acts—and the quest to unmask the secrets of passion and love is not likely to end soon. But romance gives up its mysteries grudgingly. And in some ways, we like it like that.

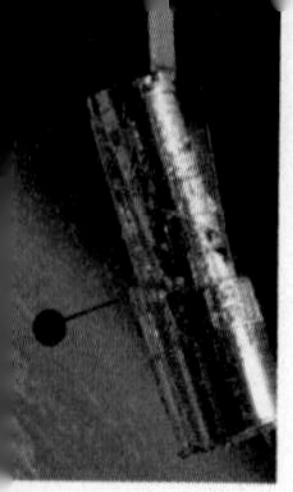

How to write to inform

These steps for the process of informative writing may not progress as neatly as this chart might suggest. Writing is not an assembly-line process. As you write, you are constantly reading what you have written and rethinking.

Keep your readers in mind while you are writing, and if you don't know who your readers might be, imagine someone. What questions might that person have? Where would they appreciate a more detailed explanation?

1 ASSESS THE WRITING TASK

- Read the assignment, carefully noting key words.
- Determine what kind of writing is required. Who are the potential readers?
- Find the limits of your topic. What do you not need to cover? How far do you need to go in breaking down your explanations?
- Review class notes and textbooks; talk to instructor and peers.
- Search for topic ideas in Web subject directories and your library's online catalog.

2 CHOOSE A TOPIC AND WRITE A THESIS

- Within the scope of the assignment, explore what interests you.
- Ask yourself, "Who else will be interested in this topic?"
- Make a list of issues, questions, or problems associated with the topic area.
- Make idea maps about possible topics.
- Discuss possible choices with your peers, coworkers, or instructor.
- Ask questions:
  What happened? What do people need to know?
  Who is my audience?
  How can I connect with them on this topic?
- Narrow your topic. When you learn more about your topic, you should be able to identify one aspect or concept that you can cover thoroughly.
- Write a working thesis that describes what you plan to report or explain.
- If you are unsure if you can follow through with your thesis, do additional research and revise your thesis.

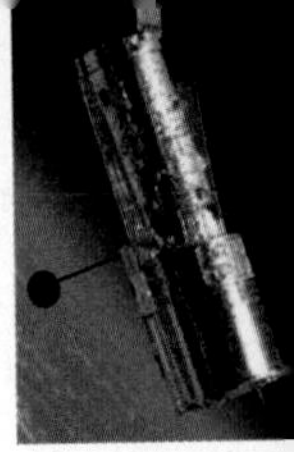

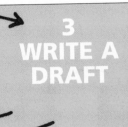

3 WRITE A DRAFT

- Write your revised thesis and main points.
- Think about how you will organize your main points.
- Make a working outline that lists the sections of your essay.
- Draft an introduction that will make readers interested in your subject.
- Build the organization by identifying the topic of each paragraph.
- Draft a conclusion that does more than summarize.
- Write an engaging title.
- If you have statistical information to present, consider using charts or graphs.

4 REVISE, REVISE, REVISE

- Reorganize your ideas for clarity.
- Add detail or further explanation where needed.
- Cut material that distracts from your thesis.
- Check that all key terms are defined.
- Frame your report with an introduction that interests readers and a conclusion that makes a point or raises an interesting question.
- Check that any sources are appropriately quoted or summarized and that they are documented correctly.
- Revise the title to be more accurate and to make readers more interested.
- Review the visual presentation of your report for readability and maximum impact.

5 SUBMITTED VERSION

- Make sure your finished writing meets all formatting requirements.

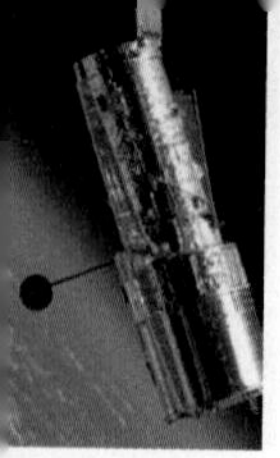

1: Assess the writing task

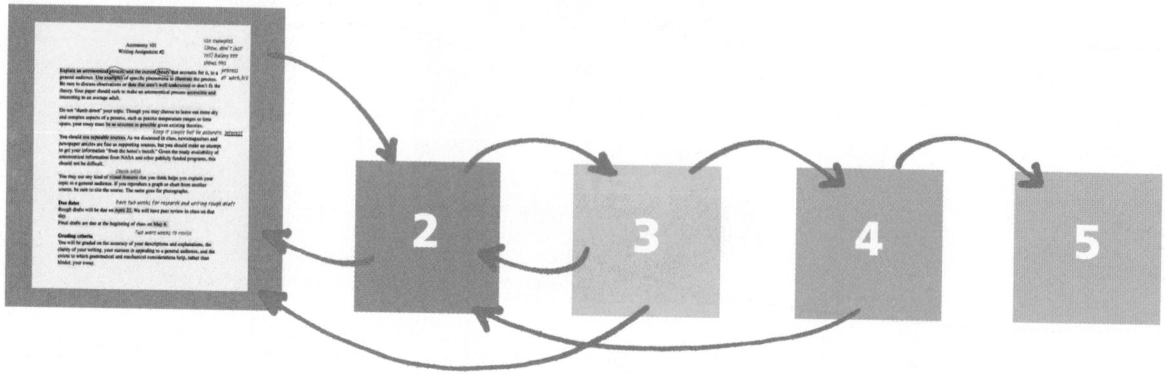

Analyze the assignment

Read your assignment slowly and carefully. Mark off any information about the length specified, date due, formatting, and other requirements. You can attend to this information later. At this point you want to zero in on the subject you will write about and how you will approach that subject.

What kind of writing is required?

Look for key words such as *analyze, compare and contrast, define, discuss,* or *explain*. Often these key words will help you in determining what direction to take. Highlight key words in all questions and commands.

Analyze — Find connections among a set of facts, events, or things, and make them meaningful.

Compare and contrast — Examine how two or more things are alike and how they differ.

Define — Make a claim about how something should be defined, according to features that you set out.

Discuss — Summarize what is known about a particular subject or issue, including research findings.

Explain — Go into detail about how something works or make an unfamiliar subject comprehensible.

Is the audience specified?

If the audience is mentioned in the assignment, how much will they know about your subject? How much background will you need to provide? What attitudes are they likely to have about your subject?

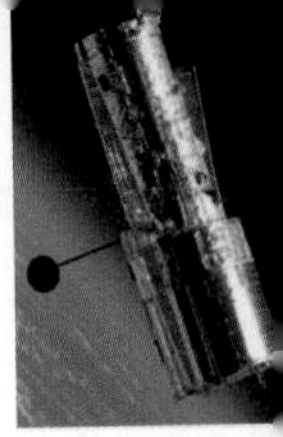

Find a topic

Sometimes you know immediately what you want to write about, but most often, it takes some time to find the right topic. Think first about what is most interesting to you.

What do you know about the general topic?

A good first step is to make an inventory of what you know. Make a list of possible ideas. After you write down as many ideas as you can, go back through the list and place a star beside the ideas that seem most promising.

What ideas can you find in your course notes, class discussions, and your textbooks?

Often you need to look no further than your course materials for possible topics. Think about subjects raised in lectures, in class discussions, or in your textbooks for potential ideas.

What can you find in a database or online library catalog?

Subject directories on databases and your library's online catalog can be valuable sources of potential topics. See Chapter 15.

What might you find on the Web?

Google searches and other search engines often turn up promising ideas to pursue. Yahoo has a subject directory that breaks down large topics into subtopics. See Chapter 15.

What might you find doing field research?

Sometimes the information you need cannot be found in libraries or on the Web, and you have to collect the information firsthand through interviews, surveys, or observations.

Write Now

Explore possible topics

1. Make a list of concepts in your courses. Textbooks usually highlight key concepts, so use them and your course notes to develop your list.
2. Put a check beside the concepts that look most interesting to write about or the ones that mean the most to you.
3. Put a question mark beside the concepts that you don't know much about. If you choose one of these concepts, you will probably have to do in-depth research—by talking to people, by using the Internet, or by going to the library.
4. Select a possible concept. Write nonstop for five minutes about why this concept is interesting to you and how it affects you and other people.

Writer at work

Astronomy 101
Writing Assignment #2

Use examples (Show, don't just tell) Galaxy 999 shows this process at work

Explain an astronomical process, and the current theory that accounts for it, to a general audience. Use examples of specific phenomena to illustrate the process. Be sure to discuss observations or data that aren't well understood or don't fit the theory. Your paper should seek to make an astronomical process accessible and interesting to an average adult.

Do not "dumb down" your topic. Though you may choose to leave out more dry and complex aspects of a process, such as precise temperature ranges or time spans, your essay must be as accurate as possible given existing theories.

Keep it simple but be accurate. Interest

You should use reputable sources. As we discussed in class, newsmagazines and newspaper articles are fine as supporting sources, but you should make an attempt to get your information "from the horse's mouth." Given the ready availability of astronomical information from NASA and other publicly funded programs, this should not be difficult.

Check NASA

You may use any kind of visual features that you think helps you explain your topic to a general audience. If you reproduce a graph or chart from another source, be sure to cite the source. The same goes for photographs.

Due dates

Have two weeks for research and writing rough draft

Rough drafts will be due on April 22. We will have peer review in class on that day.
Final drafts are due at the beginning of class on May 6.

Two more weeks to revise

Grading criteria

You will be graded on the accuracy of your descriptions and explanations, the clarity of your writing, your success in appealing to a general audience, and the extent to which grammatical and mechanical considerations help, rather than hinder, your essay.

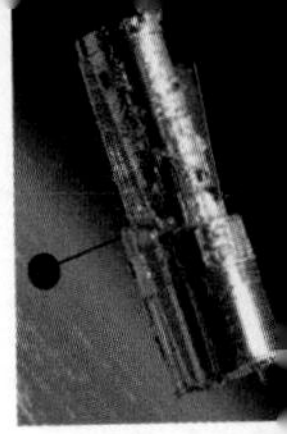

Assess the assignment
Lakshmi Kotra wrote a report in response to this assignment in her Introduction to Astronomy course. She made the following notes and observations to help determine what her essay needed to accomplish, and to explore how she might find a good topic.

Highlight key words
Lakshmi began by highlighting the words in the assignment that gave her specific information about the writing tasks she was to perform.

Identify goals
Then, she made notes on the assignment sheet to specify what she needed to do.

Note time frame
She also made notes about the time frame she has to work in.

Plan strategy
Lakshmi made notes about possible sources for her paper. Then she sketched out a brief time line to follow.

SOURCES

- *Go back over lecture notes—Unit 3 was easiest for me to understand so may be best for a general audience?*
- *Review theories—what makes an idea a theory; who decides what is the accepted theory?*
- *See book also, esp. Table of contents, for topic ideas.*
- *Library subject index*
- *Online subject index*
- *Check NASA archives online for good pictures. Maybe categories there would help too.*
- *Ask Dr. Jenson if we can do something we haven't covered in class yet.*

****Get to the library by Friday so topic is ready over the weekend. See if Karen wants to go too. Check reference librarian hours first, just in case.*

- *Outline over the weekend so I have next week to ask Dr. Jenson for help with the rough draft, if I need it.*
- *Visuals will help make the essay interesting and appealing to a general audience, and also can help explain. So maybe pick two or three topics and then look at NASA images and other visuals to see what is available. This should help narrow down my choices.*

2: Choose a topic and write a thesis

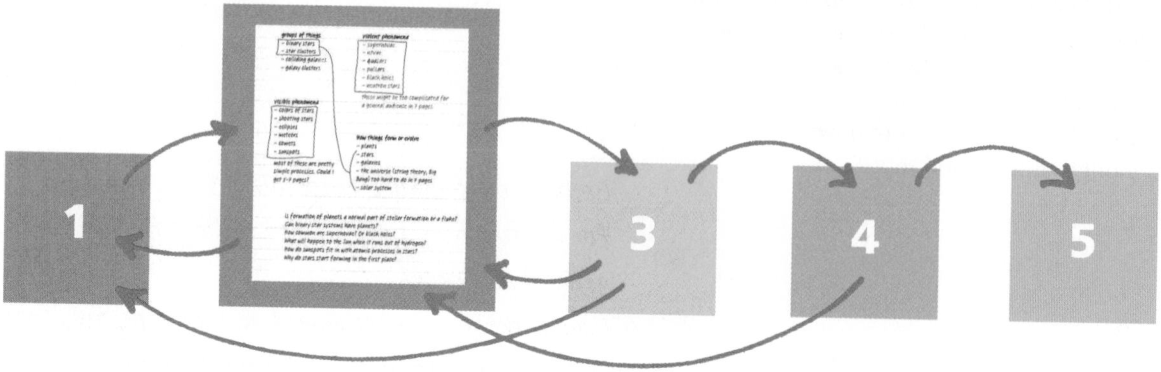

Connect your ideas

After you have done preliminary research and collected ideas, it's time to list possible topics and begin making connections. Circle the most interesting possibilities.

Choose a topic you will enjoy writing about

Writing is fun when you discover new things along the way. Choose a topic you want to explore. If your topic isn't interesting for you, it likely won't be for your readers either.

Choose a topic that your readers will enjoy reading about

Readers may ask, "Why are you telling me this?" Your subject should be interesting to your readers. If the subject isn't one that is immediately interesting, think about ways you can make it so.

Choose a topic that either you know something about or for which you can find the information you need

A central difficulty with writing to inform is determining where to stop. The key to success is to limit the topic. Choose a topic for which you can find the information you need and which you can cover thoroughly in the space you have. If you choose an unfamiliar topic, you must be strongly committed to learning much about it in a short time.

Narrow your topic and write a thesis

Look for ways of dividing large topics into smaller categories, and select one that is promising.

1. What is your topic exactly? (Try to state your answer in specific terms.)
2. What points do you want to make about your topic?
3. What exactly is your purpose in this project? To inform? explain? compare?
4. Develop a working thesis that draws on your answers to questions 1 and 2 and that reflects the purpose you described in your answer to question 3.

Staying on Track

Evaluate your thesis

Your thesis should fulfill the assignment

If your assignment is informative, your purpose is not to argue something is good or bad (see Chapter 11), not to argue for a position (see Chapter 12), and not to argue for change (see Chapter 13).

OFF TRACK

"The electoral college is an antiquated system that results in unfair election results."

(evaluates rather than informs)

ON TRACK

"Considering the huge impact the electoral college system has on American presidential elections, it is surprising that few people understand how it actually works."

Your thesis should be interesting

If your readers already know everything that you have to say, you will bore them. Likewise, your thesis should be significant. Readers will care little about what you have to say if they find your subject trivial.

OFF TRACK

"There are many steps involved before a bill becomes a law."

(vague, bland)

ON TRACK

"Only a tiny fraction of the bills proposed in Congress will ever become laws, and of those, most will accrue so many bizarre amendments and riders that they will barely resemble the original document."

Your thesis should be focused

You cannot tell the story of the Cold War in five pages. Narrow your thesis to a topic you can treat in depth.

OFF TRACK

"Many new products were developed in the 1950s to support the boom in housing construction."

(possibly interesting if particular products are described)

ON TRACK

"The rush to create new housing for returning WWII veterans in the 1950s resulted in many houses that are now extremely hazardous to live in."

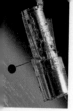

Writer at work

groups of things
- binary stars
- star clusters
- colliding galaxies
- galaxy clusters

violent phenomena
- supernovae
- novae
- quasars
- pulsars
- black holes
- neutron stars

these might be too complicated for a general audience in 7 pages

visible phenomena
- colors of stars
- shooting stars
- eclipses
- meteors
- comets
- sunspots

most of these are pretty simple processes. Could I get 5–7 pages?

How things form or evolve
- plants
- stars
- galaxies
- the universe (string theory, Big Bang) too hard to do in 7 pages
- solar system

Is formation of planets a normal part of stellar formation or a fluke?
Can binary star systems have planets?
How common are supernovae? Or black holes?
What will happen to the Sun when it runs out of hydrogen?
How do sunspots fit in with atomic processes in stars?
Why do stars start forming in the first place?

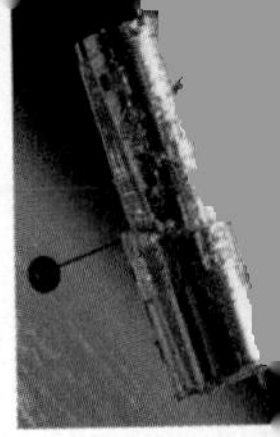

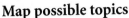

Map possible topics

Lakshmi Kotra began by reviewing her class notes and her textbooks. She also looked in the library's online catalog subject index and an online subject index. She listed all the possible topics she came across in these sources. Then she made an idea map of the topics that appealed to her, clustering types of theories, and adding new ones as they occurred to her. She made a few notes on some of her topic areas, describing how well they would meet the needs of her assignment. And she jotted down questions she had about some topics as well.

Narrow the search

Lakshmi narrowed her search by considering how complicated a topic she wanted to take on. Since she had to explain the theory to a general audience, she ruled out topics like black holes and string theory. She noticed that stellar processes showed up several times in her lists of interesting topics.

GRIN — GREAT IMAGES IN NASA

- Browse by Subject
- Browse by Center
- Search by Keywords
- Frequent Questions
- How to Use GRIN
- Copyright Information

National Aeronautics and Space Administration

NASA Center: Hubble Space Telescope Center
Image # : PR95-44A
Date : 04/01/1995

Title

The Eagle Nebula

Full Description

These eerie, dark pillar-like structures are columns of cool interstellar hydrogen gas and dust that are also incubators for new stars. The pillars protrude from the interior wall of a dark molecular cloud like stalagmites from the floor of a cavern. They are part of the "Eagle Nebula" (also called M16 -- the 16th object in Charles Messier's 18th century catalog of "fuzzy" objects that aren't comets), a nearby star-forming region 7,000 light-years away in the constellation Serpens. Ultraviolet light is responsible for illuminating the convoluted surfaces of the columns and the ghostly streamers of gas boiling away from their surfaces, producing the dramatic visual effects that highlight the three dimensional nature of the clouds. The tallest pillar (left) is about a light-year long from base to tip. As the pillars themselves are slowly eroded away by the ultraviolet light, small globules of even denser gas buried within the pillars are uncovered. These globules have been dubbed "EGGs." EGGs is an acronym for "Evaporating Gaseous Globules," but it is also a word that describes what these objects are. Forming inside at least some of the EGGs are embryonic stars, stars that abruptly stop growing when the EGGs are uncovered and they are separated from the larger reservoir of gas from which they were drawing mass. Eventually, the stars themselves emerge from the EGGs as the EGGs themselves succumb to photoevaporation. The picture was taken on April 1, 1995 with the Hubble Space Telescope Wide Field and Planetary Camera 2. The color image is constructed from three separate images taken in the light of emission from different types of atoms. Red shows emission from singly-ionized sulfur atoms. Green shows emission from hydrogen. Blue shows light emitted by doubly- ionized oxygen atoms.

Identify the topic

Lakshmi settled on stellar formation as a theory that interested her and which she felt confident she could explain in layman's terms. Her preliminary research also indicated there was a wealth of observational data and photos that she could use in her report.

Find images and get source information

Lakshmi wanted to include photographs of star formation, and on NASA's Web site she located images that she could use legally. She carefully recorded all the information she would need to find the images again and to document the images in her paper.

AUTHOR: U.S. National Aeronautics and Space Administration

DATE: April 1, 1995

PAGE TITLE: The Eagle nebula.

SITE TITLE: Great Images in NASA

DATE OF RETRIEVAL: April 5, 2008

URL: http://grin.hq.nasa.gov/ABSTRACTS/GPN-000987.html

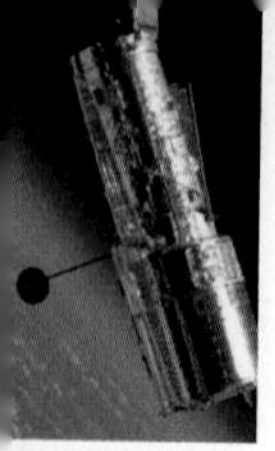

3: Write a draft

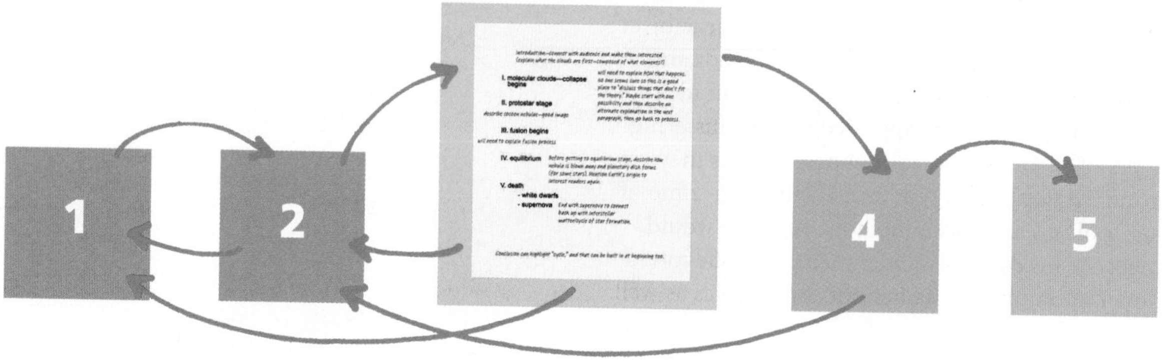

Organize your information

Gather your notes and other materials. Think about how you want to convey the information to your readers.

- If your subject matter occurs over time, you might want to use a chronological order.
- If you need to discuss several aspects, you likely will need to identify key concepts and think about how they relate to each other. An idea map can help you to determine these relationships.
- If you are comparing two or more things, you will want to think about how these things are similar and how they are different.

Make a working outline

A working outline is a tool that you can use as you write your first draft. The more detailed it is, the better. (If you would prefer to write a complete, formal outline before drafting your essay, by all means do so.) To make your outline, follow these steps:

1. List the sections of your essay, in the order that you expect them to appear.
2. Write two or three complete sentences describing the content and purpose of each section.
3. Now, review your outline. Does the project as you have described it here achieve the purpose you intend it to?

Think about a title

An effective title motivates your readers to want to read what you have written. Be as specific as you can.

Consider the use of visuals

Would a table or chart be helpful? photographs? a map? Do you need headings and subheadings?

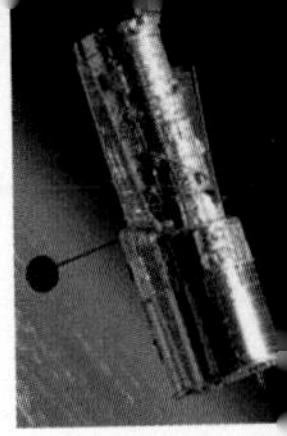

Write an effective introduction and conclusion

Write an effective introduction

Get off to a fast start. Cut to the chase: no empty sentences or big generalizations at the beginning.

OFF TRACK

"Because we all live such busy, hectic lives in these modern times, everyone wants to know why we must wait for hours and hours at the airport before boarding a flight."

(boring, predictable beginning—a signal that the paper will be dull)

ON TRACK

"It's a traveler's worst nightmare: the long line of people at the security gate, snaking back and forth across the waiting area. What exactly goes on in an airport screening area, and how does it help to keep us safe?"

Write an effective conclusion

Remember that a summary of what you have just written is the weakest way to conclude. Think of something interesting for your reader to take away such as an unexpected implication or a provocative example.

OFF TRACK

"In conclusion, we have seen how peer-to-peer file sharing works."

(ineffective; says only that the paper is finished)

ON TRACK

"The peer-to-peer file sharing process is relatively simple. Unfortunately, in many cases it is also illegal. It is ironic that a technology intended to help people has resulted in turning many of them into *de facto* criminals."

(ends with a significant point, which helps readers remember the paper)

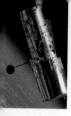

Writer at work

Lakshmi Kotra began with the following rough outline of the process she planned to write about.

Introduction—connect with audience and make them interested (explain what the clouds are first—composed of what elements?)

I. molecular clouds—collapse begins

will need to explain HOW that happens. No one seems sure so this is a good place to "discuss things that don't fit the theory." Maybe start with one possibility and then describe an alternate explanation in the next paragraph, then go back to process.

II. protostar stage

describe cocoon nebulae—good image

III. fusion begins

will need to explain fusion process

IV. equilibrium

Before getting to equilibrium stage, describe how nebula is blown away and planetary disk forms (for some stars). Mention Earth's origin to interest readers again.

V. death

- white dwarfs
- supernova

End with supernova to connect back up with interstellar matter/cycle of star formation.

Conclusion can highlight "cycle," and that can be built in at beginning too.

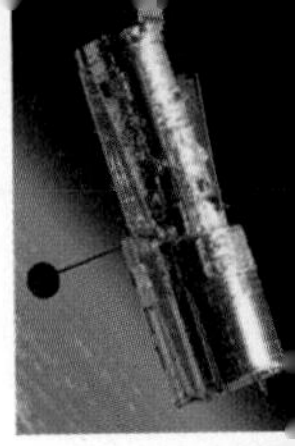

Think about organization

Lakshmi recognized that the process she was describing naturally lent itself to chronological, or time-order, organization, because one thing has to happen after another for a star to form. However, she found that she had to "break out" from the simple time line of stellar formation at some points, to explain in more detail or to trace multiple possibilities.

Make notes on how to develop the subject

She made notes on her outline indicating where she would step away from the chronological pattern to do this explaining. As she considered how she wanted to end her essay, she realized the idea of a "life cycle" for stars could point back toward the essay's beginning. This strategy helped her focus her thesis.

Connect with readers

Lakshmi realized that stellar formation would probably seem like a distant and forbidding topic to a general audience, so she thought carefully about making a connection with her readers. She began by trying out some different ways to introduce her essay. Here are some of her initial attempts and the comments she made on them. Lakshmi decided to work with the last of these openings and see how well she could integrate it with the rest of her essay.

Stars have a complex and fascinating life cycle. Saying it's fascinating doesn't make it fascinating to readers.

Have you ever looked up at the stars at night and wondered why they are there? Vague. Kind of sounds like I'm going to talk about religious or spiritual issues.

Astronomers have spent many years studying the life cycle of stars. So? Anyway, I just want to talk about what they've found, not how long it took them.

If "sunshine on your shoulders" makes you happy, you will be even happier to know that the sun will keep shining for at least another 8 billion years. Too corny. Does anyone even remember that song? Anyway, "happy" isn't the way I want readers to feel. But using a familiar phrase might be good.

"Twinkle, twinkle little star. How I wonder what you are." Good—more personal than "Have you ever looked up at the stars and wondered . . ." Astronomers wonder too. That could be the connection between them and scientists' work. More familiar song, also.

4: Revise, revise, revise

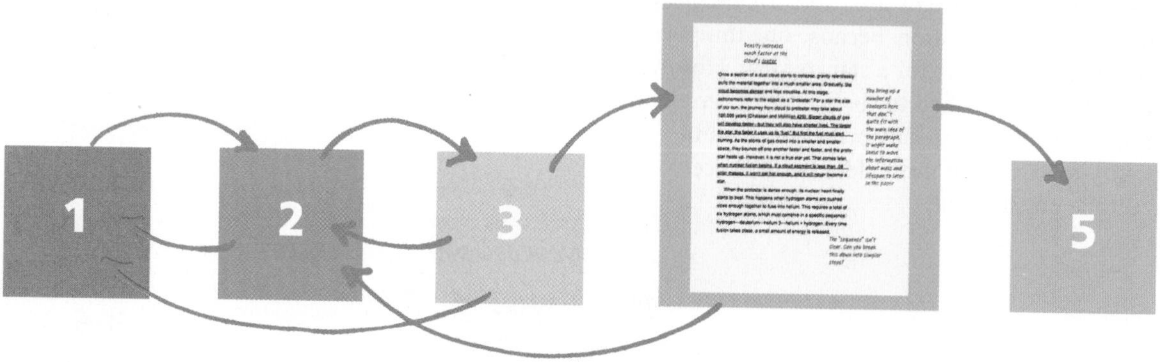

Skilled writers know that the secret to writing well is rewriting. Even the best writers often have to revise several times to get the result they want. You also must have effective strategies for revising if you're going to be successful. The biggest trap you can fall into is starting off with the little stuff first. Leave the small stuff for last.

Does your paper or project meet the assignment?

- Look again at your assignment. Does your paper or project do what the assignment asks?
- Look again at the assignment for specific guidelines, including length, format, and amount of research. Does your work meet these guidelines?

Is your title specific?

- Vague titles suggest dull treatment of the topic. Can you make your title more accurate?

Does your writing have a clear focus?

- Does your project have an explicitly stated thesis? If not, is your thesis clearly implied?
- Is each paragraph related to your thesis?
- Do you get off the track at any point by introducing other topics?
- Are your main points adequately developed?
- Do you support your main points with reasons and evidence?
- Can you add more examples and details that would help to explain your main points?

Is your organization effective?

- Is the order of your main points clear to your reader?
- Are there any places where you find abrupt shifts or gaps?
- Are there sections or paragraphs that could be rearranged to make your draft more effective?

Is your introduction effective?

- Do you have any general statements that you might cut to get off to a faster start?

	• Can you think of a vivid example that might draw in readers? • Can you use a striking fact to get readers interested? • Does your introduction make clear where you are headed?
Is your conclusion effective?	• Conclusions that only summarize tend to bore readers. Does your conclusion add anything new to what you've said already? • Can you use the conclusion to discuss further implications? • Have you left your audience with a final provocative idea that might invite further discussion?
Do you represent yourself effectively?	• To the extent you can, forget for a moment that you wrote what you are reading. What impression do you have of you, the writer? • Does "the writer" create an appropriate tone? • Has "the writer" done his or her homework?
Is the writing project visually effective?	• Is the font attractive and readable? • Are the headings and visuals effective?
Save the editing for last.	When you have finished revising, edit and proofread carefully.

Staying on Track

Reviewing your draft

Give yourself plenty of time for reviewing your draft. For detailed information on how to participate in a peer review, how to review it yourself, and how to respond to comments from your classmates, your instructor, or a campus writing consultant, see pages 24–28.

Some good questions to ask yourself when reviewing informative writing	• Are the explanations in the essay easy to follow? • Are there gaps or places where you feel you need more information? • Are any unusual or discipline-specific words defined for readers? • Can the reader construct a clear picture of what the essay describes? • Is the essay interesting enough to catch readers' attention and keep them reading?

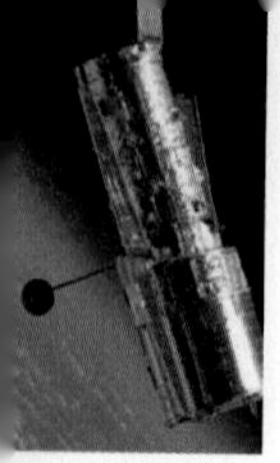

Writer at work

Density increases much faster at the cloud's center

Once a section of a dust cloud starts to collapse, gravity relentlessly pulls the material together into a much smaller area. Gradually, the cloud becomes denser and less cloudlike. At this stage, astronomers refer to the object as a "protostar." For a star the size of our sun, the journey from cloud to protostar may take about 100,000 years (Chaisson and McMillan 429). Bigger clouds of gas will develop faster—but they will also have shorter lives. The larger the star, the faster it uses up its "fuel." But first the fuel must start burning. As the atoms of gas crowd into a smaller and smaller space, they bounce off one another faster and faster, and the protostar heats up. However, it is not a true star yet. That comes later, when nuclear fusion begins. If a cloud segment is less than .08 solar masses, it won't get hot enough, and it will never become a star.

You bring up a number of concepts here that don't quite fit with the main idea of the paragraph. It might make sense to move the information about mass and lifespan to later in the paper

When the protostar is dense enough, its nuclear heart finally starts to beat. This happens when hydrogen atoms are pushed close enough together to fuse into helium. This requires a total of six hydrogen atoms, which must combine in a specific sequence: hydrogen—deuterium—helium 3—helium + hydrogen. Every time fusion takes place, a small amount of energy is released.

The "sequence" isn't clear. Can you break this down into simpler steps?

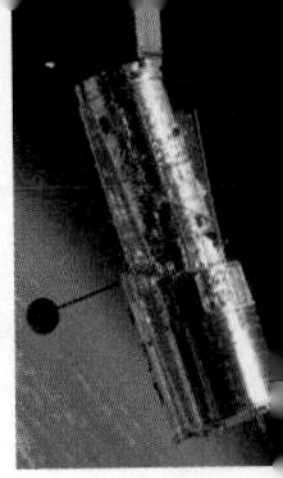

Read carefully your instructor's comments
Lakshmi Kotra gave a copy of her first draft to her instructor for feedback. She used his comments to guide her revision of the essay.

Determine a plan for revision in light of your instructor's comments
Based on her instructor's comments, Lakshmi decided to shift some information on the rates at which stars burn nuclear fuel from an earlier section of the paper to her later discussion of the fates of stars with different masses. This strategy also allowed her to flesh out the description of "brown dwarfs"—starlike objects that do not develop into stars.

Act on specific comments
She also took her instructor's advice about simplifying her explanation of hydrogen fusion.

Read your paper aloud to catch mistakes and awkward phrasing
Lakshmi also read her essay aloud to help identify spelling errors and missing or poorly chosen words.

Visit your writing center
Finally, Lakshmi visited her school's writing center. She asked for specific help in making the paper accessible for an audience without a scientific background. Working with a consultant, she recognized the need to define scientific terms, like *nebulae, protostar,* and *equilibrium,* that might not be familiar to a general audience.

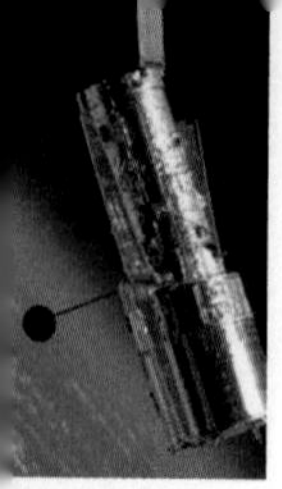

5: Submitted version

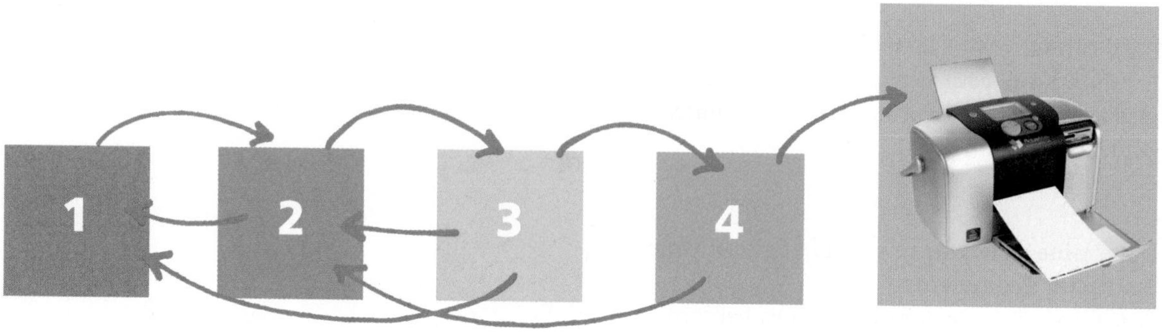

Kotra 1

Lakshmi Kotra

Professor Jenson

Astronomy 101

6 May 2008

The Life Cycle of Stars

"Twinkle, twinkle, little star; how I wonder what you are." This old nursery rhyme may not seem profound, but it echoes some of the biggest questions astronomers puzzle over: What are stars made of? How do they form? How are they born and how do they die? Current theories of star formation answer some of these questions, but not all of them. We do know that, even though stars are separated from one another by vast amounts of space, their life cycles are intertwined.

Twinkling stars are born in dark, cold clouds of dust and gas called nebulae. These clouds consist mainly of hydrogen, and may be as cold as 10 degrees Kelvin (Chaisson and McMillan 427). Nebulae are very dense compared to the near-vacuum of interstellar space. But something must concentrate this dust and gas even more if a star is to

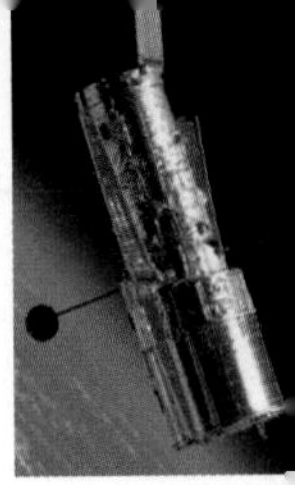

Kotra 2

form. This first part of the star-forming process is not fully understood. Some force has to cause a portion of the nebula to begin collapsing. Magnetism and rotation are two forces already at work in most clouds, but astronomers have long thought that these forces are more likely to counteract the collapsing force of gravity (Chaisson and McMillan 427). However, new research may have found a solution to this problem. In some clouds, magnetic fields may cancel out some or all of the rotational force. This reorganization would allow gravity to begin collapsing the star (Farivar).

Another theory is that a shock wave from some outside event or object might trigger the collapse of a cloud. The Eagle Nebula provides a good illustration of this theory. Ultraviolet radiation from super-hot stars in the nebula has been observed bombarding the surrounding dust and gas. The radiation has stripped away a lot of dust but left dense columns of cloud where stars are believed to be forming. The impact of this "stellar wind" may have also triggered the star formation. Smaller clumps of denser gas are contracting within the columns, taking their first step on the journey to stardom (see fig. 1).

Once a section of a dust cloud starts to collapse, gravity relentlessly pulls the material together into a much smaller area. Gradually, the center of the cloud becomes denser and less cloudlike. At this stage, astronomers refer to the object as a "protostar." For a star the size of our sun, the journey from cloud to protostar may take about 100,000 years (Chaisson and McMillan 429). As the atoms of gas crowd into a smaller and smaller space, they bounce off one another faster and faster, and the protostar heats up. However, it is not a true star yet. That comes later, when nuclear fusion begins. For now,

Kotra 3

Fig. 1. Eagle Nebula
The columns of interstellar gas in the Eagle Nebula are incubators for new stars (US, NASA, "Eagle").

the developing protostar is still surrounded by a shroud of dust that hides it from view. This dust mantle is called a cocoon nebula. Some protostars can be detected by the infrared glow of their cocoon nebulae (Chaisson and McMillan 435-36).

Over millions of years, the protostar continues to grow and change, like a butterfly in its cocoon. Gravity keeps compacting it, making it smaller in size and denser. When the protostar is dense enough, its nuclear heart finally starts to beat. This happens when hydrogen atoms are pushed close enough together to fuse into helium. The fusion process involves several steps. First, two hydrogen atoms will fuse to form an atom of deuterium, or heavy hydrogen. When a third hydrogen atom joins the deuterium atom, an isotope called helium 3 results. Finally,

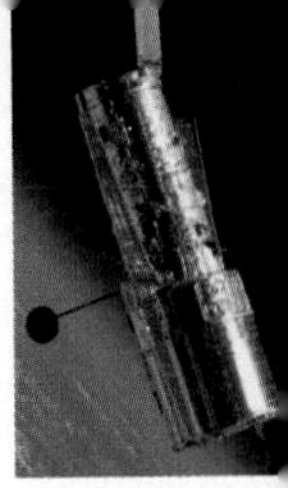

Kotra 4

when two helium 3 atoms fuse together, an atom of regular helium plus two of hydrogen are created. But the crucial part of this process is that, every time fusion takes place, a small amount of energy is released. The radiation emitted from the fusion of hydrogen into helium is what makes the majority of stars shine. Fusion radiation from the Sun lights our planet in the daytime, makes the moon shine at night—and gives you sunburn.

Hydrogen atoms must be moving at extremely high speeds in order to fuse. Another way to say this is that the temperature in the core of a protostar must be very high for fusion to take place: at least 10 million degrees Kelvin (Chaisson and McMillan 431). Now nuclear forces, not just gravity's grip, are controlling the star's development. In fact, these two forces will compete throughout the star's life. Gravity tries to collapse the star, while the pressure of its fast-moving, superheated atoms pushes it outward. As long as the two forces balance each other, the star will remain stable. Astronomers call this state "equilibrium."

During the intense heating at the end of the protostar stage, and when hydrogen fusion is beginning, intense radiation streams off the young star. The dust and gas that have surrounded the protostar are swept away by this energy bombardment, and the star emerges from its cocoon. This phenomenon can be observed visually in NGC 4214. Young stars in this nebula are pouring out radiation that has created "bubbles" in the surrounding gas. Brighter and older stars have pushed away more of the dust and gas. The bubbles around these stars are bigger than those around younger or cooler stars in the nebula (see fig. 2).

Kotra 5

Sometimes, not all of a protostar's dust cocoon blows away. According to one theory, you can look around our own solar system and see the remnants of the dust that once surrounded our Sun. In fact, you are standing on some of it. The Earth and the rest of the planets in our solar system are believed to have formed from a disk of dust and gas left over after the sun formed. The reasons this happens are not entirely clear, but astronomers now think that many stellar systems have planetary disks around them. The Orion Nebula provides some confirmation of this theory. There, astronomers have observed many glowing disks of dust, called "proplyds." They think these disks are actually young stars surrounded by material that will eventually form a system of orbiting planets (see fig. 3).

Fig. 2. Star Formation
Clusters of new stars form from interstellar gas and dust in galaxy NGC 4214 (US, NASA, "Star").

Kotra 6

The size of the original dust cloud a star is born from will also determine how it dies. Some protostars don't quite have what it takes to become a star. Clumps of dust and gas that are smaller than .08 solar masses never get hot enough to begin fusing hydrogen (Chaisson and McMillan 433). These "brown dwarfs" produce infrared radiation, but they never shine visibly.

True stars burn through their nuclear fuel at different rates. The larger the star, the faster its fuel is fused. Smaller stars, like our Sun, are called "dwarf stars." If they began life with less than eight times the mass of our Sun, they will quietly burn hydrogen for perhaps ten billion years. Toward the end of their lives, as they begin to run out of fuel,

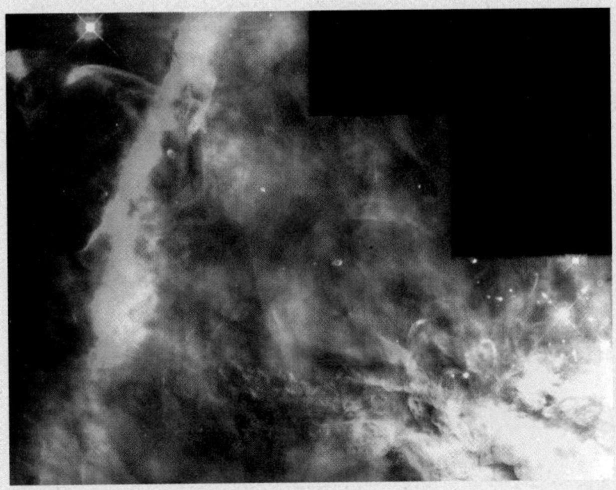

Fig. 3. Orion Nebula
This composite photo of the Orion nebula assembled from images taken by the Hubble Space Telescope shows the beginnings of new solar systems surrounding young stars (US, NASA, "Orion").

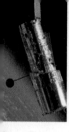

Kotra 7

they will swell briefly into red giant stars, fusing their helium into carbon, and cooling substantially. Finally, they will subside into "white dwarf" stars, about the size of the planet earth. Provided they do not have nearby neighboring stars that might interact with them, white dwarfs gradually dim and cool, until they go dark altogether (Chaisson and McMillan 459). This cooling process is what astronomers predict will some day happen to our Sun.

A star of more than about eight solar masses has a shorter but much more spectacular life. It will fuse all its available fuel in well under one billion years—perhaps in as little as one million years. When a giant star has run through all its available nuclear fuel, it develops a core of iron atoms, which cannot be fused into anything else. When this core has grown to about 1.4 solar masses, the star will explode in a supernova. All that will be left of the original star is a dark neutron star or black hole (Chaisson and McMillan 475). But the shock wave from the supernova may go on to trigger new star formation in dust clouds nearby. In this way, dying stars contribute to the birth of new ones, and the life cycle of stars continues.

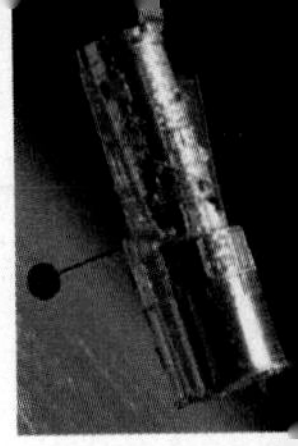

Kotra 8

Works Cited

Chaisson, Eric, and Steve McMillan. *Astronomy Today*. 6th ed. Upper Saddle River: Prentice, 2008. Print.

Farivar, Cyrus. “Galactic Map Aids Stellar Formation Theory.” *Daily Californian*. Daily Californian, 23 Jan. 2002. Web. 8 Apr. 2008.

United States. National Aeronautics and Space Adm. “The Eagle Nebula.” Photograph. *Great Images in NASA*. 1. Apr. 1995. Web. 8 Apr. 2008.

---. ---. “Fireworks of Star Formation Light Up a Galaxy.” Photograph. *Great Images in NASA*. 6 Jan. 2000. Web. 8 Apr. 2008.

---. ---. “The Orion Nebula.” Photograph. *Great Images in NASA*. 20 Nov. 1995. Web. 8 Apr. 2008.

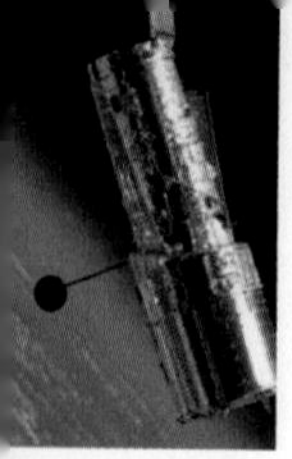

Projects

No matter how diverse its forms, successful informative writing begins with the basics.

- What do readers already know about a subject?
- What do readers need to know about a subject?
- What kind of writing is best suited for particular readers? a Web site? a brochure? an article? or something else?

You'll do many kinds of informative writing in your life after college. The following projects are common informative writing tasks.

Instructions

Be aware that instructions are much harder to write than most people expect. They usually require a lot of detail, yet if they are too complex, people will be confused or intimidated. After all, how many times have you glanced at an instruction booklet for a new appliance, set it aside, and just started pushing buttons?

Think of a fairly simple device you have learned to use, like an iPod or a software application.

Imagine a friend who wants to learn to use the same device. How could you simply and accurately instruct him or her?

Write a one- or two-page set of instructions explaining how to perform a simple task, such as creating a play list on your iPod, using your school's Web-based email service, or changing the toner cartridge in your printer. When you are finished, have a friend volunteer to try out your instructions. How easy is it to follow them? Do they work?

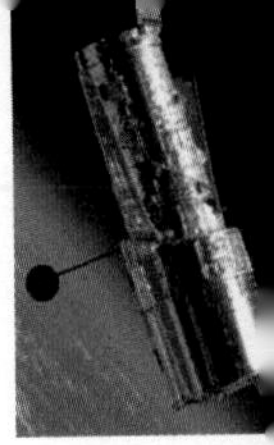

Profile

Find several written profiles of people at your school—these might be your school president, a coach, and an award-winning student. Profiles often appear in school newspapers, on school Web sites, and in news reports about events on campus.

Read the profiles and note what information is included about each person, and what is left out.

- Are the profiles all written for the same audience?
- How does the information in each profile vary depending on the intended audience?

Choose someone else to write a profile about—a classmate, a staff member you have worked with, or even yourself— and interview that person. Choose someone you find interesting. A custodial worker or fellow student can be just as interesting as a college president, depending on the details you select to write about. Model your profile on the examples you have read.

Think carefully about the audience you wish to appeal to. How can you interest them in your subject?

Report

Think of a subject you know a great deal about but most other people, especially those who are your intended readers, do not.

Your subject might come from your life experience

- What's it like to grow up on a family farm?
- What's it like to be an immigrant to the United States?

Your hobbies

- What's the best way to train for a marathon?
- How can you avoid injuries in sports by stretching?

Your personal interests

- Why everyone over age 20 should pay attention to cholesterol

A place that you have found fascinating, or a subject you have studied in college

- The misunderstood nature of conceptual art
- Breakthroughs in nanotechnology in the near future.

Consider what will likely be most interesting about your subject to your readers.

Engage your readers with a provocative title and a thesis that will challenge them to think about your subject in new ways.

Aim for a report of 700–1000 words or about 3–5 double-spaced pages.

9 Rhetorical Analyses

Every piece of writing, every painting, every building, every movie, every new product, every advertisement, is a response to what came before it.

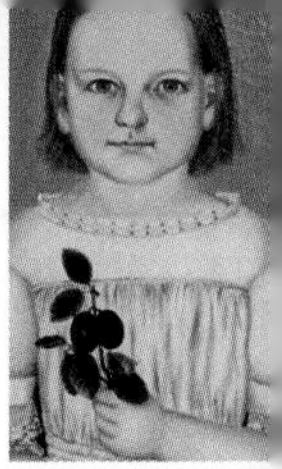

CHAPTER CONTENTS

Writing to analyze

Critical reading and viewing are essential skills for all kinds of writing. Analysis is a more specific aim where those critical reading and viewing skills are applied to particular subjects. Analysis involves dividing a whole into parts that can be studied both as individual entities and as parts of the whole.

Rhetorical analysis is a kind of analysis that divides a whole into parts to understand how an act of speaking or writing conveys meaning. Thus the goal of a rhetorical analysis is to understand how a particular act of writing or speaking influenced particular people at a particular time.

Visual analysis is closely related to rhetorical analysis. The tools of rhetorical analysis have been applied to understanding how other human creations make meaning, including art, buildings, photographs, dance, memorials, advertisements—any kind of symbolic communication.

Literary analysis takes into account elements of literature such as plot, character, and setting, paying particular attention to language and metaphor. The goal of literary analysis is to interpret a literary text and support that interpretation with evidence or, more simply, to make a discovery about a text that you share with your readers.

Text and context

A rhetorical, visual, or literary analysis may be concerned with either text or context, but often it examines both. Textual analysis focuses on the features of a text—the words and evidence in a speech, the images and patterns in a picture, and so on. For a textual analysis, ask

- What is the subject?
- What is the author's claim or what are the main ideas?
- What is the medium of the text? a newspaper? Web site? scholarly journal? a photograph? a short story?
- What appeals are used? What are the author's credentials, and how does he represent himself? What facts or evidence does he present? What values does he share with you and the rest of his audience? What emotions does he try to evoke?
- How is the text organized?
- What kind of style does the author use? Formal or informal, satirical or humorous? Are any metaphors used?

Contextual analysis reconstructs the cultural environment, or context, that existed when a particular rhetorical event took place, and then depends on that recreation to produce clues about persuasive tactics and appeals. For a contextual analysis, ask

- Who is the author? What else has she written or said on this subject? Who does she borrow from or quote? What motivated her to address this issue?
- Who is the audience? What are the occasion and forum for writing? Would the argument have been constructed differently if it had been presented in a different medium? What motivated the newspaper, magazine, or other venue to publish it?
- What is the larger conversation? When did the text appear? Why did it appear at that particular moment? Who or what might this text be responding to?

The statue of Castor stands at the entrance of the Piazza del Campidoglio in Rome. A textual analysis focuses on the statue itself. The size and realism of the statue makes it a masterpiece of classical Roman sculpture.

A contextual analysis focuses on the surroundings and the history of the statue. Legend has Castor and his twin brother Pollux, the mythical sons of Leda, assisting Romans in an early battle. Romans built a large temple in the Forum to honor them. The statues of Castor and Pollux were uncovered in sixteenth-century excavations and brought in 1583 to stand at the top of the Cordonata, a staircase designed by Michelangelo as part of a renovation of the Piazza del Campidoglio commissioned by Pope Paul III Farnese in 1536.

Working Together

Analyze text and context

In a group of three or four students

Find several examples of verbal and visual texts. These might be ads you have seen on television or heard on the radio, photos or editorials in the student newspaper, or Web sites.

- What is the context in which this text was produced?
- How was the creator of the text attempting to influence or persuade the audience? What appeals are made?
- In the visual texts, what connections or associations is the reader invited to create?
- In the verbal texts, what claims and reasons are explicitly stated?

Writing a rhetorical analysis

People often use the term *rhetoric* to describe empty language. "The Governor's speech was just a bunch of rhetoric," you might say, meaning that the Governor offered noble-sounding words but no real ideas. But rhetoric originated with a much more positive meaning. According to Aristotle, rhetoric is "the art of finding in any given case the available means of persuasion." Rhetoric is concerned with producing effective pieces of communication.

Rhetoric can also be used to interpret or analyze. Students of rhetoric know not only how to produce effective communication, but also how to understand communication. The two skills complement each other: Becoming a better writer makes you a better analyst, and becoming a better analyst makes you a better writer. For an example of rhetorical analysis, see pages 186–189.

Components of a rhetorical analysis

What is the author's purpose?	**Identify the purpose.** Some texts have an obvious purpose; for example, an ad wants you to buy something. But texts can have more than one purpose. A politician who accuses an opponent of being corrupt may also be making a case for her own honesty.
Who is the audience?	**Examine the audience.** The most effective texts are ones that are tailored specifically for an audience. What can you determine about the actual audience's values, attitudes, and beliefs? How does the author create an audience in the text by making assumptions about what the audience believes?
Who is the author of my text?	**Examine the author**. How did the author come to this subject? Is the author an expert or an outsider?
What is the background of my text?	**Examine the context**. What else has been said or written on this topic? What was going on at the time that influenced this text?
Which rhetorical appeals are used in my text?	**Analyze rhetorical appeals.** Aristotle set out three primary tactics of argument: appeals to the emotions and deepest held values of the audience (pathos), appeals based on the trustworthiness of the speaker (ethos), and appeals to good reasons (logos).
How does the language and style contribute to the purpose?	**Examine the language and style**. Is the style formal? informal? academic? Does the writer or speaker use humor or satire? What metaphors are used?

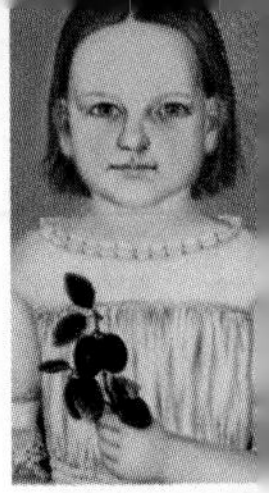

Keys to rhetorical analysis

Choose a text that you care about	Your paper will require close multiple readings of the text. Your interest (or lack of interest) in your text will come through in your paper.
Write a descriptive title	The title of your essay should indicate the focus of your analysis.
Check your thesis	Make sure your thesis is sensible and realistic as well as being supported by evidence and examples in the text.
Interrogate evidence	Look closely at the evidence supporting the writer's claims. Is it convincing? Are there gaps? Can it be interpreted in a different way? Is counterevidence acknowledged?
Examine underlying values, attitudes, and beliefs	When a writer or speaker neglects the audience's values, attitudes, and beliefs, the text is rarely persuasive.
Identify fallacies	Be aware when only one side of the story is being presented, when claims and accusations are grossly exaggerated, and when complex issues are oversimplified. See pages 14–15.
Identify relationships	An effective rhetorical analysis makes connections, showing how strategies in the text are responses to other texts and the larger context.
Recognize complexity	Many texts cannot be reduced to a sound bite. Successful rhetorical analyses often read between the lines to explain why a statement may be ironic or what is not being said. Readers appreciate being shown something they may not otherwise have noticed.

Writing a visual analysis

We are bombarded by images on a daily basis. They compete for our attention, urge us to buy things, and guide us on our way home from work. These visual texts frequently attempt to persuade us; to make us think, feel, or act a certain way. Yet we rarely stop to consider how they do their work.

Visual texts leave room for the audience to interpret to a greater degree than many verbal texts, which make them particularly rich subjects for analysis.

Components of a visual analysis

What kind of visual is it?	**Describe what you see.** Is it a single image, part of a series, a sign, a building, or something else? What are the conventions for this kind of visual?
What is the image about?	**Consider the subject.** What does the image depict? What is the setting? What is the purpose? Are words connected with the image?
How is the image arranged?	**Analyze the composition.** What elements are most prominent? Which are repeated? Which are balanced or in contrast to each other? Which details are important?
What is the context?	**Examine the context.** Who created the image? When and where did it first appear? Can you determine why it was created?
What visuals are like it?	**Look for connections.** What is the genre? What kind of visual is it? What elements have you seen before? Which remind you of other visuals?

Keys to visual analysis

Choose a visual text that you care about	If an image or other visual text means something to you, you will find it easier to analyze.
Pay close attention to details	Identify the key details that keep the viewer's attention and convey meaning. Also, examine the point of view—the viewer's perspective of the subject.
Provide a frame for understanding	You will need to provide a context for understanding a visual text, giving a sense of how it is a response to events and trends going on at the time and how it was initially understood.
Go beyond the obvious	A successful visual analysis gets readers to make connections and see aspects that they otherwise would not have noticed.

Stone Cold
Steve Austin #1
PRETTY BELLE
PREMIUM CALIFORNIA CITRUS
Clementine
CHEVROLET
5V00715
Panasonic
protecting your purchase

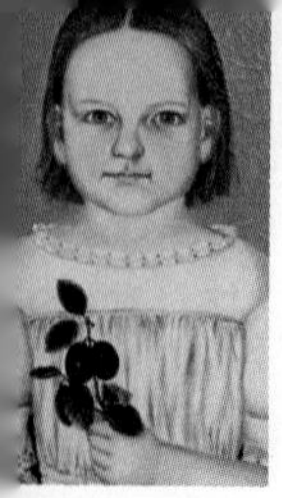

An effective analysis

A successful analysis can be generally textual or contextual in nature. But the two approaches are not mutually exclusive—in fact, most analysts consider the details of the text, but also attend to the particulars of context as well.

theguardian

Straight from the Heart
Tim Collins

On July 11, 2005, a woman named Marie Fatayi-Williams made an immensely moving speech in London at the site where her son Anthony had been killed in a terrorist bombing four days earlier. Her speech was reported in numerous media outlets. *The Guardian,* a British newspaper, printed Fatayi-Williams's speech on July 13, with an analysis and commentary by Tim Collins. Collins considers the factors that make Fatayi-Williams's speech so powerful, and places it in a larger context of responses to terrorism.

Caught in the spotlight of history, set on the stage of a very public event, Marie Fatayi-Williams, the mother of Anthony Fatayi-Williams, 26 and missing since Thursday, appeals for news of her son. Her words are a mixture of stirring rhetoric, heartfelt appeal and a stateswoman-like vision, and so speak on many levels to the nation and the world. Her appeal is a simple one—where is my son? If he has been killed, then why? Who has gained?

Collins points out the appeal to pathos—the beliefs and values of the audience—that lies at the heart of Fatayi-Williams's speech.

Marie has found herself, as I did on the eve of the invasion of Iraq, an unwitting voice, speaking amid momentous events. Her appeal, delivered on Monday not far from Tavistock Square, where she fears her son died in the bomb attack on the number 30 bus, gives a verbal form to the whirlpool of emotions that have engulfed society as the result of last week's bombings. I suspect Marie, like myself, had no idea that her words would find such wide recognition, have fed such an acute hunger for explanation, have slaked such a thirst for expression of the sheer horror of Thursday's events.

Collins identifies the genre of the speech, which is usually crafted for a specific occasion. Marie's speech is remarkable because it is spontaneous.

This kind of speech is normally the preserve of the great orators, statesmen and playwrights, of Shakespeare, Churchill or Lincoln. It is often a single speech, a soliloquy or address from the steps of the gallows, that explains, inspires, exhorts and challenges. But always such addresses are crafted for effect and consciously intended to sway and influence, and often, as in the case of Shakespeare's Henry V, they are set in the mouth

of a long dead hero or delivered by wordsmiths who are masters of their craft. It is rare in history that such oratory is the genuine article, springing from the heart and bursting forth to an unwitting audience. In Marie's case, her speech gains its power as a vehicle of grief and loss, and of the angst of a mother who yearns for her beloved son. In my case it was the opposite emotion from which I drew inspiration—an appeal to understand, to empathize, to give courage and purpose. I was motivated by a need to warn and teach as well as to encourage. Marie's motivation is a reflection on loss and that most powerful of all emotions, a mother's love.

The form the address takes is as poignant as the language used. There is an initial explanation of the extraordinary circumstances of the loss, a cri de coeur for the innocent blood lost, a rejection of the act by its comparison to the great liberators, and the assertion that her loss is all our loss in the family of humanity. It ends with her personal grief for her flesh and blood, her hopes and pride. The language echoes verses of the Bible as well as from the Koran. It has raw passion as well as heart-rending pathos.

Several rhetorical techniques used in the speech connect it to a larger historical tradition.

With only a photograph of her son and a sheet of paper as a prompt, Marie's words burst out with as much emotion as anger. Her speech stands in stark contrast to the pronouncements of politicians, prepared by aides and delivered from copious notes. It is indeed the raw originality and authentic angst that give the delivery such impact, the plea such effect. No knighted veteran of the Royal Shakespeare Company could deliver such an address without hours or even days of rehearsal. I know from my own experience that only momentous events can provoke such a moment, only raw emotion can inspire such a spontaneous plea. I am often asked how long it took me to write my speech, delivered to my regiment, the Royal Irish, on the eve of the invasion of Iraq on March 19, 2003, at Fort Blair Mayne camp in the Kuwaiti desert. My answer is simple—not one moment. There was no plan; I spoke without notes. For me there was only the looming specter of actual warfare and the certainty of loss and killing, and I was speaking to myself as well as to my men. I suspect for Marie there was only the yawning black void of loss, the cavern left behind in her life caused by the loss of a son who can never be replaced.

Collins's own experience informs his understanding of what Fatayi-Williams might have been feeling. His empathy helps assure his audience that he is qualified to comment on the meaning of her speech.

What, then, can we take from this? Marie's appeal is as important as it is momentous. Her words are as free from hatred as they are free from self-interest; it is clear that no man can give her her heart's desire—her son. I was also struck by the quiet dignity of her words, the clarity of her view and the weight of her convictions. She does not condemn, she appeals; her words act as an indictment of all war and violence, not just acts of terror but also the unnecessary aggression of nation states. Her message is simple: here is a human who only wanted to give, to succeed and to make his mother proud. Where is the victory in his death? Where is the progress in his destruction? In her own words: "What inspiration can senseless slaughter provide?"

Collins examines how Marie creates her ethos, which convinces her audience of her sincerity and lack of malice.

I am certain that Marie's appeal will go down as one of the great speeches of our new century. It will give comfort to the families and friends of the dead and injured, both of this act and no doubt, regrettably, of events still to come. It should act as a caution to statesmen and leaders, a focus for public grief and, ultimately, as a challenge to, as well as a condemnation of, the perpetrators.

Collins sees Fatayi-Williams's directness as perhaps the most important aspect of her speech. She responds to historic events in a way that personalizes them and shows their human cost.

Marie is already an icon of the loss of Thursday July 7. Having travelled from Africa to find a better life, Anthony Fatayi-Williams carried the hopes and pride of his family. Now, as his mother has traveled to London, arguably one of the most cosmopolitan and integrated cities in the world, and standing nearby a wrecked icon of that city, a red double-decker bus, she has made an appeal which is as haunting as it is relevant, as poignant as it is appealing. It is a fact that such oratory as both Marie and I produced is born of momentous events, and inspired by hope and fears in equal measure.

But Marie's appeal is also important on another level. I have long urged soldiers in conflict zones to keep communicating with the population in order to be seen as people—it is easier to kill uniforms than it is to kill people. On July 7 the suicide bombers attacked icons of a society that they hated more than they loved life, the red London bus and the tube. Marie's speech has stressed the real victims' identities. They are all of us.

Marie's speech

Marie Fatayi-Williams

This is Anthony, Anthony Fatayi-Williams, 26 years old, he's missing and we fear that he was in the bus explosion ... on Thursday. We don't know. We do know from the witnesses that he left the Northern line in Euston. We know he made a call to his office at Amec at 9.41 from the NW1 area to say he could not make [it] by the tube but he would find alternative means to work.

Since then he has not made any contact with any single person. Not New York, not Madrid, not London. There has been widespread slaughter of innocent people. There have been streams of tears, innocent tears. There have been rivers of blood, innocent blood. Death in the morning, people going to find their livelihood, death in the noontime on the highways and streets.

They are not warriors. Which cause has been served? Certainly not the cause of God, not the cause of Allah because God Almighty only gives life and is full of mercy. Anyone who has been misled, or is being misled to believe that by killing innocent people he or she is serving God should think again because it's not true. Terrorism is not the way, terrorism is not the way. It doesn't beget peace. We can't deliver peace by terrorism, never can we deliver peace by killing people. Throughout history, those people who have changed the world have done so without violence, they have won people to their cause through peaceful protest. Nelson Mandela, Martin Luther King, Mahatma Gandhi, their discipline, their self-sacrifice, their conviction made people turn towards them, to follow them. What inspiration can senseless slaughter provide? Death and destruction of young people in their prime as well as old and helpless can never be the foundations for building society.

My son Anthony is my first son, my only son, the head of my family. In African society, we hold on to sons. He has dreams and hopes and I, his mother, must fight to protect them. This is now the fifth day, five days on, and we are waiting to

know what happened to him and I, his mother, I need to know what happened to Anthony. His young sisters need to know what happened, his uncles and aunties need to know what happened to Anthony, his father needs to know what happened to Anthony. Millions of my friends back home in Nigeria need to know what happened to Anthony. His friends surrounding me here, who have put this together, need to know what has happened to Anthony. I need to know, I want to protect him. I'm his mother, I will fight till I die to protect him. To protect his values and to protect his memory.

Innocent blood will always cry to God Almighty for reparation. How much blood must be spilled? How many tears shall we cry? How many mothers' hearts must be maimed? My heart is maimed. I pray I will see my son, Anthony. Why? I need to know, Anthony needs to know, Anthony needs to know, so do many other unaccounted for innocent victims, they need to know.

It's time to stop and think. We cannot live in fear because we are surrounded by hatred. Look around us today. Anthony is a Nigerian, born in London, worked in London, he is a world citizen. Here today we have Christians, Muslims, Jews, Sikhs, Hindus, all of us united in love for Anthony. Hatred begets only hatred. It is time to stop this vicious cycle of killing. We must all stand together, for our common humanity. I need to know what happened to my Anthony. He's the love of my life. My first son, my first son, 26. He tells me one day, "Mummy, I don't want to die, I don't want to die. I want to live, I want to take care of you, I will do great things for you, I will look after you, you will see what I will achieve for you. I will make you happy." And he was making me happy. I am proud of him, I am still very proud of him but I need to now where he is, I need to know what happened to him. I grieve, I am sad, I am distraught, I am destroyed.

He didn't do anything to anybody, he loved everybody so much. If what I hear is true, even when he came out of the underground he was directing people to take buses, to be sure that they were OK. Then he called his office at the same time to tell them he was running late. He was a multi-purpose person, trying to save people, trying to call his office, trying to meet his appointments. What did he then do to deserve this? Where is he, someone tell me, where is he?

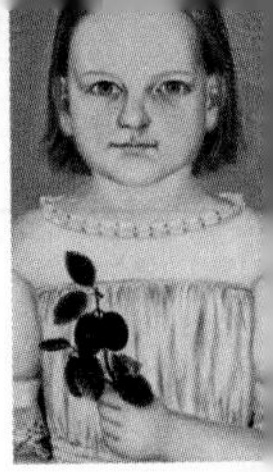

Explore Current Issues

Analyzing the rhetoric of the gay marriage debate

On May 15, 2008, the California Supreme Court handed down a decision that legalized gay marriage in the state, based on the ruling that denying same-sex couples the same rights as different-sex couples was unconstitutional. Conservative and religious groups called the judges activist and liberal and accused them of bending to social and political pressure in going against the intentions of the framers of the state constitution.

Andrew Sullivan, a gay, conservative political commentator argues instead that the law *had* to adapt—the judges' apparent change of mind was not ideological but instead "empirical...based on increased knowledge of who gay people are." He continues:

> Once you absorb this knowledge, this evidence, this truth, legislative schemes which arbitrarily separate gay people from straight people—and put gay relationships in a separate and unequal box—seem grossly unfair, and certainly a violation of the equality promised in various state constitutions. I think that's what has really happened in the two decades I've been arguing about this. We have altered our view of homosexuality. And the alteration is not one of degree but of kind. And so the law must adapt. Maybe it has happened too quickly for easy cultural digestion. But it is inevitable if we are not now to replace knowledge with fear, and inclusion with, yes, prejudice.

Write about it

1. What is Sullivan's position in the debate over whether or not the California Supreme Court was right to make same-sex marriage? What are the reasons he gives to support this position?
2. What strategies other than appeals to logic does he use to build his argument? In other words, how does he appeal to his audience's values? Their emotions? How does he present himself as a credible voice for this position?
3. Why is Sullivan making this argument? What is at stake for him? What is at stake for his audience?
4. Summarize the position that Sullivan is arguing against. What is at stake for those who support this position? Does Sullivan attempt to address these concerns?

How to read analyses

Make notes as you read, either in the margins, if it is your own copy, or on paper or a computer file. Circle any words or references that you don't know and look them up.

What kind of analysis is it?	• Is it a rhetorical analysis? a literary analysis? an analysis of a visual? an analysis of an object?
Where did it come from?	• Who wrote the analysis? • What do you know about the writer's background that might have influenced the analysis?
Who is the intended audience?	• What clues do you find about whom the writer had in mind as the readers? • What does the writer assume that the readers already know about the subject? • What new knowledge is the writer providing?
What is the focus of the analysis?	• What does the writer have to say about the context or background? • What does the writer have to say about how the text or object is composed?
What is the significance of the analysis?	• Does the writer make specific claims? • What did you learn or come to understand differently by reading the analysis?
How is it composed?	• How does the writer represent herself or himself? • How would you characterize the style? • If there are any photographs or other graphics, what information do they contribute?

The Collapse of Big Media: The Young and the Restless

(ESSAY)

David T. Z. Mindich

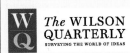

The WILSON QUARTERLY
SURVEYING THE WORLD OF IDEAS

David T. Z. Mindich, a former assignment editor at CNN, is a professor of journalism and mass communication at St. Michael's College in Colchester, Vermont, and the author of *Tuned Out: Why Americans under 40 Don't Follow the News* (2005). "The Collapse of Big Media: The Young and the Restless" was published in the *Wilson Quarterly* in spring 2005.

Return to these questions after you have finished reading.

Analyzing and Connecting

1. Mindich's essay is an audience analysis in which he concludes that "Most of the young people I interviewed had almost no measurable interest in political news." First, from your experience do you agree with Mindich's claim? If you do agree, does having no measurable interest in political news mean that young people are not interested in news in general?
2. Make a log for one entire day on all the news you read, watch, or listen to: newspapers, radio, television news broadcasts, comedy reporting of news like *The Daily Show*, comic monologues commenting on events, news flashes at the bottom of other television programs, news on the Web, blogs, and personal news sources such as email. Make notes about what the news contained, and keep track of the time you spent reading, viewing, or listening. On the next day total the time for each category. Bring your analysis to class to compare with other students' totals. Do the results for the entire class surprise you in any way?
3. Mindich speaks of the decline in newspaper readership and television news viewing as a cultural crisis. Do you believe this trend is something to worry about? Why or why not?
4. In the next-to-last paragraph, Mindich makes proposals that news should be a part of the school curriculum, high school seniors should take a civics test, and broadcasters should be required to produce a certain amount of children's news programming. Do you support these proposals? What suggestions do you have to raise the civic awareness of young people?

Finding Ideas for Writing

Watch the NBC, CBS, or ABC evening news and make a list of the ads. Then watch *The Daily Show* or another comedy news program and make a list of the ads. Write a paragraph in which you compare the lists. What can you infer about the audiences for each program from the ads? What age group is being targeted? Are men or women being targeted? What income level?

The Collapse of Big Media: The Young and the Restless

When news executives look at the decline over the past few decades in the number of people who read or watch the news, they're scared silly. But then they reassure themselves that the kids will come around. Conventional wisdom runs that as young men and women gain the trappings of adulthood—a job, a spouse, children, and a house—they tend to pick up the news habit, too. As CBS News president Andrew Heyward declared in 2002, "Time is on our side in that as you get older, you tend to get more interested in the world around you." Unfortunately for Heyward and other news executives, the evidence suggests that young people are not picking up the news habit—not in their teens, not in their twenties, not even in their thirties.

When they aren't reassuring themselves, editors and publishers are lying awake at night thinking about the dismaying trends of recent decades. In 1972, nearly half of 18-to-22-year-olds read a newspaper every day, according to research conducted by Wolfram Peiser, a scholar who studies newspaper readership. Today, less than a quarter do. That younger people are less likely to read than their elders is of grave concern, but perhaps not surprising. In fact, the baby boomers who came of age in the 1970s are less avid news consumers than their parents were. More ominous for the future of the news media, however, is Peiser's research showing that a particular age cohort's reading habits do not change much with time; in other words, as people age, they continue the news habits of their younger days. Thus, the real danger, Peiser says, is that cohort replacement builds in a general decline in newspaper reading. The deleterious effects of this phenomenon are clearly evident: In 1972, nearly three-quarters of the 34-to-37 age group read a paper daily. Those thirtysomethings have been replaced by successive crops of thirtysomethings, each reading less than its predecessor. Today, only about a third of this group reads a newspaper every day. This means that fewer parents are bringing home a newspaper or discussing current events over dinner. And fewer kids are growing up in households in which newspapers matter.

A similar decline is evident in television news viewership. In the past decade, the median age of network television news viewers has crept up from about 50 to about 60.

Tune in to any network news show or CNN, and note the products hawked in the commercials: The pitches for Viagra, Metamucil, Depends, and Fixodent are not aimed at teenyboppers. Compounding the problem of a graying news audience is the proliferation of televisions within the typical household, which diminishes adult influence over what's watched. In 1970, six percent of all sixth graders had TVs in their bedrooms; today that number is an astonishing 77 percent. If you are in sixth grade and sitting alone in your room, you're probably not watching Peter Jennings.

One of the clearest signs of the sea change in news viewing habits was the uproar following the appearance last fall by Jon Stewart, host of *The Daily Show*, a parody of a news program, on CNN's *Crossfire*, a real one. With a median age of 34, *The Daily Show*'s audience is the envy of CNN, so when Stewart told *Crossfire*'s hosts that their show's predictable left/right approach to debates of current issues was "hurting America," one could have guessed that CNN bigwigs would pay attention. But who could have foreseen that CNN president Jonathan Klein would cancel *Crossfire*? "I agree wholeheartedly with Jon Stewart's overall premise," he told the *New York Times*. News executives are so desperate to get to consumers before the AARP does that they're willing to heed the advice of a comedian.

If the young (and not so young) are not reading newspapers or watching network television news, many assume that they are getting news online. Not so. Only 18 percent of Americans listed the Internet as a "primary news source" in a survey released earlier this year by the Pew Internet and American Life Project and the Pew Research Center for the People and the Press. And the theory that younger people are more reliant on the Internet for news than their elders doesn't hold up. Certainly an engaged minority of young people use the Net to get a lot of news, but studies show that most use it primarily for e-mailing, instant messaging, games, and other diversions. You only need to wander into a computer lab at your local college or high school and see what the students have on their screens for the dismal confirmation of these choices.

The entertainment options competing with the news for the attention of the youth audience have multiplied exponentially. In the 1960s, there were only a handful of television stations in any given market. When Walter Cronkite shook the nation by declaring in a February 1968 report on the Vietnam War that the United States was "mired in

stalemate," he spoke to a captive audience. New York City, for example, had only seven broadcast stations. At 10:30 p.m. on the night of Cronkite's remarks, channels 4 and 11 ran movies, channels 5 and 9 had discussion shows, and channel 7 was showing *N. Y. P. D.*, a cop show. In this media universe of limited competition, nearly 80 percent of all television viewers watched the nightly news, and from the late 1960s on, Cronkite won the lion's share of the total news audience. Today, young people can choose from hundreds of stations, less than a tenth of which are devoted to news. And that's not to mention the many competing diversions that weren't available in 1968, from video games to iPods. Amid this entertainment cornucopia, the combined network news viewership has shrunk significantly—from some 50 million nightly in the 1960s to about 25 million today. (In comparison, CNN's audience is minuscule, typically no more than a million or so viewers, while public television's *NewsHour with Jim Lehrer* generally reaches fewer than three million viewers.)

The effects of this diet are evident in how little Americans know about current events. True, Americans have been extremely uninformed for a long time. Most follow public affairs only in a vague way, and many don't bother to engage at all. In the 1950s and 1960s, at the height of the Cold War, a poll revealed that only 55 percent of Americans knew that East Germany was a communist country, and less than half knew that the Soviet Union was not part of NATO, report political scientists Michael X. Delli Carpini and Scott Keeter in *What Americans Know about Politics and Why It Matters* (1996). In short, there was never a golden age of informed citizenry. But in recent decades, Americans' ignorance has reached truly stupefying levels, particularly among young adults. A series of reports published over the past two decades by the Pew Research Center for the People and the Press (and its predecessor, the Times Mirror Center) suggest that young adults were once nearly as informed as their elders on a range of political issues. From 1944 to 1968, the interest of younger people in the news as reported in opinion surveys was less than five percent below that of the population at large. Political debates and elections in the 1940s, the Army-McCarthy hearings of the 1950s, and the Vietnam War in the 1960s generated as much interest among the young as among older people. But Watergate in the 1970s was the last in this series of defining events to draw general public attention. (Decades later, in 2001, the bombing of the World Trade Center towers revived general public engagement, at least for a few weeks.) Soon after Watergate, surveys began to show flagging interest in current affairs among younger people.

There is no single explanation for this sudden break. Many of the young people I spoke with in doing my research were disaffected with the political process and believed that it was completely insulated from public pressure. Why, in that case, keep up with public affairs? The blurring line between entertainment and journalism, along with corporate consolidation of big media companies, has also bred in some minds a deep skepticism about the news media's offerings. At bottom, however, the sense of community has declined as Americans are able to live increasingly isolated lives, spending long hours commuting to work and holing up in suburban homes cocooned from the rest of the world.

The failing health of the nation's news media is not only a symptom of Americans' low levels of engagement in political life. It is a threat to political life itself. "The role of the press," writes news media critic James W. Carey, "is simply to make sure that in the short run we don't get screwed." Independent, fair, and accurate reporting is what gives "We the People" our check on power. Reporters dig up corruption and confront power; they focus the public's attention on government policies and actions that are unwise, unjust, or simply ineffective. It was the news media that exposed the Watergate burglary and cover-up engineered by Richard Nixon, sparked the investigation of the Iran-Contra affair during the watch of Ronald Reagan and George H. W. Bush, ferreted out Bill Clinton's Whitewater dealings, and turned a searchlight on George W. Bush's extrajudicial arrests of American citizens suspected of terrorism.

A shrinking audience impairs the news media's ability to carry out their watchdog role. It also permits the powers that be to undermine journalism's legitimate functions. Where was the public outrage when it was revealed that the current Bush administration had secretly paid journalists to carry its water, or when the White House denied a press pass to a real journalist, Maureen Dowd of the *New York Times*, and gave one to a political hack who wrote for purely partisan outlets using a fake identity? The whole notion of the news media as the public's watchdog, once an unquestioned article of the American civic faith, is now in jeopardy. A recent study commissioned by the John S. and James L. Knight Foundation showed that more than a third of high school students feel that newspaper articles should be vetted by the federal government before publication.

If we are entering a post-journalism age—in which the majority of Americans, young and old, have little interaction with mainstream news media—the most valuable thing we are losing is the marketplace of ideas that newspapers and news broadcasts uniquely provide, that place where views clash and the full range of democratic choices is debated. You usually don't get that on a blog. You don't get that in the left-leaning *Nation* or on right-wing talk shows. But any newspaper worth its salt, and there are plenty, presents a variety of views, including ones antithetical to its editorial page positions. These papers are hardly immune from criticism—they sometimes err, get sloppy, or succumb to partisan or ideological bias—but they do strive to be accurate and independent sources of fact and opinion, and more often than not they fulfill that indispensable public function.

America's newspapers and television news divisions aren't going to save themselves by competing with reality shows and soap operas. The appetite for news, and for engagement with civic life itself, must be nurtured and promoted, and it's very much in the public interest to undertake the task. It's not the impossible assignment it may seem. During the course of my research, I met a group of boys in New Orleans who were very unlikely consumers of news: They were saturated with television programs and video games, they were poor, and they were in eighth grade. Yet they were all reading the *New York Times* online. Why? Because one of their teachers had assigned the newspaper to them to read when they were in sixth grade, and the habit stuck. There's no reason why print and broadcast news shouldn't be a bigger part of the school curriculum, or why there shouldn't be a short civics/current affairs section on the SAT for college-bound students, or why all high school seniors shouldn't have to take a nonbinding version of the civics test given to immigrants who want to become U.S. citizens. And why shouldn't broadcasters be required to produce a certain amount of children's news programming in return for their access to the public airwaves? These are only the most obvious possibilities.

Reporters, editors, producers, and media business executives will all need to make their own adjustments to meet the demands of new times and new audiences, but only by reaching a collective judgment about the value and necessity of vigorous news media in American democracy can we hope to keep our public watchdogs on guard and in good health.

Volkswagen Beetle

(PRODUCT DESIGN)

The Volkswagen Type 1, better known as the Beetle or Bug, is the most produced car in history. From 1938 until the last original Beetle came off an assembly line in Puebla, Mexico, over twenty-one million were built. The Beetle began in Nazi Germany, when Adolf Hitler commissioned Ferdinand Porsche to produce a car for common people. Only a handful were produced before World War II started in 1939. Volkswagen was soon back in production after the war, and by 1954, the number of Beetles passed a million. Volkswagen began shipping cars to the United States at a time when American cars were big and boxy. The VW Beetle was just the opposite—small and rounded, inexpensive, and three times as fuel efficient. Beetles dominated the small-car market until Japanese imports showed up in large numbers in the mid-1970s.

More than the story of a car, however, the Beetle demonstrates how what we buy reflects cultural attitudes and values.

Return to these questions after you have finished reading.

Analyzing and Connecting

1. Volkswagen ads in the United States in the 1960s appealed to simplicity—simple shape, simple technology—which grew out of long-standing American values of honesty, economy, and lack of pretense. Look at automobile ads today, both in print and on television. What values do they appeal to?

2. Your campus may have a building that is better known by a nickname than its official name. Is the building liked or disliked by students? How does the nickname change the image of the building? For example, is it more friendly or less friendly?

3. Look up the word *bug* in the *Oxford English Dictionary*, which traces the histories of words. Your library has the print OED and may allow access through the library's Web site. How has the meaning of *bug* changed over time? Think about how *bug* is used today. For example, a common saying among computer programmers is "It's not a bug, it's a feature." Identify examples of other words such as *pimp* that have changed meanings in recent years.

4. Think of other products that we find cute and lovable. What makes them cute and lovable? Does advertising promote these associations?

Finding Ideas for Writing

The Volkswagen Beetle has a complicated and dark history. What values from the car's conceptualization were carried over into the advertising you see here? How were the negative historical associations downplayed or erased? How do today's advertisements for Volkswagen cars compare? Write a paragraph describing the associations the brand has now, and how these relate (or not relate) to the car's history.

VOLKSWAGEN BEETLE

When Adolf Hitler became Chancellor of Germany in 1933, he declared that a centerpiece of Nazism would be the motorization of the country. He asked Ferdinand Porsche to design a car that would be affordable for everyone.

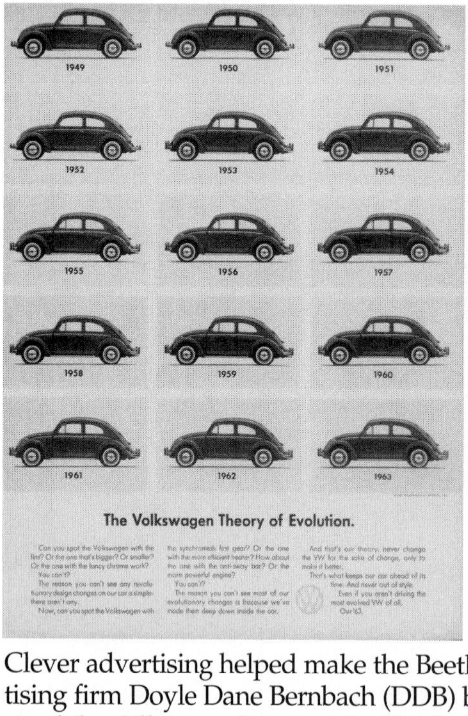

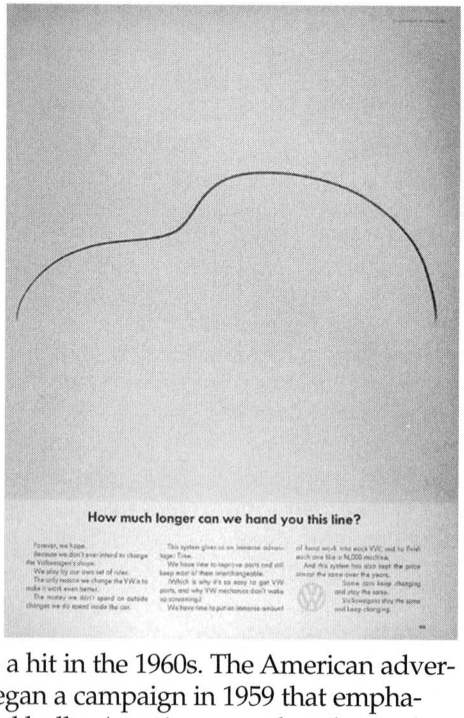

Clever advertising helped make the Beetle a hit in the 1960s. The American advertising firm Doyle Dane Bernbach (DDB) began a campaign in 1959 that emphasized the differences between the Beetle and bulky American cars that changed designs yearly.

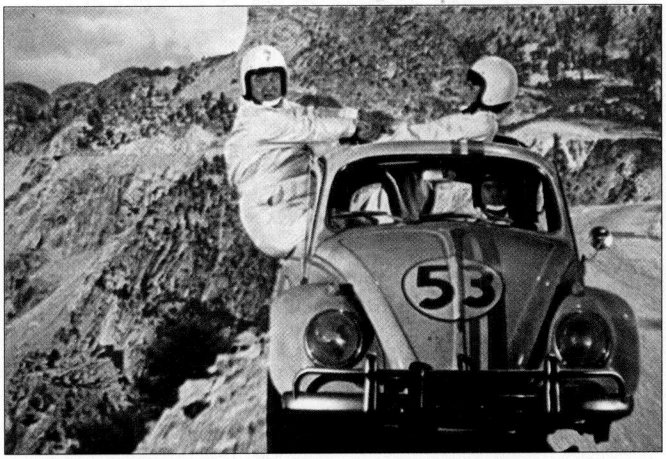
53

In 1968, Walt Disney's *The Love Bug* created a new generation of Beetle fans and led to a series of *Herbie* sequels.

OMYGAWD

Beetles became part of the counterculture of the 1960s. Many were hand-painted and customized in various ways, even adding fins that mocked American cars.

Misery has enough company.
Dare to be happy.

In 1998 Volkswagen launched the New Beetle, which benefited from the lovable image of the original Beetle.

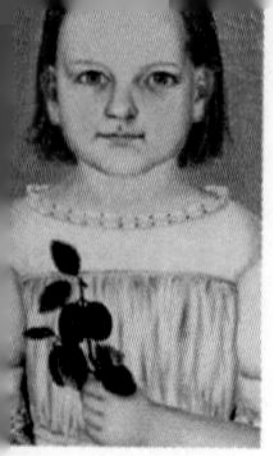

How to write a rhetorical analysis

These steps for the process of writing a rhetorical analysis may not progress as neatly as this chart might suggest. Writing is not an assembly-line process.

As you write, be open to new insights about the subject you are analyzing. Writing often generates new ideas that you can use to strengthen your analysis.

1 SELECT A TEXT TO ANALYZE

- Examine the assignment.
- Find a text.
- Make an analytical claim.
- Research the context.
- Research the author and audience.

2 ANALYZE CONTEXT AND TEXT

- Consider the medium and genre.
- Identify the main claim or claims.
- Consider the evidence.
- Analyze the appeals. How does the author establish credibility? How logical are the arguments? What values does the author appeal to?
- Situate the text in its context. Where do you find evidence that the text was responding to other texts and events?
- Consider the style and tone.

3 WRITE A DRAFT

- Briefly describe the text you are analyzing. Name the author and give information about when and where the text was published or delivered.
- Make a claim about the text.
- Analyze the context. Discuss what motivated the author to write and the author's purpose. Describe the original audience and their attitudes. Place the text in the larger "conversation" that was occurring at the time.
- Analyze the text. Identify the main claim. Analyze appeals to ethos, logos, and pathos.
- Consider your voice and tone.
- Choose a title that will interest readers.

4 REVISE, REVISE, REVISE

- Check that your paper or project fulfills the assignment.
- Make sure your analysis has a clear focus and claim.
- Check that each point of your analysis is supported with evidence.
- Make sure your voice and tone will engage readers.
- Examine your organization and think of possible better ways to organize.

5 SUBMITTED VERSION

- Make sure your finished writing meets all formatting requirements.

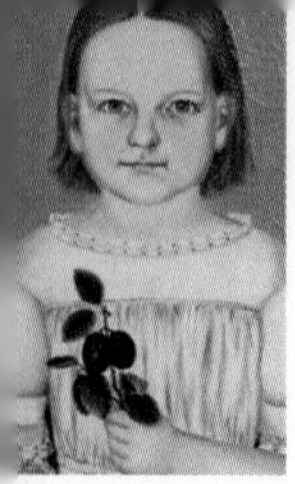

1: Select a text to analyze

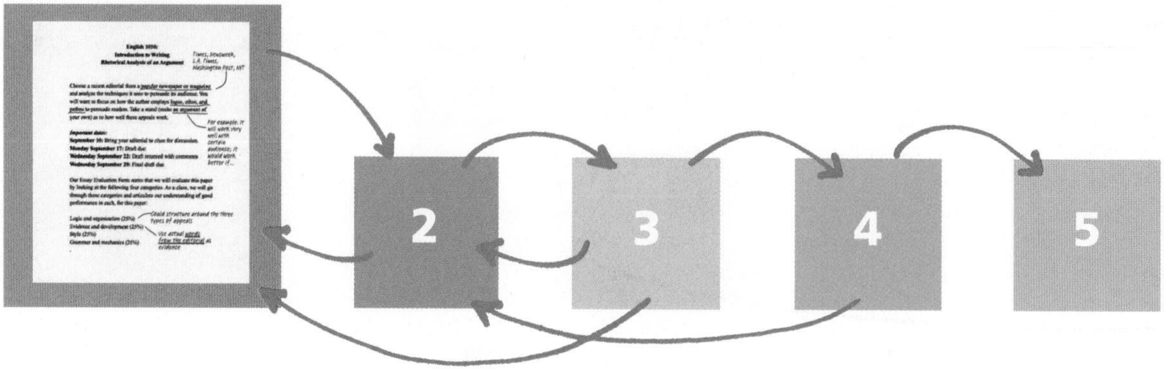

Examine the assignment

- Read your assignment slowly and carefully. Look for the key words *analyze* or *critique*. These key words tell you that you are writing an analysis.
- Make a note of any information about the length specified, date due, formatting, and other requirements. You can attend to this information later. At this point you want to zero in on the subject and your analytical claim.

Find a text to analyze

- Look for a text or image that offers an argument or opinion—one that tries to influence the thoughts, feelings, or actions of its audience.
- Newspaper editorials, activist Web sites, speeches, art, and advertisements are all good sources of texts for analysis.

Make an analytical claim

- Ask: What will my analysis reveal for readers that they might not otherwise have realized about the text?
- Think about the evidence you will need to support your claim. It may come from the text itself, or from your research into the piece's context.

Research the context

- What else was being written and said about this subject at the time the text was written?
- What events were taking place that might have influenced the author?

Research the author and audience

- Who is the author? What else has he or she said on this subject? What motivated him or her to produce this text?
- Who is the audience? Where did the text first appear (or, why was this image made or created)? Why did it appear at that particular moment?

Write Now

Find a verbal text to analyze

Find at least three examples of verbal texts that intend to persuade you in some way. They may ask you to do something specific such as buy a product or vote for a candidate or else they may aim at changing your attitude. Note what makes each text interesting and make a tentative claim.

Text	Deadspin.com blog
What makes it interesting	Takes a humorous look at sports, exposing the pretensions and lack of honesty among sports figures.
Claim	Deadspin.com represents the spirit of many blogs in going for the truth underneath layers of hype and having fun along the way.

Write Now

Find a visual text to analyze

Identify at least three visual texts for possible analysis. Look for a visual text that in some way attempts to influence the viewer—an advertisement, a public building, a statue, a controversial work of art, a dramatic photograph, a television commercial, a corporate logo, and so on. Note what makes it interesting and make a tentative claim.

Text	Logos of competing political candidates
What makes it interesting	Candidate X's logo appears much better than candidate Y's logo among people I have asked, but they cannot explain why.
Claim	Candidate X has a better logo than candidate Y because the typeface and colors of X's logo express strength, energy, and movement while those on Y's logo suggest indecision and weakness.

Writer at work

Kelsey Turner was asked to write a rhetorical analysis for her composition class. She made the following notes and observations on her assignment sheet:

English 1010:
Introduction to Writing
Rhetorical Analysis of an Argument

Times, Newsweek, L.A. Times, Washington Post, NYT

Choose a recent editorial from a popular newspaper or magazine and analyze the techniques it uses to persuade its audience. You will want to focus on how the author employs logos, ethos, and pathos to persuade readers. Take a stand (make an argument of your own) as to how well these appeals work.

For example: It will work very well with certain audience; it would work better if...

Important dates:

September 10: Bring your editorial to class for discussion.
Monday September 17: Draft due
Wednesday September 22: Draft returned with comments
Wednesday September 29: Final draft due

Our Essay Evaluation Form states that we will evaluate this paper by looking at the following four categories. As a class, we will go through these categories and articulate our understanding of good performance in each, for this paper:

Logic and organization (25%) — *Could structure around the three types of appeals*
Evidence and development (25%) — *Use actual words from the editorial as evidence*
Style (25%)
Grammar and mechanics (25%)

Kelsey found a *Washington Post* opinion piece on food banks and poverty that interested her (see pages 305–309 to read the full essay). She began by asking the questions she would need to answer to write a good rhetorical analysis (see page 154). Here are the questions and her responses:

<u>What is the author's purpose?</u>
–To make readers re-think their "generous" donations to food banks, and look at causes of hunger.

<u>Who is the audience?</u>
– Readers of Washington Post (nationwide distribution). People concerned with hunger and poverty. People who usually make gestures rather than really working for change?

<u>Who is the author?</u>
– He worked at a food bank, was very successful, became disillusioned. He understands the problem better than most people.

<u>What is the background?</u>
– It was published right before Thanksgiving, when people are thinking about having enough food as an American tradition.

<u>Which rhetorical appeals are used?</u>
– All three:

- Pathos--Appeals to readers' sympathy for those who are hungry. Describes fatigue of donors and volunteers with current system. Makes volunteering and donating seem foolish and possibly harmful.
- Ethos--His background. He assumes readers will agree that it is better to empower people and that we shouldn't patronize them just to make ourselves feel generous.
- Logos-- Paints the bigger picture of poverty, of which hunger is just one part. But he goes back and forth between saying maybe food is given to people who don't need it, and then saying the more food we give, the more people need it. It seems like the meaning of "need" changes.

The pathos appeals are the strongest and most noticeable, but the ethos of the author probably works the best to persuade people.
<u>How does the language and style contribute to the purpose?</u>
– Words like "play," and "pep rally," are associated with frivolous activities. They belittle the actions of food pantry workers and donors. Author makes food-givers feel kind of stupid or self-interested and short-sighted. Like they are making the problem worse. Blaming them, almost.

2: Analyze context and text

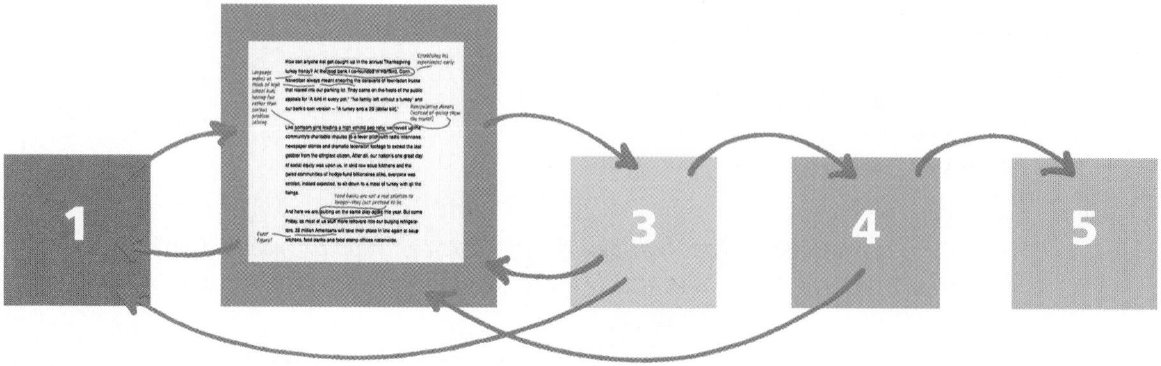

Consider the medium and genre

- What is the medium?
- What is the genre of the piece? Is it an editorial? a speech? an advertisement?

Consider the main claim or claims

- Summarize the claim, or describe the subject.

Consider the evidence

- Note all the reasons and evidence given to support the claim.

Analyze the appeals

- How is the author presented? As a credible, trustworthy person?
- How logical are the arguments? Are there any logical fallacies?
- What emotions, if any, does the author appeal to?
- How effective is each one of these appeals and techniques? How effective are they all together? Why are they effective or not effective?

Situate the text in its context

- Where do you find evidence that this text was responding to other texts and events?
- What does this text contribute to the ongoing conversation of which it is part?

Consider the style and tone

- How would you characterize the style? Is the style formal? informal? academic?
- How would you characterize the tone? Does the writer or speaker use humor or satire?
- How is language used to influence the audience? repetition? contrast? particular word choices? What metaphors are used?

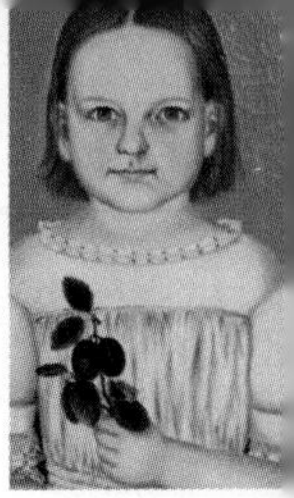

Writer at work

Kelsey Turner read her chosen editorial carefully several times, making notes in the margins about the rhetorical appeals she saw being used.

Establishes his experiences early.

How can anyone not get caught up in the annual Thanksgiving turkey frenzy? At the food bank I co-founded in Hartford, Conn., November always meant cheering the caravans of fowl-laden trucks that roared into our parking lot. They came on the heels of the public appeals for "A bird in every pot," "No family left without a turkey" and our bank's own version -- "A turkey and a 20 [dollar bill]."

Language makes us think of high school kids having fun rather than serious problem solving.

Manipulating donors (Instead of giving them the truth?)

Like pompom girls leading a high school pep rally, we revved up the community's charitable impulse to a fever pitch with radio interviews, newspaper stories and dramatic television footage to extract the last gobbler from the stingiest citizen. After all, our nation's one great day of social equity was upon us. In skid row soup kitchens and the gated communities of hedge-fund billionaires alike, everyone was entitled, indeed expected, to sit down to a meal of turkey with all the fixings.

Food banks are not a real solution to hunger—they just pretend to be.

And here we are, putting on the same play again this year. But come Friday, as most of us stuff more leftovers into our bulging refrigerators, 35 million Americans will take their place in line again at soup kitchens, food banks and food stamp offices nationwide.

Exact figure?

Finally, Kelsey developed a position that could serve as a working thesis for her paper:

Mark Winne's essay gives good reasons for readers to stop supporting the food banking industry, but the belittling tone he uses to describe food bank donors and workers may insult or offend readers, making them less likely to agree with him.

3: Write a draft

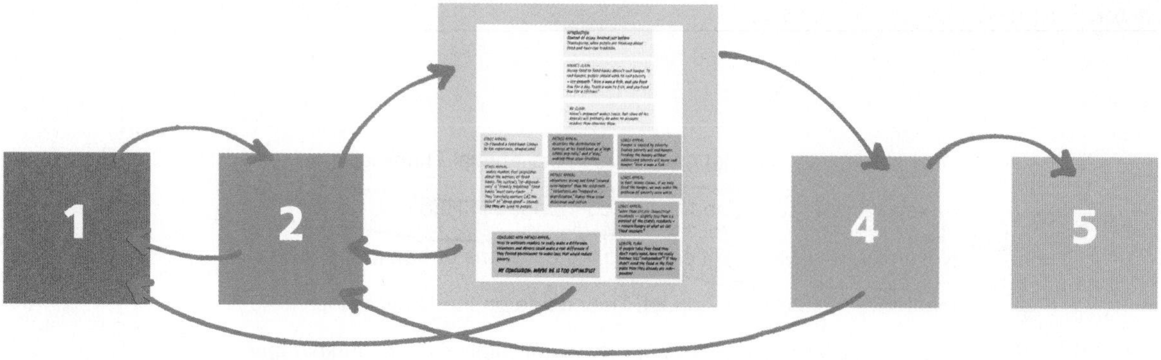

Briefly describe the text you are analyzing	• Describe the medium and genre (newspaper editorial, blog on the Web, radio interview, and so on). • Who produced it? Where and when did it first appear?
Make a claim	• Analysis adds a new dimension to a text; what will your analysis reveal for readers? Be sure your claim is not an over-generalization and can be supported by textual and contextual evidence.
Analyze the context	• Through research find out what else was being said about the subject your text discusses. • Track down any references to other texts or events.
Analyze the text	• Select the most important parts of the text to focus on. Choose elements that will show a pattern or illustrate specific techniques you want to talk about. However, be honest: do not leave out evidence that might undercut your claims. • Build a critical mass of evidence. Supply the evidence and examples to support your claim. • Make larger patterns or contrasts visible for your readers. For example, does an author seem to be appealing to two different audiences in a single essay? What parts of the work appeal to one audience? What parts appeal to the other?
Build a strong conclusion	• Don't merely summarize what you have already said. Ask yourself "Have I learned anything new in this analysis?"A conclusion can be a good place to succinctly describe a larger pattern you have been tracing in a work. Or, it may be a good place to make conjectures about other works by the same artist, about the motivations of a school or movement, or to tie your analysis of this text to other texts.

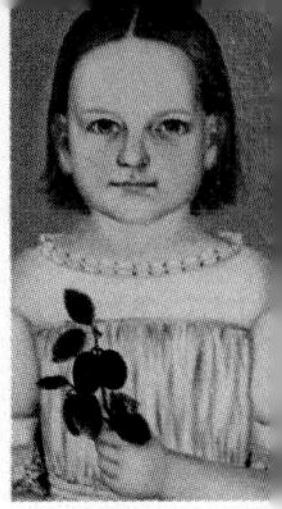

Writer at work

Kelsey used sticky notes to determine the best structure for her paper. She grouped them in different categories and changed their order until she was satisfied with the basic structure for her first draft.

INTRODUCTION
Context of essay: Printed just before Thanksgiving, when people are thinking about food and American tradition.

WINNE'S CLAIM:
Giving food to food banks doesn't end hunger. To end hunger, people should work to end poverty.
- Use proverb: "Give a man a fish, and you feed him for a day. Teach a man to fish, and you feed him for a lifetime."

MY CLAIM:
Winne's argument makes sense, but some of his appeals will probably do more to alienate readers than convince them.

ETHOS APPEAL:
Co-founded a food bank (shows he has experience, compassion)

ETHOS APPEAL:
makes readers feel suspicious about the motives of food banks. The system's "co-dependency" is "frankly troubling." Food banks "must curry favor . . ." They "carefully nurture [d] the belief" of "doing good"— sounds like they are lying to people.

PATHOS APPEAL:
describes the distribution of turkeys at his food bank as a "high school pep rally," and a "play," making them seem frivolous

PATHOS APPEAL:
volunteers giving out food "seemed even happier" than the recipients. . . Volunteers are "trapped in . . . gratification." Makes them seem delusional and selfish.

LOGOS APPEAL:
Hunger is caused by poverty. Ending poverty will end hunger. Feeding the hungry without addressing poverty will never end hunger. "Give a man a fish . . .

LOGOS APPEAL:
In fact, Winne claims, if we only feed the hungry, we may make the problem of poverty even worse.

LOGOS APPEAL:
"more than 275,000 Connecticut residents -- slightly less than 8.6 percent of the state's residents -- remain hungry or what we call 'food insecure.'"

LOGICAL FLAW:
If people take free food they don't really need, have they really become less "independent"? If they didn't need the food in the first place then they already are independent.

CONCLUDES WITH PATHOS APPEAL:
tries to motivate readers to really make a difference. Volunteers and donors could make a real difference if they forced government to make laws that would reduce poverty.

MY CONCLUSION: MAYBE HE IS TOO OPTIMISTIC?

4: Revise, revise, revise

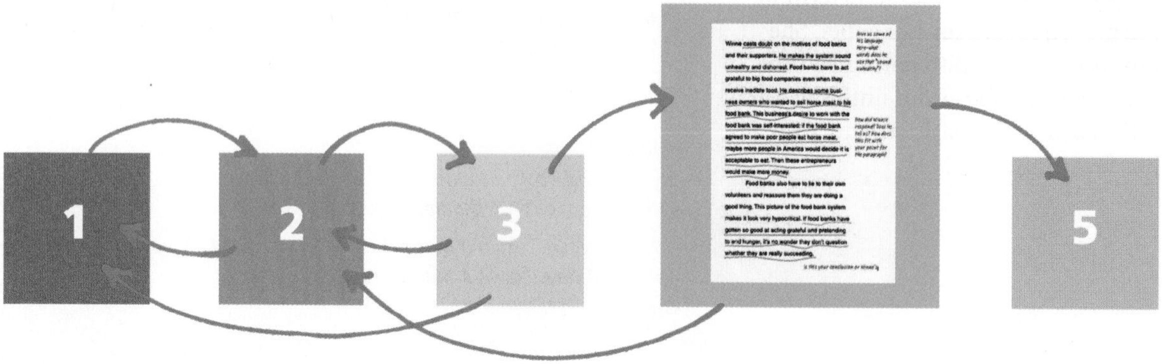

Skilled writers know that the secret to writing well is rewriting. Leave correcting errors for last.

Does your paper or project meet the assignment?	• Look again at your assignment. Does your paper or project do what the assignment asks? • Check the assignment for specific guidelines, including length, format, and amount of research. Does your work meet these guidelines?
Does your analysis have a clear purpose?	• Does it tell readers something they would not have otherwise noticed? • Do you make some kind of claim about the work you are analyzing? Is it a debatable claim?
Do you support your analysis with evidence?	• Do you provide a background about the author, intended audience, and the larger conversation surrounding the text you are analyzing? • Can you provide additional analysis to support your claims?
Is your organization effective?	• Is the order of your main points clear to your reader? • Are there any places where you find abrupt shifts or gaps? • Are there sections or paragraphs that could be rearranged to make your draft more effective?
Is the writing project visually effective?	• Is the font attractive and readable? • Are the headings and visuals effective?
Save the editing for last.	• When you have finished revising, edit and proofread carefully.

A peer review guide is on page 27.

Writer at work

Kelsey Turner received comments from her instructor on her draft. She used these comments to revise her draft.

Kelsey's instructor encouraged her to use Winne's own words instead of summarizing them

Kelsey found several points in her paper where she had included information that did not directly advance her argument. Some of these points could be moved to other sections of the paper where they fit better; others she removed entirely

Kelsey received specific feedback on an important aspect of her analysis: the shifts back and forth between her voice and Winne's. To see how she distinguished her ideas from Winne's see her submitted draft on page 328.

Winne casts doubt on the motives of food banks and their supporters. He makes the system sound unhealthy and dishonest. Food banks have to act grateful to big food companies even when they receive inedible food. He describes some business owners who wanted to sell horse meat to his food bank. This business's desire to work with the food bank was self-interested: if the food bank agreed to make poor people eat horse meat, maybe more people in America would decide it is acceptable to eat. Then these entrepreneurs would make more money.

Give us some of his language here–what words does he use that "sound unhealthy"?

How did Winnie respond? Does he tell us? How does this fit with your point for the paragraph?

Food banks also have to lie to their own volunteers and reassure them they are doing a good thing. This picture of the food bank system makes it look very hypocritical. If food banks have gotten so good at acting grateful and pretending to end hunger, it's no wonder they don't question whether they are really succeeding.

Is this your conclusion or Winne's?

5: Submitted version

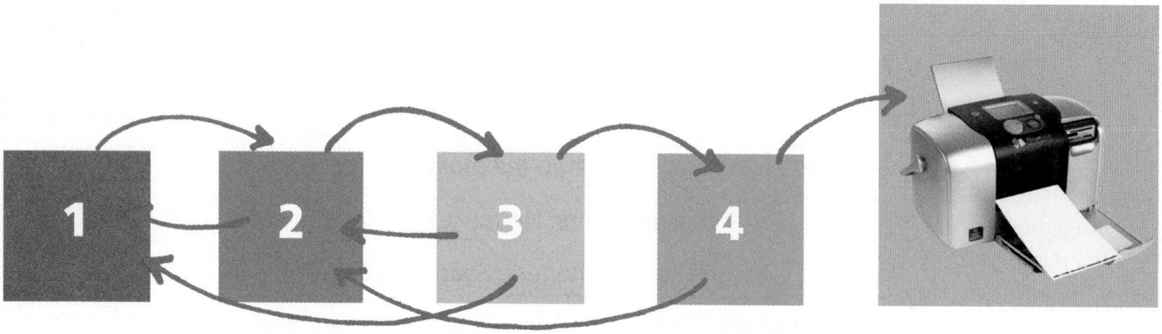

Turner 1

Kelsey Turner

Professor Perez

English 1010

29 September 2008

Biting the Hands That Feed America

Mark Winne's Thanksgiving 2007 article in the *Washington Post*, "When Handouts Keep Coming, the Food Line Never Ends," makes readers re-think their "generous" donations to food banks and pantries. Winne calls our attention instead to poverty, which causes hunger, and challenges us to end hunger by ending poverty. This challenge makes sense. After all, most of us have heard the proverb, "Give a man a fish, and you feed him for a day. Teach a man to fish, and you feed him for a lifetime." However, Winne's tone in his essay works against the logic of his argument. Even though he is a compassionate person who has spent much of his life working to feed the poor, the language he uses belittles the people who want to help. He tries to motivate readers, but he does this partly by making them feel ashamed of themselves. His frustration with the food bank system is understandable, but taking it out on casual readers diminishes sympathy for him and his cause.

Winne begins by mentioning that he co-founded a food bank in Hartford, Connecticut, which establishes a strong ethos for his argument, letting his readers

know that Winne has experience with the system he is going to criticize. If anyone should know what works and doesn't work in food-banking, it is the people who structure and run the food banks. He also establishes his compassion for the plight of the poor and hungry. Furthermore, Winne says he wants to empower the poor, not just feed them. Because America has a long tradition of self-reliant citizens who can take care of themselves, promoting self-reliance should sound like a worthy goal to most readers. Because we are a democracy, we want our citizens to be strong and self-supporting, not just well-fed.

Winne makes a simple, logical argument: Hunger is caused by poverty. Ending poverty will end hunger. Feeding the hungry without addressing poverty will never end hunger. In fact, Winne claims, if we only feed the hungry, we may make the problem of poverty even worse.

Winne uses statistics to support his case. Despite his best efforts, and those of other food bank workers, he tells us, "more than 275,000 Connecticut residents—slightly less than 8.6 percent of the state's residents—remain hungry or what we call 'food insecure.'" After Thanksgiving, "35 million Americans will take their place in line again at soup kitchens, food banks and food stamp offices nationwide." We learn that families on food stamps only receive three dollars per person per day. These numbers make a compelling appeal to our sense of logic and reason. The problem is not going away. The government's response to hunger is inadequate. Anyone who can read the *Washington Post* is smart enough to know that a three-dollar food budget might buy enough French fries to keep you alive, but it wouldn't keep you healthy for very long.

A flaw undercuts his argument, however, when he describes a scene which made him realize the "futility" of food banks: "No one made any attempt to determine whether the recipients actually needed the food, nor to encourage the recipients to seek other forms of assistance, such as food stamps." Winne implies that some of the people taking the food didn't really need it, but just took it because it was free. The lines of people grew longer, leading Winne to observe, "It may have been that a donor-recipient co-dependency had developed. Both parties were trapped in an ever-expanding web of

Turner 3

immediate gratification that offered the recipients no long-term hope of eventually achieving independence and self-reliance." If people take free food even though they don't need it, have they really become less "independent"? The fact that they didn't need the food in the first place means they already *are* independent.

Most people accept free things from time to time, but doing so doesn't automatically make us less self-reliant. Winne explains what he sees as a cause-and-effect problem—too much free food causing people to depend upon more free food—by quoting another food bank director: "The more you provide, the more demand there is." However, demand isn't the same thing as need. People may want free food, and take it when it is offered. They may even "demand" more of it when they don't get what they are expecting. But that's not the same as really needing it. Winne uses "demand" and "need" interchangeably, but he doesn't explain how people go from accepting free food they don't need, to needing free food. Do they get so used to receiving free food that they quit their jobs on the assumption that they don't need to earn money for food? Does free food make them eat more? Maybe there is some way free food can cause dependence, but Winne doesn't explain this process, and it's clearly not logical to assume that free food always makes people less self-reliant.

Winne's article was published on the Sunday before Thanksgiving when readers would be reminded of the American tradition of plentiful food. Likely many would feel sympathy for the hungry and possibly want to do something to help; however, Winne belittles and insults the generous impulses of donors and volunteers. He describes the distribution of turkeys at his food bank as a "high school pep rally" and a "play," making them seem like frivolous activities that make no real difference. This language is sure to make readers think twice before they give a turkey to their local food bank. Winne even makes them feel selfish for wanting to help. He says the volunteers giving out food "seemed even happier" than the recipients. He describes their charity as an "act of faith," and says they are "fortified by the belief that their act of benevolence was at least mildly appreciated." Like the recipients of the food, Winne says, the volunteers are "trapped in an ever-expanding web of immediate gratification." Winne makes feeding the hungry seem like a selfish act rather than an act of charity.

Turner 4

Winne attempts to make readers suspicious about the motives of food banks and their supporters. He says the system's "co-dependency" is "frankly troubling." Food banks "must curry favor with the nation's food industry, which often regards food banks as a waste-management tool." Food banks keep their own volunteers "dependent on carefully nurtured belief that they are 'doing good' by 'feeding the hungry.'" This assertion renders volunteers as dupes for large corporations who have their own motives for supporting food banks. The hypocrisy of the food bank system is what prevents people who want to help from asking "if this is the best way to end hunger, food insecurity and their root cause, poverty."

Winne concludes by trying to motivate readers to really make a difference. All the energy poured into food banks by volunteers and donors could make a real difference, he feels, if it were used to force government to make policies that would reduce poverty. One the one hand, Winne's call to action appears unrealistic given that politicians largely ignore poverty because it is not an issue that stirs voters. On the other hand, Winne does effectively contrast the power of volunteers, who could "dismantle the Connecticut state capitol brick by brick " with his earlier descriptions of the fatigue and frustration of the current system. He at least gets us to think about food banks in a way other than a feel-good story on the evening news at Thanksgiving.

Work Cited

Winne, Mark. "When Handouts Keep Coming, the Food Line Never Ends." *Washington Post* 18 Nov. 2007. late ed.: B1. Print.

Projects

Analyzing is valuable for clarifying and developing your own thinking as well as for giving your readers a broader understanding.

These projects are frequently written kinds of analyses.

Rhetorical analysis

Select a text to analyze—a speech, a sermon, an editorial, a persuasive letter, an essay, a Web site, a pamphlet, a brochure, or another kind of text.

↓

Explain briefly what kind of text it is, when and where it was first published or spoken, and its main argument.

↓

Make a claim about the text, which you support with close analysis.

↓

Analyze the context. Is the text part of a larger debate? What other texts or events does it respond to? Who is the author? What motivated the author to write this text? What can you infer about the intended audience?

↓

Analyze the appeals. What appeals to values and emotions are used? What appeals to logic are used? Do you find any logical fallacies (see pages 14–15)? Do you trust the writer?

↓

Analyze the organization and style. What are the major parts and how are they arranged? Is the style formal, informal, satirical, or something else? Are any metaphors used?

Visual analysis

Find a visual text to analyze. You might analyze a popular consumer product, a public building, advertising, art, or a map.

Make a claim about the visual text. Support your claim with close analysis. Describe key features.

Analyze the context. Where and when was the visual created? What was the purpose? Who created it? What can you infer about the intended audience?

Analyze the visual text. What kind of visual is it? What is the medium? How is it arranged? How would you characterize the style? Are any words connected?

Critical literary analysis

Read carefully a short story or other literary text. Map out the plot. What is the conflict and how is it resolved?

Examine the characterization, including the major and minor characters. Characters are not real people, but instead they are constructed for a purpose. What role does each character perform? The setting too is a character. What role does the setting play in the story?

Consider the point of view. Does a character tell the story? Or is the narrator an all-knowing observer? Describe the language, style, and tone of the story. Identify any important images, symbols, and metaphors.

Identify the story's central theme. How does the title of the story relate to the theme?

Write an arguable thesis that connects one or more elements—characters, setting, language, metaphors, and so on—to the overall theme. A paper that begins with an engaging thesis arouses the reader's interest. Support your thesis with evidence from the text. A successful paper shares a discovery with the reader.

10 Causal Analyses

An effective causal analysis moves beyond the obvious to examine complex underlying causes.

CHAPTER CONTENTS

Writing to analyze causes

Have you ever wondered why your car is hard to start on a cold morning? Why all the shoppers in the supermarket seem to converge on the checkout stands at the same time? Why a company's stock price rises when it announces hundreds of layoffs?

Questions of causation confront us all the time. We spend much of our daily lives puzzling over them—trying to start the car, pick the best time to visit the supermarket, or buy the most valuable stock. Causal investigation also drives scientists, as they search for cures to diseases, to try to explain certain behaviors in people and animals, and attempt to predict the weather.

Answering these kinds of questions requires a causal analysis, which typically takes the form "SOMETHING causes (or does not cause) SOMETHING ELSE."

Understand how causal arguments work

Causal arguments take three basic forms.

FORM 1

One cause leads to one or more effects.

EXAMPLE

The invention of the telegraph led to the commodities market, the establishment of standard time zones, and news reporting as we know it today.

FORM 2

One effect has several causes.

EXAMPLE

Hurricanes are becoming more financially destructive to the United States because of the greater intensity of recent storms, an increase in the commercial and residential development of coastal areas, and a reluctance to enforce certain construction standards in coastal residential areas.

FORM 3

Something causes something to happen, which in turn causes something else to happen.

EXAMPLE

Making the HPV vaccination mandatory for adolescent girls will make unprotected sex seem safer, leading to greater promiscuity and resulting in more teenage pregnancies.

Methods of analyzing causes

Causal analyses can be challenging to write because any topic worth writing about is likely to be complex. Causes can be hard to identify, and there may be more than one cause behind any given phenomenon. The philosopher John Stuart Mill (1806–1873) developed four different methods for finding causes.

1 The Common Factor Method

If you look at all the cases of a phenomenon, and find a single factor that is common to all of them, that common factor is probably the cause. For example, if a number of people in your dormitory all develop symptoms of food poisoning, and it turns out they all ate the potato salad from the cafeteria salad bar the night before, the potato salad is probably the cause of their illness.

2 The Single Difference Method

This method is useful when you have two similar situations, with only one leading to an effect. Look for something that was present in one case and not the other. It is commonly used in scientific experiments under controlled conditions. You might grow a group of identical soybean plants, for example, giving them all equal amounts of light and water, but only feeding fertilizer to half of them. If the fertilized plants grow faster, the fertilizer is probably the cause.

3 Concomitant Variation

This method is also frequently used by scientists, especially when they cannot completely control the conditions they are observing. Investigators look for a similar pattern of variation between a possible cause and a possible effect. If you give different amounts of fertilizer to each soybean plant in the example, and the plants getting the most fertilizer grow the tallest, while the ones getting the least stay the smallest, a causal relationship between fertilizer and accelerated growth is likely.

4 The Process of Elimination

The more complex the set of causes behind a phenomenon, the more likely you are to use the process of elimination. Let's return to the soybean plants from the earlier example. You are fairly certain that adding fertilizer to the plants causes them to grow faster. Yet you notice that some plants have developed spots on their leaves. Some of the spotted plants get a lot of fertilizer, and some only get a little, but they all have a similar number of leaf spots, so the fertilizer is probably not the cause. Upon further investigation, you find that an absentminded professor has been emptying the remains of his diet soda into the spotted plants' pots every evening. Even though conditions among the spotted plants are not identical, it is reasonable to infer that the soda is causing the spotting. It is the only factor "left over" after you have accounted for all the others' impact on the plants.

Which method should I use?

You can use more than one of Mill's methods to evaluate possible causes. For example, the common factor and single difference methods are often combined: If everyone in your dorm who got sick had eaten the potato salad and the fruit cocktail, you would have to find someone who ate the fruit cocktail, but not the potato salad, to determine which food was the cause of illness. If anyone who ate fruit cocktail stayed healthy, you can eliminate it as a possible cause and focus on the potato salad.

Keys to causal analysis

Pay attention to effects

It's not enough to simply identify causes. In order for a causal analysis to matter, you must make clear why the effects are important. Otherwise, readers are apt to ask, "So what?" We often look for causes so that we can prevent something bad from happening, or facilitate something good. You may make the case that the film versions of *101 Dalmatians* led to an increase in the popularity of Dalmatian dogs, but your analysis gains more stature if you further explore that effect: many of the puppies bred and sold to people who saw the movie ended up in animal shelters because their new owners were not prepared for such high-energy pets.

Identify what is at stake

Because a strong causal claim may inspire people to change policies or behaviors or take other action, you will find that some members of your audience hold different stakes in the outcome of your analysis. Their stakes can influence the ways, and the degree to which, they oppose your claim. For example, although the causal link between cigarette smoke and cancer was widely accepted in scientific circles for many years, tobacco companies argued vociferously that no such link existed.

Move beyond the obvious to identify underlying causes

When people are involved, you can expect causes to be complex. Perhaps the cause you are seeking to link to an effect is only one of several causes. You'll need to address all the contributing causes, not just the one you are focusing on. A well-thought-out causal analysis will trace multiple causes and consider their cumulative effect.

Avoid mistaking correlation for causations

A common pitfall of causal analysis is confusing causation with correlation. Events can be correlated, or mutually related in some way, without one being the cause of the other. Deaths by drowning and baseball games are correlated. But does one cause the other? Or is it because both occur most frequently in the summer?

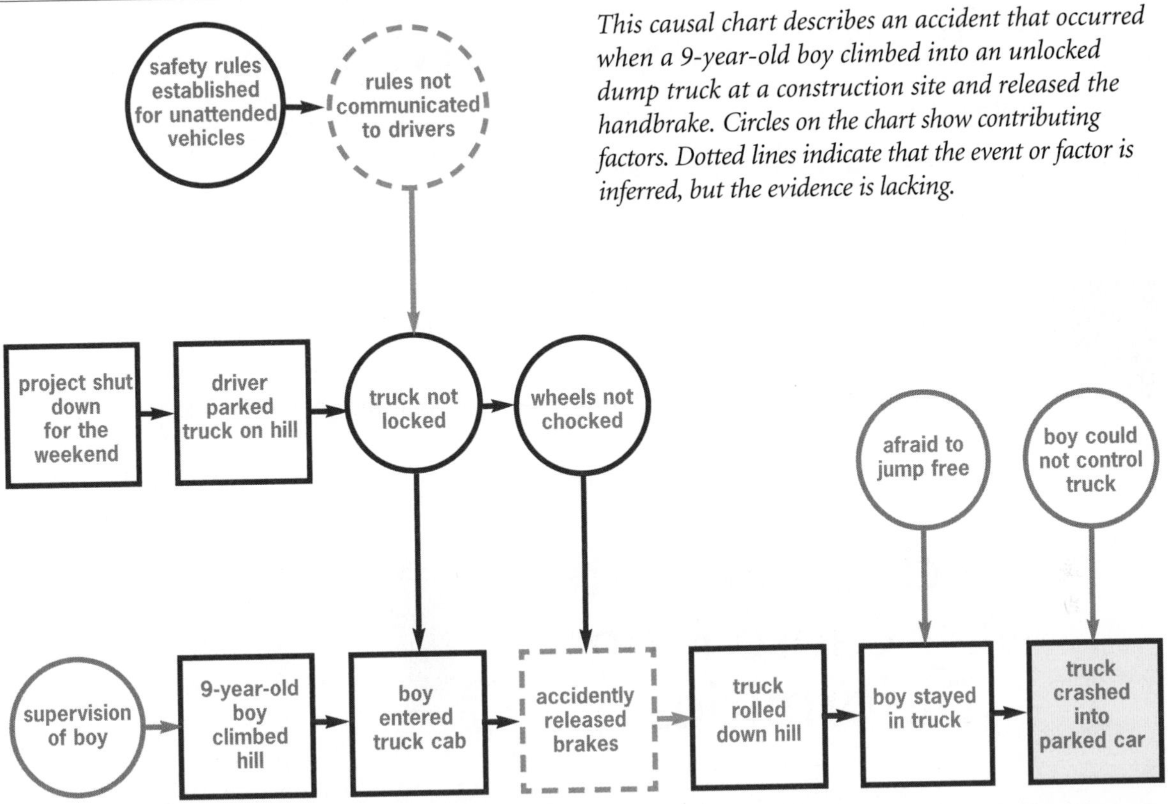

This causal chart describes an accident that occurred when a 9-year-old boy climbed into an unlocked dump truck at a construction site and released the handbrake. Circles on the chart show contributing factors. Dotted lines indicate that the event or factor is inferred, but the evidence is lacking.

Working Together

Find causes

In a group of three or four students

Brainstorm to create a list of "Why?" questions about causes. Your list might include questions such as "Why is the sky blue?" or "Why do music CDs cost $15 when DVDs of entire films, with director's cuts, outtakes, and other extras only cost $19?" Try to come up with at least ten or fifteen questions.

Working together, come up with as many possible causes for each phenomenon as you can. Use your imagination, but stay within the realm of possibility. You might want to arrange your responses from the most plausible to the least plausible.

An effective causal analysis

Effective causal analyses examine the significance of cause-and-effect relationships.

Pesticides, Parasite May Cause Frog Deformities
Stentor Danielson

Over the past ten to fifteen years, more and more frogs have been discovered with deformed, missing, or extra hind legs. Concerned about these abnormalities, scientists worldwide have been searching for the cause. In this *National Geographic* article from July 2002, science journalist Stentor Danielson looks at a careful study of the interplay between two potential causes: a waterborne parasite and common pesticides.

Pesticides, Parasite May Cause Frog Deformities

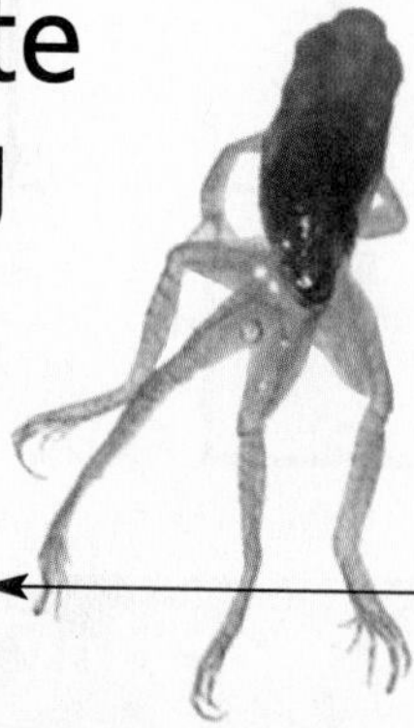

Frogs with extra legs or missing legs have been showing up with greater frequency over the past decade, and scientists have been baffled by the cause.

Danielson begins by briefly laying out the problem and by explaining how his article will add to previous discussions: new research indicates that two potential causes need to be considered together in order to get a clear picture of what is happening.

Some researchers have concluded that pesticide runoff from farms is to blame; others say a common parasite is the culprit. Now, a new study suggests that both these factors in combination have disturbed normal development in many frogs, leading to the abnormalities.

The study, published today in the *Proceedings of the National Academy of Sciences*, was based on tests in both the laboratory and the field that were designed to examine the interaction of parasites and pesticides. The research team, led by Joseph Kiesecker, found that only frogs infected by the larvae of a parasite, the trematode worm, developed deformities, but infected frogs exposed to pesticide runoff experienced much higher levels of deformities.

"It is not uncommon now for 20 to 30 percent of the frogs at many locations to have limb deformities," said Kiesecker, an assistant professor of biology at Penn State University.

Abnormalities have been documented in 52 species of amphibians, mainly frogs, in 46 U.S. states and four Canadian provinces, according to the U.S. Geological Survey. Reports of deformed frogs have been particularly common in New England and the Upper Midwest and on the Pacific coast.

Statistics provide a sense of the scope of the phenomenon. Notice the use of a government source for this information—sources which are usually credible and respected by readers.

Although there is some disagreement about what levels of deformities occur naturally in frog populations, most researchers agree that current levels are above normal.

Kiesecker and other researchers have warned that the physiological problems seen in frogs may foreshadow similar effects on humans.

At the end of this introductory section, Danielson places an important point about the issue: it could directly affect humans.

Infected by Trematodes

During its life cycle, the parasitic trematode depends on several hosts, including pond snails. Tadpoles in ponds with snails pick up trematode larvae, called cercariae. In some cases the cercariae develop into hard cysts, which interfere with the tadpole's metamorphosis into a frog. When the cysts occur in tissue that later develops into legs, the cysts disrupt the animal's normal development and cause duplicate or missing legs.

Details about one of the causes are explained step-by-step.

The trematode also affects people—although not so dramatically as in developing frogs. It's the same parasite that causes "swimmer's itch," a common ailment in people who swim in ponds and lakes. Eventually, the human immune system defeats the cercariae, leaving the victim with just a rash.

Pesticides, Parasite May Cause Frog Deformities

In tropical climates trematodes cause schistosomiasis, a disease that kills millions of people. The World Health Organization estimates that 120 million people worldwide suffer from schistosomiasis.

Kiesecker's team took tadpoles from Centre County, Pennsylvania, and placed them in six local ponds—three affected by pesticide runoff and three pesticide-free. In each

pond, the tadpoles were separated into two groups. One group was placed inside a fine mesh that kept out cercariae.

Only the tadpoles that were exposed to cercariae developed deformities. "We learned from the first field experiment that tadpoles have to be exposed to trematode infection for limb deformities to develop," Kiesecker said.

Danielson explains how an experiment was designed to isolate possible causes of the limb mutations.

Pesticide Problems

Kiesecker's team then compared the rate of infection between trematode-exposed tadpoles in the different ponds. The team discovered that rates of infection were much higher in the ponds that received pesticide runoff.

This result parallels the finding of a study in 2000 in which frogs from the same pond—that is, those experiencing the same environmental conditions—were found to have similar deformities.

To examine the effects of pesticides on cercariae development, the team conducted lab experiments on four groups of tadpoles—three groups exposed to three common pesticides and a control group. The pesticides were Atrazine, the most commonly used pesticide in North America; Malathion, a common household pesticide that also is used to control insect pests in agricultural fields; and Esfenvalerate, a synthetic pyrethroid pesticide. The tadpoles were all exposed to cercariae.

Scientists repeated the pond test under controlled laboratory conditions and got similar results, with more detailed findings. In scientific causal analysis, repeatability of results strengthens the case for causality.

When they counted the number of cysts that formed in the tadpoles, the researchers found much higher levels in the tadpoles exposed to pesticides. The team also took blood samples before and after the experiments to determine whether the tadpoles' white blood cell count—a measure of immune system health—was affected.

"The tadpoles that we exposed to pesticides had fewer of this particular kind of white blood cell compared to the tadpoles that we did not expose to pesticides, suggesting that pesticides make these animals more susceptible to parasitic infections," Kiesecker said.

Pesticides have been found to have additional harmful effects on frogs. A study published in April in the *Proceedings of the National Academy of Sciences* found that Atrazine interfered with the sexual development of male frogs in the Midwest, reducing their levels of testosterone to below the levels found in female frogs.

"Atrazine-exposed frogs don't have normal reproductive systems," said Tyrone Hayes, the leader of a team from the University of California at Berkeley. "The males have ovaries in their testes and much smaller vocal organs."

Human Impacts?

Kiesecker said society can learn a lot from the experiments because "amphibians are particularly sensitive to environmental changes that appear to be associated with the recent emergence of new diseases and resurgence of old diseases that infect humans."

Especially disturbing, he added, is that the concentrations of two of the pesticides that caused the deformities in frogs, Esfenvalerate and Atrazine, were low enough for the water to be considered safe for human consumption under Environmental Protection Agency standards.

"Frogs may be a sentinel species that is warning us about the interplay between human-caused environmental change and disease susceptibility," he said, adding: "Hopefully, people will listen."

Danielson closes by reminding readers of the possibility that the cause-and-effect relationship at work in frogs might have parallels for humans.

In other recent research on this problem, a study published in the July 1 issue of *Environmental Science & Technology* indicates that frog deformities may also occur as a result of exposure to ultraviolet (UV) radiation. At levels close to 60 percent of normal sunlight, frogs experienced deformities.

A survey of ponds in the Duluth, Minnesota, area showed that frogs in only three of 26 ponds were at risk of UV-induced deformities, because wetlands absorb a significant portion of the radiation. However, Steve Diamond of the Environmental Protection Agency's Duluth office and leader of the UV study said there may be cause for concern if human activities cause UV levels to rise.

Explore Current Issues

Is fast-food marketing contributing to childhood obesity?

Over the past few years, the connection between fast food and obesity—especially childhood obesity—has also become a part of the public's consciousness. Many chain restaurants, theme parks, and even cities such as New York have banned the use of trans fats in commercial food preparation. However, popular family movies continue to have marketing tie-ins to fast food restaurants. In 2008, for example, Burger King joined forces with two summer blockbusters, *Iron Man* and *Indiana Jones and the Kingdom of the Crystal Skull*. In *Iron Man*, a Burger King cheeseburger is the ultimate comfort food to Robert Downey Jr.'s Tony Stark.

In an open letter to George Lucas and Steven Speilberg published on Slate.com, pediatrician Rahul K. Parikh, M.D. argues that this common marketing strategy is feeding the obesity epidemic:

> Each week American kids spend a full-time job's worth of time in front of the TV, on the Web and playing video games. They will see about 40,000 ads per year, and two-thirds of those ads are for junk food and fast food. Studies show that what kids see on TV is what they tell their parents they want for supper. No doubt the Indy Double Whopper—with bacon!—will be flying off the greasy grill in short order.

Parikh ultimately blames power players in the entertainment world such as Lucas and Spielberg for this irresponsible and greedy use of their influence.

Write about it

1. Do you think marketing tie-ins of movies with fast food such as the ones Parikh criticizes are responsible for exacerbating the childhood obesity epidemic? Why or why not?
2. Who do you think is most responsible for the childhood obesity epidemic? Why? Do you think anyone in the entertainment industry is to blame for aggravating the problem? Why?
3. Which of the following might also be factors in the cause-and-effect relationship Parikh sets up? Rate these in order of relevance.
   - Increasing cost of living
   - Workers working more hours
   - Single parents
   - Food shortages
   - Increasing food costs
   - Associations people have with certain brands

Are there any you would add?

How to read causal analyses

Make notes as you read, either in the margins, if it is your copy, or on paper or a computer file. Circle any words or references that you don't know and look them up.

What is it?	• What kind of a text is it? An article? an essay? a chart? a scientific report? a Web site? an executive summary? What are your expectations for this kind of text? • What media are used? (Web sites, for example, often combine images, words, and sounds.)
Where did it come from?	• Who wrote the analysis? • Where did it first appear? In a book, newspaper, magazine, online, in a company, or in an organization?
What is the writer's thesis or main idea?	• What is the writer's topic? What effect is he or she trying to determine the cause of? • Why is this topic important? • What are the key ideas or concepts that the writer considers? • What are the key terms? How does the writer define those terms?
Who is the intended audience?	• What clues do you find about whom the writer had in mind as the readers? • What does the writer assume that the readers already know about the subject? • What new knowledge is the writer providing?
How are causes analyzed?	• What methods does the writer use to determine causation? • Does the writer consider multiple causes? • How complex is the analysis? Does the writer examine relationships between causes, or look at how one cause may arise from another? • Can you think of other causes that the writer doesn't consider?
What kinds of evidence are given?	• Is the evidence from books, newspapers, periodicals, the Web, or field research? • Is the evidence convincing that the causes given are the actual causes?
How is it composed?	• How does the writer represent herself or himself? • How would you characterize the style? • How effective is the design? Is it easy to read? • If there are any photographs, charts, or other graphics, what information do they contribute?

The Future of Marriage

(ESSAY)

Stephanie Coontz

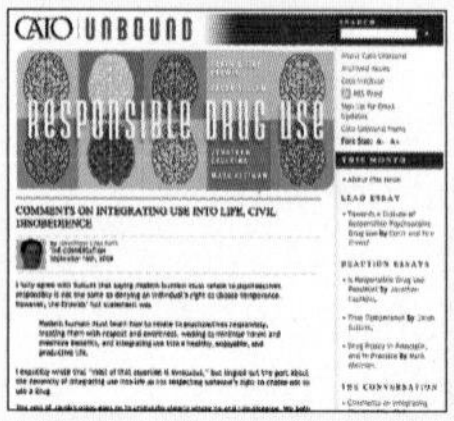

Stephanie Coontz teaches history and family studies at Evergreen State College in Olympia, Washington, and is Director of Research and Public Education for the Council on Contemporary Families. She is most recently the author of *Marriage, A History: From Obedience to Intimacy, or How Love Conquered Marriage* (2005). "The Future of Marriage" appeared January 14, 2008, on *Cato Unbound*, an online magazine-blog hybrid that presents the ideas of key thinkers and encourages public discourse.

Return to these questions after you have finished reading.

Analyzing and Connecting

1. Given the mission of *Cato Unbound*, what is the purpose of this article? Does Coontz ever state this purpose directly?

2. In her first paragraph, Coontz states: "Many people who hope to 're-institutionalize' marriage misunderstand the reasons that marriage was once more stable and played a stronger role in regulating social life." What does the phrase "re-institutionalize" mean? Why do some people want to "re-institutionalize" marriage?

3. Coontz concludes with the assertion that we need to let go of an idealized and mythical view of marriage in order to help people forge better relationships and be better parents. What other "institutions" might this philosophy apply to?

4. Think about the marriages with which you are familiar. What seems to be the greatest reason for a marriage's success? How about a marriage's failure?

Finding Ideas for Writing

This article was published on a site dedicated to public discourse. Write a paragraph response to Coontz's ideas on marriage that might appear on this site.

CATO UNBOUND

SEARCH

About Cato Unbound
Archived Issues

The Future of Marriage

Any serious discussion of the future of marriage requires a clear understanding of how marriage evolved over the ages, along with the causes of its most recent transformations. Many people who hope to "re-institutionalize" marriage misunderstand the reasons that marriage was once more stable and played a stronger role in regulating social life.

For most of history, marriage was more about getting the right in-laws than picking the right partner to love and live with. In the small-scale, band-level societies of our distant ancestors, marriage alliances turned strangers into relatives, creating interdependencies among groups that might otherwise meet as enemies. But as large wealth and status differentials developed in the ancient world, marriage became more exclusionary and coercive. People maneuvered to orchestrate advantageous marriage connections with some families and avoid incurring obligations to others. Marriage became the main way that the upper classes consolidated wealth, forged military coalitions, finalized peace treaties, and bolstered claims to social status or political authority. Getting "well-connected" in-laws was a preoccupation of the middle classes as well, while the dowry a man received at marriage was often the biggest economic stake he would acquire before his parents died. Peasants, farmers, and craftsmen acquired new workers for the family enterprise and forged cooperative bonds with neighbors through their marriages.

Because of marriage's vital economic and political functions, few societies in history believed that individuals should freely choose their own marriage partners, especially on such fragile grounds as love. Indeed, for millennia, marriage was much more about regulating economic, political, and gender hierarchies than nourishing the well-being of adults and their children. Until the late 18th century, parents took for granted their right to arrange their children's marriages and even, in many regions, to dissolve a marriage made without their permission. In Anglo-American law, a child born outside an approved marriage was a "fillius nullius"—a child of no one, entitled to nothing. In fact, through most of history, the precondition for maintaining a strong institution of marriage was the existence of an equally strong institution of illegitimacy, which denied such children any claim on their families.

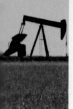

Even legally-recognized wives and children received few of the protections we now associate with marriage. Until the late 19th century, European and American husbands had the right to physically restrain, imprison, or "punish" their wives and children. Marriage gave husbands sole ownership over all property a wife brought to the marriage and any income she earned afterward. Parents put their children to work to accumulate resources for their own old age, enforcing obedience by periodic beatings.

Many people managed to develop loving families over the ages despite these laws and customs, but until very recently, this was not the main point of entering or staying in a union. It was just 250 years ago, when the Enlightenment challenged the right of the older generation and the state to dictate to the young, that free choice based on love and compatibility emerged as the social ideal for mate selection. Only in the early 19th century did the success of a marriage begin to be defined by how well it cared for its members, both adults and children.

These new marital ideals appalled many social conservatives of the day. "How will we get the right people to marry each other, if they can refuse on such trivial grounds as lack of love?" they asked. "Just as important, how will we prevent the wrong ones, such as paupers and servants, from marrying?" What would compel people to stay in marriages where love had died? What would prevent wives from challenging their husbands' authority?

They were right to worry. In the late 18th century, new ideas about the "pursuit of happiness" led many countries to make divorce more accessible, and some even repealed the penalties for homosexual love. The French revolutionaries abolished the legal category of illegitimacy, according a "love child" equal rights with a "legal" one. In the mid-19th century, women challenged husbands' sole ownership of wives' property, earnings, and behavior. Moralists predicted that such female economic independence would "destroy domestic tranquility," producing "infidelity in

CATO UNBOUND

SEARCH

EARTH & FIRE EROWID

About Cato Unbound
Archived Issues

the marriage bed, a high rate of divorce, and increased female criminality." And in some regards, they seemed correct. Divorce rates rose so steadily that in 1891 a Cornell University professor predicted, with stunning accuracy, that if divorce continued rising at its current rate, more marriages would end in divorce than death by the 1980s.

But until the late 1960s, most of the destabilizing aspects of the love revolution were held in check by several forces that prevented people from building successful lives outside marriage: the continued legal subordination of women to men; the ability of local elites to penalize employees and other community members for then-stigmatized behaviors such as remaining single, cohabiting, or getting a divorce; the unreliability of birth control, combined with the harsh treatment of illegitimate children; and above all, the dependence of women upon men's wage earning.

In the 1970s, however, these constraints were swept away or seriously eroded. The result has been to create a paradox with which many Americans have yet to come to terms. Today, when a marriage works, it delivers more benefits to its members—adults and children—than ever before. A good marriage is fairer and more fulfilling for both men and women than couples of the past could ever have imagined. Domestic violence and sexual coercion have fallen sharply. More couples share decision-making and housework than ever before. Parents devote unprecedented time and resources to their children. And men in stable marriages are far less likely to cheat on their wives than in the past.

But the same things that have made so many modern marriages more intimate, fair, and protective have simultaneously made marriage itself more optional and more contingent on successful negotiation. They have also made marriage seem less bearable when it doesn't live up to its potential. The forces that have strengthened marriage as a personal relationship between freely-consenting adults have weakened marriage as a regulatory social institution.

In the 1970s and 1980s, the collapse of the conditions that had forced most people to get and stay married led to dramatic—and often traumatic—upheavals in marriage. This was exacerbated by an

COONTZ :THE FUTURE OF MARRIAGE

economic climate that made the 1950s ideal of the male breadwinner unattainable for many families. Divorce rates soared. Unwed teen motherhood shot up. Since then, some of these destabilizing trends have leveled off or receded. The divorce rate has fallen, especially for college-educated couples, over the past 20 years. When divorce does occur, more couples work to resolve it amicably, and fewer men walk away from contact with their children. Although there was a small uptick in teen births last year, they are still almost 30 percent lower than in 1991.

Still, there is no chance that we can restore marriage to its former supremacy in coordinating social and interpersonal relationships. Even as the divorce rate has dropped, the incidence of cohabitation, delayed marriage and non-marriage has risen steadily. With half of all Americans aged 25-29 unmarried, marriage no longer organizes the transition into regular sexual activity or long-term partnerships the way it used to. Although teen births are lower than a decade ago, births to unwed mothers aged 25 and older continue to climb. Almost 40 percent of America's children are born to unmarried parents. And gay and lesbian families are permanently out of the closet.

The decline in marriage's dominating role in organizing social and personal life is not unique to America. It is occurring across the industrial world, even in countries with less "permissive" values and laws. In predominantly Catholic Ireland, where polls in the 1980s found near-universal disapproval of premarital sex, one child in three today is born outside marriage. China's divorce rate has soared more than 700 percent since 1980. Until 2005, Chile was the only country in the Western Hemisphere that still prohibited divorce. But in today's world, prohibiting divorce has very different consequences than in the past, because people no longer feel compelled to marry in the first place. Between 1990 and 2003, the number of marriages in Chile fell from 100,000 to 60,000 a year, and nearly half of all children born in Chile in the early years of the 21st century were born to unmarried couples. In Italy, Singapore, and Japan, divorce, cohabitation, and out-of wedlock births remain low by American standards, but a much larger percentage of women avoid marriage and childbearing altogether. This suggests that

we are experiencing a massive historical current that, if blocked in one area, simply flows over traditional paths of family life at a different spot.

The late 20th-century revolution in the role and function of marriage has been as far-reaching—and as wrenching—as the replacement of local craft production and exchange by wage labor and ndustrialization. Like the Industrial Revolution, the family diversity revolution has undercut old ways of organizing work, leisure, caregiving, and redistribution to dependents. It has liberated some people from restrictive, socially-imposed statuses, but stripped others of customary support systems and rules for behavior, without putting clearly defined new ones in place. There have been winners and losers in the arriage revolution, just as there were in the Industrial Revolution. But we will not meet the challenges of this transformation by trying to turn back the clock. Instead we must take two lessons away from these historical changes.

First, marriage is not on the verge of extinction. Most cohabiting couples eventually do get married, either to each other or to someone else. New groups, such as gays and lesbians, are now demanding access to marriage—a demand that many pro-marriage advocates oddly interpret as an attack on the institution. And a well-functioning marriage is still an especially useful and effective method of organizing interpersonal commitments and improving people's well-being. But in today's climate of gender equality and personal choice, we must realize that successful marriages require different traits, skills, and behaviors than in the past.

Marriages used to depend upon a clear division of labor and authority, and couples who rejected those rules had less stable marriages than those who abided by them. In the 1950s, a woman's best bet for a lasting marriage was to marry a man who believed firmly in the male breadwinner ideal. Women who wanted a "MRS degree" were often advised to avoid the "bachelor's" degree, since as late as 1967 men told pollsters they valued a woman's cooking and housekeeping skills above her intelligence or education. Women who hadn't married by age 25 were less likely to ever marry than their more traditional counterparts, and studies in the 1960s suggested that if they did marry at an older

age than average they were more likely to divorce. When a wife took a job outside the home, this raised the risk of marital dissolution.

All that has changed today. Today, men rank intelligence and education way above cooking and housekeeping as a desirable trait in a partner. A recent study by Paul Amato *et al.* found that the chance of divorce recedes with each year that a woman postpones marriage, with the least divorce-prone marriages being those where the couples got married at age 35 or higher. Educated and high-earning women are now less likely to divorce than other women. When a wife takes a job today, it works to stabilize the marriage. Couples who share housework and productive work have more stable marriages than couples who do not, according to sociologist Lynn Prince Cooke. And the Amato study found that husbands and wives who hold egalitarian views about gender have higher marital quality and fewer marital problems than couples who cling to more traditional views.

The second lesson of history is that the time has passed when we can construct our social policies, work schedules, health insurance systems, sex education programs—or even our moral and ethical beliefs about who owes what to whom—on the assumption that all long-term commitments and care-giving obligations should or can be organized through marriage. Of course we must seek ways to make marriage more possible for couples and to strengthen the marriages they contract. But we must be equally concerned to help couples who don't marry become better co-parents, to help single parents and cohabiting couples meet their obligations, and to teach divorced parents how to minimize their conflicts and improve their parenting.

The right research and policy question today is not "what kind of family do we wish people lived in?" Instead, we must ask "what do we know about how to help every family build on its strengths, minimize its weaknesses, and raise children more successfully?" Much recent hysteria to the contrary, we know a lot about how to do that. We should devote more of our energies to getting that research out and less to fantasizing about a return to a mythical Golden Age of marriage of the past.

Why Should I Be Nice To You? Coffee Shops and the Politics of Good Service

(ESSAY)

Emily Raine

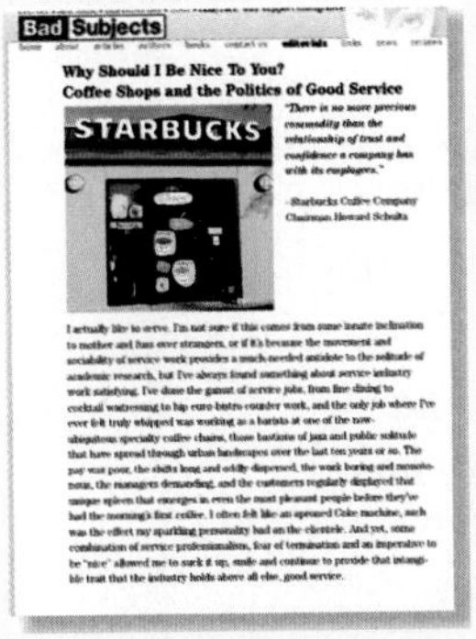

Emily Raine recently received a Masters degree in Communication Studies at McGill University in Montreal. She also writes about graffiti and street art. This essay appeared in the online journal *Bad Subjects* in 2005.

Return to these questions after you have finished reading.

Analyzing and Connecting

1. What exactly is Raine's causal argument about why work in coffee chains is worse than in other kinds of service jobs?

2. Raine mixes technical terms with informal language. For example, she says "café labor is heavily grounded in the rationalism of Fordist manufacturing principles," which is the technical term for the method of assembly-line production developed by Henry Ford. But she says she "felt like an aproned Coke machine." Look for other examples of technical and informal language. Why does she mix them?

3. Why is it important that coffee shop employees not act like individuals from the employer's perspective?

4. Have you ever worked in a restaurant, coffee shop, retail store, or another service industry? If so, how was your experience similar to or different from Raine's? If not, think about your experiences as a customer in coffee shops and similar businesses. How did the employees behave?

5. Look at the last paragraph. Raine makes a new claim that rudeness allows workers to retain their individuality. Why does she put this claim in the conclusion? Does it lead to a strong conclusion?

Finding Ideas for Writing

Think about the causal argument that Raine presents and your own experiences as an employee or as a customer at a coffee shop, restaurant, store, or other service-oriented establishment. Are there any factors she's neglecting that may change the nature of the causal relationship she's setting up? Write a one-paragraph rebuttal based on this overlooked factor.

RAINE: WHY SHOULD I BE NICE TO YOU?

eserver » bad home » bad editorials » 2006 » raza/race: why support immigrants?

Bad Subjects

home about articles authors books contact us **editorials** links news reviews

Why Should I Be Nice To You? Coffee Shops and the Politics of Good Service

"There is no more precious commodity than the relationship of trust and confidence a company has with its employees."

–Starbucks Coffee Company Chairman Howard Schultz

I actually like to serve. I'm not sure if this comes from some innate inclination to mother and fuss over strangers, or if it's because the movement and sociability of service work provides a much-needed antidote to the solitude of academic research, but I've always found something about service industry work satisfying. I've done the gamut of service jobs, from fine dining to cocktail waitressing to hip euro-bistro counter work, and the only job where I've ever felt truly whipped was working as a barista at one of the now-ubiquitous specialty coffee chains, those bastions of jazz and public solitude that have spread through urban landscapes over the last ten years or so. The pay was poor, the shifts long and oddly dispersed, the work boring and monotonous, the managers demanding, and the customers regularly displayed that unique spleen that emerges in even the most pleasant people before they've had the morning's first coffee. I often felt like an aproned Coke machine, such was the effect my sparkling personality had on the clientele. And yet, some combination of service professionalism, fear of termination and an imperative to be "nice" allowed me to suck it up, smile and continue to provide that intangible trait that the industry holds above all else, good service.

eserver » bad home » bad editorials » 2006 » **raza/race: why support immigrants?**

Bad Subjects

home about articles authors books contact us **editorials** links news reviews

Good service in coffee shops doesn't amount to much. Unlike table service, where interaction with customers spans a minimum of half an hour, the average contact with a café customer lasts less than ten seconds. Consider how specialty cafés are laid out: the customer service counter is arranged in a long line that clients move along to "use" the café. The linear coffee bar resembles an assembly line, and indeed, café labor is heavily grounded in the rationalism of Fordist manufacturing principles, which had already been tested for use in hospitality services by fast food chains. Each of the café workers is assigned a specific stage in the service process to perform exclusively, such as taking orders, using the cash registers, or handing clients cups of brewed coffee.

The specialization of tasks increases the speed of transactions and limits the duration of any one employee's interaction with the clientele. This means that in a given visit a customer might order from one worker, receive food from the next, then brewed coffee or tea from yet another, then pay a cashier before proceeding down the line of the counter, finishing the trip at the espresso machine which is always situated at its end. Ultimately, each of the café's products is processed and served by a different employee, who repeats the same preparation task for hours and attends to each customer only as they receive that one product.

Needless to say, the productive work in cafés is dreary and repetitive. Further, this style of service severely curtails interaction with the clientele, and the very brevity of each transaction precludes much chance for authentic friendliness or conversation—even asking about someone's day would slow the entire operation. The one aspect of service work that can be unpredictable—people—becomes redundant, and interaction with customers is reduced to a fatiguing eight-hour-long smile and the repetition of sentiments that allude to good service, such as injunctions to enjoy their purchases or to have a nice day. Rather than friendly exchanges with customers, barista workers' good service is reduced to a quick rictus in the customer's direction between a great deal of friendly interaction with the espresso machine.

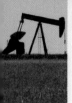

RAINE: WHY SHOULD I BE NICE TO YOU?

eserver » bad home » bad editorials » 2006 » raza/race: why support immigrants?

Bad Subjects

home about articles authors books contact us **editorials** links news reviews

As the hospitality industry really took off in the sixties, good service became one of the trademarks of its advertising claims, a way for brands to distinguish themselves from the rest of the pack. One needn't think too hard to come up with a litany of service slogans that holler the good graces of their personnel—at Starbucks where the baristas make the magic, at PSA where smiles aren't just painted on, or at McDonald's where smiles are free. Employee friendliness emerged as one of the chief distinguishing brand features of personal services, which means that the workers themselves become an aspect of the product for sale.

Our notions of good service revolve around a series of platitudes about professionalism—we're at your service, with a smile, where the customer's always right—each bragging the centrality of the customer to everything "we" do. Such claims imply an easy and equal exchange between two parties: the "we" that gladly serves and the "you" that happily receives. There is, however, always a third party involved in the service exchange, and that's whoever has hired the server, the body that ultimately decides just what the dimensions of good service will be.

Like most employees, a service worker sells labor to an employer at a set rate, often minimum wage, and the employer sells the product of that labor, the service itself, at market values. In many hospitality services, where gratuities make up the majority of employment revenue, the worker directly benefits from giving good service, which of course translates to good tips. But for the vast majority of service staff, and particularly those employed in venues yielding little or no gratuities—fast food outlets, café chains, cleaning and maintenance operations—this promises many workers little more than a unilateral imperative to be perpetually bright and amenable.

The vast majority of service personnel do not spontaneously produce an unaffected display of cheer and good will continuously for the duration of a shift. When a company markets its products on servers' friendliness, they must then monitor and control employees' friendliness, so good service is defined and enforced from above. Particularly in chains, which are premised

eserver » bad home » bad editorials » 2006 » raza/race: why support immigrants?

Bad Subjects

home about articles authors books contact us **editorials** links news reviews

upon their consistent reproduction of the same experience in numerous locations, organizations are obliged to impose systems to manage employees' interaction with their customers. In some chains, namely the fast food giants such as McDonald's and Burger King, employee banter is scripted into cash registers, so that as soon as a customer orders, workers are cued to offer, "would you like a dessert with that?" (an offer of dubious benefit to the customer) and to wish them a nice day. Ultimately, this has allowed corporations to be able to assimilate "good service"—or, friendly workers—into their overall brand image.

While cafés genuflect toward the notion of good service, their layouts and management styles preclude much possibility of creating the warmth that this would entail. Good service is, of course, important, but not if it interferes with throughput. What's more, these cafés have been at the forefront of a new wave of organizations that not only market themselves on service quality but also describe employees' job satisfaction as the seed from which this flowers.

Perhaps the most glaring example of this is Starbucks, where cheerful young workers are displayed behind elevated counters as they banter back and forth, calling out fancy Italian drink names and creating theatre out of their productive labor. Starbucks' corporate literature gushes not only about the good service its customers will receive, but about the great joy that its "partners" take in providing it, given the company's unique ability to "provide a great work environment and treat each other with respect and dignity," and where its partners are "emotionally and intellectually committed to Starbucks success." In the epigraph to this essay, Starbucks' chairman even describes the company's relationship with its workers as a commodity. Not only does Starbucks offer good service, but it attempts to guarantee something even better: good service provided by employees that are genuinely happy to give it.

Starbucks has branded a new kind of worker, the happy, wholesome, perfume-free barista. The company offers unusual benefits for service

RAINE: WHY SHOULD I BE NICE TO YOU?

workers, including stock options, health insurance, dental plans and other perks such as product discounts and giveaways. Further, they do so very, very publicly, and the company's promotional materials are filled with moving accounts of workers who never dreamed that corporate America could care so much. With the other hand, though, the company has smashed unionization drives in New York, Vancouver and at its Seattle roaster; it schedules workers at oddly timed shifts that never quite add up to full-time hours; the company pays only nominally more than minimum wage, and their staffs are still unable to subsist schlepping lattes alone.

Starbucks is not alone in marketing itself as an enlightened employer. When General Motors introduced its Saturn line, the new brand was promoted almost entirely on the company's good relations with its staff. The company's advertising spots often featured pictures of and quotes from the union contract, describing their unique partnership between manufacturer, workers and union, which allowed blue-collar personnel to have a say in everything from automobile designs to what would be served for lunch. The company rightly guessed that this strategy would go over well with liberal consumers concerned about the ethics of their purchases. Better yet, Saturn could market its cars based on workers' happiness whether personnel were satisfied or not, because very few consumers would ever have the chance to interact with them.

At the specialty coffee chains, however, consumers have to talk to employees, yet nobody ever really asks. The café service counter runs like a smooth piece of machinery, and I found that most people preferred to pretend that they were interacting with an appliance. In such short transactions, it is exceedingly difficult for customers to remember the humanity of each of the four to seven people they might interact with to get their coffees. Even fast food counters have one server who processes each customer's order, yet in cafés the workers just become another gadget in the well-oiled café machine. This is a definite downside for the employees—clients are much ruder to café staff than in any other sector of the industry I ever worked in. I found that

eserver » bad home » bad editorials » 2006 » **raza/race: why support immigrants?**

Bad Subjects

home about articles authors books contact us **editorials** links news reviews

people were more likely to be annoyed than touched by any reference to my having a personality, and it took no small amount of thought on my part to realize why.

Barista workers are hired to represent an abstract category of worker, not to act as individuals. Because of the service system marked by short customer interaction periods and a homogenous staff, the services rendered are linked in the consumer imagination to the company and not to any one individual worker. Workers' assimilation into the company image makes employees in chain service as branded as the products they serve. The chain gang, the workers who hold these eminently collegiate after-school jobs, are proscribed sales scripts and drilled on customer service scenarios to standardize interactions with customers. The company issues protocols for hair length, color and maintenance, visible piercings and tattoos as well as personal hygiene and acceptable odorific products. Workers are made more interchangeable by the use of uniforms, which, of course, serve to make the staff just that. The organization is a constant intermediary in every transaction, interjecting its presence in every detail of the service experience, and this standardization amounts to an absorption of individuals' personalities into the corporate image.

Many of the measures that chains take to secure the homogeneity of their employees do not strike us as particularly alarming, likely because similar restrictions have been in place for several hundred years. Good service today has inherited many of the trappings of the good servant of yore, including prohibitions against eating, drinking, sitting or relaxing in front the served, entering and exiting through back doors and wearing uniforms to visually mark workers' status. These measures almost completely efface the social identities of staff during work hours, providing few clues to workers' status in their free time. Contact between service workers and their customers is thus limited to purely functional relations, so that the public only see them as workers, as makers of quality coffee, and never as possible peers.

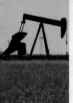

eserver » bad home » bad editorials » 2006 » raza/race: why support immigrants?

Bad Subjects

home about articles authors books contact us **editorials** links news reviews

Maintaining such divisions is integral to good service because this display of class distinctions ultimately underlies our notions of service quality. Good service means not only serving well, but also allowing customers to feel justified in issuing orders, to feel okay about being served—which, in turn, requires demonstrations of class difference and the smiles that suggest servers' comfort with having a subordinate role in the service exchange.

Unlike the penguin-suited household servant staffs whose class status was clearly defined, service industry workers today often have much more in common from a class perspective with those that they serve. This not only creates an imperative for them to wear their class otherness on their sleeves, as it were, but also to accept their subordinate role to those they serve by being unshakably tractable and polite.

Faith Popcorn has rather famously referred to the four-dollar latte as a "small indulgence," noting that while this is a lot to pay for a glass of hot milk, it is quite inexpensive for the feeling of luxury that can accompany it. In this service climate, the class status of the server and the served—anyone who can justify spending this much on a coffee—is blurry, indeed. Coffee shops that market themselves on employee satisfaction assert the same happy servant that allows politically conscientious consumers who are in many cases the workers' own age and class peers, to feel justified in receiving good service. Good service—as both an apparent affirmation of subordinate classes' desire to serve and as an enforced one-sided politeness—reproduces the class distinctions that have historically characterized servant-served relationships so that these are perpetuated within the contemporary service market.

The specialty coffee companies are large corporations, and for the twenty-somethings who stock their counters, barista work is too temporary to bother fighting the system. Mostly, people simply quit. Dissatisfied workers are stuck with engaging in tactics that will change nothing but allow them to make the best of their lot. These include minor infractions such as taking liberties with the uniforms or grabbing little bits of company time for their own pleasure,

eserver » bad home » bad editorials » 2006 » **raza/race: why support immigrants?**

Bad Subjects

home about articles authors books contact us **editorials** links news reviews

what Michel de Certeau calls *la perruque* and the companies themselves call "time theft." As my time in the chain gang wore on, I developed my own tactic, the only one I found that jostled the customers out of their complacency and allowed me to be a barista and a person.

There is no easy way to serve without being a servant, and I have always found that the best way to do so is to show my actual emotions rather than affecting a smooth display of interminable patience and good will. For café customers, bettering baristas' lots can be as simple as asking about their day, addressing them by name—any little gesture to show that you noticed the person behind the service that they can provide. My tactic as a worker is equally simple, but it is simultaneously an assertion of individual identity at work, a refusal of the class distinctions that characterize the service environment and a rebuttal to the companies that would promote my satisfaction with their system: be rude. Not arbitrarily rude, of course—customers are people, too, and nobody gains anything by spreading bad will. But on those occasions when customer or management behavior warranted a zinging comeback, I would give it.

Rudeness, when it is demanded, undermines companies' claims on workers' personal warmth and allows them to retain their individuality by expressing genuine rather than affected feelings in at-work interpersonal exchanges. It is a refusal of the class distinctions that underlie consumers' unilateral prerogative of rudeness and servers' unilateral imperative to be nice. It runs contrary to everything that we have been taught, not only about service but about interrelating with others. But this seems to be the only method of asserting one's person-hood in the service environment, where workers' personalities are all too easily reduced to a space-time, conflated with the drinks they serve. Baristas of the world, if you want to avoid becoming a green-aproned coffee dispensary, you're just going to have to tell people off about it.

How to write a causal analysis

These steps for the process of writing a causal analysis may not progress as neatly as this chart might suggest. Writing is not an assembly-line process. As you write, you are constantly reading what you have written and rethinking.

Continue thinking about causation as you write and revise. The process of writing may lead you to additional causal relationships.

1 MAKE A CAUSAL CLAIM

- Examine a social trend, law, or policy.
- Analyze problems in your neighborhood or at your school.
- Investigate natural phenomena.
- Investigate the impact of human activity on the environment.
- Think about what is at stake. What could or should change if the cause is known?
- Put your claim in the form "____ causes (or does not cause) _____."

2 THINK ABOUT THE POSSIBLE CAUSES

- What are the obvious causes?
- What are the underlying causes?
- What causes might be hidden?
- What are the causes that most people have not recognized before?
- Who is affected by what you are investigating? Do your readers have a stake in what you are analyzing?
- Look for disagreement among your sources. If they all agree on the cause, probably you won't have much to add.

3 WRITE A DRAFT

- Describe the trend, event, or phenomenon.
- Give the background your readers will need.
- If the trend or event you are analyzing is unfamiliar to your readers, explain the cause or the chain of causation.
- Another way to organize the body of your analysis is to set out the causes that have already been offered and reject them one by one. Then you can present the cause or causes that you think are the right ones.
- A third method is to look at a series of causes one by one, analyzing the importance of each.
- Do more than simply summarize in your conclusion. You might consider additional effects beyond those you have previously noted, or explain to readers any action you think should be taken based on your conclusions.
- Choose a title that will interest readers in your essay.
- Include any necessary images or tables.

4 REVISE, REVISE, REVISE

- Check that your causal analysis fulfills the assignment.
- Make sure that your claim is clear and that you have sufficient evidence to convince readers.
- Look at additional potential causes, if necessary.
- Reconsider how multiple causes might interact.
- Go further back in the causal chain, if necessary, showing how the causes you examine have their roots in other events.
- Examine the organization of your analysis and think of possible better ways to organize.
- Review the visual presentation of your analysis for readability and maximum impact.
- Proofread carefully.

5 SUBMITTED VERSION

- Make sure your finished writing meets all formatting requirements.

1: Make a causal claim

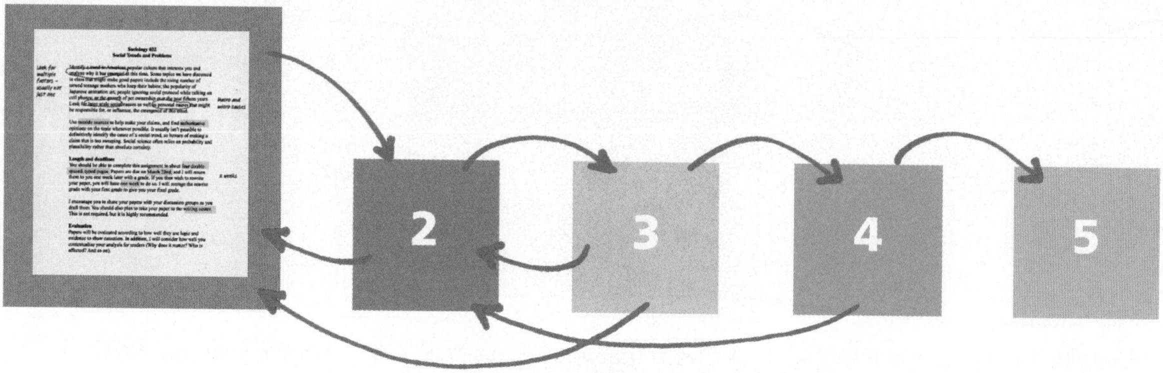

Analyze the assignment

- Read your assignment slowly and carefully. Look for key words like *causes, effect, result, impact, why*, and *influence*. These key words tell you that you are writing a causal analysis.
- Highlight any information about the length specified, date due, formatting, and other requirements. You can attend to this information later. At this point you want to give your attention to the topic and criteria you will use in your analysis.

Explore possible topics

- Make a list of fashion trends including cars, clothing, hairstyles, food, tattoos, and piercing. Look at your list and think about where and why a particular trend originates. Make notes about the origins of trends on your list.
- Make a list of social trends including music, television shows, movies, sports, exercising, childrearing, and leisure. Look at your list and think about where and why a particular trend originates. Make notes about the origins of trends on your list.
- Make a list of important historical events or discoveries that changed the course of civilization. Make notes about what led to these events or discoveries and how people's lives were changed by them.

Think about what's at stake

- Remember that people often have a stake in the outcome of a causal claim. Ask: Who will agree with me? Who will disagree, and why?
- Think about why your analysis matters. If people accept your causal claim, will anything change?

Staying on Track

Make a claim that matters

Make an arguable claim

Easy answers generally make bad arguments. If all the sources you consult agree about the cause of the effect you are interested in, there is probably no need for you to make another argument saying the same thing. Look for a phenomenon that hasn't been explained to everyone's satisfaction.

OFF TRACK

Cigarette smoke is a leading cause of lung cancer.

ON TRACK

New research indicates that childhood asthma may be linked to exposure to cockroaches.

Explain why it matters

Readers need to know why this cause-and-effect relationship is important. If we determine the cause of this phenomenon, what will change? What can we do? What might happen?

OFF TRACK

This paper will investigate the most common causes of foundation failure in U.S. residential housing.

ON TRACK

Foundation failure, especially cracked slabs, can cost anywhere from a few thousand to tens of thousands of dollars to repair. Determining the primary causes of foundation failure can help homeowners and insurers protect themselves against economic loss and inconvenience.

Write Now

Think about causal factors

1. Consider trends or problems you are familiar with—in your daily life, or in the larger world.
2. List these trends and problems on the right side of a piece of paper. On the left side, write down what you think some of the causes of the problems might be. Underline the causes that you are confident about.
3. Look over your two lists. Which topics seem most interesting to you? If an entry has many underlined causes or effects, it may be too obvious to write about.

Writer at work

Sean Booker was asked to write a paper analyzing the causes of a current trend in popular culture for a course in Social Trends and Problems. He made the following notes on his assignment sheet while his class was discussing the assignment.

Sociology 032
Social Trends and Problems

Look for multiple factors – usually not just one

Identify a trend in American popular culture that interests you and analyze why it has emerged at this time. Some topics we have discussed in class that might make good papers include the rising number of unwed teenage mothers who keep their babies; the popularity of Japanese animation art; people ignoring social protocol while talking on cell phones; or the growth of pet ownership over the past fifteen years. Look for large scale social causes as well as personal causes that might be responsible for, or influence, the emergence of this trend.

Macro and micro causes

Use outside sources to help make your claims, and find authoritative opinions on the topic whenever possible. It usually isn't possible to definitively identify the cause of a social trend, so beware of making a claim that is too sweeping. Social science often relies on probability and plausibility rather than absolute certainty.

Length and deadlines
You should be able to complete this assignment in about four double-spaced, typed pages. Papers are due on March 22nd, and I will return them to you one week later with a grade. If you then wish to rewrite your paper, you will have one week to do so. I will average the rewrite grade with your first grade to give you your final grade.

2 weeks

I encourage you to share your papers with your discussion groups as you draft them. You should also plan to take your paper to the writing center. This is not required, but it is highly recommended.

Evaluation
Papers will be evaluated according to how well they use logic and evidence to show causation. In addition, I will consider how well you contextualize your analysis for readers (Why does it matter? Who is affected? And so on).

Read the assignment closely
Sean Booker began by circling the words and phrases that indicated his analytical task. Then he highlighted information about dates and processes for the project.

Choose a topic
Sean Booker made a list of trends he might write about. After each item on his list, he made notes about why the topic would matter, and to whom. He also made preliminary observations about where he might find "authoritative opinions" on each topic, wrote down any possible causes that occurred to him at the time, and noted any other observations or questions he had about that topic. Finally, he chose one trend for further research.

POPULARITY OF ANIME
- Is it more popular with certain age groups or other demographic groups?
- Is there any scholarly/authoritative research on it? Maybe in Art History?
- I've seen tons of magazines devoted to it at the bookstore.
- Could interview Sarah about the collection she has.

POPULARITY OF RAP MUSIC
(especially among white teenagers) ** Best research possibilities**
- What percentage of sales of rap music are to white kids?
- Is it any different from white teenagers liking rock n' roll in the 50s?
- Because it annoys parents?
- Does it indicate racial tolerance?
- I know there has been research on this from an economic viewpoint.

SUV SALES
- Why do people want to drive "off-roading" cars to work every day?
- Are sales declining with rising gas prices?
- Is this even a trend any more? People are buying VWs and Mini Coopers now.

"ILLEGAL" FILE SHARING
- Why do so many people do it if it is "illegal"? (Because you get something for free.)
- What are the arguments saying that it is or isn't illegal?
- Easy answer: people are willing to "steal" in this case because there is still significant disagreement over whether it is really stealing.

2: Think about possible causes

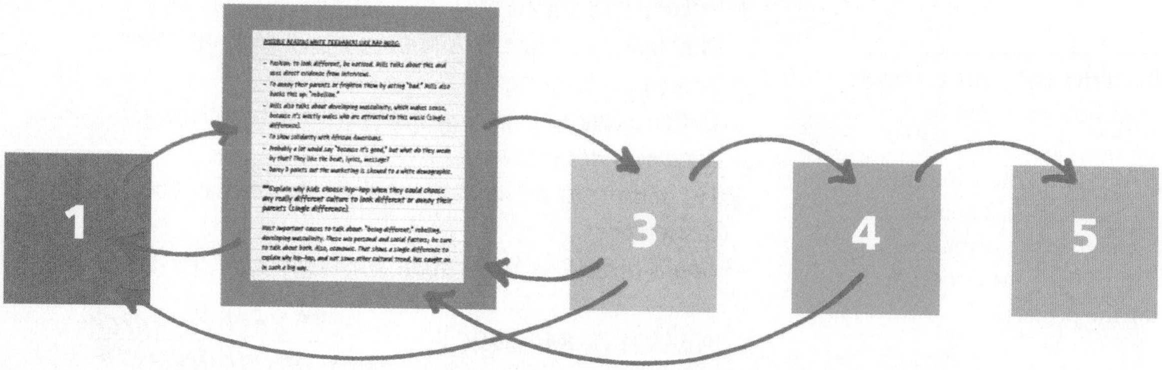

Find the obvious causes, and then dig deeper

- **What causal factors might be hidden from the general observer, and why?** Use your imagination; hidden causes require new thinking if they are to be uncovered.
- **How do various causal factors interact?** Several causes together might contribute to an effect, rather than any single cause being the determining factor.
- **What "causes the cause" that you have identified?** What prior conditions does each cause arise from? If poor attendance is a factor in drop-out rates, what causes some students to have poor attendance in the first place?

Analyze your audience

- **Think about who is affected by the phenomenon you are investigating.** Who is in a position to react to your claims, and make changes?
- **If you don't know who your audience is, do some research to find out who is interested in your topic.** Who has offered opinions or responded to previous causal claims on this topic?

Research your analysis

- **Look for some disagreement among your sources.** If they all agree on the cause, your analysis won't matter much.
- **When your sources disagree, ask why.** Does one give more weight to some pieces of evidence than to others? Do they draw different conclusions from the same evidence? Do they use Mill's methods of determining causation in different ways?
- **Be on the lookout for new potential causes, or new findings that could help you rule out potential causes.**

Writer at work

Sean Booker began his analysis by brainstorming for all the possible causes he could think of. Then, he researched the topic to find information on the causes he had listed and also to learn about other potential causes that had been put forward.

Sean Booker thought about his own experience with the trend to help define his audience. He also noted the types of audiences his sources appeared to be writing for. Finally, Sean Booker identified what he thought were the most likely causes of rap's popularity with white teenagers. He did this analysis by applying Mill's methods of determining causation and by weighing the opinions of the authoritative sources he had read.

POSSIBLE REASONS WHITE TEENAGERS LIKE RAP MUSIC:

- Fashion: to look different, be noticed. Mills talks about this and uses direct evidence from interviews.
- To annoy their parents or frighten them by acting "bad." Mills also backs this up: "rebellion."
- Mills also talks about developing masculinity, which makes sense, because it's mostly males who are attracted to this music (single difference).
- To show solidarity with African Americans.
- Probably a lot would say "Because it's good," but what do they mean by that? They like the beat, lyrics, message?
- Davey D points out the marketing is skewed to a white demographic.

**Explain why kids choose hip-hop when they could choose any really different culture to look different or annoy their parents (single difference).

Most important causes to talk about: "being different," rebelling, developing masculinity. These mix personal and social factors; be sure to talk about both. Also, economic. That shows a single difference to explain why hip-hop, and not some other cultural trend, has caught on in such a big way.

3: Write a draft

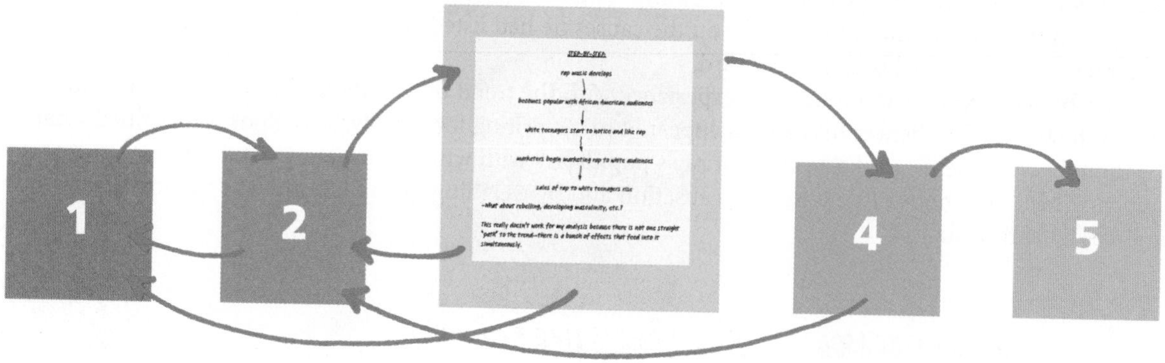

Introduce what you will be analyzing

- Describe the trend, event, or phenomenon you will be analyzing.
- Give your readers any background information they will need.
- Explain why it is important to determine the cause of this phenomenon (you can save this for the conclusion if you wish).

Describe the causal relationship

- Explain how the chain of causation works to produce the effect in question. Break down each step so readers can follow the process.
- Alternatively, set out the causes offered by other people and show how they can be ruled out. Then, introduce your own claim and demonstrate why it is superior to others'.
- A third method is to look at a series of possible causes one at a time, analyzing each and making a claim about its relative impact on a phenomenon.

Anticipate and address opposing viewpoints

- Acknowledge other stakeholders in the analysis, and consider their claims.
- Demonstrate why your claim is preferable.

Conclude by doing more than summarizing

- Spell out the importance of the analysis, if you haven't already done so.
- Consider additional effects you haven't previously discussed.
- Explain any action you think needs to be taken based on your conclusion.

Staying on Track

Look at the big picture

Don't confuse correlation with causation

Mill's method of concomitant variation might lead you to conclude that any mutual relationship between two events is causal. Remember that concomitant variation only determines cause when all other variables are accounted for.

OFF TRACK

The drop in the number of Americans living in poverty during the Clinton administration was due to a number of factors, the Welfare Reform Act being chief among them.

ON TRACK

The lower number of Americans living in poverty during the Clinton administration was due to a number of factors. How much did the Welfare Reform Act contribute to this trend? The general economic prosperity experienced by the entire country during that time probably had a greater impact. Statistics show that the primary effect of the Welfare Reform Act was to simply remove people from welfare rolls, not actually lift them out of poverty.

Identify the stakeholders in your analysis

Be especially alert for opinions about your topic from people who would be adversely affected by a different causal outcome.

OFF TRACK

Can mega-doses of vitamin C prevent colds, flu, and other illnesses? Good health is important to everyone, so we should all be interested in the news that vitamin C has many important health benefits.

ON TRACK

Can mega-doses of vitamin C prevent colds, flu, and other illnesses? The supplements industry has spent millions of dollars to convince consumers that this is the case. The industry stands to make hundreds of millions more if people believe them. But evidence from independent researchers casts some doubt on the effectiveness of mega-doses of vitamin C in preventing illness.

Writer at work

Sean Booker tested three organizational patterns for his analysis. First he looked at how describing a chain of causation could illuminate his analysis. Next, he considered examining causes one by one and eliminating them before describing the cause he thought was correct. Finally, he structured his analysis as an examination of possible causes, one by one, with accompanying discussion of each cause's relative contribution to the overall effect. This seemed to Sean Booker like the best method for making his analysis, so he used it to write his draft.

STEP-BY-STEP:

rap music develops

↓

becomes popular with African American audiences

↓

white teenagers start to notice and like rap

↓

marketers begin marketing rap to white audiences

↓

sales of rap to white teenagers rise

-What about rebelling, developing masculinity, etc.?

This really doesn't work for my analysis because there is not one straight "path" to the trend—there is a bunch of effects that feed into it simultaneously.

DISPROVING ALTERNATE CAUSES:

White kids like rap just because "it is good" and they are colorblind about music.

- Actually, they are acutely aware of the racial difference between themselves and the performers; that's part of why they like it.

White kids like rap because they feel sympathy with African American culture.

- I'm the only person who even thought of this reason. A lot of people I know who listen to rap know next to nothing about African American culture, so this is pretty clearly wrong. But what good does it do to bring it up and refute it if no one else would have even considered it as a possibility?

I guess the problem here is that there isn't a big controversy over which causes are "right." That kind of controversy would work better with this structure. It's more a question of how many different causes there might be, and how they might work together.

ONE CAUSE AT A TIME:

- Appeal of the fashion and style is one possible cause. Explain how it fills a need for white teenagers.
- Rebellion against social expectations. Explain why white kids need to do this.
- Developing masculinity. Explain how social pressures lead white male teenagers to think rap's message makes them more masculine.
- Marketing. Look at how rap is marketed to white kids, amplifying all the causes above.

This strategy is the best approach because it lets me look at all the possible causes in detail and finish with the one that sort of gathers up and amplifies the first three.

4: Revise, revise, revise

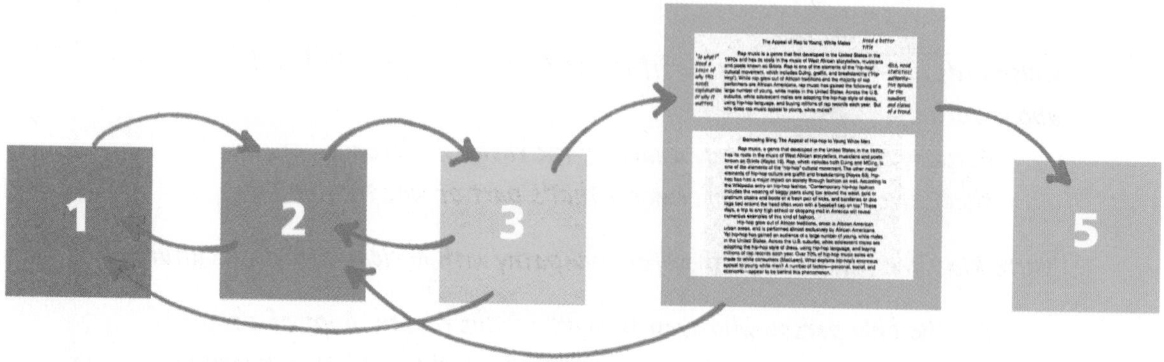

Skilled writers know that the secret to writing well is rewriting. Even the best writers often have to revise several times to get the result they want. You also must have effective strategies for revising if you're going to be successful. The biggest trap you can fall into is starting off with the little stuff first. Leave the small stuff for last.

Does your paper or project meet the assignment?

- Look again at your assignment. Does your paper or project do what the assignment asks?
- Look again at the assignment for specific guidelines, including length, format, and amount of research. Does your work meet these guidelines?

Is your causal claim arguable?

- Do enough people disagree with you to make the evaluation worthwhile?
- Who cares about this topic? Do you explain to readers why it is important?

Do you use logical means of determining causation?

- Do you examine common factors, single differences, and concomitant variations?
- Do you use more than one method whenever possible?
- Do you avoid confusing correlation with causation?

Is your evidence authoritative and convincing?

- Have you found the most accurate available information about your topic?
- Have you identified stakeholders in your analysis?
- Have you carefully examined the analysis and conclusions of people who have already expressed an opinion on this topic?

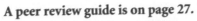

Do you address opposing views?	• Have you acknowledged the opinions of people who disagree with your claim? • Have you shown how your causal claim is preferable?
Is the writing project visually effective?	• Is the font attractive and readable? • Are the headings and visuals effective? • If you use images or tables as part of your analysis, are they legible and appropriately placed?
Save the editing for last.	When you have finished revising, edit and proofread carefully.

A peer review guide is on page 27.

Writer at work

Sean Booker talked with his peer group about his analysis, and took his draft to the writing center for a consultation. He wrote notes on the draft to help him revise, and then he made some changes to the draft. His peers particularly urged him to focus his introduction. Here is the draft of Sean Booker's introduction as he originally wrote it, with notes he made, and as he revised it for his final draft.

The Appeal of Rap to Young, White Males

Need a better title

"So what?" Need a sense of why this needs explanation or why it matters

Rap music is a genre that first developed in the United States in the 1970s and has its roots in the music of West African storytellers, musicians and poets known as Griots. Rap is one of the elements of the "hip-hop" cultural movement, which includes DJing, graffiti, and breakdancing ("Hip-Hop"). While rap grew out of African traditions and the majority of rap performers are African Americans, rap music has gained the following of a large number of young, white males in the United States. Across the U.S. suburbs, white adolescent males are adopting the hip-hop style of dress, using hip-hop language, and buying millions of rap records each year. But why does rap music appeal to young, white males?

Also, need statistics/ authoritative opinion for the numbers and claims of a trend.

Borrowing Bling: The Appeal of Hip-hop to Young White Men

Rap music, a genre that developed in the United States in the 1970s, has its roots in the music of West African storytellers, musicians and poets known as Griots (Keyes 19). Rap, which includes both DJing and MCing, is one of the elements of the "hip-hop" cultural movement. The other major elements of hip-hop culture are graffiti and breakdancing (Keyes 63). Hip-hop has had a major impact on society through fashion as well. According to the Wikipedia entry on hip-hop fashion, "Contemporary hip-hop fashion includes the wearing of baggy jeans slung low around the waist, gold or platinum chains and boots or a fresh pair of kicks, and bandanas or doo rags tied around the head often worn with a baseball cap on top." These days, a trip to any high school or shopping mall in America will reveal numerous examples of this kind of fashion.

Hip-hop grew out of African traditions, arose in African American urban areas, and is performed almost exclusively by African Americans. Yet hip-hop has gained an audience of a large number of young, white males in the United States. Across the U.S. suburbs, white adolescent males are adopting the hip-hop style of dress, using hip-hop language, and buying millions of rap records each year. Over 70% of hip-hop music sales are made to white consumers (MacLean). What explains hip-hop's enormous appeal to young white men? A number of factors—personal, social, and economic—appear to be behind this phenomenon.

Staying on Track

Reviewing your draft

Give yourself plenty of time for reviewing your draft. For detailed information on how to participate in a peer review, how to review it yourself, and how to respond to comments from your classmates, your instructor, or a campus writing consultant, see pages 24–28.

Some good questions to ask yourself when reviewing causal analysis

- Is my causal claim clear? Have I avoided oversimplifying?
- Will my audience understand why this issue is important?
- Have I accounted for the various stakeholders in this analysis?
- Have I considered all possible causes? Have I used sound logic to evaluate them?
- Have I provided evidence to support my claim?

5: Submitted version

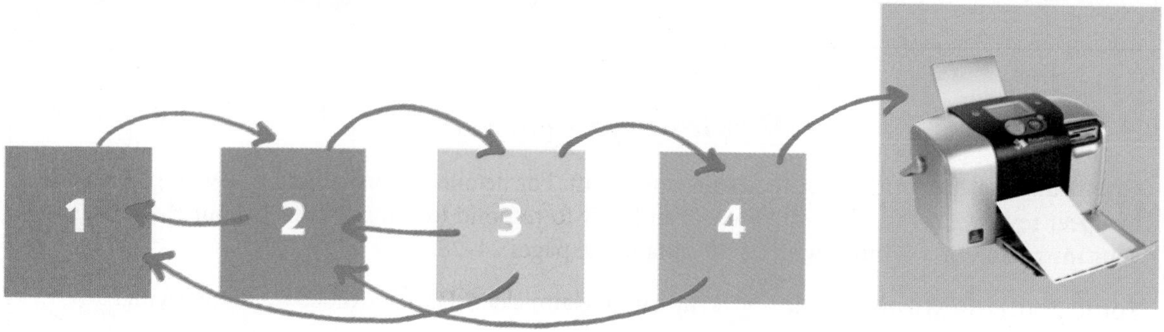

Booker 1

Sean Booker

Professor Martinez

SOC 032

22 March 2008

Borrowing Bling: The Appeal of Hip-hop to Young White Men

Rap music, a genre that developed in the United States in the 1970s, has its roots in the music of West African storytellers, musicians and poets known as Griots (Keyes 19). Rap, which includes both DJing and MCing, is one of the elements of the "Hip-Hop" cultural movement. The other major elements of hip-hop culture are graffiti and breakdancing (Keyes 63). Hip-hop has had a major impact on society through fashion as well. According to the Wikipedia entry on hip-hop, "Contemporary hip-hop fashion includes the wearing of baggy jeans slung low around the waist, gold or platinum chains and boots or a fresh pair of kicks, and bandanas or doo rags tied around the head often worn with a baseball cap on top." These days, a trip to any high school or shopping mall in America will reveal numerous examples of this kind of fashion.

Hip-hop grew out of African traditions, arose in African American urban areas, and is performed almost exclusively by African Americans. Yet hip-hop has gained an audience of a large number of young, white males in the United States. Across the U.S. suburbs, white adolescent males are adopting the hip-hop style of dress, using hip-hop

language, and downloading millions of rap records each year. Over seventy percent of hip-hop music sales are made to white consumers (MacLean). What explains hip-hop's enormous appeal to young white men? A number of factors—personal, social, and economic—appear to be behind this phenomenon.

On a personal level, hip-hop appeals to young, white males because it allows them to escape from the constraints of white society and experience the world of the rapper. Rap music details the life of the African American, sometimes describing a violent and gritty life on the street, or alternatively, a life filled with the glamour of flashy jewelry, nice cars, women, and money. Both of these world views differ vastly from the often insulated, predictable world of the young white adolescent. Professor Fiona Mills interviewed young white rap listeners for her essay "Rap and Young, White Males: Masculinity, Masking and Denial." She found that "young, white men are drawn to the escapist and exotic aspects of rap."

But hip-hop is more than an outlet for personal fantasy. It can also provide a highly defined alternative culture which appeals to the young, white man who may have trouble finding himself within white culture, or who may consciously reject white culture. The fact that hip-hop especially appeals to young men at a time in their lives when they are seeking to define themselves as adults supports this theory. For a white teenager trying desperately to establish himself as a unique person, hip-hop style may appeal because it is something he can easily recognize and emulate, and something which then sets him apart from his white peers. It is a means for situating himself in society.

Additionally, Mills explains that rap music, with its focus on sex, money, drugs and violence, builds a "hyper-masculine aura" that white adolescent males are drawn to because it gives them a model for establishing their masculinity. As Mills revealed in her study, white males often begin listening to music around age twelve or thirteen, just as they are entering adolescence and beginning to establish their masculine identities. In contrast, Mills found that African American males reported listening to rap music from a very young age. Mills suggests that the white adolescents she interviewed saw rap music "as a way of asserting their manhood by associating themselves with an overtly masculine culture—one in which femininity had no place."

Rap music also appeals to young white men because it is a way to rebel against their parents and white society in general. By associating themselves with a musical

culture that involves heavy use of profane language and often centers on violence and drugs, white males establish their rebellion against societal standards. Many teens may like rap for the simple fact that their parents do not approve of its foul language, portrayal of violence, and treatment of women.

These factors all help explain why young white men might be drawn to hip-hop and rap music and what they might gain from adopting its cultural markers. But do these factors alone explain hip-hop's enormous popularity with white consumers? There are many other types of music and culture that might appeal to white adolescents on the same grounds as hip-hop. Why has hip-hop become such a huge cultural phenomenon?

Marketing may well be the answer. Hip-hop historian and journalist Davey D has chronicled the economic pressures that led to hip-hop being marketed directly to white audiences. Historically, advertisers and record companies have cared little about young African American consumers, who typically have less disposable income than white consumers. Young white males, on the other hand, are a key demographic that all marketers pursue. As Davey D puts it, "As major corporations saw lots of white kids getting down with hip-hop, they decided to do whatever it took to appeal to what is considered a lucrative demographic. . . . What this all boiled down to was there was a premium placed on white/more affluent listeners. Many corporations simply did not want to attract a young African American clientele." To attract a white clientele, Davey D argues, record companies and promoters began putting out hip-hop acts that fed white stereotypes about African Americans. As a result, "in 2003 you have a genre of music that was born in the harshest ghettos outselling any other music and now attracting the desired Holy Grail for corporate advertisers—white folks 18-34 [translation: Generation X]."

If Davey D's argument is correct, then the popularity of hip-hop among young white men is cause for concern. While cultural crossover is in many ways a good thing and can help promote understanding among people, some feel that hip-hop is being used to manipulate consumers and even promote racial stereotypes. If true, this would be a sad statement about today's white hip-hop fans. Like white audiences at a 1920s vaudeville show, they could be exposed to a parody of African American culture and think it was the real thing.

Booker 4

Works Cited

D, Davey. "Hip Hop's Ultimate Battle: Race and the Politics of Divide and Conquer." *Davey D's Hip Hop Daily News*. N.p., 10 Jan. 2003. Web. 13 Mar. 2008.

Keyes, Cheryl Lynette. *Rap Music and Street Consciousness*. Champaign: U of Illinois P., 2002. Print.

MacLean, Natalie. "Bring on the Bling—Rappers Give Cristal and Hennessy Street Cred." *San Francisco Chronicle*. San Francisco Chronicle, 16 Dec. 2004. Web. 10 Mar. 2008.

Mills, Fiona. "Rap and Young, White Males: Masculinity, Masking and Denial." *Magazine Americana*. Americana: The Institute for the Study of American Popular Culture, Dec. 2001. Web. 13 Mar. 2008.

Projects

A causal analysis answers the question: How did something get that way? They first have to identify what that something is: an event, an object, a phenomenon, or a trend. Once they have identified the **what,** then they move to the **how** and **why**.

Causal analyses have several different purposes. Sometimes we are just curious about why something happened. In some cases, we may want to repeat something, such as the successful sales of a product. In other cases, we may want to prevent potentially bad effects from occurring. And in still other cases, we might want to forecast the future.

The following projects give you a range of opportunities for causal analysis.

Causal analysis of a trend

Identify a significant change in human behavior over a period of months or years. Why have mega-churches grown rapidly? Why has reality television become popular? Why have the wealthiest one percent of Americans grown significantly richer over the past twenty years? Why have homicide rates dropped to levels not seen since the 1960s? Why are children increasingly obese?

Determine the time span of the trend. When did it start? When did it stop? Is it still going on? You likely will need to do research.

Analyze the possible causes of the trend, arguing for the ones you think are most likely the true causes. Look for underlying and hidden causes.

Remember that providing facts is not the same thing as establishing causes, even though facts can help support your causal analysis.

Analyzing claims and stakeholders

Identify a causal relationship that is now generally accepted but was once in doubt, such as Galileo's explanation of the phases of the moon, the link between DDT and the decline of bald eagle populations, or the effects of vitamin B12 on developing fetuses.

Research the arguments that were made for and against these causal relationships. Who initially proposed the cause? What was the reaction? Who argued against them, and why? How did the causal relationship come to be accepted as real? Write a short essay outlining the stakeholders in the issue you have chosen.

Explain the arguments made for and against the now-accepted cause, and the evidence presented. Which of Mill's methods of determining causation did each party use (see page 195)? Why were the arguments of the now-accepted cause more effective?

Causal analysis of a human-influenced natural phenomenon

Find a natural phenomenon or trend that is (or may be) the result of human activity. Is the growing hole in the earth's ozone layer the result of human-produced chemicals in the atmosphere? Why have populations of American alligators rebounded in the southern United States? Are sinkholes in a Kentucky town the result of new mining activity in the area? Why are more and more bacteria developing resistance to antibiotics? Choose a topic that interests you and which you feel is important. If you think the topic is important, it will be easier to convince your audience that your analysis is important.

Research the possible causes of the phenomenon, focusing on the ones you think are most likely the true causes. Remember to look at underlying and hidden causes.

Think about possible alternative causes. Do you need to incorporate them? If you don't think they are valid causes, then you need to refute them.

Recognize that causal relationships between humans and the natural world are so complex and large in scale that it is often difficult to prove them definitively. Don't oversimplify or make sweeping claims that can't be proven.

11 Evaluations

Convincing evaluations rely on selecting criteria and supporting a claim with reasons and evidence.

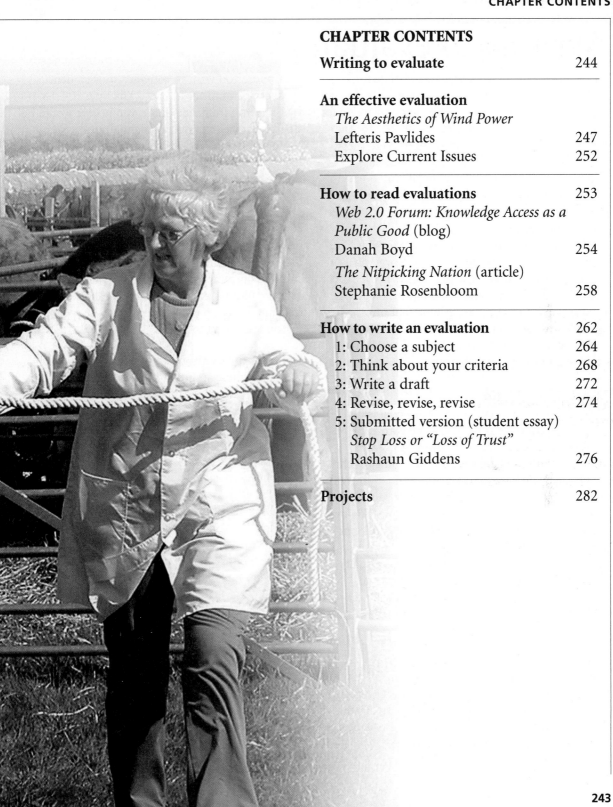

CHAPTER CONTENTS

Writing to evaluate

You make evaluations every day. You choose a favorite CD, a favorite restaurant, a favorite ring tone on your cell phone. Newspapers and Web sites feature "best of" polls that let people vote for the restaurant, movie, television show, or band they think is the "best." To some extent, these judgments are a matter of personal taste. Yet, if you look into the reasons people give for their preferences, you often find that different people use similar criteria to make evaluations.

For example, think about a restaurant you like. What are your reasons for feeling this way? Is it clean? The food fresh? The prices low? Is it convenient to your home or campus? Do you like the atmosphere? These are criteria that most people will use to judge a restaurant. That's why some restaurants are always crowded, while many others quickly go out of business.

Goals of evaluation

When you write an evaluation, your goal is usually to convince readers to agree with your judgment. Convincing other people that your judgment is sound depends on the validity of the criteria you will use to make your evaluation. Will the criteria you're using as the basis of your evaluation be convincing to other people? You may think a movie is good because it has exceptional cinematography, but an action-movie fan is less likely to go see a movie just because it is visually beautiful. Sometimes you must argue for the validity of your criteria before readers will accept them. If they don't accept your criteria, they won't agree with your conclusions.

An evaluative claim

An evaluation can be stated in the form "SOMETHING is good (or bad, the best or the worst) if measured by these criteria." Usually, the most important task when writing an evaluation is to determine the kind of criteria to use.

Suppose you want to convince your student Speakers' Committee to host a talk by a well-known filmmaker whom you believe would be a better choice than other potential speakers. You could argue that, because she is famous, the filmmaker will draw many students to her talk, thus raising the profile of the Speakers' Program, and generating more money in ticket sales. You could also argue that the filmmaker's talk would be a culturally enriching experience for students because she has made many critically acclaimed movies. You might argue that a large number of students on campus have expressed their desire to hear the filmmaker, and that the Speakers' Committee has an obligation to provide speakers the students want to hear.

Criteria for evaluation

Each of these arguments uses a different kind of criteria. An argument that the filmmaker will draw students and make money is based on **practical criteria**. An argument that her artistic achievement makes her a worthwhile speaker is based on **aesthetic criteria**. An argument that the committee is bound to consider the wishes of students is based on **ethical criteria**. These are the three basic categories of criteria for all evaluative arguments.

Things are usually judged to be good (or bad) either because they work well (practicality), because they are beautiful (aesthetics), or because they are morally fair or just (ethics). An evaluative argument may use any or all of these types of criteria, and can emphasize them in different ways. For example, if you want to convince your roommate to go to an expensive sushi restaurant, you would probably emphasize the aesthetic experience of enjoying fresh sushi in a fashionable atmosphere. You would want to downplay practical criteria like cost, especially if your roommate's budget requires that he usually dine on Ramen noodles instead of sushi.

Understand how evaluation arguments work

Evaluation arguments set out criteria and then judge something to be good or bad or best or worst according to those criteria.

Something is a good (bad, the best, the worst)______if measured by certain criteria (practicality, aesthetics, ethics).

EXAMPLE

Google Maps is the best mapping program because it is easy to use, it is accurate, and it provides entertaining and educational features such as Google Earth.

Components of evaluations

What will make a good subject to evaluate?	**Find something to evaluate.** Listing is one way to identify possible subjects for evaluation. You might list restaurants, buildings, cars, computers, and other objects. You might evaluate a film, a book, a TV show, a presidential speech, or certain policies or courses at your school.
What is my working thesis?	**Write a working thesis.** Your thesis should argue that something is good/better/best or bad/worst, successful or unsuccessful on the basis of criteria that you name.
What values are most important for my readers?	**Consider your readers**. How interesting will this topic be to your readers? What criteria will be most convincing to them?
What are the appropriate criteria for my subject?	**Choose the appropriate criteria. Practical criteria** will demand that the thing being evaluated work efficiently or lead to good outcomes (profits, satisfied customers, improved conditions, lower costs, and so on). **Aesthetic criteria** hinge on the importance and value of beauty, image, or tradition. **Ethical criteria** are used to evaluate whether something is morally right, consistent with the law and with rules of fair play.
Who would disagree with me?	**Consider other views.** Has anyone evaluated your subject before? What criteria did they use? For example, you might hate horror movies because they give you bad dreams, but many other people love them. You should consider why they have such a strong following.
What is the most engaging way to begin?	**Start fast.** You may have to give some background but get quickly to your subject.
What is the most effective way to end?	**Finish strong.** If you have not announced your stance, then you can make your summary evaluation. If your readers know where you stand, you might end with a compelling example.

Keys to evaluations

Describe briefly your subject	Your readers may be unfamiliar with what you are evaluating. Give your readers a brief description.
Explain your criteria	The importance of many criteria may not be evident to your readers. You may need to state explicitly each criterion you use and explain why it is relevant.
Be fair	Be honest about the strengths and weaknesses of what you are evaluating. Rarely is anything perfectly good or absolutely bad. Your credibility will increase if you give a balanced view.
Support your judgments with evidence	Back up your claims with specific evidence. If you write that a restaurant serves inedible food, describe examples in detail.
Define criteria for visual evaluations	Criteria for visual evaluations may require additional work to define and explain.

Working Together

What makes an effective review?

In a group of three or four students

- Look at a selection of short, amateur online reviews, such as customer book reviews at Amazon.com, consumer reviews on a site like Epinions.com, or user comments on a film at www.imdb.com.
- Select several examples of reviews that you think are persuasive and several that are not (see if you can find some persuasive reviews that you don't necessarily agree with). Share these with the rest of your group.
- As a group, discuss the following: What criteria do reviewers of similar products share? What types of criteria do the persuasive reviews use? What types do the less persuasive reviews use? Do you see any patterns that make reviews persuasive?

An effective evaluation

A successful evaluation makes a claim about the value of something. It supports its main claim with criteria that the audience will agree are important.

The Providence Journal

The Aesthetics of Wind Power

Lefteris Pavlides

People argue that wind turbines are good or bad depending on the criteria they select. Proponents of wind power argue that they produce energy without creating pollution and reduce dependence on foreign oil (practical criteria). Opponents argue that they drive down real estate values (a practical criterion), are ugly (an aesthetic criterion), and kill birds (an ethical criterion). The proposed Cape Wind project on Nantucket Sound in Massachusetts has provoked an especially contentious debate. Lefteris Pavlides, who is a professor of architecture at Roger Williams University, published this evaluation in the *Providence Journal* in March 2005.

The Aesthetics of Wind Power

by Lefteris Pavlides

"Wind turbines are not pretty," said Massachusetts Governor Romney late last year, to the applause of about half of the emotional crowd at an Army Corps of Engineers public hearing on Cape Wind Park.

The author assumes his readers are familiar with the controversy, so the evaluation begins with an opposing view—that wind turbines are bad because they are ugly.

Yet the Corps's 3,800-page report was an overwhelmingly positive evaluation of the 130 modern windmills proposed for Horseshoe Shoal, in Nantucket Sound. And despite the governor's attempt to speak for the public's aesthetic, the truth is that most people love the elegance of slow-moving giants that quietly turn wind into electricity.

Whose visual judgment matters on this issue? And how do we know that most people see modern windmills as visual assets?

Blind impartial market indicators provide indirect evidence that modern windmills are seen as beautiful. Surveys on real-estate prices and on tourism cited in the Army Corps's draft Environmental Impact Study (section 5) clearly show the strong visual appeal of modern windmills in many places around the world.

> Pavlides questions the opposing view, claiming that most people find wind turbines elegant.

A boon to real estate values and tourism

And a study of 29,000 real-estate transactions in America found that the property values of homes with views of wind turbines rose faster than those of nearby homes with no such views.

> Pavlides challenges the assertions that wind turbines lower the value of surrounding homes and harm tourism.

The Corps's report also examined surveys of visitors to sites around the globe where wind energy is well established—modern windmills in such places as Scotland, Australia and California, and off Denmark and Sweden. Installation of wind turbines increases tourism, it was found, providing evidence that most people see them as attractive additions to land- and seascapes. From Scotland to New Zealand, and from California to the Greek Isles, people pay to visit wind turbines and be photographed with them.

As a professor of architecture, I understand the visual logic of this phenomenon. I teach that forms made to move in wind—such as sailboats and Porsches—are inherently beautiful. Experts discuss the artistic qualities of aerodynamic lines and the kinetic grace of modern windmills, using such terms as proportion, contrast, rhythm and movement to express what we all experience.

> The author builds his credibility as an authority.

The aesthetics of wind power

From an abstract view, the graceful modern windmills are even more beautiful than their ancient

> He returns to aesthetic criteria and offers more evidence of the beauty of modern windmills.

counterparts. A Cape Cod sculptor recently wrote to me, "[T]he beauty of modern windmills is a joyous scene to behold. As sail boats provide visual delight while transforming air into propulsion, so will windmills that catch ambient breezes for essential power."

Non-experts in aesthetics also discuss the delight of watching windmills. An engineer with no artistic training sent me his unsolicited opinion that the Danish Horns Rev offshore wind park was "one of the most inspiring and thrilling sights seen from the Blavaand lighthouse observatory deck."

To adapt an adage, beauty is in the eye and also the mind of the beholder. Our judgment of what is beautiful is based not just on abstract qualities of form. Modern windmills, for instance, have acquired a broad range of connotations.

For some, they are worse than ugly, evoking deep fear in their enormous scale. For others, they are beyond magnificent, evoking deep religious feelings.

More common associations with modern windmills include economic benefits or threats to market share (for fossil-fuel interests); reduction of disease in the reduction of polluting emissions; and real or bogus environmental threats.

Visual delight accompanies connotations of:

- Economic benefits, such as fixed energy prices for years to come. The Army Corps reported that Cape Wind would have a significant positive impact on the local economy.
- Health benefits from reduced pollution, including fewer people with asthma and bronchitis, and fewer premature deaths. The Corps reported a probable $53 million in health savings.

The strongest arguments for wind turbines are based on practical criteria. They provide a dependable, pollution-free source of energy.

Visual blight is an impression that accompanies connotations of:

- Loss of market share. Modern windmills are a constant reminder of eroding market share for executives of coal and oil companies, such as Douglas Yearly, a former chairman of Phelps Dodge who is on the board of Marathon Oil. Mr. Yearly, who has a summer place in Cape Cod's Osterville, has spearheaded opposition to Cape Wind.

Pavlides questions the motives of some critics of wind power.

The Army Corps's report indicates that Cape Wind would produce three-quarters of the electricity needed by Cape Cod and the Islands.

Regarding wildlife, when people are told that modern windmills offer protections to animals, they see them as beautiful, while those who believe widespread misinformation about dangers to birds have reservations.

The Corps's exhaustive avian studies conclude that there is no basis for concern. Further scientific studies show that wind energy is hugely beneficial to birds and other wildlife, in that it reduces:

- acid rain, which causes regional bird extinctions by killing the snails that are critical to bird diets;
- mercury contamination, which has caused extinction of loons on the Great Lakes;
- oil spills, which kill all manner of wildlife;
- and global warming, the biggest threat of all

He counters the ethical argument of harm to birds by pointing to benefits to wildlife from reduced pollution.

There is every indication that the opposition to Cape Wind will evolve much the way public attitudes toward the Statue of Liberty evolved over a century ago. The statue's installation was resisted and delayed because, as newspapers declared, it "was neither an object of art [n]or beauty." Now an adored icon, the statue significantly raises the value of properties with views of it. It is seen as beautiful because of its sculptural qualities and also because of the freedom and human rights that it represents.

He ends with the analogy to the Statue of Liberty, which many people initially found ugly when it was installed in New York Harbor but soon grew to love.

As an architect who has been studying public perception of wind turbines, I predict that most people would similarly come to see Cape Wind's turbines as breath-givingly beautiful.

The vast majority of people around Nantucket Sound would see Cape Wind as a magnificent addition to the sound—making visible the reduction of invisible toxic gases that despoil the region's environment.

And the windmills would visually communicate, now and to future generations, our commitment to energy freedom and a disease-free environment.

New Englanders have a responsibility to express their support for this project.

Explore Current Issues

What makes a video game "smart"?

Both fans and detractors of the "Grand Theft Auto" game series know it to be extremely violent; the goal of each game in the series is essentially to use any means necessary to rise to the top of the criminal underworld of a familiar, yet fictional futuristic city. Critics of the game argue that the game flaunts crime, racial conflict, and sexual violence. Perhaps most shocking is the amorality of the game: innocent citizens as well as hardened criminals are mown down not just indiscriminately, but gleefully.

The latest installment in the series, "Grand Theft Auto IV" set sales records when it was released in late April of 2008 and garnered critical praise for its superior playability and graphics. More interestingly, however, is that "GTA IV" is being called "smart." *Salon.com* writer Farhad Manjoo argues that the richness of the story (so rich, in fact, that engaged players might be less inclined to kill random bystanders), the depth and realism of the world, the dimensionality and quirkiness of the characters, the wry humor, and the more interactive and socially based tasks and puzzles of the game will make players it call it "the smartest video game ever created."

Write about it

1. How do you think Manjoo defines the word "smart"? Why do you think this? Do you agree with this definition? Why or why not? What other word could he use instead of "smart"?
2. Which of the following criteria are useful for evaluating the content of a video game? Why?
   - Richness of story line
   - Realism
   - Violence
   - Complexity of characters
   - Types of puzzles and tasks
   - Representation of gender, class, ethnicity, and disability
   - Morality
   - Humor
3. Are any of the criteria more important than the others? If so, how would you rank them? Are there any criteria you would add?

How to read evaluations

Make notes as you read, either in the margins or on paper or a computer file. Circle any words or references that you don't know and look them up.

What is it?	• What kind of a text is it? A review? an essay? a blog? an editorial? What are your expectations for this kind of text? • What media are used? (Web sites, for example, often combine images, words, and sounds.)
Where did it come from?	• Who wrote the evaluation? • What do you know about the writer's background that might have influenced the evaluation?
What is the writer's thesis or main idea?	• What clues do you find about whom the writer had in mind as the readers? • What does the writer assume that the readers already know about the subject? • What new knowledge is the writer providing?
Who is the intended audience?	• What clues do you find about whom the writer had in mind as the readers? • What does the writer assume that the readers already know about the subject? • What new knowledge is the writer providing?
Does the writer make a clear evaluative claim?	• What exactly is the writer's evaluative claim?
What are the criteria used in the evaluation?	• Does the writer use practical criteria? aesthetic criteria? ethical criteria? (See pages 244–245.) • Does the writer argue for how these criteria apply to the subject? • Does the writer acknowledge opposing views?
How is it composed?	• How does the writer represent herself or himself? • How would you characterize the style? • If there are any photographs or other graphics, what information do they contribute?

Web 2.0 Forum: Knowledge Access as a Public Good

(BLOG)

Danah Boyd

Danah Boyd researches and writes on how teens present themselves and socialize within mediated environments, especially social networking sites on the Internet such as MySpace, YouTube, and Facebook. She also maintains a blog on social media, called *Apophenia*. In this blog, she responds to Michael Gorman's argument in the same forum that Web 2.0 is damaging to intellectual life. "Knowledge Access as a Public Good" was published in an online forum sponsored by the Encyclopedia Britannica on June 27, 2007.

Return to these questions after you have finished reading.

Analyzing and Connecting

1. Examine the language, tone, and cultural references in Boyd's argument. How do they affect the appeal of the argument?

2. Much like Stephpanie Rosenbloom's "The Nitpicking Nation" (see pages 258–261) is not so much a straightforward evaluation of Craigslist but instead a look at how people make evaluations on Craigslist, so too does Boyd's response evaluate Gorman's response to Web 2.0. Where exactly does she find strengths and weaknesses in Gorman's argument?

3. Thinking about the positive and negative aspects of Web 2.0 you gleaned from Boyd's argument, what does she consider an effective response? Does this response address both the positive negative aspects of Web 2.0 effectively? Why or why not?

4. Boyd begins her concluding paragraph with the historic phrase "I hold these truths to be self-evident." Why do you think she chooses this phrase for her conclusion? What kind of appeal does it make? Is it appropriate for her argument? Why or why not?

Finding Ideas for Writing

Boyd's argument proceeds from two large claims in the seventh paragraph. She writes:

> I want to help people gain access to information in the hopes that they can create knowledge that is valuable for everyone. I have lost faith in traditional organizations leading the way to mass access and am thus always on the lookout for innovative models to produce and distribute knowledge.

Do you agree that if people have broad access to information, they will create knowledge that is valuable to everyone? And do you agree with her claim that traditional organizations have failed in giving people mass access to information?

KNOWLEDGE ACCESS AS A PUBLIC GOOD

As a child, I believed that all educated people were wise. In particular, I placed educators and authorities on a high pedestal and I entered the academy both to seek their wisdom and to become one of them. Unfortunately, eleven years of higher education has taught me that parts of the academy are rife with many of the same problems that plague society as a whole: greed, self-absorbtion, addiction to power, and an overwhelming desire to be validated, praised, and rewarded. As Dr. Gorman laments the ills of contemporary society, I find myself nodding along. Doing ethnographic work in the United States often leaves me feeling disillusioned and numb. It breaks my heart every time a teenager tells me that s/he is more talented than Sanjaya and thus is guaranteed a slot on the next "American Idol."

The pervasive view that American society is a meritocracy makes me want to scream, but I fear as though my screams fall on deaf ears.

To cope with my frustration, I often return to my bubble. My friends all seem to come from Lake Wobegon where "the women are strong, the men are good looking, and all of the children are above average." I have consciously surrounded myself with people who think like me, share my values, and are generally quite overeducated. I feel very privileged to live in such an environment, but like all intellectuals who were educated in the era of identity politics, I am regularly racked with guilt over said privilege.

The Internet is a funny thing, especially now that those online are not just the connected elite. It mirrors and magnifies the offline world—all of the good, bad, and ugly. I don't need to travel to Idaho to face neo-Nazis. I don't need to go to Colorado Springs to hear religious views that contradict my worldview. And I don't need to go to Capitol Hill to witness the costs of power for power's sake.

If I am willing to look, there are places on the Internet that will expose me to every view on this planet, even those that I'd prefer to pretend did not exist. Most of the privileged people that I know prefer to live like ostriches, ignoring the realities of everyday life in order to sustain their privileges. I am trying not to be that person, although I find it to be a challenge.

In the 16th century, Sir Francis Bacon famously wrote that "knowledge is power." Not surprisingly, institutions that profit off of knowledge trade in power. In an era of capitalism, this equation often gets tainted by questions of profitability. Books are not published simply because they contain valued and valid information; they are published if and when the publisher can profit off of the sale of those books. Paris Hilton stands a far better chance of getting a publishing deal than most astute and thought-provoking academics. Even a higher education is becoming more inaccessible to more people at a time when a college degree is necessary to work in a cafe. $140,000 for a college education is a scary proposition, even if you want to enter

the ratrace of the white collar mega-corporations where you expect to make a decent salary. Amidst this environment, it frustrates me to hear librarians speak about information dissemination while they create digital firewalls that lock people out of accessing knowledge unless they have the right academic credentials.

I entered the academy because I believe in knowledge production and dissemination. I am a hopeless Marxist. I want to equal the playing field; I want to help people gain access to information in the hopes that they can create knowledge that is valuable for everyone. I have lost faith in traditional organizations leading the way to mass access and am thus always on the lookout for innovative models to produce and distribute knowledge.

Unlike Dr. Gorman, Wikipedia brings me great joy. I see it as a fantastic example of how knowledge can be distributed outside of elite institutions. I have watched stubs of articles turn into rich homes for information about all sorts of subjects. What I like most about Wikipedia is the self-recognition that it is always a work-in-progress. The encyclopedia that I had as a kid was a hand-me-down; it stated that one day we would go to the moon. Today, curious poor youth have access to information in an unprecedented way. It may not be perfect, but it is far better than a privilege-only model of access.

Knowledge is not static, but traditional publishing models assume that it can be captured and frozen for consumption. What does that teach children about knowledge? Captured knowledge makes sense when the only opportunity for dissemination is through distributing physical artifacts, but this is no longer the case. Now that we can get information to people faster, why should we support the erection of barriers?

In middle school, I was sent to the principal's office for correcting a teacher's math. The issue was not whether or not I was correct—I was; I was ejected from class for having the gall to challenge authority. Would Galileo have been allowed to write an encyclopedia article? The "authorities" of his day rejected his scientific claims. History has many examples of how the vetting process has failed us. Imagine all of the knowledge that was produced that was more successfully suppressed by authorities. In the era of the Internet, gatekeepers have less power. I don't think that this is always a bad thing.

Like paper, the Internet is a medium. People express a lot of crap through both mediums. Yet, should we denounce paper as inherently flawed? The Internet—and Wikipedia—change the rules for distribution and production. It means that those with knowledge do not have to retreat to the ivory towers to share what they know. It means that individuals who know something can easily share it, even when they are not formally declared as experts. It means that those with editing skills can help the information become accessible, even if they only edit occasionally. It means that multi-lingual individuals can help get information to people who speak languages

that publishers do not consider worth their time. It means that anyone with an Internet connection can get access to information traditionally locked behind the gates of institutions (and currently locked in digital vaults).

Don't get me wrong—Wikipedia is not perfect. But why do purported experts spend so much time arguing against it rather than helping make it a better resource? It is free! It is accessible! Is it really worth that much prestige to write an encyclopedia article instead of writing a Wikipedia entry? While there are certainly errors there, imagine what would happen if all of those who view themselves as experts took the time to make certain that the greatest and most broad-reaching resource was as accurate as possible.

I believe that academics are not just the producers of knowledge—they are also teachers. As teachers, we have an ethical responsibility to help distribute knowledge. We have a responsibility to help not just the 30 people in our classroom, but the millions of people globally who will never have the opportunity to sit in one of our classes. The Internet gives us the tool to do this. Why are we throwing this opportunity away? Like Dr. Gorman, I don't believe that all crowds are inherently wise. But I also don't believe that all authorities are inherently wise. Especially not when they are vying for tenure.

Why are we telling our students not to use Wikipedia rather than educating them about how Wikipedia works? Sitting in front of us is an ideal opportunity to talk about how knowledge is produced, how information is disseminated, how ideas are shared. Imagine if we taught the "history" feature so that students would have the ability to track how a Wikipedia entry is produced and assess for themselves what the authority of the author is. You can't do this with an encyclopedia. Imagine if we taught students how to fact check claims in Wikipedia and, better yet, to add valuable sources to a Wikipedia entry so that their work becomes part of the public good.

Herein lies a missing piece in Dr. Gorman's puzzle. The society that he laments has lost faith in the public good. Elitism and greed have gotten in the way. By upholding the values of the elite, Dr. Gorman is perpetuating views that are destroying efforts to make knowledge a public good. Wikipedia is a public-good project. It is the belief that division of labor has value and that everyone has something to contribute, if only a spelling correction. It is the belief that all people have the inalienable right to knowledge, not just those who have academic chairs. It is the belief that the powerful have no right to hoard the knowledge. And it is the belief that people can and should collectively help others gain access to information and knowledge.

Personally, I hold these truths to be self-evident, and I'd rather see us put in the effort to make Wikipedia an astounding resource that can be used by all people than to try to dismantle it simply because it means change.

The Nitpicking Nation

(ARTICLE)

Stephanie Rosenbloom

In addition to being a journalist for the *New York Times*, 1997 Colgate graduate Stephanie Rosenbloom began acting at a young age and has directed plays since she was a senior in high school. She writes articles about real estate and about how people adapt new technologies for their own purposes. "The Nitpicking Nation" appeared in the *New York Times* in May 2006.

Return to these questions after you have finished reading.

Analyzing and Connecting

1. In one way "The Nitpicking Nation" is not a classic evaluation but rather a look at how people make evaluations on Craigslist. But it also indirectly evaluates Craigslist. What positives and negatives of Craigslist are given?

2. Visit Craigslist.org, and compare housing and roommate ads for a city in the United States with those in a city in another country. Make a list of what is desirable and undesirable in roommates or house-sharing partners for both cities. Which criteria are the same on both lists? Which are different?

3. What criteria do you use to evaluate roommates? What makes an ideal roommate in your view?

4. Think of a product that you already own or would like to own. Enter the name of the product on Google followed by the word *review*. If you don't find many reviews, try consumersearch.com. Read several reviews and make a list of the most frequent criteria used to evaluate the product.

Finding Ideas for Writing

Rosenbloom cites Craig Newmark's belief that Craigslist operates in a "culture of trust," inspiring users to be honest. How does this culture work? Does it always work? Write a paragraph to insert into Rosenbloom's article explaining how and why this culture of trust works (or doesn't). Use your own or others' experiences with listing sites such as Craigslist, eBay, and others to provide support for your explanation.

THE NITPICKING NATION

THEY are single, gay, straight, biracial, conservative, liberal and tattooed—and they have as many preferences for a potential roommate as an online dater has for a potential lover. They are bankers, fetishists, self-declared nerds and drug users. They have old wounds and new hopes, and are willing to barter their cooking and sexual expertise for free or discounted rent.

They are all seeking and selling housing on Craigslist.org, the electronic listing service with sites in all 50 states and more than 200 worldwide. And because users pay nothing (for now) and are able to go on at length about who they are and what they want, their postings provide a sociological window into housing trends and desires across the country, from the neon cityscape of the Las Vegas Strip to the wheat fields of Wichita, Kan.

Myriad other sites provide roommate-matching services, but in the last decade Craigslist has emerged as the gold standard. It is easy to navigate, has an extensive number of listings and does not require people to complete an online sign-up sheet to view postings in their entirety. And the intimate and sometimes politically incorrect nature of Craigslist postings can make them fun to read–amusing, frank and even kinky.

Perhaps the most eyebrow-raising thing about the housing listings is the abundance of users—even young, savvy residents of anything-goes metropolises like Los Angeles and Miami—who want mellow, nonpartying roommates. Las Vegas sounds more like Snore City if you judge it by its housing listings. And New Yorkers can come off sounding square. "No parties" and "no drama" are common refrains.

There are exceptions, but even club-hopping Paris Hilton hopefuls seem to have their limits. As four women (ages 19 to 22) seeking a fifth roommate in Boston wrote, "We want a partier, not a puker."

People in their 20's often list their alma maters and request a roommate in their own age group. Cleanliness is a must, or at least "clean-ish," "decently clean" or "clean in public spaces." And spending life with a "professional" appears to be just as important to users of Craigslist's housing listings as it is to users of Match.com.

Some listings have stirred up trouble, however, and the Chicago Lawyers' Committee for Civil Rights Under Law, a nonprofit group, has filed a lawsuit in federal court against Craigslist for "publishing housing advertisements which exclude prospective tenants on the basis of race, gender, family status, marital status, national origin and religion."

A news release issued by the organization said that the Craigslist postings contained such language as "no minorities," "African-Americans and Arabians tend to clash with me so that won't work out," "ladies, please rent from me," "requirements: clean godly Christian male," "will allow only single occupancy," and "no children."

The suit is addressed on Craigslist: "Although in all likelihood this suit will be dismissed on the grounds that Internet sites cannot legally be held liable for content posted by users, Craigslist has no need to hide behind this well-established immunity."

The statement also says that Craigslist respects constitutionally protected free speech rights and that "discriminatory postings are

exceedingly uncommon, and those few that do reach the site are typically removed quickly by our users through the flagging system that accompanies each ad."

Craig Newmark, the founder of Craigslist, said that its "culture of trust" inspires users to be straightforward. In fact, some users do not even feel compelled to embellish the descriptions of their spaces, as housing advertisements commonly do. Rather, they take a certain pride in the gritty crudeness of their offerings. A small room for rent in the East Village is described as "definitely a young person's apartment" with "two small junky TV's that we have cheap antennas on, but we get the normal channels, and that is enough for us."

"There is no window," the listing says, "but you have a full-sized door."

And where else do you find housing listings that include candid photographs of the owner or leaseholder instead of the property they are advertising? (A man in Fort Lauderdale, Fla., compromised and included images of his bare room and his bare chest.)

Indeed, Craigslist is where sex and real estate can truly merge. Near Dallas, a married couple are looking for a female roommate "with benefits." A listing for Astoria, Queens, reads: "I am offering a free room for up to three months for any females who are ticklish." A single man in Los Angeles is offering foot massages and free rent to women with comely feet.

Those are some of the tamer overtures, though the majority of roommate listings are not suggestive.

But just who are the most desirable roommates?

Many people prefer women to men. There are women who feel more comfortable sharing a home with someone of the same sex, men who say they get along better with female housemates, and a few cyberspace Casanovas who want to take a shot at turning a roommate into a bedmate. Interns are also desirable, apparently because they are thought to be hard-working, responsible and willing to pay good money for cramped rooms.

But couples are sometimes lumped into a list of the unacceptable, like cigarette smoking. Over all, Democrats are more vocal than Republicans in expressing a desire not to live with the opposing party, though two "hip professional guys" found elusive harmony on Capitol Hill: "One guy is straight, and one is gay. One is a Republican, and the other is a Democrat," they wrote in a listing for a third roommate. "We appreciate and welcome diversity."

Users in the San Francisco Bay Area appear to be among the least interested in rooming with a pet. This area had the highest percentage of "no pets" listings during a key-word search last Thursday (slightly more than 16 percent of 32,295 housing listings). In Boston, about 14 percent of 45,880 listings said "no pets."

Dallas, Wyoming and Birmingham, Ala., seemed quite pet-friendly by comparison: only about 1 percent of the housing listings in each location said "no pets." But Wichita, Kan., emerged as one of the most accepting places, with less than 1 percent of the listings snubbing pets.

In some parts of the country Craigslist housing postings are an essential part of the real estate biosphere. New York is by far the leader in this regard (it had some 180,245 housing listings last Thursday).

Mr. Newmark said there were two reasons for that. "New York real estate is kind of a

blood sport," he said, "and also, because our site is free, brokers tend to post a lot of redundant ads."

He said he hoped to address that problem in a matter of weeks by beginning to charge a fee.

Although Mr. Newmark has not studied how the number of housing listings fluctuates day to day, he believes they remain fairly steady on weekdays and drop off on weekends.

Boston had 45,880 housing listings last Thursday, and the San Francisco Bay Area had 32,295. In other places like Montana and Louisville, Ky., there were just a few hundred postings, and North Dakota had fewer than 100.

The New York listings include some of the most expensive, precarious sleeping arrangements in the country. A sofa bed in the living room/kitchen of a one-bedroom apartment on 55th Street between Eighth and Ninth Avenues is $683 a month. You could get a 780-square-foot one-bedroom cottage in Savannah, Ga., for $665 a month. A couch on the West Coast, in a Los Angeles apartment belonging to three actors, is merely $400 a month and includes utilities, cable, Netflix membership, Starbucks wireless membership and wireless Internet, as well as household staples like toothpaste and shampoo.

New Yorkers are also adept at constructing what the military calls a zone of separation. A woman with an apartment at Union Square posted a photograph, not of the bedroom she wanted to rent out for $1,150 a month, but of a large divider she planned to use to create the bedroom from part of her living room.

Near Columbus Circle, a "very small, but cozy space enclosed by tall bookshelves and bamboo screens" is listed for $1,700 a month. Potential occupants are advised that they must be older than 30 and cannot wear shoes inside the apartment, smoke, consume alcohol, invite guests over or have "sleepovers."

A plethora of "no smokers" statements in the New York housing listings make it appear that the public smoking ban has infiltrated private spaces, too.

But while cigarettes are a deal breaker for some, a number of Craigslist users across the country (Denver and Boulder, Colo.; San Francisco; Boston; and Portland, Ore., to name but a few) say that they are "420 friendly," slang for marijuana use. References to 420 were nonexistent in other cities, including Little Rock, Ark.; Santa Fe, N.M.; and Boise, Idaho.

There are also myriad references to amenities, everything from the use of old record collections and video games to a trapeze suspended in a Brooklyn loft. A posting for a room for rent in Detroit lacks images of the property, though there is a photograph of the L.C.D. television.

And if nothing else, Craigslist housing postings in the United States confirm the zaniness of the hunt and provide a taste of the free-spirited, random connections that have always been part of the experience.

A posting in Asheville, N.C., says that two 21-year-old women are planning to drive almost 20 hours to Austin, Tex., this summer, where they will rent a two-bedroom apartment for $550 a month. "We are looking for one or two (yeah, you can bring a buddy) cool people to ride out there and split an apartment with us," the listing reads. "Are you up for being spontaneous?"

Would-be Jack Kerouacs, take note: they hit the road at the end of the month.

How to write an evaluation

These steps for the process of writing an evaluation may not progress as neatly as this chart might suggest. Writing is not an assembly-line process.

As you write and revise, think about how you might sharpen your criteria and better explain how they apply to what you are evaluating. Your instructor and fellow students may give you comments that help you to rethink your argument from the beginning.

1 CHOOSE A SUBJECT

- Analyze the assignment.
- Explore possible subjects by making lists. Consider which items on your list you might evaluate.
- Analyze a subject by thinking about other things like it.
- Make an evaluative claim that something is good, bad, best, or worst if measured by certain criteria.
- Think about what's at stake. If nearly everyone agrees with you, your claim probably isn't important. Why would some people disagree with you?

2 THINK ABOUT YOUR CRITERIA

- List the criteria that makes something good or bad.
- Which criteria are the most important?
- Which criteria are fairly obvious, and which will you have to argue for?
- How familiar will your readers be with what you are evaluating?
- Which criteria will they accept with little explanation, and which will they possibly disagree with?
- Research your argument by finding evidence and reliable sources.

3 WRITE A DRAFT

- Introduce the issue and give the necesary background.
- Describe each criterion and then analyze how well what you are evaluating meets that criterion.
- If you are making an evaluation according to the effects of something, describe those effects in detail.
- Anticipate where readers might question your criteria and address possible objections.
- Anticipate and address opposing viewpoints by acknowledging how others' evaluations might differ.
- Conclude with either your position, a compelling example, or what is at stake.
- Choose a title that will interest readers in your essay.

4 REVISE, REVISE, REVISE

- Check that your paper or project fulfills the assignment.
- Is your evaluative claim arguable?
- Are your criteria reasonable, and will your audience accept them?
- Is your evidence convincing and sufficient?
- Do you address opposing views?
- Review the visual presentation of your paper or project.
- Proofread carefully.

5 SUBMITTED VERSION

- Make sure your finished writing meets all formatting requirements.

1: Choose a subject

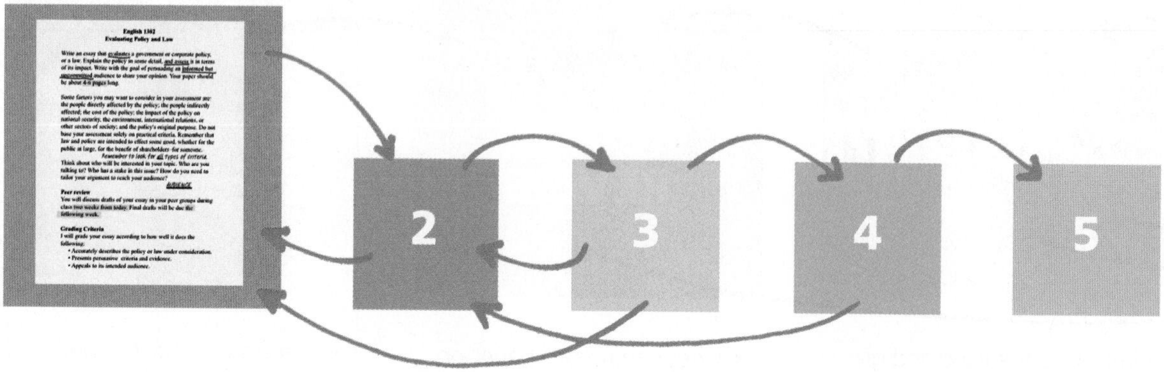

Analyze the assignment	• Read your assignment slowly and carefully. Look for key words like *evaluate, rank, review,* and *assess*. These key words tell you that you are writing an evaluative essay. • Mark off any information about the length specified, date due, formatting, and other requirements. You can attend to this information later.
Explore possible subjects by making lists	• Make a list of goods and services you consume; sports, entertainment, or hobbies you enjoy; books you have read recently; films you have seen; speeches you have heard; or policies and laws that affect you or concern you. • Consider which items on your list you might evaluate. Which are interesting to you? Which would likely interest your readers? Put checkmarks by these items. • Choose something to evaluate that is potentially controversial. You will learn the most, and interest readers most, if you build a strong evaluation that persuades your opponents to rethink their position.
Analyze a subject	• What does your subject attempt to achieve? What do other similar subjects attempt to achieve? (For example, a mountain bike is designed to climb and descend trails, but a good mountain bike will be lightweight, durable, and have good suspension.) • Who is the audience for your subject? (Mountain bikes appeal to people who prefer to ride on trails rather than pavement.)
Think about what's at stake	• Who will agree with you? Who will disagree, and why? • Think about why your evaluation matters.

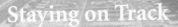

Staying on Track

Make an arguable claim

A claim that is too obvious or too general will not produce an interesting evaluation. Don't waste your time—or your readers'.

OFF TRACK
Michael Jordan was a great basketball player.

ON TRACK
Bill Russell was the best clutch player in the history of professional basketball.

OFF TRACK
Running is great exercise and a great way to lose weight.

ON TRACK
If you start running to lose weight, be aware of the risks: your body running exerts eight times its weight on your feet, ankles, legs, hips, and lower back, often causing injury to your joints. Swimming, biking, or exercise machines might be the better choice.

Write Now

Finding a subject to evaluate

1. Make a list of possible subjects to evaluate, and select the one that appears most promising.
2. Write nonstop for five minutes about what you like and dislike about this particular subject.
3. Write nonstop for five minutes about what you like and dislike about things in the same category (Mexican restaurants, world leaders, horror movies, mountain bikes, and so on).
4. Write nonstop for five minutes about what people in general like and dislike about things in this category.
5. Underline the likes and dislikes in all three freewrites. You should gain a sense of how your evaluation stacks up against those of others. You may discover a way you can write against the grain, showing others a good or bad aspect of this subject that they may not have observed.

Writer at work

Rashaun Giddens began by underlining the words and phrases that indicated his evaluative task and highlighting information about dates and processes for the project. He then made notes and list of possible subjects. He selected the military's stop loss policy, which he knew about first hand.

English 1302
Evaluating Policy and Law

Write an essay that evaluates a government or corporate policy, or a law. Explain the policy in some detail, and assess it in terms of its impact. Write with the goal of persuading an informed but uncommitted audience to share your opinion. Your paper should be about 4-6 pages long.

Some factors you may want to consider in your assessment are: the people directly affected by the policy; the people indirectly affected; the cost of the policy; the impact of the policy on national security, the environment, international relations, or other sectors of society; and the policy's original purpose. Do not base your assessment solely on practical criteria. Remember that law and policy are intended to effect some good, whether for the public at large, for the benefit of shareholders–for someone.

Remember to look for all types of criteria.

Think about who will be interested in your topic. Who are you talking to? Who has a stake in this issue? How do you need to tailor your argument to reach your audience?

AUDIENCE

Peer review
You will discuss drafts of your essay in your peer groups during class two weeks from today. Final drafts will be due the following week.

Grading Criteria
I will grade your essay according to how well it does the following:

- Accurately describes the policy or law under consideration.
- Presents persuasive criteria and evidence.
- Appeals to its intended audience.

CLAIMS COULD BE:

1. The "don't ask, don't tell" policy in the military is ineffective and discriminatory.
2. The Washington, DC, Metro is one of the best subway systems in the world.
3. The "stop loss" policy that forbids thousands of soldiers from leaving the military when their volunteer commitment ends is not an effective policy.
4. The movie *War of the Worlds* does not hold up to the original radio broadcast.
5. The current policy regarding steroid use in professional sports does not effectively deter steroid use.

FREEWRITE:

I remember the Army recruiter who came to my high school during my last year. He made a really good pitch about joining the reserves. He said it was a chance to serve our country and get a start on paying for college. That was a big one at my school because most of us had jobs in high school to pay for food and clothes. That's one thing people don't think about--even when you get a scholarship that pays tuition, you still have to eat and have a place to stay. Anyway, my cousin jumped at the chance to join. The recruiter told us 15 months of active duty, but my cousin now knows the Army can keep him much longer.

2: Think about your criteria

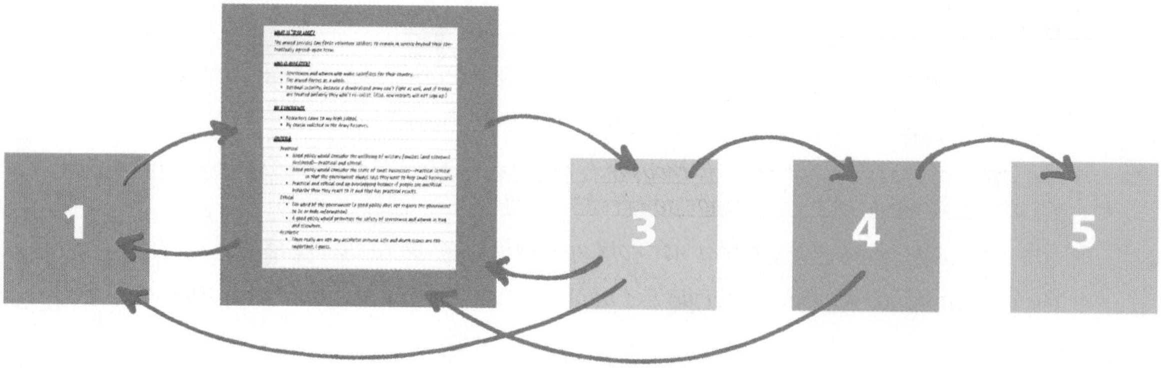

Find the obvious criteria, and then dig deeper

- Write down the criteria you already know you will use in your evaluation. For example, a good study location is quiet, well-lit, safe, and easy to get to.
- Consider other criteria you might not be aware you're using. Perhaps you gravitate toward the student union rather than the library because you are allowed to drink coffee there. Maybe you began avoiding the library when its blue and orange carpet started to hurt your eyes.
- Think about whether these criteria are practical, aesthetic, or ethical. It isn't that important for you to classify each criterion exactly; there is often overlap between these categories. But you may run into trouble with your audience if you rely too much on one type of criteria, such as aesthetics, and neglect others, like practicality, such as a beautiful chair that hurts your back.

Research your argument

- Find evidence to show how the thing you are evaluating meets or doesn't meet your criteria. If you claim that a symphony has a compelling melodic theme in the first movement, describe the passage in detail.
- Go to reliable sources to find out how others have evaluated the same thing. Do other reviewers tend to agree or disagree with you? Do they use criteria that you don't? Are they addressing the same audience you are?

Analyze your audience

- Consider which of your criteria are most likely to appeal to your audience. Which criteria might they find unconvincing or unimportant?
- How familiar will readers be with your topic? How much background information will they need?

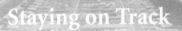

Staying on Track

Specify and argue for your criteria

Specify your criteria
Show exactly how your criteria apply to what you are evaluating.

OFF TRACK
Border collies make the best pets because they are smart, friendly, and easy to train. *[Vague; many pets are smart, friendly, and easy to train]*

ON TRACK
Border collies are ideal family pets because their intelligence and trainability enable them to fit into almost any household, no matter how crowded.

Support your criteria
Give evidence to demonstrate why your criteria are valid.

OFF TRACK
Swimming is better exercise than running because you get a better workout. *[How so?]*

ON TRACK
Health professionals maintain that for those who have access to pools or lakes, swimming is the best workout because it exercises all major muscle groups and it's not prone to causing injuries.

Don't assume your audience shares your criteria
It's easy to forget that other people have different concerns and priorities. Your challenge as a writer is finding common ground with people who think differently.

OFF TRACK
Coach X is a bad coach who should be fired because he has lost to our rival school three years in a row. *[For some fans beating the big rival is the only criterion, but not all fans.]*

ON TRACK
While coach X hasn't beaten our big rival in three years, he has succeeded in increasing attendance by 50%, adding a new sports complex built by donations, and raising the players' graduation rate to 80%.

Writer at work

Rashaun Giddens made the following notes about his evaluative claim.

WHAT IS "STOP LOSS"?

The armed services can force volunteer soldiers to remain in service beyond their contractually agreed-upon term.

WHO IS AFFECTED?

- Servicemen and women who make sacrifices for their country.
- The armed forces as a whole.
- National security, because a demoralized army can't fight as well, and if troops are treated unfairly they won't re-enlist. (Also, new recruits will not sign up.)

MY EXPERIENCE

- Recruiters came to my high school.
- My cousin enlisted in the Army Reserves.

CRITERIA

Practical

- Good policy would consider the well-being of military families (and economic livelihood)--Practical and ethical.
- Good policy would consider the state of small businesses--Practical (ethical in that the government always says they want to help small businesses).
- Practical and ethical end up overlapping because if people see unethical behavior then they react to it and that has practical results.

Ethical

- The word of the government (a good policy does not require the government to lie or hide information).
- A good policy would prioritize the safety of servicemen and women in Iraq and elsewhere.

Aesthetic

- There really are not any aesthetic criteria. Life and death issues are too important, I guess.

AUDIENCE

Who has a stake in this issue? What do they know about it? How should I appeal to them?

Military families

- Families feel direct effect.
- Military families will probably have a strong sense of duty. They are likely to feel upset if the government does not treat them fairly.

All citizens

- Citizens are responsible for the way our government treats our soldiers. Appeal to people's sense of fair play.
- Citizens have concerns on moral or ideological grounds.
- All citizens need to feel a sense of empathy with the military families; that "This could be me or my child."

BACKGROUND

People may or may not have basic knowledge of policy. Perhaps don't know the specifics or the origin (bring in the history to ground it). May not be aware of how bad it can be in the details.

TO RESEARCH

- Need to get info on how stop loss originated, when it has been used, and what impact it had. Were situations in the past comparable to now?
- Find evidence of hardships for troops. Personal anecdotes from news articles and figures about effects on enlistment.
- Find evidence and testimony about effects on families and small businesses.

3: Write a draft

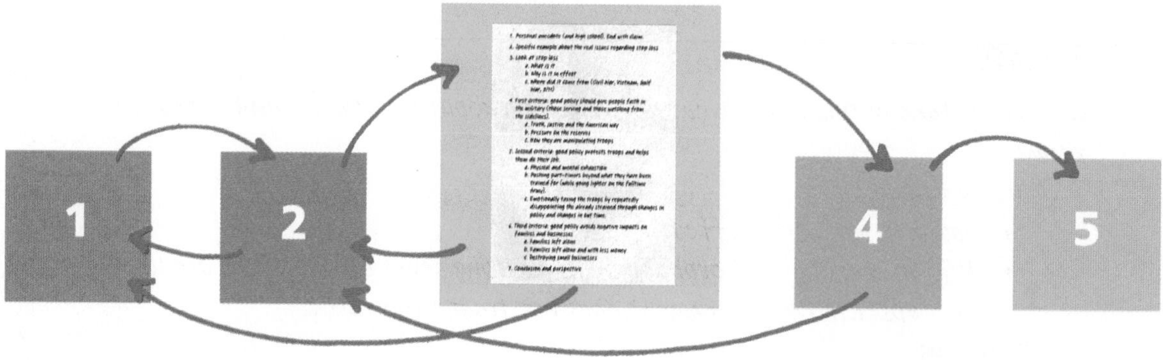

Introduce the issue	• Give your readers any background information they will need. • State your stance up front, if you wish. Some evaluations work better if the writer's judgment is issued at the beginning; sometimes, it is more effective to build up a mass of evidence and then issue your verdict at the end.
Describe your criteria and offer evidence	• Organize the criteria you present to be as effective as possible. Do you want to start with the most important one, or build up to it? Try both ways, and see which seems more convincing. • Explain each criterion and give reasons to support its use, if readers are unlikely to automatically accept it. • Analyze how well the thing you are evaluating meets each criterion. Provide specific examples.
Anticipate and address opposing viewpoints	• Acknowledge why others may have a different opinion than you do. • Demonstrate why your evaluation is better by pointing out either why your criteria are better or why you have better evidence and reasons.
Conclude with strength	• State your position at the end of your argument if you haven't done so previously. • Offer a compelling example or analogy to end your essay. • State explicitly what is at stake in your evaluation, especially if you are evaluating a policy or issue that affects many people.
Choose a title that will interest readers in your essay	• A bland, generic title like "An Evaluation of X" gives little incentive to want to read the paper.

Writer at work

Based on his lists of criteria, his conclusions about his audience, and his research, Rashaun Giddens sketched out a rough outline for his essay.

1. Personal anecdote (and high school). End with claim.
2. Specific example about the real issues regarding stop loss
3. Look at stop loss
   a. What is it
   b. Why is it in effect
   c. Where did it come from (Civil War, Vietnam, Gulf War, 9/11)
4. First criteria: good policy should give people faith in the military (those serving and those watching from the sidelines).
   a. Truth, justice and the American way
   b. Pressure on the reserves
   c. How they are manipulating troops
5. Second criteria: good policy protects troops and helps them do their job.
   a. Physical and mental exhaustion
   b. Pushing part-timers beyond what they have been trained for (while going lighter on the fulltime Army).
   c. Emotionally taxing the troops by repeatedly disappointing the already strained through changes in policy and changes in out time.
6. Third criteria: good policy avoids negative impacts on families and businesses
   a. Families left alone
   b. Families left alone and with less money
   c. Destroying small businesses
7. Conclusion and perspective

4: Revise, revise, revise

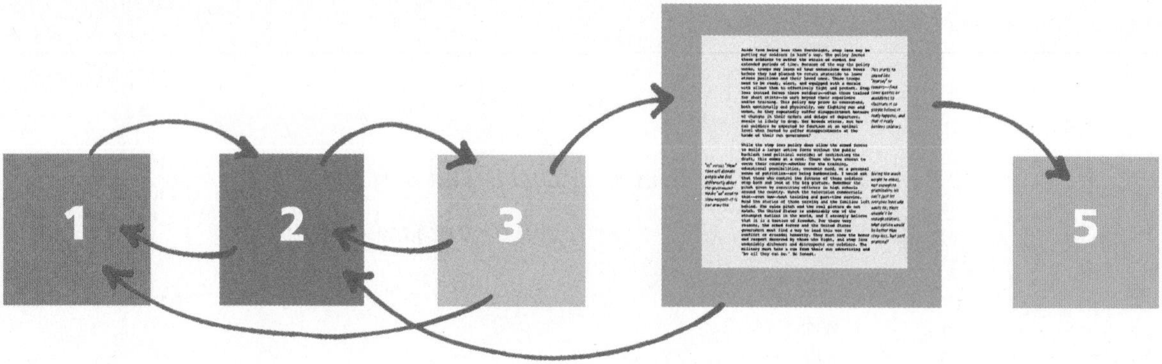

Skilled writers know that the secret to writing well is rewriting. Leave correcting errors for last.

Does your paper or project meet the assignment?	• Look again at your assignment. Does your paper or project do what the assignment asks? • Look again at the assignment for specific guidelines, including length, format, and amount of research. Does your work meet these guidelines?
Is your evaluative claim arguable?	• Do enough people disagree with you to make the evaluation worthwhile? • Does anyone but you care about this topic?
Are your criteria reasonable, and will your audience accept them?	• Do you provide compelling reasons for readers to accept your criteria for evaluation, if they weren't predisposed to do so? • Do you weight criteria appropriately, balancing aesthetic, ethical, and practical considerations in a way likely to appeal to your audience?
Is your evidence convincing and sufficient?	• Will readers believe what you say about the thing you are evaluating? What proof do you offer that it does or doesn't meet your criteria? • Are your descriptions clear and accurate?
Do you address opposing views?	• Have you acknowledged the opinions of people who disagree with you? • Where do you show why your evaluation is better?
Is the writing project visually effective?	• Is the font attractive and readable? • Are the headings and visuals effective? • If you use images or tables as part of your evaluation, are they legible and appropriately placed?
Save the editing for last.	• See guidelines for editing and proofreading on pages 24–28.

Writer at work

Working with a group of his fellow students, Rashaun Giddens made comments on his rough draft, and used them to help produce a final draft.

Aside from being less than forthright, stop loss may be putting our soldiers in harm's way. The policy forces these soldiers to suffer the strain of combat for extended periods of time. Because of the way the policy works, troops may learn of tour extensions mere hours before they had planned to return stateside to lower stress positions and their loved ones. These troops need to be ready, alert, and equipped with a morale with allows them to effectively fight and protect. Stop loss instead forces these soldiers—often those trained for short stints—to work beyond their experience and/or training. This policy may prove to overextend, both emotionally and physically, our fighting men and women. As they repeatedly suffer disappointment because of changes in their orders and delays of departure, morale is likely to drop. War breeds stress, but how can soldiers be expected to function at an optimal level when forced to suffer disappointments at the hands of their own government?

This starts to sound like "hearsay" or rumors--find some quotes or anecdotes to illustrate it so people believe it really happens, and that it really bothers soldiers.

While the stop loss policy does allow the armed forces to build a larger active force without the public backlash (and political suicide) of instituting the draft, this comes at a cost. Those who have chosen to serve their country—whether for the training, educational possibilities, economic need, or a personal sense of patriotism—are being bamboozled. I would ask that those who control the futures of these soldiers step back and look at the big picture. Remember the pitch given by recruiting officers in high schools around the country. Watch the television commercials that—even now—tout training and part-time service. Read the stories of those serving and the families left behind. The sales pitch and the real picture do not match. The United States is undeniably one of the strongest nations in the world, and I strongly believe that it is a bastion of freedom. For these very reasons, the armed forces and the United States government must find a way to lead this war (or conflict or crusade) honestly. They must show the honor and respect deserved by those who fight, and stop loss undeniably dishonors and disrespects our soldiers. The military must take a cue from their own advertising and "be all they can be." Be honest.

"Us" versus "them" tone will alienate people who feel differently about the government. Maybe "we" need to show respect—it is our army too

Giving too much weight to ethics, not enough to practicality. We can't just let everyone leave who wants to; there wouldn't be enough soldiers. What option would be better than stop loss, but still practical?

5: Submitted version

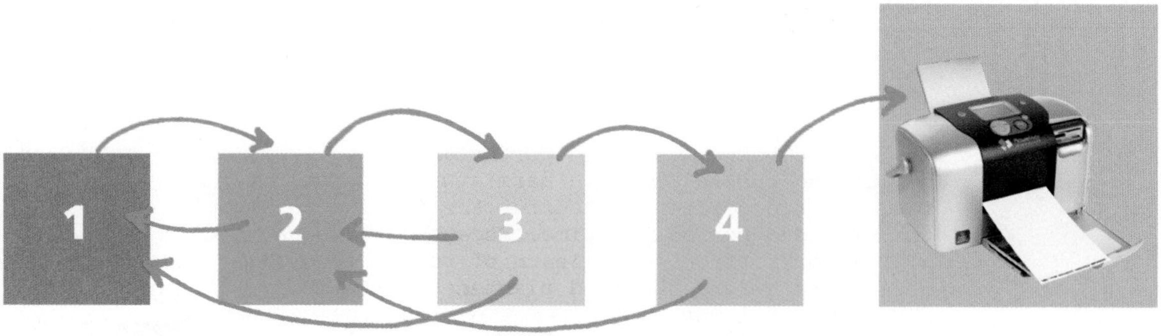

Giddens 1

Rashaun Giddens

Professor Chen

English 1302

21 April 2008

Stop Loss or "Loss of Trust"

Looking back on my high school career, my social and extracurricular lives were filled with countless highs: hanging out with my friends, prom, and varsity track to name a few. My academic career, however, was a bit shakier. So busy with what I saw then as the important things in life, I often procrastinated or altogether avoided my schoolwork. My senior year, the recruiter from the U.S. Army Reserves spoke at a school assembly. He asked that we as seniors consider the prospect of becoming "weekend warriors." In the wake of September 11, we could help protect our country and simultaneously work toward paying for a college education, which seemed like a great idea to many students. For those who could not otherwise afford college, the prospect of receiving a higher education in return for patriotism and some good hard work sounded fair enough. My life, however, took a different turn. When I received my track scholarship, I decided to head off to college right away. Many of my friends, however, heeded the call to service. So far, their realities have

been far from the lives that were pitched to them; rather, this was the beginning of a path to broken dreams and broken promises.

My cousin, moved to action by a charismatic recruiter, an Army announcement of fifteen-month active tours, and the prospect of a paid college education, chose to join the United States Army Reserves. The Army, suffering from a recruitment shortfall, had recently announced a policy that would allow recruits to serve in active duty for a mere fifteen months. For serving for just over a year, my cousin could do his national duty and put himself on a path to self-improvement. The recruiter did not, however, highlight the fine print to this new program. No one told my cousin that he could be called back to active duty for up to eight years under the government's stop loss policy. Further, no one told him that just one day after the Army announced the incentive program, an appeals court ruled that the Army could, under "stop loss," compel soldiers to remain beyond the initial eight-year obligation (Wickham).

The "stop loss" policy forces thousands of soldiers to serve beyond their volunteer enlistment contracts. The all-volunteer army—on which the government prides itself—is slowly developing into a disgruntled mass of men and women being held against their wills. These men and women wanted to serve their country and they signed what they believed were binding agreements with a trustworthy employer—the United States government—only to find that their government didn't bargain in good faith.

As far back as the Civil War, the government needed incentives to retain its troops. (Although we all want freedom, fewer actually want to put our own lives on the line in the pursuit of that goal.) Both the Union and the Confederacy needed to make tough decisions to maintain strong armed forces when soldiers' contracts were expiring. The Union chose to offer financial incentives to keep its young men in uniform, while the Confederacy instituted a series of (not so) "voluntary" reenlistment policies (Robertson). During World War II all soldiers were forced to

remain active until they reached a designated number of "points." Vietnam saw the last stage of a mandatory draft, with soldiers serving one-year tours (Hockstader). Today's military relies on "stop loss," making soldiers stay in the military after their commitment ends. Congress first gave the military the authority to retain soldiers after the Vietnam War when new volunteers were too few to replace departing soldiers. In November 2002 the Pentagon gave stop-loss orders for Reserve and National Guard units activated to fight terrorism (Robertson).

This policy is neither forthcoming, safe, nor compassionate toward those most directly impacted—the soldiers and their families. As the United States became more and more entrenched in the conflict in Iraq, the military was stretched thinner and thinner. By 2004, approximately 40% of those serving in Iraq and Afghanistan came from the ranks of the part-time soldiers: the Reserves and the National Guard (Gerard). While these individuals did know that their country could call if they enlisted, they continue to bear an inordinate burden of actual combat time, and this new policy continues to create situations further removed from the job for which they had enlisted. Recruiters often pitch the military—including the Reserves and the Guard—to young, impressionable, and often underprivileged kids. I have experienced this pitch firsthand and seen the eyes of my classmates as the recruiter promised them a better and richer tomorrow. Seeing a golden opportunity for self-respect and achievement, young men and women sign on the dotted line. Today, other young men and women are buying a bill of goods. These recruits—and those who came before them—deserve to have an honest relationship with the government they protect. As policymakers tout the all-volunteer Army, those who serve find their rights threatened. The military claims to teach soldiers respect and honor. Is misleading your employees honest?

Aside from being less than forthright, stop loss may be putting our soldiers in harm's way. The policy forces these soldiers to suffer the strain of combat for extended periods of time. Because of the way the policy works, troops may learn of

Giddens 4

tour extensions mere hours before they had planned to return stateside to lower stress positions and their loved ones. These troops need to be ready, alert, and equipped with a morale with allows them to fight effectively. Stop loss instead forces these soldiers—often those trained for short stints—to work beyond their experience and training. This policy may prove to overextend, both emotionally and physically, our fighting men and women. As they repeatedly suffer disappointment because of changes in their orders and delays of departure, morale is likely to drop. Based on reports from families, this practice has been devastating to their soldiers. Nancy Durst, wife of United States Reservist Staff Sergeant Scott Durst, told *Talk of the Nation's* Neal Conan that the military detained her husband's unit just thirty minutes before it was to board the bus scheduled to deliver it to a stateside flight. The unit was later informed that tours had been extended for another four months (Durst). War breeds stress, but how can soldiers be expected to function at an optimal level when forced to suffer disappointments at the hands of their own government?

Finally, this policy simply runs contrary to the current administration's stated interest in the preservation of family and the bolstering of small businesses. First (and most obviously), this less-than-forthright policy keeps families separated. Husbands, wives, and children find themselves separated for longer periods of time, left with uncertainty and ambiguity for comfort. How does this aid in preserving the family? Second, when the government deploys reservists, soldiers often take a severe pay cut. Forced to leave their regular jobs, soldiers—and their families—must survive on often a much smaller government wage. Stop loss extends tours of duty and consequently the economic struggles of the families in question. Third, the policy has proven detrimental to the small business owner. Men and women have used their military experience, discipline, and training to further themselves economically. America prides itself on the power of the small businessman; however, individuals such as Chief Warrant Officer Ronald Eagle have been hurt by this policy. After

Giddens 5

twenty years of service, Eagle was set to retire from the Army and focus on his aircraft-maintenance business. Instead, the Army has indefinitely moved his retirement date. As a consequence, Eagle has taken a $45,000 pay cut and wonders whether his business will survive his hiatus (Hockstader). Is this the way the government and military fight to preserve the family—emotionally and economically?

Because American men and women risk their lives in the name of bettering those of Iraqis, the military should think about how their policy affects the lives of their soldiers and those back home. While the stop loss policy does allow the armed forces to build a larger active force without the public backlash (and political suicide) of instituting the draft, this policy comes at a cost. Those who have chosen to serve their country—whether for the training, educational possibilities, economic need, or a personal sense of patriotism—are being bamboozled.

Watch the television commercials that, even now, tout training and part-time service. Read the stories of those serving and the families left behind. The sales pitch and the real picture do not match. The United States is undeniably one of the strongest nations in the world and a bastion of freedom. For these very reasons, the armed forces and the United States government, which represents all citizens, must find a way to lead this war (or conflict or crusade) honestly. If we have to pay soldiers double what they currently make in order to get them to re-enlist, we should do so. Even a draft would at least be aboveboard and honest. But we cannot continue to trick people into risking their lives for our national security. Our country must show the honor and respect deserved by those who fight, and stop loss undeniably dishonors and disrespects our soldiers. The military must take a cue from their own advertising and “be all they can be.” Be honest.

Works Cited

Durst, Nancy. Interview by Neal Conan. *Talk of the Nation*. Natl. Public Radio. WNYC, New York. 19 Apr. 2004. Radio.

Gerard, Philip. "When the Cry Was 'Over the Hill in October.'" *Charleston Gazette* 16 May 2004: 1E. *LexisNexis Academic*. Web. 6 Apr. 2008.

Hockstader, Lee. "Army Stops Many Soldiers From Quitting; Orders Extend Enlistments to Curtail Troop Shortages." *Washington Post* 29 Dec. 2003: A01. *LexisNexis Academic*. Web. 8 Apr. 2008.

Robertson, John. "The Folly of Stop Loss." *Pittsburgh Post-Gazette* 19 Dec. 2004: J1. *LexisNexis Academic*. Web. 7 Apr. 2008.

Wickham, DeWayne. "A 15-Month Enlistment? Check Army's Fine Print." *USA Today* 17 May 2005: 13A. *LexisNexis Academic*. Web. 6 Apr. 2008.

Projects

You likely have a great deal of experience making consumer evaluations, and when you have time to do your homework to compare features, quality, and price, probably you will make a good decision. For other evaluations, however, the criteria may not be obvious. Often the keys are finding the right criteria and convincing your readers that these criteria are the best ones to use.

These projects are frequently written kinds of evaluations.

Evaluate a controversial subject

Think of controversial subjects on your campus or in your community for which you can find recent articles in your campus or local newspaper. For example, is your mayor or city manager an effective leader? Is your campus recreational sports facility adequate? Is a new condominium complex built on city land that was used as a park good or bad?.

Identify what is at stake in the evaluation. Who thinks it is good or effective? Who thinks it is bad or ineffective? Why does it matter?

List the criteria that make something or someone good or bad. Which criteria are the most important? Which will you have to argue for?

Analyze your potential readers. How familiar will they be with what you are evaluating? Which criteria will they likely accept and which might they disagree with?

Write a draft. Introduce your subject and give the necessary background. Make your evaluative claim either at the beginning or as your conclusion. Describe each criterion and evaluate your subject on each criterion. Be sure to address opposing viewpoints by acknowledging how their evaluations might be different.

Evaluate a campus policy

Identify a policy on your campus that affects you. Examples include the way your school schedules classes and has students register, the way parking spaces are allotted on campus, the library's late fee and returns policy, housing or admissions policies, or rules regulating student organizations.

Consider your target audience as the readers of your campus newspaper. Who else besides you does this issue affect? What office or division of the school is responsible for the program? Who implemented it in the first place? Keep in mind that your school's administration is part of your audience.

Determine the criteria for your evaluation. Which criteria will be most important for other students? for the faculty and staff? for the administration?

Take a clear position about the policy. If you think the policy is unfair or ineffective, acknowledge why it was put into place. Sometimes good intentions lead to bad results. If you think the policy is fair or effective, explain why according to the criteria you set out. In either case, give reasons and examples to support your judgment.

Film review

Select a film to review. Choose a specific magazine, newspaper, or online publication as the place where you would publish the review. Read some reviews in that publication and notice the criteria that they use. You will need to keep the audience in mind.

Watch the film more than once and take notes. Analyze the film's genre. What makes a good horror movie? a good action-adventure movie? a good documentary? a good comedy? These will be your criteria for evaluation.

Find information on the film. The Internet Movie Database (**www.imdb.com**) is a good place to start. Look at the director's credits to find other films that he or she has done. Look at the information about the actors and locations.

Write a thesis that makes an evaluative claim: the film is a successful or unsuccessful example of its genre. Go beyond the obvious in selecting criteria. A comedy is supposed to make you laugh, but movies that are only gags tend to wear thin. Comedies that have engaging characters keep your interest. Acting often makes the difference between a good and great movie. Use evidence from the film to support your claim.

12 Arguments for a Position

Position arguments aim to change readers' attitudes and beliefs.

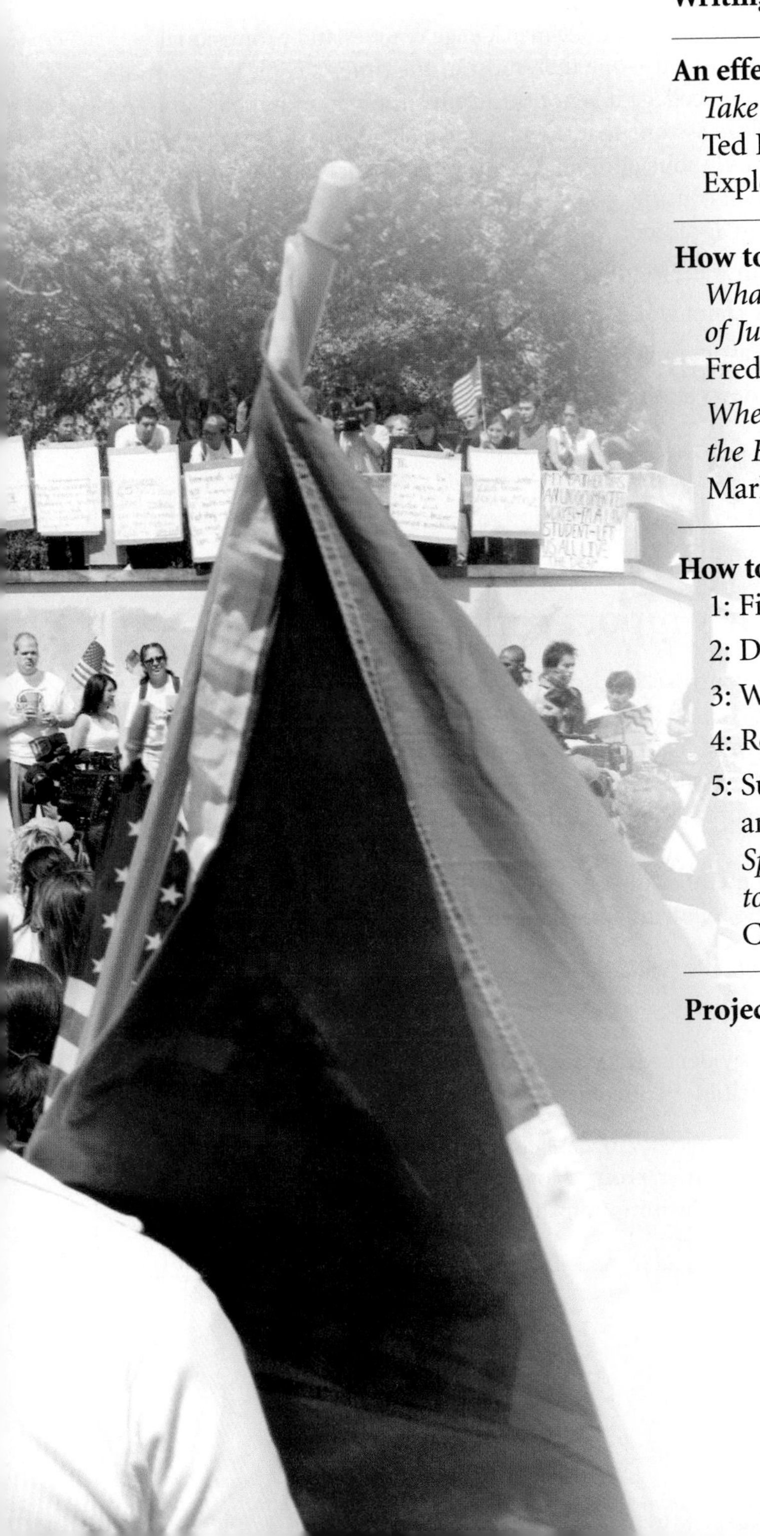

CHAPTER CONTENTS

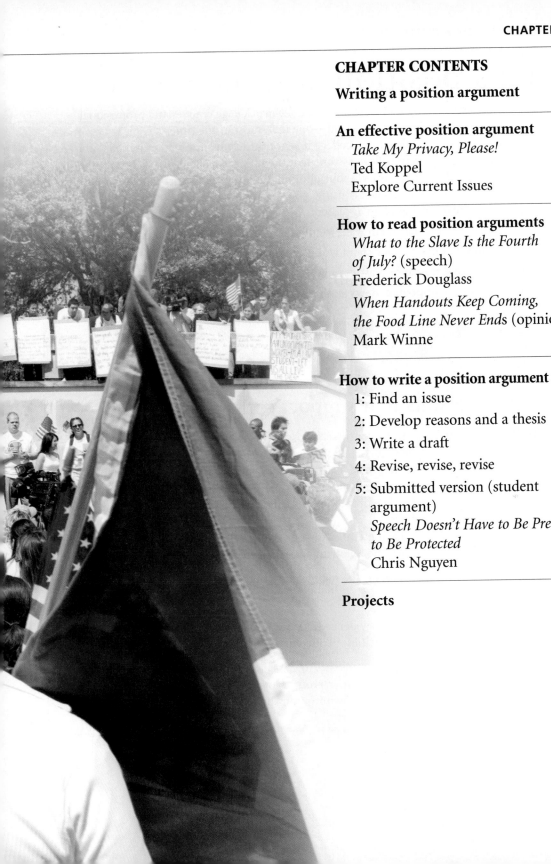

Writing a position argument

Many people think of the term *argument* as a synonym for *debate*. College courses and professional careers, however, require a different kind of argument—one that, most of the time, is cooler in emotion and more elaborate in detail than oral debate. In college it is not sufficient simply to write that "I believe this" or "It's just my opinion." Readers in college assume that if you make a claim in writing, you believe that claim. More important, a claim is rarely *only* your opinion. Because most beliefs and assumptions are shared by many people, responsible readers will consider your position seriously.

Readers in college expect the following of an argument.

- A **claim** that is interesting and makes them want to find out more about what you have to say
- At least one **good reason** that makes your claim worth taking seriously
- Some **evidence** that the good reason or reasons are valid
- Some acknowledgment of the **opposing views** and **limitations** of the claim

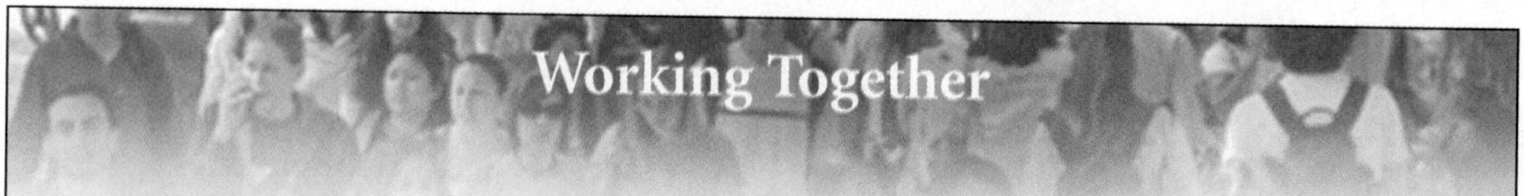

Identify reasons that support conflicting claims

In a group of three or four students

Select a controversial issue for which there are multiple points of view. You can find a list of issues at **www.dir.yahoo.com/Society_and_Culture/Issues_and_Causes/**. Explore the links for one of the issues to get a sense of the range of opinion. Then decide which Web sites will give your group a range of views on the issue.

Each member of your group will analyze two Web sites. Write down the following for each site.

- What is the main claim of the Web site?
- What reason or reasons are given?
- What evidence (facts, examples, statistics, and the testimony of authorities) is offered?

Bring your answers to class and compare them with other members of your group. How do the reasons differ for opposing claims? What assumptions underlie the reasons? How does the evidence differ?

Components of position arguments

What exactly is my issue?	**Define the issue.** Your subject should be clear to your readers. If readers are unfamiliar with the issue, you should give enough examples so they understand the issue in concrete terms.
Who are the stakeholders?	**Identify the stakeholders.** Who is immediately affected by this issue? Who is affected indirectly?
What has been written about the issue?	**Read about the issue.** Every significant issue has an extensive history of discussion involving many people and various points of view. Before you formulate a claim about an issue, become familiar with the conversation about that issue by reading.
What exactly is my stand on the issue?	**State your position.** You may want to state your thesis in the opening paragraph to let readers know your position immediately. If your issue is unfamiliar, you may want to find out more before you state your position. In any case, you should take a definite position on the issue.
What are the reasons for my position?	**Find one or more reasons.** You need to give one or more reasons for your position. List as many reasons as you can think of. Use the ones that are most convincing.
Where can I find evidence?	**Provide evidence.** In support of your reasons, provide evidence—in the form of examples, statistics, and testimony of experts—that the reasons are valid. When the issue is unfamiliar, more evidence than usual is required.
Who disagrees with my position?	**Acknowledge opposing views and limitations of the claim.** If everybody thinks the same way, then there is no need to write a position argument. Anticipate what objections might be made to your position. You can answer possible objections in two ways: that the objections are not valid or that the objections have some validity but your argument is stronger.

Understand how position arguments work

Position arguments often take two forms—definition arguments and rebuttal arguments.

Definition arguments

The continuing controversies about what art is, free speech, pornography, and hate crimes (to name just a few) illustrate why definitions often matter more than we might think. People argue about definitions because of the consequences of something being defined in a certain way.

People make definitions that benefit their interests. Early in life you learned the importance of defining actions as "accidents." Windows can be broken through carelessness, especially when you are tossing a ball against the side of the house, but if it's an accident, well, accidents just happen (and don't require punishment). Your mother or father probably didn't think breaking the window was an accident, so you had to convince Mom or Dad that you were really being careful, and the ball just slipped out of your hand. If you can get your audience to accept your definition, then usually you succeed. For this reason, definition arguments are the most powerful arguments.

For example, is graffiti vandalism? Or is it art? If you claim at least some forms of graffiti should be considered art, you need to set out criteria to define art and argue that graffiti meets those criteria.

Something = or ≠ ________

Criteria A

Criteria B

Criteria C

EXAMPLE

Graffiti is art because it is a means of self expression, it shows an understanding of design pinciples, and it stimulates both the senses and the mind.

Rebuttal arguments

Rebuttal arguments take the opposite position. You can challenge the criteria a writer uses to make a definition or you can challenge the evidence that supports a claim. Sometimes the evidence presented is incomplete or simply wrong. Sometimes you can find counterevidence. Often when you rebut an argument, you identify one or more fallacies in that argument (see pages 14–15).

Opposing claim

Bad reason 1

Bad reason 2

EXAMPLE

The great white shark gained a reputation as a "man eater" from the 1975 movie *Jaws,* but in fact attacks on humans are rare and most bites have been "test bites," which is a common shark behavior with unfamiliar objects.

Keys to position arguments

Understand your goal	A well-written and well-reasoned position argument may not change minds entirely, but it can convince readers that a reasonable person can hold this point of view. Position arguments do not necessarily have winners and losers. Your goal is to invite a response that creates a dialogue.
Be sensitive to the context	Even position arguments that have become classics and in a sense "timeless" frequently were written in response to a historical event; for example, Martin Luther King, Jr. wrote his powerful argument for civil disobedience, "Letter from Birmingham Jail," in response to a published statement by eight Birmingham clergymen. A careful analysis of a recent or historical event often provides your argument with a sense of immediacy.
Rely on careful definitions	What exactly does *freedom of speech* mean? What exactly does *privacy* mean? What exactly does *animal rights* mean? Getting readers to accept a definition is often the key to a position argument. For example, torturing animals is against the law. Animal rights activists argue that raising and slaughtering animals for food is torture and thus would extend the definition. If you can get readers to accept your definition, then they will agree with your position.
Use quality sources	Find the highest-quality sources for citing evidence. Recent sources are critical for current topics, such as the relationship of certain diets to disease.
Create credibility	You have probably noticed that many times in the course of reading, you get a strong sense of the writer's character, even if you know nothing about the person. Be honest about strengths and weaknesses and about what you don't know, and avoid easy labels. If readers trust you are sincere, they will take you seriously.
Cultivate a sense of humor and a distinctive voice	A reasonable voice doesn't have to be a dull one. Humor is a legitimate tool of argument, especially when the stakes are high and tempers are flaring.
Argue responsibly	When you begin an argument by stating "in my opinion," you are not arguing responsibly. If you don't like broccoli, it is a matter of personal taste. But if you are for or against universal health care, then it is not just your opinion. Millions of other Americans hold views similar to yours on this contested issue.

An effective position argument

Position arguments succeed when readers consider the writer's position as one to take seriously.

Take My Privacy, Please!

Ted Koppel

Ted Koppel joined ABC News in 1963 and served from 1980 until 2005 as the anchor and managing editor of *Nightline,* the first late-night network news program. He has had a major reporting role in every presidential campaign since 1964. "Take My Privacy, Please!" which appeared in June 2005 in the *New York Times,* is an example of a position argument that doesn't begin with a thesis but first gives a series of examples.

Take My Privacy, Please!

by Ted Koppel

THE PATRIOT ACT—brilliant! Its critics would have preferred a less stirring title, perhaps something along the lines of the Enhanced Snooping, Library and Hospital Database Seizure Act. But then who, even right after 9/11, would have voted for that?

Precisely. He who names it and frames it, claims it. The Patriot Act, however, may turn out to be among the lesser threats to our individual and collective privacy.

There is no end to what we will endure, support, pay for and promote if only it makes our lives easier, promises to save us money, appears to enhance our security and comes to us in a warm, cuddly and altogether nonthreatening package. To wit: OnStar, the subscription vehicle tracking and assistance system.

Koppel announces his stance and his subject in the first two paragraphs. He questions the Patriot Act and then suggests that there may be bigger threats to privacy.

Part of its mission statement, as found on the OnStar Web site, is the creation of "safety, security and peace of mind for drivers and passengers with thoughtful wireless services that are always there, always ready." You've surely seen or heard their commercials, one of which goes like this:

ANNOUNCER -- The following is an OnStar conversation. (Ring)

The OnStar commercial provides a concrete example.

ONSTAR -- OnStar emergency, this is Dwight.

DRIVER -- (crying) Yes, yes??!

ONSTAR -- Are there any injuries, ma'am?

DRIVER -- My leg hurts, my arm hurts.

ONSTAR -- O.K. I do understand. I will be contacting emergency services.

ANNOUNCER -- If your airbags deploy, OnStar receives a signal and calls to check on you. (Ring)

EMERGENCY SERVICES -- Police.

ONSTAR -- This is Dwight with OnStar. I'd like to report a vehicle crash with airbag deployment on West 106th Street.

EMERGENCY SERVICES -- We'll send police and E.M.S. out there.

In the ad, OnStar is portrayed as a technology that can save lives.

DRIVER -- (crying) I'm so scared!

ONSTAR -- O.K., I'm here with you, ma'am; you needn't be scared.

KOPPEL: TAKE MY PRIVACY, PLEASE!

Well, maybe just a little scared. Tell us again how Dwight knows just where the accident took place. Oh, right! It's those thoughtful wireless services that are always there. Always, as in any time a driver gets into an OnStar-equipped vehicle. OnStar insists that it would disclose the whereabouts of a subscriber's vehicle only after being presented with a criminal court order or after the vehicle has been reported stolen. That's certainly a relief. I wouldn't want to think that anyone but Dwight knows where I am whenever I'm traveling in my car.

Koppel uses critical thinking to question the main assumption of the ad: Is it necessarily good that OnStar always knows where you are while driving?

Of course, E-ZPass and most other toll-collecting systems already know whenever a customer passes through one of their scanners. That's because of radio frequency identification technology. In return for the convenience of zipping through toll booths, you need to have in your car a wireless device. This tag contains information about your account, permitting E-ZPass to deduct the necessary toll—and to note when your car whisked through that particular toll booth. They wouldn't share that information with anyone, either; that is, unless they had to.

Convenient technologies also keep track of our movements. Koppel gets his readers to think about what happens to personal information that is passively collected.

Radio frequency identification technology has been used for about 15 years now to reunite lost pets with their owners. Applied Digital Solutions, for example, manufactures the VeriChip, a tiny, implantable device that holds a small amount of data. Animal shelters can scan the chip for the name and phone number of the lost pet's owner. The product is now referred to as the HomeAgain Microchip Identification System.

Useful? Sure. Indeed, it's not much of a leap to suggest that one day, the VeriChip might be routinely implanted under the skin of, let's say, an Alzheimer's patient. The Food and Drug Administration approved the VeriChip for use in people last October. An Applied Digital Solutions spokesman estimates that about 1,000 people have already had a VeriChip implanted, usually in the right triceps. At the moment, it doesn't carry much information, just an identification number

that health care providers can use to tap into a patient's medical history. A Barcelona nightclub also uses it to admit customers with a qualifying code to enter a V.I.P. room where drinks are automatically put on their bill. Possible variations on the theme are staggering.

Technologies used to track pets can also track people.

And how about all the information collected by popular devices like TiVo, the digital video recorder that enables you to watch and store an entire season's worth of favorite programs at your own convenience? It also lets you electronically mark the programs you favor, allowing TiVo to suggest similar programs for your viewing pleasure. In February, TiVo announced the most frequently played and replayed commercial moment during the Super Bowl (it involves a wardrobe malfunction, but believe me, you don't want to know), drawing on aggregated data from a sample of 10,000 anonymous TiVo households. No one is suggesting that TiVo tracks what each subscriber records and replays. But could they, if they needed to? That's unclear, although TiVo does have a privacy policy. "Your privacy," it says in part, "is very important to us. Due to factors beyond our control, however, we cannot fully ensure that your user information will not be disclosed to third parties."

The popular TiVo service admits that it does not fully protect the privacy of its subscribers.

Unexpected and unfortunate things happen, of course, even to the most reputable and best-run organizations. Only last February, the Bank of America Corporation notified federal investigators that it had lost computer backup tapes containing personal information about 1.2 million federal government employees, including some senators. In April, LexisNexis unintentionally gave outsiders access to the personal files (addresses, Social Security numbers, drivers license information) of as many as 310,000 people. In May, Time Warner revealed that an outside storage company had misplaced data stored on computer backup tapes on 600,000 current and former employees. That same month, United Parcel Service picked up a box of computer tapes in New Jersey from CitiFinancial, the consumer finance subsidiary of

Numerous accidents and data thefts have given private information to unauthorized people.

KOPPEL: TAKE MY PRIVACY, PLEASE!

Citigroup, that contained the names, addresses, Social Security numbers, account numbers, payment histories and other details on small personal loans made to an estimated 3.9 million customers. The box is still missing.

Whoops!

CitiFinancial correctly informed its own customers and, inevitably, the rest of the world about the security breach. Would they have done so entirely on their own? That is less clear. In July 2003, California started requiring companies to inform customers living in the state of any breach in security that compromises personally identifiable information. Six other states have passed similar legislation.

No such legislation exists on the federal stage, however—only discretionary guidelines for financial institutions about whether and how they should inform their customers with respect to breaches in the security of their personal information.

Both the House and Senate are now considering federal legislation similar to the California law. It's a start but not nearly enough. We need mandatory clarity and transparency; not just with regard to the services that these miracles of microchip and satellite technology offer but also the degree to which companies share and exchange their harvest of private data.

Koppel hopes by this point he has raised concerns about privacy for his readers. He now gives his thesis: The public has the right to know what is being done with private information they give to companies and services.

We cannot even begin to control the growing army of businesses and industries that monitor what we buy, what we watch on television, where we drive, the debts we pay or fail to pay, our marriages and divorces, our litigations, our health and tax records and all else that may or may not yet exist on some computer tape, if we don't fully understand everything we're signing up for when we avail ourselves of one of these services.

Explore Current Issues

Can pennies really solve the world's problems?

On World Water Day, March 22, 2007, UNICEF kicked off their Tap Project, in which diners at restaurants in select cities can donate $1 for every glass of tap water they order. The money goes to clean drinking water programs around the world. A video on the Tap Project Web site promotes the program, segueing from images of people living in areas with poor drinking water to a question: "But what if . . . you could change these lives without making a change to yours?"

Pushing the convenience of giving in small amounts has long been a strategy of charitable organizations. The refrain "for only pennies a day" has inspired people of many generations to sponsor starving children and house homeless pets. However, are small monetary donations as effective as people believe? According to Larry Brilliant, writing for Slate.com's 2008 special philanthropy issue, less than one-third of the funds donated to nonprofits in 2005 actually reached the people for whom they were intended.

Write about it

1. The effectiveness of small monetary donations, or the effectiveness of monetary donations in comparison to donations of time, skills, or goods are only two issues surrounding charitable donations. Think about other issues on which people might hold different positions, such as how charitable organizations advertise, how kids are getting involved in charitable giving, and how organizations are using new technologies to raise donations.
2. What is at stake in making arguments about charitable organizations? Choose one of the issues you listed for the first question. Who is involved with this issue? What is at stake for each individual or group? Which position might each of these groups hold?
3. Think about your own patterns of charitable giving. What inspires you to give to an organization? Are you more likely to donate your time or money? Why? Write a paragraph explaining your position.

How to read position arguments

Make notes as you read, either in the margins or on paper or a computer file. Circle any words or references that you don't know and look them up.

What is it?	• What kind of a text is it? An article? an essay? a chart? a scientific report? a Web site? an executive summary? What are your expectations for this kind of text? • What media are used? (Web sites, for example, often combine images, words, and sounds.)
Where did it come from?	• Who wrote the analysis? • Where did it first appear? In a book, newspaper, magazine, online, in a company, or in an organization?
What is the writer's thesis or main idea?	• What is the writer's topic? What effect is he or she trying to determine the cause of? • Why is this topic important? • What are the key ideas or concepts that the writer considers? • What are the key terms? How does the writer define those terms?
Who is the intended audience?	• What clues do you find about whom the writer had in mind as readers? • What does the writer assume that the readers already know about the subject? • What new knowledge is the writer providing?
What are the reasons that support the claim?	• Is there one primary reason? • Are multiple reasons given? • Do you find any fallacies in the reasons (see pages 14–15)?
What kinds of evidence are given?	• Is the evidence from books, newspapers, periodicals, the Web, or field research? • Is the evidence convincing that the causes given are the actual causes?
How is it composed?	• How does the writer represent himself or herself? • How would you characterize the style? • How effective is the design? Is it easy to read? • If there are any photographs, charts, or other graphics, what information do they contribute?

What to the Slave Is the Fourth of July?

(SPEECH)

Frederick Douglass

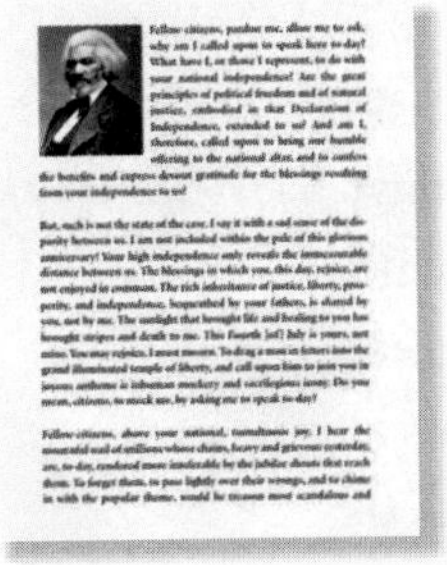

On the fifth of July, 1852, former slave Frederick Douglass spoke at a meeting of the Ladies' Anti-Slavery Society in Rochester, New York. In this series of excerpts from his lengthy oration (published shortly thereafter as a pamphlet), Douglass reminds his audience of the irony of celebrating freedom and liberty in a land where much of the population was enslaved.

Return to these questions after you have finished reading.

Analyzing and Connecting

1. Douglass spends considerable time telling his audience what points do *not* need to be argued: that a slave is human, that man is entitled to liberty, and so on. If in fact these points are agreed upon by all, why do you think Douglass spends so much time talking about them?
2. Douglass was speaking in the last few years before the American Civil War began. How did the vivid imagery in this speech likely affect listeners? Read carefully through Douglass's descriptions of the slave trade and its impact on individuals and families. What values is he appealing to?
3. What impact does Douglass's personal history have on his credibility? Would the argument in this speech have been as compelling if it had been made by someone who had never experienced slavery firsthand?
4. What words would you use to describe the overall tone of Douglass's speech? Is it angry? threatening? hopeful? pessimistic? Why do you think Douglass chose the tone he used in this argument?

Finding Ideas for Writing

Imagine you were at Douglass's speech. Write a brief newspaper article describing the event and summarizing Douglass's argument. Make sure to also describe how the audience might have reacted to Douglass as a speaker and particular passages, especially the last paragraph. What appeals was he using and how did the audience respond?

DOUGLASS: WHAT TO THE SLAVE IS THE FOURTH OF JULY?

Fellow-citizens, pardon me, allow me to ask, why am I called upon to speak here to-day? What have I, or those I represent, to do with your national independence? Are the great principles of political freedom and of natural justice, embodied in that Declaration of Independence, extended to us? And am I, therefore, called upon to bring our humble offering to the national altar, and to confess the benefits and express devout gratitude for the blessings resulting from your independence to us?

But, such is not the state of the case. I say it with a sad sense of the disparity between us. I am not included within the pale of this glorious anniversary! Your high independence only reveals the immeasurable distance between us. The blessings in which you, this day, rejoice, are not enjoyed in common. The rich inheritance of justice, liberty, prosperity, and independence, bequeathed by your fathers, is shared by you, not by me. The sunlight that brought life and healing to you has brought stripes and death to me. This Fourth [of] July is yours, not mine. You may rejoice, I must mourn. To drag a man in fetters into the grand illuminated temple of liberty, and call upon him to join you in joyous anthems is inhuman mockery and sacrilegious irony. Do you mean, citizens, to mock me, by asking me to speak to-day?

Fellow-citizens, above your national, tumultuous joy, I hear the mournful wail of millions whose chains, heavy and grievous yesterday, are, to-day, rendered more intolerable by the jubilee shouts that reach them. To forget them, to pass lightly over their wrongs, and to chime in with the popular theme, would be treason most scandalous and

shocking, and would make me a reproach before God and the world. My subject, then fellow citizens, is AMERICAN SLAVERY. I shall see, this day, and its popular characteristics, from the slave's point of view. Standing, there, identified with the American bondman, making his wrongs mine, I do not hesitate to declare, with all my soul, that the character and conduct of this nation never looked blacker to me than on this 4th of July! Whether we turn to the declarations of the past, or to the professions of the present, the conduct of the nation seems equally hideous and revolting. America is false to the past, false to the present, and solemnly binds herself to be false to the future. Standing with God and the crushed and bleeding slave on this occasion, I will, in the name of humanity which is outraged, in the name of liberty which is fettered, in the name of the constitution and the Bible, which are disregarded and trampled upon, dare to call in question and to denounce, with all the emphasis I can command, everything that serves to perpetuate slavery—the great sin and shame of America! "I will not equivocate; I will not excuse"; I will use the severest language I can command; and yet not one word shall escape me that any man, whose judgment is not blinded by prejudice, or who is not at heart a slaveholder, shall not confess to be right and just.

But I fancy I hear some one of my audience say, it is just in this circumstance that you and your brother abolitionists fail to make a favorable impression on the public mind. Would you argue more, and denounce less, would you persuade more, and rebuke less, your cause would be much more likely to succeed. But, I submit, where all is plain there is nothing to be argued. What point in the anti-slavery creed would you have me argue? On what branch of the subject do the people of this country need light? Must I undertake to prove that the slave is a man? That point is conceded already. Nobody doubts it. The slaveholders

themselves acknowledge it in the enactment of laws for their government. They acknowledge it when they punish disobedience on the part of the slave. There are seventy-two crimes in the State of Virginia, which, if committed by a black man, (no matter how ignorant he be), subject him to the punishment of death; while only two of the same crimes will subject a white man to the like punishment. What is this but the acknowledgement that the slave is a moral, intellectual and responsible being? The manhood of the slave is conceded. It is admitted in the fact that Southern statute books are covered with enactments forbidding, under severe fines and penalties, the teaching of the slave to read or to write. When you can point to any such laws, in reference to the beasts of the field, then I may consent to argue the manhood of the slave. When the dogs in your streets, when the fowls of the air, when the cattle on your hills, when the fish of the sea, and the reptiles that crawl, shall be unable to distinguish the slave from a brute, there will I argue with you that the slave is a man!

For the present, it is enough to affirm the equal manhood of the negro race. Is it not astonishing that, while we are ploughing, planting and reaping, using all kinds of mechanical tools, erecting houses, constructing bridges, building ships, working in metals of brass, iron, copper, silver and gold; that, while we are reading, writing and ciphering, acting as clerks, merchants and secretaries, having among us lawyers, doctors, ministers, poets, authors, editors, orators and teachers; that, while we are engaged in all manner of enterprises common to other men, digging gold in California, capturing the whale in the Pacific, feeding sheep and cattle on the hillside, living, moving, acting, thinking, planning, living in families as husbands, wives and children, and, above all, confessing and worshipping the Christian's God, and looking hopefully for life and immortality beyond the grave, we are called upon to prove that we are men!

Would you have me argue that man is entitled to liberty? That he is the rightful owner of his own body? You have already declared it. Must I argue the wrongfulness of slavery? Is it to be settled by the rules of logic and argumentation, as a matter beset with great difficulty, involving a doubtful application of the principle of justice, hard to be understood? How should I look to-day, in the presence of Americans, dividing, and subdividing a discourse, to show that men have a natural right to freedom? speaking of it relatively, and positively, negatively, and affirmatively. To do so would be to make myself ridiculous and offer an insult to your understanding. There is not a man beneath the canopy of heaven that does not know that slavery is wrong for him.

What, am I to argue that it is wrong to make men brutes, to rob them of their liberty, to work them without wages, to keep them ignorant of their relations to their fellow men, to beat them with sticks, to flay their flesh with the lash, to load their limbs with irons, to hunt them with dogs, to sell them at auction, to sunder their families, to knock out their teeth, to burn their flesh, to starve them into obedience and submission to their masters? Must I argue that a system thus marked with blood, and stained with pollution, is wrong? No! I will not. I have better employments for my time and strength, than such arguments would imply.

What, then, remains to be argued? Is it that slavery is not divine; that God did not establish it; that our doctors of divinity are mistaken? There is blasphemy in the thought. That which is inhuman, cannot be divine! Who can reason on such a proposition? They that can, may; I cannot. The time for such argument is past.

What, to the American slave, is your 4th of July? I answer: a day that reveals to him, more than all other days in the year, the gross injustice

and cruelty to which he is the constant victim. To him, your celebration is a sham; your boasted liberty, an unholy license; your national greatness, swelling vanity; your sounds of rejoicing are empty and heartless; your denunciations of tyrants, brass fronted impudence; your shouts of liberty and equality, hollow mockery; your prayers and hymns, your sermons and thanksgivings, with all your religious parade, and solemnity, are, to him, mere bombast, fraud, deception, impiety, and hypocrisy—a thin veil to cover up crimes which would disgrace a nation of savages. There is not a nation on the earth guilty of practices, more shocking and bloody, than are the people of these United States, at this very hour.

Behold the practical operation of this internal slave-trade, the American slave-trade, sustained by American politics and American religion. Here you will see men and women reared like swine for the market. You know what is a swine-drover? I will show you a man-drover. They inhabit all our Southern States. They perambulate the country and crowd the highways of the nation, with droves of human stock. You will see one of these human flesh-jobbers, armed with pistol, whip and Bowie-knife, driving a company of a hundred men, women, and children from the Potomac to the slave market at New Orleans. These wretched people are to be sold singly, or in lots, to suit purchasers. They are food for the cotton-field, and the deadly sugar-mill. Mark the sad procession, as it moves wearily along, and the inhuman wretch who drives them. Hear his savage yells and his blood-chilling oaths, as he hurries on his affrighted captives! There, see the old man, with locks thinned and gray. Cast one glance, if you please, upon that young mother, whose shoulders are bare to the scorching sun, her briny tears falling on the brow of the babe in her arms. See, too, that girl of thirteen, weeping, yes! weeping, as she thinks of the mother from whom she has been torn! The drove moves tardily. Heat

and sorrow have nearly consumed their strength; suddenly you hear a quick snap, like the discharge of a rifle; the fetters clank, and the chain rattles simultaneously; your ears are saluted with a scream, that seems to have torn its way to the centre of your soul! The crack you heard, was the sound of the slave-whip; the scream you heard, was from the woman you saw with the babe. Her speed had faltered under the weight of her child and her chains! that gash on her shoulder tells her to move on. Follow this drove to New Orleans. Attend the auction; see men examined like horses; see the forms of women rudely and brutally exposed to the shocking gaze of American slave-buyers. See this drove sold and separated forever; and never forget the deep, sad sobs that arose from that scattered multitude. Tell me citizens, WHERE, under the sun, you can witness a spectacle more fiendish and shocking. Yet this is but a glance at the American slave-trade, as it exists, at this moment, in the ruling part of the United States.

I was born amid such sights and scenes. To me the American slave-trade is a terrible reality. When a child, my soul was often pierced with a sense of its horrors. I lived on Philpot Street, Fell's Point, Baltimore, and have watched from the wharves, the slave ships in the Basin, anchored from the shore, with their cargoes of human flesh, waiting for favorable winds to waft them down the Chesapeake. There was, at that time, a grand slave mart kept at the head of Pratt Street, by Austin Woldfolk. His agents were sent into every town and county in Maryland, announcing their arrival, through the papers, and on flaming "hand-bills," headed CASH FOR NEGROES. These men were generally well dressed men, and very captivating in their manners. Ever ready to drink, to treat, and to gamble. The fate of many a slave has depended upon the turn of a single card; and many a child has been snatched from the arms of its mother by bargains arranged in a state of brutal drunkenness.

Allow me to say, in conclusion, notwithstanding the dark picture I have this day presented of the state of the nation, I do not despair of this country. There are forces in operation, which must inevitably work the downfall of slavery. "The arm of the Lord is not shortened," and the doom of slavery is certain. I, therefore, leave off where I began, with hope. While drawing encouragement from the Declaration of Independence, the great principles it contains, and the genius of American Institutions, my spirit is also cheered by the obvious tendencies of the age. Nations do not now stand in the same relation to each other that they did ages ago. No nation can now shut itself up from the surrounding world, and trot round in the same old path of its fathers without interference. The time was when such could be done. Long established customs of hurtful character could formerly fence themselves in, and do their evil work with social impunity. Knowledge was then confined and enjoyed by the privileged few, and the multitude walked on in mental darkness. But a change has now come over the affairs of mankind. Walled cities and empires have become unfashionable. The arm of commerce has borne away the gates of the strong city. Intelligence is penetrating the darkest corners of the globe. It makes its pathway over and under the sea, as well as on the earth. Wind, steam, and lightning are its chartered agents. Oceans no longer divide, but link nations together. From Boston to London is now a holiday excursion. Space is comparatively annihilated. Thoughts expressed on one side of the Atlantic are distinctly heard on the other. The far off and almost fabulous Pacific rolls in grandeur at our feet. The Celestial Empire, the mystery of ages, is being solved. The fiat of the Almighty, "Let there be Light," has not yet spent its force. No abuse, no outrage whether in taste, sport or avarice, can now hide itself from the all-pervading light.

When Handouts Keep Coming, the Food Line Never Ends

(OPINION)

Mark Winne

Mark Winne was the director of Connecticut's Hartford Food System from 1979 to 2003. He is the author of *Closing the Food Gap: Resetting the Table in the Land of Plenty* (2008), which examines how people from all classes obtain food: from lower income people at food pantries and convenience stores to more affluent people who tend to seek out organic and local products. Instead of the term *hunger*, Winne uses the phrase *food insecure*, which refers to a lack of access at all times to enough food for an active, healthy life. According to the USDA, 10.9% of households in the United States were food insecure at least some time during 2006. "When Handouts Keep Coming, the Food Line Never Ends" was published in the *Washington Post* on November 18, 2007.

Return to these questions after you have finished reading.

Analyzing and Connecting

1. Winne begins his article by talking about the flurry of giving that occurs during Thanksgiving. Why do you think people are more likely to make donations and volunteer during the holiday season?

2. In this article, Winne explains his position on the government's methods of dealing with poverty. In doing so, he sets up several causal relationships, the most clearly stated: "We know hunger's cause—poverty. We know its solution—end poverty." What are the others?

3. Winne is making a controversial claim—that we need to rethink our devotion to food donation. What is at stake in this claim for donors, food banks, and the poor? What is at stake for Winne in making this argument?

4. In this article, Winne provides many details—some of them potentially surprising to his audience—about the operations of food banks and of public food services. Why do you think he does this? How do these details affect his argument? his credibility?

Finding Ideas for Writing

As Winne points out, certain kinds of philanthropy continue—even though a change in policy might be more effective—because donors, whether corporations, organizations, or individuals, gain some benefit such as good public relations or even just feeling good. Write about an experience of volunteering, even if it was only an act of helping a stranger. Has this experience affected the way you feel about philanthropy? public services?

When Handouts Keep Coming, the Food Line Never Ends

How can anyone not get caught up in the annual Thanksgiving turkey frenzy? At the food bank I co-founded in Hartford, Conn., November always meant cheering the caravans of fowl-laden trucks that roared into our parking lot. They came on the heels of the public appeals for "A bird in every pot," "No family left without a turkey" and our bank's own version—"A turkey and a 20 [dollar bill]."

Like pompom girls leading a high school pep rally, we revved up the community's charitable impulse to a fever pitch with radio interviews, newspaper stories and dramatic television footage to extract the last gobbler from the stingiest citizen. After all, our nation's one great day of social equity was upon us. In skid row soup kitchens and the gated communities of hedge-fund billionaires alike, everyone was entitled, indeed expected, to sit down to a meal of turkey with all the fixings.

And here we are, putting on the same play again this year. But come Friday, as most of us stuff more leftovers into our bulging refrigerators, 35 million Americans will take their place in line again at soup kitchens, food banks and food stamp offices nationwide. The good souls who staff America's tens of thousands of emergency food sites will renew their pleas to donors fatigued by their burst of holiday philanthropy. Food stamp workers will return to their desks and try to convince mothers that they can feed their families on the $3 per person per day that the government allots them. The cycle of need—always present, rarely sated, never resolved—will continue.

Unless we rethink our devotion to food donation.

America's far-flung network of emergency food programs—from Second Harvest to tens of thousands of neighborhood food pantries—constitutes one of the largest charitable institutions in the nation. Its vast base of volunteers and donors and its ever-expanding distribution infrastructure have made it a powerful force in shaping popular perceptions of domestic hunger and other forms of need. But in the end, one of its most lasting effects has been to sidetrack efforts to eradicate hunger and its root cause, poverty.

As sociologist Janet Poppendieck made clear in her book *Sweet Charity,* there is something in the food-banking culture and its

relationship with donors that dampens the desire to empower the poor and take a more muscular, public stand against hunger.

It used to be my job to scour every nook and cranny of Hartford for food resources, and I've known the desperation of workers who saw the lines of the poor grow longer while the food bank's inventory shrank. The cutback in federal support for social welfare programs triggered by the Reagan administration in the 1980s unleashed a wave of charitable innovation and growth not seen since the Great Depression. As demand for food rose unabated—as it does to this day—our food bank's staff became increasingly adept at securing sustenance from previously unimaginable sources.

No food donation was too small, too strange or too nutritionally unsound to be refused.

I remember the load of nearly rotten potatoes that we "gratefully" accepted at the warehouse loading dock and then promptly shoveled into the dumpster once the donor was safely out of sight. One of our early food bank meetings included a cooking demonstration by a group of local entrepreneurs who were trying to develop a market for horse meat. The product's name was Cheva-lean, taken from "cheval," the French word for horse. The promoters reminded us that the French, the world's leading authorities on food, ate horse meat, implying that therefore our poor clients could certainly do the same. The only thing that topped that was when we had to secure recipes from the University of Maine to help us use the moose parts proudly presented by representatives of the Connecticut Fish and Game Division who'd been forced to put down the disoriented Bullwinkle found wandering through suburban back yards.

We did our job well, and everything grew: Over 25 years, the food bank leapfrogged five times from warehouse to ever-vaster warehouse, finally landing in a state-of-the-art facility that's the equal of most commercial food distribution centers in the country. The volunteers multiplied to 3,000 because the donations of food, much of it unfit for human consumption, required many hands for sorting and discarding. The number of food distribution sites skyrocketed from five in 1982 to 360 today.

But in spite of all the outward signs of progress, more than 275,000 Connecticut residents—slightly less than 8.6 percent of the state's

residents—remain hungry or what we call "food insecure." The Department of Agriculture puts 11 percent of the U.S. population in this category. (The department also provides state-by-state breakdowns.)

The overall futility of the effort became evident to me one summer day in 2003 when I observed a food bank truck pull up to a low-income housing project in Hartford. The residents had known when and where the truck would arrive, and they were already lined up at the edge of the parking lot to receive handouts. Staff members and volunteers set up folding tables and proceeded to stack them with produce, boxed cereal and other food items. People stood quietly in line until it was their turn to receive a bag of pre-selected food.

No one made any attempt to determine whether the recipients actually needed the food, nor to encourage the recipients to seek other forms of assistance, such as food stamps. The food distribution was an unequivocal act of faith based on generally accepted knowledge that this was a known area of need. The recipients seemed reasonably grateful, but the staff members and volunteers seemed even happier, having been fortified by the belief that their act of benevolence was at least mildly appreciated.

As word spread, the lines got longer until finally the truck was empty. The following week, it returned at the same time, and once again the people were waiting. Only this time there were more of them. It may have been that a donor-recipient co-dependency had developed. Both parties were trapped in an ever-expanding web of immediate gratification that offered the recipients no long-term hope of eventually achieving independence and self-reliance. As the food bank's director told me later, "The more you provide, the more demand there is."

My experience of 25 years in food banking has led me to conclude that co-dependency within the system is multifaceted and frankly troubling. As a system that depends on donated goods, it must curry favor with the nation's food industry, which often regards food banks as a waste-management tool. As an operation that must sort through billions of pounds of damaged and partially salvageable food, it requires an army of volunteers who themselves are dependent on the carefully nurtured belief that they are "doing good" by "feeding the

hungry." And as a charity that lives from one multimillion-dollar capital campaign to the next (most recently, the Hartford food bank raised $4.5 million), it must maintain a ready supply of well-heeled philanthropists and captains of industry to raise the dollars and public awareness necessary to make the next warehouse expansion possible.

Food banks are a dominant institution in this country, and they assert their power at the local and state levels by commanding the attention of people of good will who want to address hunger. Their ability to attract volunteers and to raise money approaches that of major hospitals and universities. While none of this is inherently wrong, it does distract the public and policymakers from the task of harnessing the political will needed to end hunger in the United States.

The risk is that the multibillion-dollar system of food banking has become such a pervasive force in the anti-hunger world, and so tied to its donors and its volunteers, that it cannot step back and ask if this is the best way to end hunger, food insecurity and their root cause, poverty.

During my tenure in Hartford, I often wondered what would happen if the collective energy that went into soliciting and distributing food were put into ending hunger and poverty instead. Surely it would have a sizable impact if 3,000 Hartford-area volunteers, led by some of Connecticut's most privileged and respected citizens, showed up one day at the state legislature, demanding enough resources to end hunger and poverty. Multiply those volunteers by three or four—the number of volunteers in the state's other food banks and hundreds of emergency food sites—and you would have enough people to dismantle the Connecticut state capitol brick by brick. Put all the emergency food volunteers and staff and board members from across the country on buses to Washington, to tell Congress to mandate a living wage, health care for all and adequate employment and child-care programs, and you would have a convoy that might stretch from New York City to our nation's capital.

But what we have done instead is to continue down a road that never comes to an end. Like transportation planners who add more lanes to already clogged highways, we add more space to our food banks in the futile hope of relieving the congestion.

We know hunger's cause—poverty. We know its solution—end poverty. Let this Thanksgiving remind us of that task.

How to write a position argument

These steps for the process of writing a position argument may not progress as neatly as this chart might suggest. Writing is not an assembly-line process.

As you write and revise you may think of additional reasons to support your position. Your instructor and fellow students may give you comments that help you to rethink your argument. Use their comments to work through your paper or project again, strengthening your content and making your writing better organized and more readable.

1 FIND AN ISSUE

- Read your assignment slowly and carefully. Note key words like *argue for* and *take a stand* that indicate the assignment requires a position argument.
- Make a list of possible issues.
- Select a possible issue.
- Read about your issue.
- Analyze your potential readers. What do your readers likely know about the issue? Where are they most likely to disagree with you?

2 DEVELOP REASONS AND A THESIS

- Take a definite position.
- Develop reasons by considering whether you can argue from a definition, compare or contrast, consider good and bad effects, or refute objections.
- Support your reasons by making observations and finding facts, statistics, and statements from authorities.
- Write a working thesis.

3 WRITE A DRAFT

- Introduce the issue and give the necessary background. Explain why the issue is important.
- Think about how readers will view you, the writer.
- If you argue from a definition, set out the criteria.
- Avoid fallacies.
- Provide evidence to support your main points.
- Address opposing views. Summarize opposing positions and explain why your position is preferable.
- Make counterarguments if necessary. Examine the facts and assumptions on which competing claims are based.
- Conclude with strength. Avoid merely summarizing. Emphasize the importance of your argument and possibly make an additional point or draw implications.
- Choose a title that will interest readers.

4 REVISE, REVISE, REVISE

- Check that your position argument fulfills the assignment.
- Make sure that your claim is arguable and focused.
- Check your reasons and add more if you can.
- Add additional evidence where reasons need more support.
- Examine the organization.
- Review the visual presentation.
- Proofread carefully.

5 SUBMITTED VERSION

- Make sure your finished writing meets all formatting requirements.

1: Find an issue

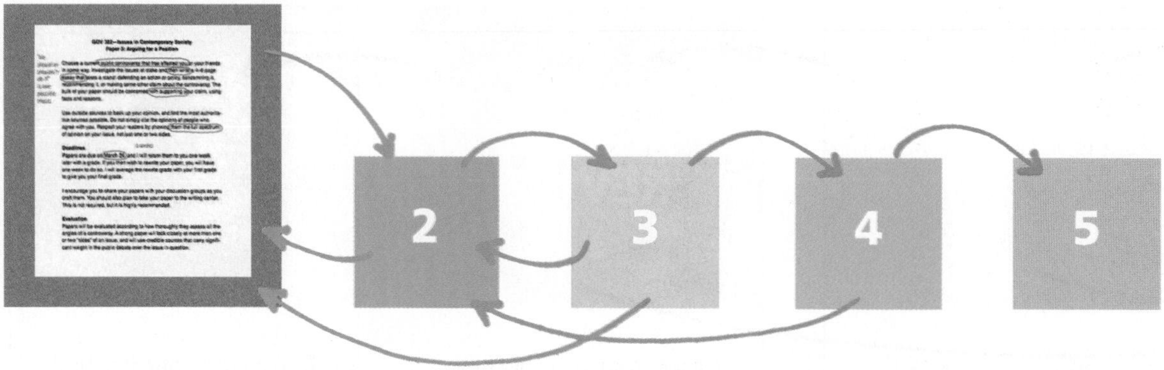

Analyze the assignment

- Read your assignment slowly and carefully. Look for key words like *argue for, take a stand,* and *write on a controversial issue.* These key words tell you that you are writing a position argument.
- Note any information about the length specified, date due, formatting, and other requirements. You can attend to this information later. At this point you want to give your attention to finding an issue if one is not specified.

Make a list of possible campus issues

Think about issues that are debated on your campus such as these.

- Should smoking be banned on campus?
- Should varsity athletes get paid for playing sports that bring in revenue?
- Should admissions decisions be based exclusively on academic achievement?
- Should knowledge of a foreign language be required for all degree plans?
- Should fraternities be banned from campuses if they are caught encouraging alcohol abuse?

Make a list of possible community issues

Think about issues that are debated in your community such as these.

- Should people who ride bicycles and motorcycles be required to wear helmets?
- Should high schools be allowed to search students for drugs at any time?
- Should bilingual education programs be eliminated?
- Should bike lanes be built throughout your community to encourage more people to ride bicycles?
- Should more tax dollars be shifted from building highways to public transportation?

Make a list of possible national and international issues

Think about national and international issues such as these.

- Should advertising be banned on television shows aimed at preschool children?
- Should the Internet be censored?
- Should the government be allowed to monitor all phone calls and all email to combat terrorism?
- Should handguns be outlawed?
- Should people who are terminally ill be allowed to end their lives?
- Should the United States punish nations with poor human rights records?

Read about your issue

- What are the major points of view on your issue?
- Who are the experts on this issue? What do they have to say?
- What major claims are being offered?
- What reasons are given to support the claims?
- What kinds of evidence are used to support the reasons?

Analyze your potential readers

- For whom does this issue matter? Whose interests are at stake?
- What attitudes and beliefs will your readers likely have about this issue?
- What key terms will you need to define or explain?
- What assumptions do you have in common with your readers?
- Where will your readers most likely disagree with you?

Write Now

Choose an issue that you care about

1. Make a list of issues that fulfill your assignment.
2. Put a checkmark beside the issues that look most interesting to write about or the ones that mean the most to you.
3. Put a question mark beside the issues that you don't know very much about. If you choose one of these issues, you will probably have to do in-depth research—by talking to people, by using the Internet, or by going to the library.
4. Select a possible issue. What is your stand on this issue? Write nonstop for five minutes about why this issue is important and how it affects you.

Writer at work

Chris Nguyen received a writing assignment in her government class, and made the following notes on her assignment sheet.

GOV 322—Issues in Contemporary Society
Paper 3: Arguing for a Position

"We should or shouldn't do X" is one possible thesis.

Choose a current public controversy that has affected you or your friends in some way. Investigate the issues at stake and then write a 4–6 page essay that takes a stand: defending an action or policy, condemning it, recommending it, or making some other claim about the controversy. The bulk of your paper should be concerned with supporting your claim, using facts and reasons.

Use outside sources to back up your opinion, and find the most authoritative sources possible. Do not simply cite the opinions of people who agree with you. Respect your readers by showing them the full spectrum of opinion on your issue, not just one or two sides.

Deadlines

2 weeks

Papers are due on March 24, and I will return them to you one week later with a grade. If you then wish to rewrite your paper, you will have one week to do so. I will average the rewrite grade with your first grade to give you your final grade.

I encourage you to share your papers with your discussion groups as you draft them. You should also plan to take your paper to the writing center. This is not required, but it is highly recommended.

Evaluation

Papers will be evaluated according to how thoroughly they assess all the angles of a controversy. A strong paper will look closely at more than one or two "sides" of an issue, and will use credible sources that carry significant weight in the public debate over the issue in question.

Read the assignment closely
Chris Nguyen began by marking information about due dates and requirements. She noted her instructor's suggestion that students might phrase their thesis in a particular way. She also wrote down her teacher's advice to avoid oversimplifying the controversy.

Choose a topic
Chris made a list of potential topics for her paper. She began by thinking of controversies she had talked about with her friends in the recent past. She chose to write about a recent event on campus, in which a number of students had been ejected from a public talk because they were wearing T-shirts critical of the speaker.

Explore the issue
Chris looked for news articles about similar events, and court proceedings that followed. As she researched, she made a list of events she wanted to compare to the event at her school. She also found references to a number of court cases, which she researched as well.

Identify key terms
Chris compiled a list of key terms to help her think about her issue.

POSSIBLE TOPICS

Should military recruiting on campus be allowed if the military discriminates against gays? What is college's responsibility to students/country?

Peer-to-peer music downloading—should it be legal?

Students thrown out of speech for wearing T-shirts—violation of free speech?

<u>NOTES</u>
Two people wearing anti-Bush T-shirts at a rally at the West Virginia Capitol were arrested for trespassing, but charges were dropped.

High school student sent home from school for wearing a T-shirt with the word "redneck" was vindicated by court ruling.

A man is arrested for trespassing in a mall for wearing a shirt he had bought there reading "Give peace a chance."

1969 Tinker v. Des Moines ISD
Supreme Court: In order to censor, a high school must show evidence of substantial disruption as a result of speech, or invasion of others' rights.

1969 Brandenburg v. Ohio
Supreme Court: to prohibit speech, it must be "directed at inciting or producing imminent lawless action" or "likely to incite or produce such action."

1986 Bethel v. Fraser
Supreme Court: vulgar speech can be prohibited at a school assembly.

1988 Hazelwood School District v. Kuhlmeier
Supreme Court: school-sponsored speech (like school papers) can be censored.

What is free speech?
What is an invasion of someone else's rights?
What is a "substantial disruption"?
What is vulgar speech?
What is school-sponsored speech? [what about protest of it?]
What is "socially inappropriate behavior"?

2: Develop reasons and a thesis

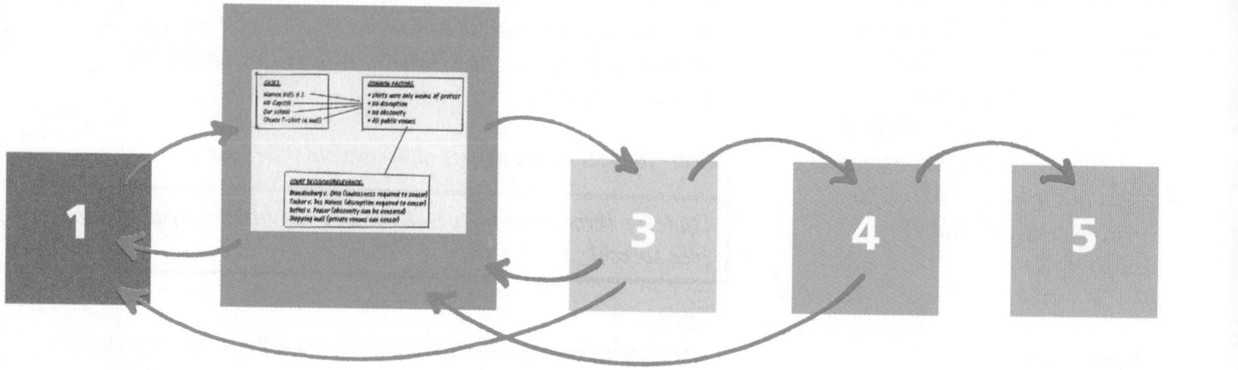

Take a definite position

- Why do you take this position? Write down the first things you think of that form your thinking on this issue.

Develop reasons

- Can you argue from a definition? Is ____ a _____? Are cheerleaders athletes? Are zoos guilty of cruelty to animals?
- Can you compare and contrast? Is ____ like or unlike ____? Should health care in the United States be more like health care in Canada? Is the war in Iraq like the Vietnam War?
- Can you argue that good things will result from your position or bad things can be avoided? Is ecotourism the long-term answer to preserving endangered rain forests?
- Can you refute objections to your position?

Support your reasons

- Can you support your reasons by going to a site and making observations?
- Can you find facts to support your reasons?
- Can you find statistics to support your reasons?
- Can you find statements from authorities to support your reasons?

Write a working thesis

- Is your thesis arguable? Statements of fact are not arguable unless the facts are disputed.

  NOT ARGUABLE: The population of the United States grew faster in the 1990s than in any previous decade because Congress increased the level of legal immigration and the government stopped enforcing most laws against illegal immigration in the interior of the country.

  ARGUABLE: Allowing a high rate of immigration helps the United States deal with the problems of an increasingly aging society and helps provide funding for millions of Social Security recipients.

  ARGUABLE: The increase in the number of visas to foreign workers in technology industries is the major cause of unemployment in those industries.

- Is your thesis specific? A thesis may be arguable but too broad to be treated adequately in a short paper.

  ARGUABLE, BUT TOO BROAD: We should take action to resolve the serious traffic problem in our city.

  ARGUABLE AND FOCUSED: The existing freight railway that runs through the center of the city should be converted to a passenger railway because it is the cheapest and most quickly implemented way to decrease traffic congestion downtown.

Staying on Track

Evaluate your thesis

Once you have a working thesis, ask these questions:

1. Is it arguable?
2. Is it specific?
3. Is it manageable in the length and time you have?
4. Is it interesting to your intended readers?

OFF TRACK

Over 60% of Americans play video games on a regular basis.

ARGUABLE? The thesis states a commonly acknowledged fact.

SPECIFIC? The thesis is a bland general statement.

MANAGEABLE? A known fact is stated in the thesis, so there is little to research. Several surveys report this finding.

INTERESTING? Video games are interesting as a cultural trend, but nearly everyone is aware of the trend.

ON TRACK

Video games are valuable because they improve children's visual attention skills, their literacy skills, and their computer literacy skills.

ARGUABLE? The thesis takes a position contrary to the usual view of video games.

SPECIFIC? The thesis gives specific reasons for the claim.

MANAGEABLE? The thesis is manageable if research can be located and observations of game playing included.

INTERESTING? The topic is interesting because it challenges conventional wisdom.

Writer at work

I believe school administrators were wrong to eject the students wearing T-shirts.

HOW TO ARGUE?????

Chris Nguyen knew how she felt, but she didn't know at first how to make a convincing case. She read more about events similar to the one that happened on her campus, and she became convinced that her school's administrators had acted improperly, and perhaps illegally, in ejecting the students. She examined the cases she had researched and drew an idea map.

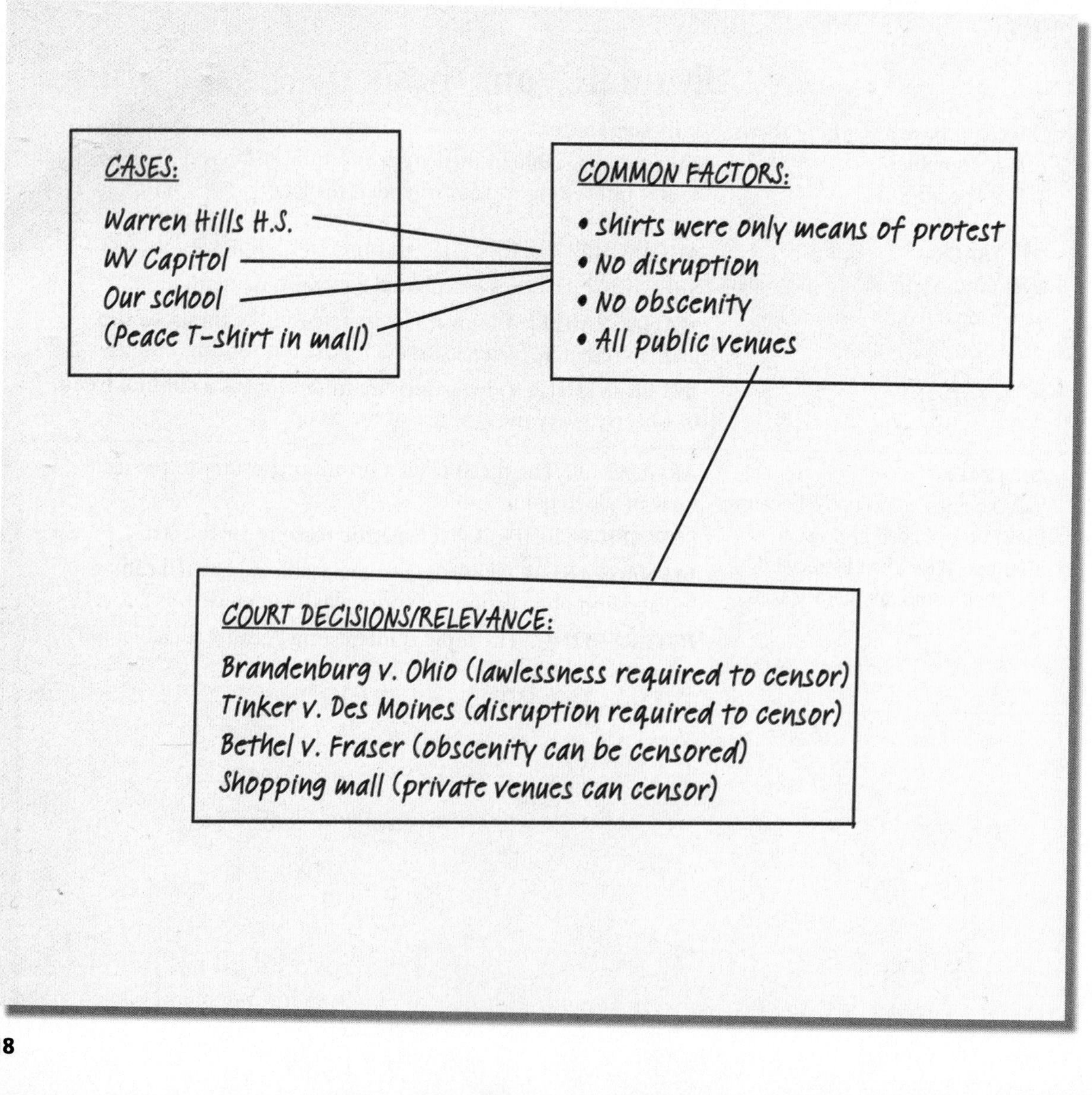
CASES:
Warren Hills H.S.
WV Capitol
Our school
(Peace T-shirt in mall)
COMMON FACTORS:
• shirts were only means of protest
• No disruption
• No obscenity
• All public venues
COURT DECISIONS/RELEVANCE:
Brandenburg v. Ohio (lawlessness required to censor)
Tinker v. Des Moines (disruption required to censor)
Bethel v. Fraser (obscenity can be censored)
Shopping mall (private venues can censor)

Chris used the idea map to define the conditions in which speech can be restricted.

CRITERIA FOR FREE SPEECH
- Cannot incite violence
- Cannot threaten violence
- Cannot be obscene (although what exactly is obscene isn't clear)
- Only on public property
- Only for adults

Ejecting students would be justified if
- The students were doing something "directed to and likely to incite imminent lawless action" NO
- They used vulgar or obscene language NO
- They were in a private venue NO
- They were minors NO

WORKING THESIS
The college was wrong to eject the six protesting students from last month's speakers' event because the students were not inciting lawless action, did not use vulgar or obscene language, were in a public venue, and were not minors.

Chris's research supported a more specific claim than the one she initially made: that the college was "wrong" to remove the students. She revised her thesis to focus on this stronger and, she thought, more interesting claim. In addition to claiming the students' right to free speech was violated, she argued that her school should apologize to the students involved. Here is the final working thesis Chris used to begin drafting her essay:

The University administration should drop trespassing charges against the six students arrested last month and offer them a formal apology, because their ejection and arrest was a violation of the students' constitutionally protected right to free speech.

3: Write a draft

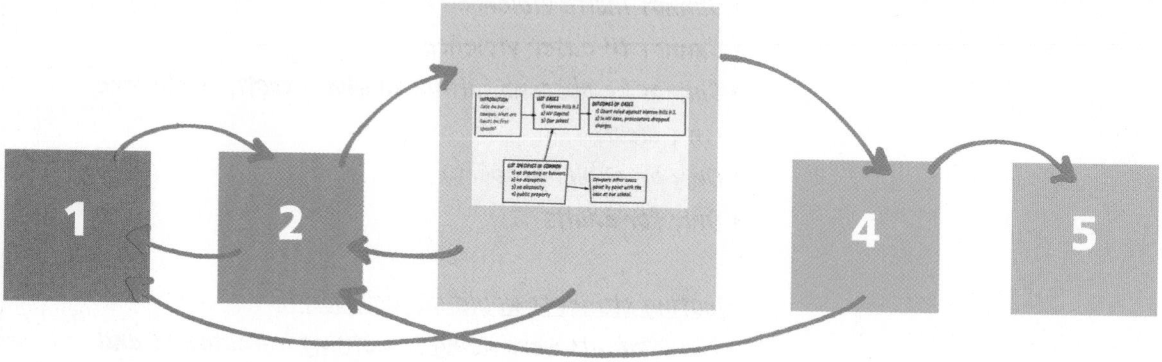

Introduce the issue	• Describe the trend, event, or phenomenon you will be analyzing. • Give your readers any background information they will need.
Think about how readers will view you, the writer	• What group or group will readers consider you a part of? At the very least, they will consider you as a college student. What assumptions will they have about you? • Think about how you can connect with your readers as you write by appealing to their sense of fairness, their core beliefs, and their sense of logic.
If you argue from a definition, set out the criteria	• Which criteria are necessary for _____ to be a _____? • Which are not necessary? • Which are most important? • Does your case in point meet all the necessary criteria?
Avoid fallacies	• Fallacies generally arise from a lack of evidence or faulty evidence. • You can find a list of fallacies on pages 14–15.
Anticipate and address opposing viewpoints	• Acknowledge other stakeholders for the issue, and consider their positions. • Explain why your position is preferable.
Make counterarguments if necessary	• Examine the facts on which a competing claim is based. Are the facts accurate, current, and a representative sample? Are sources treated fairly or taken out of context? • Examine the primary assumption of a claim that you are rejecting. Is the assumption flawed? What other assumptions are involved?

Conclude with strength	• Avoid summarizing what you have just said. • Spell out the importance of the analysis, if you haven't already done so. • Consider additional effects you haven't previously discussed. • Explain any action you think needs to be taken based on your conclusion.
Choose a title that will interest readers	• Make your title specific. • Engage your readers with the issue.

Staying on Track

Facts vs. your opinion

Distinguish facts from opinions

Find facts to support what you think. You may be surprised to find that the facts are not what you anticipated.

OFF TRACK

I believe that Americans have the best medical care in the world.

ON TRACK

On one of the most trusted indicators of health—life expectancy at birth—in 2005 the United States ranks 48th behind nearly all of Europe, Japan, Singapore, Hong Kong, and even countries like Jordan, Cuba, and Costa Rica.

OFF TRACK

It is obvious from watching television news that violent crime is on the rise.

ON TRACK

While violent crime remains the staple of local news, FBI statistics show a 24% drop in violent crimes in the United States between 1995 and 2004.

Writer at work

Chris mapped the ideas she would need to include in her paper.

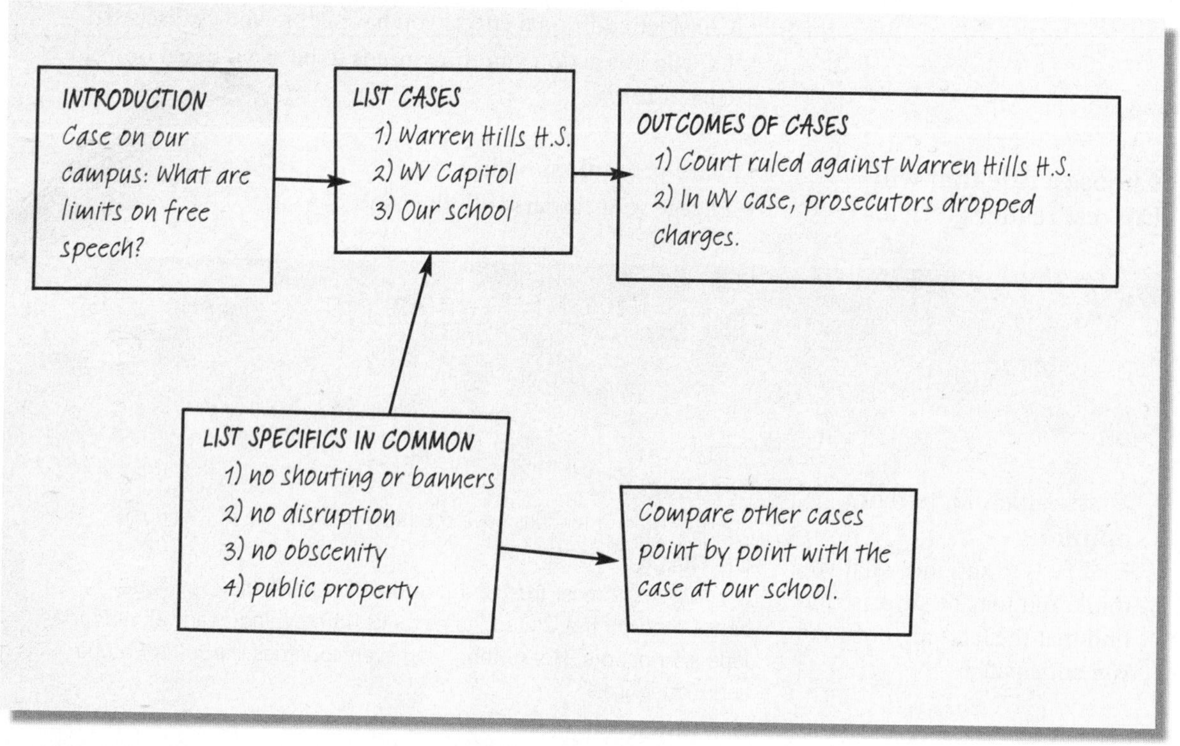
INTRODUCTION
Case on our campus: What are limits on free speech?
LIST CASES
1) Warren Hills H.S.
2) WV Capitol
3) Our school
OUTCOMES OF CASES
1) Court ruled against Warren Hills H.S.
2) In WV case, prosecutors dropped charges.
LIST SPECIFICS IN COMMON
1) no shouting or banners
2) no disruption
3) no obscenity
4) public property
Compare other cases point by point with the case at our school.

Chris began by writing the common factors in the cases because they would be the core of her paper. She would build the rest of the paper around these four factors.

These are the factors the three cases have in common:

1) *In each case, the wearers of the shirts did not express themselves in any way other than by wearing the shirts. They did not speak, shout, hold up banners or signs, or call attention to themselves in any way.*
2) *None of the events were disrupted by the shirts. Any disruption that occurred was due to the removal of the wearers by authority figures.*
3) *None of the T-shirts featured obscene language or imagery.*
4) *All took place in government-funded venues: a public school, a state capitol, and a state-funded university.*

Chris next made a working outline, which she used to write her paper.

1) start with a brief mention of our case where students were ejected

2) describe limits on free speech

3) introduce the three T-shirt cases; end with claim that ejection at our school was unconstitutional

4) list factors that the cases have in common

5) introduce standard of lawless action for restricting free speech

6) discuss the Warren Hills High School case

7) discuss the West Virginia Capitol case

8) discuss the issue of what is offensive or considered obscene

9) compare the West Virginia Capitol incident to our campus because both involve political speech

10) make the distinction between public and private venues

11) point out that all cases were at public venues

12) raise the issue of minors and point out that college students are of legal age

13) conclude with a call for an apology

4: Revise, revise, revise

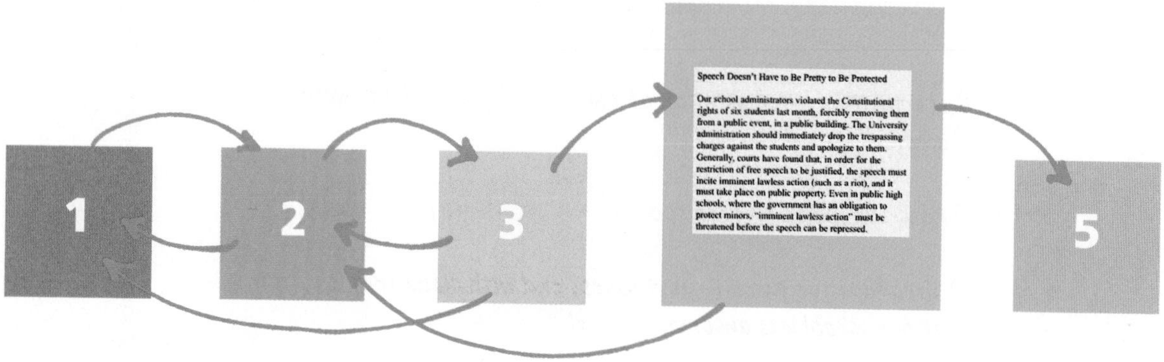

1
2
3
Speech Doesn't Have to Be Pretty to Be Protected
Our school administrators violated the Constitutional rights of six students last month, forcibly removing them from a public event, in a public building. The University administration should immediately drop the trespassing charges against the students and apologize to them. Generally, courts have found that, in order for the restriction of free speech to be justified, the speech must incite imminent lawless action (such as a riot), and it must take place on public property. Even in public high schools, where the government has an obligation to protect minors, "imminent lawless action" must be threatened before the speech can be repressed.
5

Skilled writers know that the secret to writing well is rewriting. Even the best writers often have to revise several times to get the result they want. You also must have effective strategies for revising if you're going to be successful. The biggest trap you can fall into is starting off with the little stuff first. Leave the small stuff for last.

Does your position argument fulfill the assignment?

- Look again at your assignment. Does your paper or project do what the assignment asks?
- Look again at the assignment for specific guidelines, including length, format, and amount of research. Does your work meet these guidelines?

Is your claim arguable and focused?

- Is your position arguable? Statements of fact and statements of religious belief are not arguable.
- Can you make your claim more specific to avoid ambiguous language and situations where your claim may not apply?

Are your reasons adequate?

- Are your reasons clear to your readers?
- Can you add additional reasons to strengthen your argument?
- Have you acknowledged the views of people who disagree with your position?
- Have you shown how your position is preferable?

Are your reasons supported with evidence?

- Have you found the most accurate information available about your issue?
- Can you find additional evidence in the form of examples, quotations from experts, statistics, comparisons, and on-site observations?

Is your organization effective?

- Are your reasons in the best possible order?
- Do you get off to a fast start with your title and introduction? Can you do more to gain and keep the reader's interest?
- Is your conclusion only a summary of what you have said? If so, can you think of an implication or an example that gets at the heart of the issue?

Is the writing project visually effective?

- Is the font attractive and readable?
- Are the headings and visuals effective?
- If you use images or tables as part of your analysis, are they legible and appropriately placed? Do you have captions for each?

Save the editing for last.

When you have finished revising, edit and proofread carefully.

A peer review guide is on page 27.

Writer at work

Chris Nguyen took her first draft of the essay to her school's writing center. In particular, she asked to discuss the paper's opening, which she felt was too abrupt. The consultant at the writing center suggested that one possible strategy was to move the thesis statement to the end of the introductory section. Chris found this change worked well for her essay, giving her claim more weight.

Chris had her thesis in the second sentence in her first draft. Moving it to the end of the introductory section allowed her to explain the issue of restricting free speech before announcing her position. Her revised paper begins on the next page.

Speech Doesn't Have to Be Pretty to Be Protected

Our school administrators violated the Constitutional rights of six students last month, forcibly removing them from a public event, in a public building. The University administration should immediately drop the trespassing charges against the students and apologize to them. Generally, courts have found that, in order for the restriction of free speech to be justified, the speech must incite imminent lawless action (such as a riot), and it must take place on public property. Even in public high schools, where the government has an obligation to protect minors, "imminent lawless action" must be threatened before the speech can be repressed.

5: Submitted version

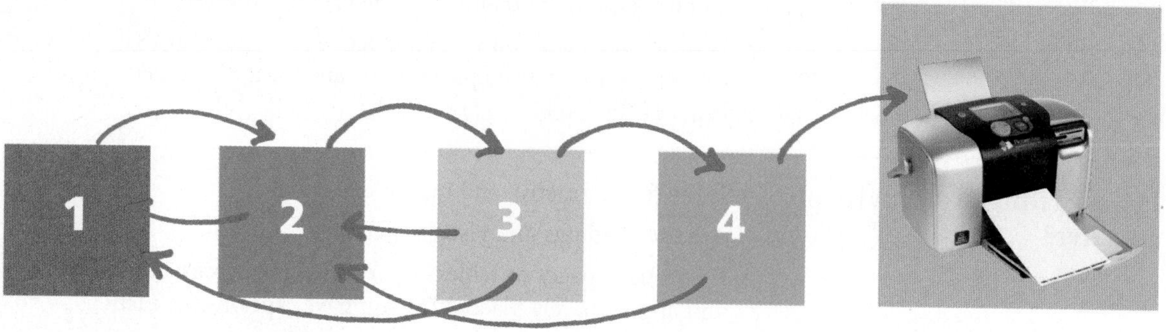

Nguyen 1

Chris Nguyen
Professor Conley
GOV 322
24 March 2008

Speech Doesn't Have to Be Pretty to Be Protected

Last month six students on our campus were ejected from a university auditorium for wearing T-shirts with "war criminal" on the front. Was the university justified in removing our fellow students who were not disruptive in any other way?

The First Amendment to the Constitution of the United States of America guarantees the right to freedom of expression. This important right is one of the foundations of our democracy. Yet many Americans do not understand what the right to free speech really means. Free speech is your right to say what you think—within limits. It is not the right to cause mayhem, or to threaten violence, or to incite others to violence. Authority figures also need to understand the limits on free speech. Generally, courts have found that, in order for the restriction of free speech to be justified, the speech must incite imminent lawless action (such as a riot), and it must take place on public property. Even in public high schools, where the government has an obligation to protect minors, "imminent lawless action" must be threatened before the speech can be repressed.

Nguyen 2

Clearly, it's not always easy to tell when restriction of free speech is justified. Consider these recent controversies over free speech:

- A student at Warren Hills Regional High School in New Jersey was suspended for wearing a T-shirt that featured the word "redneck" ("Federal Court").
- Jeff and Nicole Rank attended an official visit by President Bush at the West Virginia Capitol and were charged with trespassing when they refused to remove T-shirts that read "Love America, Hate Bush" (Bundy).
- Six students were removed from a university auditorium and charged with trespassing during a speech by former U.S. Secretary of State, Henry Kissinger, for wearing T-shirts that referred to the speaker as a "war criminal."

In the first two cases, it has been established that authorities did not have the right to curtail the speech of the people involved: a federal appeals court decided the first case in favor of the student, and the prosecutor in the second case dropped the charges, admitting that no law had been broken. If we examine the similarities and differences among these three cases, it becomes clear that in the third case, which happened on our own campus last month, the administration's ejection of the students was unconstitutional.

These are the factors the three cases have in common:

1. In each case, the wearers of the shirts did not express themselves in any way other than by wearing the shirts. They did not speak, shout, hold up banners or signs, or call attention to themselves in any way.
2. None of the events where the shirts were worn were disrupted by the shirts. Any disruption that occurred was due to the removal of the wearers by authority figures.
3. None of the T-shirts featured obscene language or imagery.
4. All took place in government-funded venues: a public school, a state capitol, and a state-funded university.

Nguyen 3

These similarities are important because they show how, in each case, the T-shirt wearers acted within their constitutionally protected right to free expression.

The first two factors above show how each of these cases fails to meet the standard of "imminent lawless action," set in the 1969 case of Brandenburg v. Ohio. In that case, the Supreme Court ruled that in order to ban forms of expression, the government had to prove the expression was "directed to and likely to incite imminent lawless action." If the act of expression did not seem likely to cause a riot, for example, it could not be restricted. Simply making people angry or uncomfortable is not justification for censorship.

In the first case, at Warren Hills High School, the only person who objected to the "redneck" T-shirt was a vice principal, who claimed the term "redneck" was offensive to minority students and violated the school's racial harassment policy ("Federal Court"). The U.S. Court of Appeals for the Third Circuit, however, ruled that the school failed to prove "that the shirt might genuinely threaten disruption or, indeed, that it violated any of the particular provisions of the harassment policy." This decision followed the precedent of another landmark case, Tinker v. Des Moines, in which the Supreme Court ruled that, even in public schools, the government must provide evidence that the speech would cause "(a.) a substantial disruption of the school environment, or (b.) an invasion of the rights of others" (Haynes).

In the second case, the government never even made a claim that the T-shirts worn by Jeff and Nicole Rank were inciting lawlessness. The only people who were upset by the Ranks' T-shirts were two Secret Service officers, who ordered the couple to remove the shirts. When they refused, the officers ordered Charleston city police to arrest them, which the police did. The Ranks were charged with trespassing ("Secret Service"). The irony of arresting U.S. citizens for standing peacefully on public, state-owned property was even clear to the prosecutor, who dropped the charges (Bundy).

Moreover, none of the cases met the test for "vulgar or obscene" language. Vulgar and obscene language can be regulated, to some extent, without violating the First Amendment. In 1986, the Supreme Court ruled in the case of Bethel v. Fraser that public school officials could prohibit vulgar speech at a school assembly. The

court said that "[T]he undoubted freedom to advocate unpopular and controversial views in schools and classrooms must be balanced against the society's countervailing interest in teaching students the boundaries of socially appropriate behavior." The vice principal in the Warren Hills Case was the only one who thought "redneck" was offensive, and the fact that the word is used constantly on television and other media shows that it is not considered obscene by society at large.

The Ranks' arrest is a better comparison to the situation at our school, because their shirts were clearly singled out for their political content, not for vulgarity. They carried a message that might have been offensive to some of the supporters of the president who were present, but under no circumstances could the content of the shirts be considered obscene. The same is true of the shirts that got my fellow students kicked out of a public event. Calling someone a war criminal is a serious accusation, but it is not obscene.

Finally, public versus private venue is an important factor in the protection of free speech. The Constitution guarantees that the state will not infringe the right to free expression. Private entities are free to do so, however. For example, protestors can be thrown out of a private meeting of club members. Even a shopping mall owner can deny entry to protesters or even people without shoes. Of course, anyone with private property also has to consider the economic impact of limiting speech. Recently a shopping mall owner had police arrest a man wearing a "Give Peace a Chance" T-shirt ("Man Arrested") that he had just bought in the mall. Not surprisingly, the mall owner received a great deal of bad publicity about this decision. Concerned citizens who felt this action by the mall owner went too far wrote letters to newspapers publicizing the act. They even wrote letters to the police who arrested the man ("Big Support"). The trespassing charges against the man were dropped. This incident illustrates how free speech is negotiated in the marketplace.

In the Ranks' case, the trespassing charges against them were dropped because they were on the statehouse grounds. How can a citizen trespass on public property? In the same vein, how can students be trespassing on their own campus? The six people arrested at our school were students, whose tuition and fees helped pay for the building they were in. What's more, the event was advertised in flyers and

Nguyen 5

newspaper ads as "free and open to the public." How can anyone be charged with trespassing at a public event?

The Warren Hills case was decided in favor of the student, even though the expression took place in a public school. As Bethel v. Fraser shows, courts generally feel that schools can take special steps to protect minors: vulgar or obscene speech can be censored, and school-sponsored forms of expression, like newspapers, can be censored. But these actions are justified because the students are minors. Presumably, they need more guidance as they learn about the boundaries of socially acceptable behavior. But most if not all college students are legally adults, so it does not make sense to say our school was "teaching students the boundaries of socially appropriate behavior" by throwing them out of a public event because of their shirts. It is not the job of a college administration to teach manners.

Our school administrators violated the Constitutional rights of six students last month. They forcibly removed them from a public event, in a public building. The students were not causing a commotion in any way before their arrests; there was no indication whatsoever that "imminent lawless action" might be provoked by their T-shirts. Because the students in this case were clearly exercising their Constitutional right to free speech, the university administration should immediately drop the trespassing charges against the students. Evidence from prior cases indicates the charges will not stand up in court in any case, so the legal battle will be a waste of money for the college. Furthermore, as an institution of learning that supposedly safeguards the free exchange of ideas, the college should offer a sincere apology to the arrested students. The administrators would send an important message to all students by doing this: Your right to free speech is respected at this school.

Nguyen 6

Works Cited

Bethel School Dist. v. Fraser. 478 US 675. Supreme Court of the US. 1986. *Supreme Court Collection.* Legal Information Inst., Cornell U Law School, n.d. Web. 7 Mar. 2008.

"Big Support for 'Peace' T-shirt Arrestees." *The Smoking Gun*. Turner Entertainment Digital Network, 25 Mar. 2003. Web. 10 Mar. 2008.

Brandenburg v. Ohio. 395 US 444. Supreme Court of the US. 1969. *Supreme Court Collection*. Legal Information Inst., Cornell U Law School, n.d. Web. 7 Mar. 2008.

Bundy, Jennifer. "Trespass Charges Dropped Against Bush Protesters." *CommonDreams.org Newscenter*. CommonDreams.org, 15 Jul. 2004. Web. 18 Mar. 2008.

"Federal Court Says NJ School Can't Ban Redneck T-shirt." *Center for Individual Rights*. Center for Individual Rights, 6 Nov. 2003. Web. 11 Mar. 2008.

Haynes, Charles C. "T-shirt Rebellion in the Land of the Free." *First Amendment*. First Amendment Center, 14 Mar. 2004. Web. 18 Mar. 2008.

"Man Arrested for 'Peace' T-shirt." *CNN.com*. Cable News Network, 4 Mar. 2003. Web. 15 Mar. 2008.

"Secret Service and White House Charged with Violating Free Speech Rights in ACLU Lawsuit." *ACLU*. American Civil Liberties Union, 14 Sep. 2004. Web. 19 Mar. 2008.

Projects

Much of what passes for position arguments on television talk shows and on talk radio is little more than shouted assertions and name calling. Arguments in writing are different in character. They are not merely statements of someone's opinion, but are reasoned arguments backed by evidence. They aim not to get in the last word but rather to advance the discussion on an issue so that all benefit from hearing different points of view. These projects are frequently written kinds of position arguments.

Position argument

Make a position claim on a controversial issue. See pages 312–313 for help on identifying an issue.

Think about what's at stake. Would everyone agree with you? Then your claim probably isn't interesting or important. If you can think of people who would disagree, then something is at stake.

Identify the key term. Often position arguments depend on the definition of the key term. What criteria are necessary for something to meet this definition? How would others benefit from a different definition?

Analyze your potential readers. How does the claim you are making affect them? How familiar are they with the issue? How likely will they be to accept your claim or the definition that underlies your claim?

Write an essay on a controversial issue that takes a stand supported by developed reasons.

Rebuttal argument

Identify a position argument to argue against. What is its main claim or claims? A fair summary of your opponent's position should be included in your finished rebuttal.

Examine the facts on which the claim is based. Are the facts accurate? Are the facts current? Can the statistics be interpreted differently? How reliable are the author's sources?

Analyze the assumptions on which the claim is based. What is the primary assumption of the claim you are rejecting? What are the secondary assumptions? How are these assumptions flawed? What fallacies does the author commit (see pages 14–15)?

Consider your readers. To what extent do your potential readers support the claim you are rejecting? If they strongly support that claim, then how do you get them to change their minds? What beliefs and assumptions do you share with them?

Write a rebuttal. Make your aim clear in your thesis statement. Identify the issue you are writing about and give background information if the issue is likely to be unfamiliar to your readers. Question the evidence and show the flaws in the argument you are rejecting. Conclude on a strong note with your counterargument or counterproposal.

Narrative position argument

Think about an experience you have had that makes an implicit causal argument. Have you ever experienced being stereotyped? Have you ever had to jump through many unnecessary bureaucratic hoops? Have you ever been treated differently because of your perceived level of income? Have you ever experienced unfair application of laws and law enforcement?

How common is your experience? If other people have similar experiences, probably what happened to you will ring true.

Describe the experience in detail. When did it happen? How old were you? Why were you there? Who else was there? Where did it happen? If the place is important, describe what it looked like.

Reflect on the significance of the event. How did you feel about the experience when it happened? How do you feel about the experience now? What long-term effects has it had on your life?

Write an essay. You might need to give some background, but if the story is compelling, often it is best to jump right in. Let the story do most of the work. Avoid drawing a simple moral lesson. Your readers should feel the same way you do if you tell your story well.

13 Proposal Arguments

Proposal arguments aim to convince others to take action for change (or not to take action).

CHAPTER CONTENTS

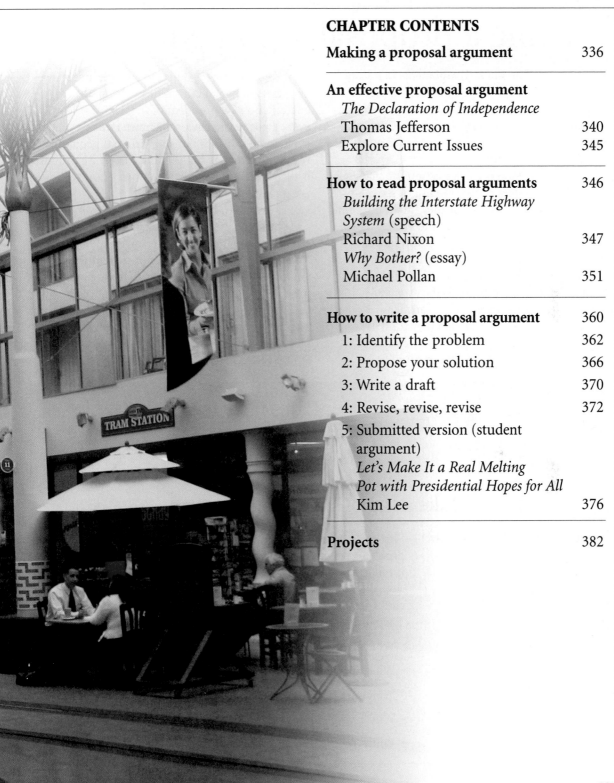

Making a proposal argument

Every day we hear and read arguments that some action should be taken. We even make these arguments to ourselves: We should exercise more; we should change our work habits. We can make many changes in our lives if we convince ourselves that the effort is worth it.

Convincing others to take action for change is always harder. Other people might not see the same problem that you see or they might not think that the problem is important. And even if they do see the same problem and think it is important, they may not want to commit the time and resources to do something about it. In the short term, at least, doing nothing is the easy choice. Nevertheless, most people aren't satisfied with doing nothing about a problem they think is important. We are impatient when we believe something is wrong or something could be improved. We expect things to change; indeed, we have even designed our political system to guarantee a new president of the nation at least every eight years. The problem we face in persuading others is not so much that people are resistant to change but that the change we propose is the right one and worthy of their effort to make it happen.

Every major construction project, every large-scale product, every major scientific endeavor starts with an argument for change—an argument to do something that we are not currently doing and to take action. Arguments for change can even involve changing an entire government (think of the Declaration of Independence). These kinds of arguments are called proposal arguments, and they take the classic form: *We should (or should not) do SOMETHING.*

Working Together

Make a list of problems to solve

In a group of three or four students

First make a list of all the things you can think of that are problems: your library closes too early for late-night study, there is too little work-study aid on your campus, your roommate is a slob, the weather stays too hot or too cold for too long, store clerks are rude, and on and on. Share your list with the group. Then discuss the following.

- Which items turned up on more than one list?
- Which problems are the most important?
- Which are possible to solve?
- Which problems are the most interesting to your group?
- Which problems are the least interesting to your group?

Understand how proposal arguments work

Proposal argumants call for some action to be taken (or not taken). The challenge for writers is to convince readers that they should take action, which usually involves their commitment of effort or money.

Someone should (or should not) do something because __________.

EXAMPLE

We should convert existing train tracks in the downtown area to a light-rail system and build a new freight track around the city because we need to relieve traffic and parking congestion downtown.

Components of proposal arguments

What exactly is the problem?

Identify the problem. Sometimes, problems are evident to your intended readers. If your city is constantly tearing up the streets and then leaving them for months without doing anything to repair them, then you shouldn't have much trouble convincing the citizens of your city that streets should be repaired more quickly. But if you raise a problem that will be unfamiliar to most of your readers, you will first have to argue that the problem exists and it is in their interest that something should be done about it.

What is my solution?

State your proposed solution. You need to have a clear, definite statement of exactly what you are proposing. Say exactly what you want others to do. You might want to place this statement near the beginning of your argument, or later, after you have considered and rejected other possible solutions.

VAGUE:
Our city should encourage all citizens to conserve water.

SPECIFIC:
Our city should provide incentives to conserve water, including offering rain barrels for the minimal cost of $10, replacing at no cost old toilets with water-efficient toilets, and providing rebates up to $500 to those who replace grass with plants that require little water.

Will my solution work?

Convince your readers that your solution will work. When your readers agree that a problem exists and a solution should be found, your next task is to convince them that your solution is the best one to resolve the problem. Many college campuses suffer from transportation and parking problems. If your campus is one of them, then your readers likely will agree that the problems exist. The question is what to do about them. One possible solution is to add a light-rail line to campus from your city's planned light-rail system. If you argue for adding a light-rail line, you must project how many people will ride it and how many car trips will be reduced.

Why is my solution better than others?

Show why your solution is better than other possible solutions. An obvious solution to a lack of parking is to build a parking garage. But parking garages also cost money, and they might even encourage more people to drive, further aggravating the traffic problem. Another solution is to provide more buses, which would not require building a light-rail line and likely would be cheaper. You must argue why rail would be preferable.

Will people be willing to implement my solution?

Demonstrate that your solution is feasible. Your solution not only has to work; it must have a realistic chance of being implemented. Can we afford it? Will it take too long to do? Will people accept it? What else might not get done? A light-rail link might be ideal for getting students to and from campus, but it would cost a great deal of money to construct. The rail proposal is feasible only if you have a concrete proposal for how it would be funded.

How can I convince my readers?

Focus on the audience. All effective writing attends to the audience, but in no form of writing is the audience more important than in arguments for change. Readers have to be convinced that "we really have a problem, and we need to do something about it." It's not enough just to get readers to agree that the problem exists. They have to believe that the problem is worth solving.

Arguments for light rail include reducing traffic, reducing air pollution, and encouraging the develoment of neighborhoods near rail routes.

Keys to proposal arguments

Convince readers that you can be trusted	To gain the trust of your readers, you first must convince them that you are well informed. You also must convince them that you are fair and sincere and that your heart is in the right place. Readers think favorably of good writers. Poor writers lose readers on all counts, even with the same ideas as a good writer.
Convince your readers that you have their best interests in mind	At the outset many readers may not have much interest in the problem you identify. If you are proposing adding bike lanes to streets in your city, you likely will need the support of people who will never use them. You could argue that if more people rode bicycles, there would be more parking places for those who drive and less air pollution for everyone.
Convince your readers with evidence	You may need a great deal of evidence for a problem that is unfamiliar to your readers. Statistics are often helpful in establishing that a problem affects many people. Likewise, you will need evidence that your solution will work and that it can be accomplished.
Emphasize what you have in common with your readers and be honest about differences	You may not share the assumptions and beliefs of your audience. Think about what may separate you from your audience and what you have in common. When you can establish common ground with your readers because you live in the same community, have similar goals, or share experiences, then you can be frank about any differences you might have. Readers appreciate honesty.
Show exactly how your proposal will have good consequences and possibly reduce bad consequences	Predicting the future is never easy. Think about how your proposal can make good things happen or reduce bad things. Has a solution similar to the one that you are proposing been tried elsewhere? Can you connect to other good consequences? For example, saving water also saves the energy required to run a water treatment plant and to pump it to a home or business.
End with strength	Remember that you want your readers to take action. If you have a powerful example, use it in the conclusion. Inspire your readers to want something better than the status quo. Leave them with a strong impression.

An effective proposal argument

Readers have to be motivated to take action to solve a problem.

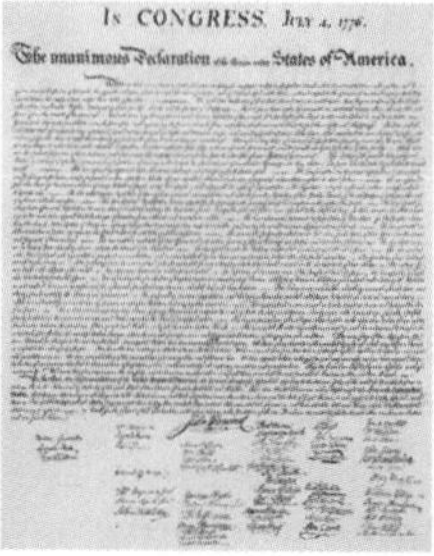
IN CONGRESS, JULY 4, 1776.
The unanimous Declaration of the thirteen united States of America.

The Declaration of Independence

Thomas Jefferson

The American Revolution had already begun with the battles of Lexington, Concord, and Bunker Hill, and George Washington had been named to head the colonial army by June 7, 1776, when the Continental Congress moved to draft a Declaration of Independence. Thomas Jefferson was given eighteen days to complete the task with the help of Benjamin Franklin and John Adams.

IN CONGRESS, JULY 4, 1776.

The unanimous Declaration of the thirteen united States of America,

When, in the Course of human events, it becomes necessary for one people to dissolve the political bands which have connected them with another, and to assume among the powers of the earth, the separate and equal station to which the laws of nature and of nature's God entitle them, a decent respect to the opinions of mankind requires that they should declare the causes which impel them to the separation.

Jefferson maintains that the drastic solution of declaring independence is justified if the problem is of great magnitude.

We hold these truths to be self-evident: That all men are created equal; that they are endowed by their Creator with certain unalienable rights; that among these are life, liberty and the pursuit of happiness. That, to secure these rights, governments are instituted among men, deriving their just powers from the consent of the governed; that, whenever any form of government becomes destructive of these ends, it is the right of the people to alter or to abolish it, and to institute new Government, laying its foundation on such principles, and organizing its powers in such form, as to them shall seem most likely to effect their safety and happiness. Prudence,

The rationale for the proposal is a definition argument. According to Jefferson, the purpose of a government is to ensure the rights of the governed. When a government fails to achieve its defined purpose—to ensure the rights of the people—the people have the right to abolish it. The British used similar arguments to justify the revolution against King James II in 1688.

indeed, will dictate that governments long established should not be changed for light and transient causes; and accordingly all experience hath shown, that mankind are more disposed to suffer, while evils are sufferable, than to right themselves by abolishing the forms to which they are accustomed. But when a long train of abuses and usurpations, pursuing invariably the same object evinces a design to reduce them under absolute despotism, it is their right, it is their duty, to throw off such government and to provide new guards for their future security. Such has been the patient sufferance of these colonies, and such is now the necessity which constrains them to alter their former systems of government. The history of the present king of Great Britain is a history of repeated injuries and usurpations, all having in direct object the establishment of an absolute tyranny over these States. To prove this, let facts be submitted to a candid world.

He has refused his assent to laws, the most wholesome and necessary for the public good.

He has forbidden his governors to pass laws of immediate and pressing importance, unless suspended in their operation till his Assent should be obtained, and, when so suspended, he has utterly neglected to attend to them.

The burden for Jefferson is to convince others of the severity of the problem—that life is intolerable under the King. He goes on to detail a long list of complaints. His goal is to prove the need for change rather than to outline how the solution will work.

He has refused to pass other laws for the accommodation of large districts of people, unless those people would relinquish the right of representation in the legislature–a right inestimable to them and formidable to tyrants only.

He has called together legislative bodies at places unusual, uncomfortable, and distant from the depository of their public Records, for the sole purpose of fatiguing them into compliance with his measures.

He has dissolved representative houses repeatedly, for opposing with manly firmness his invasions on the rights of the people.

He has refused for a long time, after such dissolutions, to cause others to be elected; whereby the legislative powers, incapable of annihilation, have returned to the people at large for their exercise; the State remaining in the mean time exposed to all the dangers of invasion from without, and convulsions within.

He has endeavored to prevent the population of these states; for that purpose obstructing the laws for naturalization of foreigners; refusing to pass others to encourage their migrations hither, and raising the conditions of new appropriations of lands.

He has obstructed the administration of justice by refusing his assent to laws for establishing judiciary powers.

He has made judges dependent on his will alone, for the tenure of their offices, and the amount and payment of their salaries.

He has erected a multitude of new offices, and sent hither swarms of officers to harass our people, and eat out their substance.

The legalistic list of charges is made more vivid by the use of metaphors such as "swarms of officers," which likens the British to a plague of insects.

He has kept among us, in times of peace, standing armies without the consent of our legislatures.

He has affected to render the military independent of and superior to the civil power.

He has combined with others to subject us to a jurisdiction foreign to our constitution, and unacknowledged by our laws; giving his assent to their acts of pretended legislation:

For quartering large bodies of armed troops among us;

For protecting them, by a mock trial, from punishment for any murders which they should commit on the inhabitants of these States;

For cutting off our trade with all parts of the world;

For imposing taxes on us without our consent;

For depriving us in many cases, of the benefits of trial by jury;

For transporting us beyond seas to be tried for pretended offences;

For abolishing the free system of English laws in a neighboring province, establishing therein an arbitrary government, and enlarging its boundaries so as to render it at once an example and fit instrument for introducing the same absolute rule into these colonies;

For taking away our charters, abolishing our most valuable laws, and altering fundamentally the forms of our governments;

For suspending our own legislatures, and declaring themselves invested with power to legislate for us in all cases whatsoever.

He has abdicated government here, by declaring us out of his protection and waging war against us.

He has plundered our seas, ravaged our coasts, burnt our towns, and destroyed the lives of our people.

He is at this time transporting large armies of foreign mercenaries to complete the works of death, desolation and tyranny, already begun with circumstances of cruelty and perfidy scarcely paralleled in the most barbarous ages, and totally unworthy the head of a civilized nation.

He has constrained our fellow citizens taken captive on the high seas to bear arms against their country, to become the executioners of their friends and brethren, or to fall themselves by their hands.

The strongest charges against the king are placed at the end of the list.

He has excited domestic insurrections amongst us, and has endeavored to bring on the inhabitants of our frontiers, the merciless Indian savages, whose known rule of warfare is an undistinguished destruction of all ages, sexes and conditions.

In every stage of these oppressions we have petitioned for redress in the most humble terms; our repeated petitions have been answered only by repeated injury. A prince,

whose character is thus marked by every act which may define a tyrant, is unfit to be the ruler of a free people.

Nor have we been wanting in attentions to our British brethren. We have warned them from time to time of attempts by their legislature to extend an unwarrantable jurisdiction over us. We have reminded them of the circumstances of our emigration and settlement here. We have appealed to their native justice and magnanimity, and we have conjured them by the ties of our common kindred to disavow these usurpations, which would inevitably interrupt our connections and correspondence. They too have been deaf to the voice of justice and of consanguinity. We must, therefore, acquiesce in the necessity, which denounces our separation, and hold them, as we hold the rest of mankind, enemies in war, in peace, friends.

To build credibility Jefferson makes a case that the colonists' frustration with the British government is justified. He argues that the colonists have tried the peaceful approach only to be rebuffed.

We, therefore, the representatives of the United States of America, in general congress, assembled, appealing to the Supreme Judge of the world for the rectitude of our intentions, do, in the name, and by authority of the good people of these colonies, solemnly publish and declare, that these united colonies are, and of right ought to be free and independent states; that they are absolved from all allegiance to the British crown, and that all political connection between them and the state of Great Britain, is and ought to be totally dissolved; and that as free and independent states, they have full power to levy war, conclude peace, contract alliances, establish commerce, and to do all other acts and things which independent states may of right do. And for the support of this declaration, with a firm reliance on the protection of Divine Providence, we mutually pledge to each other our lives, our fortunes and our sacred honor.

The proposal is that the colonies no longer have any political connection to Great Britain and possess all the rights of an independent country.

Explore Current Issues

Should the government help the Lower Ninth Ward rebuild after Katrina?

By 2007, around 56% of the population of New Orleans had returned to the city. However, only 7% of the residents of the Lower Ninth Ward came back. Residents of this devastated area have seen little rebuilding since storm waters from Hurricane Katrina overflowed the levees and flooded the city in 2005. The rebuilding that has occurred in the Lower Ninth Ward is due mainly to various religious and nonprofit organizations who have pledged to rebuild the community one house at a time. The leadership of many of these groups feels that the federal government has failed not only the city as a whole, but the Lower Ninth Ward in particular.

However, how responsible is the federal government for rebuilding New Orleans? Some, such as former Speaker of the House Dennis Hastert, feel that the government should not be involved in rebuilding the homes of people who knowingly live in a flood-prone area. Others feel that areas such as the Lower Ninth Ward should not be rebuilt, but instead demolished to make way for an entirely new New Orleans.

Those who believe that the federal government should be responsible for the rebuilding efforts argue that New Orleans is both culturally unique and economically essential to the United States. Senator Mary Landrieu has even suggested that the billions of dollars in revenue that the U.S. receives from offshore petroleum leases in Louisiana could be used for wetlands and flood protection projects. In May of 2008, the argument for federal rebuilding efforts was given more fuel when the Army Corps of engineers was found liable for the failure of the MR-GO (Mississippi River-Gulf Outlet), which routed storm surges towards New Orleans and resulted in the fateful levee breaches.

Write about it

1. If you were a spokesperson for FEMA (Federal Emergency Management Agency), what reasons would you give to residents of the Lower Ninth Ward that your agency should not be responsible for rebuilding houses in the area?
2. If you were a spokesperson for a nonprofit organization building houses in the Lower Ninth Ward, what reasons would you give to a local corporation to sponsor your work?
3. If you were a developer who wanted to remove most of the old structures in the Lower Ninth Ward and build entirely new, mixed-income multiple- and single-family dwellings, what reasons would you give the residents of that area to support this change?

How to read proposal arguments

Make notes as you read, either in the margins or on paper or a computer file. Circle any words or references that you don't know and look them up.

What is it?	• What kind of a text is it? An editorial? an essay? an advertisement? a grant proposal? a Web site? a business proposal? What are your expectations for this kind of text? • What media are used? (Web sites, for example, often combine images, words, and sounds.)
Where did it come from?	• Who wrote this material? • Where did it first appear? In a book, newspaper, magazine, online, in a company, or in an organization?
What is the problem?	• Where is the evidence for the problem? Does this evidence establish that the problem exists? • How important is the problem? • Whom does the problem affect? (These people are called the stakeholders.) • What else has been written about the problem?
What is the solution?	• What exactly is the solution that the writer proposes? • Where is the evidence for the proposed solution? Does this evidence convince you that the proposal will solve the problem? • What kinds of sources are cited? Are they from books, newspapers, periodicals, or the Web? Are they completely documented?
How feasible is the proposed solution?	• Does the writer make a case that this is practical, and will people support the solution? • If the solution costs money, where does the money come from?
How is it composed?	• How is the piece of writing organized? • How does the writer represent herself or himself? • How would you characterize the style? • How effective is the design? Is it easy to read? • If there are any photographs, charts, or other graphics, what information do they contribute?

Building the Interstate Highway System

(SPEECH)

Richard Nixon

In July 1954, President Eisenhower was scheduled to deliver a speech to the annual conference of United States Governors held at Lake George, New York, but was called away by a death in the family. Then-Vice President Richard Nixon filled in for the president and, speaking from Eisenhower's notes, unveiled a startling plan: the federal government proposed to dedicate $50 billion—an enormous sum in 1954—to create a system of interstate highways connecting the country from coast to coast, and from border to border. The proposal was electrifying news, and led directly to the creation of the Interstate Highway System we use today.

Return to these questions after you have finished reading.

Analyzing and Connecting

1. What evidence does the vice president present that the state of America's highways is indeed a problem? What are the specific problems this plan is intended to solve?
2. Traffic in many locations today is more congested than it was when Nixon delivered his speech in 1954. Some politicians today argue for building more roads. How are arguments for more roads today similar to and different from Nixon's arguments?
3. Nixon's speech was covered in the media for the general public, whose approval was needed in order for the proposal to pass through Congress into law. But the immediate audience for the speech consisted of forty-eight state governors. What gestures do you see in this speech that show the vice president and president wanted to appeal to them specifically, and understood their unique concerns?
4. Vice President Nixon delivered this speech on President Eisenhower's behalf, using Eisenhower's notes. Therefore, the occasion required Nixon both to present the president's ideas as worthy and to present himself as a credible substitute. How does he try to accomplish these goals? Is he effective? Why or why not?

Finding Ideas for Writing

How many of the problems outlined by Nixon were actually solved by the Interstate Highway System? Write a brief "progress" report in which you assess what problems have been solved and what other problems have arisen because of the Interstate Highway System.

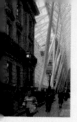

BUILDING THE INTERSTATE HIGHWAY SYSTEM

A Cabinet committee has just been established by the President to explore and to help formulate a comprehensive transportation policy for the Nation, taking into account the vital interests of carriers, shippers, the States and communities, the public at large. But more specifically, our highway net is inadequate locally, and obsolete as a national system.

To start to meet this problem at this session of the Congress, we have increased by approximately 500 million dollars the Federal monies available to the States for road development. This seems like a very substantial sum. But the experts say that 5 billion dollars a year for ten years, in addition to all current, normal expenditures, will pay off in economic growth; and when we have spent 50 billion dollars in the next ten years, we shall only have made a good start on the highways the country will need for a population of 200 million people.

A 50 billion dollar highway program in ten years is a goal toward which we can—and we should—look.

Now, let us look at the highway net of the United States as it is. What is wrong with it? It is obsolete because in large part it just happened. It was governed in the beginning by terrain, existing Indian trails, cattle trails, arbitrary section lines. It was designed largely for local movement at low speeds of one or two horsepower. It has been adjusted, it is true, at intervals to meet metropolitan traffic gluts, transcontinental movement, and increased horsepower. But it has never been completely overhauled or planned to satisfy the needs ten years ahead.

At this point in his notes, the President had a personal anecdote illustrating the problem. Thirty-five years ago this month, the Secretary of War initiated a transcontinental truck convoy to prove that the gas engine had displaced the mule, even on our relatively primitive roads. A Second

Lieutenant named Dwight Eisenhower went along as an observer. All-weather roads in the United States at that time totaled 300,000 miles. The autos and trucks numbered 7.6 million. That truck convoy left Washington July the 7th. It arrived in San Francisco on September the 5th, sixty days and 6000 breakdowns later.

Today, all-weather mileage is approximately 1.8 million as compared with 300,000 miles. But autos and trucks number more than 56 million, as compared with 7.6 million.

It is obvious, then, that the increase in mileage has lagged behind the increase in vehicles. The road system, moreover, is fundamentally the same, either haphazard or completely arbitrary in its origin, designed for local movement, in an age of transcontinental travel.

Now, what are the penalties of this obsolete net which we have today? Our first most apparent [is] an annual death toll comparable to the casualties of a bloody war, beyond calculation in dollar terms. It approaches 40,000 killed and exceeds 1.3 million injured annually.

And second, the annual wastage of billions of hours in detours, traffic jams, and so on, measurable by any traffic engineer and amounting to billions of dollars in productive time.

Third, all the civil suits that clog up our courts. It has been estimated that more than half have their origins on highways, roads and streets.

Nullification of efficiency in the production of goods by inefficiency in the transport of goods is another result of this obsolete net that we have today.

And finally, the appalling inadequacies to meet the demands of catastrophe or defense, should an atomic war come.

These penalties warrant the expenditures of billions to correct them.

Now, let us look at the highway net as it should be. The President believes that the requirements are these: a grand plan for a properly

articulated system that solves the problems of speedy, safe, transcontinental travel; intercity communication; access highways; and farm-to-market movement; metropolitan area congestion; bottlenecks; and parking.

Second, a financing proposal based on self-liquidation of each project, wherever that is possible, through tolls or the assured increase in gas tax revenue, and on Federal help where the national interest demands it.

And third, and I would emphasize this, particularly at this Conference, because I know how deeply the President believes in this principle: a cooperative alliance between the Federal government and the states so that local government and the most efficient sort of government in the administration of funds, will be the manager of its own area.

And the fourth, very probably, a program initiated by the Federal government, with State cooperation, for the planning and construction of a modern State highway system, with the Federal government functions, for example, being to advance funds or guarantee the obligations of localities or States which undertake to construct new, or modernize existing highways.

And then I would like to read to you the last sentence from the President's notes, exactly as it appears in them, because it is an exhortation to the members of this Conference: "I hope that you will study the matter, and recommend to me the cooperative action you think the Federal government and the 48 States should take to meet these requirements, so that I can submit positive proposals to the next session of the Congress."

And I know that in making this request to the Governors Conference, that the President believes it is essential that we have cooperation in this field. He believes that only with cooperation, and with the maximum of State and local initiative and control can we make a program which will deal with the problem and deal with it effectively.

Why Bother?

(ESSAY)

Michael Pollan

Michael Pollan is an author and professor of journalism at the University of California, Berkeley. His most recent book is *In Defense of Food: An Eater's Manifesto* (2008). His previous book, *The Omnivore's Dilemma: A Natural History of Four Meals*, was named one of the ten best books of 2006 by the *New York Times* and the *Washington Post*. This article appeared in a special "Green" issue of the *New York Times Magazine* in April 2008.

Return to these questions after you have finished reading.

Analyzing and Connecting

1. The success of Pollan's argument depends on his being able to grab his audience's attention, make them care about the problem at hand, and make them responsible for the solution. How does he try to achieve these goals? Do you think he is successful? Why or why not?
2. Pollan begins the article by describing his reaction to Al Gore's "puny" solution to the seemingly insurmountable problem of global warming—changing our light bulbs. How do Pollan's solutions compare? Do they seem in proportion to the problem, or are they more in proportion to what is possible? What, according to Pollan, is more important?
3. What kind of tone does Pollan set up with the title, "Why Bother?" Does he carry this tone throughout the essay? Is the tone appropriate for the argument? Why or why not? How does his tone affect his credibility with his audience?
4. Pollan again revisits Gore's request that we change our light bulbs, explaining that "Gore probably can't imagine us doing anything much more challenging, like, say, growing some portion of our own food." What is the causal relationship that Pollan sets up to explain our helplessness? How does this causal relationship support his overall argument?

Finding Ideas for Writing

Pollan mourns the downfall of the word *virtue*, asking "how did it come to pass that virtue—a quality that for most of history has generally been deemed, well, a virtue—became a mark of liberal softheadedness?" What other words have similarly lost favor, being relegated now to derogatory or ironic usage? Choose one of these words and write a short opinion piece detailing its fall from grace.

Why Bother?

Why bother? That really is the big question facing us as individuals hoping to do something about climate change, and it's not an easy one to answer. I don't know about you, but for me the most upsetting moment in *An Inconvenient Truth* came long after Al Gore scared the hell out of me, constructing an utterly convincing case that the very survival of life on earth as we know it is threatened by climate change. No, the really dark moment came during the closing credits, when we are asked to . . . change our light bulbs. That's when it got really depressing. The immense disproportion between the magnitude of the problem Gore had described and the puniness of what he was asking us to do about it was enough to sink your heart.

But the drop-in-the-bucket issue is not the only problem lurking behind the "why bother" question. Let's say I do bother, big time. I turn my life upside-down, start biking to work, plant a big garden, turn down the thermostat so low I need the Jimmy Carter signature cardigan, forsake the clothes dryer for a laundry line across the yard, trade in the station wagon for a hybrid, get off the beef, go completely local. I could theoretically do all that, but what would be the point when I know full well that halfway around the world there lives my evil twin, some carbon-footprint *doppelgänger* in Shanghai or Chongqing who has just bought his first car (Chinese car ownership is where ours was back in 1918), is eager to swallow every bite of meat I forswear and who's positively itching to replace every last pound of CO_2 I'm struggling no longer to emit. So what exactly would I have to show for all my trouble?

A sense of personal virtue, you might suggest, somewhat sheepishly. But what good is that when virtue itself is quickly becoming a term of derision? And not just on the editorial pages of the *Wall Street Journal* or on the lips of the vice president, who famously dismissed energy conservation as a "sign of personal virtue." No, even in the pages of the *New York Times* and the *New Yorker*, it seems the epithet "virtuous," when applied to an act of personal environmental responsibility, may be used only ironically. Tell me: How did it come to pass that virtue—a quality that for most of history has generally been deemed, well, a virtue—became a mark of liberal softheadedness? How peculiar, that doing the right thing by the environment—buying the hybrid, eating like a locavore—should now set you up for the Ed Begley Jr. treatment.

And even if in the face of this derision I decide I am going to bother, there arises the whole vexed question of getting it right. Is eating local or walking to work really going to reduce my carbon footprint? According to one analysis, if walking to work increases your appetite and you consume more meat or

milk as a result, walking might actually emit more carbon than driving. A handful of studies have recently suggested that in certain cases under certain conditions, produce from places as far away as New Zealand might account for less carbon than comparable domestic products. True, at least one of these studies was co-written by a representative of agribusiness interests in (surprise!) New Zealand, but even so, they make you wonder. If determining the carbon footprint of food is really this complicated, and I've got to consider not only "food miles" but also whether the food came by ship or truck and how lushly the grass grows in New Zealand, then maybe on second thought I'll just buy the imported chops at Costco, at least until the experts get their footprints sorted out.

There are so many stories we can tell ourselves to justify doing nothing, but perhaps the most insidious is that, whatever we do manage to do, it will be too little too late. Climate change is upon us, and it has arrived well ahead of schedule. Scientists' projections that seemed dire a decade ago turn out to have been unduly optimistic: the warming and the melting is occurring much faster than the models predicted. Now truly terrifying feedback loops threaten to boost the rate of change exponentially, as the shift from white ice to blue water in the Arctic absorbs more sunlight and warming soils everywhere become more biologically active, causing them to release their vast stores of carbon into the air. Have you looked into the eyes of a climate scientist recently? They look really scared.

So do you still want to talk about planting gardens?

I do.

Whatever we can do as individuals to change the way we live at this suddenly very late date does seem utterly inadequate to the challenge. It's hard to argue with Michael Specter, in a recent *New Yorker* piece on carbon footprints, when he says: "Personal choices, no matter how virtuous [N.B.!], cannot do enough. It will also take laws and money." So it will. Yet it is no less accurate or hardheaded to say that laws and money cannot do enough, either; that it will also take profound changes in the way we live. Why? Because the climate-change crisis is at its very bottom a crisis of lifestyle—of character, even. The Big Problem is nothing more or less than the sum total of countless little everyday choices, most of them made by us (consumer spending represents 70 percent of our economy), and most of the rest of them made in the name of our needs and desires and preferences.

For us to wait for legislation or technology to solve the problem of how we're living our lives suggests we're not really serious about changing—something our politicians cannot fail to notice. They will not move until we do. Indeed, to look to leaders and experts, to laws and money and grand schemes, to save us from

our predicament represents precisely the sort of thinking—passive, delegated, dependent for solutions on specialists—that helped get us into this mess in the first place. It's hard to believe that the same sort of thinking could now get us out of it.

Thirty years ago, Wendell Berry, the Kentucky farmer and writer, put forward a blunt analysis of precisely this mentality. He argued that the environmental crisis of the 1970s—an era innocent of climate change; what we would give to have back that environmental crisis!—was at its heart a crisis of character and would have to be addressed first at that level: at home, as it were. He was impatient with people who wrote checks to environmental organizations while thoughtlessly squandering fossil fuel in their everyday lives—the 1970s equivalent of people buying carbon offsets to atone for their Tahoes and Durangos. Nothing was likely to change until we healed the "split between what we think and what we do." For Berry, the "why bother" question came down to a moral imperative: "Once our personal connection to what is wrong becomes clear, then we have to choose: we can go on as before, recognizing our dishonesty and living with it the best we can, or we can begin the effort to change the way we think and live."

For Berry, the deep problem standing behind all the other problems of industrial civilization is "specialization," which he regards as the "disease of the modern character." Our society assigns us a tiny number of roles: we're producers (of one thing) at work, consumers of a great many other things the rest of the time, and then once a year or so we vote as citizens. Virtually all of our needs and desires we delegate to specialists of one kind or another—our meals to agribusiness, health to the doctor, education to the teacher, entertainment to the media, care for the environment to the environmentalist, political action to the politician.

As Adam Smith and many others have pointed out, this division of labor has given us many of the blessings of civilization. Specialization is what allows me to sit at a computer thinking about climate change. Yet this same division of labor obscures the lines of connection—and responsibility—linking our everyday acts to their real-world consequences, making it easy for me to overlook the coal-fired power plant that is lighting my screen, or the mountaintop in Kentucky that had to be destroyed to provide the coal to that plant, or the streams running crimson with heavy metals as a result.

Of course, what made this sort of specialization possible in the first place was cheap energy. Cheap fossil fuel allows us to pay distant others to process our food for us, to entertain us and to (try to) solve our problems, with the result that there is very little we know how to accomplish for ourselves. Think for a

moment of all the things you suddenly need to do for yourself when the power goes out—up to and including entertaining yourself. Think, too, about how a power failure causes your neighbors—your community—to suddenly loom so much larger in your life. Cheap energy allowed us to leapfrog community by making it possible to sell our specialty over great distances as well as summon into our lives the specialties of countless distant others.

Here's the point: Cheap energy, which gives us climate change, fosters precisely the mentality that makes dealing with climate change in our own lives seem impossibly difficult. Specialists ourselves, we can no longer imagine anyone but an expert, or anything but a new technology or law, solving our problems. Al Gore asks us to change the light bulbs because he probably can't imagine us doing anything much more challenging, like, say, growing some portion of our own food. We can't imagine it, either, which is probably why we prefer to cross our fingers and talk about the promise of ethanol and nuclear power—new liquids and electrons to power the same old cars and houses and lives.

The "cheap-energy mind," as Wendell Berry called it, is the mind that asks, "Why bother?" because it is helpless to imagine—much less attempt—a different sort of life, one less divided, less reliant. Since the cheap-energy mind translates everything into money, its proxy, it prefers to put its faith in market-based solutions—carbon taxes and pollution-trading schemes. If we could just get the incentives right, it believes, the economy will properly value everything that matters and nudge our self-interest down the proper channels. The best we can hope for is a greener version of the old invisible hand. Visible hands it has no use for.

But while some such grand scheme may well be necessary, it's doubtful that it will be sufficient or that it will be politically sustainable before we've demonstrated to ourselves that change is possible. Merely to give, to spend, even to vote, is not to do, and there is so much that needs to be done—without further delay. In the judgment of James Hansen, the NASA climate scientist who began sounding the alarm on global warming 20 years ago, we have only 10 years left to start cutting—not just slowing—the amount of carbon we're emitting or face a "different planet." Hansen said this more than two years ago, however; two years have gone by, and nothing of consequence has been done. So: eight years left to go and a great deal left to do.

Which brings us back to the "why bother" question and how we might better answer it. The reasons not to bother are many and compelling, at least to the cheap-energy mind. But let me offer a few admittedly tentative reasons that we might put on the other side of the scale:

If you do bother, you will set an example for other people. If enough other people bother, each one influencing yet another in a chain reaction of behavioral change, markets for all manner of green products and alternative technologies will prosper and expand. (Just look at the market for hybrid cars.) Consciousness will be raised, perhaps even changed: new moral imperatives and new taboos might take root in the culture. Driving an S.U.V. or eating a 24-ounce steak or illuminating your McMansion like an airport runway at night might come to be regarded as outrages to human conscience. Not having things might become cooler than having them. And those who did change the way they live would acquire the moral standing to demand changes in behavior from others—from other people, other corporations, even other countries.

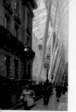

All of this could, theoretically, happen. What I'm describing (imagining would probably be more accurate) is a process of viral social change, and change of this kind, which is nonlinear, is never something anyone can plan or predict or count on. Who knows, maybe the virus will reach all the way to Chongqing and infect my Chinese evil twin. Or not. Maybe going green will prove a passing fad and will lose steam after a few years, just as it did in the 1980s, when Ronald Reagan took down Jimmy Carter's solar panels from the roof of the White House.

Going personally green is a bet, nothing more or less, though it's one we probably all should make, even if the odds of it paying off aren't great. Sometimes you have to act as if acting will make a difference, even when you can't prove that it will. That, after all, was precisely what happened in Communist Czechoslovakia and Poland, when a handful of individuals like Vaclav Havel and Adam Michnik resolved that they would simply conduct their lives "as if" they lived in a free society. That improbable bet created a tiny space of liberty that, in time, expanded to take in, and then help take down, the whole of the Eastern bloc.

So what would be a comparable bet that the individual might make in the case of the environmental crisis? Havel himself has suggested that people begin to "conduct themselves as if they were to live on this earth forever and be answerable for its condition one day." Fair enough, but let me propose a slightly less abstract and daunting wager. The idea is to find one thing to do in your life that doesn't involve spending or voting, that may or may not virally rock the world but is real and particular (as well as symbolic) and that, come what may, will offer its own rewards. Maybe you decide to give up meat, an act that would reduce your carbon footprint by as much as a quarter. Or you could try this: determine to observe the Sabbath. For one day a week, abstain completely from economic activity: no shopping, no driving, no electronics.

But the act I want to talk about is growing some—even just a little—of your own food. Rip out your lawn, if you have one, and if you don't—if you live in a high-rise, or have a yard shrouded in shade—look into getting a plot in a community garden. Measured against the Problem We Face, planting a garden sounds pretty benign, I know, but in fact it's one of the most powerful things an individual can do—to reduce your carbon footprint, sure, but more important, to reduce your sense of dependence and dividedness: to change the cheap-energy mind.

A great many things happen when you plant a vegetable garden, some of them directly related to climate change, others indirect but related nevertheless. Growing food, we forget, comprises the original solar technology: calories produced by means of photosynthesis. Years ago the cheap-energy mind discovered that more food could be produced with less effort by replacing sunlight with fossil-fuel fertilizers and pesticides, with a result that the typical calorie of food energy in your diet now requires about 10 calories of fossil-fuel energy to produce. It's estimated that the way we feed ourselves (or rather, allow ourselves to be fed) accounts for about a fifth of the greenhouse gas for which each of us is responsible.

Yet the sun still shines down on your yard, and photosynthesis still works so abundantly that in a thoughtfully organized vegetable garden (one planted from seed, nourished by compost from the kitchen and involving not too many drives to the garden center), you can grow the proverbial free lunch—CO_2-free and dollar-free. This is the most-local food you can possibly eat (not to mention the freshest, tastiest and most nutritious), with a carbon footprint so faint that even the New Zealand lamb council dares not challenge it. And while we're counting carbon, consider too your compost pile, which shrinks the heap of garbage your household needs trucked away even as it feeds your vegetables and sequesters carbon in your soil. What else? Well, you will probably notice that you're getting a pretty good workout there in your garden, burning calories without having to get into the car to drive to the gym. (It is one of the absurdities of the modern division of labor that, having replaced physical labor with fossil fuel, we now have to burn even more fossil fuel to keep our unemployed bodies in shape.) Also, by engaging both body and mind, time spent in the garden is time (and energy) subtracted from electronic forms of entertainment.

You begin to see that growing even a little of your own food is, as Wendell Berry pointed out 30 years ago, one of those solutions that, instead of begetting a new set of problems—the way "solutions" like ethanol or nuclear power inevitably do—actually beget other solutions, and not only of the kind that save carbon. Still more valuable are the habits of mind that growing a little of your own food can yield. You quickly learn that you need not be dependent on specialists to provide for yourself—that your body is still good for something and may actually be enlisted in its own support. If the experts are right, if both oil and time are running out, these are skills and habits of mind we're all very soon going to need. We may also need the food. Could gardens provide it? Well, during World War II, victory gardens supplied as much as 40 percent of the produce Americans ate.

But there are sweeter reasons to plant that garden, to bother. At least in this one corner of your yard and life, you will have begun to heal the split between what you think and what you do, to commingle your identities as consumer and producer and citizen. Chances are, your garden will re-engage you with your neighbors, for you will have produce to give away and the need to borrow their tools. You will have reduced the power of the cheap-energy mind by personally overcoming its most debilitating weakness: its helplessness and the fact that it can't do much of anything that doesn't involve division or subtraction. The garden's

season-long transit from seed to ripe fruit—*will you get a load of that zucchini?!*—suggests that the operations of addition and multiplication still obtain, that the abundance of nature is not exhausted. The single greatest lesson the garden teaches is that our relationship to the planet need not be zero-sum, and that as long as the sun still shines and people still can plan and plant, think and do, we can, if we bother to try, find ways to provide for ourselves without diminishing the world.

How to write a proposal argument

These steps for the process of writing an argument for change may not progress as neatly as this chart might suggest. Writing is not an assembly-line process.

As you write and revise, imagine that you are in a conversation with an audience that contains people who both agree and disagree with you. Think about what you would say to both and speak to these diverse readers.

1 IDENTIFY THE PROBLEM

- Read your assignment carefully and note exactly what you are being asked to do.
- Identify the problem, what causes it, and whom it affects.
- Do background research on what has been written about the problem and what solutions have been attempted.
- Describe what has been done or not done to address the problem.
- Make a claim advocating a specific change or course of action. Put the claim in this form: We should (or should not) do _____.

2 PROPOSE YOUR SOLUTION

- State your solution as specifically as you can.
- Consider other solutions and describe why your solution is better.
- Examine if the solution will have enough money and support to be implemented.
- Analyze your potential readers. How interested will your readers be in this problem? How would your solution benefit them directly and indirectly?

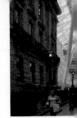

3 WRITE A DRAFT

- Define the problem. Give the background your readers will need.
- Discuss other possible solutions.
- Present your solution. Explain exactly how it will work, how it will be accomplished, and if anything like it has been tried elsewhere.
- Argue that your proposal will work. Address any possible arguments that your solution will not work.
- Describe the positive consequences of your solution and the negative consequences that can be avoided.
- Conclude with a call for action. Be specific about exactly what readers need to do.
- Write a title that will interest readers.
- Include any necessary images, tables, or graphics.

4 REVISE, REVISE, REVISE

- Recheck that your proposal fulfills the assignment.
- Make sure that your proposal claim is clear and focused.
- Add detail or further explanation about the problem.
- Add detail or further explanation about how your solution addresses the problem.
- Make sure you have considered other solutions and explain why yours is better.
- Examine your organization and think of possible better ways to organize.
- Review the visual presentation of your report for readability and maximum impact.
- Proofread carefully.

5 SUBMITTED VERSION

- Make sure your finished writing meets all formatting requirements.

1: Identify the problem

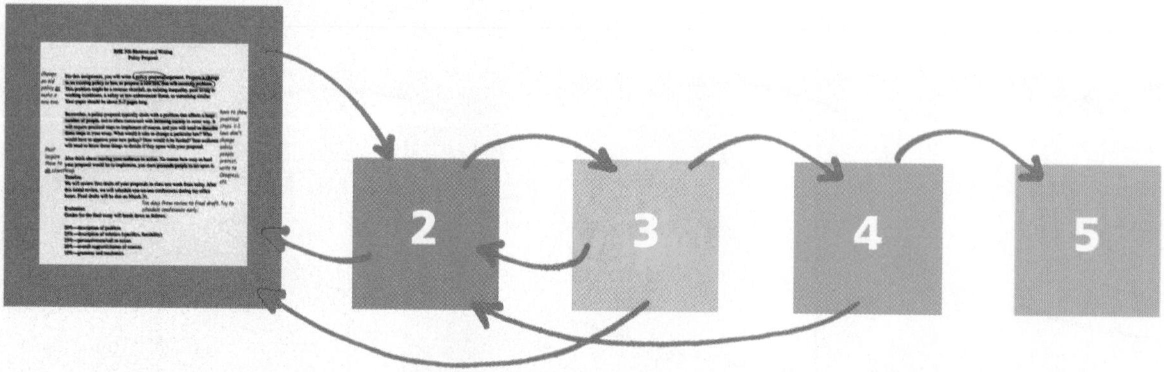

Analyze the assignment

- Read your assignment slowly and carefully. Look for the key words *propose* or *problem* and *solution*. These key words tell you that you are writing a proposal.
- Highlight any information about the length specified, date due, formatting, and other requirements. You can attend to this information later. At this point you want to zero in on the subject and your proposal claim.

Identify the problem

- What exactly is the problem?
- Who is most affected by the problem?
- What causes the problem?
- Has anyone tried to do anything about it? If so, why haven't they succeeded?
- What is likely to happen in the future if the problem isn't solved?

Do background research in online and print library sources, Web sources, government documents, experts in the field, and possibly field research such as a survey

- What has been written about the problem?
- What other solutions have been proposed?
- Where have other solutions been effective?
- Where have other solutions failed?

Make a proposal claim

- Proposal claims advocate a specific change or course of action. Put the claim in this form: We should (or should not) do ____.

Write Now

Make an idea map

When you have a number of ideas and facts about a topic, write them on sticky notes. Then post the sticky notes and move them around, so you can begin to see how they might fit together. When you find an organization that suits your subject, make a working outline from your sticky notes.

PROBLEM:
Citizens of the United States born in another country cannot run for president

EXCEPTION:
Foreign-born citizens whose parents are American citizens

REQUIRED:
2/3s majority of Congress and 2/3s of state legislatures must approve

SOLUTION:
Amend the U.S. Constitution to allow foreign-born American citizens to run for and serve as the president of the United States

HOW WOULD IT WORK?
Grass-roots campaign

WHO WOULD SUPPORT?
Probably Asian Americans, Mexican Americans, and other recent immigrant groups

WHO WOULD OPPOSE?
1) politicians afraid of angering voters
2) Americans who are afraid of foreigners

HOW LONG WOULD IT TAKE?
Probably years because of the approval process

PRO ARGUMENTS
1) Fairness
2) America's image of itself as a land of opportunity

COUNTERARGUMENT
Point out that foreign born doesn't mean untrustworthy

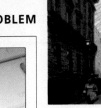

Writer at work

Kim Lee was asked to write a proposal argument for her Rhetoric and Writing course. Upon receiving the assignment, she made the following notes and observations.

RHE 306 Rhetoric and Writing
Policy Proposal

Change an old policy or make a new one.

For this assignment, you will write a policy proposal argument. Propose a change to an existing policy or law, or propose a new law, that will correct a problem. This problem might be a revenue shortfall, an existing inequality, poor living or working conditions, a safety or law-enforcement threat, or something similar. Your paper should be about 5–7 pages long.

Remember, a policy proposal typically deals with a problem that affects a large number of people, and is often concerned with bettering society in some way. It will require practical steps to implement of course, and you will need to describe these steps in your essay. What would it take to change a particular law? Who would have to approve your new policy? How would it be funded? Your audience will need to know these things to decide if they agree with your proposal.

have to show practical steps. U.S. laws don't change unless people protest, write to Congress, etc.

Must inspire them to do something.

Also think about moving your audience to action. No matter how easy or hard your proposal would be to implement, you must persuade people to act upon it.

Timeline
We will review first drafts of your proposals in class one week from today. After this initial review, we will schedule one-on-one conferences during my office hours. Final drafts will be due on March 31.

Ten days from review to final draft. Try to schedule conference early.

Evaluation
Grades for the final essay will break down as follows:

20%—description of problem
25%—description of solution (specifics, feasibility)
25%—persuasiveness/call to action
20%—overall support/citation of sources
10%—grammar and mechanics

Read the assignment closely
Kim Lee began by highlighting key words in the assignment and noting specifics about the length and due date.

POSSIBLE TOPICS

– Create a standardized form of testing for steroid use in all American sports (professional, educational, recreational).

Might be too broad. Also, the science involved might be hard to explain in 5–7 pages

– Move the U.S. capital to Nashville, Tennessee.

Too regional?

Choose a topic
Kim listed possible topics and then considered the strengths and weaknesses of each. She chose one that could be developed adequately and could motivate her audience.

– Amend the Constitution to allow foreign-born American Citizens (or naturalized citizens) to serve as president of the United States.

An issue of fair treatment.
Good for motivating audience.

– Revitalize Youngstown, Ohio, by building a tourist trade around its previous Mafioso reputation as "Little Chicago."

Could give lots of specific steps (funding, building plans, tourist info).

– Reformulate the means by which the Corporation for Public Broadcasting receives federal funds.

Would be very dry, though T.V. shows like Sesame Street could be used to provoke interest/make people want to act.

Plan research strategies
Kim made a list of possible sources of information to begin her research.

To Do:

– Search Internet for current discussion on this topic. What kinds of sites are discussing the "natural-born" clause? AmendforArnold.com, Orrin Hatch.
– Search periodicals for discussions of this topic.
– Search academic and law journals for more sophisticated discussions.
– Any books???
– What groups (political, ideological) are discussing this right now?

2: Propose your solution

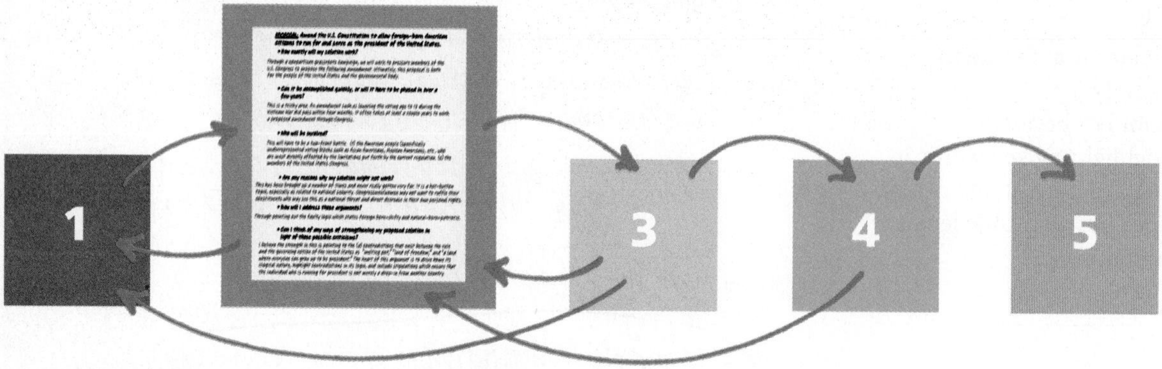

State your solution as specifically as you can

- What exactly do you want to achieve?
- How exactly will your solution work?
- Can it be accomplished quickly, or will it have to be phased in over a few years?
- Has anything like it been tried elsewhere?
- Who will be involved?
- Is it possible that your solution might not work?
- How will you address those arguments?
- Can you think of any ways of strengthening your proposed solution in light of those possible criticisms?

Consider other solutions

- What other solutions have been or might be proposed for this problem, including doing nothing?
- What are the advantages and disadvantages of those solutions?
- Why is your solution better?

Examine the feasibility of your solution

- How easy is your solution to implement?
- Will the people who will be most affected be willing to go along with it? (For example, lots of things can be accomplished if enough people volunteer, but groups often have difficulty getting enough volunteers to work without pay.)
- If it costs money, how do you propose paying for it?
- Who is most likely to reject your proposal because it is not practical enough?
- How can you convince your readers that your proposal can be achieved?

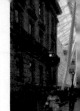

Analyze your potential readers

- Whom are you writing for?
- How interested will your readers be in this problem?
- How much does this problem affect them?
- How would your solution benefit them directly and indirectly?

Staying on Track

Acknowledging other points of view

Write for readers who may disagree with you

Proposal arguments that ignore other points of view and other possible solutions tend to convince only those who agree with you before you start writing. Your goal is to convince those who haven't thought about the problem and those who might disagree at the outset but can be persuaded. Think about why readers might disagree.

- Are they misinformed about the problem? If so, you will need to provide accurate information.
- Do they have different assumptions about the problem? If so, can you show them that your assumptions are better?
- Do they share your goals but think your solution is not the right one? If so, you will need to explain why your solution is better.

You might have to do some research to find out the views of others. If you are writing about a local problem, you may need to talk to people.

Deal fairly with other solutions and other points of view

OFF TRACK

Free tuition for all state high school graduates who attend state colleges is an idea too ridiculous to consider.
(No reason is given for rejecting an alternative solution, and those who propose it are insulted.)

ON TRACK

Free tuition for all state high school graduates is a desirable solution to get more students to attend college, but it is not likely to be implemented because of the cost. A solution targeted to low-income students similar to the HOPE scholarship program in Georgia, which is funded by state lottery money, could be implemented in our state.
(The author offers a reason for rejecting an alternative solution and proposes a solution that has some common ground with the alternative.)

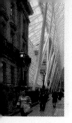

Writer at work

Kim Lee began laying out her proposal by first stating her solution as specifically as possible. She used the following list of questions to guide her proposal argument.

PROPOSAL: Amend the U.S. Constitution to allow foreign-born American citizens to run for and serve as the president of the United States.

- **How exactly will my solution work?**

Through a nonpartisan grassroots campaign, we will work to pressure members of the U.S. Congress to propose the following amendment. Ultimately, this proposal is both for the people of the United States and the governmental body.

- **Can it be accomplished quickly, or will it have to be phased in over a few years?**

This is a tricky area. An amendment such as lowering the voting age to 18 during the Vietnam War did pass within four months. It often takes at least a couple years to work a proposed amendment through Congress.

- **Who will be involved?**

This will have to be a two-front battle. (1) the American people, specifically underrepresented voting blocks such as Asian Americans, Mexican Americans, etc., who are most directly affected by the limitations put forth by the current regulation. (2) the members of the United States Congress.

- **Are any reasons why my solution might not work?**

This has been brought up a number of times and never really gotten very far. It is a hot-button topic, especially as related to national security. Congressmen/women may not want to ruffle their constituents who may see this as a national threat and direct decrease in their own personal rights.

- **How will I address those arguments?**

Through pointing out the faulty logic which states foreign born=shifty and natural-born=patriotic.

- **Can I think of any ways of strengthening my proposed solution in light of those possible criticisms?**

I believe the strength in this is pointing to the (a) contradictions that exist between the rule and the governing notion of the United States as "melting pot," "land of freedom," and "a land where everyone can grow up to be president." The heart of this argument is to drive home its illogical nature, highlight contradictions in its logic, and include stipulations which ensure that the individual who is running for president is not merely a drop-in from another country.

OTHER SOLUTIONS

- Solutions that have been discussed recently seem to differ in the length of required residence.

Not necessarily disadvantages, but have been ineffective in achieving the goal. It comes from the people and not in support of one candidate, but an idea.

FEASIBILITY

- How easy is my solution to implement?

It all depends on the people's ability to move Congress to action.

- Will the people who will be most affected be willing to go along with it?

I believe the answer is yes.

- How will we pay for it?

Again, grass roots political fundraising. A major source may be ethic/immigrant groups, etc.

- Who is most likely to reject my proposal because it is not practical enough?

Most likely (a) politicians who see support of the change as a threat to their positions (due to voter dissent) and (b) citizens who live in a state of fear.

- How can I convince my readers that my proposal can be achieved?

It must be proposed as being about the people and their ability to enact change. It is about empowerment.

POTENTIAL READERS

- Whom am I writing for?

American people (specifically the immigrant population).

- How interested will my readers be in this problem?

It is currently a hot topic and hopefully making it more personally relevant will peak interest (not just about Governor Schwarzenegger).

- How much does this problem affect them?

It withholds a basic right for them and their children.

- How would my solution benefit them directly and indirectly?

Directly, it allows for naturalized citizens to run for president (or vice president). Indirectly, it fosters a sense of pride in one's ethnic identity and helps (through visibility and legislative legitimacy) to create an image of diversity and success.

3: Write a draft

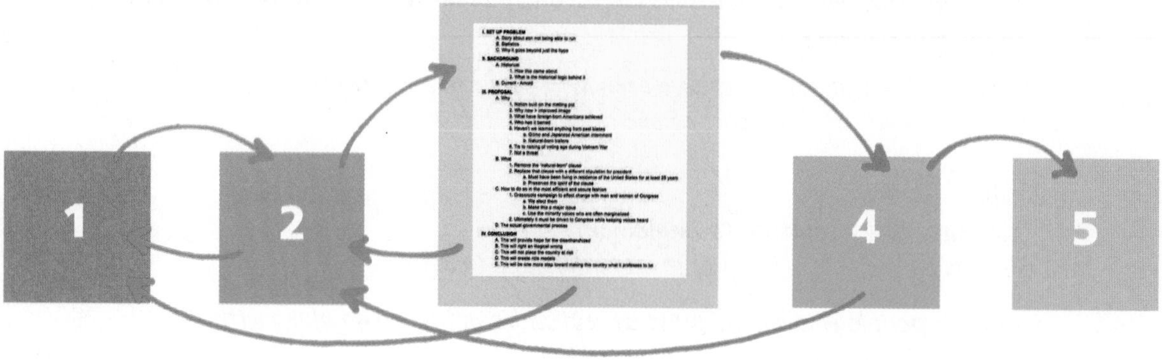

Define the problem

- Set out the issue or problem. If the problem is local, you might begin by telling about your experience or the experience of someone you know. You might need to argue for the seriousness of the problem, and you might have to give some background on how it came about.

Present your solution

- Describe other solutions that have been attempted and others that are possible. Explain why other solutions either don't solve the problem or are unrealistic.
- Make clear the goals of your solution. Many solutions cannot solve problems completely.
- Describe in detail the steps in implementing your solution and how they will solve the problem you have identified. You can impress your readers by the care with which you have thought through this problem.
- Explain the positive consequences that will follow from your proposal. What good things will happen and what bad things will be avoided if your proposal is implemented?

Argue that your solution can be done

- Your proposal for solving the problem is a truly good idea only if it can be put into practice. If people have to change the ways they are doing things now, explain why they would want to change. If your proposal costs money, you need to identify exactly where the money would come from.

Conclude with a call for action

- Make a call for action. You should put your readers in a position such that if they agree with you, they will take action. You might restate and emphasize what exactly they need to do.

Writer at work

Here is the outline that Kim Lee used to write the first draft of her proposal essay.

I. SET UP PROBLEM

- A. Story about son not being able to run
- B. Statistics
- C. Why it goes beyond just the hype

II. BACKGROUND

- A. Historical
  - 1. How this came about
  - 2. What is the historical logic behind it
- B. Current - Arnold

III. PROPOSAL

- A. Why
  - 1. Nation built on the melting pot
  - 2. Why now > improved image
  - 3. What have foreign-born Americans achieved
  - 4. Who has it barred
  - 5. Haven't we learned anything from past biases
    - a. Gitmo and Japanese American internment
    - b. Natural-born traitors
  - 6. Tie to raising of voting age during Vietnam War
  - 7. Not a threat
- B. What
  - 1. Remove the "natural-born" clause
  - 2. Replace that clause with a different stipulation for president
    - a. Must have been living in residence of the United States for at least 25 years
    - b. Preserves the spirit of the clause
- C. How to do so in the most efficient and secure fashion
  - 1. Grassroots campaign to effect change with men and women of Congress
    - a. We elect them
    - b. Make this a major issue
    - c. Use the minority voices who are often marginalized
  - 2. Ultimately it must be driven to Congress while keeping voices heard
- D. The actual governmental process

IV. CONCLUSION

- A. This will provide hope for the disenfranchised
- B. This will right an illogical wrong
- C. This will not place the country at risk
- D. This will create role models
- E. This will be one more step toward making this country what it professes to be

4: Revise, revise, revise

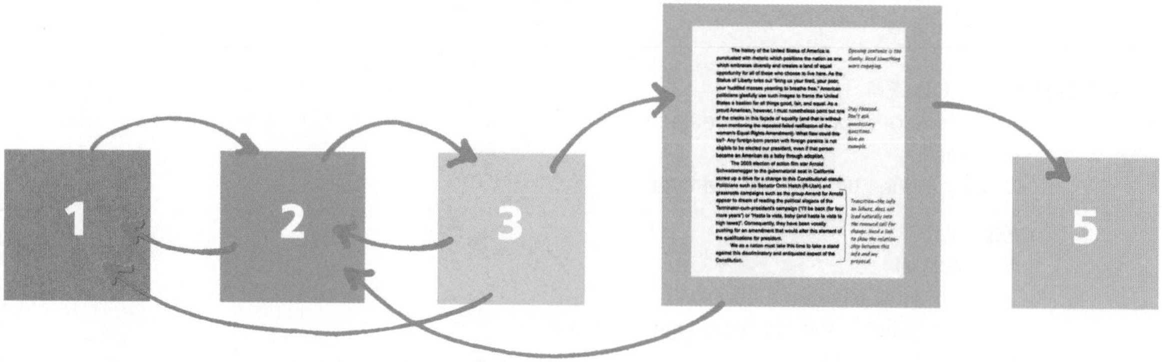

Take a break from your writing and come back to it with "fresh eyes." When you return, imagine you are someone who has never seen your proposal before. Read the proposal out loud. When you are done, ask yourself: Do I understand the problem? Does it really seem like a problem that must be dealt with? Is the solution clear? Does it seem like it is worth the trouble? Do I think it will really work? How much will it cost me, in money, effort, or inconvenience? The biggest trap you can fall into is starting off with the little stuff first. Leave the small stuff for last.

Does your paper or project meet the assignment?

- Look again at your assignment. Does your paper or project do what the assignment asks?
- Look again at the assignment for specific guidelines, including length, format, and amount of research. Does your work meet these guidelines?

Is the proposal claim clear and focused?

- Does the proposal claim address the problem?
- Does the proposal claim issue a clear call to action?

Do you identify the problem adequately?

- Do you need more evidence that the problem exists and is a serious concern?
- Will your readers find credible any sources you include? Can you think of other sources that might be more persuasive?

Is it clear how your solution will address the problem?

- Can you find more evidence that your solution will resolve the problem?
- Do you address potential objections to your solution?
- Do you provide evidence that your solution is feasible? For example, if your solution requires money, where will the money come from?

Do you consider alternative solutions?	• Do you explain why your solution is better than the alternatives?
Is your organization effective?	• Is the order of your main points clear to your reader? • Are there any places where you find abrupt shifts or gaps? • Are there sections or paragraphs that could be rearranged to make your draft more effective?
Is your introduction effective?	• Can you get off to a faster start, perhaps with a striking example? • Can you think of a better way to engage your readers to be interested in the problem you identify? • Does your introduction give your readers a sense of why the problem is important?
Is your conclusion effective?	• Does your conclusion have a call for action? • Do you make it clear exactly what you want your readers to do?
Do you represent yourself effectively?	• To the extent you can, forget for a moment that you wrote what you are reading. What impression do you have of you, the writer? • Does "the writer" create an appropriate tone? • Has "the writer" done his or her homework?
Is the writing project visually effective?	• Is the font attractive and readable? • Is the overall layout attractive and readable? • If headings are used, do they make clear what comes under each of them? • Is each photograph, chart, graph, map, or table clearly labeled? Does each visual have a caption?
Save the editing for last.	When you have finished revising, edit and proofread carefully.

A peer review guide is on page 27.

Writer at work

During peer review of her paper with fellow classmates, and in her meeting with her instructor, Kim Lee made notes on her rough draft. She used these comments to guide her revision of the essay.

The history of the United States of America is punctuated with rhetoric which positions the nation as one that embraces diversity and creates a land of equal opportunity for all of those who choose to live here. As the Statue of Liberty cries out "bring us your tired, your poor, your huddled masses yearning to breathe free," American politicians gleefully use such images to frame the United States a bastion for all things good, fair, and equal. As a proud American, however, I must nonetheless point out one of the cracks in this façade of equality ~~(and that is without even mentioning the repeated failed ratification of the women's Equal Rights Amendment). What flaw could this be?~~ Any foreign-born person with foreign parents is not eligible to be elected our president, even if that person became an American as a baby through adoption.

Opening sentence is too clunky. Need something more engaging.

Stay focused. Don't ask unnecessary questions. Give an example.

The 2003 election of action film star Arnold Schwarzenegger to the gubernatorial seat in California stirred up a drive for a change to this Constitutional statute. Politicians such as Senator Orrin Hatch (R-Utah) and grassroots campaigns such as the group Amend for Arnold appear to dream of reading the political slogans of the Terminator-cum-president's campaign: "I'll be back (for four more years") or "Hasta la vista, baby (and hasta la vista to high taxes)." Consequently, they have been vocally pushing for an amendment that would alter this element of the qualifications for president.

We as a nation must take this time to take a stand against this discriminatory and antiquated aspect of the Constitution.

Transition—the info on Schwrz. does not lead naturally into the renewed call for change. Need a link to show the relationship between this info and my proposal.

Look for ways to focus	Kim Lee responded to suggestions from her teacher and her peers to make her opening paragraph less wordy and better focused on her main point. She removed material that did not obviously inform readers about the problem she was interested in.
Check transitions	She also worked on strengthening transitions between paragraphs.
Read your paper aloud	Finally, Kim Lee read her essay aloud to check for misspelled words, awkward phrasing, and other mechanical problems.

Reviewing your draft

Give yourself plenty of time for reviewing your draft. For detailed information on how to participate in a peer review, how to review it yourself, and how to respond to comments from your classmates, your instructor, or a campus writing consultant, see pages 24–28.

Some good questions to ask yourself when reviewing an argument for change

- Do you connect the problem to your readers? Even if the problem doesn't affect them directly, at the very least you should appeal to their sense of fairness.
- Can you explain more specifically how your solution will work?
- If resources including people and money are required for your solution, can you elaborate where these resources will come from?
- Do you include other possible solutions and discuss the advantages and disadvantages of each? Can you add to this discussion?
- Does your conclusion connect with the attitudes and values of your readers in addition to making clear what you want them to do? Can you add an additional point? Can you sharpen your call to action?

5: Submitted version

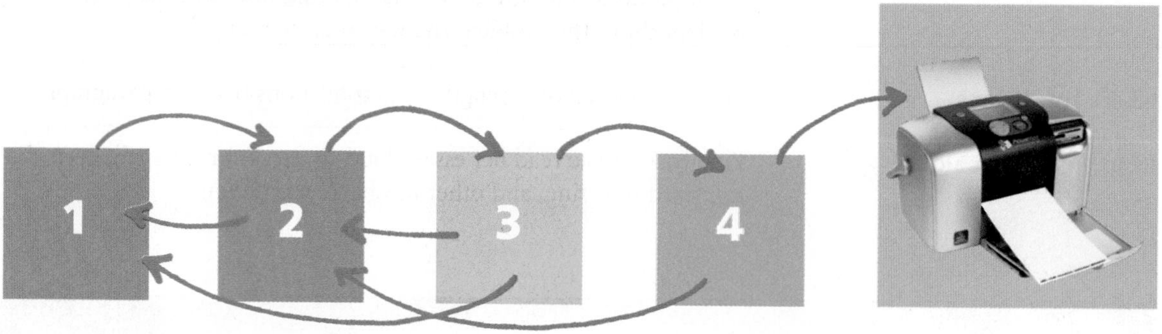

Lee 1

Kim Lee
Professor Patel
RHE 306
31 March 2008

Let's Make It a Real Melting Pot with Presidential Hopes for All

The image the United States likes to advertise is a country that embraces diversity and creates a land of equal opportunity for all. As the Statue of Liberty cries out "give me your tired, your poor, your huddled masses yearning to breathe free," American politicians gleefully evoke such images to frame the United States a bastion for all things good, fair, and equal. As a proud American, however, I must nonetheless highlight one of the cracks in this façade of equality. Imagine an infertile couple decides to adopt an orphaned child from China. They follow all of the legal processes deemed necessary by both countries. They fly abroad and bring home their (once parentless) six-month-old baby boy. They raise and nurture him, and while teaching him to embrace his ethnicity, they also teach him to love Captain Crunch, baseball, and *The Three Stooges*. He grows and eventually attends an ethnically diverse

Lee 2

American public school. One day in the fifth grade his teacher tells the class that anyone can grow up to be president. To clarify her point, she turns to the boy, knowing his background, and states, "No, you could not be president, Stu, but you could still be a senator. That's something to aspire to!" How do these parents explain this rule to this American-raised child? This scenario will become increasingly common. Senator Larry Craig of Idaho states that Americans adopt over 25,000 foreign-born children annually (Epstein A5). As the Constitution currently reads, only "natural-born" citizens may run for the offices of president and vice president. Neither these children nor the thousands of hardworking Americans who chose to make America their official homeland may aspire to the highest political position in the land. While the huddled masses may enter, it appears they must retain a second-class citizen ranking.

The "natural-born" stipulation regarding the presidency stems from the self-same meeting of minds which brought the American people the Electoral College. During the Constitutional Convention of 1787, the Congress formulated the regulatory measures associated with the office of the president. A letter sent from John Jay to George Washington during this period read as follows:

> "Permit me to hint," Jay wrote, "whether it would not be wise and seasonable to provide a strong check to the admission of foreigners into the administration of our national government; and to declare expressly that the Command in Chief of the American army shall not be given to, nor devolve on, any but a natural-born citizen." (Mathews A1)

Shortly thereafter, Article II, Section I, Clause V of the Constitution declared that "No Person except a natural born Citizen, or a Citizen of the United States at the time of

the Adoption of this Constitution, shall be eligible to the Office of President." Jill A. Pryor states in *The Yale Law Journal* that "some writers have suggested that Jay was responding to rumors that foreign princes might be asked to assume the presidency" (881). Many cite disastrous examples of foreign rule in the eighteenth century are the impetus for the "natural born" clause. For example, in 1772—only fifteen years prior to the adoption of the statute—Poland had been divided up by Prussia, Russia, and Austria, (Kasindorf). Perhaps an element of self-preservation and *not* ethnocentrism led to the questionable stipulation. Nonetheless, in the twenty-first century this clause reeks of xenophobia.

The 2003 election of action film star Arnold Schwarzenegger as governor of California stirred up movement to change this Constitutional statute. Politicians such as Senators Orrin Hatch (R-Utah) and Ted Kennedy (D-Massachusetts and Arnold's uncle by marriage) have created a buzz for ratifying a would-be twenty-eighth amendment. In addition, grassroots campaigns like "Amend for Arnold" are trying to rally popular support as they dream of the Terminator-cum-president's political slogans ("I'll be back . . . for four more years" or "Hasta la vista, baby, and hasta la vista to high taxes"). Schwarzenegger has become the face—and the bulked-up body—of the viable *naturalized* president.

We as a nation should follow the lead set by those enamored of the action star, but distance the fight from this one extremely wealthy actor. We must instead take a stand against the discriminatory practice applied to all foreign-born American citizens by this obsolete provision of the Constitution. Congress has made minor attempts to update this biased clause. The Fourteenth Amendment clarified the difference

between "natural-born" and "native born" citizens by spelling out the citizenship status of children born to American parents *outside* of the United States (Ginsberg 929). (Such a clause qualifies individuals such as Senator John McCain—born in Panama—for presidency.) This change is not enough. I propose that the United States abolish the "natural born" clause and replace it with a stipulation that allows naturalized citizens to run for president. This amendment would state that a candidate must have been naturalized and lived in residence in the United States for a period of at least twenty-five years. The present time is ideal for this change. This amendment could simultaneously honor the spirit of the Constitution, protect and ensure the interests of the United States, promote an international image of inclusiveness, and grant heretofore withheld rights to thousands of legal and loyal United States citizens.

In our push for change, we must make clear the importance of this amendment. It would not provide special rights for would-be terrorists. To the contrary, it would fulfill the longtime promises of the nation. The United States claims to allow all people to blend into the great stew of citizenship. It has already suffered embarrassment and international cries of ethnic bias as a result of political moves such as Japanese American internment and the Guantanamo Bay detention center. This amendment can help mend the national image as every American takes one more step toward equality. Naturalized citizens have been contributing to the United States for centuries. Many nameless Mexican, Irish, and Asian Americans sweated and toiled to build the American railroads. The public has welcomed naturalized Americans such as Bob Hope, Albert Pujols, and Peter Jennings into their hearts and living rooms. Individuals such as German-born Henry Kissinger and Czechoslovakian-born Madeleine Albright

Lee 5

have held high posts in the American government and served as respected aides to its presidents. The amendment must make clear that it is not about one man's celebrity. Approximately 700 foreign-born Americans have won the Medal of Honor and over 60,000 proudly serve in the United States military today (Siskind 5). The "natural-born" clause must be removed to provide each of these people—over half a million naturalized in 2003 alone—with equal footing to those who were born into citizenship rather than working for it (U.S. Census Bureau).

Since the passing of the Bill of Rights, only seventeen amendments have been ratified. This process takes time and overwhelming congressional and statewide support. To alter the Constitution, a proposed amendment must pass with a two-thirds "super-majority" in both the House of Representatives and the Senate. In addition, the proposal must find favor in two-thirds (thirty-eight) of state legislatures. In short, this task will not be easy. In order for this change to occur, a grassroots campaign must work to dispel misinformation regarding naturalized citizens and force the hands of senators and representatives wishing to retain their congressional seats. We must take this proposal to ethnicity-specific political groups from both sides of the aisle, business organizations, and community activist groups. We must convince representatives that this issue matters. Only through raising voices and casting votes can the people enact change. Only then can every American child see the possibility for limitless achievement and equality. Only then can everyone find the same sense of pride in the possibility for true American diversity in the highest office in the land.

Lee 6

Works Cited

Epstein, Edward. "Doubt About a Foreign-Born President." *San Francisco Chronicle* 6 Oct. 2004: A5. *LexisNexis Academic*. Web. 6 Mar. 2008.

Facts for Features. US Dept. of Commerce, 27 June 2005. Web. 17 Mar. 2008.

Ginsberg, Gordon. "Citizenship: Expatriation: Distinction Between Naturalized and Natural Born Citizens." *Michigan Law Review* 50 (1952): 926-29. *JSTOR*. Web. 6 Mar. 2008.

Mathews, Joe. "Maybe Anyone Can Be President." *Los Angeles Times* 2 Feb. 2005: A1. *LexisNexis Academic*. Web. 6 Mar. 2008.

Kasindorf, Martin. "Should the Constitution Be Amended for Arnold?" *USA Today* 2 Dec. 2004. *LexisNexis Academic*. Web. 8 Mar. 2008.

Pryor, Jill A. "The Natural Born Citizen Clause and Presidential Eligibility: An Approach for Resolving Two Hundred Years of Uncertainty." *The Yale Law Journal* 97.5 (1988): 881-99. Print.

Siskind, Lawrence J. "Why Shouldn't Arnold Run?" *The Recorder* 10 Dec. 2004: 5. *LexisNexis Academic*. Web. 10 Mar. 2008.

United States. Dept. of Commerce. Census Bureau. "The Fourth of July 2005."

Projects

If you want to persuade your readers to do something, you must convince them that a problem exists and that something needs to be done about it. You'll likely make the best argument for change if the problem matters to you. Most groups and organizations are faced with problems. You'll be able to argue with conviction, and you might even bring about change.

The following projects will give you experience in the kinds of proposals frequent in the workplace and in public life.

Proposal essay

Write a proposal of 1000–1250 words (about five to seven double-spaced pages) that would solve a problem that you identify.

Choose a problem with which you have personal experience, but you should also think about how many other people this problem affects. Your proposal should take them into account as part of your audience.

Find out who would be in a position to enact your proposal. How can you make your solution seem like a good idea to these people?

Propose your solution as specifically as you can. What exactly do you want to achieve? How exactly will your solution work? Has anything like it been tried elsewhere? Who will be involved?

Consider other solutions that have been or might be proposed for this problem, including doing nothing. What are the advantages and disadvantages of those solutions? Why is your solution better?

Examine how easy your solution is to implement. Will the people most affected be willing to go along with it? Lots of things can be accomplished if enough people volunteer, but groups often have difficulty getting enough volunteers to work without pay. If it costs money, how do you propose paying for it?

Reconstructing a proposal

You may not have a lot of experience writing proposals. Nevertheless, proposals have had a profound impact on your life. Almost every program, law, policy, or business that affects you had to be proposed before it became a reality.

Think of some things in your life that were proposed by people: the building where you attended high school, for example. At some point, that building was proposed as a way of solving a certain problem—perhaps your town had one old, overflowing high school, and your building was proposed to solve the overcrowding. Its location was probably chosen carefully, to avoid causing more problems with traffic, and to ensure that it was easy for students to reach.

Choose something you are familiar with that went through a proposal process. Try to reconstruct the four components of the original proposal. What problem do you think people were trying to solve? How did concerns about fairness and feasibility shape the program, building, or policy?

Outline your re-created proposal in a page or two.

Ask yourself if this policy, program, or business truly solved the problem it was intended to solve. Clearly, the proposal itself was successful, for the school was built, the law was passed, or the business was started. But how successful was the proposed solution in reality?

Teamwork: counterproposals

Find a proposal argument that you and three or four classmates are interested in. This might be a proposal to widen a road in your town, to pass a law making English the official language of your state government, or something similar.

As a group discuss the four components of the proposal as outlined in this chapter: What is the problem being addressed? What is the solution? Is it workable and fair? Is it feasible?

Then have each person in the group construct a one- or two-page counterproposal. Your counterproposals should address the same problem as the original proposal, but should offer different solutions. Your analysis of the workability, fairness, and feasibility of the original proposal will help you shape your counterproposals. Is there a way to solve the problem that is cheaper? less disruptive? more fair? less risky?

Present your counterproposals to the rest of your group, and discuss which is the most appealing. You may find that a combination of elements of the different proposals ends up being the best.

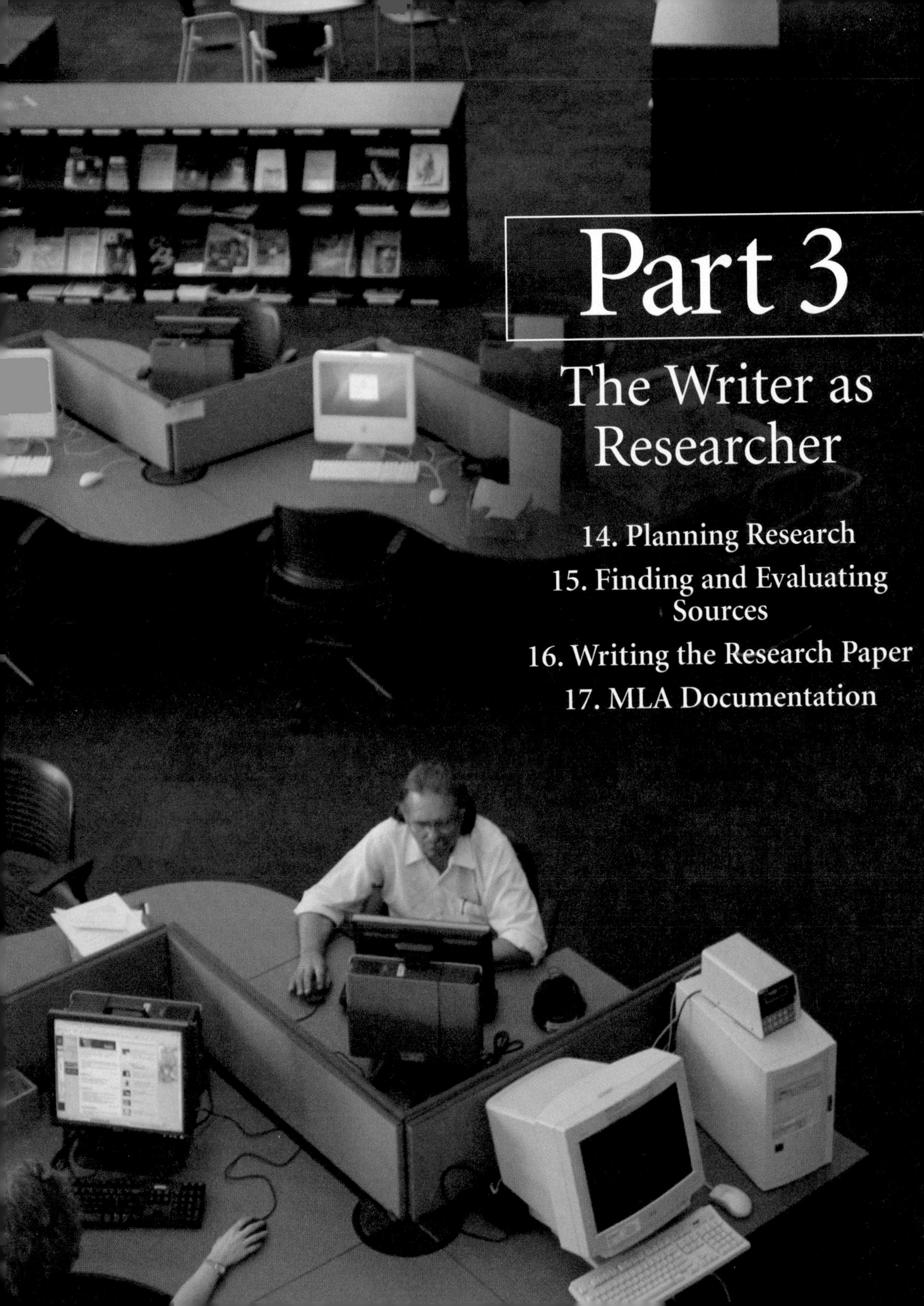

Part 3

The Writer as Researcher

14 Planning Research

Understand the different kinds of possible research and plan your strategy in advance.

Analyze the research task

If you have an assignment that requires research, look closely at what you are being asked to do. The assignment may ask you to review, compare, survey, analyze, evaluate, or prove that something is true or untrue. You may be writing for experts, for students like yourself, or for the general public. The purpose of your research and your potential audience will help guide your strategies for research.

The key is understanding what is expected of you. You are being asked to

1. Determine your goals.
2. Find a subject.
3. Ask a question about the subject.
4. Find out what has been said about this subject.
5. Make a contribution to the discussion about this subject.

Determine your goals

Often your assignment will tell you how to get started. Look for key words:

- An *analysis* or *examination* requires you to look at an issue in detail, explaining how it has evolved, who or what it affects, and what is at stake.
- A *survey* requires you to gather opinions about a particular issue, either by a questionnaire or by interviews.
- An *evaluation* requires you to make critical judgments.
- An *argument* requires you to assemble evidence in support of a claim you make.

Ask your instructor for guidance if you remain unsure what is expected.

Find a subject that interests you

When you ask meaningful questions, your research will be enjoyable. Your courses may give you some ideas about questions to ask. Personal experience is often a good source of questions related to your research topic: What was the cause of something that happened to you? Was your experience typical or atypical? How can you solve a problem you have? What do experts think about the issues that concern you? Working with a topic that has already aroused your curiosity makes it more likely that your findings will interest others.

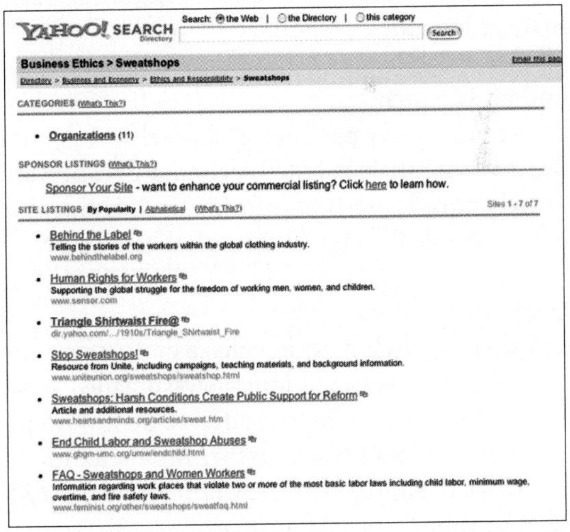

A good way to begin is by browsing a subject directory, either in your library or on the Web. Subject directories can show you many different aspects of a single topic.

[Reproduced with permission of Yahoo! Inc. Copyright © 2008 by Yahoo! Inc. YAHOO! and the YAHOO! logo are trademarks of Yahoo! Inc.]

Ask a question

Often you'll be surprised by the amount of information your initial browsing uncovers. Your next task will be to identify in that mass of information a question for your research project. This researchable question will be the focus of the remainder of your research and ultimately of your research project or paper. Browsing on the topic of solid waste recycling might lead you to a researchable question such as

- Do cities save or lose money on recycling programs?
- Why can't all plastics be recycled?
- Are Americans being persuaded to recycle more paper, aluminum, and plastic?

Focus your research question

Think about how to make your research question specific enough so that you can treat it thoroughly in a paper. Reading about your subject will help you to focus your research question.

- Why did the number of tons of recycled plastic and glass in our city peak in 2005 and decline slightly ever since?
- Should our state mandate the use of degradable plastics that decay along with kitchen and yard waste in compost heaps?
- Besides paper bags that deplete forests, what are the alternatives to plastic bags that contaminate soil in landfills and sabotage the recycling system by jamming the machinery that sorts bottles and cans?

Determine what kinds of research you need to do

Once you have formulated a research question, begin thinking about what kind of research you will need to do to address the question.

Secondary research

Most researchers rely partly or exclusively on the work of others as sources of information. Research based on the work of others is called **secondary research.** In the past this information was contained almost exclusively in collections of print materials housed in libraries, but today enormous amounts of information are available through library databases and the World Wide Web.

Primary research

Much of the research done in college creates new information through **primary research**: experiments, data-gathering surveys and interviews, detailed observations, and the examination of historical documents. Although some undergraduates do not do primary research, sometimes you may be researching a question that requires you to gather firsthand information. For example, if you are researching a campus issue such as the impact of a new library fee on students' budgets, you may need to conduct interviews, make observations, or take a survey.

Determine what you need

Is the scope of your issue . . .	Then research might include . . .
Local? (Inadequate bike lanes, local noise ordinances, school policies)	• interviews and observations • local newspapers • other local media: television, radio
Regional? (County taxes, toll road construction, watershed protection)	• some of the sources above • state government offices • regional organizations, clubs, or associations—e.g., the Newark Better Business Bureau, Brazos Valley Mothers Against Drunk Driving
National? (Federal agricultural subsidies, immigration, major league sports)	• some of the sources above • federal government offices • national organizations, clubs, or associations—e.g., the American Automobile Association • national network news on television and radio • national newspapers or magazines—e.g., the *New York Times* or *Rolling Stone*
International? (Trade imbalances, military conflicts, global climate change)	• some of the sources above • federal government offices • international agencies such as UNICEF • international news outlets such as Reuters • foreign newspapers or magazines like *Le Monde* and *der Spiegel*

You can also find sources you need by thinking about people affected by your issue and noting where it is being discussed.

Who is interested in this issue?

scientists
teachers
voters
minors
senior citizens
policy makers
stock brokers

Where would they read, write, talk, or hear about it?

scientific journals
political journals
scholarly journals
newspapers
books
Web forums
government documents

In what different media might the information appear?

online
television
radio
print
film/DVD

Set a Schedule

Use your assignment, your personal schedule, and your knowledge of the sources you'll need to schedule your research. Allow yourself some large blocks of uninterrupted time, especially during the browsing stage.

Project: Research paper for a government course, analyzing a recent financial fraud

Days until first draft is due: 17

Days 1–3:
PRELIMINARY research, one hour each evening

Days 4–6:
IN-DEPTH library research—Schedule appointment with reference librarian for periodicals search tutorial

Days 7–9:
Go over collected material, think about research question/hypothesis

Days 10–12:
Begin drafting

Days 13–14:
Revise rough draft for clarity, organization, and ideas

Days 15–16:
Follow-up research or verify questionable sources as needed

Day 17:
Fine-tune draft

Project: Paper utilizing field research for an introduction to social research course

Weeks until project due: 7

Week 1:
Research and brainstorm topics; discuss short list of possible topics/methods with professor; make final decision

Week 2:
Research survey/interview methods; design appropriate method

Week 3:
Conduct field research

Week 4:
Analyze data and do follow-up if necessary

Week 5:
Draft paper—go back to library if necessary

Week 6:
Take draft to writing center; revise

Week 7:
Proofread, fine tune, and make sure all charts and images print correctly

Draft a working thesis

Once you have done some preliminary research into your question, you need to craft a working thesis. Perhaps you have found a lot of interesting material on the home economics movement of the 1950s and 1960s. You have discovered that food companies—particularly makers of packaged foods—were deeply involved in shaping and funding the movement. As you research the question of why food companies fostered the home economics movement, a working thesis begins to emerge.

Write your topic, research question, and working thesis on a note card or sheet of paper. Keep your working thesis handy. You may need to revise it several times until the wording is precise. As you research, ask yourself, does this information tend to support my thesis? Information that does not support your thesis is still important! It may lead you to adjust your thesis, or even abandon it altogether. You may need to find another source or reason that shows your thesis is still valid.

TOPIC:
The Home Economics Movement of the 1950s and 1960s.

RESEARCH QUESTION:
Why did the major American food corporations fund the Home Economics movement of the 50s and 60s?

WORKING THESIS:
Major American food corporations invested in the development and spread of Home Economics in order to create a ready market for their products by teaching women to rely on prepared foods instead of cooking "from scratch." They used Home Economics programs to change the way Americans thought about food and cooking.

Write Now

Determine what information you need

Select one of the possible topics below or identify a topic that will work for your assignment. Write a brief list or paragraph describing the types of research that might be used to investigate the question. What kinds of information would you need? Where would you look for it?

1. How much does an average American couple spend to adopt a child from overseas?
2. What determines the price of gasoline that you pay at the pump?
3. How effective was drafting soldiers in the North and South during the Civil War?
4. Why does the U.S. Postal Service spend part of its budget to encourage stamp collecting?

15 Finding and Evaluating Sources

Know how to find and identify the best information available.

Find information in databases

You can learn how to use databases in your library with the help of a reference librarian. Your library may also have online and printed tutorials on using databases. Once you know how to access the databases you need, you can work from computers in other locations.

Most databases are by subscription only and must be accessed through your library's Web site, but a few like Google Scholar are free to everyone.

Academic Search Premier and Academic Search Complete	Provides full text articles for thousands of scholarly publications, including social sciences, humanities, education, computer sciences, engineering, language and linguistics, literature, medical sciences, and ethnic studies journals.
ArticleFirst	Indexes journals in business, the humanities, medicine, science, and social sciences.
EBSCOhost Research Databases	Gateway to a large collection of EBSCO databases, including Academic Search Premier and MasterFILE Premier.
Expanded Academic ASAP	Indexes periodicals from the arts, humanities, sciences, social sciences, and general news, with full-text articles and images.
Factiva	Provides news and business information from over 10,000 sources including the *Wall Street Journal.*
FirstSearch	Offers millions of full-text articles from many databases.
Google Scholar	Searches scholarly literature according to criteria of relevance.
InfoTrac OneFile	Contains millions of full-text articles on a wide range of academic and general interest topics.
JSTOR	Provides scanned copies of scholarly journals.
LexisNexis Academic	Provides full text of a wide range of newspapers, magazines, government and legal documents, and company profiles from around the world.
OmniFile Full Text	Provides full-text articles, indexes, and abstracts for most subjects.

Construct effective searches

To use databases effectively, make a list of keywords in advance.

Select a database

Your next decision is to choose a database to begin your research. Newspapers might include stories on local deer populations and changes in hunting policy. Popular journals such as *Field and Stream* might have articles on national trends in deer hunting, and might also summarize scholarly research on the subject. Scholarly journals, perhaps in the field of wildlife biology, would contain articles about formal research into the effects of deer hunting on population density, average size and weight of animals, range, and other specific factors.

To find newspaper stories, begin with LexisNexis Academic. To find popular and scholarly journal articles, go Academic Search Premier, Academic Search Complete, EBSCOhost, Expanded Academic ASAP, FirstSearch, or InfoTrac OneFile.

Evaluate database sources

Databases collect print sources and put them in digital formats. Evaluate database sources the same way you evaluate print sources.

1. **Source:** Is the source a scholarly or popular journal?
2. **Author:** What are the author's qualifications?
3. **Timeliness:** How current is the source?
4. **Evidence:** Where does the evidence come from?
5. **Biases:** Can you detect particular biases?
6. **Advertising:** Is advertising prominent?

Evaluate for relevance

Even reliable sources may not pertain to your topic. Consider the relevance of each source for your subject.

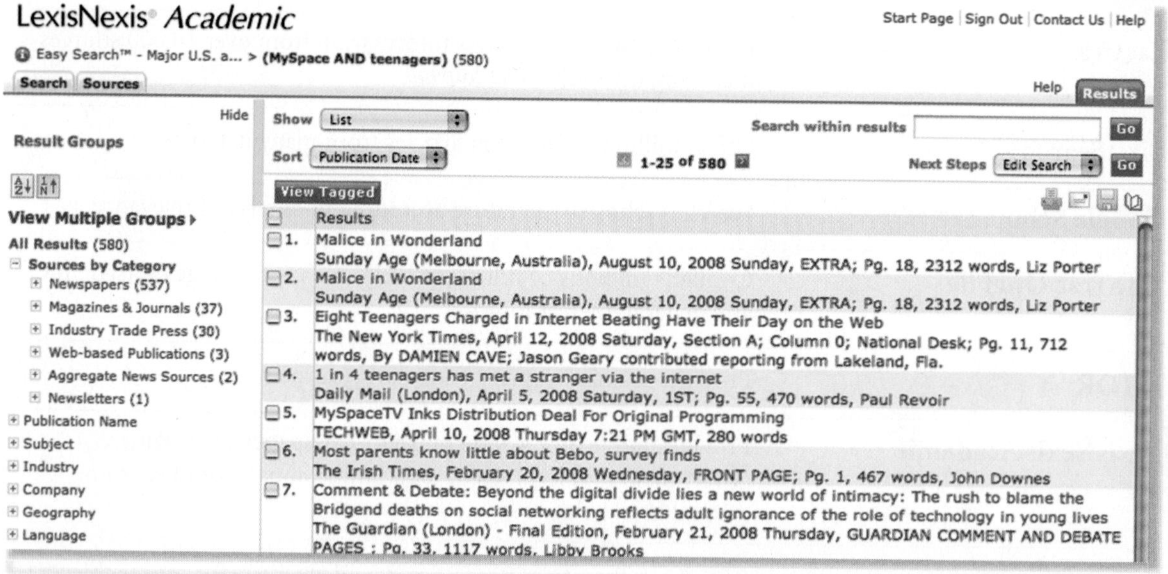

Results of a search on LexisNexis for MySpace AND teenagers. If your topic is the danger of predators taking advantage of younger teenagers on MySpace, probably articles 1, 4, 6, and 7 would be the first ones to examine.

Locate elements of a citation

To cite a source from a database, you will need the

- Author if listed
- Title of article
- Name of periodical
- Volume and issue number (for journals)
- Date of publication (and edition for newspapers)
- Section (for newspapers) and page numbers
- Name of database
- Medium of publication (*Web*)
- Date of access (the day you found the article in the database)

A sample article from the Academic Search Premier search for "steroids" and "high school." The confusing part of citing this example is distinguishing between the database and the vendor. The vendor's name often appears at the top of the screen, making the vendor's name look like the name of the database. In this case, EBSCO is the vendor—the company that sells your library access to Academic Search Premier and many other databases. Often you have to look carefully to find the name of the database.

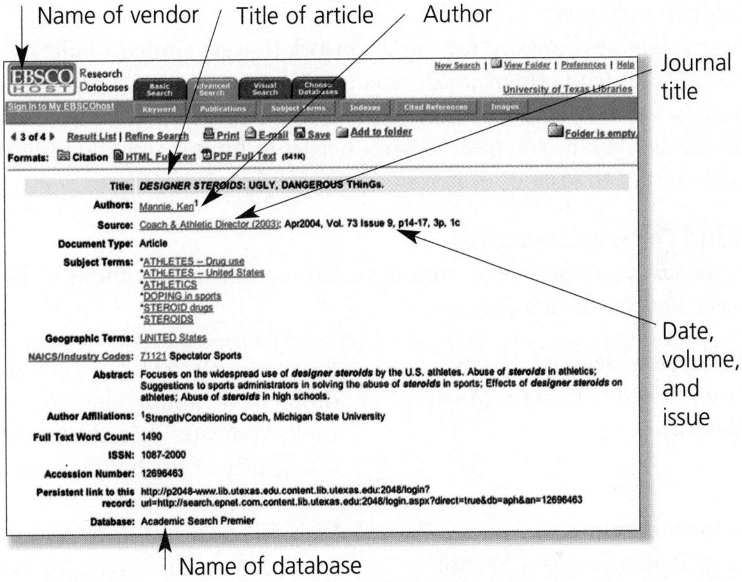

A citation for an article that you find on a database looks like this in MLA style:

> Mannie, Ken. "Designer Steroids: Ugly, Dangerous Things." *Scholastic Coach and Athletic Director* 73.9 (2004): 14–17. *Academic Search Premier*. Web. 26 July 2008.

Working Together

Compare databases

In a group of three or four students

Identify keywords for your research topic, and use the same keywords for searches on three or more databases. If the search yields too many items, use AND to connect the terms or add another keyword plus AND. Copy the results from each search and paste this into a file. Which database turned up more items? Which turned up more scholarly articles? Which turned up more articles in popular journals? Which will be most helpful for your research topic?

Find information on the Web

Because anyone can publish on the Web, there is no overall quality control and there is no system of organization as you would find in a library. Nevertheless, the Web offers you some resources for current topics that would be difficult to find in a library. The keys to success are knowing where you are most likely to find current and accurate information about the particular question you are researching, and knowing how to access that information.

Search engines

Search engines designed for the Web work in ways similar to library databases and your library's online catalog, but with one major difference. Databases typically do some screening of the items they list, but search engines potentially take you to every Web site that isn't password protected—millions of pages in all. Consequently, you have to work harder to limit searches on the Web; otherwise you can be deluged with tens of thousands of items.

Kinds of search engines

A search engine is a set of programs that sort through millions of items at incredible speed. There are four basic kinds of search engines.

1. Keyword search engines (e.g., Ask.com, Google, MSN, Yahoo!)	Keyword search engines give different results because they assign different weights to the information they find. Google, for example, ranks Web sites according to how many other sites link to them and the quality of the linking sites.
2. Web directories (e.g., Britannica.com, Yahoo! Directory)	Web directories classify Web sites into categories and are the closest equivalent to the cataloging system used by libraries. On most directories professional editors decide how to index a particular Web site. Web directories also allow keyword searches.
3. Metasearch agents (e.g., Dogpile, HotBot, Metacrawler)	Metasearch agents allow you to use several search engines simultaneously. While the concept is sound, metasearch agents are limited by the number of hits they can return and their inability to handle advanced searches.
4. Specialized search engines (e.g., Froogle [shopping], Google Scholar [academic], Monster.com [jobs], Baidu [regional for China], WebMD [medicine])	Specialized search engines have been developed in recent years for specific subjects.

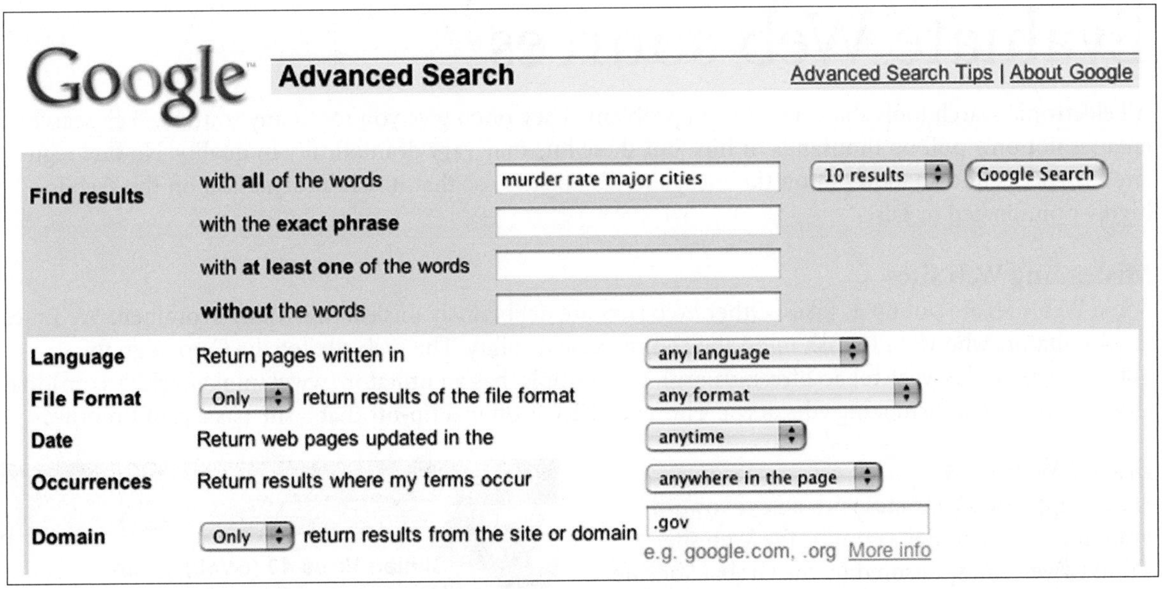

An advanced search on Google for government sites only (.gov).

Advanced searches

Search engines often produce too many hits and are therefore not always useful. If you look only at the first few items, you may miss what is most valuable. The alternative is to refine your search. Most search engines offer you the option of an advanced search, which gives you the opportunity to limit numbers.

The advanced searches on Google and Yahoo! give you the options of using a string of words to search for sites that contain (1) all the words, (2) the exact phrase, (3) any of the words, or (4) that exclude certain words. They also allow you to specify the language of the site, the date range, the file format, and the domain. For example, government statistics on crime are considered the most reliable, so if you want to find statistics on murder rates, you can specify the domain as .gov in an advanced search.

Discussion forums, groups, and blogs

The Internet allows you to access other people's opinions on thousands of topics. The Groups section of Google (groups.google.com) has an archive of several hundred million messages that can be searched. Much of the conversation on these sites is undocumented and highly opinionated, but you can still gather important information about people's attitudes and get tips about other sources, which you can verify later.

Web logs, better known as blogs, also are sources of public opinion. Several tools have been developed to search blogs: Bloglines, Google Blog Search, Technorati, and IceRocket. Blogs are not screened and are not considered authoritative sources, but blogs can sometimes lead you to quality sources.

Evaluate Web sources

All electronic search tools share a common problem: They often give you too many sources. Web search engines not only pull up thousands of hits, but these hits may vary dramatically in quality. No one regulates or checks information put on the Web, and it's no surprise that much information on the Web is highly opinionated or false.

Misleading Web sites

Some Web sites are put up as jokes. Other Web sites are deliberately misleading. Many prominent Web sites draw imitators who want to cash in on the commercial visibility. The Web site for the Campaign for Tobacco-Free Kids (www.tobaccofreekids.org), for example, has an imitator (www.smokefreekids.com) that sells software for antismoking education. The .com URL is often a tip-off that a site has a profit motive.

Biased Web sites

Always approach Web sites with an eye toward evaluating content. For example, the Web site Thinktwice.com, sponsored by the Global Vaccine Institute, opposes the vaccination of children. On the site you can find claims that the polio vaccine administered to millions in the United States causes cancer because it was contaminated with Simian Virus 40. Always look for other sources for verification. The U.S. Centers for Disease Control publishes fact sheets on the latest information about diseases and their prevention, including one on polio vaccine and Simian Virus 40.

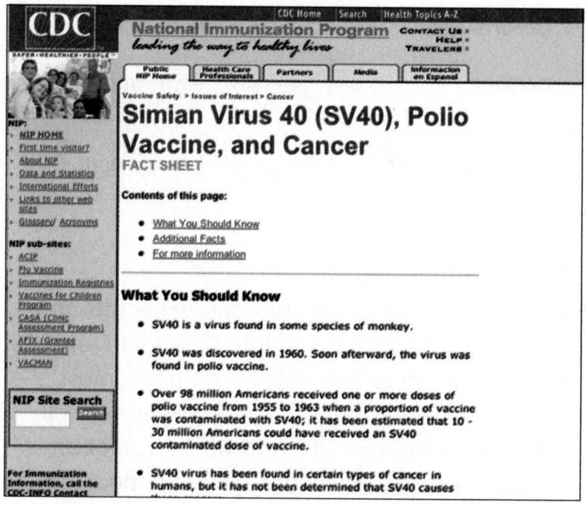

Fact sheet on Simian Virus 40, Polio Vaccine, and Cancer from the Centers for Disease Control (http://www.cdc.gov/nip/vacsafe/concerns/cancer/sv40-polio-cancer-facts.htm).

Locate elements of a citation

To cite a Web site you will need

- Author if listed
- Title of the work (in italics unless part of a larger work)
- Title of the overall Web site (in italics if distinct from the work)
- Version of the site (if relevant)
- Publisher or sponsor of the site (if no publisher is given, use *N.p.*)
- Date of publication (if no date is given, use *n.d.*)
- Medium of publication (Web)
- Date of access

Ogintz, Eileen. "Hiking Italy's Amalfi Coast." *CNN.com*. Cable News Network, 1 July 2008. Web. 3 July 2008.

A citation for a Web page looks like this in MLA style.

Criteria for evaluating Web sources

The criteria for evaluating print sources can be applied to Web sources if the special circumstances of the Web are acknowledged. For example, when you find a Web page by using a search engine, often you go deep into a complex site without having any sense of the context for that page. To evaluate the credibility of the site, you would need to examine the home page, not just the specific page you saw first.

Source	Look for the site's ownership in the Web address. If a Web site doesn't indicate ownership, then you have to make judgments about who put it up and why. The suffix can offer clues: .gov is used by government bodies, and .edu by educational institutions, generally colleges and universities. These sites are generally more reliable than .com sites.
Author	Often Web sites give no information about their authors other than an e-mail address, if that. In such cases it is difficult or impossible to determine the author's qualifications. Look up the author on Google. If qualifications are listed, is the author an expert in the field?
Timeliness	Many Web pages do not list when they were last updated; thus you cannot determine their currency.
Evidence	The accuracy of any evidence found on the Web is often hard to verify. The most reliable information on the Web stands up to the tests of print evaluation, with clear indication of the sponsoring organization and the sources of any factual information.
Biases	Many Web sites announce their viewpoint on controversial issues, but others conceal their attitude with a reasonable tone and seemingly factual evidence such as statistics. Citations and bibliographies do not ensure that a site is reliable. Look carefully at the links and sources cited.
Advertising	Many Web sites are infomercials aimed at getting you to buy a product or service. While they might contain useful information, they are no more trustworthy than other forms of advertising.

Wikipedia

Wikipedia is not considered a reliable source of information for a research paper by many instructors and the scholarly community in general. The problem with Wikipedia is not so much that erroneous information exists on Wikipedia but that the content changes frequently. There is no guarantee that what you find on Wikipedia today will still be there tomorrow. Many Wikipedia entries, however, do list reliable sources that you can consult and cite in a research paper.

Find visual sources online

You can find images published on the Web using Google and other search engines that allow you to specify searches for images. For example, if you are writing a research paper on invasive plant species, you might want to include an image of kudzu, an invasive vine common in the American South. In Google, choose Images and type *kudzu* in the search box. You'll find a selection of images of plant, including several from the National Park Service.

Three major search engines are designed specifically to find images.

- Google Image Search (images.google.com). The most comprehensive image search tool.
- Picsearch (www.picsearch.com). Provides thumbnails of images linked to the source on the Web.
- Yahoo Search (images.search.yahoo.com). Has tools to limit results on the Advanced Search similar to Google.

Other useful visual sites for visual resources include

- *Statistical Abstract of the United States* (www.census.gov/compendia/statab/). Contains statistical data represented in charts and graphs.
- Directory of map sites (www.lib.utexas.edu/maps/map_sites/map_sites.html).

Kudzu
Pueraria montana var. *lobata* (Willd.) Maesen & S. Almeida
Pea family (Fabaceae)
NATIVE RANGE: Asia
DESCRIPTION: Kudzu ia a climbing, semi-woody, perennial vine in the pea family. Deciduous leaves are alternate and compound, with three broad leaflets up to 4 inches across. Leaflets may be entire or deeply 2-3 lobed with hairy margins. Individual flowers, about 1/2 inch long, are purple, highly fragrant and borne in long hanging clusters. Flowering occurs in late summer and is soon followed by production of brown, hairy, flattened, seed pods, each of which contains three to ten hard seeds.

Kudzu was planted widely in the South to reduce soil erosion but has itself become a major pest, smothering native trees and plants.

Follow copyright requirements

Just because images are easy to download from the Web does not mean that you are free to use every image you find. Look for the image creator's copyright notice and suggested credit line. This notice will tell you if you can reproduce the image. You should acknowledge the source of any image you use.

In many cases you will find a copyright notice that reads something like this, "Any use or re-transmission of text or images in this Web site without written consent of the copyright owner constitutes copyright infringement and is prohibited." You must write to the creator to ask permission to use an image from a site that is not in the public domain, even if you cannot find a copyright notice.

Write Now

Evaluate Web sites

Hoaxbusters (http://hoaxbusters.ciac.org/) provides an index of Internet hoaxes sorted into categories. Read several of the hoaxes, and select one to explore further. To evaluate your site use the criteria for evaluating Web sources on the opposite page. On which criteria does it fail to be reliable?

Next do a Google search for Ritalin, a commonly prescribed drug for attention deficit disorder (ADD) and attention deficit hyperactivity disorder (ADHD). You will find that the drug is quite controversial. Look at five different Web sites. Which sites do you find most reliable and the least reliable?

Find books

Nearly all college libraries now shelve books according to the Library of Congress Classification System, which uses a combination of letters and numbers to give you the book's unique location in the library. The Library of Congress call number begins with a letter or letters that represent the broad subject area into which the book is classified.

The Library of Congress system groups books by subject, and you can often find other items relevant to your search shelved close to the particular one you are looking for. You can search the extensive Library of Congress online catalog (catalog.loc.gov) to find out how your subject might be indexed, or you can go straight to your own library's catalog and conduct a subject search. The call number will enable you to find the item in the stacks. You will need to consult the locations guide for your library to find the book on the shelves.

When you find a book in your library catalog, take time to notice the subject headings under which it is indexed. For example, if you locate Jeff Hawkins's *On Intelligence*, you will probably find it cross-listed under several subject categories, including

```
Brain
Intellect
Artificial intelligence
Neural networks (Computer science)
```

Browsing within these categories, or using some of their keywords in a new search, may lead you to more useful sources.

Find journal articles

Like books, scholarly journals provide in-depth examinations of subjects. The articles in scholarly journals are written by experts, and they usually contain lists of references that can guide you to other research on a subject. In contrast, articles in popular magazines like *Newsweek, Rolling Stone,* and *People* are typically written by journalists. Some instructors frown on using popular magazines, but these journals can be valuable for researching current opinion on a particular topic.

Searching for articles in scholarly journals and popular magazines works much the same way as searching for books. Indexes for scholarly journals and magazines are available on your library's Web site. Databases increasingly contain the full text of articles, allowing you to read and copy the contents onto your computer. Others give you a citation to a print journal, which you then have to find on a shelf in your library.

Your library has a list of databases and indexes by subject. Find this subject index either on your library's Web site or in the reference section of your library. Follow these steps to find articles:

1. Select an index appropriate to your subject. (For researching multiple sclerosis, you might start with Health Reference Center, MEDLINE, and PsycINFO.)
2. Search the index using relevant subject heading(s). (You could start with multiple sclerosis and then combine MS with other terms to narrow your search.)
3. Print or copy the complete citation to the article(s).
4. Print or copy the full text if it is available.
5. If the full text is not available, check the periodicals holdings to see if your library has the print journal.

Your library will probably have printed handouts or information on the Web that tell you which specialized index to use for a particular subject. Ask a librarian who works at the reference or information desk to help you.

Evaluate print sources

Whether you use print or online sources, a successful search will turn up many more items than you can expect to use in your final product. You have to make a series of decisions about what is important and relevant. Return to your research question and working thesis (see Chapter 14) to determine which items are relevant.

How reliable are your sources? Books are expensive to print and distribute, so book publishers generally protect their investment by providing some level of editorial oversight. Print sources in libraries have an additional layer of oversight because someone has decided that a book or journal is worth purchasing and cataloging. Web sites, in contrast, can be put up and changed quickly, so information can be—and often is—posted thoughtlessly.

But print sources contain their share of biased, inaccurate, and misleading information. Over the years librarians have developed a set of criteria for evaluating print sources.

Source	Who published the book or article? Scholarly books and articles in scholarly journals are reviewed by experts in the field before they are published. They are generally more reliable than popular magazines and books, which tend to emphasize what is entertaining at the expense of comprehensiveness.
Author	Who wrote the book or article? What are the author's qualifications?
Timeliness	How current is the source? If you are researching a fast-developing subject such as vaccines for Asian bird flu, then currency is very important. Currency might not be as important for a historical subject, but even historical figures and events are often reinterpreted.
Evidence	Where does the evidence come from: facts, interviews, observations, surveys, or experiments? Is the evidence adequate to support the author's claims?
Biases	Can you detect particular biases of the author? How do the author's biases affect the interpretation offered?
Advertising	Is advertising a prominent part of the journal or newspaper? How might the ads affect what gets printed?

Write Now

Evaluate information

Think of three or four different types of writing you have read recently: a novel, textbook, blog, letter, flyer, comic book, or online review. Evaluate each source according to the criteria above. Which item is the most reliable? For what purpose? Which is the least reliable?

16 Writing the Research Paper

Thorough reasearch gives you a wealth of ideas and information to communicate.

Plan your organization

Review your goals and thesis

Before you begin writing your paper, review the assignment and your goals (see Chapter 14). Your review of the assignment will remind you of your purpose, your potential readers, your stance on your subject, and the length and scope you should aim for.

By now you should have formulated a working thesis, which will be the focus of your paper. You should also have located, read, evaluated, and taken notes on enough source material to write your paper. At this stage in the writing process, your working thesis may be rough and may change as you write your draft, but having a working thesis will help keep your paper focused.

Determine your contribution

A convincing and compelling research paper does not make claims based solely on the word of the writer. It draws on the expertise and reputations of others as well. Thus it is critical to show your readers which elements of your paper represent your original thinking.

Determine exactly what you are adding to the larger conversation about your subject.

- Who do you agree with?
- Who do you disagree with?
- What can you add to points you agree with?
- What original analysis or theorizing do you have to offer?
- What original findings from field research do you have to offer?

Determine your main points and group your findings

Look back over your notes and determine how to group the ideas you researched. Decide what your major points will be, and how those points support your thesis. Group your research findings so that they match up with your major points.

Now it is time to create a working outline. Always include your thesis at the top of your outline as a guiding light. Some writers create formal outlines with roman numerals and the like; others compose the headings for the paragraphs of their paper and use them to guide their draft; still others may start writing and then determine how they will organize their draft when they have a few paragraphs written. Experiment and decide which method works best for you.

Avoid plagiarism

You know that copying someone else's paper word for word or taking an article off the Internet and turning it in as yours is plagiarism. That's plain stealing, and people who take that risk should know that the punishment can be severe. But plagiarism also means using the ideas, melodies, or images of someone else without acknowledging them, and it is important to understand exactly what defines plagiarism.

What you don't have to document

Fortunately, common sense governs issues of academic plagiarism. The standards of documentation are not so strict that the source of every fact you cite must be acknowledged. Suppose you are writing about the causes of maritime disasters and you want to know how many people drowned when the *Titanic* sank on the early morning of April 15, 1912. You check the *Britannica Online* Web site and find that the death toll was around 1,500. Since this fact is available in many other reference works, you would not need to cite *Britannica Online* as the source.

But let's say you want to challenge the version of the sinking offered in the 1998 movie *Titanic*, which repeats the usual explanation that the *Titanic* side-swiped an iceberg, ripping a long gash along the hull that caused the ship to go down. Suppose that, in your reading, you discover that a September 1985 exploration of the wreck by an unmanned submersible did not find the long gash previously thought to have sunk the ship. The evidence instead suggested that the force of the collision with the iceberg broke the seams in the hull, allowing water to flood the ship's watertight compartments. You would need to cite the source of your information for this alternative version of the *Titanic*'s demise.

What you do have to document

For facts that are not easily found in general reference works, statements of opinion, and arguable claims, you should cite the source. You should also cite the sources of statistics, research findings, examples, graphs, charts, and illustrations. For example, if you state that the percentage of obese children aged 6 to 11 in the United States rose from 4% in 1974 to 15% in 2000, you need to cite the source.

As a reader you should be skeptical about statistics and research findings when the source is not mentioned. When a writer does not cite the sources of statistics and research findings, there is no way of knowing how reliable the sources are or whether the writer is making them up.

From the writer's perspective careful citing of sources lends credibility. If you take your statistics from a generally trusted source, your readers are more likely to trust whatever conclusions or arguments you are presenting. When in doubt, always document the source.

Be careful when taking notes and copying material online

The best way to avoid unintentional plagiarism is to take care to distinguish source words from your own words.

- Don't mix words from the source with your own words. If you copy anything from a source when taking notes, place those words in quotation marks and note the page number(s) where those words appear.
- Write down all the information you need for each source.
- If you copy words from an online source, take special care to note the source. You could easily copy online material and later not be able to find where it came from.
- Photocopy printed sources and print out online sources. Having printed copies of sources allows you to double-check later that you haven't used words from the source by mistake and that any words you quote are accurate.

Quote sources without plagiarizing

Effective research writing builds on the work of others. You can summarize or paraphrase the work of others, but often it is best to let the authors speak in your text by quoting their exact words. Indicate the words of others by placing them inside quotation marks.

Most people who get into plagiarism trouble lift words from a source and use them without quotation marks. Where the line is drawn is easiest to illustrate with an example. In the following passage, Steven Johnson takes sharp issue with the metaphor of surfing applied to the Web:

> The concept of "surfing" does a terrible injustice to what it means to navigate around the Web. . . . What makes the idea of cybersurf so infuriating is the implicit connection drawn to television. Web surfing, after all, is a derivation of channel surfing—the term thrust upon the world by the rise of remote controls and cable panoply in the mid-eighties. . . . Applied to the boob tube, of course, the term was not altogether inappropriate. Surfing at least implied that channel-hopping was more dynamic, more involved, than the old routine of passive consumption. Just as a real-world surfer's enjoyment depended on the waves delivered up by the ocean, the channel surfer was at the mercy of the programmers and network executives. The analogy took off because it worked well in the one-to-many system of cable TV, where your navigational options were limited to the available channels.
>
> But when the term crossed over to the bustling new world of the Web, it lost a great deal of precision. . . . Web surfing and channel surfing are genuinely different pursuits; to imagine them as equivalents is to ignore the defining characteristics of each medium. Or at least that's what happens in theory. In practice, the Web takes on the greater burden. The television imagery casts the online surfer in the random, anesthetic shadow of TV programming, roaming from site to site like a CD player set on shuffle play. But what makes the online world so revolutionary is the fact that there are connections between each stop on a Web itinerant's journey. The links that join those various destinations are links of association, not randomness. A channel surfer hops back and forth between different channels because she's bored. A Web surfer clicks on a link because she's interested.
>
> Steven Johnson. *Interface Culture: How New Technology Transforms the Way We Create and Communicate.* New York: Harper, 1997. 107–09. Print.

If you were writing a paper or putting up a Web site that concerned Web surfing, you might want to mention the distinction that Johnson makes between channel surfing and surfing on the Web. You could then expand on the distinction.

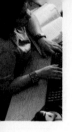

Use quotation marks for direct quotations

If you quote directly, you must place quotation marks around all words you take from the original:

> One observer marks this contrast: "A channel surfer hops back and forth between different channels because she's bored. A Web surfer clicks on a link because she's interested" (Johnson 109).

Notice that the quotation is introduced and not just dropped in. This example follows Modern Language Association (MLA) style, where the citation–(Johnson 109)–goes outside the quotation marks but before the final period. In MLA style, source references are made according to the author's last name, which refers you to the full citation in the list of works cited at the end. Following the author's name is the page number where the quotation can be located. (Notice also that there is no comma after the name.)

Attribute every quotation

If the author's name appears in the sentence, cite only the page number, in parentheses:

> According to Steven Johnson, "A channel surfer hops back and forth between different channels because she's bored. A Web surfer clicks on a link because she's interested" (109).

Quoting words that are quoted in your source

If you want to quote material that is already quoted in your source, use single quotes for that material:

> Steven Johnson uses the metaphor of a Gothic cathedral to describe a computer interface: "'The principle of the Gothic architecture,' Coleridge once said, 'is infinity made imaginable.' The same could be said for the modern interface" (42).

Summarize and paraphrase sources without plagiarizing

Summarizing

When you summarize, you state the major ideas of an entire source or part of a source in a paragraph or perhaps even a sentence. The key is to put the summary in your own words. If you use words from the source, you have to put those words within quotation marks.

PLAGIARIZED

Steven Johnson argues in *Interface Culture* that the concept of "surfing" is misapplied to the Internet because channel surfers hop back and forth between different channels because they're bored, but Web surfers click on links because they're interested.

[Most of the words are lifted directly from the original; see page 407.]

ACCEPTABLE SUMMARY

Steven Johnson argues in *Interface Culture* that the concept of "surfing" is misapplied to the Internet because users of the Web consciously choose to link to other sites while television viewers mindlessly flip through the channels until something catches their attention.

Paraphrasing

When you paraphrase, you represent the idea of the source in your own words at about the same length as the original. You still need to include the reference to the source of the idea. The following example illustrates what is not an acceptable paraphrase.

PLAGIARIZED

Steven Johnson argues that the concept of "surfing" does a terrible injustice to what it means to navigate around the Web. What makes the idea of Web surfing infuriating is the association with television. Web surfing and channel surfing are truly different activities; to imagine them as the same is to ignore their defining characteristics. A channel surfer skips around because she's bored while a Web surfer clicks on a link because she's interested (107-09).

Even though the source is listed, this paraphrase is unacceptable. Too many of the words in the original are used directly here, including much or all of entire sentences.

When a string of words is lifted from a source and inserted without quotation marks, the passage is plagiarized. Changing a few words in a sentence is not a paraphrase. Compare these two sentences:

SOURCE

Web surfing and channel surfing are genuinely different pursuits; to imagine them as equivalents is to ignore the defining characteristics of each medium.

UNACCEPTABLE PARAPHRASE

Web surfing and channel surfing are truly different activities; to imagine them as the same is to ignore their defining characteristics.

The paraphrase takes the structure of the original sentence and substitutes a few words. It is much too similar to the original.

A true paraphrase represents an entire rewriting of the idea from the source

ACCEPTABLE PARAPHRASE

Steven Johnson argues that "surfing" is a misleading term for describing how people navigate on the Web. He allows that "surfing" is appropriate for clicking across television channels because the viewer has to interact with what the networks and cable companies provide, just as the surfer has to interact with what the ocean provides. Web surfing, according to Johnson, operates at much greater depth and with much more consciousness of purpose. Web surfers actively follow links to make connections (107-09).

Even though there are a few words from the original in this paraphrase, such as *navigate* and *connections*, these sentences are original in structure and wording while accurately conveying the meaning of the source.

Frame each paraphrase

Each paraphrase should begin by introducing the author and conclude with a page reference to the material that is paraphrased.

Incorporate quotations

Quotations are a frequent problem area in research papers. Review every quotation to ensure that each is used effectively and correctly.

- Limit the use of long quotations. If you have more than one blocked quotation on a page, look closely to see if one or more can be paraphrased or summarized.
- Check that each quotation supports your major points rather than making major points for you. If the ideas rather than the original wording are what's important, paraphrase the quotation and cite the source.
- Check that each quotation is introduced and attributed. Each quotation should be introduced and the author or title named. Check for verbs that signal a quotation: Smith *claims*, Jones *argues*, Brown *states.*
- Check that you cite the source for each quotation. You are required to cite the sources of all direct quotations, paraphrases, and summaries.
- Check the accuracy of each quotation. It's easy to leave out words or mistype a quotation. Compare what is in your paper to the original source. If you need to add words to make the quotation grammatical, make sure the added words are in brackets.
- Read your paper aloud to a classmate or a friend. Each quotation should flow smoothly when you read your paper aloud. Put a check beside rough spots as you read aloud so you can revise later.

When to quote directly and when to paraphrase

Use direct quotations when the original wording is important.

DIRECT QUOTATION

Smith notes that

> Although the public grew to accept film as a teaching tool, it was not always aware of all it was being taught. That was because a second type of film was also being produced during these years, the "attitude-building" film, whose primary purpose was to motivate, not instruct. Carefully chosen visuals were combined with dramatic story lines, music, editing, and sharply drawn characters to create powerful instruments of mass manipulation. (21)

Prose quotations longer than four lines (MLA) or forty words (APA) should be indented one inch in MLA style or one-half inch in APA style. Shorter quotations should be enclosed within quotation marks.

PARAPHRASE

Smith points out that a second kind of mental hygiene film, the attitude-building film, was introduced during the 1940s. It attempted to motivate viewers, whereas earlier films explicitly tried to teach something. The attitude-building films were intended to manipulate their audiences to feel a certain way (21).

PARAPHRASE COMBINED WITH QUOTATION

In his analysis of the rise of fascism in twentieth-century Europe, George Mosse notes that the fascist movement was built on pre-existing ideas like individualism and sacrifice. It "scavenged" other ideologies and made use of them. "Fascism was a new political movement but not a movement which invented anything new," Mosse explains (xvii).

In the second example, the original wording provides stronger description of the attitude-building films. The direct quotation is a better choice.

Often, you can paraphrase the main idea of a lengthy passage and quote only the most striking phrase or sentence.

Verbs that introduce quotations and paraphrases

acknowledge	claim	emphasize	offer
add	comment	explain	point out
admit	compare	express	refute
advise	complain	find	reject
agree	concede	grant	remark
allow	conclude	illustrate	reply
analyze	contend	imply	report
answer	criticize	insist	respond
argue	declare	interpret	show
ask	describe	maintain	state
assert	disagree	note	suggest
believe	discuss	object	think
charge	dispute	observe	write

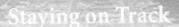

Staying on Track

Quotations don't speak for themselves

OFF TRACK

Don't rely on long quotations to do the work of writing for you.

> Richard Lanham writes:
>
> > Economics . . . studies the allocation of scarce resources. Normally we would think that the phrase "information economy," which we hear everywhere nowadays, makes some sense. It is no longer physical stuff that is in short supply, we are told, but information about it. So, we live in an "information economy." but information is not in short supply in the new information economy. We're drowning in it. What we lack is the human attention needed to make sense of it all. (xi)
>
> Lanham goes on to say:
>
> > "Rhetoric" has not always been a synonym for humbug. For most of Western history, it has meant the body of doctrine that teaches people how to speak and write and, thus, act effectively in public life. Usually defined as "the art of persuasion," it might as well have been called "the economics of attention." It tells us how to allocate our central scarce resource, to invite people to attend to what we would like them to attend to. (xii-xiii)

These quotations are picked up out of context and dropped into the paper. Readers have no clue about why they are relevant to the writer's text.

ON TRACK

When sources are used effectively, they are woven into the fabric of a research project but still maintain their identity.

Most of the source is paraphrased, allowing the discussion to be integrated into the writer's text. The writer centers on how two key concepts, the "information economy" and "rhetoric," are reinterpreted by Richard Lanham. Only those words critical to representing Lanham's position are quoted directly.

> In *The Economics of Attention*, Richard Lanham begins by pointing out that the "information economy" stands traditional economics on its head because there is no shortage of information today. Instead Lanham argues that attention is what is in short supply and that the discipline of rhetoric can help us to understand how attention is allocated. Rhetoric historically has meant the art and study of speaking and writing well, especially for participating in public life. Lanham maintains that what rhetoric has really been about is what he calls "the economics of attention" (xii). The central goal of rhetoric, according to Lanham, is "to invite people to attend to what we would like them to attend to" (xii-xiii).

Incorporate visuals

Here are a few guidelines to keep in mind for incorporating visual sources into your research paper.

- Use visuals for examples and supporting evidence, not for decoration. For example, if the subject of your research is Internet crime in San Francisco, including a picture of the Golden Gate Bridge is irrelevant and will detract from your paper.
- Refer to images and other graphics in the body of your research paper. Explain the significance of any images or graphics in the body of your paper.
- Respect the copyright of visual sources. You may need to request permission to use a visual from the Web.
- Get complete citation information. You are required to cite visual sources in your list of works cited just as you are for other sources.
- Describe the content of the image or graphic in the caption.

Façade of the Last Judgment, Orvieto, Italy, c. 1310–1330. Medieval churches frequently depicted Christ as a judge, damning sinners to hell.

Write Now

Summarize, paraphrase, and quote directly

Read this quotation and then

- Write a summary of it;
- Write a paraphrase of it;
- Incorporate a direct quotation from it into a sentence.

There is no strife, no prejudice, no national conflict in outer space as yet. Its hazards are hostile to us all. Its conquest deserves the best of all mankind, and its opportunity for peaceful cooperation may never come again. But why, some say, the moon? Why choose this as our goal? And they may well ask why climb the highest mountain? Why, 35 years ago, fly the Atlantic? Why does Rice play Texas?

We choose to go to the moon. We choose to go to the moon in this decade and do the other things, not because they are easy, but because they are hard, because that goal will serve to organize and measure the best of our energies and skills, because that challenge is one that we are willing to accept, one we are unwilling to postpone, and one which we intend to win, and the others, too. (President John F. Kennedy, September 12, 1962).

Review your research project

Read your project aloud and put checks in the margin in places where you think it sounds rough or might need more development. When you finish, try to imagine yourself as a reader who doesn't know much about your subject or has a different viewpoint. What could you add to benefit that reader?

Reviewing another student's research project

Read through a paper twice. The first time you read through a paper, concentrate on comprehension and overall impressions. On your second reading show the writer where you got confused or highlight parts that were especially good by adding comments in the margins.

Questions for reviewing a research project

- Does the title describe the subject of the paper? Does it create interest in the subject?
- Are the introductory paragraphs effective and relevant to the paper that follows?
- Is the thesis clearly stated in the beginning paragraphs of the paper?
- Does the writer offer support for the thesis from a variety of valid and reliable sources?
- Does the paper go into enough detail to support the thesis, and are the details relevant to the thesis?
- Do the arguments presented in the paper flow logically? Is the paper well organized?
- Is the tone of the paper consistent throughout? Is the word choice varied and appropriate throughout?
- Did you have to read some parts more than once to fully understand them?
- Are quotations properly introduced and integrated into the text?
- Are all facts and quotations that are not common knowledge documented?
- Is the documentation in the correct form?
- Is the paper free of errors of grammar and punctuation?

Revise your research project

From your review and possibly reviews of other students, make a list of changes you might make. Start with the large concerns—reorganizing paragraphs, cutting unnecessary parts, and adding new sections. When you have finished revising, edit and proofread carefully.

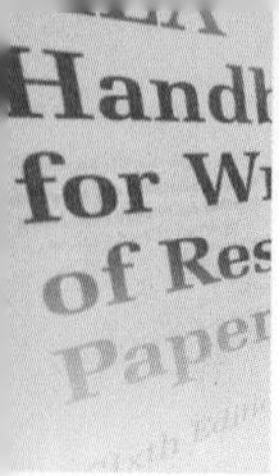

17 MLA Documentation

MLA is the preferred style in the humanities and fine arts.

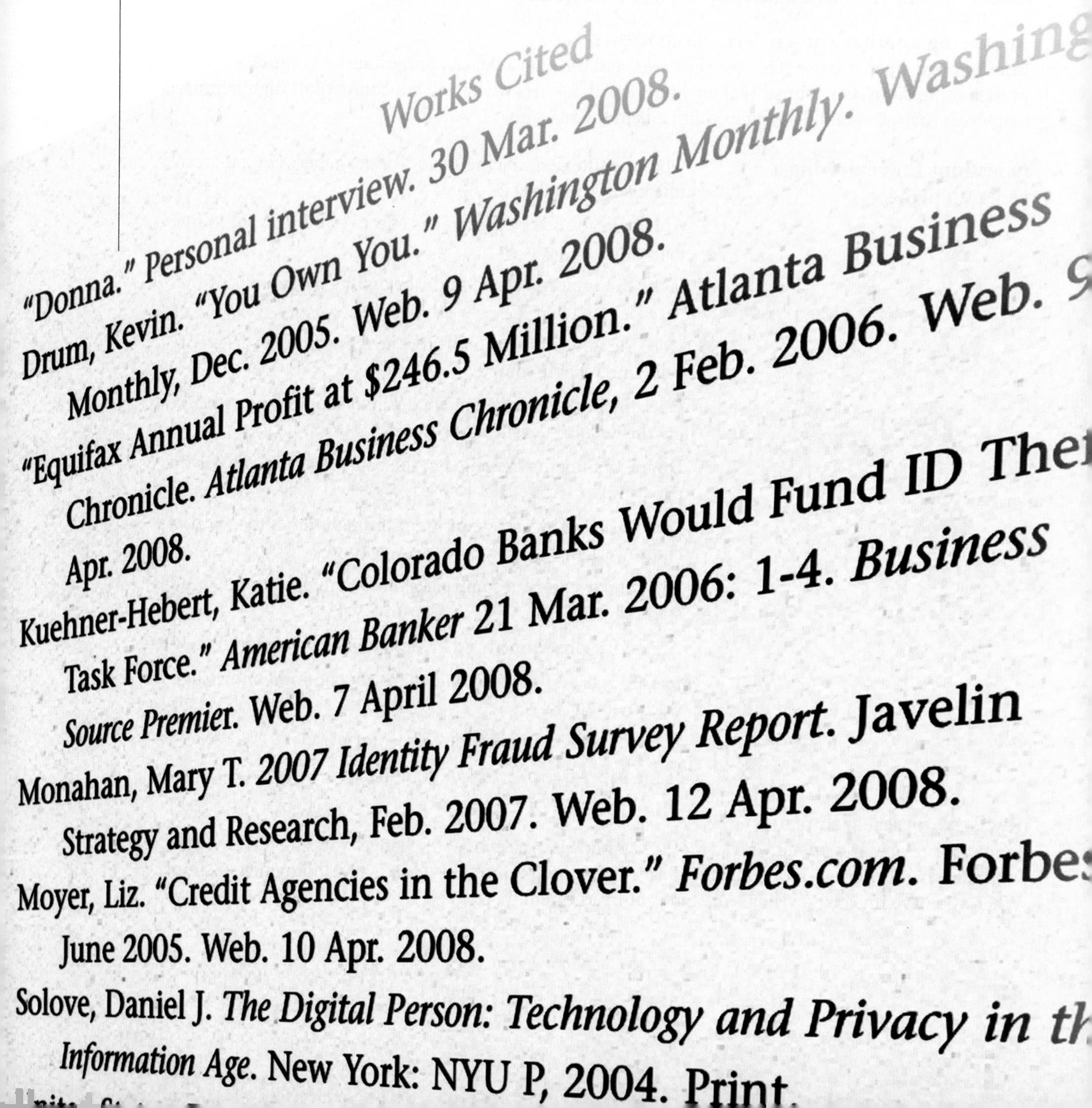

CHAPTER CONTENTS

If you have questions that the examples in this chapter do not address, consult the *MLA Handbook for Writers of Research Papers*, 7th ed. (2009), and the *MLA Style Manual and Guide to Scholarly Publishing*, 3rd ed. (2008).

Elements of MLA documentation

In MLA style, quotations, summaries, and paraphrases from outside sources are indicated by in-text citations in parentheses. When readers find a parenthetical reference in the body of a paper, they can turn to the list of works cited at the end of the paper to find complete publication information for the cited source.

Walker 3

. . . But how important is face-to-face interaction to maintaining good, "social" behavior in a group?

Describing humans as "innate mind readers," one observer argues that "our skill at imagining other people's mental states ranks up there with our knack for language and our opposable thumbs" (Johnson 196). The frequency of "flame wars" on Internet message boards and list serves, however, indicates that our innate skill at reading minds isn't always accurate. Some crucial information must be lacking in these forums that causes people to misread others' mental states.

The writer quotes a passage from page 196 of Johnson's book.

Walker 5

Works Cited

Darlin, Damon. "'Wall-E': An Homage to Mr. Jobs." *New York Times*. New York Times, 29 June 2008. Web. 7 July 2008.

Johnson, Steven. *Emergence: The Connected Lives of Ants, Brains, Cities, and Software.* New York: Scribner, 2001. Print.

"Listen to the Brain Drain." *Irish Times* 24 June 2008, final ed.: 17. *LexisNexis Academic*. Web. 8 July 2008.

The reader can find the source by looking up Johnson's name in the list of works cited. The information there can be used to locate the book, to check whether the writer accurately represents Johnson, and to see how the point quoted fits into Johnson's larger argument.

Entries in the works-cited list

The list of works cited is organized alphabetically by authors or, if no author is listed, the first word in the title other than *a*, *an*, or *the*. MLA style uses four basic forms for entries in the list of works cited: books, periodicals (scholarly journals, newspapers, magazines), online sources, and database sources.

1. WORKS-CITED ENTRIES FOR BOOKS

Entries for books have three main elements:

1. Author's name.

2. *Title of book.*

3. Publication information.

Sterling, Bruce. *Shaping Things.* Cambridge: MIT P, 2005. Print.

1. Author's name.
- List the author's name with the last name first, followed by a period.

2. Title of book.
- Find the exact title on the title page, not the cover.
- Separate the title and subtitle with a colon.
- Italicize the title and put a period at the end.

3. Publication information.
- The place (usually the city) of publication,
- The name of the publisher,
- The date of publication,
- The medium of publication (Print).

Use a colon between the place of publication and the publisher's name (using accepted abbreviations), followed by a comma and then the publication date.

2. WORKS-CITED ENTRIES FOR PERIODICALS

Entries for periodicals have three main elements:

1. Author's name.

2. "Title of article."

3. Publication information.

Danielewicz, Jane. "Personal Genres, Public Voices." *College Composition and Communication* 59.3 (2008): 420-50. Print.

1. Author's name.
- List the author's name with the last name first, followed by a period.

2. "Title of article."
- Place the title of the article inside quotation marks.
- Insert a period before the closing quotation mark.

3. Publication information.
- Italicize the title of the journal.
- For scholarly journals follow the title immediately with the volume and issue number.
- List the date of publication, in parentheses, followed by a colon.
- List the inclusive page numbers, separated by a hyphen, followed by a period.
- Give the medium of publication.

3. WORKS-CITED ENTRIES FOR WEB SOURCES

Publications on the Web vary widely. For works other than newspapers, magazines, and other journals published on the Web, include the following components if you can locate them. Include a URL only if your readers probably cannot find the source without it.

1. Author's name.

2. "Title of work."

3. *Title of overall Web site.*

4. Version or edition used.

5. Publisher or sponsor of the site,

6. Date of publication.

7. Medium of publication *(Web).*

8. Date of access.

Dalenberg, Alex. "University of Arizona Looks Beyond Mars Mission." *CNN.com.* Cable News Network, 2 July 2008. Web. 24 July 2008.

1. Author's name
- List the author's or editor's name if you can find it; otherwise begin with the title of the work.

2. "Title of work."
- Place the title of work inside quotation marks if it is part of a larger Web site.

3. Title of overall Web site.
- Italicize the name of the overall site if it is different from 2.

4. Version or edition used.
- Some Web sites are updated, so list the version if you find it (e.g., 2006 edition).

5. Publisher or sponsor of the site,
- Follow the publisher's or sponsor's name with a comma. If not available, use *N.p.*

6. Date of publication.
- Use day, month, and year if available; otherwise use *n.d.*

7. Medium of publication (*Web*).

8. Date of access.
- List the day, month, and year you accessed the source.

4. WORKS-CITED ENTRIES FOR DATABASE SOURCES

Basic entries for database sources have five main elements.

1. Author's name.

2. Print publication information.

3. *Name of database.*

4. Medium of publication *(Web).*

5. Date of access.

Hede, Jesper. "Jews and Muslims in Dante's Vision." *European Review* 16.1 (2008): 101-14. *Academic Search Premier*. Web. 14 Sept. 2008.

1. Author's name
- List the author's or editor's name with the last name first, followed by a period.

2. Print publication information.
- Give the print publication information in standard format, in this case for a periodical.

3. Name of database.
- Italicize the name of the database, followed by a period.

4. Medium of publication.
- For all database sources, the medium of publication is Web.

5. Date of access.
- List the date you accessed the source (day, month, and year).

In-text citations in MLA style

1. Author named in your text

Put the author's name in a signal phrase in your sentence.

> Sociologist Daniel Bell called this emerging U.S. economy the "postindustrial society" (3).

---

2. Author not named in your text

> In 1997, the Gallup poll reported that 55% of adults in the United States think secondhand smoke is "very harmful," compared to only 36% in 1994 (Saad 4).

---

3. Work by one author

The author's last name comes first, followed by the page number. There is no comma.

> (Bell 3)

---

4. Work by two or three authors

The authors' last names follow the order of the title page. If there are two authors, join the names with *and.* If there are three, use commas between the first two names and a comma with *and* before the last name.

> (Francisco, Vaughn, and Lynn 7)

---

5. Work by four or more authors

You may use the phrase *et al.* (meaning "and others") for all names but the first, or you may write out all the names. Make sure you use the same method for both the in-text citations and the works-cited list.

> (Abrams et al. 1653)

---

6. Work by no named author

Use a shortened version of the title that includes at least the first important word. Your reader will use the shortened title to find the full title in the works-cited list.

> A review in *The New Yorker* of Ryan Adams's new album focuses on the artist's age ("Pure" 25).

Notice that "Pure" is in quotation marks because it refers to the title of an article. If it were a book, the short title would be in italics.

7. Work by a group or organization

Treat the group or organization as the author. Try to identify the group author in the text and place only the page number in the parentheses.

> According to the *Irish Free State Handbook*, published by the Ministry for Industry and Finance, the population of Ireland in 1929 was approximately 4,192,000 (23).

8. Quotations longer than four lines

NOTE: When using indented ("block") quotations of longer than four lines, the period appears *before* the parentheses enclosing the page number.

> In her article "Art for Everybody," Susan Orlean attempts to explain the popularity of painter Thomas Kinkade:
>
> > People like to own things they think are valuable. . . .The high price of limited editions is part of their appeal: it implies that they are choice and exclusive, and that only a certain class of people will be able to afford them—a limited edition of people with taste and discernment. (128)
>
> This same statement could possibly also explain the popularity of phenomena like PBS's *Antiques Roadshow.*

If the source is longer than one page, provide the page number for each quotation, paraphrase, and summary.

9. Web sources including Web pages, blogs, podcasts, wikis, videos, and other multimedia sources

MLA prefers that you mention the author in the text instead of putting the author's name in parentheses.

> Andrew Keen ironically used his own blog to claim that "blogs are boring to write (yawn), boring to read (yawn) and boring to discuss (yawn)."

If you cannot identify the author, mention the title in your text.

10. Work in an anthology

Cite the name of the author of the work within an anthology, not the name of the editor of the collection. Alphabetize the entry in the list of works cited by the author, not the editor. For example, Melissa Jane Hardie published the chapter "Beard" in *Rhetorical Bodies*, a book edited by Jack Selzer and Sharon Crowley.

> In "Beard," Melissa Jane Hardie explores the role assumed by Elizabeth Taylor as the celebrity companion of gay actors including Rock Hudson and Montgomery Clift (278-79).

Note that Hardie, not Selzer and Crowley, is named in parenthetical citations.

> (Hardie 278-79)

11. Two or more works by the same author

Use the author's last name and then a shortened version of the title of each source.

> The majority of books written about coauthorship focus on partners of the same sex (Laird, *Women* 351).

Note that *Women* is italicized because it is the name of a book.

12. Different authors with the same last name

If your list of works cited contains items by two or more different authors with the same last name, include the initial of the first name in the parenthetical reference. Note that a period follows the initial.

> Web surfing requires more mental involvement than channel surfing (S. Johnson 107).

13. Two or more sources within the same sentence

Place each citation directly after the statement it supports.

> Many sweeping pronouncements were made in the 1990s that the Internet is the best opportunity to improve education since the printing press (Ellsworth xxii) or even in the history of the world (Dyrli and Kinnaman 79).

14. Two or more sources within the same citation

If two sources support a single point, separate them with a semicolon.

> (McKibbin 39; Gore 92)

15. Work quoted in another source

When you do not have access to the original source of the material you wish to use, put the abbreviation *qtd. in* (quoted in) before the information about the indirect source.

> National governments have become increasingly what Ulrich Beck, in a 1999 interview, calls "zombie institutions"—institutions which are "dead and still alive" (qtd. in Bauman 6).

16. Literary works

To supply a reference to literary works, you sometimes need more than a page number from a specific edition. Readers should be able to locate a quotation in any edition of the book. Give the page number from the edition that you are using, then a semicolon and other identifying information.

> "Marriage is a house" is one of the most memorable lines in *Don Quixote* (546; pt. 2, bk. 3, ch. 19).

Books in MLA-style works cited

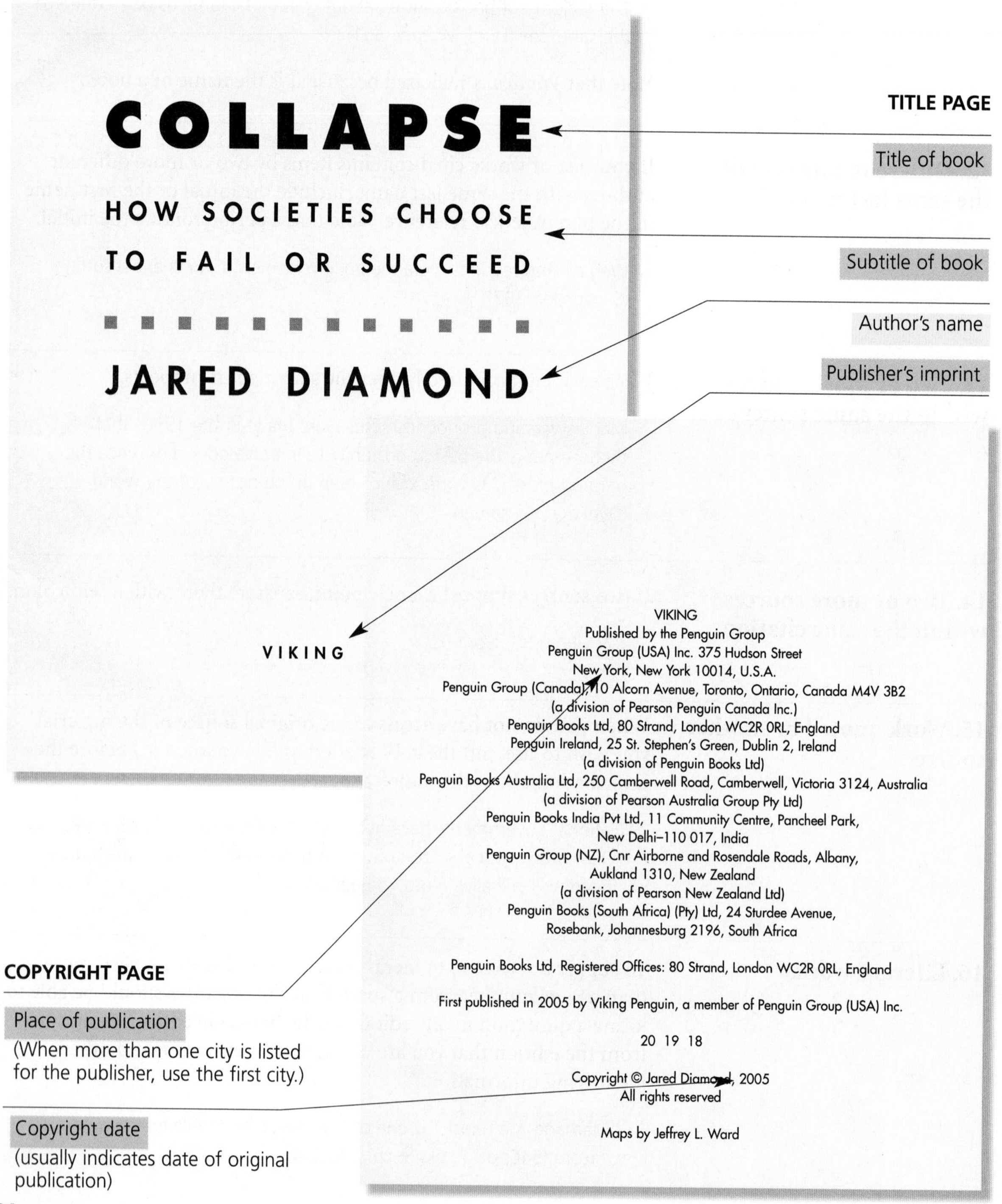
COLLAPSE
HOW SOCIETIES CHOOSE TO FAIL OR SUCCEED
JARED DIAMOND
VIKING
TITLE PAGE
Title of book
Subtitle of book
Author's name
Publisher's imprint
VIKING
Published by the Penguin Group
Penguin Group (USA) Inc. 375 Hudson Street
New York, New York 10014, U.S.A.
Penguin Group (Canada), 10 Alcorn Avenue, Toronto, Ontario, Canada M4V 3B2
(a division of Pearson Penguin Canada Inc.)
Penguin Books Ltd, 80 Strand, London WC2R 0RL, England
Penguin Ireland, 25 St. Stephen's Green, Dublin 2, Ireland
(a division of Penguin Books Ltd)
Penguin Books Australia Ltd, 250 Camberwell Road, Camberwell, Victoria 3124, Australia
(a division of Pearson Australia Group Pty Ltd)
Penguin Books India Pvt Ltd, 11 Community Centre, Pancheel Park,
New Delhi–110 017, India
Penguin Group (NZ), Cnr Airborne and Rosendale Roads, Albany,
Aukland 1310, New Zealand
(a division of Pearson New Zealand Ltd)
Penguin Books (South Africa) (Pty) Ltd, 24 Sturdee Avenue,
Rosebank, Johannesburg 2196, South Africa
Penguin Books Ltd, Registered Offices: 80 Strand, London WC2R 0RL, England
First published in 2005 by Viking Penguin, a member of Penguin Group (USA) Inc.
20 19 18
Copyright © Jared Diamond, 2005
All rights reserved
Maps by Jeffrey L. Ward
COPYRIGHT PAGE
Place of publication
(When more than one city is listed for the publisher, use the first city.)
Copyright date
(usually indicates date of original publication)

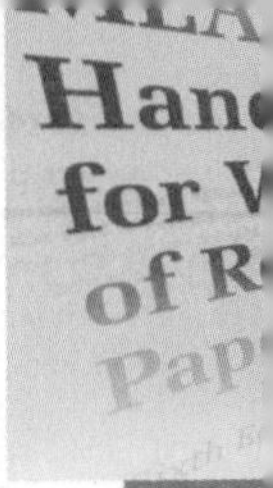

Diamond, Jared. *Collapse: How Societies Choose to Fail or Succeed.* New York: Viking, 2005. Print.

1. Author's or editor's name

- The author's last name comes first, followed by a comma and the first name.
- For edited books, put the abbreviation *ed.* after the name, preceded by a comma:

  Kavanaugh, Peter, ed.

2. Book title

- Use the exact title, as it appears on the title page (not the cover).
- Italicize the title.
- All nouns, verbs, pronouns, adjectives, and subordinating conjunctions, and the first word of the title are capitalized. Do not capitalize articles, prepositions, or coordinating conjunctions unless they are the first word of the title.

3. Publication information

Place of publication

- If more than one city is given, use the first.
- For cities outside the United States add an abbreviation of the country or province if the city is not well known.

Publisher

- Omit words such as Press, Publisher, and Inc.
- For university presses, use UP:

  New York UP

- Shorten the name. For example, shorten W.W. Norton & Co. to Norton.

Date of publication

- Give the year as it appears on the copyright page.
- If no year is given, but can be approximated, put a c. ("circa") and the approximate date in brackets: [c. 1999].
- Otherwise, put *n.d.* ("no date"):

  Boston: Harvard UP, n.d.

Medium of publication

- Print.

Sample works-cited entries for books

ONE AUTHOR

17. Book by one author

The author's last name comes first, followed by a comma, the first name, and a period.

> Doctorow, E. L. *The March*. New York: Random, 2005. Print.

18. Two or more books by the same author

In the entry for the first book, include the author's name. In the second entry, substitute three hyphens and a period for the author's name. List the titles of books by the same author in alphabetical order.

> Grimsley, Jim. *Boulevard.* Chapel Hill: Algonquin, 2002.
> ---. *Dream Boy.* New York: Simon, 1995. Print.

MULTIPLE AUTHORS

19. Book by two or three authors

The second and subsequent authors' names appear first name first. A comma separates the authors' names. If all are editors, use eds. after the names.

> Cruz, Arnaldo, and Martin Manalansan, eds. *Queer Globalizations: Citizenship and the Afterlife of Colonialism.* New York: New York UP, 2002. Print.

20. Book by four or more authors

You may use the phrase *et al.* (meaning "and others") for all authors but the first, or you may write out all the names. You need to use the same method in the in-text citation as you do in the works-cited list.

> Britton, Jane et al. *The Broadview Anthology of Expository Prose.* New York: Broadview, 2001. Print.

ANONYMOUS AND GROUP AUTHORS

21. Book by an unknown author

Begin the entry with the title.

> *The Baseball Encyclopedia.* 10th ed. New York: MacMillan; 1996. Print.

22. Book by a group or organization

Treat the group as the author of the work.

> United Nations. *The Charter of the United Nations: A Commentary.* New York: Oxford UP, 2000. Print.

23. Religious texts

The New Oxford Annotated Bible. Ed. Bruce M. Metzger and Roland E. Murphy. New York: Oxford UP, 1991. Print.

EDITIONS, REPRINTS, AND ILLUSTRATED BOOKS

24. Book with an editor

List an edited book under the editor's name if your focus is on the editor. Otherwise, cite an edited book under the author's name.

Lewis, Gifford, ed. *The Big House of Inver*. By Edith Somerville and Martin Ross. Dublin: Farmar, 2000. Print.

25. Reprinted works

For works of fiction that have been printed in many different editions or reprints, give the original publication date after the title.

Wilde, Oscar. *The Picture of Dorian Gray*. 1890. New York: Norton, 2001. Print.

26. Illustrated book or graphic narrative

After the title of the book, give the illustrator's name, preceded by the abbreviation *Illus.* If the emphasis is on the illustrator's work, place the illustrator's name first, followed by the abbreviation *illus.*, and list the author after the title, preceded by the word *By*.

Strunk, William, Jr., and E. B. White. *The Elements of Style Illustrated*. Illus. Maira Kalman. New York: Penguin, 2005. Print.

PARTS OF BOOKS

27. Introduction, Foreword, Preface, or Afterword

Give the author and then the name of the specific part being cited. If the author for the whole work is different, put that author's name after the word *By*. Place inclusive page numbers at the end.

Benstock, Sheri. Introduction. *The House of Mirth*. By Edith Wharton. Boston: Bedford-St. Martin's, 2002. 3-24. Print.

28. Single chapter written by same author as the book

Ardis, Ann. "Mapping the Middlebrow in Edwardian England." *Modernism and Cultural Conflict: 1880-1922*. Cambridge: Cambridge UP, 2002. 114-42. Print.

29. Selection from an anthology or edited collection

Sedaris, David. "Full House." *The Best American Nonrequired Reading 2004*. Ed. Dave Eggers. Boston: Houghton, 2004. 350-58. Print.

Periodicals in MLA-style works cited

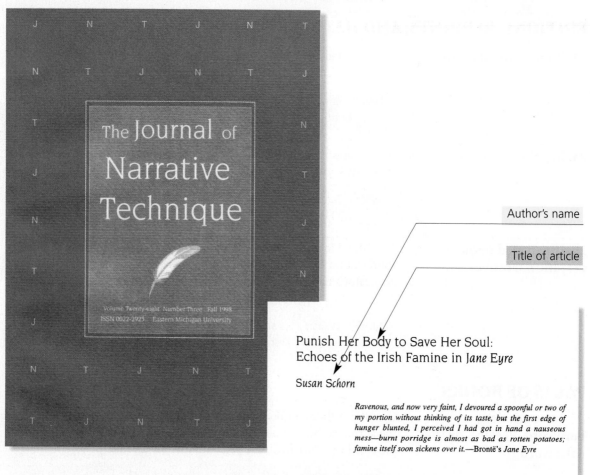

Author's name

Title of article

Name of journal, volume number, issue number, date of publication, page numbers

Punish Her Body to Save Her Soul:
Echoes of the Irish Famine in *Jane Eyre*

Susan Schorn

> *Ravenous, and now very faint, I devoured a spoonful or two of my portion without thinking of its taste, but the first edge of hunger blunted, I perceived I had got in hand a nauseous mess—burnt porridge is almost as bad as rotten potatoes; famine itself soon sickens over it.*—Brontë's *Jane Eyre*

In 1846, the second year of the Irish Potato Famine, Charles Trevelyan, Assistant Secretary in charge of the relief of Ireland, stated "The great evil with which we are to contend is not the physical evil of famine, but the moral evil of the selfish, perverse and turbulent character of the people" (Clarity). That same year, Charlotte Brontë penned the following speech for the character of Mr. Brocklehurst in her novel *Jane Eyre*: "Oh, madam, when you put bread and cheese, instead of burnt porridge, into these children's mouths, you may indeed feed their vile bodies, but you little think how you starve their immortal souls!" The similarity between the sentiment and policy of these two men, one fictional, one very real indeed, is no coincidence. Both express ideas that were then common currency with regard to "the Irish Problem." The connections between starvation, moral improvement, discipline, and nationality were familiar ones in Victorian England, and Brontë's use of this public, political sentiment in her novel—and of numerous other images borrowed from accounts of the

The Journal of Narrative Technique 28.3 (Fall 1998): 350–365. Copyright © 1998 by *The Journal of Narrative Technique.*

Schorn, Susan. "'Punish Her Body to Save Her Soul': Echoes of the Irish Famine in *Jane Eyre*." *The Journal of Narrative Technique* 28.3 (1998): 350-65. Print.

1. Author's or editor's name
- The author's last name comes first, followed by a comma and the first name.

2. Title of article
- Use the exact title, which appears at the top of the article.
- Put the title in quotation marks. If a book title is part of the article's title, italicize the book title. If a title requiring quotation marks is part of the article's title, use single quotation marks around it.
- All nouns, verbs, pronouns, adjectives, and subordinating conjunctions, and the first word of the title are capitalized. Do not capitalize articles, prepositions, or coordinating conjunctions unless they are the first word of the title.

3. Publication information

Name of journal
- Italicize the title of the journal.
- Abbreviate the title of the journal if it commonly appears that way.

Volume, issue, and page numbers
- For scholarly journals give the volume number and issue number. Place a period between the volume and issue numbers: "28.3" indicates volume 28, issue 3.
- Some scholarly journals use issue numbers only.
- Give the page numbers for the entire article, not just the part you used.

Date of publication
- For magazines and journals identified by the month or season of publication, use the month (or season) and year in place of the volume.
- For weekly or biweekly magazines, give both the day and month of publication, as listed on the issue. Note that the day precedes the month and no comma is used.

Medium of publication
- Print.

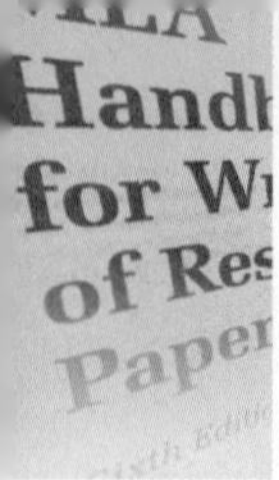

Sample works-cited entries for periodicals

JOURNAL ARTICLES

30. Article by one author

Mallory, Anne. "Burke, Boredom, and the Theater of Counterrevolution." *PMLA* 118.2 (2003): 224-38. Print.

31. Article by two or three authors

Higgins, Lorraine D., and Lisa D. Brush. "Personal Experience Narrative and Public Debate: Writing the Wrongs of Welfare." *College Composition and Communication* 57.4 (2006): 694-729. Print.

32. Article by four or more authors

You may use the phrase *et al.* (meaning "and others") for all authors but the first, or you may write out all the names.

Breece, Katherine E. et al. "Patterns of mtDNA Diversity in Northwestern North America." *Human Biology* 76.1 (2004): 33-54. Print.

PAGINATION IN JOURNALS

33. Article in a scholarly journal

After the title of the article, give the journal name in italics, the volume and issue number, the year of publication in parentheses, a colon, the inclusive page numbers, and the medium of publication.

Duncan, Mike. "Whatever Happened to the Paragraph?" *College English* 69.5 (2007): 470-95. Print.

34. Article in a scholarly journal paginated by issue that uses only issue numbers

Some scholarly journals use issue numbers only. List the issue number after the name of the journal.

McCall, Sophie. "Double Vision Reading." *Canadian Literature* 194 (2007): 95-97. Print.

MAGAZINES

35. Monthly or seasonal magazines

Use the month (or season) and year in place of the volume. Abbreviate the names of all months except May, June, and July.

Barlow, John Perry. "Africa Rising: Everything You Know about Africa Is Wrong." *Wired* Jan. 1998: 142-58. Print.

36. Weekly or biweekly magazines

Give both the day and month of publication, as listed on the issue.

Toobin, Jeffrey. "Crackdown." *New Yorker* 5 Nov. 2001: 56-61. Print.

NEWSPAPERS

37. Newspaper article by one author

The author's last name comes first, followed by a comma and the first name.

> Marriott, Michel. "Arts and Crafts for the Digital Age." *New York Times* 8 June 2006, late ed.: C13. Print.

38. Article by two or three authors

The second and subsequent authors' names are printed in regular order, first name first:

> Davis, Howard, June Allstead, and Jane Mavis. "Rice's Testimony to 9/11 Commission Leaves Unanswered Questions." *Dallas Morning News* 9 Apr. 2004, final ed.: C5. Print.

39. Newspaper article by an unknown author

Begin the entry with the title.

> "The Dotted Line." *Washington Post* 8 June 2006: final ed.: E2. Print.

REVIEWS, EDITORIALS, LETTERS TO THE EDITOR

40. Review

If there is no title, just name the work reviewed.

> Mendelsohn, Daniel. "The Two Oscar Wildes." Rev. of *The Imporatnce of Being Earnest,* dir. Oliver Parker. *The New York Review of Books* 10 Oct. 2002: 23-24. Print.

41. Editorial

> "Stop Stonewalling on Reform." Editorial. *Business Week* 17 June 2002: 108. Print.

42. Letter to the editor

> Patai, Daphne. Letter. *Harper's Magazine* Dec. 2001: 4. Print.

Web sources in MLA-style works cited

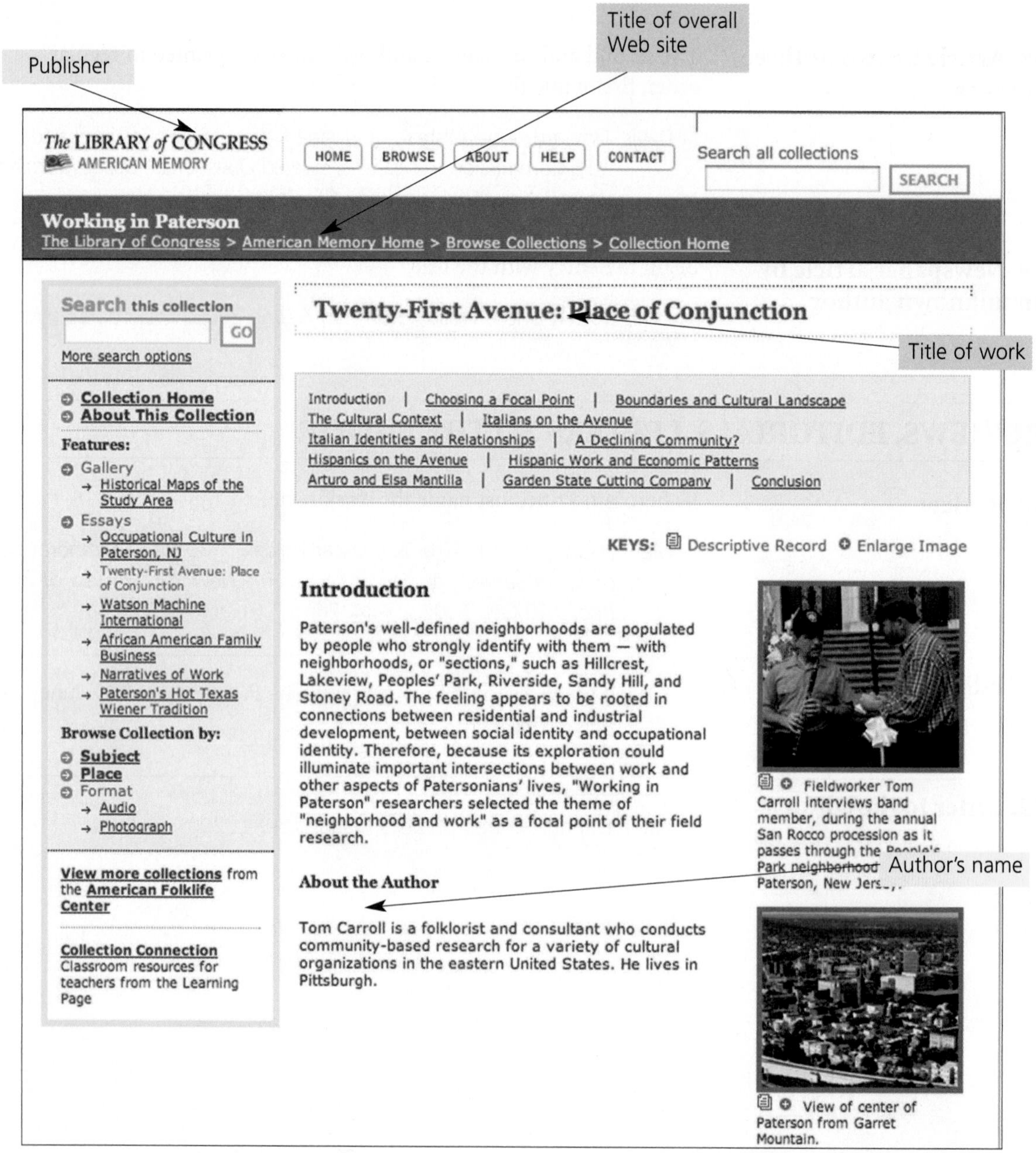

Carrol, Tom. "Twenty-First Avenue: Place of Conjunction." *Working in Patterson*. Lib. of Cong., n.d. Web. 14 Mar. 2009.

1. Author's name
- Authorship is often difficult to determine for Web sources. If you know the author or creator, follow the rules for books and periodicals.
- If you cannot identify the author or creator, begin with the title.

2. Title of work and title of overall Web site
- Place the title of the work inside quotation marks if it is part of a larger Web site.
- Untitled works may be identified by a label (e.g., *Home page, Introduction*). List the label in the title slot without quotations marks or italics.
- Italicize the name of the overall site if it is different from the work.
- The name of the overall Web site will usually be found on its index or home page. If you can not find a link back to the home page, look at the URL for clues. You can work backward through the URL by deleting sections (separated by slashes) until you come to the home page.
- Some Web sites are updated; list the version if you find it (e.g., *Vers, 1.2*).

3. Publication information
- List the publisher's or sponsor's name followed by a comma. If it isn't available, use *N.p.*
- List the date of publication by day, month, and year if available. If you cannot find a date, use *n.d.*
- Give the medium of publication *(Web).*
- List the date you accessed the site by day, month, and year.

When do you list a URL?

MLA style no longer requires including URLs of Web sources. URLs are of limited value because they change frequently and they can be specific to an individual search. Include the URL as supplementary information only when your readers probably cannot locate the source without the URL.

Sample works-cited entries for Web sources

ONLINE PUBLICATIONS

43. Publication by a known author

If you know the author or creator, follow the rules for periodicals and books.

> Boerner, Steve. "Leopold Mozart." *The Mozart Project: Biography*. The Mozart Project, 21 Mar. 1998. Web. 30 Oct. 2008.

44. Publication by an anonymous author

If a work has no author's or editor's name listed, begin the entry with the title.

> "State of the Birds." *Audubon*. National Audubon Society, 2008. Web. 19 Aug. 2008.

45. Publication on the Web with print publication data

Include the print publication information. Then give name of the Web site or database in italics, the medium of publication (*Web*), and the date of access (day, month, and year).

> Kirsch, Irwin S., et al. *Adult Literacy in America*. Darby: Diane, 1993. *Google Scholar*. Web. 30 Oct. 2008.

46. Government publication on the Web

Government publications are issued in many formats. If you cannot locate the author of the document, given the name of the government and agency that published it.

> United States. Dept of Health and Human Services. *Salmonellosis Outbreak in Certain Types of Tomatoes*. 5 July 2008. *U.S. Food and Drug Administration Site*. Web. 30 July 2008.

ONLINE PERIODICALS

47. Article in a scholarly journal

Some scholarly journals are published on the Web only. List articles by author, title, name of journal in italics, volume and issue number, and year of publication. If the journal does not have page numbers, use *n. pag.* in place of page numbers. Then list the medium of publication (*Web*) and the date of access (day, month, and year).

> Fleckenstein, Kristie. "Who's Writing? Aristotelian Ethos and the Author Position in Digital Poetics." *Kairos* 11.3 (2007): n. pag. Web. 6 Apr. 2008.

48. Article in a newspaper

The first date is the date of publication, the second is the date of access.

> Brown, Patricia Leigh. "Australia in Sonoma." *New York Times*. New York Times, 5 July 2008. Web. 3 Aug. 2008.

49. Article in a popular magazine

Follow the publisher's name with a comma. If no publisher is available, use *n.p.*

> Brown, Patricia Leigh. "The Wild Horse Is Us." *Newsweek*. Newsweek, 1 July 2008. Web. 3 July 2008.

ONLINE BOOKS AND SCHOLARLY PROJECTS

50. Online book

If the book was printed and then scanned, give the print publication information. Then give the name of the database or Web site in italics, the medium of publication (*Web*), and the date of access (day, month, and year).

> Prebish, Charles S. and Kenneth K. Tanaka. *The Faces of Buddhism in America*. Berkeley: U of California P, 2003. *eScholarship Editions*. Web. 22 May 2008.

51. Document within a scholarly project

Give the print information, then the title of the scholarly project or database, the medium of publication (*Web*), and the date of access (day, month, and year).

> "New York Quiet." *Franklin Repository* 5 Aug. 1863, 1. *Valley of the Shadow*. Web. 23 Feb. 2008.

LIBRARY DATABASE

52. Work from a library database

Begin with the print publication information, but omit the medium of original publication (*Print*). Give the name of the database in italics, the medium of publication (*Web*), and the day, month, and year you accessed the source.

> Mortensen, Daniel E. "The Loci of Cicero." *Rhetorica* 26.1 (2008): 31-56. *Academic Search Complete*. Web. 21 Sept. 2008.

Other sources in MLA-style works cited

53. E-mail

Give the name of the writer, the subject line, a description of the message, the date, and the medium of delivery.

> Ballmer, Steve. "A New Era of Business Productivity and Innovation." Message to Microsoft Executive E-mail. 30 Nov. 2006. E-mail.

54. Blog

If there is no sponsor or publisher for the blog, use *N.p.*

> Arrington, Michael. "Think Before You Voicemail." *TechCrunch*. N.p., 5 July 2008. Web. 10 Sept. 2008.

55. Personal home page

List *Home page* without quotation marks in place of the title. If no date is listed. use *n.d.*

> Graff, Harvey J. Home page. Dept. of English, Ohio State U, n.d. Web. 15 Nov. 2008.

56. Sound recording

List the composer, performer, composer, or group first, depending on which you wish to emphasize. Place a comma between the publisher and the date. Indicate the medium after the date.

> McCoury, Del, perf. "1952 Vincent Black Lightning." By Richard Thompson. *Del and the Boys*. Ceili, 2001. CD.

57. Film

Begin with the title in italics. List the director, the distributor, the date, and the medium. Other data, such as the names of the screenwriters and performers, is optional.

> *Wanted*. Dir. Timur Bekmambetov. Perf. James McAvoy, Angelina Jolie and Morgan Freeman. Universal, 2008. Film.

58. Video or DVD

Follow the same format for films.

> *No Country for Old Men*. Dir. Ethan Coen and Joel Coen. Perf. Tommy Lee Jones, Javier Bardem and Josh Brolin. Paramount, 2007. DVD.

59. Television or radio program

Provide the title of the episode or segment, followed by the title of the program and series (if any). After the titles, list any performers, narrators, directors, or others who might be pertinent. Then give the name of the network, call numbers and city for any local station, the broadcast date, and the medium of reception (*television or radio*).

> "Kaisha." *The Sopranos*. Perf. James Gandolfini, Lorraine Bracco, and Edie Falco. HBO. 4 June 2006. Television.

Visual sources in MLA-style works cited

60. Cartoon

Trudeau, Garry. "Doonesbury." Comic Strip. *Washington Post* 21 Apr. 2008. C15. Print.

61. Advertisement

Nike. Advertisement. ABC. 8 Oct. 2008. Television.

62. Map, graph, or chart

Treat a map, graph, or chart as an anonymous book, but add the appropriate descriptive label. List *Map* after the name of the map.

Greenland. Map. Vancouver: International Travel Maps, 2004. Print.

63. Painting, sculpture, or photograph

Give the artist's name first if available, the title of the work in italics, the medium of composition, the name of the institution that houses the work and the city, or the name of the collection. In the text, mentioning the work and the artist is preferable to a parenthetical citation.

Manet, Edouard. *Olympia*. 1863. Oil on canvas. Musée d'Orsay, Paris.

VISUAL SOURCES ON THE WEB

64. Video on the Web

Video on the Web often lacks a creator and a date. Begin the entry with a title if you cannot find a creator. Use *n.d.* if you cannot find a date.

Wesch, Michael. *A Vision of Students Today*. *YouTube*. YouTube, 2007. Web. 28 May 2008.

65. Work of art on the Web

Gardner, Alexander. *The Home of a Rebel Sharpshooter, Gettysburg*. 1863. Prints and Photographs Div., Lib of Cong. *Selected Civil War Photographs*. Web. 5 Dec. 2008.

66. Map on the Web

"Lansing, Michigan." Map. *Google Maps*. Google, 3 Nov. 2008. Web. 3 Nov. 2008.

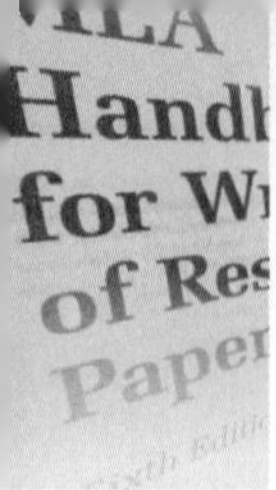

Sample MLA paper

Include your last name and page number as page header, beginning with the first page, 1/2″ from the top.

Abukar 1

George Abukar

Professor Hernandez

English 1102

5 May 2008

It's Time to Shut Down the Identity Theft Racket

Center the title. Do not underline the title, put it inside quotation marks, or type it in all capital letters.

For many college students, a credit rating is something you'll start to worry about after you graduate and get a job. A friend of mine, whom I'll call "Donna," has never had a credit card in her life, and protecting her credit rating was the last thing on her mind her junior year. That is, until she started getting disturbing calls from debt collectors accusing her of not paying her credit card bill.

Indent each paragraph five spaces (1/2″ on the ruler in your word processing program).

The first few times she got these calls, Donna explained to the callers that she didn't have a credit card and didn't know what account they were talking about. Then one debt collector threatened to tell Donna's boss about her bad debts and take her to court. Donna got scared.

It took several days of phone calls to her parents, her bank, the police, and a credit-reporting agency before Donna found out what was going on. During spring break of her sophomore year, Donna had lost her wallet at a beach in South Carolina. She got a new driver's license from the Department of Motor Vehicles when she returned home, but she didn't report the lost wallet to the police because it didn't have any money or credit cards in it.

Specify 1″ margins all around. Double-space everything.

But whoever found Donna's wallet used her driver's license information to apply for a credit card, and got one, with Donna's name on it. He or she used the card to rack up several thousand dollars in bills, mostly for clothes and stereo equipment. When this criminal didn't pay the bill, the creditors came looking for Donna instead.

It's bad enough that someone stole Donna's identity. What was worse, to her, was that none of the people who should have helped stop the crime did. The credit card company that issued the card did not bother to check the applicant's identity. The

MLA style does not require a title page. Check with your instructor to find out whether you need one.

Abukar 2

credit reporting agencies did nothing to help her get the bad information off her files. In fact, even after she has filled out forms for all three national credit reporting agencies, asking to have the information about the unpaid credit card bills removed from her file, the bad debts are still showing up. Donna worries that she will never have a clean credit record, and that she'll have trouble buying a house or car after she graduates. "All this information about me has been falsified," Donna said in an interview, "and I don't even get to set the record straight." Only the credit reporting agencies have the ability to do that, and since they do not stand to make any money from helping Donna, they are in no hurry to do it.

As long as credit-reporting agencies are protected from the effects of identity theft, they will not take steps to protect consumers. Therefore, I propose that the United States Congress pass federal legislation making credit-reporting agencies liable for damages when their actions or negligence lead to loss from identity theft.

Akubar states his thesis in this paragraph after he has described the problem using the example of Donna.

This legislation is necessary because identity theft is out of control. In 2007 there were 8.4 million adult victims of identity theft in the United States for a total loss of $49.3 billion (Monahan). The great majority of victims learn of identity theft when they become victims; very few are alerted by proactive businesses. Clearly, identity theft is a huge and expensive problem. What is being done to prevent it?

Mostly, consumers are being told to protect themselves. The United States Federal Trade Commission has an entire Web site devoted to telling consumers how to minimize their risk of identity theft. Some of their advice is obvious, like "Keep your purse or wallet in a safe place at work." Some tips are more obscure: "Treat your mail and trash carefully." Some assume that people have a lot more time, patience, and knowledge than they really do:

> Ask about information security procedures in your workplace or at businesses, doctor's offices or other institutions that collect your personally identifying information. Find out who has access to your

Quotations of more than four lines should be indented 1" or ten spaces.

Abukar 3

> personal information and verify that it is handled securely. Ask about the disposal procedures for those records as well. Find out if your information will be shared with anyone else. If so, ask how your information can be kept confidential. *(Identity Theft: Minimizing)*.

Do not include a page number for items without pagination, such as Web sites.

Not many people are prepared to spend twenty minutes grilling the checkout person at Old Navy when she asks for their phone number. But even if someone takes all these steps and avoids even a simple mistake like Donna made by losing her wallet, is that enough.

Daniel J. Solove, in his book *The Digital Person: Technology and Privacy in the Information Age*, argues that it is not. "The underlying cause of identity theft," he says, "is an architecture that makes us vulnerable to such crimes and unable to adequately repair the damage" (115). He notes that

Introduce blocked quotations rather than just dropping them into the text.

> We are increasingly living with digital dossiers about our lives, and these dossiers are not controlled by us but by various entities, such as private-sector companies and the government. These dossiers play a profound role in our existence in modern society. The identity thief taps into these dossiers and uses them, manipulates them, and pollutes them. The identity thief's ability to so easily access and use our personal data stems from an architecture that does not provide adequate security to our personal information and that does not afford us with a sufficient degree of participation in its collection, dissemination, and use. (115)

Do not place blocked quotations within quotation marks.

Solove's proposal for reducing identity theft is to change the structure, or "architecture," of the systems we use to collect and store personal information. He recommends giving individuals more control over their personal information and requiring the companies that use that information to inform

For other examples of papers using MLA documentation, see pages 140–147, 326–331, and 376–381.

Works Cited

"Donna." Personal interview. 30 Mar. 2008.

Drum, Kevin. "You Own You." *Washington Monthly*. Washington Monthly, Dec. 2005. Web. 9 Apr. 2008.

"Equifax Annual Profit at $246.5 Million." *Atlanta Business Chronicle*. Atlanta Business Chronicle, 2 Feb. 2006. Web. 9 Apr. 2008.

Kuehner-Hebert, Katie. "Colorado Banks Would Fund ID Theft Task Force." *American Banker* 21 Mar. 2006: 1-4. *Business Source Premie*r. Web. 7 April 2008.

Monahan, Mary T. *2007 Identity Fraud Survey Report*. Javelin Strategy and Research, Feb. 2007. Web. 12 Apr. 2008.

Moyer, Liz. "Credit Agencies in the Clover." *Forbes.com*. Forbes, June 2005. Web. 10 Apr. 2008.

Solove, Daniel J. *The Digital Person: Technology and Privacy in the Information Age*. New York: NY UP, 2004. Print.

United States. Dept. of Commerce. Federal Trade Commission. *Identity Theft Survey Report*. McLean: Synovate, 2004. Print.

---. ---. *Identity Theft: Minimizing Your Risk*. US Dept. of Commerce, 2005. Web. 15 Apr. 2008.

Center "Works Cited" on a new page.

Double-space all entries. Indent all but the first line in each entry one-half inch.

Alphabetize entries by the last names of the authors or by the first important word in the title if no author is listed.

Italicize the titles of books and periodicals.

If an author has more than one entry, list the entries in alphabetical order by title. Use three hyphens in place of the author's name for the second and subsequent entries.

Go through your text and make sure all the sources you have used are in the list of works cited.

Photo Credits

p. 8: Oona Curley; **p. 40:** Oona Curley; **p. 60:** Time & Life Pictures/Getty Images; **p. 62:** Xen/Alamy; **p. 67:** Frank Capri/Hulton/Getty Images; **p. 92:** NASA; **p. 119:** Getty Images; **p. 161:** AP Images; **p. 163:** Ted Soqui/Corbis; **p. 172 (top):** Hoffmann/Getty Images; **p. 172 (bottom left):** Gaslight Ad Archives; **p. 172 (bottom right):** Volkswagen AG; **p. 173 (top left):** Photofest; **p. 173 (bottom):** © 2006 Volkswagen of America, Inc.; **p. 202:** Helene Rogers/Alamy; **p. 252:** Reuters/Corbis; **p. 295:** Unicef; **p. 298:** National Archives; **p. 305:** Vario images GmbH & Co.KG/Alamy; **p. 347:** Wally McNamee/Corbis; **p. 386:** Oona Curley.

Unless otherwise credited, all photos © Lester Faigley Photos.

Text Credits

danah boyd, "Web 2.0 Forum: Knowledge Access as a Public Good," *Britannica Blog,* June 2007. Reprinted with permission from the *Britannica Blog,* copyright © 2007 by Encyclopaedia Britannica, Inc.

Tim Collins, "Straight from the Heart" from *The Guardian,* July 13, 2005. Copyright © Tim Collins 2005. Reprinted by permission.

Lee Connell, "My Dropout Boyfriend Kept Dropping In," *New York Times,* June 1, 2008. Copyright © 2008 The New York Times. All rights reserved. Used by permission and protected by the Copyright Laws of the United States. The printing, copying, redistribution, or retransmission of the material without express written permission is prohibited.

Stephanie Coontz, "The Future of Marriage," *Cato Unbound,* January 14, 2008. Copyright © 2008 by Cato Institute. Reproduced with permission of Cato Institute via Copyright Clearance Center.

Stentor Danielson "Pesticides, Parasite May Cause Frog Deformities," *National Geographic News,* July 9, 2002. Reprinted by permission of the National Geographic Society.

EBSCO. Screen images from EBSCO Database are used by permission of EBSCO Publishing.

Sue Kunitomi Embrey, "Some Lines for a Younger Brother." Originally published in *Gidra,* Vol. II, No. 5, May 1970. Copyright © 1970 by Sue Kunitomi Embrey. Reprinted by permission.

Lori Gottlieb, "How Do I Love Thee?" *Atlantic Monthly,* March 2006. Reprinted by permission of the author.

Ted Koppel, "Take My Privacy Please!" *New York Times,* June 13, 2005. Copyright © 2005 by The New York Times Co. Reprinted with permission.

LexisNexis Copyright 2009, LexisNexis, a division of Reed Elsevier Inc. All Rights Reserved. LexisNexis and the Knowledge Burst logo are registered trademarks of Reed Elsevier Properties Inc. and are used with the permission of LexisNexis.

David T.Z. Mindich, "The Collapse of the Media: The Young and the Restless," *The Wilson Quarterly,* Spring 2005. Reprinted by permission of the author.

Lefteris Pavlides, "The Aesthetics of Wind Power," *Providence Journal,* March 7, 2005. Reprinted by permission of the author.

Michael Pollan, "Why Bother?" Reprinted by permission of International Creative Management, Inc. Copyright © 2008 by Michael Pollan. First appeared in *New York Times Magazine.*

Emily Raine, "Why Should I Be Nice to You? Coffee Shops and the Politics of Good Service" from *Bad Subjects,* Issue 74, December 2005. Reprinted by permission of the author.

Stephanie Rosenbloom, "The Nitpicking Nation," *The New York Times,* May 7, 2006. Copyright © 2006 The New York Times. All rights reserved. Used by permission and protected by the Copyright Laws of the United States. The printing, copying, redistribution, or retransmission of the material without express written permission is prohibited.

Chip Walter, "Affairs of the Lips: Why We Kiss," *Scientific American Mind,* February/March 2008. Reprinted with permission. Copyright © 2008 by Scientific American, Inc. All rights reserved.

Samuel Wilson, "*The Emperor's Giraffe*" The Emperor's Giraffe. Copyright © 1999 by Westview Press. Reprinted by permission of Westview Press, a member of Perseus Books Group.

Mark Winne, "When Handouts Keep Coming, the Food Line Never Ends," *Washington Post,* November 18, 2007, Reprinted by permission of the author.

YAHOO! Ince. Reproduced with permission of Yahoo! Inc. Copyright © 2008 by Yahoo! Inc. YAHOO! and the YAHOO! logo are trademarks of Yahoo! Inc.

Index

ADDITIONAL READINGS FROM *MAJOR THEMES FOR MODERN WRITERS,* BY HARVEY S. WIENER

contents

From *Major Themes for Modern Writers* by Harvey S. Wiener.

rhetorical contents

Description

Narration

Illustration

Comparison and Contrast

Process

Cause and Effect

Classification

Definition

Argumentation

preface

Major Themes for Modern Writers adds a distinctive perspective to the Penguin Academics series, which with its several composition texts has brought great essays to freshman readers and their instructors. As its title affirms, this text organizes its more than sixty readings according to major themes, central issues that face the citizens of the twenty-first century. At its core this volume asserts that powerful ideas do not exist in a vacuum and that multiple perspectives on a subject help us better understand its nuances and range of possibilities. Further, the book insists that using thematically organized selections as the basis for a writing course enriches the intellectual experience of beginning college students and energizes their efforts to produce clear, thoughtful, and dynamic essays of their own.

Innumerable themes emerge as we consider the complex world we live in, certainly, and *Major Themes for Modern Writers* makes no claim of exclusivity: the themes categorized here are by no means the only themes one could choose to examine. Yet this book identifies what most people would agree are critical challenges in our effort to understand our lives and environment. Family, education, work, law and justice, gender, science and technology, language, and human values: these are the book's organizing principles.

In Chapter 1, "Introduction: Reading and Writing About Major Themes," students will find a useful approach to the tasks of critical reading and informed writing. Here one can explore a variety of methods that inform the fundamental tasks in any writing course. Students can learn strategies for reading with attention and focus; and they can investigate strategies for developing strong essays, from advanced planning, to writing a thesis, to choosing appropriate rhetorical strategies, among others.

At the start of each of eight subsequent thematic chapters, a brief but compelling introduction raises some of the theme's dimensions. Before each selection, a head note provides insights into the author's life and works. After each selection, under the heading **For Thinking, Discussing, and Writing**, four sharply focused questions guide an understanding and appreciation of the author's key points. At chapter's end, under the heading **Connecting Ideas**, a few items help readers and writers integrate and contest some of the notions presented around the theme. Trusting students to initiate their own questions and challenges and honoring the instructor's efforts to identify key elements as she sees them, we have kept pedagogy to a bare minimum.

The text offers essays that not only bring vigorous thinking to an important topic but also represent quality writing—good craftsmanship that students can emulate as they attempt their own essays. The selections throughout provide a range of approaches and cross the boundaries of time and geography. For example, George Orwell's frequently anthologized "A Hanging" first appeared more than fifty years ago, yet no attempt to understand law and justice is complete without considering Orwell's brilliantly understated and beautifully constructed critique of capital punishment. And a 2006 piece, "Continuing the Search for Kinder Executions" by Mark Essig yanks the issue into today's consciousness, where state-sponsored penalty by death finds both wide support and searing contempt among people all over the world. Orwell's perspective as a citizen of Great Britain emanates from his years of foreign service in India; Essig, born and reared in the United States, lives in Los Angeles and wrote his doctoral thesis on forensic toxicology.

Major Themes for Modern Writers does not shrink from controversy in attempting to cut as wide a swath as possible within its stated chapter themes. Selections address such issues as gay parenting, the return of the sweatshop to America's manufacturing sector, voter apathy, the failures of feminism, global warming, the excesses of cyberspace, the uses of torture, animal rights, and the right to die. Yet controversy is not a defining tenet of the book; rather, the text aims through variety and range of viewpoints to engage readers to consider thoughtfully the prominent themes that test our humanity and guide the ways we live our lives.

No book exists without the help and support of loyal colleagues, friends, and family. I give my thanks to the following instructors who lent their invaluable feedback to this mansucript: Claudia Milstead, Missouri Valley College; Fred D'Astoli, College of the Canyons; Tina Zigon, Southwest Texas State University; Dr. Nancy Remler, Armstrong

Atlantic State University; Sandi Hubnik, University of Texas at Arlington; Diane Carr, Midlands Technical College; Dr Adam Fischer, Bowie State University; and Craig Franson, University of Oregon. Lauren Finn at Longman provided astute editorial guidance and the support of an informed, conscientious reader and lover of books. Carmen O'Donnell watched over the book at its major points of production, both before and after the text went to print. Saul Adam Wiener, now a doctoral student at Fordham University, worked diligently to collect vital information on the many authors represented here. And my wife Barbara Koster Wiener accepted yet another deadline-driven project with her typical patience, love, and support.

Harvey S. Wiener
City University of New York
LaGuardia Community College

CHAPTER 1

Introduction: Reading and Writing About Major Themes

Critical Reading

Anything involving the human mind is complex, and reading is among the most complex of the mind's activities. Neurobiologists, sociologists, computer scientists—in all fields today, researchers seek to understand the phenomenon of reading in physical, cultural, and linguistic terms. Yet you might say, "I've been reading since I was six—so what's the big deal?" That's true enough: reading has become so much of a habit for many of us that it feels as if we do it without thinking.

And that's a problem. We become passive readers, a bit distracted, a bit apathetic, and we don't consider and use what reading demands of the human mind, all of it pretty much: the part that gathers facts, the part that looks at parts and relations, the part that judges, responds emotionally, compares, applies, and so on. College demands *critical reading*, a high level of awareness and interaction when you examine any text. Being a critical reader means reading actively, setting your mind to extract whatever you can of importance from what you see on a page.

Critical readers make connections between what they have read and what they are reading now. The philosophy of this book takes root in the idea that neither readers nor writers exist in a context-free milieu, and that means that any piece of writing has a broad and deep relevance to a larger world of ideas. Even when a writer has a very specific audience in mind, the larger audience beyond centuries and geography establishes an expansive intellectual environment. We have no evidence that Shakespeare, writing for rowdy Elizabethan theatergoers, gave even a fleeting thought to his impact over time and space. And yet today, more than four hundred years after his phenomenal output, he still talks to modern readers across the globe.

Critical readers are curious about the interconnections among themes and ideas expressed by a variety of reflective thinkers. By presenting the selections according to theme, *Major Themes for Modern Writers* attempts to make your reading more informed through multiple perspectives on major issues. At the outset you know that all the readings in a given chapter offer a take on a topic that all the other writers in the chapter are approaching from varied points of view. None of your reading is in a vacuum, then, and if you keep the theme of each chapter in mind as you read, you'll find that your efforts are more informed than they otherwise might be. That the readings in this book already appear in a thematic context will help you make connections, and each chapter ends with just a few items to remind you of how you can view some of the selections in a comprehensive framework.

But the possibilities for weighing one piece of writing against another transcend the thematic units established chapter by chapter, and you should be awake to the possibilities of associations between as well as within chapters, as well as to the larger world of books and ideas beyond this text. When readers attempt to link ideas across a broad spectrum of thinkers, they engage in an elevated level of critical thought, which, in fact, is one of the hallmarks of a well-educated person.

You know, of course, that different people think in different ways, and so there are no hard and fast rules on how to start your investigation of a piece of writing, even with the kind of thematic context provided here. But practiced thinkers do find certain techniques invaluable for making sense as they read.

Perhaps the most important advice to offer is your need to engage the text by questioning what you read. True, questions always surround reading in college. Textbooks and teachers pose questions constantly—asking you for facts, analyses, and judgments. Often these questions stimulate thinking, but unless you become part of the question-generating process, you can feel alienated from it. It's not enough simply to respond to someone else's questions: you have to learn to pose them yourself. In this way the questions become yours. You have a way of connecting with whatever you're reading. After all, many texts do not come with appended questions—an article on AIDS in a respected medical journal, an editorial in your local newspaper on poor day care, an essay on military reform in *Harper's* or the *Atlantic* or some other highly regarded periodical. The many books your instructors assign as supplements to your textbooks often do not provide questions to highlight key concepts that you should learn. And how can you evaluate your own writing draft by draft unless you approach it with a questioning attitude: Is my point clear? Have I provided appropriate detail? Does my introduction hold the reader's attention?

In a sense the whole act of reading is a giant question: What does this mean? Again and again as our minds engage the written word, we must ask this question. Yet too often, especially in course reading supported by textbooks, we stop asking and simply follow a bunch of commands, accepting the questions at the end of a piece as the only needed guidelines for understanding.

Certainly you'll find some post-reading questions in this text—but these are meant as much as models for your own questioning strategies as prods for thinking and writing about the text before you. You should very deliberately question these questions and reformulate them, as needed, as you proceed in order to get the most from what you read and what you write.

Keeping in mind the essential intellectual tool of questioning what you read, as you approach your career as a college reader, you can benefit from following a series of steps to help you establish your own style of investigation.

Previewing

Approaching a reading in some ways is like approaching anything new. We instinctively ask ourselves, *What is this*? Or, *Where am I*? Or, *What can I figure out rapidly*? We look it over quickly at first. We wonder, *Have I seen anything like this before? What can I understand right away*? We try to determine what the surface of a thing can tell us in advance of what lies within.

Using previewing as a way of helping them read resolutely, thoughtful readers decide in advance a purpose for their reading; and they draw on their prior knowledge as an aid to encountering the text. What is *previewing*? Just as you might think, it means *viewing before*. And that means taking stock, ahead of your reading the piece fully, of what it might be attempting, why you're reading it in the first place. And what role does *prior knowledge* play? If you can make even a small connection from your past experiences or reading with the unread selection before you and the theme it reflects as stated in the chapter title, you'll be amazed at how much that connection will help you engage the text. Ask yourself what you know about the topic, what you believe, maybe why you believe it.

Before you read in Chapter 3, "What Is Education," Judith Ortiz Cofer's "The Patterson Public Library," for example, a quick flashback to your own library days—good or bad—will help you link your own thoughts to the pending essay and make you more attentive to it. What was your neighborhood library like? How did you get there? What did the building look like? How does a library resonate with the chapter theme, "What Is Education?" Just a few questions like these help set up your mind for attentive access to the selection. If asked your purpose in reading, you might be tempted to respond, "It's required." But that doesn't get you very far, other than to prick some resentment and to put you in the laconic camp of passive readers. You do have to determine what your own particular purpose is in reading. Are you reading to learn new facts and data? New concepts and vocabulary? To delight in a piece of fiction? To prepare for an examination? For a lecture or class discussion? To find an idea for a research paper? To learn new rhetorical techniques to advance your own writing? To see how the piece relates to the chapter theme? No doubt there are other purposes as well. And of course, these are neither mutually exclusive nor set in stone: you can have more than one purpose and can shift your purpose as you read.

Here are some steps to take before you actually read a selection.

- State in your own mind why you are reading the piece.
- Glance at the selection's title and weigh it for a moment.
- Check the writer's name and any information supplied about the writer's life.

- Consider the headings or subtitles, the introductory paragraph, the ending.
- Examine any illustrations, tables, charts, graphs, and photographs.
- If the reading is from a textbook, study a head note or marginal notes by the writers or questions after a chapter.

Yes, observe these strategies before you read: experienced readers take many of these steps before plowing through a selection. Previewing—a quick sizing up—makes sense as a first step in reading anything. Don't worry that investigating the text in an orderly fashion before reading it will take away the joy of reading the piece "naturally," from start to finish. A reflective preview will simply give you a good start, ensuring that you gather some basics to help you make sense of the piece straight away.

Take for example the selection in Chapter 6 called "Why Should Males Exist?" The previewing reader has a field day with a piece like this! In approaching the selection at the outset, you'd have to wonder what the title possibly could mean. Is this an attack on men in general, the writer having lived a life of abuse in a household ruled by men? Is it a piece rooted in science, perhaps, where the writer will make a claim for female dominance in the natural world and the weak role men play as mates and fathers? After all, the title does say "male" not "men," and "male" includes other species than the human. Is this perhaps a humorous essay about all the problems men cause in the world—the title sounds preposterous, doesn't it, almost silly?

So why does the reader want to read this piece? If the essay is about disagreeable relations with men, the notion of a proposed world without them should pique your interest. Could anyone be serious about questioning the existence of males? If the piece has some scientific basis, your prior knowledge should tell you that from what you learned in biology males are important in propagation, at the very least. So maybe the writer will challenge your previously held assumptions, and maybe you could learn something about procreation.

In previewing, you'd want to look at the notes that appear before the selection (page 205). Information about the writer and the essay might give you some further insights. Matt Ridley, as you can see, writes about scientific topics; the head note says that in one book he explores the role of genes in human development. You can infer from this information that the piece you're about to read will have some scientific underlay. And the note says further that the piece will examine "the male animal and his role in propagation and evolution." Looking at the first sentence in the essay, you can tell from the informal language that this piece may have some humorous elements: if "men are at the root of a lot of the world's troubles," the engaged reader surely will want to read more.

All this mental activity should occur before your actual reading—venturing guesses about what the piece will deal with, getting your mind ready to absorb it by setting a purpose for reading, tapping in to your prior knowledge. Through advance thought, you can become an active reader, ready to extract essential meaning from the essay.

Notes and Reading Journals

Years of anxiety about marking up schoolbooks often train us to read with pencils and pens in our pockets or pocketbooks and not between our thumbs and forefingers. But the human mind can't hold onto enough of what comes its way. The truth is that even the best memories need prods to recall. Writing things down remains the best way to hold onto information. And writing helps us to organize and reflect on information, to shape and examine ideas. As you read, then, even as you preview, have a pen or pencil in hand. If you own the book, you may want to get into the habit of taking notes in the margins. Many people find it useful to underline important ideas, use asterisks to identify key concepts, place checkmarks beside special phrasing—the systems vary from person to person. Some make an index in the back of the book with key words and page numbers on which the words appear. Many use the margins for recording brief summaries or reflections, connecting points to other points within the reading itself, or to points in other readings or experience. Again, there are no hard and fast rules for taking notes in a book. Use your good sense and develop a system that works for you. Claim the text with a pencil or pen; find your own shorthand system to ask questions (???), agree (!!!), challenge. Circle, star, underline, double-underline, highlight.

Some readers like to take notes in notebooks instead of taking notes in the book itself. Some like to keep notebooks in addition to book notes—even if you take notes in books as you read, maintaining a notebook for reading can serve you well as a learner and thinker. Whether you call it a log, journal, diary, or notebook; whether it's on paper or on a computer monitor, these personal volumes help you interact with the text in a sustained way and join the reading to your life and mind.

For many readers, a journal can remain a steady life companion. Many people—teenagers, travelers, writers—keep free-form journals, recording day's events, thoughts, longings, secrets, or a mix of these. Scientists, musicians, historians, nurses, doctors and people in all professions and disciplines keep records of their thoughts and actions. Readers from all walks of life keep notebooks in which they record any number of things from their reading—incandescent phrases, interesting facts, compelling ideas and arguments, their own responses to these. Major thinkers like the great seventeenth-century poet, John Milton, kept what were called chapbooks—handwritten excerpts, word for word, that excited and stimulated them from books they read. Copying out your favorite passages from essays, stories, and books is a marvelous way of making a text your own.

Keeping a reading journal supports inquiry; it counters the temptation to read passively, drawing us into the text and into our thinking.

Thesis and Themes

The notion of understanding a text is nowhere so profoundly affected as in a reader's efforts to determine the writer's thesis or theme. *What is the main point here?:* you should learn to ask that question regularly about anything you read. All active readers keep that question as a beacon to their journey through a text. Sometimes the writer will say exactly what the point is, perhaps in the title, perhaps in the introductory paragraph, perhaps elsewhere. Timothy Harper's piece on page 86, "They Treat Girls Differently, Don't They?" lets you know straight off from the title what the writer's thesis is. When Leon Botstein writes this in the first paragraph of his essay on page 97:

> *The most pressing concern for the future of the American high school is correcting the fatal flaw in the way we educate adolescents, revealed through its inability to deliver excellence evenhandedly over the past 40 years,*

we know exactly what the essay will deal with. But often you have to determine the thesis or theme of a piece on your own by adding up direct statements, hints, and implications and by stating the main point in your own words. Particularly in short stories, poems, and novels, but also in complex essays, memoirs, and reports, the mind of the reader and the informing sentences of the writer must interact to peel away elements in order to reveal the theme. You should demand of yourself that you attempt to state the theme or thesis of everything you read and that you use your journal to record it.

Purpose and Audience

As you can imagine, writers may have many reasons for writing, and they may overlap. In "The Spider and the Wasp" (page 311), Alexander Petrunkevitch states his purpose with the utmost precision:

> *The case I propose to describe here is that of the tarantula spiders and their archenemy, the digger wasps of the genus* pepsis.

But not many writers tell you so directly what their purpose is, and you must attempt to uncover it as a means for better understanding. Some writers intend, for example, to entertain, others to inform, challenge, protest, describe, tell a story, persuade, or incite to action. A writer's purpose always links directly to the audience, and so experienced readers often consider both side by side. The writer's purpose and sense of the intended reader will influence the writing dramatically. You'll figure out that Petrunkevitch aims to reach fairly educated readers: his piece appeared in *Scientific American*, a popular monthly magazine. But his essay would follow very different strategies had he set out to write about the habits of spiders and wasps for a class of fifth graders or a convention of entomologists or a group of pest control experts. Thesis, purpose, language, and structure (see below)—the writer's audience significantly influences these elements.

Language

The notion of language haunts all writers, and the choice of the best word in any sentence can move from intense concentration to torment in the writer's practice. Words have both denotative and connotative meaning, and serious writers aim for words that carry the absolutely right associations, enhance the thesis and purpose, and reach the targeted audience. When David Blankenhorn chooses the word *deadbeat* for the title of his essay "The Deadbeat Dad" (page 61), we only can imagine how he must have labored to find the perfect word to convey the negative role he wants to identify and then challenge. "Absent," "cheap," "unnecessary," "stingy," "uninvolved"—as tempting and as valid as these alternate adjectives might be for the essay's context, none conveys the colloquial negativity of "deadbeat" for a divorced father who won't pay for his children's support.

In any successful piece of writing, each word and combination of words advance the writer's point, and you should consider how those words create images in your mind. How does the level of vocabulary affect the piece? Is the word choice right for the selection and its intended audience? How do the degrees of general and specific language interact? Why does the writer use emotionally charged or emotion-free words? How has the complexity or simplicity of the vocabulary influenced the writer's assertions? What happens to the meaning of a key sentence if you substitute for one or two words synonyms with even slightly different connotations?

Structure and Organization

A world of rhetorical strategies: a writer faces many options in organizing and developing a piece, and its structure plays an important part in the success of an essay. The critical reader pays careful attention to the shape of the selection and how the writer has achieved the desired ends. In the selection by Blankenhorn mentioned in previous paragraphs, the writer uses a combination of rhetorical patterns. He establishes categories of fathers—Unnecessary Father, Old Father, and New Father among them—and by means of *classification* and *definition* identifies the qualities of each. In addition, he draws on the strategy of *comparison and contrast* to weigh the qualities of the Deadbeat Dad in relation to another type of father, the New Father. An active reader thinks about why Blankenhorn chooses these patterns and how they help him achieve his ends.

And, for any selection, in addition to thinking about the basic organizing patterns of the writing, the active reader considers how the introduction and conclusion frame the subject, about the way that the sentences hold together, about how the writer unifies the ideas so that they all relate to the fundamental point.

Many writers and readers find that their reading journals are invaluable for taking notes on technique. Notes on craft and organization can provide you with resources for your own writing—tips on how or how not to organize and express ideas as you write. Build the habits of inquiry in relation to the writer's craft. Develop the practice of jotting down not only facts and summaries, but also the riches of method.

Record remarkable strategies—effective transitions, great opening lines, special phrasing, and so on. Jot down page references in case you want to come back to the selection again. Considering a writer's technique and organization provides rich opportunities to expand your understanding of writing.

Details and Evidence

One of the hallmarks of all effective writing is the nature and quality of detail that the writer uses to support assertions. As with the other elements laid out in this introduction, details and evidence link directly to thesis, purpose, and audience.

In narratives and descriptions, often in the service of argumentative essays, we look for concrete sensory language, words and images alive with sound, smell, color, action, and sensations of touch. In Chapter 5, when George Orwell in "A Hanging" identifies the man soon to fall victim to capital punishment (page 163), the essay soars with sentience:

> *One prisoner had been brought out of his cell. He was a Hindu, a puny wisp of a man, with a shaven head and vague liquid eyes. He had a thick, sprouting moustache, absurdly too big for his body, rather like the moustache of a comic man on the films. . . .*
>
> *Eight o'clock struck and a bugle call, desolately thin in the wet air, floated from the distant barracks. . . .*

Writers marshalling details to argue a point will often draw on the language of data—numbers, statistics, case studies. Note the march of numbers that solidifies one of Sasha Abramsky's points in "When They Get Out" (page 194):

> *Since 1985 America's prison population, not counting the more than half a million people in jails at any one time, has increased by about six or seven percent yearly. Truth-in-sentencing laws mandate that many prisoners serve 85 percent of their sentences before being eligible for parole; all the same, figures over the past decade indicate that on average more than 40 percent of prison inmates are released in any given year. Assuming that these statistical relationships remain constant, we can make certain predictions. In 1995 a total of 463,284 inmates were released. To use a worst case scenario, some 660,000 will be released in 2000, some 887,000 in 2005, and about 1.2 million in 2010. . . .*

The writer puts flesh on the numbers by following the cases of particular prisoners, like Robert Scully, caught in California's cycle of maximum-security punishment and prison release. Scully "was placed in a 'security housing unit cell,' where close to twenty-three hours a day he was deprived all human interaction" and after five years "reemerged . . . by now a human time bomb."

Often writers will draw on expert testimony, quotations, and paraphrases taken from the writing or speech of authorities or important players in the writer's field of interest. The citations not only provide essential detail so that the reader knows how the writer has shaped his own opinion, but they also allow the writer to comment on the expert's words, to concur with or expand upon or dismiss or dispute them, among other options. Barbara Kingsolver, in her essay "Stone Soup," cites Stephanie Coontz, the author of *The Way We Never Were*, to bolster her own argument that judging a family's values "by its tidy symmetry" is not appropriate. Later she cites Constance Ahrons who writes in *The Good Divorce* about "the binuclear family." Both these writers help Kingsolver lend credence to her assertions in the essay.

Even when the selection demands the march of figures and statistics, good writers never forget the power of a well-placed image or metaphor. Abramsky writes about a drive to an isolation unit in the Huntsville, Texas, prison complex: "Surrounding the car was a landscape of rolled razor-wire fences, surveillance cameras, bleak watchtowers, and gray concrete buildings." The imagery makes immediate the general point that high security prisons, whatever their merits, are tormenting places. Even the external environment is forbidding and, in Abramsky's essay, the surroundings serve as a powerful initial image for the terrors that lie within the "metallic-blue and Plexiglas doors" of the Huntsville facility.

The validity of most writing in no small part depends on the quality and relevance of details the writer uses to support his or her position, and the critical reader must ascertain the writer's strengths here. Analyze the kinds of details that the writer has used. Determine which images seem most original and indelible. Identify the most impressive citations. Formal research papers require a systematic citation format accepted by scholars in various professions and promulgated by national organizations such as the American Psychological Association and the Modern Language Association. Less formal writing, such as selections from many of the journals and magazines used as sources for this book, will not follow the conventions of scholarly research, not provide a list of works cited, a bibliography, or detailed parenthetical citations with page references and publication data. Instead, writers of more informal pieces will name their sources more casually, as in the examples offered from Kingsolver's piece.

Tone

Tone—the writer's attitude toward the subject—influences and is influenced by thesis, audience, purpose, language, structure, and supporting detail, the elements we've explored previously in this introduction. Tone tells you how the writer feels about the topic and, ultimately, how he wants you to feel about it. For example, the very title of Will Durst's essay in Chapter 5, "Happy National Apathy Day," tells you that irony will control the tone of this selection. How do you know? Well, we usually use "happy" in this sense to celebrate a joyous occasion (happy birthday, happy Thanksgiving, happy Valentine's Day). Who would argue seriously that in a nation defined by democratic principles national apathy is worthy of celebration? Yet by the ironic title and the tonal equivalents throughout the short piece—"Don't vote," Durst says at the essay's opening, "You don't have to. No one's going to make you. This isn't the Soviet Union in the '50s"—the writer makes readers sit up and take notice. Durst had many options in producing this essay of complaint about American citizens' bad record of voting. He could have chosen a coolheaded factual approach, showing how voters decreased dramatically over the years. He could have written a diatribe against American voters, expressing his shock and anger. He could have approached the topic analytically, seeking only to explain why voters have abandoned the polls. He could have written in a gently humorous vein, poking fun at the stay-at-homes on Election Day. He could have used a tone of sentimentality, recalling the good old days when citizens were *real* Americans and did their civic duty at the election booth!

Aware of the writer's tone, you can avoid the pitfalls of being forced to take positions before you've had a chance to weigh them carefully, and you can be especially attentive to subtle appeals to emotion and sentimentality that can obscure your view on an issue.

The habit of reading critically, from the basics of facts and details to the matters of craft, ensures solid skills and a foundation for knowledge and understanding denied the passive reader. The practice of critical reading transforms us from flaccid readers to active thinkers, who can mine text for understanding, appreciation, and action.

Informed Writing

Writing as much as reading comes alive when it is the product of active engagement. Getting into the habit of a lively exchange with yourself and others around writing tasks and challenges will mean the difference between writing that is vital to you and writing that is mechanical, done just to finish the assignment.

What follows is a series of proven strategies that most writers find extremely useful when they have to produce a piece of work. Here are two important suggestions at the outset. The first is that not all writers observe all these tactics all the time, and you should use only those that make sense to you and your writing method. The second is that these strategies do not follow each other in a linear fashion. Don't think of these recommendations as a first-you-do-this and then-you-do-that enterprise. As an example, in the first item explored below, you see that you need to establish and limit your topic; but you'll probably find that you will modify it, subtly perhaps, many times as you progress. We remind you to consider your purpose and audience before we move to a discussion on developing a thesis, but these probably proceed at the same time, one influencing the other and all three working together. Remember the interactions among these strategies and you'll remember to be flexible enough to make changes as needed as you prepare for and write your drafts.

Your Subject

Clarifying for yourself what your task is will help you get started. Most initial thoughts on a topic are much too general to be productive, and many assignments directly from your instructor or textbook, too, lack specificity. As a result you have to figure out how you can extract a limited topic from whatever the assignment looks like at first blush. Professional writers do this all the time. A magazine writer, for instance, gets an assignment to do a piece on women's fashion and decides to limit it by writing about a fashion trend, such as body decorations—body paint, body jewelry, removable tattoos. An essayist wants to write about crime in America, so, after efforts like those we describe below, she limits it to shoplifting among teenage girls in affluent suburbs. Different people have different ways of phrasing things, and, no matter what the assignment is and who makes it, the assignment often benefits from the writer's rephrasing of it in an effort to limit the field to something manageable.

You might find it useful to limit your topic in stages, moving from the general to the specific, as illustrated in the box below.

Limiting Your Topic

General	*More Limited*	*Limited Further*
Women's fashions	New trends in women's fashions	Body decorations—body paint, body jewelry, removable tattoos
Crime in America	Girls' suburban crime	Shoplifting among teenage girls in affluent suburbs
Politics	The lure of the Democratic Party	Why I am a Democrat
Concerts	Promoting concerts	Promoting "nostalgia" concerts to the over-thirty set
Sports	High school football	What makes a good coach for high school football

The important issue of topic selection requires some further attention. Your instructor may have assigned, "Write an essay to explain your politics"—no doubt a worthy activity. Yet stated in that way, it is much too broad to manage in an essay. Restate the assignment as a question. "Why Am I a Democrat?" or "How Did I Get to Be Green?" or "Who Gave Me My Political Beliefs?" Rephrasing a topic into a limiting question can convert a broad assignment into an exploration, replacing duty with enthusiasm. Again, don't view this stage of your writing as etched in stone; as you continue your thinking and exploration, you might change your topic considerably. But you have to start somewhere, and the practices we've indicated are proven topic starters for beginners and professionals alike.

When you rephrase the assignment, stating it as a question, you're really making your first pass at developing the topic. Put your limited topic on top of your blank page or blank screen so it's there to guide you as you work. Every time you lose heart or purpose, there's your topic in front of you—in your own words—to draw you back.

Prewriting Strategies

We all have different habits as writers, different ways of coping with the ongoing demands of writing and the particular assignments that crop up regularly. But all serious writers pause once they have even a slim lead on their topics to consider just what they know about it before they begin. Prior knowledge, as we have pointed out in regard to critical reading (see page 4), no matter how insubstantial, is an excellent starting point for understanding the task you're facing.

Like previewing (page 3), *prewriting*—a variety of tasks you can perform prior to starting your assignment—can help jog loose thoughts about the topic locked away somewhere in your mind.

- *Prewriting for Discovery*

How do you get going once you've made a tentative stab at a topic? How do you figure out what to draw on from your own experiences, readings, television watching, or movie going that might help you figure out which way to approach a topic? Some people are able to harness their prior knowledge, even conceptualize papers, in their minds, without writing. But this is rare. Most people do well with some kind of written activity to stimulate their efforts. The box below identifies and defines some of the prewriting practices that can help you find out what you're thinking about the topic.

Prewriting Strategies

Jotting Down Ideas	Write down your thoughts in a list or scratch outline.
Brainstorming	Raise as many questions as you can about the topic and use the questions as springboards for finding answers that can help you produce a good essay. The journalists' questions—who, what, where, when, how, and why—are very useful here.
Non-stop Writing	Fill a page with your unedited thoughts for a set time period—ten minutes, say—the point being to free associate on the topic.
Drawing a Subject Tree or Map	Track your ideas visually by connecting them with lines, arrows, or other shapes to move your thoughts along and to link them.
Making an Outline	Use the structure of an outline with headings and subheadings to help you flesh out the topic logically.

Whichever of these works for you—for many people it's a combination of activities—they help you tap your wellspring of prior knowledge on a topic. In all activities preliminary to actual writing, writers are taking stock of what they know, where their interests lie, where they need to plug gaps and find information and opinions to relate to in their own writing, and more. Again, keeping a notebook as you work is as valuable to writing as it is to reading. And your reading journal can serve as an excellent jump-off point for your writing,

For example, let's say you're jotting down ideas for a paper on entertainment, and you come up with the list below:

Prewriting: List of Ideas on Entertainment

```
Cineplexes
Drive-ins
Batman
King Kong
Harry Potter movies
Expensive
```

Even from such a short and seemingly random list prepared as freewriting, you can find your way into a topic. What does the list tell you? Hints of possible interests—*Batman, King Kong, Harry Potter.* Clearly, the list suggests an interest in film, and by the films named, fantasy-adventure films. But observe also *cineplexes* and *drive-ins*: these suggest an interest in movie environments, where films are shown to audiences. And *expensive*: perhaps an interest in costs is worth pursuing for this writer. Which of the three subjects—fantasy-adventure films, movie environments, costs—interests the writer most? Looking at a prewriting list in this way will help you hone and limit your topic. And the task becomes intellectually exciting and engaging because you're responding to the ideas you yourself generated. You're in charge. Think of your writing assignment as a list of tasks, and it feels leaden—pick topic; write thesis; do research. But getting started by exploring your knowledge and interests leaves you energized to execute a plan that can produce a successful piece of writing.

- *Finding More Information*

One of the great revelations about prewriting, other than finding out what you know about the topic in a preliminary way, is finding out what you don't know. Here, too, all writers confront this reality of knowledge gaps. How to fill them? Try asking yourself these kinds of questions as you zero in on your topic:

Expanding What You Know: Key Questions to Ask Yourself

- What do my own experiences tell me about the topic?
- What have I read—or can I read now—that will give me insights into my topic?
- What can I learn from friends, family, teachers, and other thoughtful people that can help me with the topic?
- What other sources, such as films, radio or television talk shows, computer programs, and Web pages can help me with the topic?

These questions are both reflective and directional. They tell you what you have to think about, as in the first question. To answer it you have to contemplate your past and bring from it the experiences that you can use to shape an essay. But the questions also tell you what you have to *do* as you prepare to write. They tell you to talk with people—anyone you can find, really—about your topic as you're weighing it in your mind. Conversation yields productive insights, and talking about the topic in advance of writing will help you shape your own thoughts.

The questions tell you to go to the library or to cyberspace when you've reached a dead end or even when you're pumped up about where your topic is going but you know you don't have enough information about it. Browse the online or card catalog. Go to the bookshelves. Check newspaper microfiche. Look at encyclopedias and other reference books. Use a Web browser like Google to identify more information than you'll ever use from the World Wide Web. Do a search with your limited topic as the key word.

The questions tell you not only to think about the media and any relevant information you've gleaned from them but also to stay alert to current offerings. Check the film, radio, and television listings in your local newspaper, and read the reviews of new productions. Your college may have a film series with just the perfect film related to your topic. Go to the video store and rent something relevant for home viewing.

The point here, of course, is to expand what you know so that you can give substance to your ideas and draw upon these resources as evidence or details once you get your essay going.

Purpose and Audience

As with the appropriate strategies for critical reading, you have to consider your purpose and audience, but from the perspective of someone planning to write rather than read. Topic in hand, the writer must determine why she is writing this particular paper—other than the fact that her instructor assigned it, of course. For the developing paper on entertainment, for example, the writer has a number of choices, based on the prewriting list you examined above. The writer could:

- Analyze the characteristics of modern fantasy-adventure films.
- Explore why drive-in movies have faded in popularity.
- Argue that multiplex theaters are poorly managed, unappealing substitutes for the old-fashioned single-film movie houses.
- Argue that high admission costs for movie house entry are driving away important audiences.

You've seen lists of options like this before: a writer—this time it's you—may want to entertain, inform, challenge, protest, describe, tell a story, persuade, or incite to action.

Purpose and audience work hand in hand. Audience, of course, means the readers for whom you are writing. Certainly your most direct audience will be one of your instructors. But don't let the need to submit a paper blind you to considering a broader audience. You should be writing for your fellow students as well as your teacher; many teachers will insist that students share drafts as they develop a final copy of their work. Will friends or family members read what you have to say? Would you serve your purpose of arguing for a return to small movie theaters if you wrote your argument as a letter to the president of one of the multiplex companies or as a letter to the editor of a local newspaper? Your instructor may ask you to experiment with diversified audiences. How different your paper would be if you were explaining common features of fantasy-adventure films to readers of the best selling fantasy-adventure magazine for teenagers as opposed to upper-level film school students as opposed to actors in a new television series called *Fantasy-Adventure House*. In each case the audience will influence your presentation dramatically.

Thesis

Your papers in college will require that you have a main point, often called a *thesis*. Simply having a topic is not enough; you need to make an assertion about it. As you weigh your main point, you will want to write down possibilities. Look at each possible thesis. Ask yourself which is most do-able, engaging, interesting. But know that your thesis can change as you work with the paper and move through drafts.

The student writing about entertainment settled on the topic of fantasy-adventure films, and decided to examine the two versions of *King Kong*, the black-and-white film of 1933 and the more recent color spectacular of 2005. (She eliminated the 1976 remake in an effort to limit the topic.) Look at the thesis sentence that evolved as she thought about her topic, spoke with other people, did research—in short, followed many of the recommendations made here in previous pages.

Thesis Sentence

- The two versions of *King Kong* reached wide audiences in theaters all over the country.
- Both versions of *King Kong* are very successful fantasy-adventure movies.
- Despite the enormous budget and sophisticated special effects of the 2005 version of *King Kong*, the black-and-white film of 1933 is a scarier fantasy-adventure film than its remake.

Notice how the first example is just a statement of fact—the stance is indisputable—and includes no assertion by the writer. This paper won't go very far with such a weak thesis. The second example provides an opinion, but ultimately the writer rejected this thesis sentence. The example may be true and may affirm the writer's attitude toward the topic, but most readers would concede the point and not dispute it. Why argue in favor of a position most readers would agree with? The last example makes a potent assertion that the writer will have to prove to readers; many people would disagree with the contention here, and the writer would have to find a way to convince readers that the point was valid.

A good thesis is usually debatable, and it's wise to build your thesis around a debatable point. If your thesis doesn't express an opinion you may have trouble focusing your paper and making the ideas unified and coherent. *Unity* means that all the ideas in the essay develop one main idea, the idea expressed in the thesis. Anything that doesn't contribute to this main idea is extraneous and doesn't belong in the paper. *Coherence* means that the sentences stick together, well integrated and in a clear order with smooth transitions.

Not all papers require a single thesis sentence—you may choose to express the thesis over two or more sentences, or you may choose to leave out a thesis sentence, expecting the reader to mine one from the clarity of your ideas and the force of your presentation. But most papers do benefit from the clear expression of a thesis, usually in the first paragraph of an essay. If you choose not to include a thesis sentence, you should at least be able to express one, that is, to state the thesis if someone asks you.

Organization and Development

Some writers, without much planning, can execute well-structured papers with ample development. But we don't recommend it. Most of us have to plan our writing. We face the question, "How will I organize my essay"? Remember that there is no right way. You pick one way, or a combination of ways, and live with it for this paper. Next paper you can return to a topic or approach you didn't select.

Many people find a scratch outline valuable. An outline at this stage is different from the outline you may have used in prewriting for your essay. At this point, your outline can help you organize the information you may have gathered and suggest both the general framework of your approach and the nature of individual paragraphs. But you don't need to follow an outline slavishly. With word processing, you can easily shift sentences around in your prewriting by cutting and pasting. Those without the joys of the computer can use scissors and paste to organize details that belong together but show up apart on the written page. Often a full outline produced after you write an essay can help you see how well your points connect logically.

You have a variety of rhetorical modes to consider as you plan your paper. Will you describe? Narrate? Provide examples and illustrations? Analyze a process or causes and effects? Show comparisons and contrasts? Classify? Define an important concept? Or, some well-integrated combination of these? Argumentative papers particularly can draw on many of these strategies together. Your audience, thesis, and purpose will help you decide on how to proceed with an appropriate rhetorical arrangement.

For the paper on fantasy-adventure films, note how the writer might use a variety of rhetorical strategies, depending on the ultimate thesis and purpose:

Rhetorical Strategy	*Writer's Purpose*
Description	To show the physical features of the monster King Kong
Narration	To tell the story of what happened on the set of *King Kong* during filming
Illustration	To give examples of weak special effects in the remake of the movie
Process Analysis	To show step by step how designers and animators create movie monsters like King Kong
Comparison and Contrast	To examine similarities and differences between the two versions of *King Kong*
Classification	To establish categories of fright in the *King Kong* movies—the animation, the settings, the actors' performances, for instance
Cause and Effect Analysis	To explain why *King Kong* is so popular with teenagers
Definition	To define the fantasy-adventure film in an extended definition and show how *King Kong* fits the definition
Argumentation	To argue that the 1933 version of *King Kong* is a scarier fantasy-adventure film than the 2005 version

You can tell how the writer's purpose automatically will suggest rhetorical approaches. No one ever sits down to write a comparison–contrast essay; but, many writers would use comparison and contrast to make the point strong and clear. Obviously the student writer chose argumentation as the dominant mode for her essay, but she certainly could draw on some of the other strategies in a "mixed-modes" presentation.

Drafting

Most successful papers require a process involving many stages so that a fuzzy idea becomes pages of clear and purposeful prose. Think about what's involved in the process. You've already considered many of the first steps—exploring the topic, assessing and building up your knowledge, deciding on a thesis, weighing audience and purpose, and determining a plan. But this is only the beginning.

Once you have a topic, a thesis based on it, and a plan in place, you will start writing. Most writers find it useful to engage in the following activities toward a finished product:

- write a rough draft
- read and talk about the draft
- show it to others
- re-draft
- edit
- write another draft and maybe another
- proofread (the final step)

Be prepared for writing to take time and energy.

As you already must know, the computer has made the drafting process much less painful than in the past. Years ago, writers' drafts, handwritten or typed, often looked like disaster zones—words written over other words, arrows pointing from one paragraph to another, heavy cross-outs and marginal additions, just to name a few—before the tedious process of copying the paper over word-for-word. Computer word processing makes it simple to move words and paragraphs with a click of a mouse, and you can revise easily. Yet you still might benefit from printing out a draft and making handwritten changes, then returning to the computer to alter the draft on your screen. Many writers like the physical change in writing environment from keyboard to pencil or pen and then back again.

Observing a professional writer at work in the drafting process is instructive. William Zinsser, whose book about writing for the *New York Times* has been called a classic in its field, offers invaluable advice to writers about the need to avoid careless clutter. The two two-paragraph excerpts below from *On Writing Well* show the drafting process in action. In the first sample, you see a typed copy representing the fourth or fifth rewrite for the first edition of Zinsser's popular book. Rife with changes and corrections, it looks like a rough draft, doesn't it? In the second sample, you see how the paragraphs actually appeared in the sixth edition of his book (1998).

is too dumb or too lazy to keep pace with the ~~writer's~~
train of thought. My sympathies are ~~entirely~~ with him.
~~He's not so dumb.~~ If the reader is lost. It is generally

because the writer ~~of the article~~ has not been careful enough to keep him on the ~~proper~~ path.

This carelessness can take any number of ~~different~~ forms. Perhaps a sentence is so excessively ~~long and~~ cluttered that the reader, hacking his way through ~~all~~ the verbiage. Simply doesn't know what it ~~the writer~~ means. Perhaps a sentence has been so shoddily constructed that the reader could read it in any of several ~~two or three different~~ ways. ~~He thinks he knows what the writer is trying to say, but he's not sure.~~ Perhaps the writer has switched pronouns in mid-sentence. Or ~~perhaps he~~ has switched tenses, so the reader loses track of who is talking ~~to whom~~ or ~~exactly~~ when the action took place. Perhaps Sentence B is not a logical sequel to Sentence A—the writer, in whose head the connection is ~~perfectly~~ clear, has not bothered to provide ~~given enough thought to providing~~ the missing link. Perhaps the writer has used an important word incorrectly by not taking the trouble to look it up. ~~and make sure.~~ He may think that "sanguine" and "sanguinary" mean the same thing, but ~~I can assure you that~~ the difference is a bloody big one. ~~to the reader.~~ The reader ~~He~~ can only ~~try to~~ infer xxxx (speaking of big differences) what the writer is trying to imply.

Faced with these ~~such a variety of~~ obstacles, the reader is at first a remarkably tenacious bird. He ~~tends to~~ blames himself — he obviously missed something, ~~he thinks,~~ and he goes back over the mystifying sentence, or over the whole paragraph, piecing it out like an ancient rune, making guesses and moving on. But he won't do this for long. ~~He will soon run out of patience.~~ The writer is making him work too hard, ~~harder than he should have to work~~ and the reader will look for one ~~a writter~~ who is better at his craft.

It won't do to say that the reader is too dumb or too lazy to keep pace with the train of thought. If the reader is lost, it's usually because the writer hasn't been careful enough. The carelessness can take any number of forms. Perhaps a sentence is so excessively cluttered that the reader, hacking through the verbiage, simply doesn't know what it means. Perhaps a sentence has been so shoddily constructed that the reader could read it in several ways. Perhaps the writer has switched pronouns in midsentence, or has switched tenses, so the reader loses loses track of who is talking or when the action took place. Perhaps Sentence B is not a logical sequel to Sentence A; the writer, in whose head the connection is clear, hasn't bothered to provide the missing link. Perhaps the writer has used a word incorrectly by not taking the trouble to look it up. He or she may think "sanguine" and "sanguinary" mean the same thing, but the difference is a bloody big one. The reader can only infer (speaking of big differences) what the writer is trying to imply.

Faced with such obstacles, readers are at first tenacious. They blame themselves—they obviously missed something, and they go back over the mystifying sentence, or over the whole paragraph, piecing it out like an ancient rune, making guesses and moving on. But they won't do this for long. The writer is making them work too hard, and they will look for one who is better at the craft.

Zinsser made significant changes from draft to draft. He worked from a page of typescript and made the kind of messy alterations that show a serious writer at work. One can only imagine how many drafts he produced in order to produce the latest edition.

Make sure that you follow the three most important words of advice you'll ever hear about your writing efforts—revise, revise, revise.

CHAPTER 2

All in the Family

WE USE THE WORD *FAMILY* TO MEAN A GROUP OF related items, like plant family or food family; we use the word family to identify a group of people sharing common ancestry; we use the word family to aggregate languages descending from the same parent language. The periodic table of elements lists in vertical columns chemical substances in the same family, such as chlorine, bromine, and fluorine. A mafia don is the head of a crime family. The widespread and varied use of the word no doubt reflects the pervasive human need to express likenesses and strong connections physically, but also emotionally.

But it is in the context of our daily human relations, perhaps, that our regular use of the word betrays our profound dependence on one another. What, in fact, do we mean by the word *family* at the most basic level? Certainly, family is a hard notion to pin down, and all the more worthy of our inquiry.

Once upon a time, many people had a fixed notion of family—mother, father, children, grandparents, aunts and uncles, who lived together or nearby or even far away but certainly kept up regular contact governed by codes of behavior and responsibility passed on through generations. Perhaps your own family experience mirrors these features. Families loved each other, respected each other, prayed together, and dined together. In years past, representational media reinforced (some would say invented!) this view, from Norman Rockwell's homey paintings of Americans at work or at the dinner table; to photographs of mother-father-sister-brother units in magazine advertisements for automobiles, new houses, and home baking products (among many others); to the warm and joyous lives depicted in such television staples as *Leave It to Beaver, Father Knows Best, The Brady Bunch, Ozzie and Harriet,* and *The Cosby Show.* Odd as it may seem, one writer in this chapter, Mary Cantwell, bemoans the good family life in "The Burden of a Happy Childhood."

Today's television families are more eclectic than those of a previous era. In *Two and a Half Men*, for example, a father, an uncle, and a pre-teen make up the family unit. The group of single, then married, people living close together in *Friends* (still in regular video returns) puts a spin on the family unit unfamiliar to viewers in the early decades of television's ascendancy. And at the other end of television's family life spectrum, the turbulent world of the soap opera, rife with infidelity, betrayal, divorce, and mean-spirited relatives, haunts the airwaves during the day. Bubbling with histrionic excesses, soap operas draw an unorthodox, if not downright dark, background to the typical American family shown in evening programming.

Although a view of family perfection still prevails for many in our society, the course and pace of life in the twenty-first century challenge these conventions. The varied family structures of the daytime soaps seem more accurate than—or at least as accurate as—the traditional families celebrated during prime time. Single-parent families with mother or father not present, grandparents or uncles or aunts rearing children for absent parents, interracial families, foster families, homeless families, families riven by divorce, families headed by gay parents, families with children adopted from halfway round the globe—all defy the traditions of the last few centuries.

The selections in this chapter offer multiple perspectives on family by a wide swath of writers. In "The Children of Divorce," Judith Wallerstein and Sandra Blakeslee look at the effects of broken homes on youngsters. Karen S. Peterson takes you close to the lives of gay family units in "Looking Straight at Gay Parents." You may not agree with what they or others in this chapter have to say, but the pieces certainly will challenge you to consider your own views. As you read, keep an open mind to the possibilities and restraints in evolving family units and to the joys and limits of conventional family structures.

E. B. WHITE

Once More to the Lake

E. B. White (1899–1985) was born in Mt. Vernon, New York, and was a widely known, award-winning essayist whose work appeared for more than 50 years in The New Yorker. *He also authored several books, including the children's works* Stuart Little *and* Charlotte's Web. *In this essay, written in 1941, White recalls his visits to a Maine lake as a child and a subsequent visit with his son.*

1 One summer, along about 1904, my father rented a camp on a lake in Maine and took us all there for the month of August. We all got ringworm from some kittens and had to rub Pond's Extract on our arms and legs night and morning, and my father rolled over in a canoe with all his clothes on; but outside of that the vacation was a success and from then on none of us ever thought there was any place in the world like that lake in Maine. We returned summer after summer—always on August 1 for one month. I have since become a salt-water man, but sometimes in summer there are days when the restlessness of the tides and the fearful cold of the sea water and the incessant wind that blows across the afternoon and into the evening make me wish for the placidity of a lake in the woods. A few weeks ago this feeling got so strong I bought myself a couple of bass hooks and a spinner and returned to the lake where we used to go, for a week's fishing and to revisit old haunts.

2 I took along my son, who had never had any fresh water up his nose and who had seen lily pads only from train windows. On the journey over to the lake I began to wonder what it would be like. I wondered how time would have marred this unique, this holy spot—the coves and streams, the hills that the sun set behind, the camps and the paths behind the camps. I was sure that the tarred road would have found it out, and I wondered in what other ways it would be desolated. It is strange how much you can remember about places like that once you allow your mind to return into the grooves that lead back. You remember one thing, and that suddenly reminds you of another thing. I guess I remembered clearest of all the early mornings, when the lake was cool and motionless, remembered how the bedroom smelled of the lumber it was made of and of the wet woods whose scent entered through the screen. The partitions in the camp were thin and did not extend clear to the top of the rooms, and as I was always the first up I would dress

softly so as not to wake the others, and sneak out into the sweet outdoors and start out in the canoe, keeping close along the shore in the long shadows of the pines. I remembered being very careful never to rub my paddle against the gunwale for fear of disturbing the stillness of the cathedral.

3 The lake had never been what you would call a wild lake. There were cottages sprinkled around the shores, and it was in farming country although the shores of the lake were quite heavily wooded. Some of the cottages were owned by nearby farmers, and you would live at the shore and eat your meals at the farmhouse. That's what our family did. But although it wasn't wild, it was a fairly large and undisturbed lake and there were places in it that, to a child at least, seemed infinitely remote and primeval.

4 I was right about the tar: it led to within half a mile of the shore. But when I got back there, with my boy, and we settled into a camp near a farmhouse and into the kind of summertime I had known, I could tell that it was going to be pretty much the same as it had been before—I knew it, lying in bed the first morning, smelling the bedroom and hearing the boy sneak quietly out and go off along the shore in a boat. I began to sustain the illusion that he was I, and therefore, by simple transposition, that I was my father. This sensation persisted, kept cropping up all the time we were there. It was not an entirely new feeling, but in this setting it grew much stronger. I seemed to be living a dual existence. I would be in the middle of some simple act, I would be picking up a bait box or laying down a table fork, or I would be saying something, and suddenly it would be not I but my father who was saying the words or making the gesture. It gave me a creepy sensation.

5 We went fishing the first morning. I felt the same damp moss covering the worms in the bait can, and saw the dragonfly alight on the tip of my rod as it hovered a few inches from the surface of the water. It was the arrival of this fly that convinced me beyond any doubt that everything was as it always had been, that the years were a mirage and that there had been no years. The small waves were the same, chucking the rowboat under the chin as we fished at anchor, and the boat was the same boat, the same color green and the ribs broken in the same places, and under the floorboards the same fresh-water leavings and débris—the dead helgramite, the wisps of moss, the rusty discarded fishhook, the dried blood from yesterday's catch. We stared silently at the tips of our rods, at the dragonflies that came and went. I lowered

the tip of mine into the water, tentatively, pensively dislodging the fly, which darted two feet away, poised, darted two feet back, and came to rest again a little farther up the rod. There had been no years between the ducking of this dragonfly and the other one—the one that was part of memory. I looked at the boy, who was silently watching his fly, and it was my hands that held his rod, my eyes watching. I felt dizzy and didn't know which rod I was at the end of.

6 We caught two bass, hauling them in briskly as though they were mackerel, pulling them over the side of the boat in a businesslike manner without any landing net, and stunning them with a blow on the back of the head. When we got back for a swim before lunch, the lake was exactly where we had left it, the same number of inches from the dock, and there was only the merest suggestion of a breeze. This seemed an utterly enchanted sea, this lake you could leave to its own devices for a few hours and come back to, and find that it had not stirred, this constant and trustworthy body of water. In the shadows, the dark, water-soaked sticks and twigs, smooth and old, were undulating in clusters on the bottom against the clean ribbed sand, and the track of the mussel was plain. A school of minnows swam by, each minnow with its small individual shadow, doubling the attendance, so clear and sharp in the sunlight. Some of the other campers were in swimming, along the shore, one of them with a cake of soap, and the water felt thin and clear and unsubstantial. Over the years there had been this person with the cake of soap, this cultist, and here he was. There had been no years.

7 Up to the farmhouse to dinner through the teeming, dusty field, the road under our sneakers was only a two-track road. The middle track was missing, the one with the marks of the hooves and the splotches of dried, flaky manure. There had always been three tracks to choose from in choosing which track to walk in; now the choice was narrowed down to two. For a moment I missed terribly the middle alternative. But the way led past the tennis court, and something about the way it lay there in the sun reassured me; the tape had loosened along the backline, the alleys were green with plantains and other weeds, and the net (installed in June and removed in September) sagged in the dry noon, and the whole place steamed with midday heat and hunger and emptiness. There was a choice of pie for dessert, and one was blueberry and one was apple, and the waitresses were the same country girls, there having been no passage of time, only the illusion of it as in a dropped curtain—the waitresses were still fifteen; their hair had been washed,

that was the only difference—they had been to the movies and seen the pretty girls with the clean hair.

8 Summertime, oh, summertime, pattern of life indelible, the fade-proof lake, the woods unshatterable, the pasture with the sweetfern and the juniper forever and ever, summer without end; this was the background, and the life along the shore was the design, the cottagers with their innocent and tranquil design, their tiny docks with the flagpole and the American flag floating against the white clouds in the blue sky, the little paths over the roots of the trees leading from camp to camp and the paths leading back to the outhouses and the can of lime for sprinkling, and at the souvenir counters at the store the miniature birch-bark canoes and the postcards that showed things looking a little better than they looked. This was the American family at play, escaping the city heat, wondering whether the newcomers in the camp at the head of the cove were "common" or "nice," wondering whether it was true that the people who drove up for Sunday dinner at the farmhouse were turned away because there wasn't enough chicken.

9 It seemed to me, as I kept remembering all this, that those times and those summers had been infinitely precious and worth saving. There had been jollity and peace and goodness. The arriving (at the beginning of August) had been so big a business in itself, at the railway station the farm wagon drawn up, the first smell of the pine-laden air, the first glimpse of the smiling farmer, and the great importance of the trunks and your father's enormous authority in such matters, and the feel of the wagon under you for the long ten-mile haul, and at the top of the last long hill catching the first view of the lake after eleven months of not seeing this cherished body of water. The shouts and cries of the other campers when they saw you, and the trunks to be unpacked, to give up their rich burden. (Arriving was less exciting nowadays, when you sneaked up in your car and parked it under a tree near the camp and took out the bags and in five minutes it was all over, no fuss, no loud wonderful fuss about trunks.)

10 Peace and goodness and jollity. The only thing that was wrong now, really, was the sound of the place, an unfamiliar nervous sound of the outboard motors. This was the note that jarred, the one thing that would sometimes break the illusion and set the years moving. In those other summertimes all motors were inboard; and when they were at a little distance, the noise they made was a sedative, an ingredient of summer sleep. They were one-cylinder and two-cylinder engines, and some

were make-and-break and some were jump-spark, but they all made a sleepy sound across the lake. The one-lungers throbbed and fluttered, and the twin-cylinder ones pulled and purred, and that was a quiet sound, too. But now the campers all had outboards. In the daytime, in the hot mornings, these motors made a petulant, irritable sound; at night, in the still evening when the afterglow lit the water, they whined about one's ears like mosquitoes. My boy loved our rented outboard, and his great desire was to achieve single-handed mastery over it, and authority, and he soon learned the trick of choking it a little (but not too much), and the adjustment of the needle valve. Watching him I would remember the things you could do with the old one-cylinder engine with the heavy flywheel, how you could have it eating out of your hand if you got really close to it spiritually. Motorboats in those days didn't have clutches, and you would make a landing by shutting off the motor at the proper time and coasting in with a dead rudder. But there was a way of reversing them, if you learned the trick, by cutting the switch and putting it on again exactly on the final dying revolution of the flywheel, so that it would kick back against compression and begin reversing. Approaching a dock in a strong following breeze, it was difficult to slow up sufficiently by the ordinary coasting method, and if a boy felt he had complete mastery over his motor, he was tempted to keep it running beyond its time and then reverse it a few feet from the dock. It took a cool nerve, because if you threw the switch a twentieth of a second too soon you would catch the flywheel when it still had speed enough to go up past center, and the boat would leap ahead, charging bull-fashion at the dock.

11 We had a good week at the camp. The bass were biting well and the sun shone endlessly, day after day. We would be tired at night and lie down in the accumulated heat of the little bedrooms after the long hot day and the breeze would stir almost imperceptibly outside and the smell of the swamp drift in through the rusty screens. Sleep would come easily and in the morning the red squirrel would be on the roof, tapping out his gay routine. I kept remembering everything, lying in bed in the mornings—the small steamboat that had a long rounded stem like the lip of a Ubangi, and how quietly she ran on the moonlight sails, when the older boys played their mandolins and the girls sang and we ate doughnuts dipped in sugar, and how sweet the music was on the water in the shining night, and what it had felt like to think about girls then. After breakfast we would go up to the store and the

things were in the same place—the minnows in a bottle, the plugs and spinners disarranged and pawed over by the youngsters from the boys' camp, the Fig Newtons and the Beeman's gum. Outside, the road was tarred and cars stood in front of the store. Inside, all was just as it had always been, except there was more Coca-Cola and not so much Moxie and root beer and birch beer and sarsaparilla. We would walk out with the bottle of pop apiece and sometimes the pop would backfire up our noses and hurt. We explored the streams, quietly, where the turtles slid off the sunny logs and dug their way into the soft bottom; and we lay on the town wharf and fed worms to the tame bass. Everywhere we went I had trouble making out which was I, the one walking at my side, the one walking in my pants.

12 One afternoon while we were there at that lake a thunderstorm came up. It was like the revival of an old melodrama that I had seen long ago with childish awe. The second-act climax of the drama of the electrical disturbance over a lake in America had not changed in any important respect. This was the big scene, still the big scene. The whole thing was so familiar, the first feeling of oppression and heat and a general air around camp of not wanting to go very far away. In mid-afternoon (it was all the same) a curious darkening of the sky and a lull in everything that had made life tick; and then the way the boats suddenly swung the other way at their moorings with the coming of a breeze out of the new quarter, and the premonitory rumble. Then the kettle drum, then the snare, then the bass drum and cymbals, then crackling light against the dark, and the gods grinning and licking their chops in the hills. Afterward the calm, the rain steadily rustling in the calm lake, the return of light and hope and spirits, and the campers running out in joy and relief to go swimming in the rain, their bright cries perpetuating the deathless joke about how they were getting simply drenched, and the children screaming with delight at the new sensation of bathing in the rain, and the joke about getting drenched linking the generations in a strong indestructible chain. And the comedian who waded in carrying an umbrella.

13 When the others went swimming, my son said he was going in, too. He pulled his dripping trunks from the line where they had hung all through the shower and wrung them out. Languidly, and with no thought of going in, I watched him, his hard little body, skinny and bare, saw him wince slightly as he pulled up around his vitals the small, soggy, icy garment. As he buckled the swollen belt, suddenly my groin felt the chill of death.

FOR THINKING, DISCUSSING, AND WRITING

1. Why does White return to the lake?
2. White refers to the lake as "this holy spot." What makes it "holy"? How does the religious connotation help you to understand his point? What other words and phrases in the selection also suggest mystery or wonder?
3. How would you describe the writer's relation with his son? Give examples to support your point. How typical is White's relation with his son when you compare it to relations between sons and fathers you know? Is White ever envious of his son? Why might he be?
4. What descriptive elements do you find clearest and (or) most original? Make a list of a few sensory images that give you a good picture of the lake. Note the writer's use of color, sound, and smell to evoke the scene. Then, write an essay about White's style as a writer.

MARY CANTWELL

The Burden of a Happy Childhood

Mary Cantwell (1932–2000), born in Providence, Rhode Island, was an editor and a writer. She is the author of American Girl: Scenes from a Small-Town Childhood *(1992),* Manhattan, When I Was Young *(1995), and* Speaking with Strangers *(1998). She writes in this essay of the enduring memories of a childhood lodged in a white clapboard house across the street from a little beach.*

1 Every time I described the house to friends—the two porches, the bay windows, the balcony over the front door, the stone tubs on either side of the front steps that, before they crumbled, always held geraniums—they said, "It sounds wonderful."

2 "No, it's not wonderful," I'd protest. "It's too narrow, even if it runs deep, and why in a town of beautiful houses my grandfather had to buy that one…." Then I'd stop, partly because no amount of words could disabuse my listeners of the notion that all big Victorian houses resembled the charmer in "Meet Me in St. Louis," and partly out of guilt. How could I say such things about three tall stories of

white clapboard that had housed my grandparents, a widowed great-aunt, an aunt, the husband she acquired at 56, my parents, my sister, myself and, on occasion, whatever distant relatives were passing through.

3 Oh, yes, I forgot. Until I was 19, there was a cocker spaniel named Judy and in my earliest childhood a series of canaries, all of which were named Dickie and all of which flew away because my aunt trusted them to stay on their perches when she cleaned their cages out of doors.

4 My grandfather bought the house in 1920. My mother's wedding reception was in the backyard, my aunt's, when she finally married, on the first floor, my sister's, on the second. I remember coffins in the first-floor bay window (there is nothing like an old-fashioned New England upbringing to acquaint you with life's realities) and, in the same place, the narrow bed in which my father died. It was there so he could have a view of the main street. My grandmother and I loved that view. When I was little we would sit in the window, she in her rocker, I in a hard cut-velvet-upholstered chair, and monitor the passersby.

5 The house was across the street from a little beach, and after our morning dip our grandfather sluiced my sister and me with the garden hose. Years later my aunt's husband sluiced my daughters and, eventually, my niece after their dips. In my grandfather's day the garden was beautiful. After his death my grandmother, who was not one for gardening, said there was nothing nicer than a nice green lawn. Perhaps there isn't, but I have always missed his rosebushes and peonies and his patches of sweet william and pansies.

6 Recently, after 77 years as one family's residence, the house was sold. "How dreadful for you!" friends said. Not at all. What in my childhood had been not only my home but also my fortress, because outside of it lurked every grade-school classmate who didn't like me, had become my prison. As long as it was the place to which I fled whenever my life as an adult became too hard to bear, I was immured in childhood. I was also incapable of calling the apartments in which I lived with my husband and, later, my children "home." Home was where members of my family, some of whom were long gone, were forever baking apple pies, smoking pipes while patting the dog, reading *The Providence Evening Bulletin* and crocheting elaborate bedspreads.

7 An unhappy childhood can cripple, but so can one as blessed as mine. You go through life with the sense that something has been mislaid, something you think that, with luck, you can find again. Only you can't, because what you're looking for is unconditional love. My family was too strict to spoil a child, but I knew, even before I knew the words, that they would betray me only by dying. As long as they lived, my cradle would never fall.

8 If you're smart you give up the search early on, but that is hard when the house in which you lived your joy is still yours for the wandering. Furthermore, the ghost I met in every room was not that of a grandparent or the father who died when I was 20 but of my past self. In most particulars she was pretty much the person I am today. But I have lost forever, and mourn, the innocence that had her greeting every morning as if it were the world's first.

9 Today, though, the house is gone and with it a sadness I wore as a turtle wears its shell. The old radiators are in the side yard and a big hose is hanging out the third-floor window. Its buyers are updating the heating system, gutting the attic. The door on which I had painted "Artist's Den, Keep Out" has disappeared, and once the painters move in, my family's fingerprints will disappear too. But when its new occupants first toured the house, the real-estate agent reported that they said it had "good vibes." So the family that once owned it is still there, not only in my memory but in its laths and beams and solid—oh, so solid—foundation.

FOR THINKING, DISCUSSING, AND WRITING

1. Cantwell frames the essay with two descriptions of the house: the first, in the opening sentence, deals essentially with externals; the second, in the final sentence, speaks of "its laths and beams and solid—oh, so solid—foundation." How do these descriptions help you understand Cantwell's point? Why does she describe her childhood home as a "fortress" and a "prison"?
2. How does Cantwell feel about her family? How do you know? Why did her father want his deathbed facing the main street? Why are there coffins in the front window?
3. How does Cantwell define *home* in paragraph 6? How does it compare with your own definition?
4. In paragraph 7, Cantwell writes, "An unhappy childhood can cripple, but so can one as blessed as mine." Write a paper in which you either agree or disagree with the thought behind this statement.

KAREN S. PETERSON

Looking Straight at Gay Parents

Karen S. Peterson writes for American periodicals, including the Chicago Sun-Times *and* USA Today, *in which this piece appeared on March 10, 2004. She writes here about the coming birth of a baby in 2004 and the family that will care for the child: the gay man who is the biological father, the man's partner, the gay woman who carried the child, and this woman's partner as well.*

1 When Kim Musheno, 39, gives birth to her second son next month, her lesbian partner will be in the birthing room.

2 If their current plan holds up, Victor Zaborsky, 38, the gay man who is the baby's biological father, will be there, too. And so will Joseph Price, 32, Zaborsky's gay partner. Price is the biological father of Musheno's first child, now 3.

3 Zaborsky knows it all seems quite complicated. "We are forging new territory here. There are no role models."

4 But there is certainly controversy. As President Bush calls for a constitutional amendment to ban gay marriages, a pivotal issue in the culture wars is getting renewed attention: gay parenting.

5 Buried beneath the debate on gay marriage is the question of just what being raised in a gay family means for children. On one side are gay couples such as these two who are staking out a place in mainstream society, seeking all that entails, including children.

6 "Times have changed," says Musheno, whose baby is due in April. Her friendships are based more on parenting than on an identity as a lesbian, she says. "I have more straight friends than I do gay. As you become a parent, you look for other parents."

7 "We are good people," says Catherine Alston, 44, who has been Musheno's partner for eight years. "We have good values. And we will raise sons with good values."

8 On the other side of the cultural divide are those who think gay couples are not forming "families" at all but weakening a pillar of society: the traditional unit of Mom, Dad and kids. The two-parent, heterosexual model is still considered the gold standard for children.

9 "We believe that common sense and a vast body of social-science evidence show children are better off when they are raised by their own

biological, married mother and father," says Peter Sprigg of the Family Research Council, which champions traditional marriage and family. "We think it is a great mistake to deliberately create motherless and fatherless families through homosexual parenting."

10 As with most things in the debate over gay parenting, just how many gay families there are is hard to pin down. Gary Gates, a demographer with the Urban Institute, has analyzed 2000 Census data and estimates that there are 100,000 female same-sex couples and 67,000 male same-sex couples with at least one child under 18 in the home. In his book due in April, *The Gay and Lesbian Atlas*, he estimates that 250,000 children are being raised by same-sex couples.

11 Those numbers are probably low, says Bob Witeck of Witeck-Combs Communications, a marketing firm that specializes in the gay community. Using a variety of surveys and studies, he says a conservative estimate is about 3 million children being raised by gay parents.

Concern for the Kids

12 In the 1960s and '70s, the children of gays were often the product of a heterosexual marriage that ended. The kids were then brought into a parent's new homosexual relationship.

13 Those gay parents often had been through a painful coming-out process and a bitter divorce, says David Jolliffe, 47, of Washington, D.C. Most did not think about having more children.

14 In today's "more mature culture," Joliffe says, gay adults "can decide what we want to do personally, and we have the willingness, desire and ability" to have families.

15 Jolliffe and his partner have gone the route favored by many gay men: adoption. "Being a dad is the best thing that ever happened to me," Jolliffe says. He and his partner adopted Manuel, now 6, who had lived in an orphanage in Guatemala for two years.

16 "There are a lot of children who need families and love and a parent's protection and guidance," he says. "I think that can be provided by people regardless of their sexual orientation."

17 Today's lesbian moms increasingly are having their own biological babies through artificial insemination. That was the method chosen by Musheno.

18 The two gay men who are the biological fathers of her children live in Washington, D.C. The men are actively involved parents and have helped create an extended "core family" for Alec and will do the same for the baby, Zaborsky says.

19 The parenting base is the women's modest, three-bedroom home complete with dog, cat and enough toys stacked around to stock a small store.

20 When Musheno and Alston decided they wanted kids, they rejected the idea of an anonymous donor and found Price through a friend. And when a second child was an option, his partner, Zaborsky, decided he would love to be a dad, too.

21 Complex as it may seem, it all works quite well except for occasional head-butting, Price says. He thinks Musheno has a tendency to "pamper Alec too much. When he falls down, she wants to rush over and make sure he is OK. I know he will be fine."

22 They both defer to the women, though. Alston has adopted Musheno's child; the women are the legal parents.

23 Musheno does have some qualms that Alec's playmates may ridicule him for being different when he is older. "But he could be ridiculed for anything, like being too short."

24 She will be very present at the boys' schools, she says. "I will be the cupcake-bringing mom. My strategy is to be very involved."

25 But that may not be enough to protect children, says Abigail Garner, 31, of Minneapolis, whose new book, *Families Like Mine: Children of Gay Parents Tell It Like It Is*, is due March 30. Garner interviewed the adult children of 50 homosexual, bisexual and transgender parents—people who look and act like members of the opposite sex.

26 Garner's mother remained actively in her life after a divorce when Garner was 5. But she was raised largely under the influence of her gay father, whom she adores, and his partner.

27 Her book details a strong defense of gay parents. But Garner, who is heterosexual, also cautions that these kids face special challenges and do not, in spite of what many believe, necessarily turn out the same as everyone else.

28 They often feel a need to be perfect, she says. Garner wanted "to present myself as being very successful for fear that if I had any flaws, immediately the assumption would be it was because my father was gay."

29 As a child she worried that her father might be attacked by a homophobe, and that "if the wrong person found out he was gay," she could somehow be taken away from him.

Homophobia Inevitable

30 No matter how liberal their environment, the kids will experience homophobia, she says. It is not confusing to a 3-year-old to "have two mommies who adore their kids. What gets confusing as children grow up is what they will hear from people every day: 'That is not possible. You can't have a family like that.' When the core of your family is challenged every day, that is a great disconnect, a very confusing message for a child."

31 A fact sheet from the American Psychiatric Association says "no one knows what causes heterosexuality, homosexuality or bisexuality." Nonetheless, Garner says, it is often difficult for a gay child of a gay parent to "come out" to his or her own family. The gay parent may be viewed by society as "recruiting" a child to homosexuality.

32 Courtney Puckett, 24, of San Francisco is the lesbian child of a beloved lesbian mother. She says there is still some "internalized homophobia" within the gay community, gays who still believe "that heterosexual parents are the gold standard."

33 The hardest person to come out to, she says, was her mother, who wanted to "uphold a standard of heterosexuality. My mother wanted to prove she could raise a 'normal' child."

34 There is precious little research on the children of gay families compared with that done on the children from heterosexual unions. The studies are often small, conflicting and controversial. One of the most cited overviews of research was done by two University of Southern California sociologists. Peers reviewed their article for 18 months before its publication in the *American Sociological Review* in 2001.

35 In terms of most measures of child well-being, such as mental health and cognitive development, the study overall found results "at least as positive as children with heterosexual parents," says co-author Judith Stacey. But the report also challenges "the predominant claim that the sexual orientation of parents does not matter at all."

36 "Only a handful of studies track children to adulthood," cautions Stacey, now at New York University.

37 In one small British study, the analysis found children raised by lesbians were no more likely to identify themselves as homosexual than those brought up in heterosexual households.

38 The analysis touches on the third rail of gay parenting research: sexual behavior. The British study said young girls raised by lesbians were more apt to be sexually adventurous than those raised by heterosexual parents and more likely to have had intimacy with a same-sex

partner. Boys raised by lesbians, however, were less sexually adventurous than those raised in straight households.

39 New research on gay families is underway, Stacey says. The most one can say so far is "we need more data."

40 Musheno, Alston, Zaborsky and Price are not waiting for more data. "We were not sure how well this would work out when we started," Musheno says. "You gamble whenever you have a child. But we are all very close, very much involved, one big happy family."

FOR THINKING, DISCUSSING, AND WRITING

1. What are the arguments on the two sides in the controversy over gay parenting? Which do you consider the stronger argument? Why?
2. What do the numbers of gay families reveal to you? How did children of the '60s and '70s come to live with a gay parent? How is today's "more mature society" influencing the formation of gay families?
3. What special challenges do children of gay couples face? How might homophobia affect the child? What is significant about Abigail Garner's book? How does citing the book help Peterson's argument? What does the writer indicate as the problem with much of the research on gay parenting?
4. How would the people in your city or town feel about a gay family such as the one revealed here living in its midst? Why would they feel the way they do, do you think? What arguments would most people use in evaluating this untraditional family? What are your own feelings about the matter? Write an essay in which you address some of these questions.

HENRY LOUIS GATES JR.

In the Kitchen

Henry Louis Gates Jr. (1950–) was born in Keyser, West Virginia. An expert on African-American culture and literature, in 1981 Gates found, authenticated, and published one of the first known novels written by an African American, Harriet E. Wilson's Our Nig *(1859), which led to his further rediscovery of lost works. Gates has written works of criticism such as* Figures in Black: Words, Signs, and the "Racial" Self *(1987) and* The Signifying Monkey: A Theory of African-American Literary Criticism *(1988). Currently Gates is the W. E. B. DuBois Professor of the Humanities and the Director of the W. E. B. DuBois Institute for African and African*

American Research at Harvard University and Editor-in-Chief of the Oxford African American Studies Center, the first comprehensive scholarly online resource in the field of African American Studies and Africana Studies. His National Book Award winning memoir, Colored People (1995)*, reflects on his childhood in pre-civil rights era West Virginia. Here Gates brings to life kitchen scenes with his mother and her clientele, men and women who came to have their hair "done."*

1 We always had a gas stove in the kitchen, in our house in Piedmont, West Virginia, where I grew up. Never electric, though using electric became fashionable in Piedmont in the sixties, like using Crest toothpaste rather than Colgate, or watching Huntley and Brinkley rather than Walter Cronkite. But not us: gas, Colgate, and good ole Walter Cronkite, come what may. We used gas partly out of loyalty to Big Mom, Mama's Mama, because she was mostly blind and still loved to cook, and could feel her way more easily with gas than with electric. But the most important thing about our gas-equipped kitchen was that Mama used to do hair there. The "hot comb" was a fine-toothed iron instrument with a long wooden handle and a pair of iron curlers that opened and closed like scissors. Mama would put it in the gas fire until it glowed. You could smell those prongs heating up.

2 I liked that smell. Not the smell so much, I guess, as what the smell meant for the shape of my day. There was an intimate warmth in the women's tones as they talked with my Mama, doing their hair. I knew what the women had been through to get their hair ready to be "done," because I would watch Mama do it to herself. How that kink could be transformed through grease and fire into that magnificent head of wavy hair was a miracle to me, and still is.

3 Mama would wash her hair over the sink, a towel wrapped around her shoulders, wearing just her slip and her white bra. (We had no shower—just a galvanized tub that we stored in the kitchen—until we moved down Rat Tail Road into Doc Wolverton's house, in 1954.) After she dried it, she would grease her scalp thoroughly with blue Bergamot hair grease, which came in a short, fat jar with a picture of a beautiful colored lady on it. It's important to grease your scalp real good, my Mama would explain, to keep from burning yourself. Of course, her hair would return to its natural kink almost as soon as the hot water and shampoo hit it. To me, it was another miracle how hair so "straight" would so quickly become kinky again the second it even approached some water.

4 My Mama had only a few "clients" whose heads she "did"—did, I think, because she enjoyed it, rather than for the few pennies it brought in. They would sit on one of our red plastic kitchen chairs, the kind with the shiny metal legs, and brace themselves for the process. Mama would stroke that red-hot iron—which by this time had been in the gas fire for half an hour or more—slowly but firmly through their hair, from scalp to strand's end. It made a scorching, crinkly sound, the hot iron did, as it burned its way through kink, leaving in its wake straight strands of hair, standing long and tall but drooping over at the ends, their shape like the top of a heavy willow tree. Slowly, steadily, Mama's hands would transform a round mound of Odetta kink into a darkened swamp of everglades. The Bergamot made the hair shiny; the heat of the hot iron gave it a brownish-red cast. Once all the hair was as straight as God allows kinks to get, Mama would take the well-heated curling iron and twirl the straightened strands into more or less loosely wrapped curls. She claimed that she owed her skill as a hairdresser to the strength in her wrists, and as she worked her little finger would poke out, the way it did when she sipped tea. Mama was a southpaw, and wrote upside down and backward to produce the cleanest, roundest letters you've ever seen.

5 The "kitchen" she would all but remove from sight with a handheld pair of shears, bought just for this purpose. Now, the kitchen was the room in which we were sitting—the room where Mama did hair and washed clothes, and where we all took a bath in that galvanized tub. But the word has another meaning, and the kitchen that I'm speaking of is the very kinky bit of hair at the back of your head, where your neck meets your shirt collar. If there was ever a part of our African past that resisted assimilation, it was the kitchen. No matter how hot the iron, no matter how powerful the chemical, no matter how stringent the mashed-potatoes-and-lye formula of a man's "process," neither God nor woman nor Sammy Davis Jr. could straighten the kitchen. The kitchen was permanent, irredeemable, irresistible kink. Unassimilably African. No matter what you did, no matter how hard you tried, you couldn't dekink a person's kitchen. So you trimmed it off as best you could.

6 When hair had begun to "turn," as they'd say—to return to its natural kinky glory—it was the kitchen that turned first (the kitchen around the back, and nappy edges at the temples). When the kitchen started creeping up the back of the neck, it was time to get your hair done again.

7 Sometimes, after dark, a man would come to have his hair done. It was Mr. Charlie Carroll. He was very light-complected and had a ruddy nose—it made me think of Edmund Gwenn, who played Kris Kringle in *Miracle on 34th Street.* At first, Mama did him after my brother, Rocky, and I had gone to sleep. It was only later that we found out that he had come to our house so Mama could iron his hair—not with a hot comb or a curling iron but with our very own Proctor-Silex steam iron. For some reason I never understood, Mr. Charlie would conceal his Frederick Douglass-like mane under a big white Stetson hat. I never saw him take it off except when he came to our house, at night, to have his hair pressed. (Later, Daddy would tell us about Mr. Charlie's most prized piece of knowledge, something that the man would only confide after his hair had been pressed, as a token of intimacy. "Not many people know this," he'd say, in a tone of circumspection, "but George Washington was Abraham Lincoln's daddy." Nodding solemnly, he'd add the clincher: "A white man told me." Though he was in dead earnest, this became a humorous refrain around our house—"a white man told me"—which we used to punctuate especially preposterous assertions.)

8 My mother examined my daughters' kitchens whenever we went home to visit, in the early eighties. It became a game between us. I had told her not to do it, because I didn't like the politics it suggested—the notion of "good" and "bad" hair. "Good" hair was "straight," "bad" hair kinky. Even in the late sixties, at the height of Black Power, almost nobody could bring themselves to say "bad" for good and "good" for bad. People still said that hair like white people's hair was "good," even if they encapsulated it in a disclaimer, like "what we used to call 'good.'"

9 Maggie would be seated in her high chair, throwing food this way and that, and Mama would be cooing about how cute it all was, how I used to do just like Maggie was doing, and wondering whether her flinging her food with her left hand meant that she was going to be left-handed like Mama. When my daughter was just about covered with Chef Boyardee Spaghetti-O's, Mama would seize the opportunity: wiping her clean, she would tilt Maggie's head to one side and reach down the back of her neck. Sometimes Mama would even rub a curl between her fingers, just to make sure that her bifocals had not deceived her. Then she'd sigh with satisfaction and relief: No kink . . . yet. Mama! I'd shout, pretending to be angry. Every once in a while, if no one was looking, I'd peek, too.

10 I say "yet" because most black babies are born with soft, silken hair. But after a few months it begins to turn, as inevitably as do the seasons or the leaves on a tree. People once thought baby oil would stop it. They were wrong.

11 Everybody I knew as a child wanted to have good hair. You could be as ugly as homemade sin dipped in misery and still be thought attractive if you had good hair. "Jesus moss," the girls at Camp Lee, Virginia, had called Daddy's naturally "good" hair during the war. I know that he played that thick head of hair for all it was worth, too.

12 My own hair was "not a bad grade," as barbers would tell me when they cut it for the first time. It was like a doctor reporting the results of the first full physical he has given you. Like "You're in good shape" or "Blood pressure's kind of high—better cut down on salt."

13 I spent most of my childhood and adolescence messing with my hair. I definitely wanted straight hair. Like Pop's. When I was about three, I tried to stick a wad of Bazooka bubble gum to that straight hair of his. I suppose what fixed that memory for me is the spanking I got for doing so: he turned me upside down, holding me by my feet, the better to paddle my behind. Little *nigger*, he had shouted, walloping away. I started to laugh about it two days later, when my behind stopped hurting.

14 When black people say "straight," of course, they don't usually mean literally straight—they're not describing hair like, say, Peggy Lipton's (she was the white girl on *The Mod Squad*), or like Mary's of Peter, Paul & Mary fame; black people call that "stringy" hair. No, "straight" just means not kinky, no matter what contours the curl may take. I would have done *anything* to have straight hair—and I used to try everything, short of getting a process.

15 Of the wide variety of techniques and methods I came to master in the challenging prestidigitation of the follicle, almost all had two things in common: a heavy grease and the application of pressure. It's not an accident that some of the biggest black-owned companies in the fifties and sixties made hair products. And I tried them all, in search of that certain silken touch, the one that would leave neither the hand nor the pillow sullied by grease.

16 I always wondered what Frederick Douglass put on *his* hair, or what Phillis Wheatley put on hers. Or why Wheatley has that rag on her head in the little engraving in the frontispiece of her book. One thing is for

sure: you can bet that when Phillis Wheatley went to England and saw the Countess of Huntingdon she did not stop by the Queen's coiffeur on her way there. So many black people still get their hair straightened that it's a wonder we don't have a national holiday for Madame C. J. Walker, the woman who invented the process of straightening kinky hair. Call it Jheri-Kurled or call it "relaxed," it's still fried hair.

17 I used all the greases, from sea-blue Bergamot and creamy vanilla Duke (in its clear jar with the orange-white-and-green label) to the godfather of grease, the formidable Murray's. Now, Murray's was some *serious* grease. Whereas Bergamot was like oily jello, and Duke was viscous and sickly sweet, Murray's was light brown and *hard*. Hard as lard and twice as greasy, Daddy used to say Murray's came in an orange can with a press-on top. It was so hard that some people would put a match to the can, just to soften the stuff and make it more manageable. Then, in the late sixties, when Afros came into style, I used Afro Sheen. From Murray's to Duke to Afro Sheen: that was my progression in black consciousness.

18 We used to put hot towels or washrags over our Murray-coated heads, in order to melt the wax into the scalp and the follicles. Unfortunately, the wax also had the habit of running down your neck, ears, and forehead. Not to mention your pillowcase. Another problem was that if you put two palmfuls of Murray's on your head your hair turned white. (Duke did the same thing.) The challenge was to get rid of that white color. Because if you got rid of the white stuff you had a magnificent head of wavy hair. That was the beauty of it: Murray's was so hard that it froze your hair into the wavy style you brushed it into. It looked really good if you wore a part. A lot of guys had parts *cut* into their hair by a barber, either with the clippers or with a straight-edge razor. Especially if you had kinky hair—then you'd generally wear a short razor cut, or what we called a Quo Vadis.

19 We tried to be as innovative as possible. Everyone knew about using a stocking cap, because your father or your uncle wore one whenever something really big was about to happen, whether sacred or secular: a funeral or a dance, a wedding or a trip in which you confronted official white people. Any time you were trying to look really sharp, you wore a stocking cap in preparation. And if the event was really a big one, you made a new cap. You asked your mother for a pair of her hose, and cut it with scissors about six inches or so from the open end—the end with

the elastic that goes up to the top of the thigh. Then you knotted the cut end, and it became a beehive-shaped hat, with an elastic band that you pulled down low on your forehead and down around your neck in the back. To work well, the cap had to fit tightly and snugly, like a press. And it had to fit that tightly because it was a press: it pressed your hair with the force of the hose's elastic. If you greased your hair down real good, and left the stocking cap on long enough, voilà: you got a head of pressed-against-the-scalp waves. (You also got a ring around your forehead when you woke up, but it went away.) And then you could enjoy your concrete do. Swore we were bad, too, with all that grease and those flat heads. My brother and I would brush it out a bit in the mornings, so that it looked—well, "natural." Grown men still wear stocking caps—especially older men, who generally keep their stocking caps in their top drawers, along with their cufflinks and their see-through silk socks, their "Maverick" ties, their silk handkerchiefs, and whatever else they prize the most.

20 A Murrayed-down stocking cap was the respectable version of the process, which, by contrast, was most definitely not a cool thing to have unless you were an entertainer by trade. Zeke and Keith and Poochie and a few other stars of the high-school basketball team all used to get a process once or twice a year. It was expensive, and you had to go somewhere like Pittsburgh or D.C. or Uniontown—somewhere where there were enough colored people to support a trade. The guys would disappear, then reappear a day or two later, strutting like peacocks, their hair burned slightly red from the lye base. They'd also wear "rags"—cloths or handkerchiefs—around their heads when they slept or played basketball. Do-rags, they were called. But the result was straight hair, with just a hint of wave. No curl. Do-it-yourselfers took their chances at home with a concoction of mashed potatoes and lye.

21 The most famous process of all, however, outside of the process Malcolm X describes in his *Autobiography*, and maybe the process of Sammy Davis Jr., was Nat King Cole's process. Nat King Cole had patent-leather hair. That man's got the finest process money can buy, or so Daddy said the night we saw Cole's TV show on NBC. It was November 5, 1956. I remember the date because everyone came to our house to watch it and to celebrate one of Daddy's buddies' birthdays. Yeah, Uncle Joe chimed in, they can do shit to his hair that the average Negro can't even *think* about—secret shit.

22 Nat King Cole was *clean*. I've had an ongoing argument with a Nigerian friend about Nat King Cole for twenty years now. Not about whether he could sing—any fool knows that he could—but about whether or not he was a handkerchief head for wearing that patent-leather process.

23 Sammy Davis Jr.'s process was the one I detested. It didn't look good on him. Worse still, he liked to have a fried strand dangling down the middle of his forehead, so he could shake it out from the crown when he sang. But Nat King Cole's hair was a thing unto itself, a beautifully sculpted work of art that he and he alone had the right to wear. The only difference between a process and a stocking cap, really, was taste; but Nat King Cole, unlike, say, Michael Jackson, looked *good* in his. His head looked like Valentino's head in the twenties, and some say it was Valentino the process was imitating. But Nat King Cole wore a process because it suited his face, his demeanor, his name, his style. He was as clean as he wanted to be.

24 I had forgotten all about that patent-leather look until one day in 1971, when I was sitting in an Arab restaurant on the island of Zanzibar surrounded by men in fezzes and white caftans, trying to learn how to eat curried goat and rice with the fingers of my right hand and feeling two million miles from home. All of a sudden, an old transistor radio sitting on top of a china cupboard stopped blaring out its Swahili music and started playing "Fly Me to the Moon," by Nat King Cole. The restaurant's din was not affected at all, but in my mind's eye I saw it: the King's magnificent sleek black tiara. I managed, barely, to blink back the tears.

FOR THINKING, DISCUSSING, AND WRITING

1. Which elements of Gates's mother's work on hair do you find most vivid? Where has the writer appealed most successfully to the language of the senses so that readers can see and feel the kitchen as Gates remembers it?
2. In what ways is the focus on hair a reflection of black American culture?
3. What does the discussion of black celebrities contribute to the essay?
4. Two well-known theatrical productions—the musicals *Hair* and *Hairspray* (a film version reached movie theaters in 2007)—help reaffirm the central role of hair in the way we think of ourselves; and newspapers and magazines with their endless advertisements about hair products regularly assert that hair is a major component of our appearance. Write an essay on hair as a cultural touchstone in today's society.

BARBARA KINGSOLVER

Stone Soup

Barbara Kingsolver (1955–) is an essayist and novelist whose works most often deal with the lives of middle-class Americans. She has published stories in Homeland *(1989) and poetry in* Another America *(1994), and the novels* Animal Dreams *(1990),* Pigs in Heaven *(1993),* The Poisonwood Bible *(1998), and* Prodigal Summer *(2000). Her nonfiction works include* Holding the Line: Women in the Great Arizona Mine Strike of 1983 *(1989) and* High Tide in Tucson: Essays for Now or Never *(1995) and* Animal, Vegetable, Miracle: A Year of Food Life *(2007). Her work has also appeared in a number of periodicals, including* Smithsonian *magazine, the* New York Times Book Review, *and the* Progressive. *In "Stone Soup" she challenges the conventional view of home life so popular in the American identity and asks us to "let go the fairy tale of families functioning perfectly in isolation."*

1 In the catalog of family values, where do we rank an occasion like this? A curly-haired boy who wanted to run before he walked, age seven now, a soccer player scoring a winning goal. He turns to the bleachers with his fists in the air and a smile wide as a gap-toothed galaxy. His own cheering section of grown-ups and kids all leap to their feet and hug each other, delirious with love for this boy. He's Andy, my best friend's son. The cheering section includes his mother and her friends, his brother, his father and stepmother, a stepbrother and stepsister, and a grandparent. Lucky is the child with this many relatives on hand to hail a proud accomplishment. I'm there too, witnessing a family fortune. But in spite of myself, defensive words take shape in my head. I am thinking: I dare *anybody* to call this a broken home.

2 Families change, and remain the same. Why are our names for home so slow to catch up to the truth of where we live?

3 When I was a child, I had two parents who loved me without cease. One of them attended every excuse for attention I ever contrived, and the other made it to the ones with higher production values, like piano recitals and appendicitis. So I was a lucky child too. I played with a set of paper dolls called "The Family of Dolls," four in number, who came with the factory-assigned names of Dad, Mom, Sis, and Junior. I think you know what they looked like, at least before I loved them to death and their heads fell off.

4 Now I've replaced the dolls with a life. I knit my days around my daughter's survival and happiness, and am proud to say her head is

still on. But we aren't the Family of Dolls. Maybe you're not, either. And if not, even though you are statistically no oddity, it's probably been suggested to you in a hundred ways that yours isn't exactly a real family, but an impostor family, a harbinger of cultural ruin, a slapdash substitute—something like counterfeit money. Here at the tail end of our century, most of us are up to our ears in the noisy business of trying to support and love a thing called family. But there's a current in the air with ferocious moral force that finds its way even into political campaigns, claiming there is only one right way to do it, the Way It Has Always Been.

5 In the face of a thriving, particolored world, this narrow view is so pickled and absurd I'm astonished that it gets airplay. And I'm astonished that it still stings.

6 Every parent has endured the arrogance of a child-unfriendly grump sitting in judgment, explaining what those kids of ours really need (for example,"a good licking"). If we're polite, we move our crew to another bench in the park. If we're forthright (as I am in my mind, only, for the rest of the day), we fix them with a sweet imperious stare and say, "Come back and let's talk about it after you've changed a thousand diapers."

7 But it's harder somehow to shrug off the Family-of-Dolls Family Values crew when they judge (from their safe distance) that divorced people, blended families, gay families, and single parents are failures. That our children are at risk, and the whole arrangement is messy and embarrassing. A marriage that ends is not called "finished," it's called *failed.* The children of this family may have been born to a happy union, but now they are called *the children of divorce.*

8 I had no idea how thoroughly these assumptions overlaid my culture until I went through divorce myself. I wrote to a friend: "This might be worse than being widowed. Overnight I've suffered the same losses—companionship, financial and practical support, my identity as a wife and partner, the future I'd taken for granted. I am lonely, grieving, and hard-pressed to take care of my household alone. But instead of bringing casseroles, people are acting like I had a fit and broke up the family china."

9 Once upon a time I held these beliefs about divorce: that everyone who does it could have chosen not to do it. That it's a lazy way out of marital problems. That it selfishly puts personal happiness ahead of family integrity. Now I tremble for my ignorance. It's easy, in fortunate

times, to forget about the ambush that could leave your head reeling: serious mental or physical illness, death in the family, abandonment, financial calamity, humiliation, violence, despair.

10 I started out like any child, intent on being the Family of Dolls. I set upon young womanhood believing in most of the doctrines of my generation: I wore my skirts four inches above the knee. I had that Barbie with her zebra-striped swimsuit and a figure unlike anything found in nature. And I understood the Prince Charming Theory of Marriage, a quest for Mr. Right that ends smack dab where you find him. I did not completely understand that another whole story *begins* there, and no fairy tale prepared me for the combination of bad luck and persistent hope that would interrupt my dream and lead me to other arrangements. Like a cancer diagnosis, a dying marriage is a thing to fight, to deny, and finally, when there's no choice left, to dig in and survive. Casseroles would help. Likewise, I imagine it must be a painful reckoning in adolescence (or later on) to realize one's own true love will never look like the soft-focus fragrance ads because Prince Charming (surprise!) is a princess. Or vice versa. Or has skin the color your parents didn't want you messing with, except in the Crayola box.

11 It's awfully easy to hold in contempt the straw broken home, and that mythical category of persons who toss away nuclear family for the sheer fun of it. Even the legal terms we use have a suggestion of caprice. I resent the phrase "irreconcilable differences," which suggests a stubborn refusal to accept a spouse's little quirks. This is specious. Every happily married couple I know has loads of irreconcilable differences. Negotiating where to set the thermostat is not the point. A nonfunctioning marriage is a slow asphyxiation. It is waking up despised each morning, listening to the pulse of your own loneliness before the radio begins to blare its raucous gospel that you're nothing if you aren't loved. It is sharing your airless house with the threat of suicide or other kinds of violence, while the ghost that whispers, "Leave here and destroy your children," has passed over every door and nailed it shut. Disassembling a marriage in these circumstances is as much *fun* as amputating your own gangrenous leg. You do it, if you can, to save a life—or two, or more.

12 I know of no one who really went looking to hoe the harder row, especially the daunting one of single parenthood. Yet it seems to be the most American of customs to blame the burdened for their destiny. We'd like so desperately to believe in freedom and justice for all, we can hardly

name that rogue bad luck, even when he's a close enough snake to bite us. In the wake of my divorce, some friends (even a few close ones) chose to vanish, rather than linger within striking distance of misfortune.

13 But most stuck around, bless their hearts, and if I'm any the wiser for my trials, it's from having learned the worth of steadfast friendship. And also, what not to say. The least helpful question is: "Did you want the divorce, or didn't you?" Did I want to keep that gangrenous leg, or not? How to explain, in a culture that venerates choice: two terrifying options are much worse than none at all. Give me any day the quick hand of cruel fate that will leave me scarred but blameless. As it was, I kept thinking of that wicked third-grade joke in which some boy comes up behind you and grabs your ear, starts in with a prolonged tug, and asks, "Do you want this ear any longer?"

14 Still, the friend who holds your hand and says the wrong thing is made of dearer stuff than the one who stays away. And generally, through all of it, you live. My favorite fictional character, Kate Vaiden (in the novel by Reynolds Price), advises: "Strength just comes in one brand—you stand up at sunrise and meet what they send you and keep your hair combed."

15 Once you've weathered the straits, you get to cross the tricky juncture from casualty to survivor. If you're on your feet at the end of a year or two, and have begun putting together a happy new existence, those friends who were kind enough to feel sorry for you when you needed it must now accept you back to the ranks of the living. If you're truly blessed, they will dance at your second wedding. Everybody else, for heaven's sake, should stop throwing stones.

16 Arguing about whether nontraditional families deserve pity or tolerance is a little like the medieval debate about left-handedness as a mark of the devil. Divorce, remarriage, single parenthood, gay parents, and blended families simply are. They're facts of our time. Some of the reasons listed by sociologists for these family reconstructions are: the idea of marriage as a romantic partnership rather than a pragmatic one; a shift in women's expectations, from servility to self-respect and independence; and longevity (prior to antibiotics no marriage was expected to last many decades—in Colonial days the average couple lived to be married less than twelve years). Add to all this, our growing sense of entitlement to happiness and safety from abuse. Most would agree these are all good things. Yet their result—a culture in which

serial monogamy and the consequent reshaping of families are the norm—gets diagnosed as "failing."

17 For many of us, once we have put ourselves Humpty-Dumpty-wise back together again, the main problem with our reorganized family is that other people think we have a problem. My daughter tells me the only time she's uncomfortable about being the child of divorced parents is when her friends say they feel sorry for her. It's a bizarre sympathy, given that half the kids in her school and nation are in the same boat, pursuing childish happiness with the same energy as their married-parent peers. When anyone asks how *she* feels about it, she spontaneously lists the benefits: our house is in the country and we have a dog, but she can go to her dad's neighborhood for the urban thrills of a pool and sidewalks for roller-skating. What's more, she has three sets of grandparents!

18 Why is it surprising that a child would revel in a widened family and the right to feel at home in more than one house? Isn't it the opposite that should worry us—a child with no home at all, or too few resources to feel safe? The child at risk is the one whose parents are too immature themselves to guide wisely; too diminished by poverty to nurture; too far from opportunity to offer hope. The number of children in the U.S. living in poverty at this moment is almost unfathomably large: twenty percent. There are families among us that need help all right, and by no means are they new on the landscape. The rate at which teenage girls had babies in 1957 (ninety-six per thousand) was twice what it is now. That remarkable statistic is ignored by the religious right—probably because the teen birth rate was cut in half mainly by legalized abortion. In fact, the policy gatekeepers who coined the phrase "family values" have steadfastly ignored the desperation of too-small families, and since 1979 have steadily reduced the amount of financial support available to a single parent. But, this camp's most outspoken attacks seem aimed at the notion of families getting too complex, with add-ons and extras such as a gay parent's partner, or a remarried mother's new husband and his children.

19 To judge a family's value by its tidy symmetry is to purchase a book for its cover. There's no moral authority there. The famous family comprised of Dad, Mom, Sis, and Junior living as an isolated economic unit is not built on historical bedrock. In *The Way We Never Were*, Stephanie Coontz writes, "Whenever people propose that we go back to the traditional family, I always suggest that they pick a ballpark date for the family

they have in mind." Colonial families were tidily disciplined, but their members (meaning everyone but infants) labored incessantly and died young. Then the Victorian family adopted a new division of labor, in which women's role was domestic and children were allowed time for study and play, but this was an upper-class construct supported by myriad slaves. Coontz writes, "For every nineteenth-century middle-class family that protected its wife and child within the family circle, there was an Irish or German girl scrubbing floors . . . a Welsh boy mining coal to keep the home-baked goodies warm, a black girl doing the family laundry, a black mother and child picking cotton to be made into clothes for the family, and a Jewish or an Italian daughter in a sweatshop making 'ladies' dresses or artificial flowers for the family to purchase."

20 The abolition of slavery brought slightly more democratic arrangements, in which extended families were harnessed together in cottage industries; at the turn of the century came a steep rise in child labor in mines and sweatshops. Twenty percent of American children lived in orphanages at the time; their parents were not necessarily dead, but couldn't afford to keep them.

21 During the Depression and up to the end of World War II, many millions of U.S. households were more multigenerational than nuclear. Women my grandmother's age were likely to live with a fluid assortment of elderly relatives, in-laws, siblings, and children. In many cases they spent virtually every waking hour working in the company of other women—a companionable scenario in which it would be easier, I imagine, to tolerate an estranged or difficult spouse. I'm reluctant to idealize a life of so much hard work and so little spousal intimacy, but its advantage may have been resilience. A family so large and varied would not easily be brought down by a single blow: it could absorb a death, long illness, an abandonment here or there, and any number of irreconcilable differences.

22 The Family of Dolls came along midcentury as a great American experiment. A booming economy required a mobile labor force and demanded that women surrender jobs to returning soldiers. Families came to be defined by a single breadwinner. They struck out for single-family homes at an earlier age than ever before, and in unprecedented numbers they raised children in suburban isolation. The nuclear family was launched to sink or swim.

23 More than a few sank. Social historians corroborate that the suburban family of the postwar economic boom, which we have recently

selected as our definition of "traditional," was no panacea. Twenty-five percent of Americans were poor in the mid-1950s, and as yet there were no food stamps. Sixty percent of the elderly lived on less than $1,000 a year, and most had no medical insurance. In the sequestered suburbs, alcoholism and sexual abuse of children were far more widespread than anyone imagined.

24 Expectations soared, and the economy sagged. It's hard to depend on one other adult for everything, come what may. In the last three decades, that amorphous, adaptable structure we call "family" has been reshaped once more by economic tides. Compared with fifties families, mothers are far more likely now to be employed. We are statistically more likely to divorce, and to live in blended families or other extra-nuclear arrangements. We are also more likely to plan and space our children, and to rate our marriages as "happy." We are less likely to suffer abuse without recourse, or to stare out at our lives through a glaze of prescription tranquilizers. Our aged parents are less likely to become destitute, and we're half as likely to have a teenage daughter turn up a mother herself. All in all, I would say that if "intact" in modern family-values jargon means living quietly desperate in the bell jar, then hip-hip-hooray for "broken." A neat family model constructed to service the Baby Boom economy seems to be returning gradually to a grand, lumpy shape that human families apparently have tended toward since they first took root in the Olduvai Gorge. We're social animals, deeply fond of companionship, and children love best to run in packs. If there is a *normal* for humans, at all, I expect it looks like two or three Families of Dolls, connected variously by kinship and passion, shuffled like cards and strewn over several shoeboxes.

25 The sooner we can let go the fairy tale of families functioning perfectly in isolation, the better we might embrace the relief of community. Even the admirable parents who've stayed married through thick and thin are very likely, at present, to incorporate other adults into their families—household help and baby-sitters if they can afford them, or neighbors and grandparents if they can't. For single parents, this support is the rock-bottom definition of family. And most parents who have split apart, however painfully, still manage to maintain family continuity for their children, creating in many cases a boisterous phenomenon that Constance Ahrons in her book *The Good Divorce* calls the "binuclear family." Call it what you will—when ex-spouses beat swords into plowshares and jump up and down at a soccer game together, it makes for happy kids.

26 Cinderella, look, who needs her? All those evil stepsisters? That story always seemed like too much cotton-picking fuss over clothes. A childhood tale that fascinated me more was the one called "Stone Soup," and the gist of it is this: Once upon a time, a pair of beleaguered soldiers straggled home to a village empty-handed, in a land ruined by war. They were famished, but the villagers had so little they shouted evil words and slammed their doors. So the soldiers dragged out a big kettle, filled it with water, and put it on a fire to boil. They rolled a clean round stone into the pot, while the villagers peered through their curtains in amazement.

27 "What kind of soup is that?" they hooted.

28 "Stone soup," the soldiers replied. "Everybody can have some when it's done."

29 "Well, thanks," one matron grumbled, coming out with a shriveled carrot. "But it'd be better if you threw this in."

30 And so on, of course, a vegetable at a time, until the whole suspicious village managed to feed itself grandly.

31 Any family is a big empty pot, save for what gets thrown in. Each stew turns out different. Generosity, a resolve to turn bad luck into good, and respect for variety—these things will nourish a nation of children. Name-calling and suspicion will not. My soup contains a rock or two of hard times, and maybe yours does too. I expect it's a heck of a bouillabaisse.

FOR THINKING, DISCUSSING, AND WRITING

1. Why does Kingsolver open the essay with a description of Andy's soccer game? To what degree does this description help support her point? Is her comment that Andy's family is "delirious with love for this boy" an overstatement? Why or why not?
2. What are some of the "ambushes" that Kingsolver cautions us may threaten to upset our plans for a happy marriage? What others can you think of? How does she define "irreconcilable differences"? How does she define "nonfunctioning marriage"?
3. What does the writer identify as being a "normal" family for humans? What might the changing definitions of family indicate about changes occurring in our culture? What other social structures can you think of that also have undergone a change in definition?
4. Write an essay in which you attempt to answer these two powerful questions that Kingsolver raises in paragraph 18: "Why is it surprising that a child would revel in a widened family and the right to feel at home in more than one house? Isn't it the opposite that should worry us—a child with no home at all, or too few resources to feel safe?"

JUDITH S. WALLERSTEIN
AND SANDRA BLAKESLEE

The Children of Divorce

Judith S. Wallerstein, who was born in New York City, is a psychiatric social worker specializing in the effects of divorce on families. Senior lecturer emerita at the School of Social Welfare at the University of California at Berkeley, she is the author of many professional articles and co-author of Surviving the Breakup: How Children and Parents Cope with Divorce *(1980).*

Born in New York City, Sandra Blakeslee (1943–) is a science writer for the New York Times. *She is a member of the National Association of Science Writers.*

In this selection from their book Second Chances: Men, Women, and Children a Decade after Divorce *(1989), the writers highlight some of the effects of divorce on children.*

1 The experience of divorce is entirely different for parents and for children. Many people have wanted to believe that what is good for adults will be good for their children. It is seductively simple to think that a child's psychological problems are mainly a reflection of family problems—as if children were not people with reactions of their own, separate from those of adults. As a parent puts his or her life together in the post-divorce years, they say, the children will inevitably improve. Because an unhappy woman often has a hard time being a good mother, they argue, it follows that a happy woman will be a good mother.

2 But this argument just does not jibe with my experience. It is often true that an unhappy adult finds it hard to be a nurturing parent for unhappiness can deplete the adult's capacity to provide the care and understanding that children need. But it does not follow that a happy or happier adult will necessarily become a better parent. The "trickle down" theory is not relevant to parent-child relationships. As exciting love affair or a gratifying career advance may make for a much happier adult, but there is no reason to expect that the adult's greater happiness will lead to a greater sensitivity or greater concern for his or her children. To the contrary, circumstances that enrich an adult's life can easily make that adult less available to children. Unfortunately, the genuine love and tenderness between adults in a second marriage is not always shared with the children who come from a previous marriage.

3 Although the decision to divorce is rarely mutual, adults generally do agree about the state of the marriage. It is uncommon—although it surely happens—for one spouse to be genuinely surprised when the other presses for divorce. Most of the time both adults acknowledge, openly or secretly, that there are flaws and tensions in a marriage on the brink. They may disagree about how to remedy those troubles, but they rarely disagree that the troubles exist. Children, however, can be quite content even when their parents' marriage is profoundly unhappy for one or both partners. Only one in ten children in our study experienced relief when their parents divorced. These were mostly older children in families where there had been open violence and where the children had lived with the fear that the violence would hurt a parent or themselves. Even so, few children truly expect their parents to divorce. When there is fighting in the household, children hope against hope that the fighting will vanish, and they look forward to a more peaceful time. They do not prepare themselves for divorce, and when they are told that a divorce is imminent, many refuse to believe it.

4 Divorce is a different experience for children and adults because the children lose something that is fundamental to their development—the family structure. The family comprises the scaffolding upon which children mount successive developmental stages, from infancy into adolescence. It supports their psychological, physical, and emotional, ascent into maturity. When that structure collapses, the children's world is temporarily without supports. And children, with a vastly compressed sense of time, do not know that the chaos is temporary. What they do know is that they are dependent on the family. Whatever its shortcomings, children perceive the family as the entity that provides the support and protection that they need. With divorce, that structure breaks down, leaving children who feel alone and very frightened about the present and the future.

5 The human newborn is one of the most helpless creatures on earth. Human children need their parents far longer than any other animal species, and children are tragically aware of this fact—they know how absolutely dependent they are on adults. Accordingly, they have a very primitive, very real fear of being left on their own. A child's immediate reaction to divorce, therefore, is fear. When their family breaks up, children feel vulnerable, for they fear that their lifeline is in danger of being cut. Their sense of sadness and loss is profound. A five-year-old enters my office and talks about divorce with the comment "I've come

to talk about death." Children grieve over the loss of the family, the loss of the parent who has left home, and the imagined loss of both parents. Their grief may even seem unrelated to the relationship that they had with the parent who left—children cry over parents that they were close to and parents who were distant.

6 Children are profoundly concerned not only for themselves but for the welfare of their parents. It is upsetting to see a parent in tears. A ten-year-old girl says, "Mom thinks no one worries about her. But I do!" Children long intensely for the parent who has left home and worry that he or she might never come back. One seven-year-old was told that his father had moved to Oakland. "Where is Oakland?" wailed the boy. "Is Oakland in Mexico? Where is Mexico?"

7 Children of all ages feel intensely rejected when their parents divorce. When one parent leaves the other, the children interpret the act as including them. "He left Mom. He doesn't care about me." Or "She left Dad. I must not be what she wanted."

8 Children get angry at their parents for violating the unwritten rules of parenthood—parents are supposed to make sacrifices for children, not the other way around. Some keep their anger hidden for years out of fear of upsetting parents or for fear of retribution and punishment; others show it. Little children may have temper tantrums; older children may explode, like the fifteen-year-old girl in our study who put her fist through a wall. Related to the anger is a sense of powerlessness. Children feel that they have no say, no way to influence this major event in their lives. Despite ongoing fantasies that things will magically get better, they cannot prevent divorce, fix it, rescue mom or dad, or rescue the marriage. No one gives priority to their wishes, concerns, and fears.

9 Children feel intense loneliness. It amazes me how little support they get at this time, even from grandparents. Divorce is an acute, painful, long-remembered experience that children must often negotiate with the sense that they are alone in the world. All supports, even their parents, seem to fall away. There may be no one to talk to, nowhere to turn. A child will remember for many years the neighbor down the block who was kind during the divorce. In our study, fewer than 10 percent of the children had any adult speak to them sympathetically as the divorce unfolded.

10 Loyalty conflicts, sometimes flipping from one parent to the other and back again, are a common experience for children of divorce. Many children conceptualize divorce as a fight between two teams, with the

more powerful side winning the home turf, and will root for different teams at different times. Even when children are encouraged not to take sides, they often feel that they must. However, when they do take sides to feel more protected, they also feel despair because they are betraying one parent over the other. If they do not take sides, they feel isolated and disloyal to both parents. There is no solution to their dilemma.

11 Many children feel guilty, and some feel that it is their duty to mend the marriage. One seven-year-old believed for five years that she caused her parents' divorce because she failed to deliver a message from one parent to the other. A little boy thought it was his fault because his dog was noisy.

12 The devastation children feel at divorce is similar to the way they feel when a parent dies suddenly, for each experience disrupts close family relationships. Each weakens the protection of the family; each begins with an acute crisis followed by disequilibrium that may last several years or longer; and each introduces a chain of long-lasting changes that are not predictable at the outset. But divorce may well be a more difficult tragedy for the child to master psychologically.

13 Loss due to death is final; the dead person cannot be retrieved. Only a very young child or someone with a psychotic illness can deny, for any length of time, the finality of death. Moreover, death always has an identifiable calendar date and usually a clear cause, no matter how long and drawn out or unanticipated it might be. The impact of divorce is different. Finality is not present in the same way as in death, and children logically assume that the divorce can be undone at any time. Divorce is often preceded by several separations, each of which may seem decisive but turn out not to be final. These can confuse children and lead them to expect reconciliation, if not immediately, then eventually. Moreover, divorce is usually a partial loss, and most children tend to see the departed parent for many years afterward. As a result, children who experience divorce are more likely to feel a persistent, gnawing sense that the loss of the intact family is not final; maybe it can be repaired. People who divorce can remarry. People who separate can rejoin. Thus children's capacity to cope with divorce is very much decreased by the uncertainty of the event itself, by its elusive causes, and by what children regard and keep alive as its potential reversibility. Perhaps the most important factor in keeping alive children's hope for reconciliation is their intense need to think of their parents as mutually affectionate and together.

14 This feeling can endure for decades. A middle-aged woman whose parents had divorced thirty years earlier sought counseling from a female psychologist on my staff for her periodic depressions. After a while, she confessed that she was also seeing a male psychologist at another location. Her fervent wish was to bring both psychologists together in one room, to have them hold hands, with her present, so that they might symbolically restore the intact family that she had lost when she was five years old. We had a difficult time persuading this intelligent but depressed woman that staging her fantasy would not cure her depression.

15 Second chances hold different meanings for parents and for children. For adults, there is a chance to fall in love, to make a better choice, and to succeed in another relationship or a second marriage. There is the chance to achieve new dignity, to undo a mistake, to redefine one's adulthood, one's goals, and to make use of what was learned during the first marriage. There is an opportunity for psychological growth and a chance to be a better parent, with or without a new partner.

16 Children do not perceive divorce as a second chance, and this is part of their suffering. They feel that their childhood has been lost forever. Divorce is a price *they* pay, as forfeiture to their parents' failures, jeopardizing their future lives. But children of divorce do have second chances, in the very futures they are worried about. In the years after divorce, especially in adolescence and later as they enter young adulthood, children have opportunities to negotiate different and better solutions in their own lives and to reinterpret their earlier experiences in light of newfound maturity. They may re-create the kinds of traumatic relationships that they witnessed in their parents' marriage or, as they consciously or unconsciously dredge up past hurts, they may master longstanding fears of repeating their parents' mistakes. They have a chance to choose better and to resolve the unresolved issues of a childhood that included the trauma of divorce. Many children are able to do just this. Sadly, many others fail.

17 I was surprised to discover that the severity of a child's reactions at the time of the parents' divorce does not predict how that child will fare five, ten, and even fifteen years later. All of our programs for children of divorce make the opposite assumption—if we help children acknowledge or recognize their feelings at the time, they'll do better in the years to come. But from what we saw ten and fifteen years later, this is not the case. Some of the most troubled, depressed, and fretful children in our study turned out fine ten years later, while some of the least troubled,

seemingly content, and calmest children were in poor shape ten and fifteen years later. *One cannot predict longterm effects of divorce on children from how they react at the outset.* This new finding has important implications for the mental health and legal professions. Much of our energy and effort is focused on the crisis of divorce rather than the long term. But as we talked to our families through the years, we began to think of the post-divorce period as a tapestry made of many threads, with no one thread accounting for all that we saw. As the years went by, we discovered that themes and patterns shifted with each developmental stage. A color that showed little at the outset might later come to dominate the design.

FOR THINKING, DISCUSSING, AND WRITING

1. What reasons do the writers give for asserting that "the experience of divorce is entirely different for parents and for children"? Why would many people want "to believe that what is good for adults will be good for their children"?
2. The writers compare the child's experience of death to the child's experience of divorce. How effective is the comparison in helping the writers make their point?
3. The writer refers to the "unwritten rules of parenthood." Do you think there are rules for parenthood? What are they? If there are "unwritten rules for parenthood," are there also "unwritten rules for childhood"? What might they be?
4. The writers suggest that divorce is often more traumatic for the child than for the adults involved. Nevertheless, it is unreasonable to believe that divorce in our society will cease to exist as an option. Write an essay in which you indicate what you think are legitimate reasons for dissolving a marriage in which children are involved. Try to focus on the needs of the children and the parents.

DAVID BLANKENHORN

The Deadbeat Dad

David Blankenhorn (1955–) was born in Germany and educated in the United States. Blankenhorn is the chair of the National Fatherhood Initiative, a fatherhood rights activist group, and he is founder and president of the Institute for American Values, a private, nonpartisan organization devoted to contributing intellectually to the renewal of marriage and family life. His most recent publication, The Future of Marriage *(2007), addresses the debate about the definition of marriage as posed by gay rights advocates. This essay, which comes from his book* Fatherless America *(1995), explores the role of fathers in today's society and offers a perspective on the father who doesn't meet financial obligations to his family.*

1 The Deadbeat Dad is a bad guy. He is morally culpable. He is a criminal and belongs in jail. He is the reigning villain of our contemporary fatherhood script. His visage, framed by a Wanted poster, makes the cover of *Newsweek*: "Deadbeat Dads: Wanted for Failure to Pay Child Support." At the Child Guidance Center in Akron, Ohio, a little girl writes this imaginary letter to her dad:

> *Dear Dad,*
>
> *I wish you the worst Father's Day ever. And if you don't pay, you don't get love. Oh yeah, by the way, my mom makes less money than you. . . . I hate you.*

2 The Deadbeat Dad is a bad guy because he refuses to pay. Of course, he has also abandoned his children and the mother of his children. Yet in contemporary cultural terms that character trait is secondary. The main issue is not abandonment. The main issue is payment. Accordingly, the main societal imperative, as Senator Daniel Patrick Moynihan succinctly puts it, is to "make the daddies pay."

3 If we cannot enforce good fatherhood, the script goes, we ought to enforce child-support payments. Besides, for children, money is the true bottom line. Testifying before the U.S. House Select Committee on Children, Youth, and Families, Andrew J. Cherlin of Johns Hopkins University concludes that "the major problem the children have in a single-parent family is not the lack of a male image, but rather the lack of a male income."

4 In our cultural model of the Deadbeat Dad, the core issue is money absence, not father absence. This belief is widely shared among the experts. In July 1993, for example, the Census Bureau reported a 60 percent increase in out-of-wedlock childbearing since 1982. To the *New York Times* editorial board, the deeper meaning of this trend was clear: "As the number of unwed mothers grows, so does the number of deadbeat dads." Accordingly, our society's principal response to unwed childbearing must be "a more vigorous effort to track down fathers who refuse to pay support."

5 Meet the Deadbeat Dad of the 1990s: the last traditional breadwinner in the experts' story of fatherhood. For him only, fatherhood is measured in dollars. For the New Father, of course, that old breadwinner role is a thing of the past. But for the Deadbeat Dad, the breadwinner role is alive and well: the one role that society demands that he play, even as he resists. For the New Father, breadwinning thwarts fatherhood. For the Deadbeat Dad, breadwinning defines fatherhood.

6 In several respects, the Deadbeat Dad and the New Father are opposites. One is the best, the other is the worst. One lives with his child, the other does not. One repudiates the traditional male role, the other is a caricature of the traditional male role: absent, but expected to pay.

7 Yet underneath these differences, the Deadbeat Dad and the New Father share this fundamental trait: as cultural models, both derive from the idea that fatherhood is superfluous. The essence of the New Father model is the erasure of fatherhood as a gendered social role for men—fatherhood reduced to genderless parenting skills. The essence of the Deadbeat Dad model is that absent fathers can be fathers by writing checks—fatherhood reduced to the size of a wallet. Neither model incorporates fatherhood as a distinctive social role. Both models view men as problems to be overcome. At bottom, both models presuppose an increasingly fatherless society.

8 In this sense, the Deadbeat Dad is less a new departure than a variation on a theme. In cultural terms, he is the next-door neighbor of both the New Father and the Unnecessary Father. Despite the differences, these three guys all recognize one another. Here is the basis of their mutual recognition: None of them, as men and fathers, is an irreplaceable caregiver for his children. Indeed, here is the most concise definition of the Deadbeat Dad: the Unnecessary Father who refuses to pay.

The Bad Understudy

9 The Unnecessary Father, the Old Father, and the New Father are the three leading characters of our contemporary fatherhood script. They are the stars. They get most of the attention.

10 The Unnecessary Father is a star because he is the chorus. He comments on every scene, he explains all the action. Both the Old Father and New Father are biological fathers. Moreover, both live with their children and thus can perform the daily tasks of

fatherhood. In short, they qualify as leading characters in the script largely because both of them combine biological fatherhood with social fatherhood.

11 The remaining five characters in the script do not meet this threshold test. They are the fatherhood understudies. They are either biological but not social fathers, or social but not biological fathers. They are almost fathers, sort-of fathers. The three biological fathers—the Deadbeat Dad, the Visiting Father, and the Sperm Father—do not live with their children and thus cannot care for them on a routine, daily basis. The Stepfather lives with children, but not his children. The Nearby Guy—the boyfriend, the friend—is not a biological father and he may or may not live with children, though he increasingly finds himself playing what passes for a fatherly social role.

12 Accordingly, each of these understudy roles represents the growing disembodiment and dispersal of fatherhood in our society. Each embodies the splitting apart of fatherhood from father. More specifically, as cultural models, each of these fathers has lost, or failed to attain, the core prerequisites of good-enough fatherhood. The evidence is overwhelming: To be a good-enough father, a man must reside with his child and sustain a parental alliance with the mother of his child. In cultural terms, these five minor fatherhood roles are understudies, almost-fathers, precisely because their fatherhood is unsupported by these twin foundations.

13 At the same time, however, all five of these roles are growing in social importance. They characterized increasing proportions of men. With each passing year, these understudy fathers become more present, more vital, in the lives of children. In this sense, they are becoming the fathers in our increasingly fatherless society.

14 Of these five understudies, the Deadbeat Dad role is by far the thinnest, the most widely known, and the most vilified. It is a small role for bad men. It is a specialty role, defined by minimal expectations and severely limited possibilities. To date, it is not even a speaking role. The point is not to say something but rather to do something: pay. Finally, our culture's view of this role is governed by an assumption of bad faith. As a phrase of speech, a "Deadbeat Dad" is our society's only popular label for parents that is overtly pejorative.

15 No other family behavior, and no other family policy issue, has generated such an urgent societal consensus on what is to be done. Extracting payments from Deadbeat Dads is now a regnant priority in

our society, uniting liberals and conservatives, Republicans and Democrats, elite opinion and popular sentiment. In the 1992 presidential campaign, for example, applause lines about Deadbeat Dads emerged in the stump speeches of both George Bush and Bill Clinton, constituting arguably the only issue in the campaign on which they publicly agreed.

16 The Deadbeat Dad is also increasingly visible in the popular culture. He is the subject of popular books, magazine features, and made-for-television movies. Even the *National Enquirer*, ever alert to its social responsibilities, has launched a Deadbeat Dad series—"Help find the cruel louse who deserted his four children"—which enlists the participation of readers in "hunting down and capturing some of the most wanted deadbeat dads in America."

17 The Deadbeat Dad has emerged as our principal cultural model for ex-fathers, for obviously failed fathers. As a cultural category, the Deadbeat Dad has become our primary symbol of the growing failure of fatherhood in our society. We demonize him in part because he reminds us of our fatherlessness. He represents loss. He forces us to reduce our expectations. Consequently, we vilify him, we threaten him—we demand that he pay—largely because he so clearly embodies the contemporary collapse of good-enough fatherhood.

18 Yet the content of our demand illustrates both the depth of our pessimism and the lowering of our standards. We do not ask this guy to be a father. That would be utopian, impossible. We ask him to send a check. Instead of demanding what is owed, we demand money.

19 We respond to the Deadbeat Dad by denying and pretending. If only we could get tough with these guys, that would fix what is broken. Get them to pay. That would help the children. That would relieve the taxpayer. Here, finally, is a family policy we can all agree on.

20 But this strategy is a fantasy. It is based not on evidence but on wishful thinking. To date, the strategy of tracking down Deadbeat Dads has failed even on its own terms: It has not improved the economic well-being of the typical fatherless child. Yet the real failure runs far deeper. From the child's perspective, child-support payments, even if fully paid, do not replace a father's economic provision. More fundamentally, they do not replace a father.

21 Our current Deadbeat Dad strategy fails even to acknowledge our society's spreading crisis of family fragmentation and declining child well-being. For what is broken in our society is not the proper police

procedures to compel small child-support payments from reluctant men. What is broken is fatherhood.

22 Andrew Cherlin, then, muddles the issue completely. First, he imagines that, in the home, "a male income" and "a male image" are two separate things. Fundamentally, they are not. Consequently, his preference for the former over the latter is all but meaningless. But let us imagine, with Cherlin, that the two could be separated. He still gets the issue backward. The "major problem" in fatherless homes is not "the lack of a male income" (though that certainly is a problem). The major problem is "the lack of a male image"—that is, the lack of a father. To pretend otherwise is simply to pretend that money is important, but fathers are not.

23 Ultimately, the solution to the growing problem of Deadbeat Dads is not jail cells, Most Wanted posters, job-training programs, interstate computer networks, or IRS agents. At best, these are Band-Aids on an infected wound. At worst, they are a form of denial—a self-defeating strategy intended to excuse our drift toward fatherlessness. The only solution to the problem of Deadbeat Dads is fatherhood.

FOR THINKING, DISCUSSING, AND WRITING

1. What characteristics does the writer attribute to the "New Father"? Why is he called "Father" while the Deadbeat Dad is "Dad"? Why is "extracting payment from Deadbeat Dads…a regnant priority in our society"? Should we continue to extract payment from deadbeat dads? Why or why not? What does Blankenhorn mean by the last sentence of his essay: "The only solution to the problem of Deadbeat Dads is fatherhood"? By breaking down fatherhood into narrowly defined categories, Blankenhorn suggests that our society often sees gender roles as one dimensional. Do you agree? Why or why not?
2. Blankenhorn is writing about fatherhood in the 1990s (see paragraph 5). In what ways are his assertions still valid in the twenty-first century? Or do you find them invalid? Why?
3. How does the title of the essay arouse the reader's interest? Suppose the title were "Fathers Who Don't Pay." How would that title, compared with Blankenhorn's, serve the purposes of the essay?
4. Write an essay in which you lay out what you see as the essential elements of fatherhood—that is, of being a successful father in today's world.

JUDITH WARNER

The Parent Trap

Judith Warner is the author, with Howard Dean, of You Have the Power: How to Take Back Our Country and Restore Democracy to America *(2004); of* Perfect Madness: Motherhood in the Age of Anxiety *(2005); and of the best-selling biography* Hillary Clinton: The Inside Story *(1999). A former special correspondent for* Newsweek *in Paris, she reviews books for the* New York Times *and has written about politics and women's issues for magazines including the* New Republic *and* Elle. *Warner is also the host of "The Judith Warner Show" on XM Satellite Radio.*

In this essay, Warner questions the progress women have made after Betty Friedan, a major figure in the feminist movement in America, argued in The Feminine Mystique *for women to reach their "full human potential." Friedan's death on February 4, 2006, stimulated Warner to write this piece.*

1 I First encountered *The Feminine Mystique* in college, in 1986. We read it not in women's studies, but in a class on intellectual history; and indeed, from the vantage point of a young woman coming of age in the mid-1980s, the world that Betty Friedan depicted—a world in which a married woman couldn't get a job without her husband's permission, couldn't open a checking account and couldn't get credit in her own name—seemed like ancient history.

2 And yet, five years ago, as I settled, for the first time, into a life where I worked minimal hours, spent maximal time with my children and was almost entirely dependent on my husband's salary and health benefits, ancient history became a current affair. I lived surrounded by women whose lives were much like mine, and the sentences that swirled around me on the playground stirred memories of thoughts and phrases I'd read long before.

3 The voices coalesced into a chorus of discontent that haunted me until one evening, after my daughters had gone to sleep, I went through a pile of boxes and dug up my old copy of Ms. Friedan's book. This time, as it had for many of the homemakers who read it when it was published in 1963, *The Feminine Mystique* felt horribly familiar. Looking back convinced me that we needed to start working toward a different future.

4 You could say that the "plight" of 21st-century stay-at-home moms—or part-time working moms like me—is vastly different from "the problem that has no name" experienced by the women of

Ms. Friedan's generation, and in one key respect you'd be right: Girls and women today are no longer kept from pursuing their educational dreams and career aspirations. They're no longer expected to abandon their jobs when they marry and—in theory—are no longer considered "unnatural" if they keep working when they have children.

5 We women have, in many very real ways, at long last made good on Ms. Friedan's dream that we would reach "our full human potential—by participating in the mainstream of society." But, for mothers in particular, at what cost? With what degree of exhaustion? And with what soul-numbing sacrifices made along the way?

6 The outside world has changed enormously for women in these past 40 years. But home life? Think about it. Who routinely unloads the dishwasher, puts away the laundry and picks up the socks in your house? Who earns the largest share of the money? Who calls the shots?

7 The answer, for a great many families, is the same as it was 50 years ago. That's why when I read the obituaries of Ms. Friedan, who died on Saturday, I was sad, but also depressed: their recounting of her description of the lives of women in the 1950s sounded just too much like the lives of women today.

8 Although it often seems anecdotally to be true that domestic tasks and power are pretty evenly divided in families where both parents are working full time, the statistics argue quite differently. The fact is, no matter how time- or sleep-deprived they are, working women today do upwards of 70 percent of household chores for their families. The gender caste system is still alive and well in most of our households. After all, no one really wants to do the scrubbing and folding and chauffeuring and mopping and shopping and dry-cleaner runs. (I'm leaving child-minding out of this; in a happily balanced life, it doesn't feel like a chore.) Once the money for outsourcing runs dry, it's the lower-status member of the household who does these things. It is the lower-status member of the household who is called a "nag" when she repeatedly tries to get other members of the household to share in doing them.

9 This is just one indication that the feminist "revolution" that was supposed to profoundly reshape women's lives remains incomplete. Another is the fact that there are no meaningful national policies to make satisfying work and satisfying family life anything but mutually exclusive for most men and women.

10 Ms. Friedan herself anticipated this issue, in the final pages of *The Feminine Mystique,* when she called for changing "the rules of the game" of society at large. In 1970, she came back to this thought, arguing that if we

did "not only end explicit discrimination but build new institutions," then the women's movement would prove to be "all talk." Thirty-six years later, with women having flooded the professions and explicit gender discrimination outlawed, the institutions of our society simply have not changed to embrace and accommodate the new realities of women's lives.

11 The problems of home life seem to me now to be an all but hopeless conundrum. Yet the enduring failure of our social institutions to realize the larger promises of the women's movement is something we can address, straightforwardly and comparatively easily. We owe it to Betty Friedan, to our daughters and to ourselves.

12 Ms. Friedan said last year, "We are a backward nation when it comes to things like childcare and parental leave." That's just the beginning. We need universal preschool, more and better afterschool programs, and policies to promote part-time work options that don't force parents to forgo benefits, fair pay and career prospects.

13 We desperately need leadership on these issues. Without it, our national commitment to family values is truly "all talk."

FOR THINKING, DISCUSSING, AND WRITING

1. What differences does Warner see between the twenty-first–century woman and the woman who lived in Freidan's time, the mid-1960s and 1970s? What is your response to the writer's observations?
2. Warner raises a series of provocative questions in paragraph 5. How would you answer them?
3. Warner comments that "the gender caste system is still alive and well in most of our households." Based on your own observations, why might you agree or disagree with her statement.
4. How would childcare and parental leave, if widely available, influence family dynamics, do you think? Write an essay in which you explore this notion.

CONNECTING IDEAS: All in the Family

1. How has this chapter influenced your view of family? Which essay did you find particularly challenging? Why?
2. The selections deal with both conventional and unconventional family structures. Which essays would you place in which category? Why?
3. Write an essay in which you define the word *family*. Draw upon the essays in this chapter to help make your points.

3 CHAPTER

What Is Education?

THROUGH THE AGES AND UP TO THE PRESENT MOMENT some of the most intense debates in Western civilization have centered on the goals and strategies of education.

In contemporary America the education machine chugs on relentlessly, like a self-powered locomotive that is apt to change course noisily and unpredictably on an unknown track. More than 60 million students fill the nation's classrooms; over 4 million teachers, administrators, and other school personnel attend to these students' needs. At a recent count more than 112,000 schools and 3,600 colleges and universities managed the formal education of the nation's students. Home schooling for children represents another major educational activity. Mothers and fathers who are troubled by certain curricular content (Darwin? sex education?) and (or) hostile school environments and (or) who are simply fed up with intractable educational bureaucracies are teaching their children at the kitchen table. In addition, an endless array of online courses and programs in our technology-driven society has expanded the educational context dramatically—we cannot even count the number of people directly involved in education, either on the giving or the receiving end. Learning, the enlightened citizen has come to see, is a lifelong effort. Like the novelist Frank Conroy, we believe that "education doesn't end until life ends, because you never know when you're going to understand something you hadn't understood before."

In the late 1990s, America spent almost 7.5 percent of its annual gross domestic product on formal public education. That jolting figure represents more than half a trillion dollars each year, or about $8,000 per student. Is this cause for celebration or despair? Are we wise enough as a nation to have targeted such vast resources to the educational enterprise? Or are we foolish spendthrifts, tossing money to the wind and seeing little evidence that the expense produces any lasting value? And have we given anything but lip service to the self taught, the school of Hard Knocks, the university of the world—generally nonstructured and unplanned—in understanding what education is and how people learn? In this chapter, Malcolm X in "Prison Studies" explains how initiative and hard work helped him teach himself how to read—without much help from outsiders.

Everyone, being educated in some way, has thoughts and opinions on education in this country. Newspapers as well as television and radio broadcasts regularly harangue the educational establishment. Some newspapers publish the names of failing students and failing schools. We read about charter schools, secondary schools on college campuses, magnet schools, special talent schools—all efforts in the name of innovation and reform. Leon Botstein, the president of Bard College, tells us that "the high school has outlived its usefulness to the point of catastrophe" and recommends radical changes in his essay here. What are we to make of the myriad viewpoints on education, its value, and varied delivery? The thoughtful reader and thinker must raise deliberative questions in order to make sense of the issues. But one thing is certain: education lies at the heart of modern existence. Most Americans see education as inalienable, essential to democratic life, and intrinsic to our value system.

JUDITH ORTIZ COFER

The Paterson Public Library

Judith Ortiz Cofer (1952–) is a native of Puerto Rico who currently teaches at the University of Georgia at Athens. She has published several volumes of poetry, including Terms of Survival *(1987), as well as an essay collection,* Silent Dancing *(1990). Her novel* The Line of the Sun *(1989) was nominated for a Pulitzer Prize.* The Latin Deli *(1993), from which this selection comes, is a collection of essays about biculturalism and the creative process. A collection of her poetry,* A Love Story Beginning in Spanish, *appeared in 2005. In this selection she explores the role of her city's public library as a major force in her education.*

1 It was a Greek temple in the ruins of an American city. To get to it I had to walk through neighborhoods where not even the carcasses of rusted cars on blocks nor the death traps of discarded appliances were parted with, so that the yards of the borderline poor, people who lived not in a huge building, as I did, but in their own decrepit little houses, looked liked a reversed archaeological site, incongruous next to the pillared palace of the Paterson Public Library.

2 The library must have been built during Paterson's boom years as the model industrial city of the North. Enough marble was used in its construction to have kept several Michelangelos busily satisfied for a lifetime. Two roaring lions, taller than a grammar school girl, greeted those brave enough to seek answers there. Another memorable detail about the façade of this important place to me was the phrases carved deeply into the walls—perhaps the immortal words of Greek philosophers—I could not tell, since I was developing astigmatism at that time and could only make out the lovely geometric designs they made.

3 All during the school week I both anticipated and feared the long walk to the library because it took me through enemy territory. The black girl Lorraine, who had chosen me to hate and terrorize with threats at school, lived in one of the gloomy little houses that circled the library like beggars. Lorraine would eventually carry out her violence against me by beating me up in a confrontation formally announced through the school grapevine so that for days I lived with a panic that has rarely been equaled in my adult life, since now I can get grown-ups to listen to me, and at that time disasters had to be a fait accompli for a teacher or a parent to get involved. Why did Lorraine hate me? For reasons neither one of us fully understood at the time. All I remember was that our sixth grade teacher seemed to favor me, and her way of showing it was by having me tutor "slow" students in spelling and grammar. Lorraine, older and bigger than myself, since she was repeating the grade, was subjected to this ritual humiliation, which involved sitting in the hallway, obviously separated from the class—one of us for being smart, the other for the opposite reason. Lorraine resisted my efforts to teach her the basic rules of spelling. She would hiss her threats at me, addressing me as

You little spic. Her hostility sent shudders through me. But baffling as it was, I also accepted it as inevitable. She would beat me up. I told my mother and the teacher, and they both reassured me in vague adult terms that a girl like Lorraine would not dare get in trouble again. She had a history of problems that made her a likely candidate for reform school. But Lorraine and I knew that the violence she harbored had found a target: me—the skinny Puerto Rican girl whose father was away with the navy most of the time and whose mother did not speak English; I was the perfect choice.

4 Thoughts like these occupied my mind as I walked to the library on Saturday mornings. But my need for books was strong enough to propel me down the dreary streets with their slush-covered sidewalks and the skinny trees of winter looking like dark figures from a distance: angry black girls waiting to attack me.

5 But the sight of the building was enough to reassure me that sanctuary was within reach. Inside the glass doors was the inexhaustible treasure of books, and I made my way through the stacks like the beggar invited to the wedding feast. I remember the musty, organic smell of the library, so different from the air outside. It was the smell of an ancient forest, and since the first books that I read for pleasure were fairy tales, the aroma of transforming wood suited me as a prop.

6 With my pink library card I was allowed to check out two books from the first floor—the children's section. I would take the full hour my mother had given me (generously adding fifteen minutes to get home before she sent my brother after me) to choose the books I would take home for the week. I made my way first through the world's fairy tales. Here I discovered that there is a Cinderella in every culture, that she didn't necessarily have the white skin and rosy cheeks that Disney had given her, and that the prince they all waited for could appear in any color, shape, or form. The prince didn't even have to be a man.

7 It was the way I absorbed fantasy in those days that gave me the sense of inner freedom, a feeling of power and the ability to fly that is the main reward of the writer. As I read those stories I became not only the characters but their creator. I am still fascinated by the idea that fairy tales and fables are part of humankind's collective unconscious—a familiar theory that acquires concreteness in my own writing today, when I discover over and over that the character I create or the themes that recur in my poems and in my fiction are my own

versions of the "types" I learned to recognize very early in my life in fairy tales.

8 There was also violence in these stories: villains decapitated in honorable battle, goblins and witches pursued, beaten, and burned at the stake by heroes with magic weapons, possessing the supernatural strength granted to the self-righteous in folklore. I understood those black-and-white duels between evil and justice. But Lorraine's blind hatred of my person and my knee-liquefying fear of her were not so clear to me at that time. It would be many years before I learned about the politics of race, before I internalized the awful reality of the struggle for territory that underscored the lives of blacks and Puerto Ricans in Paterson during my childhood. Each job given to a light-skinned Hispanic was one less job for a black man; every apartment leased to a Puerto Rican family was one less place available to blacks. Worst of all, though the Puerto Rican children had to master a new language in the schools and were often subjected to the scorn and impatience of teachers burdened with too many students making too many demands in a classroom, the blacks were obviously the ones singled out for "special" treatment. In other words, whenever possible they were assigned to special education classes in order to relieve the teacher's workload, mainly because their black English dialect sounded "ungrammatical" and "illiterate" to our white Seton Hall University and City College-educated instructors. I have on occasion become angry at being treated like I'm mentally deficient by persons who make that prejudgment upon hearing an unfamiliar accent. I can only imagine what it must have been like for children like Lorraine, whose skin color alone put her in a pigeonhole she felt she had to fight her way out of every day of her life.

9 I was one of the lucky ones; as an insatiable reader I quickly became more than adept at the use of the English language. My life as a navy brat, moving with my family from Paterson to Puerto Rico every few months as my father's tours of duty demanded, taught me to depend on knowledge as my main source of security. What I learned from books borrowed from the Greek temple among the ruins of the city I carried with me as the lightest of carry-on luggage. My teachers in both countries treated me well in general. The easiest way to become a teacher's pet, or *la favorita*, is to ask the teacher for books to read—and I was always looking for reading material. Even my mother's romantic novels by Corin Tellado and her *Buenhogar* (Spanish *Good Housekeeping* magazine) were not safe from my insatiable word hunger.

10 Since the days when I was stalked by Lorraine, libraries have always been an adventure for me. Fear of an ambush is no longer the reason why I feel my pulse quicken a little when I approach a library building, when I enter the stacks and inhale the familiar smell of old leather and paper. It may be the memory of the danger that heightens my senses, but it is really the expectation that I felt then and that I still feel now about books. They contained most of the information I needed to survive in two languages and in two worlds. When adults were too busy to answer my endless questions, I could always *look it up*; when I felt unbearably lonely, as I often did during those early gypsy years traveling with my family, I read to escape and also to connect: you can come back to a book as you cannot always to a person or place you miss. I read and reread favorite books until the characters seemed like relatives or friends I could see when I wanted or needed to see them.

11 I still feel that way about books. They represent my spiritual life. A library is my sanctuary, and I am always at home in one. It is not surprising that in recalling my first library, the Paterson Public Library, I have always described it as a temple.

12 Lorraine carried out her threat. One day after school, as several of our classmates, Puerto Rican and black, circled us to watch, Lorraine grabbed a handful of my long hair and forced me to my knees. Then she slapped my face hard enough that the sound echoed off the brick walls of the school building and ran off while I screamed at the sight of blood on my white knee socks and felt the throbbing on my scalp where I would have a bald spot advertising my shame for weeks to come.

13 No one intervened. To this crowd, it was one of many such violent scenes taking place among the adults and the children of people fighting over a rapidly shrinking territory. It happens in the jungle and it happens in the city. But another course of action other than "fight or flight" is open to those of us lucky enough to discover it, and that is channeling one's anger and energy into the development of a mental life. It requires something like obsessiveness for a young person growing up in an environment where physical labor and physical endurance are the marks of a survivor—as is the case with minority peoples living in large cities. But many of us do manage to discover books. In my case, it may have been what anthropologists call a cultural adaptation. Being physically small, non-English-speaking, and always the new kid on the block, I was forced to look for an alternative mode to survival in Paterson. Reading books empowered me.

14 Even now, a visit to the library recharges the batteries in my brain. Looking through the card catalog reassures me that there is no subject that I cannot investigate, no world I cannot explore. Everything that is is mine for the asking. Because I can read about it.

FOR THINKING, DISCUSSING, AND WRITING

1. Cofer remarks that "books represent my spiritual life" and that reading gave her "the sense of inner freedom, a feeling of power." What does she mean by these statements? What role did the Paterson Public Library itself play in her freedom and spiritual life?
2. What relation does the writer have with Lorraine? How did Lorraine use the school "grapevine" to intimidate Cofer? How does Lorraine's use of a racial epithet contribute to our understanding of the writer's point?
3. The essay asserts that in Paterson a struggle exists between African Americans and Puerto Ricans. What is the nature of this struggle? Why does it exist, do you think? Where else might you find such a struggle? Why do you think so?
4. Cofer writes that a course of action other than "fight or flight" is "channeling one's anger and energy into the development of a mental life." How could someone go about accomplishing this objective? Write an essay to explain Cofer's comment and its relevance to your own life and the lives of people you know.

JAMES THURBER

University Days

James Thurber (1894–1961) was born in Columbus, Ohio, and attended Ohio State University. A well-known newspaperman, humorist, and essayist, Thurber published much during his lifetime, including the books The Owl in the Attic *(1931),* My Life and Hard Times *(1933),* My World—And Welcome to It *(1942), and* The Thurber Album *(1952). Among his most famous works is the short story "The Secret Life of Walter Mitty" (1939). In this selection from his autobiography, Thurber links a series of anecdotes about his days as a student at Ohio State University.*

1 I passed all the other courses that I took at my university, but I could never pass botany. This was because all botany students had to spend several hours a week in a laboratory looking through a microscope at

plant cells, and I could never see through a microscope. I never once saw a cell through a microscope. This used to enrage my instructor. He would wander around the laboratory pleased with the progress all the students were making in drawing the involved and, so I am told, interesting structure of flower cells, until he came to me. I would just be standing there. "I can't see anyting," I would say. He would begin patiently enough, explaining how anybody can see through a microscope, but he would always end up in a fury, claiming that I could *too* see through a microscope but just pretended that I couldn't. "It takes away from the beauty of flowers anyway," I used to tell him. "We are not concerned with beauty in this course," he would say. "We are concerned solely with what I may call the *mechanics* of flars." "Well," I'd say, "I can't see anything." "Try it just once again," he'd say, and I would put my eye to the microscope and see nothing at all, except now and again a nebulous milky substance—a phenomenon of maladjustment. You were supposed to see a vivid, restless clockwork of sharply defined plant cells. "I see what looks like a lot of milk," I would tell him. This, he claimed, was the result of my not having adjusted the microscope properly, so he would readjust it for me, or rather, for himself. And I would look again and see milk.

2 I finally took a deferred pass, as they called it, and waited a year and tried again. (You had to pass one of the biological sciences or you couldn't graduate.) The professor had come back from vacation brown as a berry, bright-eyed, and eager to explain cell-structure again to his classes. "Well," he said to me, cheerily when we met in the first laboratory hour of the semester, "we're going to see cells this time, aren't we?" "Yes, sir," I said. Students to right of me and to left of me and in front of me were seeing cells; what's more, they were quietly drawing pictures of them in their notebooks. Of course, I didn't see anything.

3 "We'll try it," the professor said to me, grimly, "with every adjustment of the microscope known to man. As God is my witness, I'll arrange this glass so that you see cells through it or I'll give up teaching. In twenty-two years of botany, I—" He cut off abruptly for he was beginning to quiver all over, like Lionel Barrymore,[1] and he genuinely wished to hold onto his temper; his scenes with me had taken a great deal out of him.

[1] Lionel Barrymore (1878–1954) was one of America's premier actors.

4 So we tried it with every adjustment of the microscope known to man. With only one of them did I see anything but blackness or the familiar lacteal opacity, and that time I saw, to my pleasure and amazement, a variegated constellation of flecks, specks, and dots. These I hastily drew. The instructor, noting my activity, came back from an adjoining desk, a smile on his lips and his eyebrows high in hope. He looked at my cell drawing. "What's that?" he demanded, with a hint of a squeal in his voice. "That's what I saw," I said. "You didn't, you didn't, you *didn't*!" he screamed, losing control of his temper instantly, and he bent over and squinted into the microscope. His head snapped up. "That's your eye!" he shouted. "You've fixed the lens so that it reflects! You've drawn your eye!"

5 Another course that I didn't like, but somehow managed to pass, was economics. I went to that class straight from the botany class, which didn't help me any in understanding either subject. I used to get them mixed up. But not as mixed up as another student in my economics class who came there direct from a physics laboratory. He was a tackle on the football team, named Bolenciecwcz. At that time Ohio State University had one of the best football teams in the country, and Bolenciecwcz was one of its outstanding stars. In order to be eligible to play it was necessary for him to keep up in his studies, a very difficult matter, for while he was not dumber than an ox he was not any smarter. Most of his professors were lenient and helped him along. None gave him more hints in answering questions or asked him simpler ones than the economics professor, a thin, timid man named Bassum. One day when we were on the subject of transportation and distribution, it came Bolenciecwcz's turn to answer a question. "Name one means of transportation," the professor said to him. No light came into the big tackle's eyes. "Just any means of transportation," said the professor. Bolenciecwcz sat staring at him. "That is," pursued the professor, "any medium, agency, or method of going from one place to another." Bolenciecwcz had the look of a man who is being led into a trap. "You may choose among steam, horsedrawn, or electrically propelled vehicles," said the instructor. "I might suggest the one which we commonly take in making long journeys across land." There was a profound silence in which everybody stirred uneasily, including Bolenciecwcz and Mr. Bassum, Mr. Bassum abruptly broke this silence in an amazing manner. "Choo-choo-choo," he said, in a low voice, and turned instantly scarlet. He glanced appealingly around the room. All of us, of

course, shared Mr. Bassum's desire that Bolenciecwcz should stay abreast of the class in economics, for the Illinois game, one of the hardest and most important of the season, was only a week off. "Toot, toot, too-tooooooot!" some student with a deep voice moaned, and we all looked encouragingly at Bolenciecwcz. Somebody else gave a fine imitation of a locomotive letting off steam. Mr. Bassum himself rounded off the little show. "Ding, dong, ding, dong," he said, hopefully. Bolenciecwcz was starting at the floor now, trying to think, his great brow furrowed, his huge hands rubbing together, his face red.

6 "How did you come to college this year, Mr. Bolenciewcz?" asked the professor. "*Chuffa* chuffa, *chuffa* chuffa."

7 "M' father sent me," said the football player.

8 "What on?" asked Bassum.

9 "I git an 'lowance," said the tackle, in a low, husky voice, obviously embarrassed.

10 "No, no," said Bassum. "Name a means of transportation. What did you *ride* here on?"

11 "Train," said Bolenciecwcz.

12 "Quite right," said the professor. "Now, Mr. Nugent, will you tell us—"

13 If I went through anguish in botany and economics—for different reasons—gymnasium work was even worse. I don't even like to think about it. They wouldn't let you play games or join in the exercises with your glasses on and I couldn't see with mine off. I bumped into professors, horizontal bars, agricultural students, and swinging iron rings. Not being able to see, I could take it but I couldn't dish it out. Also, in order to pass gymnasium (and you had to pass it to graduate) you had to learn to swim if you didn't know how. I didn't like the swimming pool, I didn't like swimming, and I didn't like the swimming instructor, and after all these years I still don't. I never swam but I passed my gym work anyway, by having another student give my gymnasium number (978) and swim across the pool in my place. He was a quiet, amiable blond youth, number 473, and he would have seen through a microscope for me if we could have got away with it, but we couldn't get away with it. Another thing I didn't like about gymnasium work was that they made you strip the day you registered. It is impossible for me to be happy when I am stripped and being asked a lot of questions. Still, I did better than a lanky agricultural student who was cross-examined just before I was. They asked each student what college he was in—that is, whether Arts, Engineering, Commerce, or

Agriculture. "What college are you in?" the instructor snapped at the youth in front of me. "Ohio State University," he said promptly.

14 It wasn't that agricultural student but it was another a whole lot like him who decided to take up journalism, possibly on the ground that when farming went to hell he could fall back on newspaper work. He didn't realize, of course, that that would be very much like failing back full-length on a kit of carpenter's tools. Haskins didn't seem cut out for journalism, being too embarrassed to talk to anybody and unable to use a typewriter, but the editor of the college paper assigned him to the cow barns, the sheep house, the horse pavilion, and the annual husbandry department generally. This was a genuinely big "beat," for it took up five times as much ground and got ten times as great a legislative appropriation as the College of Liberal Arts. The agricultural student knew animals, but nevertheless his stories were dull and colorlessly written. He took all afternoon on each of them, on account of having to hunt for each letter on the typewriter. Once in a while he had to ask somebody to help him hunt. "C" and "L," in particular, were hard letters for him to find. His editor finally got pretty much annoyed at the farmer-journalist because his pieces were so uninteresting. "See here, Haskins," he snapped at him one day, "why is it we never have anything hot from you on the horse pavilion? Here we have two hundred head of horses on this campus—more than any other university in the Western Conference except Purdue—and yet you never get any real lowdown on them. Now shoot over to the horse barns and dig up something lively." Haskins shambled out and came back in about an hour; he said he had something. "Well, start it off snappily," said the editor. "Something people will read." Haskins set to work, and in a couple of hours brought a sheet of typewritten paper to the desk; it was a two-hundred-word story about some disease that had broken out among the horses. Its opening sentence was simple but arresting. It read: "Who has noticed the sores on the tops of the horses in the animal husbandry building?"

15 Ohio State was a land grant university and therefore two years of military drill was compulsory. We drilled with old Springfield rifles and studied the tactics of the Civil War even though the World War was going on at the time. At 11 o'clock each morning thousands of freshmen and sophomores used to deploy over the campus, moodily creeping up on the old chemistry building. It was good training for the kind of warfare that was waged at Shiloh but it had no connection with what was going on in Europe. Some people used to think there was German

money behind it, but they didn't dare say so or they would have been thrown in jail as German spies. It was a period of muddy thought and marked, I believe, the decline of higher education in the Middle West.

16 As a soldier I was never any good at all. Most of the cadets were glumly indifferent soldiers, but I was no good at all. Once General Littlefield, who was commandant of the cadet corps, popped up in front of me during regimental drill and snapped, "You are the main trouble with this university!" I think he meant that my type was the main trouble with the university but he may have meant me individually. I was mediocre at drill, certainly—that is, until my senior year. By that time I had drilled longer than anybody else in the Western Conference, having failed at military at the end of each preceding year so that I had to do it all over again. I was the only senior still in uniform. The uniform which, when new, had made me look like an interurban railway conductor, now that it had become faded and too tight made me look like Bert Williams[2] in his bellboy act. This had a definitely bad effect on my morale. Even so, I had become by sheer practice little short of wonderful at squad maneuvers.

17 One day General Littlefield picked our company out of the whole regiment and tried to get it mixed up by putting it through one movement after another as fast as we could execute them: squads right, squads left, squads on right into line, squads right about, squads left front into line, etc. In about three minutes one hundred and nine men were marching in one direction and I was marching away from them at an angle of forty degrees, all alone. "Company, halt!" shouted General Littlefield. "That man is the only man who has it right!" I was made a corporal for my achievement.

18 The next day General Littlefield summoned me to his office. He was swatting flies when I went in. I was silent and he was silent too, for a long time, I don't think he remembered me or why he had sent for me, but he didn't want to admit it. He swatted some more flies, keeping his eyes on them narrowly before he let go with the swatter. "Button up your coat!" he snapped. Looking back on it now I can see that he meant me although he was looking at a fly, but I just stood there. Another fly came to rest on a paper in front of the general and began rubbing it's hind legs together. The general lifted the swatter cautiously. I moved restlessly and the fly flew away. "You startled him!" barked General

[2] Bert Williams (1874?–1922) was an African American who starred in vaudeville.

Littlefield, looking at me severely. I said I was sorry. "That won't help the situation!" snapped the General, with cold military logic. I didn't see what I could do except offer to chase some more flies toward his desk, but I didn't say anything. He stared out the window at the faraway figures of co-eds crossing the campus toward the library. Finally, he told me I could go. So I went. He either didn't know which cadet I was or else he forgot what he wanted to see me about. It may have been that he wished to apologize for having called me the main trouble with the university; or maybe he had decided to compliment me on my brilliant drilling of the day before and then at the last minute decided not to. I don't know. I don't think about it much any more.

FOR THINKING, DISCUSSING, AND WRITING

1. What kind of college student was Thurber seem to be? What evidence supports your point? Are there any classes he enjoys? How do you know?
2. Which elements in the incidents Thurber relates do you find most humorous? How does he achieve the humorous effects?
3. Thurber reports on his campus-related military training. How does he feel about it? What is the role of the military on campuses today? How do students feel about participating in the military through their campus's sponsorship? How do these opinions and attitudes compare with those of Thurber and his colleagues?
4. Thurber comments that "I think he [General Littlefield] meant that my type was the main trouble with the university but he may have meant me individually." Thurber suggests that there may sometimes be a conflict between the liberating possibilities of education and the ways in which institutions like schools sometimes insist that people conform. Write a paper in which you examine this conflict and try to come up with a solution to it.

MALCOLM X

Prison Studies

Born in Omaha, Nebraska, as Malcolm Little, Malcolm X (1925–1965) was a religious activist and civil rights leader as well as a prominent figure in the African-American Muslim community. Imprisoned for robbery in 1961, he educated himself while behind bars. Always a controversial figure, Malcolm X was assassinated in New York City in 1963. In this essay he chronicles some of his efforts to attack his ignorance "by being able to study intensely sometimes as much as fifteen hours a day."

1 Many who today hear me somewhere in person, or on television, or those who read something I've said, will think I went to school far beyond the eighth grade. This impression is due entirely to my prison studies.

2 It had really begun back in the Charlestown Prison, when Bimbi first made me feel envy of his stock of knowledge. Bimbi had always taken charge of any conversation he was in, and I had tried to emulate him. But every book I picked up had few sentences which didn't contain anywhere from one to nearly all of the words that might as well have been in Chinese. When I just skipped those words, of course, I really ended up with little idea of what the book said. so I had come to the Norfolk Prison Colony still going through only book-reading motions. Pretty soon, I would have quit even these motions, unless I had received the motivation that I did.

3 I saw that the best thing I could do was get hold of a dictionary—to study, to learn some words. I was lucky enough to reason also that I should try to improve my penmanship. It was sad. I couldn't even write in a straight line. It was both ideas together that moved me to request a dictionary along with some tablets and pencils from the Norfolk Prison Colony school.

4 I spent two days just riffling uncertainly through the dictionary's pages. I'd never realized so many words existed! I didn't know which words I needed to learn. Finally, to start some kind of action, I began copying.

5 In my slow, painstaking, ragged handwriting, I copied into my tablet everything printed on that first page, down to the punctuation marks.

6 I believe it took me a day. Then, aloud, I read back, to myself, everything I'd written on the tablet. Over and over, aloud, to myself, I read my own handwriting.

7 I woke up the next morning, thinking about those words—immensely proud to realize that not only had I written so much at one time, but I'd written words that I never knew were in the world. Moreover, with a little effort, I also could remember what many of these words meant. I reviewed the words whose meanings I didn't remember. Funny thing, from the dictionary first page right now, that "aardvark" spring to my mind. The dictionary had a picture of it, a

longtailed, long-eared, burrowing African mammal, which lives off termites caught by sticking out its tongue as an anteater does for ants.

8 I was so fascinated that I went on—I copied the dictionary's next page. And the same experience came when I studied that. With every succeeding page, I also learned of people and places and events from history. Actually the dictionary is like a miniature encyclopedia. Finally the dictionary's A section had filled a whole tablet—and I went on into the B's. That was the way I started copying what eventually became the entire dictionary. It went a lot faster after so much practice helped me to pick up handwriting speed. Between what I wrote in my tablet, and writing letters, during the rest of my time in prison I would guess I wrote a million words.

9 I suppose it was inevitable that as my word-base broadened, I could for the first time pick up a book and read and now begin to understand what the book was saying. Anyone who has read a great deal can imagine the new world that opened. Let me tell you something; from then until I left that prison, in every free moment I had, if I was not reading in the library, I was reading on my bunk. You couldn't have gotten me out of books with a wedge. Between Mr. Muhammad's teachings, my correspondence, my visitors—usually Ella and Reginald—and my reading of books, months passed without my even thinking about being imprisoned. In fact, up to then, I never had been so truly free in my life. . . .

10 As you can imagine, especially in a prison where there was heavy emphasis on rehabilitation, an inmate was smiled upon if he demonstrated an unusually intense interest in books. There was a sizable number of well-read inmates, especially the popular debaters. Some were said by many to be practically walking encyclopedias. They were almost celebrities. No university would ask any student to devour literature as I did when this new world opened to me, of being able to read and *understand*.

11 I read more in my room than in the library itself. An inmate who was known to read a lot could check out more than the permitted maximum number of books. I preferred reading in the total isolation of my own room.

12 When I had progressed to really serious reading, every night at about ten P.M. I would be outraged with the "lights out." It always seemed to catch me right in the middle of something engrossing.

13 Fortunately, right outside my door was a corridor light that cast a glow into my room. The glow was enough to read by, once my eyes

adjusted to it. So when "lights out" came, I would sit on the floor where I could continue reading in that glow.

14 At one-hour intervals the night guards paced past every room. Each time I heard the approaching footsteps, I jumped into bed and feigned sleep. And as soon as the guard passed, I got back out of bed onto the floor area of that light-glow, where I would read for another fifty-eight minutes—until the guard approached again. That went on until three or four every morning. Three or four hours of sleep a night was enough for me. Often in the years in the streets I had slept less than that.

15 I have often reflected upon the new vistas that reading opened to me. I knew right there in prison that reading had changed forever the course of my life. As I see it today, the ability to read awoke inside me some long dormant craving to be mentally alive. I certainly wasn't seeking any degree, the way a college confers a status symbol upon its students. My homemade education gave me, with every additional book that I read, a little bit more sensitivity to the deafness, dumbness, and blindness that was afflicting the black race in America. Not long ago, an English writer telephoned me from London, asking questions. One was, "What's your alma mater?" I told him, "Books." You will never catch me with a free fifteen minutes in which I'm not studying something I feel might be able to help the black man. . . .

16 Every time I catch a plane, I have with me a book that I want to read—and that's a lot of books these days. If I weren't out here every day battling the white man, I could spend the rest of my life reading, just satisfying my curiosity—because you can hardly mention anything I'm not curious about. I don't think anybody ever got more out of going to prison than I did. In fact, prison enabled me to study far more intensively than I would have if my life had gone differently and I had attended some college. I imagine that one of the biggest troubles with colleges is there are too many distractions, too much panty-raiding, fraternities, and boola-boola and all of that. Where else but in prison could I have attacked my ignorance by being able to study intensely sometimes as much as fifteen hours a day?

FOR THINKING, DISCUSSING, AND WRITING

1. What does Malcolm imply when he says that people who come into contact with him "will think I went to school far beyond the eighth grade"? Why does Malcolm answer the question about his alma mater with the single word "Books"?

2. The writer says that he "spent two days just riffling uncertainly through the dictionary." and he refers to his "slow, painstaking, ragged handwriting." Why does he characterize his actions and writing in this manner? What effect(s) do you think he is trying to achieve?
3. Malcolm tells us that because of his reading, "months passed without my even thinking about being imprisoned. In fact, up to then, I had never been so truly free in my life." In what way is he "truly free"? How can books free people? What does this observation suggest about the value of education?
4. Obviously there are many kinds of education, and clearly, Malcolm X was "educated," to some extent, on the street (see paragraph 14) before he went to prison. What connection does he make between reading and education in general? What is the Interrelation between book learning and street learning? Write an essay to explore these questions.

TIMOTHY HARPER

They Treat Girls Differently, Don't They?

Timothy Harper (1950–) is a journalist and author who writes on education, technology, and society for a number of popular and professional publications. He teaches at Columbia University's Graduate School of Journalism. With his daughter Elizabeth Harper as coauthor he wrote Your Name in Print: A Teen's Guide to Getting Published for Fun, Profit, and Academic Success *(2005). In this selection from* Sky Magazine *he asserts that, "Boys get more attention in the classroom than girls."*

1 Boys get more attention in the classroom than girls. There's no doubt about it. Reams of studies show that teachers, from preschool to grade school, interact more with males than with females. Especially in grade school, boys are called on more often. They get more constructive criticism, and they're asked more challenging questions.

2 A landmark study by the American Association of University Women found that when science teachers need help with demonstrations in front of their classes, four out of five times they call on a boy rather than a girl.

3 Those are the facts. What those facts mean, however, is not so clear. Some parents and teachers believe studies on classroom gender bias are misleading. Others believe they show that girls are being shortchanged by American education.

4 An important point to keep in mind from the outset is that gender bias does not start in school. What happens in classrooms, good or bad, is a reflection of society at large. All of us—parents, teachers, administrators and students—have our baggage. Indeed, one of the remarkable aspects of the debate over classroom gender bias is the reluctance to blame anyone, especially teachers. Even the most vocal critics say teachers typically are not aware of the ways they show their own bias against girls; when it is pointed out, teachers are surprised and consciously try to treat boys and girls more equally.

5 While it is not within the scope of this article to suggest how to remedy a centuries-old cultural bias that generally favors males over females—in school, in the family and on the job—there are some things that educators, students and parents can do to counteract gender bias in the classroom.

6 Critics warn that classroom gender bias hurts girls in very real ways. They argue that when girls enter kindergarten they are just as outgoing as boys, and almost as interested in math and science. By the end of high school, according to studies, girls are more likely to suffer from low self-esteem and less likely to be taking courses in chemistry, calculus, computers and other science and technology fields that hold such great growth potential in the twenty-first century. Boys gain confidence and competence; girls lose it. Boys learn that school is a place of opportunity. Girls are taught that it is a place of constraints.

7 "I don't think teachers mean for it to happen—they don't realize there's gender bias in their own classrooms," observes Ellen Silber, director of the Institute for the Education of Women and Girls at Marymount College in Tarrytown, New York. Silber, whose research and consulting include teacher training and parent awareness programs, says teachers who are videotaped are surprised to see that they call on boys more often. "But blame is not the point," she notes. "Girls are being conditioned to think that boys are smarter, or that boys need more attention because they're pains in the neck."

8 Indeed, blame is not the issue for those of us who have young children. We don't want to raise boys who think they are automatically in charge, whether in the classroom today or in the boardroom tomorrow.

And we don't want to raise daughters who think they must wait to speak until all the boys are finished, or who might have been great scientists if only physics and chemistry hadn't been "boy subjects."

9 David Sadker, a professor of education at American University, did a number of studies with his late wife, Myra, showing gender bias to be deep-rooted in American classrooms. Their studies show that from grade school through graduate school, boys are more likely to shout out answers or otherwise make comments without being called on. Typically, teachers answered the boys who called out, but chastised the girls who called out with comments such as "Please raise your hand if you want to speak." Today, Sadker frets that a cure for cancer might be "locked in the mind" of a girl who never pursued the kind of science education that would unlock it.

10 Not everyone, of course, agrees that classroom gender bias is such a big problem. Diane Ravitch, the former assistant secretary of the U.S. Department of Education and now a research scholar at New York University, says we should instead be celebrating "the successful conquest of American education by girls and women." In 1970, she says, women accounted for barely 40 percent of the college students in the United States; today it's 55 percent. Women earned less than 10 percent of the law and medical degrees awarded in 1970; today, they make up nearly 50 percent of the enrollment in U.S. law schools and colleges of medicine.

11 Yes, boys get more attention than girls, but some say that doesn't mean teachers are biased against girls. David Murray, director of research for the Washington-based Statistical Assessment Service, a private, non-profit think tank that tries to debunk science myths, says, "The reality is that boys are far more disruptive, and what they get is more negative attention."

12 He says boys are more often found at the extremes of all types of performance, good and bad. Boys score higher on the Scholastic Aptitude Test and win more National Merit honors but also are more likely to have learning disabilities, drug or alcohol problems, and trouble with the law. Girls get better grades, are less likely to drop out of high school and are more likely to got to college and get a degree.

13 Pat O'Reilly, professor of education in the field of developmental psychology and head of educational studies at the University of Cincinnati, agrees that many teachers call on boys more—because they have shorter attention spans, and the teachers are trying to keep them

involved and interested. (Boys are also three times as likely to receive a diagnosis of attention-deficit learning disorders.) "How does this affect girls? They feel less involved and sometimes feel left out," says O'Reilly. "One of the ways we plan to deal with this issue is to encourage teachers to stop calling on the first person who raises a hand, because boys are more apt to raise their hands—even if it means the embarrassment and risk of the wrong answer.

14 "Maybe boys are more confident than girls . . . we're not quite sure. Girls tend to think about an answer before they respond. We are training teachers to be more patient and to wait a minute before they call on a student. We need to make sure that girls become more confident and we need to teach boys to think before they speak."

15 For whatever reason, boys and girls seem to learn differently. Boys are more individualistic and competitive. They create hierarchies and function well in them. Girls are less competitive and more willing to cooperate. Instead of creating hierarchies, they find ways to collaborate. For some educators and parents, the answer is to segregate boys and girls, though single-sex schools or classes may not be constitutional under recent court rulings.

16 Legal or not, I wouldn't want my daughter to attend special single-sex science classes. What message will that send her about boys? And I wouldn't want my son to be left in a classroom of boys. Is that going to teach him to empathize with girls? I want my daughter to be able to compete with the boys, and my son to be able to collaborate with the girls. The easy answer, of course, is for us to make education better for everybody. But how?

17 From assorted experts and studies, here is a list of recommendations for parents and teachers concerned about gender bias in the classroom.

Parents, at Home:

18 ■ Ask your daughter (and son) to draw a picture of a scientist. If she (or he) draws a man—most do—talk about how more and more girls are doing well in science studies and growing up to become scientists, too.

19 ■ Listen to your daughter. Girls' voices are naturally softer and girls are often less aggressive about speaking up, so you may have to draw her out. Don't criticize. She should know that her thoughts, feelings, opinions and experiences are valuable both to you and to herself.

20 ■ Encourage your daughter not to limit herself academically. Find mentors—older girls or women within or outside your family—whose academic and career achievements can serve as role models, and who are willing to talk to your daughter about their experiences and views.

21 ■ Play sports and engage in other physical activities, such as hiking or cycling, with your daughter. Encourage her to participate in sports—organized community or school teams and neighborhood pickup or playground games. If you put up a hoop for her in the driveway, she'll probably go out to shoot baskets.

22 ■ Encourage your daughter to keep a journal or diary, and to write and talk about her experiences and reactions to events large and small. Ask her for her opinion and for an explanation or defense of her point of view.

23 ■ If your daughter thinks a teacher is being unfair, in terms of calling on boys or anything else, encourage her to speak to the teacher. Many kids are too uneasy to do this, but many teachers are too busy to notice slights—real or imagined—unless a student speaks up.

24 ■ Criticize the media. Talk about the way women are portrayed on television and radio and in movies, magazines, newspapers and elsewhere. Why did that character do or say that? Is anyone really that silly? What would you have done?

Parents, at School:

25 ■ Talk to teachers. Let them know you're concerned about the issue of gender bias. Ask whether your daughter speaks up in class. How does she respond to teachers' questions? Does she initiate discussions and talk about what she thinks?

26 ■ Ask teachers what they think of your daughter. If they tend to use words such as "kind," "nice," "quiet" and "conscientious," let teachers know you're just as interested in your daughter's acquiring skills and developing talents as you are in her being a "good girl."

27 ■ Visit the classroom for an hour or two. Keep track of examples of competitive and collaborative learning and combinations of the two. Count the times teachers address boys vs. girls: responding to them when they call out, answering questions, calling on them, asking them easy or tough questions.

28 ■ Grade the teachers' comments: How much of what they say is disciplinary? Is the criticism constructive? Are the questions complex and challenging? Is the praise for girls more about being nice and

getting work in on time? Is praise for boys more about initiative and ideas? Are boys rewarded for calling out while girls are reprimanded?

29 ■ Talk to other parents. Compare notes, share concerns. Groups of parents are more likely to get a positive reaction, whether it's a teacher's promise to be more aware of gender bias or a principal's agreement to call a meeting or have a program on gender bias.

Teachers:

30 ■ Visit each other's classrooms, and talk about gender bias. Keep track of how other teachers relate to boys and girls, respectively. Record each other, either on audio- or videotape, and then go back and analyze the tapes.

31 ■ Don't always call on the first student to call out or raise a hand.

32 ■ Make sure to call on the quiet people, boys or girls, even if they don't raise their hands.

33 ■ Recruit role models from the community, both men and women, willing to come to the classroom and talk about their school and work experiences.

34 ■ Mix lectures and ask-and-answer reviews with exercises where students work in teams, collaborating instead of competing. Make sure different kids are appointed as the leaders for different team exercises and take turns speaking for the group.

35 ■ Give students a chance to speak to you privately about concerns they may not want to raise in front of the whole class.

FOR THINKING, DISCUSSING, AND WRITING

1. Do you agree that "what happens in classroom, good or bad, is a reflection of society at large"? Why or why not? What evidence does the writer provide to support his point?
2. Where, according to Harper, does gender bias begin? Do you agree? Why or why not? The writer says that "one of the remarkable aspects of the debate over classroom gender bias is the reluctance to blame anyone." Why does he think it is "remarkable"? Do you think it is? Why or why not?
3. Examine Harper's list of recommendations for parents and teachers concerned with classroom gender bias. Are the recommendations achievable? Which more than others? Why?
4. In paragraph 6 the writer states that "boys learn that school is a place of opportunity. Girls are taught that it is a place of constraints." Do you agree?

Why or Why not? What kinds of constraints might exist for girls? What kinds of opportunities for boys? What are some reasons critics give for boys receiving more attention than girls in the classroom? Do the reasons make sense to you? Why or why not?

SHELBY STEELE

Indoctrination Isn't Teaching

Shelby Steele (1946–), currently a research fellow at the Hoover Institute, is a writer and teacher. He won the 1991 National Book Critics Circle Award for general nonfiction, and his essays have appeared in Harper's, *the* American Scholar, *and the* New York Times. *He is also the author of* The Content of Our Character: A New Vision of Race in America *(1990),* The End of Oppression *(1997). and* A Dream Deferred; The Second Betrayal of Black Freedom in America. *In 2004, he won the National Humanities Medal. In this essay Steele focuses on black English as a function of "one of the most seductive and dangerous ideas in American education: self-esteem."*

1 At the heart of the furor over black English is one of the most seductive yet dangerous ideas in all of American education: self-esteem.

2 It is an idea with two parts. The first is the post-'60s notion that self-esteem is not only a condition for learning but is also as important a goal in the education of minority students as academic mastery itself. The second part is the belief that self-esteem comes as much from group identity as from individual academic success. Over time, this link between self-esteem and identity has caused the education of many minority children, particularly blacks, to be based more on identity enhancement than on high academic expectations.

3 This idea is the centerpiece of a strategy of racial reform that might be called indirection. By this strategy, minority problems are never directly addressed. Instead, they are understood and approached indirectly through their root causes, which are always said to flow from America's history of racism.

4 By forcing the discussion of minority problems into the area of root causes, indirection deflects us away from problem-solving and into yet another negotiation of who owes what to whom. This is not to say that black problems don't have root causes or that racism is not

one of them. The point is that indirection is an ingenious opportunism that makes root causes the only ones with a powerful claim on society's resources.

5 "Ebonics" is a case in point. It directs us away from the problem—the poor academic performance of black children—by emphasizing self-esteem and weak racial identity as the root causes of the problem, the only causes that truly matter. In the interest of self-esteem, of protecting black children from racial shame, ebonics makes broken English the equivalent of standard English. To further bolster identity, it is said that this form of speech has an African origin, despite the lack of evidence.

6 In the world of education, it is assumed that the self-esteem difficulties of black children stem from racial victimization. So, by making poor academic performance a problem of self-esteem and identity, ebonics invokes America's history of racism as the true root cause. Now we no longer have students with academic deficits; we have racial victims, identity victims.

7 Of course it is true that racial victimization—if only its legacy—plays some role in the poor performance of these students. But ebonics seeks to make victimization the only cause that counts. Its purpose is to shift responsibility for the problem away from the people who suffer it and onto society.

8 By seeing racial identity as the main source of the self-esteem of black children, we are left with little more than identity enhancement as a way to improve their performance. So when we find inner-city black children who are in desperate academic shape, we use their very desperation to justify a program of identity enhancement.

9 In Oakland, black English is transformed into a language with African roots. In Los Angeles, there is talk of expanding a small ebonics program to reach all 92,000 African-American students in the school district. In Milwaukee, two schools are devoted to Afrocentric teaching. In Detroit, Baltimore, and other cities there are all-black military-style academies and all-male classrooms.

10 Almost everywhere there is an unquestioned belief in role-model theory—matching black students with black teachers, often by sex as well. Now there is the idea that we can match racial identities with "styles of learning."

11 Teaching that is directed primarily as the group identity of at-risk black students offers an imagery of racial glory, which is a

kind of propaganda. This puts the black child in a rather absurd position. To garner the self-esteem to do well in school, he must believe that Egyptians flew to work in little gliders or that he has his own racial learning style. He must conform to an ideology in order to be smart.

12 The poor academic performance of black students should be approached directly, with a strong commitment to academic rigor. Nothing special should be done about their self-esteem or their racial identity. The focus of their education should shift from being to doing, from identity to academic mastery. They should be treated with warm human respect, but also with the understanding that high expectations are the only show of respect they will believe in the long run. They don't need rigor as much as they deserve it.

FOR THINKING, DISCUSSING, AND WRITING

1. Steele asserts that certain claims about ebonics lack sufficient evidence and yet people persist in believing them. What exactly is *ebonics*? Does Steele present any counterevidence, or does he simply assume his audience will agree with him? Do you agree with him? Why or why not?
2. Steele says that many people believe that "self-esteem comes as much from group identity as from individual academic success." What do you think about this point? Could his statement account for the popularity of gangs among teenagers? Discuss your reasons for agreeing or disagreeing.
3. Steele assails "the unquestioned belief in role-model theory"—that is, the idea that students learn better from members of their own sex or race. Do you agree with this point? Why or why not?
4. Write an essay in which you evaluate Steele's assertion in his title: "Indoctrination Isn't Teaching." Why might you agree or disagree with him? What kinds of lessons are, in fact, taught by "indoctrination"?

KATIE ROIPHE

Campus Climate Control

Katie Roiphe (1968–) holds a PhD in English literature from Princeton University. She writes regularly about the American scene. She is the author of The Morning After *(1993),* Last Night in Paradise *(1997), and* Uncommon

Arrangements: Seven Portraits of Married Life in London Literary Circles 1910–1939 (2007). *In this selection Roiphe deals with the issue of supervision and responsibility on today's college campuses. What is the role of adult authority in a world of young adult students?*

1 I remember the butter pats that covered the soaring ceiling of my freshman dining hall. They were the first sign that I had entered a world utterly devoid of adults. I remember my best friend passing out from inhaling nitrous oxide. I remember someone I know falling drunkenly off a fire escape, and ending up in the hospital. I remember groups of us breaking into the pool at night and swimming naked. This was not 1967. This was 1990.

2 By the time I arrived at college, the ideal of adult authority had been chipped away and broken down by a previous generation—by Watergate and Vietnam and drugs. And though we would have died rather than admit it, without it some of us were feeling lost. We had the absolute, shimmering freedom that had been dreamed up for us during the 60's. We had the liberating knowledge that no one cared what we did.

3 But it wasn't making us as happy as it was supposed to. I remember moments of exultation walking through the pink campus at dawn, but I also remember moments of pure terror.

4 During a particularly wild period of my senior year, a professor looked up from my essay on Robert Lowell's falling-out-of-love poetry, glanced at the violet circles under my eyes and said, "You really need to get some sleep." I stood there in my ripped jeans. I felt suddenly reassured. The adult world, where people wake up in the morning, pay their bills and take out the trash, was still intact.

5 It, therefore does not surprise me that students now want universities to act "in loco parentis" again, and that slightly perplexed baby-boom administrators are trying to find ways to accommodate them. Some of the practical ideas being floated around campuses seem absurd. Alcohol-free, adult-supervised student centers? Students will mock them. But they may serve a function by their mere existence.

6 Parents of teenagers are always embarrassing to adolescents, and institutions acting in loco parentis will also be embarrassing. The alcohol-free, adult-supervised student centers (or trips to the theater with professors, or more resident advisers) are simply signs of an adult presence. They offer tangible monuments to an authority that you can avoid or rebel against, but that nonetheless exists. You can find it on a campus map.

7 I remember the stories my mother told of climbing into her dorm room, wedging open the window, when she got back after curfew. Part of the thrill of rules, the perverse allure, is that they can be broken. Even when students are deliberately ignoring them, the fact of their existence is comforting. Rules give order to our chaos; they give us some sort of structure for our wildness so that it doesn't feel so scary.

8 At the heart of the controversy over whether colleges should act in loco parentis is the question of whether college students are adults or children, and of course they are neither. They are childish and sophisticated, naive and knowing, innocent and wild, and in their strange netherworld, they need some sort of shadow adult, some not-quite-parent to be there as a point of reference.

9 That said, some new rules being considered on campuses seem extreme—like the rule at Lehigh that there can be no campus parties without a chaperone. Surely there must be a way of establishing a benign and diffuse adult presence without students having to drink and dance and flirt and pick people up around actual adults.

10 Many students, including the one quoted in the *New York Times* heralding "the return to the era of Donna Reed,[1]" seem to like the superficial wholesomeness of the '50s. But what about the attitudes that informed it, like the sexism that tainted any college girl who enjoyed sex?

11 There must be a way to create some sort of structure without romanticizing or fetishizing the '50s. There must be a way of bringing back an adult presence on college campuses without treating students like children, a way of correcting the excesses of the sexual revolution without throwing away all of its benefits.

12 Americans are always drawn to extreme ideologies, to extremes of freedom or repression, of promiscuity or virginity, of wildness or innocence, but may be there is a middle ground, somewhere closer to where people want to live their actual lives. A university without butter pats on the ceiling, or 10 o'clock curfews.

FOR THINKING, DISCUSSING, AND WRITING

1. Consider the questions suggested by the title of Roiphe's piece. What exactly is *climate control*? What does it mean when applied to the atmosphere of a house or apartment, a business, an airplane, or an

[1] Donna Reed was a television performer who symbolized the surface righteousness and respectability of the '50s era in America.

automobile? Consider the word *climate*—and then the word *control*. What possible meanings can these words have separately? What might Roiphe have in mind when she links the phrase *climate control* with the word *campus*? What do you think climate control means in this context?

2. What are some of the escapades Roiphe recalls from her college days of the 1990s? What had eroded the idea of adult authority on campus by the time she arrived at college? What does "in loco parentis" mean? Why is Roiphe not surprised that college students today want their schools to act in loco parentis? According to her, are college students adults or children?
3. Do you agree with Roiphe that campus rules are important—even if one ignores or breaks them—simply because their presence is reassuring? Or do you think that rules serve a larger purpose? Explain your response.
4. Are the writer's recommendations about finding a middle ground feasible, do you think? Why or why not? In asserting her point here, she offers no example of what such a middle ground might be. What middle-ground proposal could you make for "bringing back an adult presence on college campuses without treating students like children"? How would your idea affect your own campus? Write an essay to explore these issues.

LEON BOTSTEIN

Curtailing High School: A Radical Proposal

Leon Botstein (1946–) is the president of Bard College in Annandale-on-Hudson in New York state, and he is the music director of the American Symphony Orchestra and the Jerusalem Symphony Orchestra. A classically trained violinist, his musical talents receive wide praise. He also takes a passionate interest in education—witness his book Jeffferson's Children: Education and the Promise of American Culture *(1977). In 1999 he edited* The Compleat Brahms *and in 2006 published* The History of Listening. *In this piece, Botstein argues against keeping students in high school as long as we do currently in America.*

1 The most pressing concern for the future of the American high school is correcting the fatal flaw in the way we educate adolescents, revealed through its inability to deliver excellence evenhandedly over the past 40 years. It is that failure from which we must learn. The high school

has outlived its usefulness to the point of catastrophe, not only with respect to those least privileged who live in the inner cities and poor rural districts of America. It has also let down the children of families with sufficient incomes to move to suburbia in hopes of finding superior public education there.

2 The primary cause for the inadequacy of high school rests with irreversible changes in adolescent development. The current system of public education was designed when the onset of puberty was three years later than it is today. Over the past century, the age of physical maturation has steadily dropped as a result of immunization and nutritional standards. Before World War II, 18, the traditional age of high school graduation, was two or three years after maturation. That age also coincided with the onset of adult sexual activity. In the beginning of the 21st century, 16-year-old Americans are, in development and behavior, comparable to the 18-year-olds of a century ago. High school was designed to deal with large children. It is now faced with young adults whose adult behavior has already begun.

3 Neither the personnel, the buildings, the schedule nor the curriculum of high school can satisfy the presumptions of adulthood that today's high school age adolescents legitimately bring with them. The issue is not whether today's adolescents are more mature because of earlier development. The fact is they are *able* to act as adults whether they do so responsibly or not. They are treated by our consumer society as adults; the fashion industry and Hollywood recognize their role as consumers. Modern transportation and communication have given adolescents the freedom of movement we associate with adulthood. Neither community nor home effectively limits their freedom of movement.

4 Plans to extend the high school education to five years, or to expand the degree-granting range, fly in the face of social and biological facts. The freedom in learning, the dignity of serious study and the access to the deep command of subject matter that adulthood and higher education require are not available in the American high school today, nor can they be created within the current high school framework. The Advanced Placement courses that are taught, for example, are largely substandard and inferior to what is available in most colleges. The definition of what constitutes the Advanced Placement curriculum is dictated not by the teacher, but by a private testing agency. No university or college of standing permits such a

system to define its standards. The professional preparation, autonomy and academic freedom characteristic of the faculty in American higher education do not exist and cannot flourish within the walls of the American high school. Yet these qualities are essential to the high standards in science, mathematics, history and all other subjects to which adolescents can aspire.

5 The future of the American high school rests with shifting its existing curriculum and practices to younger students and reforming these practices as the shift takes place. In other words, during the next decade, we should rationalize our education system into a two-part elementary and secondary system that ends at age 16. Already it is estimated that more than 1 million young Americans complete their high school education outside the walls of the high school. The majority of college-bound seniors admit that their final year of high school is a waste of time. Increasingly, that criticism is being leveled at the last two years. The high school should, therefore, replace the junior high school and refocus its energies on a younger population, from the ages of 13 to 16.

6 In place of a high school that ends at age 18, the education system should offer multiple options for those between 16 and 19. With a high school diploma, a 16-year-old could choose to attend a community college, to enter a four-year college, or to engage in work, internships or other alternatives to formal school, as well as perhaps national service. We must maintain the democratic pattern of the American educational system by allowing individuals to start college at any time, not necessarily immediately after completing high school. The most important gain from shifting high school graduation to age 16 would be that we would no longer "infantilize" older adolescents and retard their intellectual development.

FOR THINKING, DISCUSSING, AND WRITING

1. How, according to Botstein, has the inadequacy of America's high school system revealed itself? What would we gain (according to the writer) if we adopted his suggestions to reform it?
2. Has Botstein convinced you that his suggestion for ending high school early is a good one? Why or why not?
3. What evidence does Botstein offer to support his argument that teenagers have changed over the years? How effective is this evidence?

4. Write an essay about what is *right* with today's high schools. Refute any of Botstein's arguments that you don't find convincing. Draw on your own experience as well as on research about the effects of high school education on American society.

JAMES ATLAS

Making the Grade

James Atlas (1949–) was born in Chicago. A critic as well as an editor and journalist, his essays appear frequently in the New Yorker. *He is the author of biographies of poet Delmore Schwartz (1977) and novelist Saul Bellow (2007).* The Book Wars *(1990) was an examination of literature instruction at the university level. A memoir,* My Life in the Middle Ages: A Survivor's Tale, *appeared in 2005. In this essay for the* New Yorker, *Atlas weighs the responsibilities of parents whose young children attend private school and wonders if he and his wife are up to the job of being obsessed "with every detail of our children's lives."*

1 At three o'clock on a drizzly weekday afternoon. I stand on the corner of Madison and Ninety-sixth in an orange nylon vest, with a whistle hanging around my neck, clutching a walkie-talkie and scanning the street for signs of trouble—gangs of teenage thugs, lurkers in raincoats, any ripple of urban disorder that could menace the homebound journey of the boys of St. Bernard's School. I'm on Safety Patrol. Armed with a pamphlet of instructions on "What to Do in Case of an Emergency," I'm in a state of wary preparation, and so is my partner on this blustery day—a cardiologist, whose son is in my son's class, and who has probably left a few bypass candidates lying in intensive care, waiting for a pig's valve to be installed in their chests, while he's out making Carnegie Hill safe for our children.

2 I like wearing this vest and hearing the self-important crackle of the walkie-talkie as I stride about the Upper East Side, bantering with mothers and nannies and tradesmen like a neighborhood cop on the beat. It imbues me with an aura of authority. And kids do get assaulted from time to time: just a few months ago, there was an incident near Nightingale-Bamford, my daughter's school, four blocks away. But sometimes I wonder why, in addition to the huge tuition I'm paying, I have to suit up in the vestments of a crossing guard in the middle of a

workday and trudge up and down Madison Avenue for two hours in the rain. "I give them fifteen thousand long ones a year," one mother complained to me. "I have to put on a bright-orange mommy poncho, too?"

3 I'm back in the office by five—not too bad, really. (I've been known to come back at this hour from a long lunch.) But the next afternoon I'm supposed to be on duty again, attending a meeting of the school Library Committee. Boy, am I busy! What with serving as a sommelier at the Fathers Who Cook dinner, attending "the first Class VII Parents in Action Meeting," lacing up my kids' Chargers on Great Skate Night at Wollman Rink, attending a performance of "Iolanthe," and hawking raffle tickets for the school fund drive door to door in our building, who has time for work? Sometimes I fret. Which stocks are tanking while the broker from Goldman, Sachs is at his daughter's basketball game? What perp is on the loose while the district attorney organizes the Father-Daughter Breakfast? Can the citizenry of New York City afford to have the parents of school-age children keeping these indentured-servant hours?

4 On Parents' Night at Nightingale, the headmistress delivered a stern tripartite admonition: make sure your children read; make sure they don't get overscheduled; and, lastly, stay home more. Be there for them. Fine: I'm sick of going out. But how can I stay home when I have to attend the annual Fathers' Dinner at the University Club and the Parents' Potluck Supper? Then, there's the New Parents' Breakfast, and C.A.F.E.—Cultural Awareness for Everyone night. "My daughter walks in the door from school, and I'm rushing off to a Parents-and-Partnership Tea," one mother says. "The whole thing is nuts."

5 It's a full-time job, being a parent these days. You're always on. "Every time I drop my kid off at school, I feel as if I'd just been to a cocktail party," a Spence dad says. The rules are: no jogging suit, no rumpled shirt, no spotted corduroys. The other day, I was standing on the corner with my son at seven-thirty in the morning, waiting for a crosstown bus and munching on a doughnut, when another dad pulled up in his Range Rover and offered us a ride. As I slid in next to him, admiring his nailhead suit, I noticed with horror the dusting of powdered sugar on my sweatpants. What would the parents of St. Bernard's think of me? Would my slovenliness hurt my kid's reputation at school? We're all in this together.

6 The obsession with every detail of our children's lives is largely a private-school phenomenon. My parents rarely entered the public schools in the Midwest where I got my education. I'm certain they

attended the fourth-grade performance of "Snow White and the Seven Dwarfs" at Ravinia School (I had the part of Dopey, and wore one of my mother's silk stockings on my head); and I believe I can reliably place them at Field Day, cheering me on in the hundred-yard dash. But that's about it. They never showed up on Parents' Visiting Day, the way I do, cramming into an overheated classroom on the Upper East Side with thirty other parents who've taken the morning off to audit a class discussion on slave conditions in the Old South. There *was* no Parents' Day. "My mother only went to school to vote," a mother from Michigan confirms.

7 And there weren't all these parent-teacher conferences, either—these Get to Know Your Children's Teacher Nights. I'd he surprised if my parents even knew my teachers' names. That was the joy of it: back in the fifties and sixties, the relationships you had with your teachers were your own business. "Wasn't everyone you know saved by that one English teacher who gave you a glimpse of a better life?" asks a mother who grew up in a New England mill town and now works in publishing. "Mine would invite me over for espresso after school and give me books to read." I had one of those, too—a fierce-eyed woman with a burning love of Dylan Thomas. She once appeared at my door when I was home sick and sat at the kitchen table with me correcting the page proofs of *Word Mosaic*, the school literary magazine. Today, she'd probably be afraid of getting sued for sexual harassment of a minor. And where was my mother during this editing session? Out.

8 I'm not saying they weren't good parents. It's just that they were largely absent—the norm in those days, when kids bicycled to school unsupervised and idled away their afternoons in front of the neighborhood candy store without their parents' having to worry that they would be kidnapped by some crazed child molester out on parole. The world was safe—or safer, anyway, than it is now. As for the neighborhood candy store, it has gone the way of the soda fountain and the drive-in movie. When I was ten years old, I hung out at Strauss's, where you could buy a strip of Candy Buttons—dabs of candy on a scroll of white paper—for five cents; thirty-seven years later, I stop in at Canard, the gourmet-food shop around the corner from my daughter's school, to pick up an afterschool snack of petits fours and designer lollipops: the bill comes to twelve ninety-five.

9 Field trips have changed, too. My children come home and report that they've attended a lecture on Egyptian hieroglyphics at the

Metropolitan Museum or a master violin class at Carnegie Hall; parents are expected to serve as chaperones on these excursions. The only field trip I can recall going on as a child was to Dewey's Dairy Farm: I patted a cow. There were no mothers on the bus.

10 Where were our parents, anyway? The dads arrived home late for dinner after a long commute, their bulging briefcases filled with work; the mothers did errands all day, or sweated in the laundry room making piles of sock balls. It didn't bother me that they weren't around: solitude was sweet. Today, sitting at the counter of Starbucks in my orange vest on a coffee break, I have a memory of the last time I wore one: forty years ago, when I was a patrol boy in Highland Park, Illinois, wielding a big red "Stop" sign at an intersection several blocks from school. After the last kid crossed, I dawdled up the empty street, legally late and happy to be alone. Alone: that's how I remember my childhood. "A yellow school bus took us to school and took us home, we played in the back yard by ourselves," a father who grew up on Long Island recalls. "My parents had their own lives to live. Their goal was linoleum on the floor." More than a few parents of my generation report their own parents' bewilderment over our neurotic absorption in our children: Why do you make such a big deal over how your kids *feel* all the time? I never worried about how you felt, I worried about how *I* felt."

11 There certainly wasn't so much equipment back then. On Fridays, I lug to school a duffelbag stuffed with gear for my son's hockey practice: shoulder pads, knee pads, elbow pads, mouth guard, helmet, padded pants, crotch cup, jersey, gloves. An astronaut could suit up faster. Wrestling his bag onto the bus, I think back to my own hockey days, in a public grammar school: the rink was a rough oval of splintered wooden boards and bumpy ice. My uniform consisted of a nylon ski parka, a hockey stick, and a pair of plastic shin guards. The games were pickup, and ended when it was dark. I walked home with my skates tied together by the laces and dangling from the end of my stick like a hobo's bundle. I was happy.

12 "The era of the child," as sociologists refer to our offspring-centered age, is fairly new. For centuries, no one paid much attention to children. Too many died, for one thing. American frontier parents, knowing that maybe two-thirds of their children weren't going to make it, developed a prophylactic indifference. In Europe, neglect was a given. As Philippe

Ariés documents in his classic "Centuries of Childhood," children in the Middle Ages were relegated to the lowly status of beggars. In pre-Revolutionary France, children were third-class citizens: they weren't to be heard *or* seen. Hustled off to a wet nurse in the provinces the minute they were born, they returned home at the age of three or four and disappeared into the scullery to be looked after by the help; on formal occasions they were decked out in elaborate costumes and briefly paraded in front of their parents before being remanded to the servants. The novelty of Rousseau's famous book "Émile, ou de l'Éducation" was its radical argument that parents *should* notice their children. "What is this rich man, this busy father, doing?" Rousseau taunted, deploring the use of tutors as surrogate parents. "Paying another man to discharge those duties which are peculiarly his. Venal soul! Can you believe money will buy your son another father?"

13 By the nineteenth century, the notion that families should have a little as possible to do with children had been institutionalized in the rise of the boarding school. Ariés explains, "The school was substituted for society in which all the ages were mingled together; it was called upon to mould children on the pattern of an ideal human type." To this day, the chartering classes in Britain maintain a laissez-faire attitude toward their children's education. A friend whose three daughters attend the posh Dragon School, in Oxford, invokes a household rule: "No attending a play unless the child has ten lines or more."

14 It's only in America that—to cite the title of the famous Delmore Schwartz story—"The Child Is the Meaning of This Life." We've made a fetish out of schooling. Partly, I think, this has to do with the general fanaticism of Americans: getting it right, or trying to, is a dottily endearing national trait. Whether it's marriage or children or health or religion, we're compulsively pragmatic. In our child-rearing, this "perfectibility of man" aspiration manifests itself in a whole array of goods and services: private coaching sessions to boost S.A.T. scores, camps for the overweight, manners tutoring for the Park Avenue set. I have in hand a brochure from the Barclay Classes, which offer instruction in the "practice of good manners" and "all phases of ballroom dancing." You can even send your children to a hotel in Florida where they're taught how to invest in the stock market. When I was nine years old, my grandma Rae gave me five shares of Motorola. "Hey, Mom, it's up a third!" I'd cry, poring over the stock pages of the *Sun-Times* as I gobbled Wheaties in our breakfast nook.

15 Of course, it's easy to make fun of all this nervous striving on behalf of our children, but we have reason to worry. As Olivier Bernier noted in "Pleasure and Privilege," his brilliant history of late-eighteenth-century Europe and America, "middle-class children would one day be expected to earn money and further the family fortunes: they had to be educated accordingly." The children of Park Avenue are probably safe for another generation or two of drowsing over their Latin conjugations, but my kids *have* to succeed. There's no trust fund, no financial safety net. "A lot of people out there are one step away from being downsized," says Dr. Robert Evans, a psychologist and school consultant based in Wellesley, Massachusetts; his specialty is parents in the nineties. "This is the first time that white-collar families have had the economic worries that blue-collar parents have always had. You know that Bob Dylan line? 'Twenty years of schoolin' and they put you on the day shift.'" No wonder those of us caught in the middle—somewhere between the privileged and the working classes—care so much about which nursery school our kids attend: where they are at the age of four can determine where they are at the age of forty. (This is why France and England don't share our pedagogic mania: the more rigid the class structure, the more indifferent a society is to education.)

16 But it's not just fear of falling through the middle-class safety net that makes us pushy, it's who we are. The parents of the nineties are the children of the sixties. We have insanely high expectations, and our kids represent another sphere in which to achieve. One school administrator complains, "I'm amazed that parents will call me up and demand that their children change sections: 'I want Johnny in Level 1 Math!' Never mind that Johnny can't *do* Level 1 Math." The parents' attitude is, Hey, we're paying for this. "They have a greater sense of entitlement," the administrator says. "They want more bang for their buck."

17 I can see why. Membership in the Leadership Gift Club at my daughter's school will cost you from nineteen hundred and twenty dollars for the 1920 Founders Society all the way up to fifteen thousand for the 75th Anniversary Circle. Private schools actually list your donation in a pamphlet, classified by how much you gave. (Thank God for the $1–$499 category.) You're supposed to participate in auctions and benefits—"An Evening on Broadway," "The Saturday Jamboree"—designed to extract still more cash. And then my wife and I pay out somewhere between forty-five and seventy-five dollars several times a year so that our daughter can attend "charity dances." The money goes to good

causes—community-service centers and children's-cancer wards—but a quick run-through on the calculator tots up almost another thousand a year in the debit column. At least we're spared on Grandparents' Visiting Day, when pitches are made to *our* parents, half of whom have probably just finished paying off the debt they accumulated while they were putting us through school, and need whatever small nest egg remains to pay for the nursing home. Sometimes I get the feeling that the militant emphasis on school togetherness is just another way of priming the donation pump. (In fairness, tuition doesn't cover the costs at these schools; it generally falls several thousand dollars short per student—a million dollars a year short, all told, at my son's school. "Endowment income and annual giving of remarkable proportions make up the rest," the headmaster of St. Bernard's wrote in an elegant letter accompanying this year's fee schedule.)

18 Forking over all this dough doesn't get you off the hook. An admissions officer told me, "I've added a question to the application: What kind of parents are they going to be? Are they going to be active parents, or are they just going to be *nudges*?" The pressure to maintain a high profile is hard to ignore—especially for mothers. "You're punished if you don't show up at school functions," one high-powered-lawyer mom said to me bitterly. "There's this kind of accusatory 'Why wasn't she at the mailing on Thursday?'" The mothers who don't work feel threatened by the ones who do; the ones who do feel guilty. "The less time they spend with their children, the more they need to believe they're in control," an administrator says. "It's like, 'No, I didn't see my child today, but I spoke to her French teacher.'" Parents don't establish rules at home, Dr. Evans notes. They're lax about "boundary-setting." And the less they discipline their children the more likely they are to call in a lawyer as soon as there's a conflict: "If a kid comes home and complains, 'Miss Smith was mean to me,' the parent no longer says, in the old-fashioned way, 'What did you do to Miss Smith?' but 'What did Miss Smith do?' They're not prepared to have a child work out a difficult situation on his own."

19 This parental hyper-involvement isn't confined to the weird precincts of Manhattan. It's a class thing. At Francis Parker, a private school on the North Side of Chicago, parental attendance at "morning exes" (morning exercises, or the nineties version of assembly) is virtually required. Celebrated Parker parents—among them the diva Catherine Malfitano and the movie critic Gene Siskel—are recruited

for question-and-answer sessions in the school cafeteria. In L.A., where thirty or forty children are competing for each place in high-prestige toddler groups, the family applies as a unit. "It's what the parents bring to the party," a producer says. "There are cadres of mothers who 'do' school. That's their career—and they're just as aggressive about it as any studio head."

20 Public-school families have the opposite problem. The schools are going broke, and parents are an ever-diminishing presence. The publicity literature of the National PTA is defiantly upbeat, featuring a clutch of beaming kids on the cover of its annual report, but the graph of "membership in millions" tells a different story: it's down from 11.93 in 1960 to 7.02 in 1990. Most working parents don't have time for the PTA—they're too busy making ends meet.

21 Public schools in prosperous neighborhoods seem to be exempt from this trend. "We're all big volunteers," one mother who lives on Chicago's affluent North Shore told me. The school lunches are served by parents; the teams are coached by the dads. But the parents don't do these things just out of enthusiasm; they're helping to compensate for the lack of government funds. "It's about dwindling dollars and escalating costs," the Chicago mother says. "The teachers' salaries consume eighty per cent of the budget. Who's paying for foreign-language programs? The PTA!"

22 I shouldn't complain: the education I'm paying so dearly for is far superior to the one I had. When I drop off my daughter at school and see the girls trooping through the doors in their navy-blue skirts, their backpacks crammed with Latin and French textbooks, I'm stunned by how crisp and professional the place is. It wasn't like this at my old grammar school, with its gloomy corridors and dust-bowl athletic field, the El train rumbling past. My daughter can rattle off the causes of the Revolutionary War; her best friend produced an oral report on Islamic medicine in the Middle Ages. "She comes home and talks about 'Great Expectations,'" a Brearley dad says in bewilderment. "Last night, her homework assignment was to write a theme on class-consciousness in Victorian England—in 'Dickensian style'!" I memorized the names of the Presidents and nearly burned our house down baking fake parchment paper in the oven.

23 The children aren't the only ones who benefit. Despite my doubts about whether I'm up to the job, my kids' schools have become my

surrogate community. One of the anomalies of New York life is how atomized it feels. Church and synagogue don't command our attention; apartment-building lobbies are no substitute for the back-yard fence. And so many of us are from somewhere else; we've forfeited the natural network of the extended family. As a result, we're forced to fall back on our own resources. What all these feverish school activities do is remove us from the isolation of the nuclear family. They've created a new arena of social life. "School provides you with an instant club," a journalist with a child at Dalton says. "I was the kind of person who never joined a clique in school. Now I get to be part of this warm, fuzzy group."

24 I have to admit, there's something comforting about the extracurricular rituals—the outings and conferences and parties. To huddle in the bleachers as an Arctic wind whips across the tundra of Central Park in January, the fathers clutching cups of coffee and muttering into their cell phones, a mom tending the nets as the boys skate up and down the ice in a jostling pack, gives you a bonding high. But I also have a suspicion that something has been lost. Childhood is so regimented now. Pickup baseball games have been replaced by organized after-school sports, with squads of "professional" coaches shepherding the kids to practices and drills. There's the West Side Soccer League, the Cavaliers Athletic Club, the St. Bernard's Tennis Clinic. On Saturday mornings, the kids attend art classes at the Museum of Modern Art or Children's Concerts at Avery Fisher Hall. And they can't just go: you have to sign them up, buy tickets for them, enroll them. It's as if experience itself had become privatized.

25 I wonder if, in our zeal to shield our kids, we haven't shielded them too well. They're in such a rarefied atmosphere that they don't get what regular life is really like—they don't know kids from the other side of the tracks, or "bad kids" (the ones we called "hoods"), or the pleasures thrown up by unstructured time. A few weeks ago, I picked up my daughter at midnight after a dance at the Mark Hotel, on East Seventy-seventh Street. She had spent the day shopping for a black silk evening bag to go with her outfit. Inside the Mark, a rock band was going full tilt; go-go dancers outfitted in red silk were dancing among the tables, leading a conga line of thirteen-year-olds in Dr. Seuss hats. The party-favor bag dispensed to each guest was stuffed with gold-lamé sunglasses, fancy balloons, a leather CD pouch. What did I do on Saturday night when I was thirteen? I went to the Plant Room in the basement of the Y.M.C.A. and did the Twist while Chubby Checker blasted away on a cheap record-player.

26 Nostalgia can be a distorting emotion. I can't pretend that the family gathered around our dinner table and passing the meat loaf was ideal, or that it was a happy adolescent who loitered in the park at the end of our street unsupervised on summer nights, watching the distant lights of Chicago shimmer on Lake Michigan. But I remember the idleness as dreamlike. I'm haunted by an image in John Updike's "Self-Consciousness," from a passage where he dawdles in the classroom, finishing an illustration for the school's mimeographed (mimeographed!) monthly: "Dusk was gathering in the tall windows that needed a window pole to close, here in this emptied school building, where the overhead lights floated like deflated moons and my cartoon turkey or Santa Claus was building, slow line by line, white cut into soft warm blue." No parents looking over your shoulder, no teachers offering advice—in short, no organized activities. Just a boy sitting by himself at his desk after school, drawing a picture. It's an experience my kids will never know.

FOR THINKING, DISCUSSING, AND WRITING

1. What benefits does Atlas enumerate from his children's private school education? Why does he say that in public schools "parents are an ever-diminishing presence"?
2. How, according to Atlas, did parents past cultures—such as those on the American frontier and in nineteenth-century British families—deal with their children's education?
3. How do the personal narrative and descriptive details—especially at the beginning but throughout the essay as well—contribute to the effectiveness of the essay?
4. Atlas remarks that being a parent these days is "a full-time job." He suggests in several places that modern parents are "obsessed" with every detail of their children's lives. Write an essay in which you either agree or disagree with his point. How does the world today put special demands on parents who want to rear their children well?

CONNECTING IDEAS: What Is Education?

1. Race, ethnicity, gender, and economic standing have a profound effect on education—and vice versa. Examine some of the selections in this chapter and propose a connection among these issues. Argue your point by making specific references to the texts you have chosen.

2. Several pieces in this chapter reveal atypical or unconventional approaches to education. Write an essay in which you analyze some of these approaches and explain why you agree or disagree with them as viable options for teaching and learning.
3. If James Thurber ("University Days") and Katie Roiphe ("Campus Climate Control") could have a conversation about higher education, what do you think they would talk about? Write an essay to explain your conclusions.

CHAPTER 4

A Life of Work, a Quest for Wealth

NO ONE CAN SAY WHEN PHYSICAL LABOR, ONCE SIMPLY required for human survival, turned into the concept of "work" with its human components of self-gratification and personal fulfillment on the one hand and boredom and tedium on the other. Ernest Hemingway, one of America's most famous novelists, echoes a predominant outlook on work since the early days of our nation. "Work," he wrote, "could cure almost anything." In almost absolute opposition to what we call the Protestant work ethic, Karl Marx, the renowned Russian philosopher, proclaimed that work under capitalism as we know it, for much of the world's population, is no more than wage slavery. You'll see these opposite views reflected to some degree in Linda Hogan's "Waking Up the Rake" and William Branigin's "Sweatshops Are Back," two essays in this chapter.

Yet the modern world largely agrees with the values implicit in Hemingway's view: work hard and the good life awaits. Think for a moment about how jobs and financial payoff for work well done have become a central force in our society. The media report regularly on the incredible fortunes of the wealthy: Bill Gates, Microsoft's creator and leader, reportedly the world's wealthiest man; Warren Buffett and Malcolm Forbes, financiers and business moguls; Hollywood's magic circle of multi-million-dollar-a-picture actors like Tom Cruise and Julia

Roberts; major league sports figures like Alex Rodriguez and Barry Bonds with multiyear contracts for unimaginable amounts. (Through the end of 2005 Bonds earned more than $153 million, with Rodriguez not far behind.) The title of a bestselling book in the late '90s, *The Millionaire Next Door*, says it all perhaps: the possibility and actuality of wealth lie just at the end of our reach. For better or worse, jobs and their promise dominate educational purpose: many of our efforts at educating people survive only in a job context within the even narrower sphere of money-making and wealth accumulation. You'll be interested to read about the shameful overindulgence Quentin Hardy, another essayist here, sees among the rich and superrich in "Showing Off."

Despite our devotion to work, financial reward, and wealth, many communities and nations still struggle with a survival-level existence. The countries in Africa cannot feed their populations; famine in North Korea fills the news; devastation from the tsunami in Asia and the hurricanes in Louisiana have paralyzed what we would consider the normal development of work for reward. Unemployed young men line the streets in developing nations—no jobs, no skills, not much future. Additionally, the realities of work emerge from a variety of competing perspectives, like labor diasporas, labor rights and safety, child labor, resurgent sweatshops, illegal immigrant labor, women in the workplace. Although technology and trade arrangements connect nations on our ever-shrinking globe, work opportunities for the underprivileged are few and far between.

In chat groups and on websites around the world, people question the practices of multinational corporations employing under-aged and often abused child workers in regions of poverty to create luxuries for moneyed youth in the affluent society. In boardrooms, executives question old formulas of employment; in classrooms and journals, academics question old notions of wealth and capital, seeking new definitions for our new era. When is enough too much? Can a baseball player really be worth so many times more for his services than a nurse or a physician or a teacher? Can we justify a rock star's annual income in the millions when medical research units close down for want of funds and health care quality declines? Or are these simply the realities of a capitalist society blessed with progress and the good life for a large percentage but not all of its citizens?

As readers and writers who are also present or future members of the workforce and participants in careers and professions, we cannot ignore the great implications of our engagement in the debate. The writers in this chapter try to make sense of the realities of wealth and work, and offer a forum for participation in the ongoing query into work and how it shapes individual, national, and global life.

WILLIAM BRANIGIN

Sweatshops Are Back

William Branigin (1952–) is a staff writer for the Washington Post, *where he was the Southeast Asian correspondent until 1995. In 2000, the Center for Immigration Studies presented him with the Eugene Katz Award For Excellence in the Coverage of Immigration for informed and fair reporting on the topic. Branigin in this essay revisits working conditions long thought to have faded from the American scene.*

1 After an arduous trek across the border from her native Mexico, Aurora Blancas made her way to New York City and took the first job she could find: sweeping floors and packaging clothes sewn by other illegal immigrants at a sweatshop in the garment district.

2 No experience—or documents—necessary.

3 "I started working the same day I asked for the job," she says. "The boss asked me my name and how old I was. Nothing more."

4 But unlike her fellow workers, Blancas, 28, did not accept quietly the exploitation and abuse that followed when she was hired last summer to work in the dilapidated Eighth Avenue building.

5 Although her willingness to speak out makes Blancas unusual, the place that employed her and the conditions she found there are not.

6 Despite a ledger of laws against them and periodic pledges by government and business leaders to crack down, sweatshops have made a remarkable comeback in America, evolving from a relative anomaly into a commonplace, even indispensable, part of the U.S. garment industry.

7 They have also evolved almost entirely into a phenomenon of immigrants. According to federal investigators and union officials, most such factories are owned by newcomers from Asia, who often exploit other immigrants, many of them illegal, either from Asia or Latin America. Typically, both the workers and the employers see themselves as victims of a system dominated by increasingly powerful major retailers.

8 In Blancas's case, the owner of the 14th-floor shop in which she worked is a South Korean immigrant whose clothes are sold to suppliers of such stores as Wal-Mart and Kmart. According to Blancas and another former worker, he refused to pay the minimum wage or overtime to his three dozen, mostly female employees. The workers typically toiled at their sewing machines and presses for up to 60 hours a week in a room with wires hanging from the ceiling, three small fans that served as the only source of ventilation and no fire exits. Wages, usually paid in cash to avoid taxes, often were arbitrarily cut or delayed if the owner ran short of funds. Employees who missed a day would be illegally "fined" $30, on top of losing a day's pay.

9 When workers made mistakes, the owner's wife would scream at them, throw garments in their faces and sometimes pull their hair or hit them. One newly arrived young woman was summarily fired for yawning on the job.

10 Last July, after Blancas demanded higher wages and brought the sweatshop to the attention of a garment workers union, she was fired.

11 Whether operating openly in decrepit buildings in New York or Los Angeles or hidden away illegally in people's homes in Dallas, sweatshops violate labor and tax laws amid cutthroat competition for orders that filter down from the retailers.

12 The return of the kind of sweatshops that flourished early this century—and were thought to have been largely eliminated—reflects fundamental changes in the garment industry and, more broadly, in American society. The shops have become part of a vast underground economy, shielded by an overlay of laissez-faire practices and tacit accommodations.

13 Clothing designers and retailers depend on the sweatshops for fast delivery and big profit margins. Unions, hopeful of eventually organizing these workers, appear to be more interested in preserving manufacturing jobs than driving them out of business. Large pools of illegal immigrants are so anxious for work that they accept the shops' meager wages and are often too fearful to complain. Consumers keep gravitating toward the lowest prices they can find. And government agencies do not field enough investigators or cooperate sufficiently with each other to pursue the shops effectively and enforce the laws that would eradicate them.

14 Helping sweatshops to thrive have been technological advances that allow retailers to determine instantly what is selling and to order

more of it. This allows stores to limit inventory and avoid getting stuck with large volumes of unpopular apparel. But it also requires quick turnaround, which favors domestic manufacturers. The pressures on these manufacturers to produce garments quickly and still compete with cheap foreign imports have tended to drive down wages and working conditions among the sewing shops that lie at the bottom of the industry.

15 Yet, there is no shortage of workers for these jobs because of a broader change in American society: increasing waves of legal and illegal immigration since the 1970s and growing concentrations of immigrants in cities such as Los Angeles and New York.

16 The sweatshops' revival also reflects a weakening of unions in the garment industry in recent years, in part because of their difficulties in trying to organize workers who are here illegally in the first place. For them, even a sub-minimum wage in the United States generally beats what they could earn in their homelands.

17 Although the clandestine nature of much of the industry has made it hard to track, recent federal studies point to a rise in the number of U.S. sweatshops and a worsening of their conditions.

18 Union and Labor Department officials estimate that minimum wage and overtime violations, two of the basic parameters that define a sweatshop, prevail in more than half the 22,000 U.S. sewing businesses. Many also pay their workers "off the books" to avoid various local, state and federal taxes.

19 The sweatshop conditions described by Blancas are "typical of the bottom of the industry," says Jeff Hermanson, director of the Garment Workers' Justice Center, a branch of the Union of Needletrades, Industrial and Textile Employees.

20 "Physical abuse is unfortunately quite common, and there's always the yelling," he says. The long hours, low wages and lack of benefits often found in Korean-owned sweatshops are also routine in shops run by Chinese and Latino owners, he says.

21 In New York, a garment center where much of the industry's changing dynamics play out, Koreans own up to 40 percent of the city's roughly 4,000 contract sewing shops. Chinese immigrants own almost all the rest. Yet, the Korean-owned shops have attracted relatively more attention from labor investigators, mostly because they tend to hire Latino workers, who are less reluctant to complain than Asian employees.

22 Chinese-owned shops tend to hire only other Chinese, says Maria Echaveste, administrator of the Labor Department's wage and hour division. In some cases, she says, workers have expressed fear for their lives if they reveal labor violations. Many Chinese sweatshop workers are believed to be indentured servants toiling under a form of debt bondage to pay off the heavy cost of being smuggled into the United States.

23 "The workers lie to us," one investigator says. "In Chinese shops, the falsification of records is absolutely down to a science. It's almost impossible to break unless the shop goes out of business. It's only then that workers tell us those were not the hours and rates they worked."

24 In the Korean-owned shops, poor working conditions are often exacerbated by the lack of a common language between the Koreans and their mostly young, female Latino employees.

25 "They [the Korean owners] think they can make themselves understood by yelling," says Hermanson of the Garment Workers' Justice Center, which tries to organize workers and defend them in disputes with shop owners. The result, especially when owners hit their workers, is an "atmosphere of terror and intimidation," he says.

26 The Korean Apparel Manufacturers Association says it has been trying to get its 400 member companies in New York to pay at least the minimum wage. Most now do so, the group says. But these owners are themselves victims of punishing market forces, the group argues.

27 "The problem for the sewing companies is that the minimum wage goes higher and higher, and the price from manufacturers stays the same or goes down," says a spokeswoman for the association who gave her name only as Hung.

28 She acknowledges that some owners treat their workers harshly but says most do not. As for the illegal aliens among them, she concedes, "That's a problem."

29 For Blancas, trouble started almost immediately after she was hired by a shop called New Young Fashions. The owner, Kim Young Han, paid her less than the $160 a week she says she was promised. She worked six days a week, starting at 7:30 a.m. and finishing at 6 p.m. each weekday. Her pay averaged $2.54 an hour, according to figures compiled by the workers' center.

30 When she found out what the minimum wage was and told her co-workers they should be getting at least $4.25 an hour, "they were

astonished," but refused to back her in a confrontation with the owner and his Korean wife, Blancas says.

31 "They were robbing us," she says. "I was very angry . . . I said, 'Talk, *compañeors*, talk,' but they were terrified. The [owner's wife] told me to shut up and leave, and the others just kept quiet."

32 Her co-workers, most of them fellow Mexicans and Ecuadorans, feared being deported as illegal aliens if they complained, Blancas says.

33 Interviewed at his factory, Kim said he had resolved all of his employees' complaints and that he is now complying with labor laws.

34 After Blancas was fired from New Young Fashions, the workers' center helped her recover some of her back wages. She later found work in another garment shop that pays more, though still not the minimum wage. She took a second job in a store.

35 Blancas says she left her home in Mexico City to seek work in the United States because her husband had died in a car accident a year earlier and she needed to support her young son. She crossed the border with an uncle, who also works in a sweatshop, and trekked all night over hills to reach a road that would set them on their way to New York.

36 Bertha Morales, a 25-year-old Ecuadoran who worked in another Korean-owned sweatshop, says she was sent by her boss to help out at New Young Fashions one day and was shocked by what she saw. At one point, she said in an interview, the owner's wife struck a worker on the back for sewing buttons incorrectly. Other workers described similar punishment, and one told of an incident in which the boss grabbed her hair and pulled on it.

37 One new employee, a 19-year-old woman from Nicaragua, was summarily fired by the owner's wife for yawning and left the shop in tears, Morales says.

38 Sweatshops such as Kim's lie at the bottom of what the Labor Department describes as a garment industry "food chain" beneath layers of suppliers, designers and middlemen, who compete fiercely for orders from the big retailers at the top.

39 It is a system that regulators and union officials say effectively insulates the big-name stores and fashion labels, allowing them to profess shock and ignorance of sweatshop conditions in which their clothes were sewn.

40 Major retailers, such as J.C. Penney, Sears and Wal-Mart, have quality-control inspectors who regularly visit work sites, and they know how much it costs to produce a garment at the minimum wage, a Labor

Department official says. But under a 60-year-old law, the retailers can be held liable only if they had "direct knowledge" of labor violations involved in producing their goods.

41 The system also adds markups far in excess of the actual cost of the labor and material that went into the garments.

42 Retailers say too many variables go into the final price of a garment to generalize about any of them, but Labor Department and union officials estimate that labor typically accounts for less than 3 percent of the U.S. retail price of clothing made in domestic sweatshops and as little as one-half of 1 percent for garments sewn abroad.

43 Because of the pressures weighing on those at the low end of the industry, shop owners such as Kim Young Han believe that they, too, are victims of the system.

44 Sitting at his worn desk in a corner of the shop floor, Kim blames his problems on creditors, saying he is owed thousands of dollars by garment manufacturers who had subcontracted several large jobs to him. He produces letters to them demanding payment and threatening "legal action." All are written in longhand; he does not have a typewriter.

45 Wearing jeans and a denim shirt, the lean, craggy-faced Kim, 61, says he had been a lecturer at a junior college in Seoul before coming to the United States years ago to study for a doctoral degree in linguistics under Noam Chomsky. Although that alone makes him a rarity among sweatshop owners, union officials say his violations of labor laws were all too familiar.

46 Asked about the specific allegations against him by the garment workers union, Kim becomes visibly upset and pleads for understanding.

47 "Help me, please," he begs. "I'm in trouble."

48 Seemingly on the verge of tears, Kim complains of having to compete with cheap imports and denies making any windfall profits. "I want to close my factory," he laments over the din of sewing machines and a radio blaring Spanish songs. "The market's no good. . . . No hope at my age."

49 The National Retail Federation, which represents 2,000 major U.S. retailers, in turn blames sweatshop conditions on subcontractors such as Kim.

50 "The retailers don't employ these workers," says Pamela Rucker, a spokeswoman for the federation. "The retailers many times are at least two or three steps removed from the problem." She asserts, "It's not the

retailers who are reaping the benefits from these criminal activities. It's the greedy subcontractors."

51 Shops at the bottom of the industry often go out of business, relocate and open under new names. Some fail altogether, never to reappear. But despite decades of lawmaking against them—and a public campaign by the Clinton administration following the 1995 exposure of a virtual slave-labor garment factory in Los Angeles—the system designed to eradicate the sweatshops has largely failed, union activists say.

52 Local, state and federal agencies charged with enforcing labor, immigration and tax laws have often failed to work together, allowing shop owners and workers to slip through the cracks of the system. Under a directive renewed by Mayor Rudolph W. Giuliani, a strong supporter of immigration, New York authorities are prohibited from sharing information with the Immigration and Naturalization Service.

53 At the direction of the administration and Congress, the INS has thrown the bulk of its resources at the southwestern border to prevent illegal immigrants from crossing into the United States from Mexico. Nationwide, only about 1,700 INS investigators are assigned to the interior of the country, and they spend less than 20 percent of their time enforcing immigration law at work sites of all kinds, according to the agency.

54 In a special effort in New York last year, INS agents arrested 1,824 illegal aliens during inspections of 150 work sites, most of them garment shops. However, because of lack of detention space, almost all were released on their own recognizance and told to return for court hearings.

55 "The percentage that shows up is minute," says Russ Bergeron, an INS spokesman. Most simply find another job in the underground economy, and many return to work at the same shops where they were arrested.

56 Ironically, labor groups such as the Garment Workers' Justice Center also play a part in keeping the sweatshops in business. Among the literature the center distributes, for example, are fliers in English, Spanish and Korean that advise shop owners how to fend off searches by INS and Labor Department agents.

57 The fliers encourage employers to challenge inspection on grounds of discrimination and use legal stalling tactics that the INS says often

enable them to fabricate employment eligibility records. Fliers in Spanish urge workers to "remain silent" when asked about their nationality, birth place or entry into the United States.

58 The union says its main aim is to protect workers and preserve their jobs, regardless of their immigration status. When faced with labor violations, the justice center usually tries to work out a solution with the employer without government involvement.

59 Critics call the policy misguided. "If you're trying to defend a living standard, the minimum wage and Social Security and deal with legitimate companies," one independent labor activist argues, "helping these sweatshops exist would seem to be counterproductive."

60 For some garment workers, the punishment for exposing sweatshop conditions comes from their employers. After complaining about what she saw at New Young Fashions while filling in there last year, Bertha Morales was fired by her own Korean boss, who was a friend of Kim's.

61 Others, including two illegal immigrant sisters from Mexico, say workers do not tell authorities about labor violations and physical abuse out of fear that their shops will then be raided by immigration agents.

62 In the case of another outspoken worker, the consequences of going public—or at least the perception of those effects—became evident after she appeared at a forum on sweatshops in Arlington, Va., last summer. The worker, Nancy Penaloza, 29, said she had labored in Korean-owned sweatshops in New York for nine years, working up to 66 hours a week in filthy conditions. In her current job, she said, she sewed high-quality women's suits, earning $6 apiece for garments that usually sell for $120 or more at stores such as J.C. Penney and Ann Taylor.

63 "I get paid off the books," Penaloza told the forum. "Even though I am working legally, my boss doesn't pay any taxes or Social Security. . . . I never get a vacation. I never even get a whole weekend off." She said she works in constant fear, not only of her temperamental boss but of the "big rats and mice" that continually crawl over her feet.

64 A day after she spoke, INS agents raided her factory and arrested most of her co-workers, who were illegal immigrants, Penaloza says. Three days after that, a Labor Department wage inspector showed up. Although she is sure the INS raid was a coincidence, because she did not name her employer at the forum, her co-workers blamed it on her.

65 A former secretary in Mexico, she says she originally crossed the border as an illegal alien herself, then, "became legal" a couple of years ago.

66 She says her Korean boss routinely smacks his workers in the head when they make mistakes. He also orders them to tell the Labor Department that they are receiving their proper wages and overtime, she says, and that is what they did during the latest inspection.

67 "The workers are afraid," Penaloza says. "They don't want to lose their jobs."

68 And so, she says, "they lied to the inspector," thus perpetuating a cycle that helps the industry to survive.

FOR THINKING, DISCUSSING, AND WRITING

1. What is a "sweatshop"? Where does the term come from? How do the sweatshops represent "fundamental changes in the garment industry"?
2. Branigin indicates that many immigrants are being exploited by other immigrants. Do you think that the immigrant owners of sweatshops have an obligation to take better care of their workers because of their shared experiences? Why or why not?
3. What role do you think unions and the government play in preventing sweatshops from thriving?
4. Write an essay about how to eliminate sweatshops from the American scene—or how it is impossible to eliminate them.

QUENTIN HARDY

Showing Off

Quentin Hardy is Silicon Valley Bureau Chief for Forbes, *a major magazine for business leaders. Hardy is a regular on "Forbes on Fox," a weekly business news show on Fox News Channel, and he hosts numerous panels on technology and business at events around the United States. In this essay, he points out that "the rich and powerful show a chronic tendency to wretched excess."*

1 In 1,000 years, creeds are born and die. Empires arise and crumble. But there is at least one constant: The rich and powerful show a chronic tendency to wretched excess.

2 Not just the usual variety, either, like that seen today in a sumptuous summer place in the Hamptons or the outlandish goods sold in a Neiman Marcus catalog. Against the great overconsumers of the millennium, even the late Malcolm Forbes, who flew 600 people to Morocco for his 70th birthday, seems like a relative piker.

3 Consider the Holy Roman emperor at the start of the millennium, Otto III, who commissioned what is still reckoned the world's most valuable book, a big illuminated gospel with a gold-and-ivory binding containing several hundred jewels. The manuscript has 29 full-page images from the life of Christ, plus a facing pair of paintings that show acolytes looking up in adoration at . . . Otto III. With cases like that at the start of the millennium, there is little in the way of progress in this history. There are a wealth of examples from all over, however—and possibly a couple of lessons for the budding wastrels who will doubtless follow.

4 Provided they are up to the challenge. For home decoration, how can one match Jayavarman VII of Angkor, who in 1190 built himself a huge four-sided tower so he could look out on 250 colossal stone images of himself, idealized as Buddha?

5 Imelda Marcos had lots of shoes, but she never wore a hat like Suleiman the Magnificent took to his 1532 assault on Vienna. The Turk rode under a solid gold-helmet holding four crowns, with 270 assorted rubies, diamonds, pearls and emeralds, plus a plume of rare feathers. He had a matching saddle, too.

6 Some excess—the urge to do normal things in an outsize way—has a purpose. Suleiman, for example, was strictly a turban man at home, but his European-style helmet showed he could outdress the locals (even the pope had just three crowns).

7 But many great acts of overdoing things have been for self-aggrandizement. The sun-worshipping religion of the Aztecs generally liked a few human sacrifices a day, but the 1486 festival inaugurating the reign of Ahuitzol saw 80,000 prisoners' hearts offered up, presumably to show that he could sacrifice more than any of his predecessors.

8 For some rich people, excess is a way of demonstrating that they're above all the trifling demands of everyday life—like work. Chinese foot binding showed that the woman did not have to toil in fields to help make ends meet. In 14th-century Europe, the rich wore voluminous gowns called *houppelande* with sleeves that covered the hands, showing the wearer had people who picked things up for him (after a few decades, the Catholic Church objected to the excess of cloth).

9 In other cases, people just need to show that they have more than the next potentate. In 1820, India's Prince of Baroda was forbidden by the British Raj to increase his daily number of cannon salutes, so instead he had his forts' cannons made from solid gold, each weighing 280 pounds.

10 Some customs must have struck the uninitiated as just plain odd. When Louis Antoine de Bougainville of France sailed to the islands off New Guinea in 1767, what could a European have made of the local habit of gift giving to one's worst enemy, who in turn is obligated to give back even more? The object of the ritual, which sometimes lasted years, was to bankrupt someone by an excess of forced generosity. Meanwhile, Peter the Great's funeral for a favorite court dwarf in 1715 had lines of ecclesiastics, followed by 24 pairs of male and female dwarves arranged by height, followed by the Russian czar and his ministers. The rest of Europe must have looked askance, since excessive dwarf collecting had been out of vogue for decades.

11 Wretched excess at times has had unintended consequences. By 1258, Henry III was outspending his income at a ratio of 5 to 1, loading up on paintings, jewels and England's first elephant. Eventually, the barons and Londoners rebelled, and their battle gave rise to England's first parliament. Similarly, the ostentatious high Renaissance decoration of Rome by Pope Alexander VI (Rodrigo Borgia when he was a layman) so shocked Martin Luther in 1510 that he went home and started the Protestant Reformation. (Borgia's excessive church building did, however, guarantee Rome several centuries of tourist income.)

12 Some recent examples of excess are distinctly nostalgic. In 1977, Jean-Bedel Bokassa had himself declared emperor of the Central African Empire by faithfully duplicating the coronation of Napoleon Bonaparte. This one-day re-enactment ran about $25 million, about three-quarters of his country's annual export earnings. The $150 million duplication of St. Paul's cathedral that Felix Houphouet-Boigny built in the Ivory Coast in the 1980s was another blast from the past.

13 The explosion of wealth and democratization in recent centuries has required excessive creativity for those who really need to show off in a big way. There have been so many yachts, led by the great ships of Cornelius Vanderbilt and J. P. Morgan, that mere size has given way to excess in details—why else would Aristotle Onassis have covered the stools in his ship's salon with the skin of whale scrotum?

14 The rise of mass media in recent times has made wretched excess even more of a spectator sport, which seems to encourage the consumers. At the turn of this century, the stock speculator Diamond Jim Brady grew so famous for eating that he once made a public display of consuming a 12-course meal, plus three extra helpings of favorites like

larded fowl, a gallon of orange juice and most of a five-pound box of chocolates. Some onlookers cheered, while others took bets on whether this would be the meal that killed him. The famous eater not only survived, but continued to enjoy a barrel of oysters every three days.

15 Electronic media made it possible for Japan's Ryoei Saito to give a worldwide press conference following his 1991 purchase of a Van Gogh and a Renoir for a total of $185 million. When he said he planned to be cremated with the paintings, however, the global howl made him back down.

16 Still, he could easily claim to have lived up to the credo of the outrageously rich: You can't get enough of a good thing. Or anything else, maybe.

FOR THINKING, DISCUSSING, AND WRITING

1. What are a few of the purposes excess serves for some rich people, according to Hardy? Which excesses named here do you find most surprising? Why?
2. What do you understand "wretched excess" to mean? How effective do you find the choice of phrase in advancing the essay's point about the very rich?
3. What picture of the rich emerges from this essay? How do we define "rich" in our society? How do most of us feel about the rich? Why do so many of us aspire to be rich? What conflicts concerning the question of wealth do you see in American culture?
4. Write an argumentative essay on whether or not there ought to be limits on individual wealth in a democratic society. Be sure to use illustrations to develop your argument.

JOHN UPDIKE

A Sense of Change

John Updike (1932–), prolific American novelist, short story writer, poet, and critic, was born in Pennsylvania and graduated from Harvard in 1954. A contributor for much of his career to the New Yorker, *Updike is prolific best known as a novelist. His novels include* Rabbit, Run *(1960),* Couples *(1968),* The Witches of Eastwick *(1984),* Rabbit Redux *(1971),* Rabbit Is Rich *(1981),* Rabbit at Rest *(1990), and* Terrorist *(2006). In this selection written in 1999, he reflects on the value of money—coins in particular—in a society with changing attitudes.*

1 I was shocked when, a few years ago, my stepson, still a college lad of modest means, handed me the stray change on his bureau top—perhaps two dollars' worth—because he did not like to have it jangling in his pocket. Gratefully, even greedily, I accepted the handful of pennies, nickels, dimes, and quarters. To me, once, these coins were huge in value, if not as huge as the fabled "cartwheels"—silver dollars—that now and then rolled as far east from the Western states as Pennsylvania. One of the advantages of having been a child in the Depression is that it takes very little money to gladden the heart. The Lincoln pennies we used to collect in piggy banks and glass ashtrays were not negligible: five would buy a Hershey bar, six a Tastykake, one a licorice stick, eleven (including a wartime tax) a child's ticket to the movies. Two hundred of them, dutifully accumulated over months and packaged in four paper wrappers holding fifty each, could be exchanged at the Whitner's Department Store book counter for an album of cartoons from *Collier's* or an agreeably lightweight novel by Thorne Smith or P. G. Wodehouse. The wrappers were solemnly broken open and each penny respectfully counted by the saleswoman. Now spare pennies sit like a puddle of sludge in a dish on the counter of the post office or the convenience store, and sometimes a salesclerk, rather than bother counting out four cents in change, blithely hands you a nickel.

2 Copper Lincoln cents—pale zinc-coated steel for a year of the war—figure in my earliest impressions of money, although an old Indian Head, discontinued in 1909, would still turn up in the thirties. Lincoln pennies are being minted ninety years later, the longest-lived of American coins and the first non-commemorative ones to bear a President's image. The other coins of my childhood have slowly ebbed from circulation: the Buffalo nickel (1913–38), crowded to the rim, obverse and reverse, with its heroic representations of Manifest Destiny's two victims, the defeated Indian and his all but exterminated pet prey; the Mercury dime (1916–45), so called because Miss Liberty wears an anomalous winged headdress atop her icy female profile, a profile that originally belonged, we children of Berks County did not realize, to Elsie Kachel Moll, from Reading, who had married another local, the poet Wallace Stevens, and during their seven years in Manhattan had posed for not only the iconic head on the dime but the full-length Miss Liberty on the fifty-cent piece; and the Standing Liberty quarter (1916–30), whose figure (not Elsie Stevens's) was criticized for showing too much naked flesh and was more heavily draped

in the second year of its issue. This coin, as it yielded to the Washington quarter, first minted in 1932, was treasured by small boys because, if it was turned upside down and partly covered with a knowing thumb, the wings and head of the flying eagle on the reverse became striding legs and a penis. By the time the Walking Liberty half-dollar (1916–47), with its full-length sashaying lady about to put her foot on a rising sun, gave way to Ben Franklin and the Liberty Bell, I, at the age of fifteen, had ceased to hold coinage so close to my face and to count on it for erotic insight. Half-dollars were less rare then than now—men accustomed to carrying pocket watches and pocket knives did not shun big coins—but a child seldom gained possession of one, unless it was to mark a holiday or a birthday. Fifty cents was a lot of money.

3 These metallic tokens projected a potent magic. My best friend, a lawyer's son, had a little tin box of money that, when I visited his home, he used to show me with an avid, ceremonial secrecy. My own, more meagre hoards resided in relatively frivolous piggy banks, most important a grinning, red-tongued Mickey Mouse guarding a slotted treasure chest whose bottom could be opened with a key. I had won the bank in a third-grade spelling bee—the clinching word, I think, was "lonely"—and this quaint repository's disappearance, somewhere in the second half of the century, constitutes one of the inconsolable losses of my life.

4 Money, which is now so preponderantly a matter of electronic notation, or else a breezy riffle of twenty-dollar bills cast down by an A.T.M., was in those hard-up times an earthy outgrowth, like the sparkling diamonds that the dwarfs pile up in Disney's "Snow White." My family—my possibly incomplete impression was—deposited my father's salary, received in cash in a small tan envelope, in a red-and-white "Recipe" box that sat on top of the icebox. To dip into it, I had to get a kitchen chair to stand on, and my withdrawals were supervised; indeed, everyone's withdrawals from it were announced, like the stations on a train journey. When the box was empty, we were out of money.

5 My father, as a schoolteacher in charge of basketball admissions, used to bring home the cash receipts, and I often watched him count them—the various denominations of coins mounting in slick stacks that, when they reached a certain height, were deftly slipped into a paper cylinder, which was then smartly tamped at both ends. When I tried it, the coins ran away, over the edge of the table onto the carpet

and even beyond, a coin often ending upright on its edge in a floor crack way over in a corner. This willful, kinetic quality of metal money I notice now at the poker table, where a quarter tossed into the pot will unaccountably wobble to its feet, as it were, and travel clear across the table as if seeking another master.

6 The sensuous pleasure of handling money carries into the very thought of it. "Pennies from Heaven" was a song, and "We're in the Money" another. American millionaires—Ford and Rockefeller and, upholding Pennsylvania's honor, Andrew Carnegie and Andrew Mellon—were folk heroes, Paul Bunyans of cash. The millions who for a coin or two went to the movies did not seem to begrudge the tuxedoed personas of Louis Calhearn and Eugene Pallette and Guy Kibbee their pillared estates, their lawns and swimming pools, their buffed and chauffeured English limousines, their beautiful giddy daughters in chiffon and pearls. To see such well-endowed lives projected in black-and-white on a big silver screen was itself pleasurable, like feeling coins swim through your fingers or imagining—in many a crime movie—a suitcase full of bundled bills. The American masses of the Depression had not quite lost the feudal ability to identify with an overlord's riches, alleviating their own poverty with vicarious enjoyment of an aristocracy's assets. The men and women who drudged their lives away in the local factories—most prominently, Wyoming's Berkshire Knitting Mills, fondly known as the Berkie—shared in the pith of a great enterprise, though their share, Marxists would point out, was insufficient. American society's refusal to crack beneath the dire load of the Depression owed something to an imaginative wealth that, via the movies, solaced the masses with debonair images of luxury. Images were in a way superior to the real thing, if we believed those Hollywood comedies in which the rich were often foolish and not infrequently miserable: they suffered from ulcers, financial reversals, and the discontents of excessive propriety; they were hostages to their fortunes, and prey to complications from which ordinary men were exempt. Our hearts went out to them, and their happy endings became ours. Movies, mediating between Myrna Loy and the twelve-dollar-a-week shopgirl, spun a web of trust, of sympathetic connection, like the bonds of patriotism and brand name loyalty.

7 A coin, too, bespeaks trust, passing from hand to hand as an abstract signifier of value. Coins were once worth their weight in silver or gold;

opportunists clipped their edges and passed them on for the face amount. Then the underpinning of real metallic worth was removed, and the value inhered in nothing more than a general consent. A "pretend" level of wealth was invented, less substantial but also less perishable and cumbersome than food or clothing or jewelry. This lightly worn immutability accounts for some of the fascination that money holds. Like that of words and feelings, money's value is impalpable. Yet money lasts, it doesn't flit by. Nor does it ask anything of its possessor. It melts, like ice cream, but very slowly, in the warmth of inflation. It has endurance and extension. These little disks and shallow sculptures enlist us in a conspiracy of users; a penny from a child's hand is worth just what it is from a grownup's. Getting and spending confer an instant dignity.

8 In that penny-proud world of my childhood, paper and cardboard play money carried the pretense to an even airier level. Whole afternoons went by in the counterfeit transactions of Monopoly. The war brought food tokens—little hard cardboard disks, red and blue—and stamps, and War Bonds, urged upon the public by movie stars and heroes and President Roosevelt himself, as immutable as the profile on a coin. Before the Depression, my grandfather had invested in stocks and bonds and lost most of his money; now all of us, children included, were hustled by the wartime emergency back into an economy of credit and certificates, a giant trusting of the government to see us through and pay back its debt. My adulthood's slow divorce from hard cash was under way.

9 To one who acquired his sense of money in the Depression, any payment, however modest—fifty-five dollars, say, for a poem, or a hundred for a reprint permission—seems impressive. My allowance was thirty-five cents a week, my father's salary was twelve hundred dollars a year. Measured by these sustenance sums, nineties remunerations appear huge; I often must resist the impulse to send back checks to editors and lecture agencies on the ground that I am being grossly overpaid. On the other hand, nineties expenses are a constant outrage. Four hundred and fifty dollars for one night in a hotel! Seventy-five dollars for a theatre ticket! Two million dollars for a condo on an airshaft! Thirty-three cents for a three-cent stamp! Eighty cents—can you believe it?—for a nickel candy bar! It is like going to Italy, except that these are not lire but almighty American dollars. "The almighty dollar," "sound as a dollar," "another day, another dollar"—even the sayings

from my childhood have been devalued by inflation. I simply cannot afford to live, it daily seems to me as I size up 1999 prices in the dollars of 1939. No, not the dollars; a Lilliputian in Brobdingnag, I still think in terms of 1939 quarters, dimes, nickels, and pennies. Or am I, hoisting up onto the counter a nickel that feels as hefty as a millstone, the Brobdingnagian?

FOR THINKING, DISCUSSING, AND WRITING

1. Updike begins the essay with the words "I was shocked." Why? How do these words help you understand the point he is trying to make? Why does he accept the coins from his stepson "gratefully, even greedily"? How much have prices changed in the few years since Updike wrote this piece?
2. How did people in the era of the writer's childhood respond to the value of money? How do people today respond to it? How do you account for the differences, if any?
3. Updike tells us that he received a toy bank as a prize for winning a spelling bee in school. Can you imagine a prize like that being given today? Why or why not? What kinds of prizes do we frequently award to children today? What, if anything, does this say about our value system?
4. Write an essay in which you argue for or against this point: "People today don't know the value of money as well as people in the past knew it."

CHARLOTTE ALLEN

The Return of the Happy Housewife

Charlotte Allen lives in Washington, D.C. Her writing has appeared in the Atlantic, *the* Washington Post, *the* Los Angeles Times *(in which this selection appeared), and other publications. A graduate of Stanford and Harvard, she held a Woodrow Wilson fellowship. She is the author of* The Human Christ: The Search for the Historical Jesus *(1998). Allen co-edits the InkWell blog for the Independent Women's Forum. In this piece she challenges conventional feminist theory to argue in favor of "stay-at-home" wives who, she asserts, are happy with traditional marital arrangements.*

1 Betty Friedan, it seems, died just in time to roll over in her grave.

2 A new study by two University of Virginia sociologists concludes that stay-at-home wives whose husbands are the primary family breadwinners don't suffer from "the problem that has no name," as Friedan famously wrote in 1963. In fact, the majority of fulltime homemakers don't experience any kind of special problem, according to professors W. Bradford Wilcox and Stephen L. Nock, who analyzed data from a huge University of Wisconsin survey of families, conducted during the 1990s.

3 Here are the figures, published in this month's issue of the journal Social Forces: 52% of wives who don't work outside the home reported they were "very happy" with their marriages, compared with 41% of wives in the workforce.

4 The more traditional a marriage is, the sociologists found, the higher the percentage of happy wives. Among couples who have the husband as the primary breadwinner, who worship together regularly and who believe in marriage as an institution that requires a lifelong commitment, 61% of wives said they were "very happy" with their marriages. Among couples whose marriage does not have all these characteristics, the percentage of happy wives dips to an average of 45.

5 Lest you think the statistics come out this way because tradition-minded women happen to like tradition-minded wedlock—or they're just brainwashed by their churches—you're wrong. In an unpublished second paper, Wilcox sifted through the survey data and discovered that even wives who describe themselves as feminists report being happier with traditional marital arrangements in which they stay home with the kids and their husbands provide for them.

6 "They might think of themselves as progressives and believe in gender equality, but the same pattern holds for them," Wilcox said.

7 One more surprise: Even for wives who work full time outside the home, the key to marital happiness isn't splitting household chores and child care down the middle with their husbands. It's much simpler: an affectionate and appreciative husband who believes, along with his wife, that marriage is forever. Sociologists call it "emotion work"—husbands talking to their wives, being understanding and supportive, spending quality time in the form of romantic evenings for two, walking hand-in-hand on the beach and so forth.

8 "It's far more important than who does the dishes and folds the laundry," Wilcox said.

9 These findings fly in the face of what feminist scholars have been telling us for more than four decades about what is wrong with contemporary marriage and how to fix it. Friedan's prescription was that wives should pursue careers outside the home. Alix Kates Shulman's "marriage contract" holds that spouses should agree that, say, the husband change the sheets on alternate weeks. And Judith Warner complains that full-time homemaking amounts to a "gender caste system" in which the "lower-status member" has to do the mopping and scrubbing. In short, feminists in academia and the media say that what married women really need is financial independence from their husbands—and getting their husbands to do at least half the housework.

10 The problem is that husbands, although they do help out around the house more than they did half a century ago, have been notoriously unamenable to 50-50 splits in household tasks. Wives—and working wives—in the United States still do more than 70% of the housework, according to one study.

11 Nonetheless, feminist academics urge wives to push their husbands even harder in the chores wars. In an article in the American Prospect, scholar Linda R. Hirshman advised new brides to employ behavior-modification techniques on their husbands: "If women never start playing the household-manager role, the house will be dirty, but the realities of the physical world will trump the pull of gender ideology. Either the other adult in the family will take a hand or the children will grow up with robust immune systems."

12 Other feminist scholars pooh-pooh the idea of marriage as a lifelong commitment. Writing in the Washington Post, Stephanie Coontz, a family history professor at Evergreen State University in Washington state, contended that "we cannot afford to construct our social policies, our advice to our own children and even our own emotional expectations around the illusion that all commitments, sexual activities and care-giving will take place in a traditional marriage. That series has been canceled."

13 The study by Wilcox and Nock found exactly the opposite: 57% of wives who (for religious reasons or otherwise) strongly believed in until-death-do-us-part marriage said they were very happily wed, compared with 44% among those who believe that couples should divorce when they fall out of love.

14 Furthermore, increasing numbers of married women, especially those with small children, have been quietly dropping out of the labor

force in favor of more traditional arrangements. In 1998, about 59% of married women with children under 12 months and living with their husbands worked outside the home—an all-time high, according to the Census Bureau. Six years later, the figure was 55%.

15 Until five years ago, social scientists assumed that the feminist revolution of the 1970s was so thorough and unstoppable that the percentage of mothers in the workforce would continue to rise inexorably until it reached close to 100. The phenomenon of the corporate lawyer who opts to bake cookies with her children and let her husband provide the financial security alarms feminists, but numbers from the Census Bureau suggest that her type is part of a continuing trend. The high-water mark also was 1998 for labor-force participation of mothers with children under 12 months who had both bachelor's degrees (67%) and graduate or professional degrees (74%). By 2004, the percentages had fallen to 60% and 70%, respectively.

16 The study by Wilcox and Nock suggests that happy marriages, even among irreligious dual-career couples, don't depend on utopian social engineering or the restructuring of gender roles. The important thing isn't how much housework a wife does but whether her husband makes her feel, through gratitude and affection, that her contribution to the household is as important and valuable as his own. That means both sides putting aside selfishness.

17 Many husbands don't easily express their feelings, but many wives have to give something too. They can start by realizing that their spouses who slay dragons so the family can live in comfort also make sacrifices that deserve recognition.

FOR THINKING, DISCUSSING, AND WRITING

1. Why does Allen start the essay with a reference to Betty Friedan? (See also "The Parent Trap," page 67.) In what ways are Friedan's beliefs central to your understanding of Allen's essay?
2. How has Allen used statistics to advance her argument? Who are the authorities she cites? In what ways has she used writers who oppose her own position? See what you can find out about the data analysts and other writers named here—W. Bradford Wilcox, Stephen L. Nock, Alix Kates Shulman, Judith Warner (See Warner's essay in Chapter 2), Linda R. Hirschman, and Stephanie Coontz.
3. Allen has written elsewhere that "the academic and intellectual establishment is in the grip of a poisonous feminist ideology." What

does she mean by this comment? How does the statement have relevance to the argument in this essay? Do you agree with Allen?

4. Write an essay in which you compare and contrast the value of stay-at-home wives and working wives. Take a position on which you think contributes more to a happy marriage and explain why you think so.

GARY SOTO

Black Hair

Gary Soto (1952–) grew up in Fresno, California, where his family were migrant farm workers. He published his first volume of poetry, The Elements of San Joaquin, *in 1977. He won the National Book Award in 1985 for* Living Up the Street: Narrative Recollections, *in which this essay appears. His most recent book is* Buried Onions *(2006), a novel. Currently Soto lives in Berkeley, California, and he serves as Young People's Ambassador for the California Rural Legal Assistance (CRLA) and the United Farm Workers of America (UFW). In this essay he explores his attitudes toward work as a seventeen-year-old runaway working at a tire factory.*

1 There are two kinds of work: One uses the mind and the other uses muscle. As a kid I found out about the latter. I'm thinking of the summer of 1969 when I was a seventeen-year-old runaway who ended up in Glendale, California, to work for Valley Tire Factory. To answer an ad in the newspaper I walked miles in the afternoon sun, my stomach slowly knotting on a doughnut that was breakfast, my teeth like bright candles gone yellow.

2 I walked in the door sweating and feeling ugly because my hair was still stiff from a swim at the Santa Monica beach the day before. Jules, the accountant and part owner, looked droopily through his bifocals at my application and then at me. He tipped his cigar in the ashtray, asked my age as if he didn't believe I was seventeen, but finally after a moment of silence, said, "Come back tomorrow. Eight-thirty."

3 I thanked him, left the office, and went around to the chain link fence to watch the workers heave tires into a bin; others carted uneven stacks of tires on hand trucks. Their faces were black from tire dust and when they talked—or cussed—their mouths showed a bright pink.

4 From there I walked up a commercial street, past a cleaners, a motorcycle shop, and a gas station where I washed my face and hands;

before leaving I took a bottle that hung on the side of the Coke machine, filled it with water, and stopped it with a scrap of paper and a rubber band.

5 The next morning I arrived early at work. The assistant foreman, a potbellied Hungarian, showed me a timecard and how to punch in. He showed me the Coke machine, the locker room with its slimy shower, and also pointed out the places where I shouldn't go: The ovens where the tires were recapped and the customer service area, which had a slashed couch, a coffee table with greasy magazines, and an ashtray. He introduced me to Tully, a fat man with one ear, who worked the buffers that resurfaced the white walls. I was handed an apron and a face mask and shown how to use the buffer: Lift the tire and center, inflate it with a footpedal, press the buffer against the white band until cleaned, and then deflate and blow off the tire with an air hose.

6 With a paint brush he stirred a can of industrial preserver. "Then slap this blue stuff on." While he was talking a co-worker came up quietly from behind him and goosed him with the air hose. Tully jumped as if he had been struck by a bullet and then turned around cussing and cupping his genitals in his hands as the other worker walked away calling out foul names. When Tully turned to me smiling his gray teeth, I lifted my mouth into a smile because I wanted to get along. He has to be on my side, I thought. He's the one who'll tell the foreman how I'm doing.

7 I worked carefully that day, setting the tires on the machine as if they were babies, since it was easy to catch a finger in the rim that expanded to inflate the tire. At the day's end we swept up the tire dust and emptied the trash into bins.

8 At five the workers scattered for their cars and motorcycles while I crossed the street to wash at a burger stand. My hair was stiff with dust and my mouth showed pink against the backdrop of my dirty face. I then ordered a hotdog and walked slowly in the direction of the abandoned house where I had stayed the night before. I lay under the trees and within minutes was asleep. When I woke my shoulders were sore and my eyes burned when I squeezed the lids together.

9 From the backyard I walked dully through a residential street, and as evening came on, the TV glare in the living rooms and the headlights of passing cars showed against the blue drift of dusk. I saw two children coming up the street with snow cones, their tongues darting at the packed ice. I saw a boy with a peach and wanted to stop him, but felt

embarrassed by my hunger. I walked for an hour only to return and discover the house lit brightly. Behind the fence I heard voices and saw a flashlight poking at the garage door. A man on the back steps mumbled something about the refrigerator to the one with the flashlight.

10 I waited for them to leave, but had the feeling they wouldn't because there was the commotion of furniture being moved. Tired, even more desperate, I started walking again with a great urge to kick things and tear the day from my life. I felt weak and my mind kept drifting because of hunger. I crossed the street to a gas station where I sipped at the water fountain and searched the Coke machine for change. I started walking again, first up a commercial street, then into a residential area where I lay down on someone's lawn and replayed a scene at home—my Mother crying at the kitchen table, my stepfather yelling with food in his mouth. They're cruel, I thought, and warned myself that I should never forgive them. How could they do this to me.

11 When I got up from the lawn it was late. I searched out a place to sleep and found an unlocked car that seemed safe. In the back seat, with my shoes off, I fell asleep but woke up startled about four in the morning when the owner, a nurse on her way to work, opened the door. She got in and was about to start the engine when I raised my head up from the back seat to explain my presence. She screamed so loudly when I said "I'm sorry" that I sprinted from the car with my shoes in hand. Her screams faded, then stopped altogether, as I ran down the block where I hid behind a trash bin and waited for a police siren to sound. Nothing. I crossed the street to a church where I slept stiffly on cardboard in the balcony.

12 I woke up feeling tired and greasy. It was early and a few street lights were still lit, the east growing pink with dawn. I washed myself from a garden hose and returned to the church to break into what looked like a kitchen. Paper cups, plastic spoons, a coffee pot littered on a table. I found a box of Nabisco crackers which I ate until I was full.

13 At work I spent the morning at the buffer, but was then told to help Iggy, an old Mexican, who was responsible for choosing tires that could be recapped without the risk of exploding at high speeds. Every morning a truck would deliver used tires, and after I unloaded them Iggy would step among the tires to inspect them for punctures and rips on the side walls.

14 With a yellow chalk he marked circles and Xs to indicate damage and called out "junk." For those tires that could be recapped, he said

"goody" and I placed them on my hand truck. When I had a stack of eight I kicked the truck at an angle and balanced them to another work area where Iggy again inspected the tires, scratching Xs and calling out "junk."

15 Iggy worked only until three in the afternoon, at which time he went to the locker room to wash and shave and to dress in a two-piece suit. When he came out he glowed with a bracelet, watch, rings, and a shiny fountain pen in his breast pocket. His shoes sounded against the asphalt. He was the image of a banker stepping into sunlight with millions on his mind. He said a few low words to workers with whom he was friendly and none to people like me.

16 I was seventeen, stupid because I couldn't figure out the difference between an F 78 14 and 750 14 at sight. Iggy shook his head when I brought him the wrong tires, especially since I had expressed interest in being his understudy. "Mexican, how can you be so stupid?" he would yell at me, slapping a tire from my hands. But within weeks I learned a lot about tires, from sizes and makes to how they are molded in iron forms to how Valley stole from other companies. Now and then we received a truckload of tires, most of them new or nearly new, and they were taken to our warehouse in the back where the serial numbers were ground off with a sander. On those days the foreman handed out Cokes and joked with us as we worked to get the numbers off.

17 Most of the workers were Mexican or black, though a few redneck whites worked there. The base pay was a dollar sixty-five, but the average was three dollars. Of the black workers, I knew Sugar Daddy the best. His body carried two hundred and fifty pounds, armfuls of scars, and a long knife that made me jump when he brought it out from his boot without warning. At one time he had been a singer, and had cut a record in 1967 called *Love's Chance*, which broke into the R and B charts. But nothing came of it. No big contract, no club dates, no tours. He made very little from the sales, only enough for an operation to pull a steering wheel from his gut when, drunk and mad at a lady friend, he slammed his Mustang into a row of parked cars.

18 "Touch it," he smiled at me one afternoon as he raised his shirt, his black belly kinked with hair. Scared, I traced the scar that ran from his chest to the left of his belly button, and I was repelled but hid my disgust.

19 Among the Mexicans I had few friends because I was different, a *pocho* who spoke bad Spanish. At lunch they sat in tires and laughed over burritos, looking up at me to laugh even harder. I also sat in tires

while nursing a Coke and felt dirty and sticky because I was still living on the street and had not had a real bath in over a week. Nevertheless, when the border patrol came to round up the nationals, I ran with them as they scrambled for the fence or hid among the tires behind the warehouse. The foreman, who thought I was an undocumented worker, yelled at me to run, to get away. I did just that. At the time it seemed fun because there was no risk, only a goodhearted feeling of hide-and-seek, and besides it meant an hour away from work on company time. When the police left we came back and some of the nationals made up stories of how they were almost caught—how they out-raced the police. Some of the stories were so convoluted and unconvincing that everyone laughed *mentiras*, especially when one described how he overpowered a policeman, took his gun away, and sold the patrol car. We laughed and he laughed, happy to be there to make up a story.

20 If work was difficult, so were the nights. I still had not gathered enough money to rent a room, so I spent the nights sleeping in parked cars or in the balcony of a church. After a week I found a newspaper ad for room for rent, phoned, and was given directions. Finished with work, I walked the five miles down Mission Road looking back into the traffic with my thumb out. No rides. After eight hours of handling tires I was frightening, I suppose, to drivers since they seldom looked at me; if they did, it was a quick glance. For the next six weeks I would try to hitchhike, but the only person to stop was a Mexican woman who gave me two dollars to take the bus. I told her it was too much and that no bus ran from Mission Road to where I lived, but she insisted that I keep the money and trotted back to her idling car. It must have hurt her to see me day after day walking in the heat and looking very much the dirty Mexican to the many minds that didn't know what it meant to work at hard labor. That woman knew. Her eyes met mine as she opened the car door, and there was a tenderness that was surprisingly true—one for which you wait for years but when it comes it doesn't help. Nothing changes. You continue on in rags, with the sun still above you.

21 I rented a room from a middle-aged couple whose lives were a mess. She was a school teacher and he was a fireman. A perfect set up, I thought. But during my stay there they would argue with one another for hours in their bedroom.

22 When I rang at the front door both Mr. and Mrs. Van Deusen answered and didn't bother to disguise their shock at how awful I

looked. But they let me in all the same. Mrs. Van Deusen showed me around the house, from the kitchen and bathroom to the living room with its grand piano. On her fingers she counted out the house rules as she walked me to my room. It was a girl's room with lace curtains, scenic wallpaper of a Victorian couple enjoying a stroll, canopied bed, and stuffed animals in a corner. Leaving, she turned and asked if she could do laundry for me and, feeling shy and hurt, I told her no; perhaps the next day. She left and I undressed to take a bath, exhausted as I sat on the edge of the bed probing my aches and my bruised places. With a towel around my waist I hurried down the hallway to the bathroom where Mrs. Van Deusen had set out an additional towel with a tube of shampoo. I ran the water in the tub and sat on the toilet, lid down, watching the steam curl toward the ceiling. When I lowered myself into the tub I felt my body sting. I soaped a wash cloth and scrubbed my arms until they lightened, even glowed pink, but still I looked unwashed around my neck and face no matter how hard I rubbed. Back in the room I sat in bed reading a magazine, happy and thinking of no better luxury than a girl's sheets, especially after nearly two weeks of sleeping on cardboard at the church.

23 I was too tired to sleep, so I sat at the window watching the neighbors move about in pajamas, and, curious about the room, looked through the bureau drawers to search out personal things—snapshots, a messy diary, and a high school yearbook. I looked up the Van Deusen's daughter, Barbara, and studied her face as if I recognized her from my own school—a face that said "promise," "college," "nice clothes in the closet." She was a skater and a member of the German Club; her greatest ambition was to sing at the Hollywood Bowl.

24 After a while I got into bed and as I drifted toward sleep I thought about her. In my mind I played a love scene again and again and altered it slightly each time. She comes home from college and at first is indifferent to my presence in her home, but finally I overwhelm her with deep pity when I come home hurt from work, with blood on my shirt. Then there was another version: Home from college she is immediately taken with me, in spite of my work-darkened face, and invites me into the family car for a milkshake across town. Later, back at the house, we sit in the living room talking about school until we're so close I'm holding her hand. The truth of the matter was that Barbara did come home for a week, but was bitter toward her parents for taking in boarders (two others besides me). During that time she spoke to me only

twice: Once, while searching the refrigerator, she asked if we had any mustard; the other time she asked if I had seen her car keys.

25 But it was a place to stay. Work had become more and more difficult. I not only worked with Iggy, but also with the assistant foreman who was in charge of unloading trucks. After they backed in I hopped on top to pass the tires down by bouncing them on the tailgate to give them an extra spring so they would be less difficult to handle on the other end. Each truck was weighed down with more than two hundred tires, each averaging twenty pounds, so that by the time the truck was emptied and swept clean I glistened with sweat and my T-shirt stuck to my body. I blew snot threaded with tire dust onto the asphalt, indifferent to the customers who watched from the waiting room.

26 The days were dull. I did what there was to do from morning until the bell sounded at five; I tugged, pulled, and cussed at tires until I was listless and my mind drifted and caught on small things, from cold sodas to shoes to stupid talk about what we would do with a million dollars. I remember unloading a truck with Hamp, a black man.

27 "What's better than a sharp lady?" he asked me as I stood sweaty on a pile of junked tires. "Water. With ice," I said.

28 He laughed with his mouth open wide. With his fingers he pinched the sweat from his chin and flicked at me. "You be too young, boy. A woman can make you a god."

29 As a kid I had chopped cotton and picked grapes, so I knew work. I knew the fatigue and the boredom and the feeling that there was a good possibility you might have to do such work for years, if not for a lifetime. In fact, as a kid I imagined a dark fate: To marry Mexican poor, work Mexican hours, and in the end die a Mexican death broke and in despair.

30 But this job at Valley Tire Company confirmed that there was something worse than field work, and I was doing it. We were all doing it, from foreman to the newcomers like me, and what I felt heaving tires for eight hours a day was felt by everyone—black, Mexican, redneck. We all despised those hours but didn't know what else to do. The workers were unskilled, some undocumented and fearful of deportation, and all struck with an uncertainty at what to do with their lives. Although everyone bitched about work, no one left. Some had worked there for as long as twelve years; some had sons working there. Few quit; no one was ever fired. It amazed me that no one gave up when the border patrol jumped from their vans,

baton in hand, because I couldn't imagine any work that could be worse—or any life. What was out there, in the world, that made men run for the fence in fear?

31 Iggy was the only worker who seemed sure of himself. After five hours of "junking" he brushed himself off, cleaned up in the washroom, and came out gleaming with an elegance that humbled the rest of us. Few would look him straight in the eye or talk to him in our usual stupid way because he was so much better. He carried himself as a man should—with that old world "dignity"—while the rest of us muffed our jobs and talked dully about dull things as we worked. From where he worked in his open shed he would now and then watch us with his hands on his hips. He would shake his head and click his tongue in disgust.

32 The rest of us lived dismally. I often wondered what the others' homes were like; I couldn't imagine that they were much better than our work place. No one indicated that his outside life was interesting or intriguing. We all looked defeated and contemptible in our filth at the day's end. I imagined the average welcome at home: Rafael, a Mexican national who had worked at Valley for five years, returned to a beaten house of kids who were dressed in mismatched clothes and playing kick-the-can. As for Sugar Daddy, he returned home to a stuffy room where he would read and reread old magazines. He ate potato chips, drank beer, and watched TV. There was no grace in dipping socks into a wash basin where later he would wash his cup and plate.

33 There was no grace at work. It was all ridicule. The assistant foreman drank Cokes in front of the newcomers as they laced tires in the afternoon sun. Knowing that I had a long walk home, Rudy, the college student, passed me waving and yelling "Hello" as I started down Mission Road on the way home to eat out of cans. Even our plump secretary got into the act by wearing short skirts and flaunting her milky legs. If there was love, it was ugly. I'm thinking of Tully and an older man whose name I can no longer recall fondling one another in the washroom. I had come in cradling a smashed finger to find them pressed together in the shower, their pants undone and partly pulled down. When they saw me they smiled their pink mouths but didn't bother to push away.

34 How we arrived at such a place is a mystery to me. Why anyone would stay for years is even a deeper concern. You showed up, but

from where? What broken life? What ugly past? The foreman showed you the Coke machine, the washroom, and the yard where you'd work. When you picked up a tire, you were amazed at the black it could give off.

FOR THINKING, DISCUSSING, AND WRITING

1. How does Soto's definition of work at the beginning of the selection alert you to the point he is making? Do you accept his categories? Why or why not?
2. Would you have hired Soto as he appeared at seventeen? Why or why not? Would you have rented him a room? Why or why not? Are you surprised that he went on to become a writer and teacher? Why or why not?
3. In what ways is Soto different from his co-workers? How does he cope with his alienation? How does he communicate it in his actions? How do his attempts to belong help provide structure to the essay? In what ways does he try to deal with the differences?
4. In the final paragraph, Soto asks, "Why would anyone stay?" Why do you think people work at a place like Valley Tire Factory? Write an essay to construct a satisfactory answer to this question.

RICHARD FLORIDA

Where the Brains Are

Richard Florida (1957–) is the Hirst Professor of Public Policy at George Mason University located in Fairfax, Virginia, just outside Washington, D.C. Born in Newark, New Jersey, Florida has a PhD from Columbia University. An economist and sociologist interested in social theory, he is known for his book The Rise of the Creative Class *(2002). His most recent book is* The Flight of the Creative Class *(2005). In this essay from* the Atlantic's *October 2006 issue, he shows how the educated elite in America is relocating to a small number of metropolitan regions.*

1 America's social fabric has been regularly reshaped by great migrations—of pioneers westward, of immigrants and farmers to rising industrial cities, of African Americans from the rural South to the urban North, of families outward from cities to suburbs to exurbs.

2 Today, a demographic realignment that may prove just as significant is under way: the mass relocation of highly skilled, highly educated, and highly paid Americans to a relatively small number of metropolitan regions, and a corresponding exodus of the traditional lower and middle classes from these same places. Such geographic sorting of people by economic potential, on this scale, is unprecedented. I call it the "means migration."

3 The divergence of housing prices nationwide illustrates the means migration powerfully. Home values go up and down, but according to an analysis by the economists Joseph Gyourko, Chris Mayer, and Todd Sinai, since 1950 a handful of "superstar cities" (including central cities and their suburbs) has emerged nationwide—places where growth in housing prices has consistently and rapidly outpaced the average national increase, and where growth in housing supply is limited. You could probably guess most of them—cities such as San Francisco, Los Angeles, Seattle, Boston, and Denver; the affluent suburbs of Manhattan; innovation centers such as Silicon Valley, Austin, and the Research Triangle in North Carolina.

4 Many of these city-regions may well be in the midst of housing bubbles today, but that shouldn't distract us from a larger truth. In the long run, the price of real estate is the best available indicator of the "effective demand" for a particular place, and these places have been pulling away from the pack for decades. Superstar cities are, by their nature, exclusionary, and there is good reason to believe they will become more so in the future.

5 The means migration can be seen even more clearly in the increasing geographic concentration of college graduates. According to research by Christopher Berry of the University of Chicago and Edward Glaeser of Harvard, in 1970 human capital was distributed relatively evenly throughout the United States. Nationally, 11 percent of the population over twenty-five years old had a college degree, and that figure ranged between 9 percent and 13 percent in fully half of America's 318 metropolitan regions. In Washington, D.C., 18 percent of the residents had finished college; in Cleveland, only 4 percent had finished.

6 Over the past three decades, the percentage of Americans holding a college degree has more than doubled, reaching 27 percent by 2004, but as the maps below show, those gains have not been evenly spread. For instance, about half of the residents of Washington, D.C., and San

Francisco now have college degrees—versus 14 percent and 11 percent in Cleveland and Detroit respectively. The trends for graduate degrees show a similar pattern. In Washington, D.C., and Seattle, more than 20 percent of the adult population had an advanced degree in 2004, compared with 5 percent in Cleveland, 4 percent in Detroit, and 2 percent in Newark. In the downtown neighborhoods of high-powered cities, the concentration of well-educated people is even greater. In 2000, more than two-thirds of the residents of down-town Chicago and of Midtown Manhattan, for example, held college degrees. Most rural and many suburban areas, meanwhile, are being left behind. Significantly, young graduates are flocking in ever-greater numbers to the "means metros," where they often live in penury until either making it or being forced out by the high cost of living.

7 What's behind this phenomenon? Some of the reasons for it are essentially aesthetic—many of the means metros are beautiful, energizing, and fun to live in. But there is another reason, rooted in economics: increasingly, the most talented and ambitious people *need* to live in a means metro in order to realize their full economic value.

8 The physical proximity of talented, highly educated people has a powerful effect on innovation and economic growth—in fact, the Nobel Prize–winning economist Robert Lucas declared the multiplier effects that stem from talent clustering to be the *primary* determinant of growth. That's all the more true in a postindustrial economy dependent on creativity, intellectual property, and high-tech innovation.

9 Places that bring together diverse talent accelerate the local rate of economic evolution. When large numbers of entrepreneurs, financiers, engineers, designers, and other smart, creative people are constantly bumping into one another inside and outside of work, business ideas are more quickly formed, sharpened, executed, and—if successful—expanded. The more smart people, and the denser the connections between them, the faster it all goes.

10 The local cultures of most, if not all, means metros have facilitated the establishment of many loose connections among people of diverse talents, lifestyles, and social circles (as opposed to a few tight connections within homogenous groups). They are socially tolerant and open to new ways of thinking. Job switching is common, as is periodic unemployment, and free agents find plenty of common spaces in

which to work and meet. The soup is continuously stirred, and newcomers are assimilated easily.

11 But the means metros also have a larger and simpler advantage over other regions: a head start. For a variety of historical reasons—the presence of great universities is usually one—the means metros already have a high concentration of highly talented people. And as more such people are added, their multiplier effect on growth seems to keep increasing. That's true not just for economic growth in the aggregate, but for individual incomes and opportunities as well.

12 Yet the opportunities do not exist for everyone. In both early agricultural and industrial economies, overall population growth was the key to economic growth, and economic growth meant opportunities across the board. But in a creative, postindustrial economy, that's no longer true. Changing technology, increased trade, and the ability to outsource routine functions have made highly skilled workers less reliant on the colocation of the unskilled and moderately skilled. What matters today isn't where most people settle, but where the *greatest number of the most-skilled* people does. Because the return on colocation among the ablest is so high, and because high-end incomes are rising so fast, it makes sense for these workers to continue to bid up real estate and accept other costs that traditional middle-class workers and families cannot afford. As traditional middle-class households are displaced by smaller, higher-income households, population can decline even as economic growth continues. America's most successful cities may increasingly be inhabited by a core of wealthy workers leading highly privileged lives, catered to by an underclass of service workers living in far-off suburbs.

13 Some of today's means metros could fall back eventually as housing prices and living costs rise, and new ones could emerge. But there are powerful reasons to believe that the wealth disparity between some city-regions and others will continue to grow, and perhaps even accelerate, thanks to the snowball effect of talent attraction. "This spatial sorting," says Gyourko, "will affect the nature of America as much as the rural-urban migration of the late nineteenth century did." Accommodating that sorting will be one of the great political and cultural challenges of the next generation.

THE MIGRATION OF COLLEGE GRADUATES
Since 1970, college graduates have flocked to select American cities

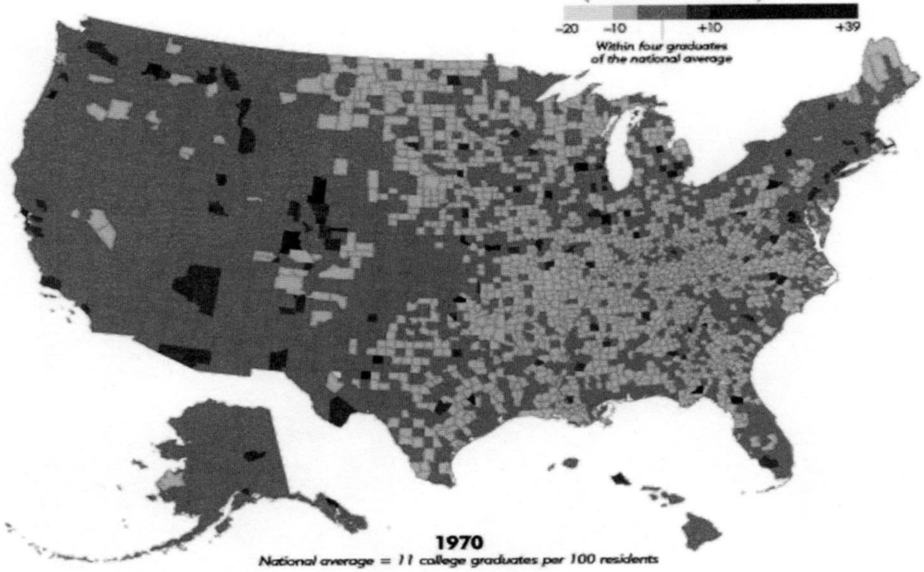

1970
National average = 11 college graduates per 100 residents

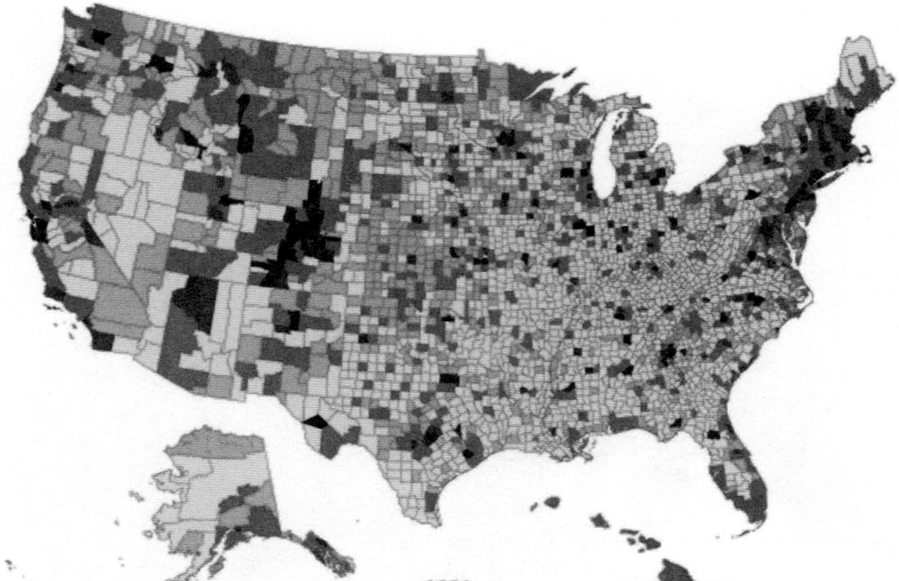

2000

National average = 24 college graduates per 100 residents

The Uneven Fortunes of America's Cities

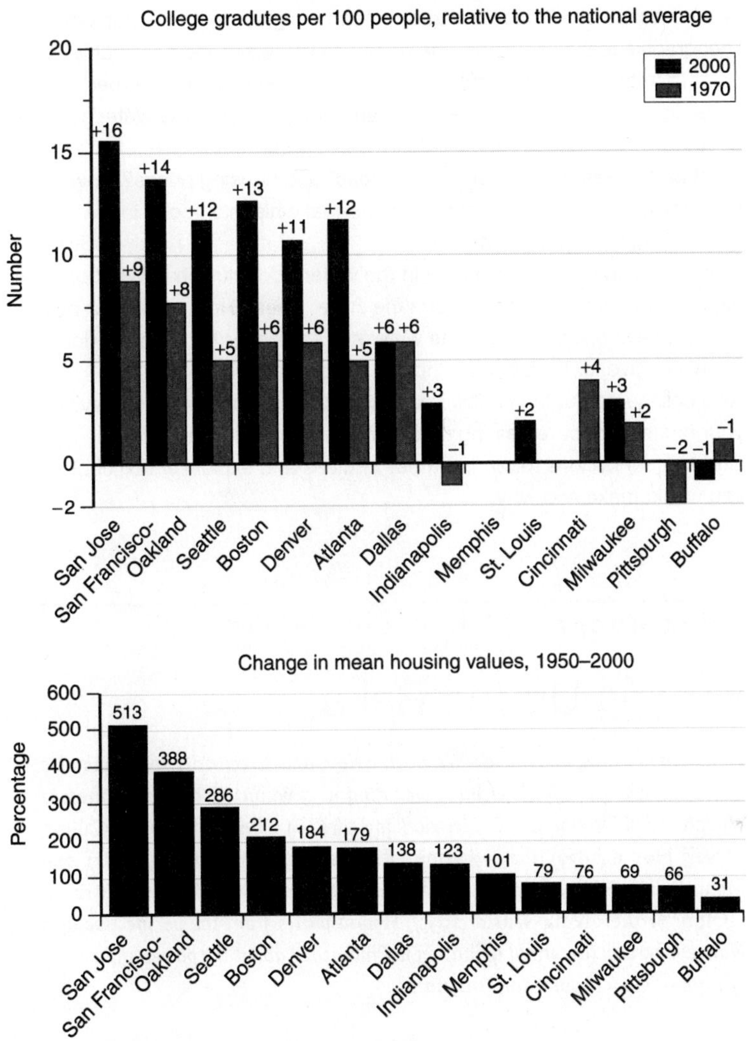

Education figures based on 1970 Standard Metropolitan Statistical Area (MSA) definitions; housing values based on 1990 Primary MSA definitions.

FOR THINKING, DISCUSSING, AND WRITING

1. What exactly does Florida mean by "means migration"? How does the "geographic realignment" that he mentions in the second paragraph differ from the kinds of population migrations that you have learned about in the past? How do the maps and graph support the writer's points?
2. What is the relation between "super cities" and housing prices? How does the price of housing help the writer make his main point in the essay? What is a "means metro"?
3. How do college graduates figure in the writer's conclusions? What often happens to them when they reach the super cities? How does your own experience support or refute the writer's assertion? What reasons does the writer give for the phenomenon of means migration?
4. As a college graduate in a few years, you will face the option of leaving your home town or remaining there. Write an essay in which you explore your options regarding these choices and explain which choice you would make and why.

LINDA HOGAN

Waking Up the Rake

Linda Hogan (1947–) is a teacher, poet, writer, and screenwriter who has also worked at a variety of other jobs, including as a volunteer at the Minnesota Wildlife Rehabilitation Clinic. Her work includes the collection of poems Calling Myself Home *(1979), the collection of stories* The Big Woman *(1987), and* Mean Spirit: A Novel *(1990). In this selection from* Dwellings: A Spiritual History of the Living World *(1995), Hogan writes from the perspective of a Native American (her tribal affiliation is Chickasaw) about the power and beauty of work—"Work is our altar," she states.*

1 In the still dark mornings, my grandmother would rise up from her bed and put wood in the stove. When the fire began to burn, she would sit in front of its warmth and let down her hair. It had never been cut and it knotted down in two long braids. When I was fortunate enough to be there, in those red Oklahoma mornings, I would wake up with her, stand behind her chair, and pull the brush through the long strands of her hair. It cascaded down her back, down over the chair, and touched the floor.

2 We were the old and the new, bound together in front of the snapping fire, woven like a lifetime's tangled growth of hair. I saw my future in her body and face, and her past was alive in me. We were morning people, and in all of earth's mornings the new intertwines with the old. Even new, a day itself is ancient, old with earth's habit of turning over and over again.

3 Years later, I was sick, and I went to a traditional healer. The healer was dark and thin and radiant. The first night I was there, she also lit a fire. We sat before it, smelling the juniper smoke. She asked me to tell her everything, my life spoken in words, a case history of living, with its dreams and losses, the scars and wounds we all bear from being in the world. She smoked me with cedar smoke, wrapped a sheet around me, and put me to bed, gently, like a mother caring for her child.

4 The next morning she nudged me awake and took me outside to pray. We faced east where the sun was beginning its journey on our side of earth.

5 The following morning in red dawn, we went outside and prayed. The sun was a full orange eye rising up the air. The morning after that we did the same, and on Sunday we did likewise.

6 The next time I visited her it was a year later, and again we went through the same prayers, standing outside facing the early sun. On the last morning I was there, she left for her job in town. Before leaving, she said, "Our work is our altar."

7 Those words have remained with me.

8 Now I am a disciple of birds. The birds that I mean are eagles, owls, and hawks. I clean cages at the Birds of Prey Rehabilitation Foundation. It is the work I wanted to do, in order to spend time inside the gentle presence of the birds.

9 There is a Sufi saying that goes something like this: "Yes, worship God, go to church, sing praises, but first tie your camel to the post." This cleaning is the work of tying the camel to a post.

10 I pick up the carcasses and skin of rats, mice, and of rabbits. Some of them have been turned inside out by the sharp-beaked eaters, so that the leathery flesh becomes a delicately veined coat for the inner fur. It is a boneyard. I rake the smooth fragments of bones. Sometimes there is a leg or shank of deer to be picked up.

11 In this boneyard, the still-red vertebrae lie on the ground beside an open rib cage. The remains of a rabbit, a small intestinal casing, holds

excrement like beads in a necklace. And there are the clean, oval pellets the birds spit out, filled with fur, bone fragments and now and then, a delicate sharp claw that looks as if it were woven inside. A feather, light and soft, floats down a current of air, and it is also picked up.

12 Over time, the narrow human perspective from which we view things expands. A deer carcass begins to look beautiful and rich in its torn redness, the muscle and bone exposed in the shape life took on for a while as it walked through meadows and drank at creeks.

13 And the bone fragments have their own stark beauty, the clean white jaw bones with ivory teeth small as the head of a pin still in them. I think of medieval physicians trying to learn about our private, hidden bodies by cutting open the stolen dead and finding the splendor inside, the grace of every red organ, and the smooth, gleaming bone.

14 This work is an apprenticeship, and the birds are the teachers. Sweet-eyed barn owls, such taskmasters, asking us to be still and slow and to move in time with their rhythms, not our own. The short-eared owls with their startling yellow eyes require the full presence of a human. The marsh hawks, behind their branches, watch our every move.

15 There is a silence needed here before a person enters the bordered world the birds inhabit, so we stop and compose ourselves before entering their doors, and we listen to the musical calls of the eagles, the sound of wings in air, the way their feet with sharp claws, many larger than our own hands, grab hold of a perch. Then we know we are ready to enter, and they are ready for us.

16 The most difficult task the birds demand is that we learn to be equal to them, to feel our way into an intelligence that is different from our own. A friend, awed at the thought of working with eagles, said, "Imagine knowing an eagle." I answered her honestly, "It isn't so much that we know the eagles. It's that they know us."

17 And they know that we are apart from them, that as humans we have somehow fallen from our animal grace, and because of that we maintain a distance from them, though it is not always a distance of heart. The places we inhabit, even sharing a common earth, must remain distinct and separate. It was our presence that brought most of them here in the first place, nearly all of them injured in a clash with the human world. They have been shot, or hit by cars, trapped in leg hold traps, poisoned, ensnared in wire fences. To ensure their survival,

they must remember us as the enemies that we are. We are the embodiment of a paradox; we are the wounders and we are the healers.

18 There are human lessons to be learned here, in the work. Fritjof Capra wrote: "Doing work that has to be done over and over again helps us to recognize the natural cycles of growth and decay, of birth and death, and thus become aware of the dynamic order of the universe." And it is true, in whatever we do, the brushing of hair, the cleaning of cages, we begin to see the larger order of things. In this place, there is a constant coming to terms with both the sacred place life occupies, and with death. Like one of those early physicians who discovered the strange, inner secrets of our human bodies, I'm filled with awe at the very presence of life, not just the birds, but a horse contained in its living fur, a dog alive and running. What a marvel it is, the fine shape life takes in all of us. It is equally marvelous that life is quickly turned back to the earth-colored ants and the soft white maggots that are time's best and closest companions. To sit with the eagles and their flutelike songs, listening to the longer flute of wind sweep through the lush grasslands, is to begin to know the natural laws that exist apart from our own written ones.

19 One of those laws, that we carry deep inside us, is intuition. It is lodged in a place even the grave-robbing doctors could not discover. It's a blood-written code that directs us through life. The founder of this healing center, Sigrid Ueblacker, depends on this inner knowing. She watches, listens, and feels her way to an understanding of each eagle and owl. This vision, as I call it, directs her own daily work at healing the injured birds and returning them to the wild.

20 "Sweep the snow away," she tells me. "The Swainson's hawks should be in Argentina this time of year and should not have to stand in the snow."

21 I sweep.

22 And that is in the winter when the hands ache from the cold, and the water freezes solid and has to be broken out for the birds, fresh buckets carried over icy earth from the well. In summer, it's another story. After only a few hours the food begins to move again, as if resurrected to life. A rabbit shifts a bit. A mouse turns. You could say that they have been resurrected, only with a life other than the one that left them. The moving skin swarms with flies and their offspring, ants, and a few wasps, busy at their own daily labor.

23 Even aside from the expected rewards for this work, such as seeing an eagle healed and winging across the sky it fell from, there are others.

An occasional snake, beautiful and sleek, finds its way into the cage one day, eats a mouse and is too fat to leave, so we watch its long muscular life stretched out in the tall grasses. Or, another summer day, taking branches to be burned with a pile of wood near the little creek, a large turtle with a dark and shining shell slips soundlessly into the water, its presence a reminder of all the lives beyond these that occupy us.

24 One green morning, an orphaned owl perches nervously above me while I clean. Its downy feathers are roughed out. It appears to be twice its size as it clacks its beak at me, warning me: stay back. Then, fearing me the way we want it to, it bolts off the perch and flies, landing by accident onto the wooden end of my rake, before it sees that a human is an extension of the tool, and it flies again to a safer place, while I return to raking.

25 The word "rake" means to gather or heap up, to smooth the broken ground. And that's what this work is, all of it, the smoothing over of broken ground, the healing of the severed trust we humans hold with earth. We gather it back together again with great care, take the broken pieces and fragments and return them to the sky. It is work at the borderland between species, at the boundary between injury and healing.

26 There is an art to raking, a very fine art, one with rhythm in it, and life. On the days I do it well, the rake wakes up. Wood that came from dark dense forests seems to return to life. The water that rose up through the rings of that wood, the minerals of earth mined upward by the burrowing tree roots, all come alive. My own fragile hand touches the wood, a hand full of my own life, including that which rose each morning early to watch the sun return from the other side of the planet. Over time, these hands will smooth the rake's wooden handle down to a sheen.

27 Raking. It is a labor round and complete, smooth and new as an egg, and the rounding seasons of the world revolving in time and space. All things, even our own heartbeats and sweat, are in it, part of it. And that work, that watching the turning over of life, becomes a road into what is essential. Work is the country of hands, and they want to live there in the dailiness of it, the repetition that is time's language of prayer, a common tongue. Everything is there, in that language, in the humblest of labor. The rake wakes up and the healing is in it. The shadows of leaves that once fell beneath the tree the handle came from are in that labor, and the rabbits that passed this way, on the altar of our work. And when the rake wakes up, all earth's gods are reborn and they dance and sing in the dusty air around us.

FOR THINKING, DISCUSSING, AND WRITING

1. What does the description of Hogan's grandmother add to the piece? The selection begins with Hogan's grandmother waking up and ends with a discussion of "waking up the rake." How does the idea of waking serve as a metaphor? How does the metaphor inform the piece?
2. Why does Hogan go into such detail about the carcasses of dead animals? Does her fascination seem in any way morbid to you? Why or why not?
3. Why does Hogan infuse her somewhat mundane and simple work with a kind of grandeur? How can people turn ordinary jobs into something special?
4. In an essay explain and analyze Hogan's view of work and compare and contrast it with prevalent attitudes about work in our age.

WILLIAM DERESIEWICZ

The Dispossessed

William Deresiewicz, who teaches English at Yale, is the author of Jane Austen and the Romantic Poets *(2005). A regular contributor to the* New York Times Book Review, *the* Nation, *and the* American Scholar *(where this article appeared in the winter 2006 issue), Deresiewicz has a PhD from Columbia University. His current project,* Friendship: A Cultural History from Jane Austen to Jennifer Aniston, *traces the impact of modernity on the ways that friendship has been imagined and practiced in Great Britain and the United States over the past two centuries, as illustrated through the arts and insights from the social sciences. In this essay he shows how people first stopped noticing members of the working class, and then convinced themselves that the working class doesn't exist.*

1 Sometimes you don't realize that something's been missing—it doesn't matter how big it is—until, for a moment or two, it isn't. About 10 years ago, I was listening to an interview with the choreographer Bill T. Jones, who had just published his memoirs. Jones is gay and black, and when the interviewer asked him what his father had thought about his becoming a dancer, Jones, somewhat testily, said something like, "You don't understand. This wasn't a *middle*-class family. The goal wasn't to become a professional: the goal was to better yourself." The first thing that hit me about this was that it had nothing to do with race

or sexuality. The second thing that hit me was that it had everything to do with class, specifically the working class—which, I suddenly realized, I never heard anyone talk about. A little while later, I read a profile of Roseanne Barr in *The New Yorker.* Only middle-class women care about feminism, Barr claimed. Working-class women already have power, because they're the ones in charge at home.

2 Working-class career expectations, working-class family structures: two things I knew nothing about. Each revelation gratified me with the feeling of learning something interesting and important and new, but together they enraged me with the recognition that the reason they felt new, the reason I was so abysmally ignorant about this world that lay all around me—the American working class—was that such knowledge had been withheld from me by my culture. It's not just that I'm middle class myself. I'm white, too, but mainstream culture (popular entertainment, the news media) has exposed me to a steady stream of images and information about blacks. I suspect that American gentiles also know quite a lot about Jews. But the working class is American culture's great lost continent.

3 There are exceptions: Roseanne's show was one, Michael Moore's *Roger & Me* (as well as the whole persona he's constructed) is another, as was the recent HBO series *Family Bonds.* But much of what was seen as important and "edgy" in those productions was their working-class subject matter, which shows how rare any serious, extended, or sympathetic popular treatment of the working class now is. (Analogous things could be said about Bruce Springsteen, or novelists like Richard Russo and Russell Banks, or the *New York Times's* recent multipart series on class in America. Imagine how superfluous it would have been for the *Times* to do a series about race or sexuality, topics that permeate half the stories it publishes.) Among mainstream films of the last decade, *Mystic River* and *Good Will Hunting* come to mind, but far more typical is the kind of thing we got in *Million Dollar Baby,* where the heroine's family was presented as loutish, contemptible trailer trash, or on the *Simpsons,* where Homer's working-class characteristics (and he seems to be the working-class breadwinner of a middle-class family) are played strictly for laughs. There are working-class *characters* all over the place: cops on detective shows, nurses and orderlies on doctor shows, and so forth. But it's the nature of such dramas to present people only in terms of their jobs, asking few or no questions about the rest of their lives. Look at a show or a movie that takes you into its characters' homes, and you'll find that the homes you're being taken into are

almost always middle or upper class, even when the characters belong to that vast, imaginary social group we might call the pseudo–working class, people with working-class jobs but middle-class lifestyles, like the Simpsons or the Gilmore girls or those lucky kids on *Friends*.

4 What we don't have in this country, in other words, is anyone like Mike Leigh, who makes art out of working-class lives by refusing to prettify them. We no longer have anyone, among our major novelists, like Steinbeck or Dos Passos. We don't even have any TV shows like *The Honeymooners* or *All in the Family*, whose frank depictions of the material conditions of working-class life (think of the Kramdens' kitchen, with its bridge table and two chairs) didn't prevent them from achieving a monumental universality. When we do get the rare serious mainstream treatment of working-class life, it comes from a middle-class observer like Barbara Ehrenreich. So why is it that the only working-class person anyone will pay attention to these days is a middle-class journalist masquerading as one? More fundamentally, why is it that the working class is treated as an exotic species, while the middle class, which it heavily outnumbers, is regarded as normal and normative?

5 It's not hard to begin to answer these questions. First, the people who get paid to create mainstream culture—journalists, editors, writers, producers—are, ipso facto, members of the middle class. As social mobility slows, more and more of them originate in that class. The middle class is not only what they know and identify with, it often seems to be the only thing they're aware of. Today's army of cultural commentators, who speak so confidently about the way "we" live now—the crazy hours, the overscheduled kids, the elite colleges and nursery schools—mistake their tiny world of urban and university-town professionals for the whole of society. Second, as TV's creation of a pseudo–working class suggests, looking at the real one is kind of a bummer. Just as everyone on TV has to be beautiful, so does everyone have to have money, or at least live like they do. Nobody wants to watch a show about some fat guy struggling to make the rent. Finally and most important, we simply don't talk about class at all anymore. Why should we, when we're all supposedly part of a single one, the great middle? What we talk about is race and sexuality. (Or in the academy, race, gender, and sexuality, the great triumvirate. The humanities, despite their claim to transformative significance, have all but forgotten about class.) Instead of Steinbeck and Dos Passos, we have Toni Morrison, Maxine Hong Kingston, Oscar Hijuelos, Jhumpa Lahiri, and Michael Cunningham.

6 It was Morrison, in fact, who provided one of the most telling indications of our loss of the working class as an imaginative category, her famous anointment of Bill Clinton as our "first black president": "Clinton displays almost every trope of blackness: single-parent household, born poor, working-class, saxophone-playing, McDonald's-and-junk-food-loving boy from Arkansas." At least Morrison still employs the term *working class*, but it's still merely a secondary category for her. If it weren't, she would have seen that what those attributes really added up to wasn't that Clinton was black (or "black"), but that he was our first *working-class* president, if not ever, then in a while, and our most flamboyantly so in a *long* while. But of course working-class attributes are going to look like tropes of blackness. Just about the only images we have of the working class are images of black people, understood *as* black people. In fact, many of the things we think of as characteristically black are really true of the working class as a whole (and aren't true of middle-class blacks). Consider the realm of family structure: having children at an early age, having them outside of marriage, raising them as a single parent, raising them with the help of an older relative—and not being stigmatized by your community for doing any of these things. It's an old American story: race becomes a surrogate for class, which is to say, a way of not thinking about it at all.

7 On the rare occasions when we do think about class, our fixation on race makes us confuse the working class with the poor, as the response to the Katrina disaster demonstrated. For an interval that proved predictably brief, Americans started talking about class again, but we still missed the true picture. For one thing, our discussion of poverty was all too quickly subsumed, again, into a discussion about race. (It's funny how few images we saw of poor, dispossessed whites, though many such people must have existed.) More important is that most of the blacks we saw wandering the highways or abandoned at the Convention Center were surely not the truly indigent (the homeless, the unemployed); they were laborers and waitresses and hospital workers and maids, members of New Orleans's socially cohesive and culturally vibrant working-class black communities. These are the same communities that are now struggling for the right to rebuild themselves, struggling to get the rest of us to acknowledge that their neighborhoods were more than just slums. The people who lived in these communities may have looked dirty and disheveled on TV, and some of them may have acted desperately at times, but how would you

have looked, and how would you have acted after four or five days in those circumstances? Yet so deeply has the notion of a working class been pushed to the recesses of our consciousness, and so powerful is the link in our minds between poverty and race, that when we're shown a working-class black, we see a poor person—and when we're shown a working-class white, we don't see anything at all.

8 What is the working class? As a first approximation, I'd suggest that a member of the working class is someone who receives and hourly wage. (There are exceptions both ways: airline pilots on the one hand, secretaries on the other.) The virtue of this definition is that it not only excludes the true middle class—professionals, managers, and small-business owners—it also reminds us that working-class people have a very different relationship to their work and their workplace than do those who earn a salary. By this criterion, the working class comprises about 80 percent of the American workforce. Even if one claims that the cop or fireman or unionized factory worker, who might well live in the suburbs and drive a big car, actually belongs to the middle class, the working class still comprises a large majority of the country. (Besides, as Paul Krugman recently argued in a *New York Times* column on the wage-and-benefit squeeze in the auto industry, a lot of those factory workers—the "working middle class"—will find themselves squarely back in the working class soon anyway.) The poor may literally be "invisible in America," as the subtitle of David K. Shipler's recent book puts it, out of sight in the human garbage heaps of ghettos and trailer parks, but the great bulk of the working class—which is to say, most of America—is invisible only because "we" aren't seeing what's right in front of our faces: the people who serve our food, ring up our purchases, fix our cars, change our bedpans.

9 It's as if the vast space between the poor and the middle class didn't exist. The term *working class* has been erased from our political discourse, replaced by *working poor* and the insidious *working families.* *Working poor* is a valuable term, because it reminds us how meagerly many jobs pay these days and belies the notion of what used to be called the *idle poor.* But *working poor* is not at all the same as *working class*, though the trailer-trash stereotype would have us think so. Some working-class people are poor, but the great majority are not, they just aren't well-off enough to be middle class. *Working families* isn't the same as *working class*, either. Whether in the mouth of a Clinton or a Bush, the term is designed to treat the working and middle classes as a monolith.

By conflating the two (the doctor struggling to pay for his kids to go to Harvard, the cashier struggling to pay for medicine), the term eliminates the working class as a political as well as a cultural category.

10 But class hasn't completely dropped out of our political discourse. In fact, it's made a comeback of late, only in a particularly devious new guise, our new ruling paradigm of red state vs. blue state—where ideology is rewritten as region (Republicans are from red states, Democrats from blue), region as culture (red-staters drink beer, blue-staters drink wine), and culture as class, though only implicitly (what do you think *beer* and *wine* really mean?). Fifty-seven million people voted for John Kerry in the last election; to speak as if all of them were Chardonnay-sipping professors, or even professionals, is ridiculous. Simple arithmetic tells us that millions of them were members of the working class. But according to the dominant syllogism, if Kerry voters are effete elitists while Bush voters are "ordinary Americans" (the closest anyone comes to actually saying *working class* anymore) then the working class looks like the stereotypical Bush voter: rural, Southern, conservative, nationalist, and fundamentalist—in other words, redneck. This is as gross an oversimplification as imagining that the middle class is composed exclusively of leftist academics. But absent any other or better images of the working class, the redneck myth not only means that Republicans get to present themselves as champions of the working class while ostensibly denying its existence (as Thomas Frank has argued in *What's the Matter with Kansas?*), it also means that the true character of the working class, in all its enormous breadth and diversity, remains hidden.

11 It remains hidden, in particular, from the working class itself, among whom the redneck myth does in fact seem to be taking hold. I lived in Portland, Oregon, last year, a heavily working-class town, and I was struck by the affinity the working class there seems to feel with Southern culture. (Country Music Television, for example, is part of the basic cable package.) The South is the one place where the white working class doesn't hide itself, as the essayist Richard Rodriguez recently noted, and its leading cultural expressions—country music and NASCAR—are becoming those of the white working class as a whole. This southernization of the working class surely owes a lot to the red-state/blue-state nonsense, to the ascendancy of southern Republicans, and to the scarcity of other kinds of working-class images.

12 But it also owes a lot to the decline of organized labor. I've suggested that working-class images haven't always been so hard to find in the mainstream, and it's no accident that their virtual disappearance over the

past few decades has coincided with that decline. Fifty years ago, more than one in three American workers were unionized; today, one in eight is. Along with a huge loss in political power has come the loss of a confident, self-conscious, working-class culture. Not only were workers visible to the classes above them, they had their own voices, their own cultural institutions, their own sense of who they were and what they did; in short, they weren't dependent on the middle class to define them. People used to speak of the "dignity of labor," and the phrase meant that being a worker was something to be proud of, that the working class saw itself as something more than a collection of people who couldn't make it, that it had its own traditions and values, constituted its own community.

13 I've spent a lot of time thinking about the working class in the 10 years since those inciting recognitions. I've kept my eyes open to whatever I could glean from the media and from my immediate surroundings. I've had long talks on the subject with my wife, who spent many years in a working-class environment, and with a former student, who grew up in one. I've come to believe not only that the working class constitutes a coherent culture very different from the middle-class one that's presented to us as natural and universal, but that that culture possesses a genuine set of virtues. *New York Times* columnist David Brooks has been singing the praises lately of bourgeois values like industry, temperance, prudence, and thrift. I have nothing against these things, especially since, as a member of the middle class, I practice them myself. But industry, temperance, prudence, and thrift are not the be-all and end-all of the good life. In fact, they are apt to be accompanied by a countervailing array of bourgeois vices, like narrowness, prudery, timidity, and meanness, not to mention hypocrisy and self-conceit.

14 As for the working class, I'll grant, for the sake of argument, that its vices tend to be the negative of bourgeois values, that working-class people are, compared to the middle class, less temperate, prudent, thrifty, and industrious (though that last seems a rather unfair description of people who do manual labor, work two jobs, or put up with forced overtime). But by the same token, working-class life breeds its own virtues: loyalty, community, stoicism, humility, and even tolerance. Not that every working-class person is a paragon of these virtues; like Brooks, I'm trying to articulate the general contours of a class culture as it arises from the facts of everyday existence. If only because of their limited possibilities in life, working-class people care more about their families and their friends and the places they're from than they do about their careers. Because they haven't been taught to believe that they're entitled to the best of

everything, they take what life brings them without whining or self-pity. Because they don't preen themselves on where they went to school or what kind of job they have, they don't act like they're better than everyone else. And when it comes right down to it, they aren't any more prejudiced than the middle class, and may even be less so. Middle-class prejudices are just more respectable—in fact, they tend to be directed against the working class itself—as well as more carefully concealed. What's more, while the middle class espouses tolerance, working-class people, because they can't simply insulate themselves from those they don't like with wads of money, are much more likely, in practice, to live and let live. Maybe what this country needs are fewer bourgeois values and more proletarian ones.

FOR THINKING, DISCUSSING, AND WRITING

1. Deresiewicz names dozens of writers, politicians, and media figures to make his argument. What is the value of all these references to the main point of the essay? Make a list of the people whose names you don't recognize and try to determine who they are and why the writer mentions them.
2. What distinction does the writer make between the middle class and the working class? The working class and the working poor?
3. Deresiewicz explains in paragraph 4 the reasons that "the working class is treated like an exotic species." Do you find his explanation valid? Why or why not? What elements of his analysis might you challenge?
4. The writer's sentiments come down clearly on the side of the working class, as opposed to the middle class. Write an essay in which you analyze Deresiewicz's views of either of these classes and explain why you might agree or disagree with him.

CONNECTING IDEAS: A Life of Work

1. Using some of the relevant essays in this chapter, write and essay that examines the role of poverty in the development of a person's view of work and its rewards and failings.
2. What is your philosophy of work and its place in your life? How does it compare with the philosophies expounded by writers in this chapter?
3. Gary Soto, Linda Hogan, and William Branigin all deal with the minority experience in regard to work. How are the revelations in their essays related exclusively to being a member of a minority group in America? What elements in the essays contribute to your Impression? Write an essay that responds to these questions.

CHAPTER 5

Law, Justice, and the Democratic Way

WHAT IS A JUST SOCIETY? AMERICANS, STALWARTS OF democracy and government through national suffrage, have long prided themselves on the notion of liberty and its concomitant opposition to capricious rules and inbred judiciaries corrupted in other nations by monarchies and dictatorships. The laws of our country, influenced in principle at least by a robust political system, aim at fairness and equality for all citizens.

Yet to judge by current events, it seems that many people in America see government as an evil to be avoided rather than an avenue for sustaining life in a just world. Election data, political party registration, and obedience to the law in our modern world have an appallingly negative cast. Voters decrease in numbers from one presidential election to another; citizens seeking to influence government through active participation in the two-party system decline annually; violations of basic laws shock us regularly with their brazen challenges to accepted modes of human conduct. Exercising the rights, privileges, and obligations of an enlightened electorate seems of little interest to many men and women today. You'll read an ironic response in this chapter to some of these realities in "Happy National Apathy Day" by Will Durst.

Oddly enough, although law, government, and politics seem to be losing their hold on the American electorate, some important contradictions challenge any hasty conclusion about our indifference to these key elements of an enlightened citizenry. First, to judge from the increasing numbers of lawyers sitting for and passing statewide bar exams and the numbers of laws passing through varied legislatures in local and national government, we certainly are more and more litigious as a society. Laws, law suits, and lawyers abound. One may fairly ask to what effect, certainly. In what ways are the laws helping us create an orderly society and develop just governments serving people's needs? Why have our laws and penal systems not prevented terrorism here and abroad? Why has legislation not successfully protected the indigent? Why do our societies continue to spawn more and more horrifying acts of violence—the unimaginable massacre of students and teachers at Virginia Tech on April 16, 2007, just one example in our age. The United States is the only Western industrialized country that through a legitimate legal system still relies on capital punishment, supposedly as a deterrent to heinous crimes, yet any abatement of such crimes over the centuries seems modest. You'll want to read Mark Essig's brief but haunting essay about the forms of capital punishment and our largely unsuccessful efforts to find painless executions. George Orwell in "A Hanging" and Edward I. Koch in "Death and Justice" provide wildly different views on the death penalty and should help you think through your own response to this volatile issue.

Another contradiction to the claim that people are not interested in the notions of law, justice, government, and politics lies in the hold these institutions have on our imaginations. Novels about courtrooms, jurors, police work, and sentencing regularly earn best-seller status. Think of the instant success in our day of books by John Grisham (*The Pelican Brief, The Chamber, The Last Juror, The Runaway Jury*), for example, or Scott Turow (*The Laws of Our Fathers, Presumed Innocent, The Burden of Proof*): the titles alone attest to the legal and political system's viability as fodder for popular fiction. From Charlie Chan to Perry Mason to the lawyers and detectives and district attorneys on the *Law and Order* franchise—movies and television shows thrive on tales of justice foiled or rewarded.

As you consider the issues of justice and government, you need to weigh along with the writers in this chapter the true responsibilities, obligations, and privileges of citizens in a democratic society—and the nature of the laws that govern it and the politics that sustain it. We need to evaluate regularly how to enforce our laws and whether our legal system is efficient, fair, and humane. Law—the rules and regulations that promote a society's stability and aims for justice; government —the administration of public policy; and politics—the policies, goals, or affairs of government or the groups or parties within it: in a democracy these entities form the basis for societies and sustain and nurture a progressive community. These are threads in a complex tapestry of human need, all responsible for protecting society against its own dangers and helping us live in peace and security.

GEORGE ORWELL

A Hanging

*George Orwell (1903–1950) is the pen name of Eric Blair. He was born in Bengal, India, in 1903; his parents were members of the British Civil Service in India. In the mid-1930s, like many left-wing intellectuals and writers, he went to Spain to fight against Fascist forces led by the ultimately victorious General Franco. Orwell was seriously wounded in the Spanish Civil War. He became famous in the early years of the Cold War for two prophetic, satirical books fed by his experiences with Communism, books that brilliantly attack totalitarian forms of government—*Animal Farm *(1945) and* Nineteen Eighty-Four *(1949). This selection is one of a group of influential essays by Orwell that explore issues of broad concern to modern readers. In "A Hanging," he shows the brutal indifference to capital punishment shown by bureaucrats.*

1 It was in Burma, a sodden morning of the rains. A sickly light, like yellow tinfoil, was slanting over the high walls into the jail yard. We were waiting outside the condemned cells, a row of sheds fronted with double bars, like small animal cages. Each cell measured about ten feet by ten and was quite bare within except for a plank bed and a pot of drinking water. In some of them brown silent men were squatting at the inner bars, with their blankets draped round them. These were the condemned men, due to be hanged within the next week or two.

2 One prisoner had been brought out of his cell. He was a Hindu, a puny wisp of a man, with a shaven head and vague liquid eyes. He had a thick, sprouting moustache, absurdly too big for his body, rather like the moustache of a comic man on the films. Six tall Indian warders were guarding him and getting him ready for the gallows. Two of them

stood by with rifles with fixed bayonets, while the others handcuffed him, passed a chain through his handcuffs and fixed it to their belts, and lashed his arms tight to his sides. They crowded very close about him, with their hands always on him in a careful, caressing grip, as though all the while feeling him to make sure he was there. It was like men handling a fish which is still alive and may jump back into the water. But he stood quite unresisting, yielding his arms limply to the ropes, as though he hardly noticed what was happening.

3 Eight o'clock struck and a bugle call, desolately thin in the wet air, floated from the distant barracks. The superintendent of the jail, who was standing apart from the rest of us, moodily prodding the gravel with his stick, raised his head at the sound. He was an army doctor, with a grey toothbrush moustache and a gruff voice. "For God's sake hurry up, Francis," he said irritably. "The man ought to have been dead by this time. Aren't you ready yet?"

4 Francis, the head jailer, a fat Dravidian in a white drill suit and gold spectacles, waved his black hand. "Yes sir, yes sir," he bubbled. "All iss satisfactorily prepared. The hangman iss waiting. We shall proceed."

5 "Well, quick march, then. The prisoners can't get their breakfast till this job's over."

6 We set out for the gallows. Two warders marched on either side of the prisoner, with their files at the slope; two others marched close against him, gripping him by arm and shoulder, as though at once pushing and supporting him. The rest of us, magistrates and the like, followed behind. Suddenly, when we had gone ten yards, the procession stopped short without any order or warning. A dreadful thing had happened—a dog, come goodness knows whence, had appeared in the yard. It came bounding among us with a loud volley of barks, and leapt round us wagging its whole body, wild with glee at finding so many human beings together. It was a large woolly dog, half Airedale, half pariah. For a moment it pranced round us, and then, before anyone could stop it, it had made a dash for the prisoner, and jumping up tried to lick his face. Everyone stood aghast, too taken aback even to grab at the dog.

7 "Who let that bloody brute in here?" said the superintendent angrily. "Catch it, someone!"

8 A warder, detached from the escort, charged clumsily after the dog, but it danced and gambolled just out of his reach, taking everything as part of the game. A young Eurasian jailer picked up a handful of gravel

and tried to stone the dog away, but it dodged the stones and came after us again. Its yaps echoed from the jail walls. The prisoner, in the grasp of the two warders, looked on incuriously, as though this was another formality of the hanging. It was several minutes before someone managed to catch the dog. Then we put my handkerchief through its collar and moved off once more, with the dog still straining and whimpering.

9 It was about forty yards to the gallows. I watched the bare brown back of the prisoner marching in front of me. He walked clumsily with his bound arms, but quite steadily, with that bobbing gait of the Indian who never straightens his knees. At each step his muscles slid neatly into place, the lock of hair on his scalp danced up and down, his feet printed themselves on the wet gravel. And once, in spite of the men who gripped him by each shoulder, he stepped slightly aside to avoid a puddle on the path.

10 It is curious, but till that moment I had never realised what it means to destroy a healthy, conscious man. When I saw the prisoner step aside to avoid the puddle, I saw the mystery, the unspeakable wrongness, of cutting a life short when it is in full tide. This man was not dying, he was alive just as we were alive. All the organs of his body were working—bowels digesting food, skin renewing itself, nails growing, tissues forming—all toiling away in solemn foolery. His nails would still be growing when he stood on the drop, when he was falling through the air with a tenth of a second to live. His eyes saw the yellow gravel and the grey walls, and his brain still remembered, foresaw, reasoned—reasoned even about puddles. He and we were a party of men walking together, seeing, hearing, feeling, understanding the same world; and in two minutes, with a sudden snap, one of us would be gone—one mind less, one world less.

11 The gallows stood in a small yard, separate from the main grounds of the prison, and overgrown with tall prickly weeds. It was a brick erection like three sides of a shed, with planking on top, and above that two beams and a crossbar with the rope dangling. The hangman, a grey-haired convict in the white uniform of the prison, was waiting beside his machine. He greeted us with a servile crouch as we entered. At a word from Francis the two warders, gripping the prisoner more closely than ever, half led, half pushed him to the gallows and helped him clumsily up the ladder. Then the hangman climbed up and fixed the rope round the prisoner's neck.

12 We stood waiting, five yards away. The warders had formed in a rough circle round the gallows. And then, when the noose was fixed, the prisoner began crying out on his god. It was a high, reiterated cry of "Ram! Ram! Ram! Ram!", not urgent and fearful like a prayer or a cry for help, but steady, rhythmical, almost like the tolling of a bell. The dog answered the sound with a whine. The hangman, still standing on the gallows, produced a small cotton bag like a flour bag and drew it down over the prisoner's face. But the sound, muffled by the cloth, still persisted, over and over again: "Ram! Ram! Ram! Ram! Ram!"

13 The hangman climbed down and stood ready, holding the lever. Minutes seemed to pass. The steady, muffled crying from the prisoner went on and on, "Ram! Ram! Ram!" never faltering for an instant. The superintendent, his head on his chest, was slowly poking the ground with his stick; perhaps he was counting the cries, allowing the prisoner a fixed number—fifty, perhaps, or a hundred. Everyone had changed colour. The Indians had gone grey like bad coffee, and one or two of the bayonets were wavering. We looked at the lashed, hooded man on the drop, and listened to his cries—each cry another second of life; the same thought was in all our minds: oh, kill him quickly, get it over, stop that abominable noise!

14 Suddenly the superintendent made up his mind. Throwing up his head he made a swift motion with his stick. "Chalo!" he shouted almost fiercely.

15 There was a clanking noise, and then dead silence. The prisoner had vanished, and the rope was twisting on itself. I let go of the dog, and it galloped immediately to the back of the gallows; but when it got there it stopped short, barked, and then retreated into a corner of the yard, where it stood among the weeds, looking timorously out at us. We went round the gallows to inspect the prisoner's body. He was dangling with his toes pointed straight downwards, very slowly revolving, as dead as a stone.

16 The superintendent reached out with his stick and poked the bare body; it oscillated, slightly. "*He's* all right," said the superintendent. He backed out from under the gallows, and blew out a deep breath. The moody look had gone out of his face quite suddenly. He glanced at his wristwatch. "Eight minutes past eight. Well, that's all for this morning, thank God."

17 The warders unfixed bayonets and marched away. The dog, sobered and conscious of having misbehaved itself, slipped after them.

We walked out of the gallows yard, past the condemned cells with their waiting prisoners, into the big central yard of the prison. The convicts, under the command of warders armed with lathis, were already receiving their breakfast. They squatted in long rows, each man holding a tin pannikin, while two warders with buckets marched round ladling out rice; it seemed quite a homely, jolly scene, after the hanging. An enormous relief had come upon us now that the job was done. One felt an impulse to sing, to break into a run, to snigger. All at once everyone began chattering gaily.

18 The Eurasian boy walking beside me nodded towards the way we had come, with a knowing smile: "Do you know, sir, our friend (he meant the dead man), when he heard his appeal had been dismissed, he pissed on the floor of his cell. From fright—Kindly take one of my cigarettes, sir. Do you not admire my new silver case, sir? From the boxwallah, two rupees eight annas. Classy European style."

19 Several people laughed—at what, nobody seemed certain.

20 Francis was walking by the superintendent, talking garrulously: "Well, sir, all hass passed off with the utmost satisfactoriness. It was all finished—flick! like that. It iss not always so—oah, no! I have known cases where the doctor wass obliged to go beneath the gallows and pull the prisoner's legs to ensure decease. Most disagreeable!"

21 "Wriggling about, eh? That's bad," said the superintendent.

22 "Ach, sir, it iss worse when they become refractory! One man, I recall, clung to the bars of hiss cage when we went to take him out. You will scarcely credit, sir, that it took six warders to dislodge him, three pulling at each leg. We reasoned with him. 'My dear fellow,' we said, 'think of all the pain and trouble you are causing to us!' But no, he would not listen! Ach, he wass very troublesome!"

23 I found that I was laughing quite loudly. Everyone was laughing. Even the superintendent grinned in a tolerant way. "You'd better all come out and have a drink," he said quite genially. "I've got a bottle of whisky in the car. We could do with it."

24 We went through the big double gates of the prison, into the road. "Pulling at his legs!" exclaimed a Burmese magistrate suddenly, and burst into a loud chuckling. We all began laughing again. At that moment Francis's anecdote seemed extraordinarily funny. We all had a drink together, native and European alike, quite amicably. The dead man was a hundred yards away.

FOR THINKING, DISCUSSING, AND WRITING

1. What is Orwell's thesis in this essay? State it in your own words. Where in the essay does the writer himself come closest to stating what you think is the thesis? Why does Orwell place it where he does?
2. Why does Orwell never directly criticize capital punishment? Why has he chosen to address the topic without provocative and inflammatory language?
3. Which sensory details in the essay do you find most indelible? How has Orwell used description, narration, and dialog to good effect?
4. Write an essay in which you comment on this statement from "A Hanging": "I saw the mystery, the unspeakable wrongness, of cutting a life short when it is in full tide."

EDWARD I.KOCH

Death and Justice

Edward I. Koch (1924–) was born in New York City. He served in Congress and was mayor of that city for twelve years. He is a writer, recently of the play Murder on 34th Street, *and is a radio and television commentator. Responding to two state-sponsored executions of violent criminals in 1984, Koch wrote this strong defense of the death penalty for the* New Republic.

1 Last December a man named Robert Lee Willie, who had been convicted of raping and murdering an 18-year-old woman, was executed in the Louisiana state prison. In a statement issued several minutes before his death, Mr. Willie said: "Killing people is wrong. . . . It makes no difference whether it's citizens, countries, or governments. Killing is wrong." Two weeks later in South Carolina, an admitted killer named Joseph Carl Shaw was put to death for murdering two teenagers. In an appeal to the governor for clemency, Mr. Shaw wrote: "Killing is wrong when I did it. Killing is wrong when you do it. I hope you have the courage and moral strength to stop the killing."

2 It is a curiosity of modern life that we find ourselves being lectured on morality by cold-blooded killers. Mr. Willie previously had been convicted of aggravated rape, aggravated kidnapping, and the murders of a Louisiana deputy and a man from Missouri. Mr. Shaw committed another murder a week before the two for which he was executed, and

admitted mutilating the body of the 14-year-old girl he killed. I can't help wondering what prompted these murderers to speak out against killing as they entered the death-house door. Did their new-found reverence for life stem from the realization that they were about to lose their own?

3 Life is indeed precious, and I believe the death penalty helps to affirm this fact. Had the death penalty been a real possibility in the minds of these murderers, they might well have stayed their hand. They might have shown moral awareness before their victims died, and not after. Consider the tragic death of Rosa Velez, who happened to be home when a man named Luis Vera burglarized her apartment in Brooklyn. "Yeah, I shot her," Vera admitted. "She knew me, and I knew I wouldn't go to the chair."

4 During my 22 years in public service, I have heard the pros and cons of capital punishment expressed with special intensity. As a district leader, councilman, congressman, and mayor, I have represented constituencies generally thought of as liberal. Because I support the death penalty for heinous crimes of murder, I have sometimes been the subject of emotional and outraged attacks by voters who find my position reprehensible or worse. I have listened to their ideas. I have weighed their objections carefully. I still support the death penalty. The reasons I maintain my position can be best understood by examining the arguments most frequently heard in opposition.

5 1. *The death penalty is "barbaric."* Sometimes opponents of capital punishment horrify with tales of lingering death on the gallows, of faulty electric chairs, or of agony in the gas chamber. Partly in response to such protests, several states such as North Carolina and Texas switched to execution by lethal injection. The condemned person is put to death painlessly, without ropes, voltage, bullets, or gas. Did this answer the objections of death penalty opponents? Of course not. On June 22, 1984, the *New York Times* published an editorial that sarcastically attacked the new "hygienic" method of death by injection, and stated that "execution can never be made humane through science." So it's not the method that really troubles opponents. It's the death itself they consider barbaric.

6 Admittedly, capital punishment is not a pleasant topic. However, one does not have to like the death penalty in order to support it any more than one must like radical surgery, radiation, or chemotherapy in order to find necessary these attempts at curing cancer. Ultimately we

may learn how to cure cancer with a simple pill. Unfortunately, that day has not yet arrived. Today we are faced with the choice of letting the cancer spread or trying to cure it with the methods available, methods that one day will almost certainly be considered barbaric. But to give up and do nothing would be far more barbaric and would certainly delay the discovery of an eventual cure. The analogy between cancer and murder is imperfect, because murder is not the "disease" we are trying to cure. The disease is injustice. We may not like the death penalty, but it must be available to punish crimes of cold-blooded murder, cases in which any other form of punishment would be inadequate and, therefore, unjust. If we create a society in which injustice is not tolerated, incidents of murder—the most flagrant form of injustice—will diminish.

7 2. *No other major democracy uses the death penalty.* No other major democracy—in fact, few other countries of any description—are plagued by a murder rate such as that in the United States. Fewer and fewer Americans can remember the days when unlocked doors were the norm and murder was a rare and terrible offense. In America the murder rate climbed 122 percent between 1963 and 1980. During that same period, the murder rate in New York City increased by almost 400 percent, and the statistics are even worse in many other cities. A study at M.I.T. showed that based on 1970 homicide rates a person who lived in a large American city ran a greater risk of being murdered than an American soldier in World War II ran of being killed in combat. It is not surprising that the laws of each country differ according to differing conditions and traditions. If other countries had our murder problem, the cry for capital punishment would be just as loud as it is here. And I daresay that any other major democracy where 75 percent of the people supported the death penalty would soon enact it into law.

8 3. *An innocent person might be executed by mistake.* Consider the work of Adam Bedau, one of the most implacable foes of capital punishment in this country. According to Mr. Bedau, it is "false sentimentality to argue that the death penalty should be abolished because of the abstract possibility that an innocent person might be executed." He cites a study of the 7,000 executions in this country from 1893 to 1971, and concludes that the record fails to show that such cases occur. The main point, however, is this. If government functioned only when the possibility of error didn't exist, government wouldn't function at

all. Human life deserves special protection, and one of the best ways to guarantee that protection is to assure that convicted murderers do not kill again. Only the death penalty can accomplish this end. In a recent case in New Jersey, a man named Richard Biegenwald was freed from prison after serving 18 years for murder; since his release he has been convicted of committing four murders. A prisoner named Lemuel Smith, who, while serving four life sentences for murder (plus two life sentences for kidnapping and robbery) in New York's Green Haven Prison, lured a woman corrections officer into the chaplain's office and strangled her. He then mutilated and dismembered her body. An additional life sentence for Smith is meaningless. Because New York has no death penalty statute, Smith has effectively been given a license to kill.

9 But the problem of multiple murder is not confined to the nation's penitentiaries. In 1981, 91 police officers were killed in the line of duty in this country. Seven percent of those arrested in the cases that have been solved had a previous arrest for murder. In New York City in 1976 and 1977, 85 persons arrested for homicide had a previous arrest for murder. Six of these individuals had two previous arrests for murder, and one had four previous murder arrests. During those two years the New York police were arresting for murder persons with a previous arrest for murder on the average of one every 8.5 days. This is not surprising when we learn that in 1975, for example, the median time served in Massachusetts for homicide was less than two-and-a-half years. In 1976 a study sponsored by the Twentieth Century Fund found that the average time served in the United States for first-degree murder is ten years. The median time served may be considerably lower.

10 4. *Capital punishment cheapens the value of human life.* On the contrary, it can be easily demonstrated that the death penalty strengthens the value of human life. If the penalty for rape were lowered, clearly it would signal a lessened regard for the victims' suffering, humiliation, and personal integrity. It would cheapen their horrible experience, and expose them to an increased danger of recurrence. When we lower the penalty for murder, it signals a lessened regard for the value of the victim's life. Some critics of capital punishment, such as columnist Jimmy Breslin, have suggested that a life sentence is actually a harsher penalty for murder than death. This is sophistic nonsense. A few killers may decide not to appeal a death sentence, but the overwhelming

majority make every effort to stay alive. It is by exacting the highest penalty for the taking of human life that we affirm the highest value of human life.

11 5. *The death penalty is applied in a discriminatory manner.* This factor no longer seems to be the problem it once was. The appeals process for a condemned prisoner is lengthy and painstaking. Every effort is made to see that the verdict and sentence were fairly arrived at. However, assertions of discrimination are not an argument for ending the death penalty but for extending it. It is not justice to exclude everyone from the penalty of the law if a few are found to be so favored. Justice requires that the law be applied equally to all.

12 6. *Thou Shalt Not Kill.* The Bible is our greatest source of moral inspiration. Opponents of the death penalty frequently cite the sixth of the Ten Commandments in an attempt to prove that capital punishment is divinely proscribed. In the original Hebrew, however, the Sixth Commandment reads, "Thou Shalt Not Commit Murder," and the Torah specifies capital punishment for a variety of offenses. The biblical viewpoint has been upheld by philosophers throughout history. The greatest thinkers of the 19th century—Kant, Locke, Hobbes, Rouseau, Montesquieu, and Mill—agreed that natural law properly authorizes the sovereign to take life in order to vindicate justice. Only Jeremy Bentham was ambivalent. Washington, Jefferson, and Franklin endorsed it. Abraham Lincoln authorized executions for deserters in war-time. Alexis de Tocqueville, who expressed profound respect for American institutions, believed that the death penalty was indispensable to the support of social order. The United States Constitution, widely admired as one of the seminal achievements in the history of humanity, condemns cruel and inhuman punishment, but does not condemn capital punishment.

13 7. *The death penalty is state-sanctioned murder.* This is the defense with which Messrs. Willie and Show hoped to soften the resolve of those who sentenced them to death. By saying in effect, "You're no better than I am," the murderer seeks to bring his accusers down to his own level. It is also a popular argument among opponents of capital punishment, but a transparently false one. Simply put, the state has rights that the private individual does not. In a democracy, those rights are given to the state by the electorate. The execution of a lawfully condemned killer is no more an act of murder than is legal imprisonment an act of kidnapping. If an individual forces a neighbor to pay him

money under threat of punishment, it's called extortion. If the state does it, it's called taxation. Rights and responsibilities surrendered by the individual are what give the state its power to govern. This contract is the foundation of civilization itself.

14 Everyone wants his or her rights, and will defend them jealously. Not everyone, however, wants responsibilities, especially the painful responsibilities that come with law enforcement. Twenty-one years ago a woman named Kitty Genovese was assaulted and murdered on a street in New York. Dozens of neighbors heard her cries for help but did nothing to assist her. They didn't even call the police. In such a climate the criminal understandably grows bolder. In the presence of moral cowardice, he lectures us on our supposed failings and tries to equate his crimes with our quest for justice.

15 The death of anyone—even a convicted killer—diminishes us all. But we are diminished even more by a justice system that fails to function. It is an illusion to let ourselves believe that doing away with capital punishment removes the murderer's deed from our conscience. The rights of society are paramount. When we protect guilty lives, we give up innocent lives in exchange. When opponents of capital punishment say to the state: "I will not let you kill in my name," they are also saying to murderers: "You can kill in your *own* name as long as I have an excuse for not getting involved."

16 It is hard to imagine anything worse than being murdered while neighbors do nothing. But something worse exists. When those same neighbors shrink back from justly punishing the murderer, the victim dies twice.

FOR THINKING, DISCUSSING, AND WRITING

1. What is Koch's stand on the death penalty? How, according to the writer, have many people responded to his position?
2. What seven points does Koch raise by way of explaining "the arguments most frequently heard in opposition" to the death penalty? How does Koch answer the objections? How could you refute his seven arguments?
3. The writer dismisses with citations and expert testimony the argument advanced by many who oppose the death penalty: "an innocent person might be executed by mistake." What is your position on this point? How has Koch convinced you—or not convinced you—that this element of the argument is invalid?

4. Apparently Koch and other like-minded people have convinced legislators across the country to support capital punishment: many states, including New York State, now allow the death penalty. Write an essay about the issue of capital punishment as "state-sanctioned murder" or "state-sanctioned justice."

MARK ESSIG

Continuing the Search for Kinder Executions

Born and reared in St. Louis, Mark Essig (1965–) has lived in Virginia, upstate New York, Manhattan, and Brooklyn, and currently resides in Los Angeles. He has a PhD from Cornell and wrote his thesis on the history of forensic toxicology. He is the author of Edison & the Electric Chair *(2004) and* Inventing America: The Life of Benjamin Franklin *(2006). "I work at the intersection of technology and death," Essig says. "There are worse ways to understand America." In this piece he reviews the ways we have attempted to execute condemned criminals in a humane manner.*

1 In Tennessee, it is a crime to euthanize a cat with pancuronium bromide, but this doesn't stop the state from using it to execute condemned criminals. Because the drug paralyzes muscles but does not affect nerves, it may leave its victims wide awake but immobilized as they painfully suffocate. So prisoners' advocates and medical experts are now trying to persuade Tennessee—and the nearly 30 other states that use the drug—to choose different poisons for lethal injection, thereby bringing euthanasia protocols for humans in line with those for domestic animals.

2 And so continues the uniquely American habit of tinkering with the machinery of death. For the past century and a half, America's capital punishment debate has resembled a strange game of leapfrog: opponents of the death penalty claim that the current method, whatever it may be, is barbaric, which prompts capital-punishment supporters to refine that method or develop a new one.

3 Although 19th-century Americans tended to believe that justice and order demanded the ultimate sanction, they were often shaken by

graphic accounts of the pain suffered by hanged men. In 1876, after an especially gruesome hanging, Maine abolished capital punishment. Inspired by this victory, opponents of the death penalty began to emphasize the cruelty of the gallows. But their effort was self-defeating: by claiming that the problem with hanging was the suffering of the condemned, they simply challenged death penalty advocates to find a better way to kill.

4 First came adjustments to the gallows. Hangmen created a formula in which rope length was a function of the prisoner's weight—the heavier the victim, the shorter the drop. But such delicate calculations of anatomy and gravity often failed to add up, and many prisoners slowly strangled to death. To dull the pain, Brooklyn officials in 1847 knocked a murderer cold with ether before hanging him, but this simply highlighted the deficiencies of the gallows.

5 Then, in 1889, New York State built the first electric chair, a device championed by Thomas Edison. Edison's advocacy was inspired in part by a wicked plan to hurt his business rival, George Westinghouse—the chair was powered by Westinghouse's alternating current, and Edison hoped consumers would begin to associate AC with danger and death. But Edison had less cynical reasons as well: he was an opponent of the death penalty—"an act of foolish barbarity," he called it—and he believed that electrocution would be less barbaric than the noose. Many others agreed, and eventually 25 states and the District of Columbia installed electric chairs.

6 Electrocution remained the state of the art for three decades, until the public grew dismayed by bungled executions that required several shocks or set the prisoner on fire. Before long there was another scientific option: an airtight chamber filled with poison gas, adopted by Nevada in 1924 and then by 10 more states in the coming decades. Like all complex machines, however, these execution devices were prone to malfunction, and prisoners suffered the consequences.

7 So in 1977 Oklahoma began to poison condemned prisoners with a three-drug cocktail: sodium thiopental (to produce unconsciousness), pancuronium bromide (to paralyze the muscles) and potassium chloride (to stop the heart). Promising a clean, painless death, this protocol quickly gained widespread acceptance.

8 Until now, that is. The next step seems obvious: states will adopt a different drug regimen, which, no doubt, will soon gain critics of its own.

9 However, it seems that many death-penalty opponents are realizing that technological leapfrog is a game they can't win, and are opting out of the latest debate. Amnesty International has issued this statement: "The search for a 'humane' way of killing people should be seen for what it is—a search to make executions more palatable." In Nebraska, the only state with the electric chair as its sole method of execution, State Senator Ernie Chambers has vowed to fight any attempt to "make executions easier." He hopes that the United States Supreme Court will one day declare electrocution unconstitutional, leaving Nebraska without a valid execution law.

10 Some of the condemned themselves have even sought a more painful death in order to highlight the hypocrisy of "painless execution." In 2001, John Byrd, a convicted murderer in Ohio, requested electrocution rather than the needle; when prison workers balked at using the chair, which had been idle for nearly 40 years, the Legislature abolished electrocution and forced Mr. Byrd to die by lethal injection. Earl Bramblett, a Virginia prisoner, had more success in his protest. "I'm not going to lay down on a gurney and have them stick a needle in my arm and make it look like an antiseptic execution," he said, and he died in the electric chair on April 9.

11 For too long, defenders of capital punishment, fearing that brutal killing methods might provoke public opposition, have found unwitting allies among their adversaries, anxious to relieve the suffering of the condemned. Now death penalty opponents are realizing that scientific execution methods, ceaselessly refined, simply mask the barbarity of killing.

FOR THINKING, DISCUSSING, AND WRITING

1. What is the effect on readers of the words "kinder" and "executions" used side by side in the title? How does the title itself provide insights into the content of the essay?
2. What is Essig's main point? How does the last paragraph assert his position? Why does he wait until the last paragraph to make that assertion so forcefully?
3. What are the varied methods presented here for executing prisoners? Which, if any, do you find more humane than others? More barbaric? Why?
4. Write an essay called "Painless Execution" in which you argue for or against methods of capital punishment that can relieve the suffering of the condemned.

MARTIN LUTHER KING JR.

Letter from Birmingham Jail[1]

Martin Luther King Jr. (1929–1968) was an American religious leader and political spokesman who helped form the civil rights movement of the 1950s and 1960s. In 1964 he won the Nobel Peace Prize. King was assassinated in Memphis, Tennessee, four years later. In this letter he lays out some of the principles of civil disobedience that motivated his leadership.

MY DEAR FELLOW CLERGYMEN:

1 While confined here in the Birmingham city jail, I came across your recent statement calling my present activities "unwise and untimely." Seldom do I pause to answer criticism of my work and ideas. If I sought to answer all the criticisms that cross my desk, my secretaries would have little time for anything other than such correspondence in the course of the day, and I would have no time for constructive work. But since I feel that you are men of genuine good will and that your criticisms are sincerely set forth, I want to try to answer your statement in what I hope will be patient and reasonable terms.

2 I think I should indicate why I am here in Birmingham, since you have been influenced by the view which argues against "outsiders coming in." I have the honor of serving as president of the Southern Christian Leadership Conference, an organization operating in every southern state, with headquarters in Atlanta, Georgia. We have some eighty-five affiliated organizations across the South, and one of them is the Alabama Christian Movement for Human Rights. Frequently we share staff, educational, and financial resources with our affiliates. Several months ago the affiliate here in Birmingham asked us to be on call to engage in a nonviolent direct-action program if such were deemed necessary. We readily consented, and when the hour came we lived up to our promise. So I, along with several members of my staff,

[1] This response to a published statement by eight fellow clergymen from Alabama (Bishop C. C. J. Carpenter, Bishop Joseph A. Durick, Rabbi Milton L. Grafman, Bishop Paul Hardin, Bishop Holan B. Harmon, the Reverend George M. Murray, the Reverend Edward V. Ramage and the Reverend Earl Stallings) was composed under somewhat constricting circumstances. Begun on the margins of the newspaper in which the statement appeared while I was in jail, the letter was continued on scraps of writing paper supplied by a friendly Negro trusty, and concluded on a pad my attorneys were eventually permitted to leave me. Although the text remains in substance unaltered, I have indulged in the author's prerogative of polishing it for publication. [King's note].

am here because I was invited here. I am here because I have organizational ties here.

3 But more basically, I am in Birmingham because injustice is here. Just as the prophets of the eighth century B.C. left their villages and carried their "thus saith the Lord" far beyond the boundaries of their home towns, and just as the Apostle Paul left his village of Tarsus and carried the gospel of Jesus Christ to the far corners of the Greco-Roman world, so am I compelled to carry the gospel of freedom beyond my own home town. Like Paul, I must constantly respond to the Macedonian call for aid.

4 Moreover, I am cognizant of the interrelatedness of all communities and states. I cannot sit idly by in Atlanta and not be concerned about what happens in Birmingham. Injustice anywhere is a threat to justice everywhere. We are caught in an inescapable network of mutuality, tied in a single garment of destiny. Whatever affects one directly, affects all indirectly. Never again can we afford to live with the narrow, provincial "outside agitator" idea. Anyone who lives inside the United States can never be considered an outsider anywhere within its bounds.

5 You deplore the demonstrations taking place in Birmingham. But your statement, I am sorry to say, fails to express a similar concern for the conditions that brought about the demonstrations. I am sure that none of you would want to rest content with the superficial kind of social analysis that deals merely with effects and does not grapple with underlying causes. It is unfortunate that demonstrations are taking place in Birmingham, but it is even more unfortunate that the city's white power structure left the Negro community with no alternative.

6 In any nonviolent campaign there are four basic steps: collection of the facts to determine whether injustices exist; negotiation; self-purification; and direct action. We have gone through an these steps in Birmingham. There can be no gainsaying the fact that racial injustice engulfs this community. Birmingham is probably the most thoroughly segregated city in the United States. Its ugly record of brutality is widely known. Negroes have experienced grossly unjust treatment in the courts. There have been more unsolved bombings of Negro homes and churches in Birmingham than in any other city in the nation. These are the hard, brutal facts of the case. On the basis of these conditions, Negro leaders sought to negotiate with the city fathers. But the latter consistently refused to engage in good-faith negotiation.

7 Then, last September, came the opportunity to talk with leaders of Birmingham's economic community. In the course of the negotiations, certain promises were made by the merchants—for example, to remove the stores' humiliating racial signs. On the basis of these promises, the Reverend Fred Shuttlesworth and the leaders of the Alabama Christian Movement for Human Rights agreed to a moratorium on all demonstrations. As the weeks and months went by, we realized that we were the victims of a broken promise. A few signs, briefly removed, returned; the others remained.

8 As in so many past experiences, our hopes had been blasted, and the shadow of deep disappointment settled upon us. We had no alternative except to prepare for direct action, whereby we would present our very bodies as a means of laying our case before the conscience of the local and the national community. Mindful of the difficulties involved, we decided to undertake a process of self-purification. We began a series of workshops on nonviolence, and we repeatedly asked ourselves: "Are you able to accept blows without retaliating?" "Are you able to endure the ordeal of jail?" We decided to schedule our direct-action program for the Easter season, realizing that except for Christmas, this is the main shopping period of the year. Knowing that a strong economic-withdrawal program would be the by-product of direct action, we felt that this would be the best time to bring pressure to bear on the merchants for the needed change.

9 Then it occurred to us that Birmingham's mayoral election was coming up in March, and we speedily decided to postpone action until after election day. When we discovered that the Commissioner of Public Safety, Eugene "Bull" Connor, had piled up enough votes to be in the run-off, we decided again to postpone action until the day after the run-off so that the demonstrations could not be used to cloud the issues. Like many others, we waited to see Mr. Connor defeated, and to this end we endured postponement after postponement. Having aided in this community need, we felt that our direct-action program could be delayed no longer.

10 You may well ask, "Why direct action? Why sit-ins, marches, and so forth? Isn't negotiation a better path?" You are quite right in calling for negotiation. Indeed, this is the very purpose of direct action. Nonviolent direct action seeks to create such a crisis and foster such a tension that a community which has constantly refused to negotiate is forced to confront the issue. It seeks so to dramatize the issue that it

can no longer be ignored. My citing the creation of tension as part of the work of the nonviolent-resister may sound rather shocking. But I must confess that I am not afraid of the word "tension." I have earnestly opposed violent tension, but there is a type of constructive, nonviolent tension which is necessary for growth. Just as Socrates felt that it was necessary to create a tension in the mind so that individuals could rise from the bondage of myths and half-truths to the unfettered realm of creative analysis and objective appraisal, so must we see the need for nonviolent gadflies to create the kind of tension in society that will help men rise from the dark depths of prejudice and racism to the majestic heights of understanding and brotherhood.

11 The purpose of our direct-action program is to create a situation so crisis-packed that it will inevitably open the door to negotiation. I therefore concur with you in your call for negotiation. Too long has our beloved Southland been bogged down in a tragic effort to live in monologue rather than dialogue.

12 One of the basic points in your statement is that the action that I and my associates have taken in Birmingham is untimely. Some have asked: "Why didn't you give the new city administration time to act?" The only answer that I can give to this query is that the new Birmingham. administration must be prodded about as much as the outgoing one, before it will act. We are sadly mistaken if we feel that the election of Albert Boutwell as mayor will bring the millennium to Birmingham. While Mr. Boutwell is a much more gentle person than Mr. Connor, they are both segregationists, dedicated to maintenance of the status quo. I have hope that Mr. Boutwell will be reasonable enough to see the futility of massive resistance to desegregation. But he will not see this without pressure from devotees of civil rights. My friends, I must say to you that we have not made a single gain in civil rights without determined legal and nonviolent pressure. Lamentably, it is an historical fact that privileged groups seldom give up their privileges voluntarily. Individuals may see the moral light and voluntarily give up their unjust posture; but, as Reinhold Niebuhr[2] has reminded us, groups tend to be more immoral than individuals.

13 We know through painful experience that freedom is never voluntarily given by the oppressor; it must be demanded by the oppressed. Frankly, I have yet to engage in a direct-action campaign that was

[2] A Protestant religious leader (1892–1971).

"well timed" in the view of those who have not suffered unduly from the disease of segregation. For years now I have heard the word "Wait!" It rings in the ear of every Negro with piercing familiarity. This "Wait" has almost always meant "Never." We must come to see, with one of our distinguished jurists, that "justice too long delayed is justice denied."

14 We have waited for more than 340 years for our constitutional and God-given rights. The nations of Asia and Africa are moving with jetlike speed toward gaining political independence, but we still creep at horse-and-buggy pace toward gaining a cup of coffee at a lunch counter. Perhaps it is easy for those who have never felt the stinging darts of segregation to say, "Wait." But when you have seen vicious mobs lynch your mothers and fathers at will and drown your sisters and brothers at whim; when you have seen hate-filled policemen curse, kick, and even kill your black brothers and sisters; when you have seen the vast majority of your twenty million Negro brothers smothering in an airtight cage of poverty in the midst of an affluent society; when you suddenly find your tongue twisted and your speech stammering as you seek to explain to your six-year-old daughter why she can't go to the public amusement park that has just been advertised on television, and see tears welling up in her eyes when she is told that Funtown is closed to colored children, and see ominous clouds of inferiority beginning to form in her little mental sky, and see her beginning to distort her personality by developing an unconscious bitterness toward white people; when you have to concoct an answer for a five-year-old son who is asking: "Daddy, why do white people treat colored people so mean?"; when you take a cross-country drive and find it necessary to sleep night after night in the uncomfortable corners of your automobile because no motel will accept you; when you are humiliated day in and day out by nagging signs reading "white" and "colored"; when your first name becomes "nigger," your middle name becomes "boy" (however old you are) and your last name becomes "John," and your wife and mother are never given the respected title "Mrs."; when you are harried by day and haunted by night by the fact that you are a Negro, living constantly at tiptoe stance, never quite knowing what to expect next, and are plagued with inner fears and outer resentments; when you are forever fighting a degenerating sense of "nobodiness"—then you will understand why we find it difficult to wait. There comes a time when the cup of endurance runs over, and men are no longer willing to be plunged into

the abyss of despair. I hope, sirs, you can understand our legitimate and unavoidable impatience.

15 You express a great deal of anxiety over our willingness to break laws. This is certainly a legitimate concern. Since we so diligently urge people to obey the Supreme Court's decision of 1954 outlawing segregation in the public schools, at first glance it may seem rather paradoxical for us consciously to break laws. One may well ask: "How can you advocate breaking some laws and obeying others?" The answer lies in the fact that there are two types of laws: just and unjust. I would be the first to advocate obeying just laws. One has not only a legal but a moral responsibility to obey just laws. Conversely, one has a moral responsibility to disobey unjust laws. I would agree with St. Augustine[3] that "an unjust law is no law at all."

16 Now, what is the difference between the two? How does one determine whether a law is just or unjust? A just law is a man-made code that squares with the moral law or the law of God. An unjust law is a code that is out of harmony with the moral law. To put it in the terms of St. Thomas Aquinas:[4] An unjust law is a human law that is not rooted in eternal law and natural law. Any law that uplifts human personality is just. Any law that degrades human personality is unjust. All segregation statutes are unjust because segregation distorts the soul and damages the personality. It gives the segregator a false sense of superiority and the segregated a false sense of inferiority. Segregation, to use the terminology of the Jewish philosopher Martin Buber,[5] substitutes an "I-it" relationship for an "I-thou" relationship and ends up relegating persons to the status of things. Hence segregation is not only politically, economically and sociologically unsound, it is morally wrong and sinful. Paul Tillich[6] said that sin is separation. Is not segregation an existential expression of man's tragic separation, his awful estrangement, his terrible sinfulness? Thus it is that I can urge men to obey the 1954 decision of the Supreme Court, for it is morally right; and I can urge them to disobey segregation ordinances, for they are morally wrong.

17 Let us consider a more concrete example of just and unjust laws. An unjust law is a code that a numerical or power majority group compels a minority group to obey but does not make binding on itself. This is

[3] Early Christian church father (354–430).
[4] A renowned philosopher and Christian leader (1225–1274).
[5] (1878–1965).
[6] Another American Protestant, who was a theologian (1886–1965).

difference made legal. By the same token, a just law is a code that a majority compels a minority to follow and that it is willing to follow itself. This is *sameness* made legal.

18 Let me give another explanation. A law is unjust if it is inflicted on a minority that, as a result of being denied the right to vote, had no part in enacting or devising the law. Who can say that the legislature of Alabama which set up that state's segregation laws was democratically elected? Throughout Alabama all sorts of devious methods are used to prevent Negroes from becoming registered voters, and there are some counties in which, even though Negroes constitute a majority of the population, not a single Negro is registered. Can any law enacted under such circumstances be considered democratically structured?

19 Sometimes a law is just on its face and unjust in its application. For instance, I have been arrested on a charge of parading without a permit. Now, there is nothing wrong in having an ordinance which requires a permit for a parade. But such an ordinance becomes unjust when it is used to maintain segregation and to deny citizens the First-Amendment privilege of peaceful assembly and protest.

20 I hope you are able to see the distinction I am trying to point out. In no sense do I advocate evading or defying the law, as would the rabid segregationist. That would lead to anarchy. One who breaks an unjust law must do so openly, lovingly, and with a willingness to accept the penalty. I submit that an individual who breaks a law that conscience tells him is unjust and who willingly accepts the penalty of imprisonment in order to arouse the conscience of the community over its injustice, is in reality expressing the highest respect for law.

21 Of course, there is nothing new about this kind of civil disobedience. It was evidenced sublimely in the refusal of Shadrach, Meshach, and Abednego to obey the laws of Nebuchadnezzar,[7] on the ground that a higher moral law was at stake. It was practiced superbly by the early Christians, who were willing to face hungry lions and the excruciating pain of chopping blocks rather than submit to certain unjust laws of the Roman Empire. To a degree, academic freedom is a reality today because Socrates practiced civil disobedience.[8] In our own nation, the Boston Tea Party represented a massive act of civil disobedience.

[7] See Daniel 3.
[8] The Athenians tried the Greek philosopher Socrates for corrupting youth by his teaching methods. He was put to death.

22 We should never forget that everything Adolf Hitler did in Germany was "legal" and everything the Hungarian freedom fighters did in Hungary was "illegal." It was "illegal" to aid and comfort a Jew in Hitler's Germany. Even so, I am sure that, had I lived in Germany at the time, I would have aided and comforted my Jewish brothers. If today I lived in a Communist country where certain principles dear to the Christian faith are suppressed, I would openly advocate disobeying that country's antireligious laws.

23 I must make two honest confessions to you, my Christian and Jewish brothers. First, I must confess that over the past few years I have been gravely disappointed with the white moderate. I have almost reached the regrettable conclusion that the Negro's great stumbling block in his stride toward freedom is not the White Citizen's Counciler or the Ku Klux Klanner, but the white moderate, who is more devoted to "order" than to justice; who prefers a negative peace which is the absence of tension to a positive peace which is the presence of justice; who constantly says, "I agree with you in the goal you seek, but I cannot agree with your methods of direct action"; who paternalistically believes he can set the timetable for another man's freedom; who lives by a mythical concept of time and who constantly advises the Negro to wait for a "more convenient season." Shallow understanding from people of good will is more frustrating than absolute misunderstanding from people of ill will. Lukewarm acceptance is much more bewildering than outright rejection.

24 I had hoped that the white moderate would understand that law and order exist for the purpose of establishing justice and that where they fail in this purpose they become the dangerously structured dams that block the flow of social progress. I had hoped that the white moderate would understand that the present tension in the South is a necessary phase of the transition from an obnoxious negative peace, in which the Negro passively accepted his unjust plight, to a substantive and positive peace, in which all men will respect the dignity and worth of human personality. Actually, we who engage in nonviolent direct action are not the creators of tension. We merely bring to the surface the hidden tension that is already alive. We bring it out in the open, where it can be seen and dealt with. Like a boil that can never be cured so long as it is covered up but must be opened with all its ugliness to the natural medicines of air and light, injustice must be exposed, with all the tension its exposure creates, to the light of human conscience and the air of national opinion, before it can be cured.

25 In your statement you assert that our actions, even though peaceful, must be condemned because they precipitate violence. But is this a logical assertion? Isn't this like condemning a robbed man because his possession of money precipitated the evil act of robbery? Isn't this like condemning Socrates because his unswerving commitment to truth and his philosophical inquiries precipitated the act by the misguided populace in which they made him drink hemlock? Isn't this like condemning Jesus because his unique God-consciousness and never-ceasing devotion to God's will precipitated the evil act of crucifixion? We must come to see that, as the federal courts have consistently affirmed, it is wrong to urge an individual to cease his efforts to gain his basic constitutional rights because the quest may precipitate violence. Society must protect the robbed and punish the robber.

26 I had also hoped that the white moderate would reject the myth concerning time in relation to the struggle for freedom. I have just received a letter from a white brother in Texas. He writes: "All Christians know that the colored people will receive equal rights eventually, but it is possible that you are in too great a religious hurry. It has taken Christianity almost two thousand years to accomplish what it has. The teachings of Christ take time to come to earth." Such an attitude stems from a tragic misconception of time, from the strangely irrational notion that there is something in the very flow of time that will inevitably cure all ills. Actually, time itself is neutral; it can be used either destructively or constructively. More and more I feel that the people of ill will have used time much more effectively than have the people of good will. We will have to repent in this generation not merely for the hateful words and actions of the bad people, but for the appalling silence of the good people. Human progress never rolls in on wheels of inevitability; it comes through the tireless efforts of men willing to be co-workers with God, and without this hard work, time itself becomes an ally of the forces of social stagnation. We must use time creatively, in the knowledge that the time is always ripe to do right. Now is the time to make real the promise of democracy and transform our pending national elegy into a creative psalm of brotherhood. Now is the time to lift our national policy from the quicksand of racial injustice to the solid rock of human dignity.

27 You speak of our activity in Birmingham as extreme. At first I was rather disappointed that fellow clergymen would see my nonviolent efforts as those of an extremist. I began thinking about the fact that

I stand in the middle of two opposing forces in the Negro community. One is a force of complacency, made up in part of Negroes who, as a result of long years of oppression, are so drained of self-respect and a sense of "somebodiness" that they have adjusted to segregation; and in part of a few middle-class Negroes who, because of a degree of academic and economic security and because in some ways they profit by segregation, have become insensitive to the problems of the masses. The other force is one of bitterness and hatred, and it comes perilously close to advocating violence. It is expressed in the various black nationalist groups that are springing up across the nation, the largest and best-known being Elijah Muhammad's Muslim movement.[9] Nourished by the Negro's frustration over the continued existence of racial discrimination, this movement is made up of people who have lost faith in America, who have absolutely repudiated Christianity, and who have concluded that the white man is an incorrigible "devil."

28 I have tried to stand between these two forces, saying that we need emulate neither the "do-nothingism" of the complacent nor the hatred and despair of the black nationalist. For there is the more excellent way of love and nonviolent protest. I am grateful to God that, through the influence of the Negro church, the way of nonviolence became an integral part of our struggle.

29 If this philosophy had not emerged, by now many streets of the South would, I am convinced, be flowing with blood. And I am further convinced that if our white brothers dismiss as "rabblerousers" and "outside agitators" those of us who employ nonviolent direct action, and if they refuse to support our nonviolent efforts, millions of Negroes will, out of frustration and despair, seek solace and security in black-nationalist ideologies—a development that would inevitably lead to a frightening racial nightmare.

30 Oppressed people cannot remain oppressed forever. The yearning for freedom eventually manifests itself, and that is what has happened to the American Negro. Something within has reminded him of his birthright of freedom, and something without has reminded him that it can be gained. Consciously or unconsciously, he has been caught up by the *Zietgeist,* and with his black brothers of Africa and his brown and yellow brothers of Asia, South America and the Caribbean, the United States Negro is moving with a sense of great urgency toward the promised land

[9] Elijah Muhammed (1897–1975), became the leader of the Nation of Islam in 1934.

of racial justice. If one recognizes this vital urge that has engulfed the Negro community, one should readily understand why public demonstrations are taking place. The Negro has many pent-up resentments and latent frustrations, and he must release them. So let him march; let him make prayer pilgrimages to the city hall; let him go on freedom rides—and try to understand why he must do so. If his repressed emotions are not released in nonviolent ways, they will seek expression through violence; this is not a threat but a fact of history. So I have not said to my people, "Get rid of your discontent." Rather, I have tried to say that this normal and healthy discontent can be channeled into the creative outlet of nonviolent direct action. And now this approach is being termed extremist.

31 But though I was initially disappointed at being categorized as an extremist, as I continued to think about the matter I gradually gained a measure of satisfaction from the label. Was not Jesus an extremist for love: "Love your enemies, bless them that curse you, do good to them that hate you, and pray for them which despitefully use you, and persecute you." Was not Amos an extremist for justice: "Let justice roll down like waters and righteousness like an ever-flowing stream." Was not Paul an extremist for the Christian gospel: "I bear in my body the marks of the Lord Jesus." Was not Martin Luther an extremist: "Here I stand; I cannot do otherwise, so help me God." And John Bunyan: [10] "I will stay in jail to the end of my days before I make a butchery of my conscience." And Abraham Lincoln: "This nation cannot survive half slave and half free." And Thomas Jefferson: "We hold these truths to be self-evident, that all men are created equal. . . ." So the question is not whether we will be extremists, but what kind of extremists we will be. Will we be extremists for hate or for love? Will we be extremists for the preservation of injustice or for the extension of justice? In that dramatic scene on Calvary's hill three men were crucified. We must never forget that all three were crucified for the same crime—the crime of extremism. Two were extremists for immorality, and thus fell below their environment. The other, Jesus Christ, was an extremist for love, truth, and goodness, and thereby rose above his environment. Perhaps the South, the nation, and the world are in dire need of creative extremists.

32 I had hoped that the white moderate would see this need. Perhaps I was too optimistic; perhaps I expected too much. I suppose I should

[10] British author and preacher (1628–1688). Amos was a prophet of the Old Testament. Paul was a New Testament apostle; Martin Luther (1483–1546) was a reformer for the Protestants in Germany.

have realized that few members of the oppressor race can understand the deep groans and passionate yearnings of the oppressed race, and still fewer have the vision to see that injustice must be rooted out by strong, persistent, and determined action. I am thankful, however, that some of our white brothers in the South have grasped the meaning of this social revolution and committed themselves to it. They are still too few in quantity, but they are big in quality. Some—such as Ralph McGill, Lillian Smith, Harry Golden, James McBride Dabbs, Ann Braden, and Sarah Patton Boyle—have written about our struggle in eloquent and prophetic terms. Others have marched with us down nameless streets of the South. They have languished in filthy, roach-infested jails, suffering the abuse and brutality of policemen who view them as "dirty nigger lovers." Unlike so many of their moderate brothers and sisters, they have recognized the urgency of the moment and sensed the need for powerful "action" antidotes to combat the disease of segregation.

33 Let me take note of my other major disappointment. I have been so greatly disappointed with the white church and its leadership. Of course, there are some notable exceptions. I am not unmindful of the fact that each of you has taken some significant stands on this issue. I commend you, Reverend Stallings, for your Christian stand on this past Sunday, in welcoming Negroes to your worship service on a nonsegregated basis. I commend the Catholic leaders of this state for integrating Spring Hill College several years ago.

34 But despite these notable exceptions, I must honestly reiterate that I have been disappointed with the church. I do not say this as one of those negative critics who can always find something wrong with the church. I say this as a minister of the gospel, who loves the church; who was nurtured in its bosom; who has been sustained by its spiritual blessings and who will remain true to it as long as the cord of life shall lengthen.

35 When I was suddenly catapulted into the leadership of the bus protest in Montgomery, Alabama, a few years ago,[11] I felt we would be supported by the white church. I felt that the white ministers, priests, and rabbis of the South would be among our strongest allies. Instead, some have been outright opponents, refusing to understand

[11] Rosa Parks refused to move to the part of the bus reserved for Negroes, and in December 1955 the bus protest began.

the freedom movement and misrepresenting its leaders; all too many others have been more cautious than courageous and have remained silent behind the anesthetizing security of stained-glass windows.

36 In spite of my shattered dreams, I came to Birmingham with the hope that the white religious leadership of this community would see the justice of our cause and, with deep moral concern, would serve as the channel through which our just grievances could reach the power structure. I had hoped that each of you would understand. But again I have been disappointed.

37 I have heard numerous southern religious leaders admonish their worshipers to comply with a desegregation decision because it is the law, but I have longed to hear white ministers declare: "Follow this decree because integration is morally right and because the Negro is your brother." In the midst of blatant injustices inflicted upon the Negro, I have watched white churchmen stand on the sideline and mouth pious irrelevancies and sanctimonious trivialities. In the midst of a mighty struggle to rid our nation of racial and economic injustice, I have heard many ministers say: "Those are social issues, with which the gospel has no real concern." And I have watched many churches commit themselves to a completely otherworldly religion which makes a strange, un-Biblical distinction between body and soul, between the sacred and the secular.

38 I have traveled the length and breadth of Alabama, Mississippi, and all the other southern states. On sweltering summer days and crisp autumn mornings I have looked at the South's beautiful churches with their lofty spires pointing heavenward. I have beheld the impressive outlines of her massive religious-education buildings. Over and over I have found myself asking: "What kind of people worship here? Who is their God? Where were their voices when the lips of Governor Barnett dripped with words of interposition and nullification? Where were they when Governor Wallace gave a clarion call for defiance and hatred? [12] Where were their voices of support when bruised and weary Negro men and women decided to rise from the dark dungeons of complacency to the bright hills of creative protest?"

[12] George Wallace (1919–1998) was governor of Alabama and fought to exclude black students from the University of Alabama. Governor of Mississippi Ross Barnett (1898–1988) fought James Meredith's admission to the University of Mississippi.

39 Yes, these questions are still in my mind. In deep disappointment I have wept over the laxity of the church. But be assured that my tears have been tears of love. There can be no deep disappointment where there is not deep love. Yes, I love the church. How could I do otherwise? I am in the rather unique position of being the son, the grandson, and the great-grandson of preachers. Yes, I see the church as the body of Christ. But, oh! How we have blemished and scarred that body through social neglect and through fear of being nonconformists.

40 There was a time when the church was very powerful—in the time when the early Christians rejoiced at being deemed worthy to suffer for what they believed. In those days the church was not merely a thermometer that recorded the ideas and principles of popular opinion; it was a thermostat that transformed the mores of society. Whenever the early Christians entered a town, the people in power became disturbed and immediately sought to convict the Christians for being "disturbers of the peace" and "outside agitators." But the Christians pressed on, in the conviction that they were "a colony of heaven," called to obey God rather than man. Small in number, they were big in commitment. They were too God-intoxicated to be "astronomically intimidated." By their effort and example they brought an end to such ancient evils as infanticide and gladiatorial contests.

41 Things are different now. So often the contemporary church is a weak, ineffectual voice with an uncertain sound. So often it is an archdefender of the status quo. Far from being disturbed by the presence of the church, the power structure of the average community is consoled by the church's silent—and often even vocal—sanction of things as they are.

42 But the judgment of God is upon the church as never before. If today's church does not recapture the sacrificial spirit of the early church, it will lose its authenticity, forfeit the loyalty of millions, and be dismissed as an irrelevant social club with no meaning for the twentieth century. Every day I meet young people whose disappointment with the church has turned into outright disgust.

43 Perhaps I have once again been too optimistic. Is organized religion too inextricably bound to the status quo to save our nation and the world? Perhaps I must turn my faith to the inner spiritual church, the church within the church, as the true *ekklesia* [13] and the hope of the

[13] In the Greek New Testament, the word for the early Christian Church.

world. But again I am thankful to God that some noble souls from the ranks of organized religion have broken loose from the paralyzing chains of conformity and joined us as active partners in the struggle for freedom. They have left their secure congregations and walked the streets of Albany, Georgia, with us. They have gone down the highways of the South on tortuous rides for freedom. Yes, they have gone to jail with us. Some have been dismissed from their churches, have lost the support of their bishops and fellow ministers. But they have acted in the faith that right defeated is stronger than evil triumphant. Their witness has been the spiritual salt that has preserved the true meaning of the gospel in these troubled times. They have carved a tunnel of hope through the dark mountain of disappointment.

44 I hope the church as a whole will meet the challenge of this decisive hour. But even if the church does not come to the aid of justice, I have no despair about the future. I have no fear about the outcome of our struggle in Birmingham, even if our motives are at present misunderstood. We will reach the goal of freedom in Birmingham and all over the nation, because the goal of America is freedom. Abused and scorned though we may be, our destiny is tied up with America's destiny. Before the pilgrims landed at Plymouth, we were here. Before the pen of Jefferson etched the majestic words of the Declaration of Independence across the pages of history, we were here. For more than two centuries our forebears labored in this country without wages; they made cotton king; they built the homes of their masters while suffering gross injustice and shameful humiliation—and yet out of a bottomless vitality they continued to thrive and develop. If the inexpressible cruelties of slavery could not stop us, the opposition we now face will surely fail. We will win our freedom because the sacred heritage of our nation and the eternal will of God are embodied in our echoing demands.

45 Before closing I feel impelled to mention one other point in your statement that has troubled me profoundly. You warmly commended the Birmingham police force for keeping "order" and "preventing violence." I doubt that you would have so warmly commended the police force if you had seen its dogs sinking their teeth into unarmed, nonviolent Negroes. I doubt that you would so quickly commend the policemen if you were to observe their ugly and inhumane treatment of Negroes here in the city jail; if you were to watch them push and curse old Negro women and young Negro girls; if you were to see them slap

and kick old Negro men and young boys; if you were to observe them, as they did on two occasions, refuse to give us food because we wanted to sing our grace together. I cannot join you in your praise of the Birmingham police department.

46 It is true that the police have exercised a degree of discipline in handling the demonstrators. In this sense they have conducted themselves rather "nonviolently" in public. But for what purpose? To preserve the evil system of segregation. Over the past few years I have consistently preached that nonviolence demands that the means we use must be as pure as the ends we seek. I have tried to make clear that it is wrong to use immoral means to attain moral ends. But now I must affirm that it is just as wrong, or perhaps even more so, to use moral means to preserve immoral ends. Perhaps Mr. Connor and his policemen have been rather nonviolent in public, as was Chief Pritchett in Albany, Georgia, but they have used the moral means of nonviolence to maintain the immoral end of racial injustice. As T. S. Eliot has said, "The last temptation is the greatest treason: To do the right deed for the wrong reason."

47 I wish you had commended the Negro sit-inners and demonstrators of Birmingham for their sublime courage, their willingness to suffer, and their amazing discipline in the midst of great provocation. One day the South will recognize its real heroes. They will be the James Merediths, with the noble sense of purpose that enables them to face jeering and hostile mobs, and with the agonizing loneliness that characterizes the life of the pioneer. They will be old, oppressed, battered Negro women, symbolized in a seventy-two-year-old woman in Montgomery, Alabama, who rose up with a sense of dignity and with her people decided not to ride segregated buses, and who responded with ungrammatical profundity to one who inquired about her weariness: "My feets is tired, but my soul is at rest." They will be the young high school and college students, the young ministers of the gospel and a host of their elders, courageously and nonviolently sitting in at lunch counters and willingly going to jail for conscience' sake. One day the South will know that when these disinherited children of God sat down at lunch counters, they were in reality standing up for what is best in the American dream and for the most sacred values in our Judeo-Christian heritage, thereby bringing our nation back to those great wells of democracy which were dug deep by the founding fathers in their formulation of the Constitution and the Declaration of Independence.

48 Never before have I written so long a letter. I'm afraid it is much too long to take your precious time. I can assure you that it would have been much shorter if I had been writing from a comfortable desk, but what else can one do when he is alone in a narrow jail cell, other than write long letters, think long thoughts, and pray long prayers?

49 If I have said anything in this letter that overstates the truth and indicates an unreasonable impatience, I beg you to forgive me. If I have said anything that understates the truth and indicates my having a patience that allows me to settle for anything less than brotherhood, I beg God to forgive me.

50 I hope this letter finds you strong in the faith. I also hope that circumstances will soon make it possible for me to meet each of you, not as an integrationist or a civil rights leader but as a fellow clergyman and a Christian brother. Let us all hope that the dark clouds of racial prejudice will soon pass away and the deep fog of misunderstanding will be lifted from our fear-drenched communities, and in some not too distant tomorrow the radiant stars of love and brotherhood will shine over our great nation with all their scintillating beauty.

Yours for the cause of Peace and Brotherhood,
Martin Luther King Jr.

FOR THINKING, DISCUSSING, AND WRITING

1. What, according to King, are the four basic steps in any nonviolent campaign? Which of these steps has resulted in the jailing of the writer?
2. The writer cites many examples of what African Americans have endured over the years. How do the examples affect your reaction to the argument? He further supports his argument by citing many individuals, either by noting the statements they made or the things they did. Why does King use this strategy, do you think?
3. King says, "I submit that an individual who breaks a law that conscience tells him is unjust, and who willingly accepts the penalty of imprisonment in order to arouse the conscience of the community over its injustice, is in reality expressing the highest respect for the law." How is this true or not true? Can one respect the law by disobeying it?
4. Write an essay about nonviolent resistance. How does it contribute to a just society? What are its consequences both for the society and the people resisting the law? Contrast nonviolent, direct-action resistance as advocated by Martin Luther King Jr. with violent resistance. What does each accomplish? How should a just society deal with these two forms of behavior?

SASHA ABRAMSKY

When They Get Out

Sasha Abramsky (1972–) was born in England and studied politics, philosophy, and economics at Balliol College, Oxford. He earned his master's degree from the Columbia Graduate School of Journalism.

He has written for the London Observer, *the* Los Angeles Times, *and the* Atlantic, *which first published this piece. His most recent book,* Conned: How Millions Went to Prison, Lost the Vote, and Helped Send George W. Bush to The White House *(2006), explores felony disenfranchisement laws in America, which remove the right to vote from people while they are in prison or on parole, and the effects these laws have had on elections nationwide. Abramsky teaches in the University Writing Program at the University of California, Davis. In this essay he explores the lives of inmates released from prison.*

1 Popular perceptions about crime have blurred the boundaries between fact and politically expedient myth. The myth is that the United States is besieged, on a scale never before encountered, by a pathologically criminal underclass. The fact is that we're not. After spiraling upward during the drug wars, murder rates began falling in the mid-1990s; they are lower today than they were more than twenty years ago. In some cities the murder rate in the late twentieth century is actually lower than it was in the nineteenth century. Nonviolent property-crime rates are in general lower in the United States today than in Great Britain, and are comparable to those in many European countries.

2 Nevertheless, horror stories have led to calls for longer prison sentences, for the abolition of parole, and for the increasingly punitive treatment of prisoners. The politics of opinion-poll populism has encouraged elected and corrections officials to build isolation units, put more prisons on "lockdown" status (in which prisoners are kept in their cells about twenty-three hours a day), abolish grants that allowed prisoners to study toward diplomas and degrees, and generally make life inside as miserable as possible. Marc Mauer, the assistant director of the Sentencing Project, an advocacy group based in Washington, D.C., says, "Fifty years ago rehabilitation was a primary goal of the system." Nowadays it's not. "The situation we're in now is completely unprecedented," Mauer says. "The number going

through the system dwarfs that in any other period in U.S. history and virtually in any other country as well." In 1986, according to figures published in the *Survey of State Prison Inmates* (1991), 175,662 people were serving sentences of more than ten years; five years later 306,006 were serving such sentences. People haven't become more antisocial; their infractions and bad habits are just being punished more ruthlessly. Crime, however, is a complex issue, and responses to it that might instinctively seem sensible, or simply satisfying, may prove deeply counterproductive. Locking ever more people away will in the long run increase the number of Robert Scullys in our midst.

3 Robert Scully grew up near San Diego, in the affluent town of Ocean Beach. From a very early age he used drugs, and before he was a teenager, he had been on the streets and then in juvenile facilities run by the California Youth Authority. From heroin use and dealing he moved to robbery; by the time he was twenty-two, in the early 1980s, he was in San Quentin. In prison Scully degenerated, eventually using a contraband hacksaw blade to escape from his cell and attacking another inmate with a homemade knife.

4 At about the same time, California began opening what it called maximum-security facilities—dumping grounds for troublesome inmates. Scully wound up in solitary confinement in a prison named Corcoran. The guards there, as recently reported in the *Los Angeles Times*, are alleged to have taken it upon themselves to organize gladiatorial combat among prisoners in the exercise yard; they would sometimes break up the battles by shooting into crowds of prisoners. Scully was shot twice. He was placed in a "security housing unit" cell, where for close to twenty-three hours a day he was deprived of all human interaction. In 1990, soon after the "supermax" prison at Pelican Bay had opened in the redwood forests northeast of the old Victorian timber town of Crescent City, Scully was moved again, into a tiny bare cell with a perforated sheet-metal door and a hatch through which his food was served. In the supermax even exercise was solitary. He stayed there four years. At the time of his release, in 1994, he had spent the previous nine years in isolation. A month later he was arrested for violating parole by consorting with an armed acquaintance, and went straight back to Pelican Bay.

5 Scully re-emerged on March 24, 1995, by now a human time bomb. He was picked up by Brenda Moore, the girlfriend of a fellow

inmate, and they began driving south, along Highway 101, toward San Diego, where Scully was supposed to check in with his parole officer, They never made it. Five days later they arrived in Sebastopol, a town an hour north of San Francisco. There, late at night, they loitered around a restaurant until the owner, fearing a robbery, called the police. The pair drove off to a nearby parking lot. Soon after, as they sat in their truck, Deputy Sheriff Frank Trejo, a middle-aged grandfather looking forward to his retirement, pulled into the lot.

6 Trejo asked to see the woman's license, and as she fumbled for it, according to investigators, he suddenly found a sawed-off shotgun pointing at his face. He was made to back up until he was between the two vehicles and get on his knees, and Scully shot him in the forehead. Scully and Moore ran across a field, broke into a house, and took a family hostage. The next afternoon, with police surrounding the area, Scully negotiated his surrender.

7 Robert Scully evolved into a murderer while housed in Pelican Bay. There he experienced some of the harshest confinement conditions known in the democratic world. Highly disturbed to start with, he was kept in a sensory-deprivation box for years on end. Psychologists and psychiatrists called in by his defense team believe that he simply lost the ability to think through the consequences of his actions. He became a creature of brutal and obsessive impulse. At Scully's trial Stuart Grassian, a psychiatrist who has spent much of his career studying the effects of isolation on prisoners, and who has testified in class-action lawsuits against departments of corrections across the country, argued that sensory deprivation and social isolation had caused Scully to regress until he was a violent animal capable only of acting on instinct, with no ability to plan beyond the moment. His incarceration had created what Grassian termed "a tremendous tunnel vision." Pelican Bay Chief Deputy Warden Joe McGrath estimates that every month thirty-five inmates are, like Scully, released from isolation directly back into the community.

8 Since 1985 America's prison population, not counting the more than half a million people in jails at any one time, has increased by about six or seven percent yearly. Truth-in-sentencing laws mandate that many prisoners serve 85 percent of their sentences before being eligible for parole; all the same, figures over the past decade indicate that on average more than 40 percent of prison inmates are released in any

given year. Assuming that these statistical relationships remain constant, we can make certain predictions. In 1995 a total of 463,284 inmates were released. To use a worst-case scenario, some 660,000 will be released in 2000, some 887,000 in 2005, and about 1.2 million in 2010. Even factoring in lower release rates because of three-strikes laws and truth in sentencing, and even taking into account estimates that 60 percent of prisoners have been in prison before, there will still be somewhere around 3.5 million first-time releases between now and 2010, and America by then will still be releasing from half a million to a million people from its prisons each year (not to mention hundreds of thousands more from short stints in jail). That is an awful lot of potential rage coming out of prison to haunt our future.

9 On a gray morning in September, with the tropical storm Frances hovering over the Gulf Coast, I rode with Larry Fitzgerald, the sixty-year-old public-relations officer for the Texas Department of Criminal Justice, to a parking lot deep inside the Estelle Unit of the Huntsville complex, seventy miles north of Houston. Surrounding the car was a landscape of rolled razor-wire fences, surveillance cameras, bleak watch-towers, and gray concrete buildings. Fitzgerald told me that he was tired; the previous evening he had attended an execution, his sixtieth in the five years he had been with the department. We got out of the car and flashed our IDs at the camera. A series of heavy electronically operated doors clicked open, one after another. We went through one, and it closed behind us before a second opened. We entered a sterile hallway lit by fluorescent ceiling lights, the air smelling the way one would expect it to smell in a place where the outside had been utterly banished. There the warden and several hefty corrections officers met us, and we proceeded into the bowels of the prison, away from outdoor light, away from outdoor sounds, deep into the computer-controlled hidden hell at the heart of America's burgeoning incarceration establishment.

10 There are up to 660 men living in isolation behind the metallic-blue and Plexiglas doors of the Estelle Unit's "administrative segregation" cells, the high-security facility at Huntsville that opened in August of 1997. (Texas is currently developing five more "supermax" units that will eventually hold more than 3,000 people.) Depending on their status—there are three levels—the men get from three to seven hours of exercise a week, and from two to eight hours of visits a month. The rest of

the time they remain in their cells. "The security here," Fitzgerald told me with satisfaction, "is better than Alcatraz. Alcatraz didn't have the electronic things we have now. The art of incarceration has definitely improved." The inmates, disciplinary cases from the broader prison system, are men removed not just from the outside society but from the rest of Texas's 140,000-plus prisoners, as close to being vanished spirits as any resident of a medieval dungeon. On them is being performed one of the most astounding social experiments in America's history: isolated for about twenty-three hours a day in bathroom-sized quarters, fed through hatches in their doors, provided with virtually no sensory stimuli for months or years on end, deprived of full meals as punishment for breaking rules, made to dress in paper gowns if they dare to rip up their uniforms, many quite simply seem to go insane. While I was touring the unit, a desperate prisoner "self-mutilated," slashing at the veins in his hands until his blood spurted over the walls, the floor, and the steel seat of the cell he was in, like a peculiarly vivid Jackson Pollock painting.

11 The inmates are often tormented by headaches. Many quite clearly can no longer focus their thoughts on anything. Some weep; others obsess; the more resilient, like David Prater, a twenty-six-year-old lifer who has a degree in finance from the University of Texas, read as much and as often as possible to while away the days. But they are a minority. The average IQ of a Texas prison inmate is 92, and many do not even know how to read. From what I could tell, many of those guarding them aren't much smarter. As prisoners from the nearby low-security unit mopped up the blood from the cutting, guards made jokes about the "mutilator." An officer with the rank of captain assured me that all the inmates were psychologically assessed when they came into Estelle, that if they were mad they would be at the psychiatric unit upstate, and that since they were here, ipso facto, they weren't mad. As he completed this logical circle, the entire "Level 3" unit behind us was rent by the howls and screams of the close-to-naked inmates. It was a hideous sound that would have been familiar in the lunatic asylums of bygone centuries. For the French philosopher Michel Foucault, who explored the histories and social functions of both the asylum and the prison in Western culture, the similarity would probably have illuminated his notion that both institutions function at least in part to reassure the outside population of its "normality" in contrast to the horror caged within.

12 William Sabol, a researcher at the Urban Institute, a Washington, D.C., think tank, has recently begun studying imprisonment and release statistics for ninety metropolitan areas. Over the next few years he will focus on releases in Baltimore, a city with a very high incarceration rate, exploring the effects of release on different communities. For Sabol, the biggest concern is not that already devastated inner cities will be further damaged but that certain struggling blue-collar areas and middleclass black districts, of whose young men large numbers have been imprisoned during the war on drugs, will be unable to reabsorb the ex-cons while retaining their civic character. "When these men return," Sabol explains, "they're less likely to get jobs and there's a higher likelihood of disruption of the family. What we're interested in is will it tip the scales against those neighborhoods that are marginal?" Faced with a growing population of ex-felons, people with resources will probably flee these communities, thereby expanding the areas of devastation.

13 Since fewer than 10 percent of prisoners are sentenced to life, we can expect that more than 90 percent of prisoners will be released. Releasing over several decades millions of people who either never acquired job skills or lost their skills in prison, and who will face employers' suspicion, is almost guaranteed to produce localized but considerable economic problems. Currently, among black men aged twenty-five to thirty-four with less than a high school education, the jobless rate is around 50 percent. If those in prison and jail are included, the figure rises above 60 percent. If incarceration rates ever start to drop, and fewer people are entering prison than are being released, then according to the most basic principles of supply and demand, wage levels in areas already suffering chronically high levels of unemployment will plummet as the competition for scarce jobs increases.

14 The sociologists Bruce Western, of Princeton University, and Katherine Beckett, of Indiana University, are convinced that the economic problems of mass release actually run much deeper. In January of this year they published a paper titled "How Unregulated Is the U.S. Labor Market? The Penal System as a Labor Market Institution," in which they argued that one of the reasons America's unemployment statistics look so good in comparison with those of other industrial democracies is that 1.6 million mainly low-skilled workers—precisely the group least likely to find work in a high-tech economy—have been

incarcerated, and are thus not considered part of the labor force. Rendering such a large group of people invisible, the authors claimed, creates a numerical mirage in which unemployment statistics are as much as two percent below the real unemployment level, and which has been made possible only by what Beckett terms an American "intervention in the economy [the growth of the prison system] comparable financially to Western Europe's unemployment benefit and welfare programs." If mass imprisonment is what the urban scholar Mike Davis, in his book *Ecology of Fear*, terms "carceral Keynesianism"—using prison building and maintenance as an enormous public-works program to shore up an economy in which blue-collar jobs have been exported to the Third World—then mass release may well prove its undoing.

15 Eddie Ellis, a onetime Black Panther who was recently released after serving out a twenty-five-year sentence for murder, believes that the cities are sitting on volcanoes. Now a full-time organizer in the Harlem-based Community Justice Center, Ellis told me when we met that starting around the year 2005, New York is going to see the release of wave after wave of inmates, at the rate of about 30,000 a year, who were incarcerated after 1990. "That's when they began phasing out the programs [education in prison, vocational training, and the like]. By 1994 to 1995 they no longer existed. These are the people we're talking about coming out in such a horrendous condition. The next wave that comes out, we're looking at a serious influx of people into a few communities that not only will devastate these communities but will have a larger consequence for the whole city." The welfare reforms of 1996 drastically curtailed felons' access to welfare money, and specifically barred addicts from access to Medicaid and many drug-rehabilitation programs. Ellis predicts rising epidemics, as ex-prisoners without work or Medicaid spread TB, HIV, and hepatitis.

16 To complete a grim picture, wholesale incarceration decimates voter rolls. In all but four states prisoners convicted of felonies lose the right to vote. In more than thirty states they can reapply only when they're off parole. Those who find work while on parole will—like much of the black population of the pre-civil-rights South—be paying taxes into a political system in which they have no say. In California alone close to a quarter of a million people are disenfranchised by such laws.

17 The situation is even worse in twelve states—almost half of them southern—where a felony can result in disenfranchisement for life. The history of these disenfranchisement laws can be traced straight back to the post–Civil War South; because of the disproportionate number of black men in prison today, the laws continue to affect not just individuals but the aspirations and political influence of entire communities. In a study released last October, the Sentencing Project and Human Rights Watch, an advocacy group based in New York, reported that throughout the country two percent of adults, or approximately four million people, are disenfranchised; within the black male community the figure is 13 percent, or 1.4 million men. In seven states—Alabama, Florida, Iowa, Mississippi, New Mexico, Virginia, and Wyoming—fully a quarter of all black men are permanently ineligible to vote. In Florida alone 204,600 black men, and in Texas 156,600 black men, have lost the vote.

18 The political implications for the next century are troubling. Already the inner cities, where on average more than a quarter of young black men are disenfranchised, have seen their power as voting blocs shrivel. And since today's young are tomorrow's old, the problem can only get worse. In 1997 the Justice Department estimated that 29 percent of black males born in 1991 would spend some time in prison. Only four percent of white males would do so. In some cities in the states in which convicted felons are permanently disenfranchised, as older, pre-prison-boom blacks die out, the proportion of black men of all ages who lack the right to vote will rise to about one third by 2020. In certain parts of some southern cities—Houston, Memphis, Miami, and New Orleans, for example—it may be as many as half. Conceivably, an overwhelmingly black town could have an electoral register dominated by a white minority.

19 Quite simply, mass incarceration followed by mass release into sub-citizenship will undermine the great democratic achievements of the past half century. In effect, even if not in intent, after the brief interregnum of the civil-rights years the South, with the rest of the country in tow, is once again moving toward excluding huge numbers of African-Americans from the political process. Marc Mauer, of the Sentencing Project, says, "It's a wonder there's any black representation at all, given the numbers."

20 Recently I met several ex-prisoners in New York City who were putting their lives back together under the auspices of the Fortune

Society, a non-profit organization that runs one of the country's most successful and intensive post-release programs. Some of the people I met had done terrible things; others had merely taken foolish wrong turns. Regardless, talking with them gave each one a human face. It helped me to understand that most of these ex-cons are damaged people with hopes and fears and dreams that perhaps can be coaxed out of them in a nurturing environment like Fortune's.

21 The most extraordinary of the people I met was a thirty-nine-year-old named Edmond Taylor, who had served a total of eighteen years in a variety of New York's toughest prisons for crimes ranging from drug dealing to violent assault. Out of prison for the past couple of years, Taylor has dedicated himself to change; he works full time as a counselor, helping other prisoners to adjust to life on the outside, and he is regarded by Fortune's executive director, JoAnne Page, as one of her great success stories. Taylor came to meet me straight from counseling a distraught woman who'd been told at a job interview that the company wouldn't hire her because she had a felony conviction. He said, "If I can save just one person a year, I'm happy."

22 A highly articulate man, more capable than most of understanding what led him into violence and helped to destroy half his life, Taylor explained that he had spent nearly four years in "the box"—some of that time in Clinton Dannemora prison, near the Canadian border, for being what he described as "a vocal critic" of conditions within the prison. Describing his reaction to being released from isolation back into the general prison population, he said, "First there's fear, then there's anger, and the anger takes over. It's violent anger. Very quick. No thought of the magnitude of the consequence of the violence. An individual bumped me, rushing to get to the gym. And I rushed up behind him and hit him with a pipe. He went into coma." Taylor went straight back into the box. I asked how long it had taken him to recover from isolation. He looked surprised by the question, and said, "Honestly, I've still not recovered. I've been out of isolation five and a half years. Ms. Page is my boss. If she was to confront me when I had a lot on my mind, anger would come up before rational thought. Anger. Strike back. Now it's not so much physical as verbal. In another situation it would cause me to lose my job." Then Taylor told me a shameful secret. Shortly after he got out of prison, he was living with his brother. His brother criticized him for some of the attitudes he'd

brought out of prison with him. "I felt fed up, and I attacked him," Taylor said. "I grabbed him, choked him, lifted him off his feet, threw him to the ground. I pummeled him causing him to get several stitches above the eye. I grabbed a kitchen knife—I don't remember any of this; he told me afterward—and put it to his neck and said, 'I should kill you. I hate you.' The realization that I put my hands on my baby brother—the only person at that time who'd ever been in my corner. . ."

23 Edmond Taylor sees a future of violent chaos, with a large, uneducated army of enraged ex-cons flooding the streets of the inner cities. JoAnne Page adds, "There's an issue of critical mass. As you lock up a higher percentage of young men in a community, what happens when these guys come out, in terms of role models, crime, the safety of the community? Prisons breed global rage. People come out loaded with so much anger that they're ready to blow up at a touch." She worries that many of them, lacking jobs upon release and having no access to state support, will resort to stealing just to eat. Many will also end up homeless, with their best chance of finding shelter being to commit crimes and return to jail or prison. The Correctional Association of New York estimates that on any given day 3,800 homeless people are in prison at Rikers Island and in other New York City jails.

24 Without making contingency plans for it—without even realizing it—we are creating a disaster that instead of dissipating over time will accumulate with the years.

FOR THINKING, DISCUSSING, AND WRITING

1. What are the popular perceptions about crime that the writer says have "blurred the boundaries between fact and politically expedient myth"?
2. What statistics that Abramsky cites concerning crime and incarceration impress you most? Why are some undocumented? How does this affect their authority?
3. How does the story of Robert Scully help Abramsky make a point? What aspects about Scully's story weaken the writer's argument? Why does Abramsky alternate the stories of Robert Scully, the visit to Huntsville prison, and the interview with Eddie Ellis with statistics on incarcerated and released prisoners? What effect does the writer achieve?

4. The implicit question here is: How can a humane and democratic society deal with crime without creating a system that actually encourages crime? Write an essay to show how Abramsky tries to answer it. Then try to answer it yourself.

WILL DURST

Happy National Apathy Day

Will Durst (1954–), a political satirist who calls himself the nation's ultimate equal opportunity offender, is the host of Livelyhood *on PBS. Here he takes on the nonvoting population of America.*

1 Don't vote. You don't have to. No one's going to make you. This isn't the Soviet Union in the '50s. You won't be forced from your bed and dragged to the polls against your will. Relax. None of your friends are voting. And things are pretty good the way they are, right? If it ain't broke, don't fix it. What do you care if some barren deserted beach does or doesn't get blanketed by a thick film of 30-weight because of off-shore drilling? Find another beach. What's the big deal?

2 Don't vote; you know you don't want to. Parking is a pain, the print is so tiny, and it's always on a Tuesday—what's that all about, anyway? Besides; haven't the pollsters already told us who's going to win? Why beat your head against a wall? It's a done deal. Out of your hands. Don't even need to wash them. It'd be totally different if it actually mattered. But it's not as if we have any real choice. If voting were effective, they would have made it illegal by now.

3 Don't vote. Everyone knows the big corporations have the politicians so deep in their pockets they've got to brush the lint out of their hair before photo ops. It's common knowledge. Conventional wisdom. You'll only end up encouraging them.

4 You must have better things to do. Jog on over to the library before it gets closed down and read up on other people who never voted. Or you could work on that extra room for Grandma when Medicare fails and she has to move in. Or take a farewell trip on your local mass transit and wave bye-bye to the neighborhood rec center. That would be fun.

5 Besides, what difference does it make? One lousy little vote. A spit in the ocean. Don't worry. Be happy. Stay home. This is still a free country, last time I looked. Who cares? Not you.

FOR THINKING, DISCUSSING, AND WRITING

1. What effect does the writer achieve by opening the essay with the command "Don't vote"? Why does he begin the following two paragraphs in the same way? What other imperatives appear in the essay? How do they help you understand the writer's point?
2. What does the writer suggest about personal responsibility and social obligation? What is our obligation to vote? When, if ever, is it all right not to vote?
3. Why might you agree or disagree with Durst when he says in the first paragraph that "things are pretty good the way they are, right?" What "things" is he referring to? Explain your answer.
4. Write an essay in which you argue whether a citizen of a democratic society has an obligation to vote. Be sure to refer to Durst's essay to illustrate and develop your argument.

LANI GUINIER

The Tyranny of the Majority

Lani Guinier (1950–) is professor at Harvard Law School, the first black tenured professor in the school's history. She received her B.A. from Radcliffe College in 1971 and a J.D. from Yale. In 1993 President Clinton nominated her to head the Civil Rights Division of the Justice Department, but an outcry by conservatives against her views on voting and democracy forced him to withdraw her nomination. She has written extensively on constitutional law, voting rights, race, and gender theory. In this piece from her book The Tyranny of the Majority: Fundamental Fairness in Representative Democracy (1994) *she explores the relation between majority rule and minority rights.*

1 I have always wanted to be a civil rights lawyer. This lifelong ambition is based on a deep-seated commitment to democratic fair play—to playing by the rules as long as the rules are fair. When the rules seem unfair, I have worked to change them, not subvert them. When I was eight years old, I was a Brownie. I was especially proud of my uniform, which represented a commitment to good citizenship and good deeds. But one day, when my Brownie group staged a hatmaking contest, I realized that uniforms are only as honorable as the people who wear them. The contest was rigged. The winner was assisted by her milliner mother, who actually made the winning entry in full view of all the participants. At the time, I was too young

to be able to change the rules, but I was old enough to resign, which I promptly did.

2 To me, fair play means that the rules encourage everyone to play. They should reward those who win, but they must be acceptable to those who lose. The central theme of my academic writing is that not all rules lead to elemental fair play. Some even commonplace rules work against it.

3 The professional milliner competing with amateur Brownies stands as an example of rules that are patently rigged or patently subverted. Yet, sometimes, even when rules are perfectly fair in form, they serve in practice to exclude particular groups from meaningful participation. When they do not encourage everyone to play, or when, over the long haul, they do not make the losers feel as good about the outcomes as the winners, they can seem as unfair as the milliner who makes the winning hat for her daughter.

4 Sometimes, too, we construct rules that force us to be divided into winners and losers when we might have otherwise joined together. This idea was cogently expressed by my son, Nikolas, when he was four years old, far exceeding the thoughtfulness of his mother when she was an eight-year-old Brownie. While I was writing one of my law journal articles, Nikolas and I had a conversation about voting prompted by a *Sesame Street Magazine* exercise. The magazine pictured six children: four children had raised their hands because they wanted to play tag; two had their hands down because they wanted to play hide-and-seek. The magazine asked its readers to count the number of children whose hands were raised and then decide what game the children would play.

5 Nikolas quite realistically replied, "They will play both. First they will play tag. Then they will play hide-and-seek." Despite the magazine's "rules," he was right. To children, it is natural to take turns. The winner may get to play first or more often, but even the "loser" gets something. His was a positive-sum solution that many adult rule-makers ignore.

6 The traditional answer to the magazine's problem would have been a zero-sum solution: "The children—all the children—will play tag, and only tag." As a zero-sum solution, everything is seen in terms of "I win; you lose." The conventional answer relies on winner-take-all majority rule, in which the tag players, as the majority, win the right to decide for all the children what game to play. The hide-and-seek

preference becomes irrelevant. The numerically more powerful majority choice simply subsumes minority preferences.

7 In the conventional case, the majority that rules gains all the power and the minority that loses gets none. For example, two years ago Brother Rice High School in Chicago held two senior proms. It was not planned that way. The prom committee at Brother Rice, a boys' Catholic high school, expected just one prom when it hired a disc jockey, picked a rock band, and selected music for the prom by consulting student preferences. Each senior was asked to list his three favorite songs, and the band would play the songs that appeared most frequently on the lists.

8 Seems attractively democratic. But Brother Rice is predominantly white, and the prom committee was all white. That's how they got two proms. The black seniors at Brother Rice felt so shut out by the "democratic process" that they organized their own prom. As one black student put it "For every vote we had, there were eight votes for what they wanted. . . . [W]ith us being in the minority we're always outvoted. It's as if we don't count."

9 Some embittered white seniors saw things differently. They complained that the black students should have gone along with the majority: "The majority makes a decision. That's the way it works."

10 In a way, both groups were right. From the white students' perspective, this was ordinary decisionmaking. To the black students, majority rule sent the message: "we don't count" is the "way it works" for minorities. In a racially divided society, majority rule may be perceived as majority tyranny.

11 That is a large claim, and I do not rest my case for it solely on the actions of the prom committee in one Chicago high school. To expand the range of the argument, I first consider the ideal of majority rule itself, particularly as reflected in the writings of James Madison and other founding members of our Republic. These early democrats explored the relationship between majority rule and democracy. James Madison warned, "If a majority be united by a common interest, the rights of the minority will be insecure." The tyranny of the majority, according to Madison, requires safeguards to protect "one part of the society against the injustice of the other part."

12 For Madison, majority tyranny represented the great danger to our early constitutional democracy. Although the American revolution was fought against the tyranny of the British monarch, it soon became clear

that there was another tyranny to be avoided. The accumulations of all powers in the same hands, Madison warned, "whether of one, a few, or many, and whether hereditary, self-appointed, or elective, may justly be pronounced the very definition of tyranny."

13 As another colonist suggested in papers published in Philadelphia, "We have been so long habituated to a jealousy of tyranny from monarchy and aristocracy, that we have yet to learn the dangers of it from democracy." Despotism had to be opposed "whether it came from Kings, Lords or the people."

14 The debate about majority tyranny reflected Madison's concern that the majority may not represent the whole. In a homogeneous society, the interest of the majority would likely be that of the minority also. But in a heterogeneous community, the majority may not represent all competing interests. The majority is likely to be self-interested and ignorant or indifferent to the concerns of the minority. In such case, Madison observed, the assumption that the majority represents the minority is "altogether fictitious."

15 Yet even a self-interested majority can govern fairly if it cooperates with the minority. One reason for such cooperation is that the self-interested majority values the principle of reciprocity. The self-interested majority worries that the minority may attract defectors from the majority and become the next governing majority. The Golden Rule principle of reciprocity functions to check the tendency of a self-interested majority to act tyrannically.

16 So the argument for the majority principle connects it with the value of reciprocity: You cooperate when you lose in part because members of the current majority will cooperate when they lose. The conventional case for the fairness of majority rule is that it is not really the rule of a fixed group—The Majority—on all issues; instead it is the rule of shifting majorities, as the losers at one time or on one issue join with others and become part of the governing coalition at another time or on another issue. The result will be a fair system of mutually beneficial cooperation. I call a majority that rules but does not dominate a Madisonian Majority.

17 The problem of majority tyranny arises, however, when the self-interested majority does not need to worry about defectors. When the majority is fixed and permanent, there are no checks on its ability to be overbearing. A majority that does not worry about defectors is a majority with total power.

18 In such a case, Madison's concern about majority tyranny arises. In a heterogeneous community, any faction with total power might subject "the minority to the caprice and arbitrary decisions of the majority, who instead of consulting the interest of the whole community collectively, attend sometimes to partial and local advantages."

19 "What remedy can be found in a republican Government, where the majority must ultimately decide," argued Madison, but to ensure "that no one common interest or passion will be likely to unite a majority of the whole number in an unjust pursuit." The answer was to disaggregate the majority to ensure checks and balances or fluid, rotating interests. The minority needed protection against an overbearing majority, so that "a common sentiment is less likely to be felt, and the requisite concert less likely to be formed, by a majority of the whole."

20 Political struggles would not be simply a contest between rulers and people; the political struggles would be among the people themselves. The work of government was not to transcend different interests but to reconcile them. In an ideal democracy, the people would rule, but the minorities would also be protected against the power of majorities. Again, where the rules of decisionmaking protect the minority, the Madisonian Majority rules without dominating.

21 But if a group is unfairly treated, for example, when it forms a racial minority, *and* if the problems of unfairness are not cured by conventional assumptions about majority rule, then what is to be done? The answer is that we may need an *alternative* to winner-take-all majoritarianism. With Nikolas's help, I now call the alternative the "principle of taking turns." In a racially divided society, this principle does better than simple majority rule if it accommodates the values of self-government, fairness, deliberation, compromise, and consensus that lie at the heart of the democratic ideal.

22 In my legal writing, I follow the caveat of James Madison and other early American democrats. I explore decisionmaking rules that might work in a multi-racial society to ensure that majority rule does not become majority tyranny. I pursue voting systems that might disaggregate The Majority so that it does not exercise power unfairly or tyrannically. I aspire to a more cooperative political style of decision making to enable all of the students at Brother Rice to feel comfortable attending the same prom. In looking to create Madisonian Majorities, I pursue a positive-sum, taking-turns solution.

23 Structuring decisionmaking to allow the minority "a turn" may be necessary to restore the reciprocity ideal when a fixed majority refuses to cooperate with the minority. If the fixed majority loses its incentive to follow the Golden Rule principle of shifting majorities, the minority never gets to take a turn. Giving the minority a turn does not mean the minority gets to rule; what it does mean is that the minority gets to influence decisionmaking and the majority rules more legitimately.

24 Instead of automatically rewarding the preferences of the monolithic majority, a taking-turns approach anticipates that the majority rules, but is not overbearing. Because those with 51 percent of the votes are not assured 100 percent of the power, the majority cooperates with, or at least does not tyrannize, the minority.

25 The sports analogy of "I win; you lose" competition within a political hierarchy makes sense when only one team can win; Nikolas's intuition that it is often possible to take turns suggests an alternative approach. Take family decisionmaking, for example. It utilizes a taking-turns approach. When parents sit around the kitchen table deciding on a vacation destination or activities for a rainy day, often they do not simply rely on a show of hands, especially if that means that the older children always prevail or if affinity groups among the children (those who prefer movies to video games, or those who prefer baseball to playing cards) never get to play their activity of choice. Instead of allowing the majority simply to rule, the parents may propose that everyone take turns, going to the movies one night and playing video games the next. Or as Nikolas proposes, they might do both on a given night.

26 Taking turns attempts to build consensus while recognizing political or social differences, and it encourages everyone to play. The taking-turns approach gives those with the most support more turns, but it also legitimates the outcome from each individual's perspective, including those whose views are shared only by a minority.

27 In the end, I do not believe that democracy should encourage rule by the powerful—even a powerful majority. Instead, the ideal of democracy promises a fair discussion among self-defined equals about how to achieve our common aspirations. To redeem that promise, we need to put the idea of taking turns and disaggregating the majority at the center of our conception of representation. Particularly as we move into the twenty-first century as a more highly diversified citizenry, it is essential that we consider the ways in which voting and representational systems succeed or fail at encouraging Madisonian Majorities.

28 To use Nikolas's terminology, "it is no fair" if a fixed, tyrannical majority excludes or alienates the minority. It is no fair if a fixed, tyrannical majority monopolizes all the power all the time. It is no fair if we engage in the periodic ritual of elections, but only the permanent majority gets to choose who is elected. Where we have tyranny by The Majority, we do not have genuine democracy.

29 My life's work, with the essential assistance of people like Nikolas, has been to try to find the rules that can best bring us together as a democratic society. Some of my ideas about democratic fair play were grossly mischaracterized in the controversy over my nomination to be Assistant Attorney General for Civil Rights. Trying to find rules to encourage fundamental fairness inevitably raises the question posed by Harvard Professor Randall Kennedy in a summary of this controversy: "What is required to create political institutions that address the needs and aspirations of all Americans, not simply whites, who have long enjoyed racial privilege, but people of color who have long suffered racial exclusion from policymaking forums?" My answer, as Professor Kennedy suggests, varies by situation. But I have a predisposition, reflected in my son's yearning for a positive-sum solution, to seek an integrated body politic in which all perspectives are represented and in which all people work together to find common ground. I advocate empowering voters and their representatives in ways that give even minority voters a chance to influence legislative outcomes.

30 But those in the majority do not lose; they simply learn to take turns. This is a positive-sum solution that allows all voters to feel that they participate meaningfully in the decisionmaking process. This is a positive-sum solution that makes legislative outcomes more legitimate.

31 I have been roundly, and falsely, criticized for focusing on outcomes. Outcomes are indeed relevant, but *not* because I seek to advance particular ends, such as whether the children play tag or hide-and-seek, or whether the band at Brother Rice plays rock music or rap. Rather, I look to outcomes as *evidence* of whether all the children—or all the high school seniors—feel that their choice is represented and considered. The purpose is not to guarantee "equal legislative outcomes"; equal opportunity to *influence* legislative outcomes regardless of race is more like it.

32 For these reasons, I sometimes explore alternatives to simple, winner-take-all majority rule. I do not advocate any one procedural rule

as a universal panacea for unfairness. Nor do I propose these remedies primarily as judicial solutions. They can be adopted only in the context of litigation after the court first finds a legal violation.

33 Outside of litigation, I propose these approaches as political solutions if, depending on the local context, they better approximate the goals of democratic fair play. One such decisionmaking alternative is called cumulative voting, which could give all the students at Brother Rice multiple votes and allow them to distribute their votes in any combination of their choice. If each student could vote for ten songs, the students could plump or aggregate their votes to reflect the intensity of their preferences. They could put ten votes on one song; they could put five votes on two songs. If a tenth of the students opted to "cumulate" or plump all their votes for one song, they would be able to select one of every ten or so songs played at the prom. The black seniors could have done this if they chose to, but so could any other cohesive group of sufficient size. In this way, the songs preferred by a majority would be played most often, but the songs the minority enjoyed would also show up on the play list.

34 Under cumulative voting, voters get the same number of votes as there are seats or options to vote for, and they can then distribute their votes in any combination to reflect their preferences. Like-minded voters can vote as a solid bloc or, instead, form strategic, cross-racial coalitions to gain mutual benefits. This system is emphatically not racially based; it allows voters to organize themselves on whatever basis they wish.

35 Corporations use this system to ensure representation of minority shareholders on corporate boards of directors. Similarly, some local municipal and county governments have adopted cumulative voting to ensure representation of minority voters. Instead of awarding political power to geographic units called districts, cumulative voting allows voters to cast ballots based on what they think rather than where they live.

36 Cumulative voting is based on the principle of one person–one vote because each voter gets the same total number of votes. Everyone's preferences are counted equally. It is not a particularly radical idea; thirty states either require or permit corporations to use this election system. Cumulative voting is certainly not antidemocratic because it emphasizes the importance of voter choice in selecting public or social policy. And it is neither liberal nor conservative. Both the Reagan and Bush administrations approved cumulative voting schemes pursuant to

the Voting Rights Act to protect the rights of racial- and language-minority voters.

37 But, as in Chilton County, Alabama, which now uses cumulative voting to elect both the school board and the county commission, any politically cohesive group can vote strategically to win representation. Groups of voters win representation depending on the exclusion threshold, meaning the percentage of votes needed to win one seat or have the band play one song. That threshold can be set case by case, jurisdiction by jurisdiction, based on the size of minority groups that make compelling claims for representation.

38 Normally the exclusion threshold in a head-to-head contest is 50 percent, which means that only groups that can organize a majority can get elected. But if multiple seats (or multiple songs) are considered simultaneously, the exclusion threshold is considerably reduced. For example, in Chilton County, with seven seats elected simultaneously on each governing body, the threshold of exclusion is now one-eighth. Any group with the solid support of one-eighth the voting population cannot be denied representation. This is because any self-identified minority can plump or cumulate all its votes for one candidate. Again, minorities are not defined solely in racial terms.

39 As it turned out in Chilton County, both blacks and Republicans benefited from this new system. The school board and commission now each have three white Democrats, three white Republicans, and one black Democrat. Previously, when each seat was decided in a head-to-head contest, the majority not only ruled but monopolized. Only white Democrats were elected at every prior election during this century.

40 Similarly, if the black and white students at Brother Rice have very different musical taste, cumulative voting permits a positive-sum solution to enable both groups to enjoy one prom. The majority's preferences would be respected in that their songs would be played most often, but the black students could express the intensity of their preferences too. If the black students chose to plump all their votes on a few songs, their minority preferences would be recognized and played. Essentially, cumulative voting structures the band's repertoire to enable the students to take turns.

41 As a solution that permits voters to self-select their identities, cumulative voting also encourages cross-racial coalition building. No one is locked into a minority identity. Nor is anyone necessarily isolated by the identity they choose. Voters can strengthen their influence by forming

coalitions to elect more than one representative or to select a range of music more compatible with the entire student body's preferences.

42 Women too can use cumulative voting to gain greater representation. Indeed, in other countries with similar, alternative voting systems, women are more likely to be represented in the national legislature. For example, in some Western European democracies, the national legislatures have as many as 37 percent female members compared to a little more than 5 percent in our Congress.

43 There is a final benefit from cumulative voting. It eliminates gerrymandering. By denying protected incumbents safe seats in gerrymandered districts, cumulative voting might encourage more voter participation. With greater interest-based electoral competition, cumulative voting could promote the political turnover sought by advocates of term limits. In this way, cumulative voting serves many of the same ends as periodic elections or rotation in office, a solution that Madison and others advocated as a means of protecting against permanent majority factions.

44 A different remedial voting tool, one that I have explored more cautiously, is supermajority voting. It modifies winner-take-all majority rule to require that something more than a bare majority of voters must approve or concur before action is taken. As a uniform decisional rule, a supermajority empowers any numerically small but cohesive group of voters. Like cumulative voting, it is race-neutral. Depending on the issue, different members of the voting body can "veto" impending action.

45 Supermajority remedies give bargaining power to all numerically inferior or less powerful groups, be they black, female, or Republican. Supermajority rules empower the minority Republicans in the Senate who used the Senate filibuster procedure in the spring of 1993 to "veto" the president's proposed economic stimulus package. The same concept of a minority veto yielded the Great Compromise in which small-population states are equally represented in the Senate.

46 I have never advocated (or imagined) giving an individual member of a legislative body a personal veto. Moreover, I have discussed these kinds of exceptional remedies as the subject of court-imposed solutions only when there has been a violation of the statute and only when they make sense in the context of a particular case. I discuss supermajority rules as a judicial remedy only in cases where the court finds proof of consistent and deeply engrained polarization. It was never my

intent that supermajority requirements should be the norm for all legislative bodies, or that simple majority voting would ever in itself constitute a statutory or constitutional violation.

47 Both the Reagan and Bush administrations took a similar remedial approach to enforcement of the Voting Rights Act. In fact, it was the Reagan administration that *approved* the use of supermajority rules as a remedial measure in places like Mobile, Alabama, where the special five-out-of-seven supermajority threshold is still in place today and is credited with increasing racial harmony in that community.

48 But—and here I come directly to the claims of my critics—some apparently fear that remedies for extreme voting abuses, remedies like cumulative voting or the Mobile supermajority, constitute "quotas"—racial preferences to ensure minority rule. While cumulative voting, or a supermajority, is quite conventional in many cases and race neutral, to order it as a remedy apparently opens up possibilities of nonmajoritarianism that many seem to find quite threatening.

49 Indeed, while my nomination was pending, I was called "antidemocratic" for suggesting that majority voting rules may not fairly resolve conflict when the majority and minority are permanently divided. But alternatives to majority voting rules in a racially polarized environment are too easily dismissed by this label. As Chief Justice [Warren] Burger wrote for the Supreme Court, "There is nothing in the language of the Constitution, our history, or our cases that requires that a majority always prevail on every issue." In other words, there is *nothing inherent in democracy that requires majority rule.* It is simply a custom that works efficiently when the majority and minority are fluid, are not monolithic, and are not permanent.

50 Other democracies frequently employ alternatives to winner-take-all majority voting. Indeed, only five Western democracies, including Britain and the United States, still use single-member-district, winner-take-all systems of representation. Germany, Spain, the Netherlands, and Sweden, among other countries, elect their legislatures under some alternative to winner-take-all majority voting. As the *New Yorker*, in a comment on my nomination, observed, President Clinton was right in calling some of my ideas "difficult to defend," but only because "Americans, by and large, are ignorant of the existence, let alone the details, of electoral systems other than their own."

51 No one who had done their homework seriously questioned the fundamentally democratic nature of my ideas. Indeed, columnists who

attacked my ideas during my nomination ordeal have praised ideas, in a different context, that are remarkably similar to my own. Lally Weymouth wrote, "There can't be democracy in South Africa without a measure of formal protection for minorities." George Will has opined, "The Framers also understood that stable, tyrannical majorities can best be prevented by the multiplication of minority interests, so the majority at any moment will be just a transitory coalition of minorities." In my law journal articles, I expressed exactly the same reservations about unfettered majority rule and about the need sometimes to disaggregate the majority to ensure fair and effective representation for all substantial interests.

52 The difference is that the minority I used to illustrate my academic point was not, as it was for Lally Weymouth, the white minority in South Africa. Nor, did I write, as George Will did, about the minority of well-to-do landlords in New York City. I wrote instead about the political exclusion of the black minority in many local county and municipal governing bodies in America.

53 Yet these same two journalists and many others condemned me as antidemocratic. Apparently, it is not controversial to provide special protections for affluent landlords or minorities in South Africa but it is "divisive," "radical," and "out of the mainstream" to provide similar remedies to black Americans who, after centuries of racial oppression, are still excluded.

54 Talking about racial bias at home has, for many, become synonymous with advocating revolution. Talking about racial divisions, in itself, has become a violation of the rules of polite society.

55 We seem to have forgotten that dialogue and intergroup communication are critical to forging consensus. In my case, genuine debate was shut down by techniques of stereotyping and silencing. As Professor Randall Kennedy observes, I was "punished" as the messenger reporting the bad news about our racial situation. I dared to speak when I should have been silent.

56 My nomination became an unfortunate metaphor for the state of race relations in America. My nomination suggested that as a country, we are in a state of denial about issues of race and racism. The censorship imposed against me points to a denial of serious public debate or discussion about racial fairness and justice in a true democracy. For many politicians and policymakers, the remedy for racism is simply to stop talking about race.

57 Sentences, words, even phrases separated by paragraphs in my law review articles were served up to demonstrate that I was violating the rules. Because I talked openly about existing racial divisions, I was branded "race obsessed." Because I explored innovative ways to remedy racism, I was branded "antidemocratic." It did not matter that I had suggested race-neutral election rules, such as cumulative voting, as an alternative to remedy racial discrimination. It did not matter that I never advocated quotas. I became the Quota Queen.

58 The vision behind my by-now-notorious law review articles and my less-well-known professional commitments has always been that of a fair and just society, a society in which even adversely affected parties believe in the system because they believe the process is fair and the process is inclusive. My vision of fairness and justice imagines a full and effective voice for all citizens. I may have failed to locate some of my ideas in the specific factual contexts from which they are derived. But always I have tried to show that democracy in a heterogeneous society is incompatible with rule by a racial monopoly of any color.

59 I hope that we can learn three positive lessons from my experience. The first lesson is that those who stand for principles may lose in the short run, but they cannot be suppressed in the long run. The second lesson is that public dialogue is critical to represent all perspectives; no one viewpoint should be permitted to monopolize, distort, caricature, or shape public debate. The tyranny of The Majority is just as much a problem of silencing minority viewpoints as it is of excluding minority representatives or preferences. We cannot all talk at once, but that does not mean only one group should get to speak. We can take turns. Third, we need consensus and positive-sum solutions. We need a broad public conversation about issues of racial justice in which we seek win-win solutions to real-life problems. If we include blacks and whites, and women and men, and Republicans and Democrats, and even people with new ideas, we will all be better off.

60 Most of all, I hope we begin to consider the principle of taking turns as a means to bring us closer to the ideal of democratic fair play. [Supreme Court] Justice Potter Stewart wrote in 1964 that our form of representative self-government reflects "the strongly felt American tradition that the public interest is composed of many diverse interests, [which] . . . in the long run . . . can better be expressed by a medley of component voices than by the majority's monolithic command." In that

"strongly felt American tradition," I hope more of us aspire to govern like Madisonian Majorities through "a medley of component voices." In that "strongly felt American tradition," I hope more of us come to reject the "monolithic command" of the fixed Majority.

61 After all, government is a public experiment. Let us not forget [Supreme Court] Justice Louis Brandeis's advice at the beginning of this century: "If we guide by the light of reason, we must let our minds be bold." At the close of the same century, I hope we rediscover the bold solution to the tyranny of The Majority, which has always been more democracy, not less.

FOR THINKING, DISCUSSING, AND WRITING

1. What is the "Tyranny of the Majority"? What attributes characterize a majority that has the power—and perhaps the inclination—to tyrannize?
2. What is the utility of drawing on the words and ideas of the various Supreme Court justices? What is the effect of this strategy? How do the references help Guinier's argument?
3. How does Guinier define fair play? Do you agree or disagree with her definition? In what ways is our society focused on an "I win; you lose" philosophy? In what ways is it focused on a "positive-sum" philosophy of taking turns? Which have you experienced more? Why, do you think?
4. Write an essay that reflects your views on the relation between majority rule and minority rights. Are the two compatible? Why or why not?

STEPHEN MIHM

Does Eating Salmon Lower the Murder Rate?

Stephen Mihm (1968–) earned his PhD at New York University in 2003; currently he teaches courses on the economic, cultural, and intellectual history of eighteenth- and nineteenth-century America in the department of history at the University of Georgia. He is also the co-editor of Artificial Parts, Practical Lives: Modern Histories of Prosthetics *(2002).*

1 Most prisons are notorious for the quality of their cuisine (pretty poor) and the behavior of their residents (pretty violent). They are therefore ideal locations to test a novel hypothesis: that violent aggression is

largely a product of poor nutrition. Toward that end, researchers are studying whether inmates become less violent when put on a diet rich in vitamins and in the fatty acids found in seafood.

2 Could a salmon steak and a side of spinach really help curb violence, not just in prison but everywhere? In 2001, Dr. Joseph Hibbeln, a senior clinical investigator at the National Institutes of Health, published a study, provocatively titled "Seafood Consumption and Homicide Mortality," that found a correlation between a higher intake of omega-3 fatty acids (most often obtained from fish) and lower murder rates.

3 Of course, seeing a correlation between fatty acids and nonviolence doesn't necessarily prove that fatty acids inhibit violence. Bernard Gesch, a senior research scientist at Oxford University, set out to show that better nutrition does, in fact, decrease violence. He enrolled 231 volunteers at a British prison in his study; one-half received a placebo, while the other half received fatty acids and other supplements. Over time, the antisocial behavior (as measured by assaults and other violations) of the inmates who had been given the supplements dropped by more than a third relative to their previous records. The control group showed little change. Gesch published his results in 2002 and plans to start a larger study later this year. Similar trials are already under way in Holland and Norway.

4 What would it mean if we found a clear link between diet and violent behavior? To start with, it might challenge the notion that violence is a product of free will. "But how do you exercise that free will without using your brain?" Gesch asks. "And how, exactly, is the brain going to work properly without an adequate nutrient supply?" The belief that people choose to be violent may be irrelevant if the brain isn't firing on all cylinders. This may especially be the case for impulsive acts of violence, which are less a choice than a failure to rein in one's worst instincts.

5 Consider, for example, a study conducted by researchers in Finland. They tested prisoners convicted of violent crimes and found that they had lower levels of omega-3 fatty acids than ordinary, healthy subjects. Why? Omega-3's foster the growth of neurons in the brain's frontal cortex, the bit of gray matter that controls impulsive behavior. Having enough of these fatty acids may keep violent impulses in check. Violent criminals may not be the only ones who would benefit from more fatty acids in their diet. In a recent double-blind trial, when omega-3's were

given to people with a history of substance abuse, the symptoms of "anger" fell by 50 percent.

6 Of course, omega-3's are widely hailed these days as a miracle substance, credited with boosting health in dozens of ways. But Gesch warns against what he calls "silver bullets." The state of the evidence, he says, "doesn't allow us to pinpoint which dietary fat is responsible for changes in behavior." In his new study, he will look into whether several interdependent nutrients may play a role.

7 Gesch further adds that we shouldn't expect nutrition alone to banish violent behavior. "The brain needs to be nourished in two ways. It needs to be educated, and it needs nutrients. Both social and physical factors are important." Simply throwing fish and vegetables at violent criminals is unlikely to have a lasting effect on its own.

8 Caveats aside, there's something that many people may find unnerving about the idea of curing violent behavior by changing what people eat. It threatens to let criminals evade responsibility for their actions. Think, for example, of the infamous "Twinkie defense," in which an accused murderer's lawyer suggested that junk food was partly to blame for his client's compromised mental state. More controversial, perhaps, is the brave-new-world idea of using diet to enforce docility and conformity to the rules, a sort of state-sponsored version of that timeless parental demand to children everywhere: "Eat your vegetables."

9 Then again, we already live in a society in which parents have resorted to drugs like Ritalin to quell unwanted outbursts and impulsive behavior. And when you approach it from that perspective, changing what people eat may not be so radical after all.

FOR THINKING, DISCUSSING, AND WRITING

1. What novel hypothesis does the writer suggest regarding prison populations? What does the title of the essay contribute to the hypothesis? At first blush, the title seems humorous and somewhat silly. What effect does the title have on the reader?
2. What research studies and researchers does Mihm cite? What is the effect of citing them in the essay?
3. What, according to the writer are some problems in trying to link nutrition and behavior? Do you agree with the objections that people may raise?

4. Write an essay in which you state your views on the relation between food intake or nutrition and human behavior. You might want to focus on a single entity—sugar, meat, alcohol, or even fast food, for example.

CONNECTING IDEAS: Law, Justice, and the Democratic Way

1. Analyze the approaches to the death penalty taken by various writers in this chapter. Which argument do you find most compelling? Easy to dismiss? Resonant with your own philosophy on capital punishment?
2. How do the writers address the issue of human rights? How do King and Guinier reflect different aspects of the topic? What does Durst contribute to the conversation?
3. How has the chapter influenced your views of prisoners and the penal system in America?

6 CHAPTER

Gender Dynamics

LOOK IN MOST ENCYCLOPEDIAS AND DICTIONARIES AND you'll learn that gender—from the Latin *genus* for class or kind—is a system used by many languages to sort nouns into the categories masculine, feminine, and neuter. Other than with pronouns and a few nouns now often considered dated (saleswoman, actress, poetess, for example), English does not draw on a complex system of gender-based nouns. Yet from French to Spanish to Russian to Bantu, many languages reflect lexical gender, an assignment of different words to one class or the other—masculine or feminine.

Look behind human languages and there is, of course, a universe of people whom we also divide into the most insistent system of classification known to our species. Researchers, physicians, and social scientists have turned a critical eye on the notion of gender and how being male or female shapes us into the people we are.

Historically, in most cultures, men—and not women—dominated writing, telling for posterity the grand defining myths and tales. As a result, these texts stress differences based on gender, largely documenting and endorsing the primacy of men and the secondary status of women. Eve grew from Adam's rib; Athena, the goddess of wisdom, sprang from the head of her father, Zeus. In Judeo-Christian texts men ruled, women served. Greek mythology acknowledged male and female gods, but the ultimate power resided in Zeus, the mighty paternal figure who watched over his family of immortals.

Yet even in the old texts we see the impulse toward a more androgynous vision, one that indicates both *male* and *female* qualities in all. Genesis tells us that humankind, male and female alike, was created in the image of God. And although important Hindu documents assert that women are unimportant receptacles for the male seed, ancient Hindu texts and art also give us androgynous figures—pregnant men, females whose milk can seed the world, gods who are male and female at once. In one god, and in humans too, the traits and talents we habitually assign as male or female combine and cooperate. Although traditional texts tend to advance the notions of gender difference and traditional roles for women and men, we also find in them a blurring of the rigid classification asserting that if you are male, you are *this;* if you are female, you are *that*.

In modern life the impulses toward gender division on the one hand and gender inclusion on the other create tension. In any sphere of human activity we see debate, and sometimes battle, over gender. Ever since the American reformers founded a new republic based on the revolutionary notion of "liberty and equality for all," women have struggled to claim their birthright. Not until the twentieth century, though, were women in the United States allowed to vote. But look at the highest offices of government, the current Senate, for example, and you will still see the political remnants of "difference" thinking: Men, and largely white men at that, populate both sides of the aisle. Women have limited access to political power in this country, although many policymakers (perhaps mostly men) assert that women have made significant progress as political leaders in the last few decades.

Senator Hillary Clinton, for example, garnered considerable enthusiasm as a possible presidential candidate in the 2008 race. In the domestic sphere, the debate also looms: Ads, political speeches, greeting cards pay homage to the blessed mom who inspires us all, while in the privacy of many homes, devaluation of mothers is often the reality, with many of them working outside the home and inside it, in work weeks that are often double those of men. However, in some households men are assuming roles once thought reserved exclusively for women: They cook the family meals, do household chores, care for children, and stay home while the wife and mother works. In the workplace, in schools and colleges, in the very language we use to live our lives, gender as a defining factor in who we are as people and communities is a subject of great debate.

What *are* the differences between males and females, men and women and the rituals that surround their behavior as gendered human beings? The *wrasse*, a marine fish of the *Labridae* family, can change sexes, becoming male or female in response to reproductive exigency, suggesting that at least somewhere in the animal kingdom biology has flexibility. For humans, where does biology end and culture begin? Because certain traits may have evolved ages ago to advance our species' survival (aggression in the males so we'd have hunters, tenderness in the females so we'd have child care, some social biologists assert) must we maintain these traits in the modern era? In the 1990s, the title of a best-seller proclaimed *Men Are from Mars, Women Are from Venus*—a description not unlike that ascribed to the early cave dwellers. Indeed in this chapter both "Listening to Men" by Deborah Tannen and "All About Eve" by Cynthia Russett take on the not-so-obvious differences between men and women.

What value and risks does preserving familiar male-female profiles entail? In our homes, schools, houses of worship, clubs, government, and all the other places we live and build our lives, how might we talk about what it means to be a man or a woman? Increased acceptance of untraditional sexual preference has helped blur the lines between biology and culture. And much resistance to gay relations still strafes our society with hate. David Leavitt in "The Hate Epidemic" here writes about the deadly attack on a young Wyoming homosexual because of his sexuality. Despite vigorous opposition in some quarters, we see men and women in long-term physical and emotional relations with same-sex partners; their existence in our society has raised one of the most potent social issues of our age—the marriage or civil union of gay couples. Perhaps even more important, the whole issue of conventional marriage in general—its ceremonies, religious underpinnings, and implicit duties—is subject to intense scrutiny and discussion. In our age, some men dress and wish to be seen as women, some women dress and wish to be seen as men, and both men and women sometimes seek release from biologically determined genders that trap them. Medical procedures today virtually allow people to switch sexual identities. A remarkable 2005 film called *Transamerica*—fiction but loaded with volatile contemporary issues—traced the progress of a man (played by a female actor) turning himself into a woman both emotionally and physically.

Gender dynamics always seem to heat up discourse, conservative and liberal thinkers squaring off on each side of a rock-hard line. Yet the thoughtful reader will consider principles for discussion that enhance the exchange of ideas around the provocative issue we have tried to capture through multiple perspectives here. We should carry on this complex but essential debate with a dialogue of respect.

MATT RIDLEY

Why Should Males Exist?

Matt Ridley (1958–) is a British author and journalist who has contributed articles to several periodicals, including Smithsonian *and* Atlantic. *His books include* The Red Queen: Sex and the Evolution of Human Nature *(1994) and, most recently,* Genome: The Autobiography of a Species in 23 Chapters *(1999), in which Ridley explores genes one at a time and each one's role in human development, in addition to the social implications of genetic research. In this selection from the August 18/August 25, 1997, issue of* U.S. News and World Report, *Ridley examines some characteristics of the male animal and his role in propagation and evolution.*

1 You do not need to be a feminist to recognize that men are at the root of a lot of the world's troubles.

2 Compared with women, they are more likely to drive fast, commit murders, desert their spouses, abuse children, develop autism or hemophilia, get into fights, become alcoholics, fail at school, find modern service-sector employment uncongenial, get cancer, and die young. Now that Dolly the cloned sheep has shown us that female mammals can be produced directly from the cells of other females, the human race might well ask whether it's necessary to put up with these troubles anymore. Dolly aside, there are already many species that happily or occasionally indulge in parthenogenesis (Greek for virgin birth): Turkeys can develop (with difficulty) in unfertilized eggs. Whiptail lizards are an all-female species. Various fish, crustaceans, insects, and worms can reproduce without the male sex. Some microscopic animals, such as *bdelloid* rotifers, appear to have gone without sex for at least 40 million years. Many common plants such as dandelions are wholly asexual. These species stand as living proof that sex is unnecessary.

3 And not just unnecessary but downright wasteful: Sex means giving away 50 percent of the shares in your own offspring. A sexual

reproduction means holding on to all the equity. Companies that give away 50 percent of their equity every few years have to grow twice as fast as companies that do not, or the market will bury them. This biological paradox is so puzzling that some biologists have been tempted to chalk up sex to an accident of history. It's useless, but species like ours can't get rid of it.

4 If sex were truly useless, though, a species that *did* manage to get rid of it ought to say good riddance and return to the happy state of the rotifer. But consider the greenfly: It is perfectly able to reproduce asexually, but it reverts to sexual reproduction after only a few generations. It simply would not do so if sex did not carry some evolutionary advantage.

5 Many ideas have been advanced to explain the purpose of sex; the only one that is definitely wrong is the one still given in most textbooks—that sex is good for the species because it helps it to evolve. That would be rather like one company arguing that it's willing to take a 50 percent loss because it's helping the evolution of all other companies in the same business in the process. Few shareholders would be impressed.

6 The search for other explanations for sex starts with the observation of where sex happens and where it does not. Almost all animals and plants living in tropical rain forests and coral reefs are sexual. Many animals and plants living in temporary or unstable habitats—freshwater ponds, ephemeral forest clearings, arctic tundras, alpine meadows—do without males. This counts against several theories: First to go is the idea that sex is there to repair mutations. Animals and plants that live at high altitudes, drenched with mutation-causing ultraviolet light, are among the most likely to be asexual.

7 Second to go are a bunch of theories that explain sex as a sort of reshuffling of the genetic pack to adapt to changing environments. Yet it is precisely in *stable* environments like rain forests that sex seems most indispensable.

8 In accordance with Sherlock Holmes's famous dictum—eliminate the impossible, and whatever remains, however improbable, is the truth—many biologists now lean toward a bizarre but intriguing explanation: Sex is for combating parasites. In warm, rich, stable environments, living creatures are under continuous assault from microscopic parasites, which are constantly evolving new abilities to undermine their hosts' defenses. The hosts need to change their genes regularly if

they are to stay one step ahead. Only small, rapidly reproducing creatures living nomadically in cold or fast-changing environments can keep ahead of parasites without having sex. This idea, championed by Oxford University's William Hamilton, is known as the "Red Queen" theory, after the character in *Through the Looking Glass* who must keep running just to stay in the same place.

9 Having invented males, this theory goes, our ancestors only subsequently found other ways to put them to good use. Most birds and many fish employ males as assistant parents, sharing the duties of building nests, incubating eggs, and feeding babies. But this was not so much the purpose of sex as a byproduct of it—an attempt by females to turn the given fact of sexual reproduction to their advantage by selecting as mates males that were not total freeloaders.

10 Even seemingly destructive male behavior may be explained by this genetic war between the sexes. Male elephant seals and peacocks, for example, are the ultimate boors of the animal world. The male takes no part in child rearing after a brief insemination of the female. Indeed, such is the male elephant seal's aggressiveness that he sometimes tramples babies under foot. Except as a sperm provider, he is a liability.

11 Or is he? Think of it this way: When the female elephant seal hauls her body onto the best part of the breeding beach, she finds that she has unwittingly become the property of the biggest, strongest, healthiest, and most agile of the males. He has fought long and hard to monopolize exactly that spot. Genetically speaking, he is not a bad father at all: He is equipped with superb innate abilities, excellent disease resistance, a good brain, a well-put-together body. The long and bloody battles he has fought, the enormous muscles he has grown—females are responsible for these. It is their fault, because they have been choosing to allow the victors of battles to win their hearts for thousands of generations. Seen from this eugenic perspective, males are a sort of genetic test bed, a sieve through which the genes of the species are passed in every generation, with only the best being selected.

12 So, far from railing against the fact that men fight, take risks, die young, and treat women as property, women should apologize for it. The reason men are that way is most likely that women have bred them that way, gradually and imperceptibly over many generations, by choosing macho men as fathers for their sons.

13 Human males stand somewhere in the middle of the boorishness spectrum. They share many of the aggressive tendencies of their

fellow male primates, but they also are intimately involved in child rearing in a way that male chimpanzees and gorillas are not. A more accurate description, however, may be to say that human males combine both extremes. Again, that is the fault of females. Many seemingly monogamous birds, for example, try to have their beefcake and eat it too. The Danish biologist Anders Moller, using DNA fingerprinting to establish the paternity of nestlings, found that female barn swallows select the most nurturing male they can get as a social husband, to build the nest and rear the chicks—then often sneak around the back of the barn and cuckold him by getting sperm from a genetically superior male (as indicated in this species by his long tail).

14 This is uncomfortably close to home. Like swallows, human females have clearly been trying an evolutionary mixed strategy. They have been choosing good and faithful husbands keen on child rearing, but they also have been rewarding macho showoffs with a disproportionate share in the next generation.

15 However, men have their revenge. In most species, female behavior is little influenced by male selection, because males are sexually indiscriminate (which in turn is because sperm is cheap and quick to produce compared with eggs). Sexual selection is one-way traffic, which is why peacocks look ridiculous and peahens look normal.

16 But in humans, almost uniquely, males play the same game: They are quite selective in their choice of a mate, as much as females or even more. Their selectivity, over thousands of generations, has landed female human beings with sexually selected features—swollen breasts, narrow waists, wide hips that have no higher evolutionary purpose than to produce a next generation of females who also will be sexually attractive to men. Women would not have these features if men had not been picking on them for such a long time. Pamela Anderson Lee was made by men, just as Mike Tyson was by women.

FOR THINKING, DISCUSSING, AND WRITING

1. What are some of the negative attributes the writer says are characteristic of men?
2. In paragraph 3, Ridley mentions a "biological paradox." What is he referring to? Is it really a paradox? Why or why not? What is the meaning of the word "equity" in that same paragraph? How does it help the writer establish his point?

3. What assumptions about male and female relations does Ridley make? Are they fair ones? Why or why not? In what ways does Ridley challenge the basic assumption that sexual union is ultimately connected with the idea of love? How do his points win you over to his beliefs? In what ways does he not convince you? How fair and accurate is he when he describes the kind of man most women want? What about the kind of woman most men want? How do his notions compare and contrast with your own?
4. Ridley asks, "Why should males exist?" How successful is he in answering the question stated in the title? In what ways is the question purely rhetorical? In what ways is it a serious question? How would you answer it? Write an essay to address some of these issues.

PHYLLIS CHESLER

The Failure of Feminism

Professor Emerita of psychology and women's studies at the College of Staten Island of the City University of New York, Phyllis Chesler (1940–) is the author of the best-selling Women and Madness *(1973),* The New Antisemitism *(2003),* Women's Inhumanity to Women *(2002), and* The Death of Feminism *(2005), from which she adapted this essay for the* Chronicle of Higher Education's *October 17, 2006, issue. She serves on the Board of Scholars for Peace in the Middle East.*

1 Is feminism really dead? Well, yes and no. It gives me no pleasure, but someone must finally tell the truth about how feminists have failed their own ideals and their mandate to think both clearly and morally. Only an insider can really do this, someone who cares deeply about feminist values and goals. I have been on the front lines for nearly 40 years, and I feel called upon to explain how many feminists—who should be the first among freedom- and democracy-loving people—have instead become cowardly herd animals and grim totalitarian thinkers. This must be said, and my goal in saying it is a hopeful one. We live at a time when women can and must make a difference in the world.

2 From the start, feminism has been unfairly, even viciously, attacked. I do not want to do that without cause here. The truth is that in less than 40 years, a visionary feminism has managed to challenge, if not transform, world consciousness.

3 For example, you can find feminists on every continent who have mounted brave and determined battles against rape, incest, domestic violence, economic and professional inequality, and local "cultural" practices such as Arab honor killings, dowry burnings, female genital mutilation, as well as against the global trafficking in women and children. I don't want to minimize or simplify what feminism has accomplished.

4 In some ways, feminism has also been inclusive. Feminists are Republicans and Democrats, right-wing conservatives and left-wing radicals; feminists are both religious and anti-religious, anti-abortion and pro-abortion, anti-pornography and pro-pornography, anti-gay-marriage and pro-gay-marriage. Feminists come in all ages and colors; belong to every caste, gender, class, and religion; and live everywhere.

5 Nevertheless feminists are often perceived as marginal and irrelevant; and in some important ways the perception is accurate.

6 Today the cause of justice for women around the world is as urgent as it has ever been. The plight of both women and men in the Islamic world (and increasingly in Europe) requires a sober analysis of reality and a heroic response. World events have made feminism more important—yet at the same time, feminism has lost much of its power.

7 To my horror, most Western academic and mainstream feminists have not focused on what I call gender apartheid in the Islamic world, or on its steady penetration of Europe. Such feminists have also failed to adequately wrestle with the complex realities of freedom, tyranny, patriotism, and self-defense, and with the concept of a Just War.

8 Islamic terrorists have declared jihad against the "infidel West" and against all of us who yearn for freedom. Women in the Islamic world are treated as subhumans. Although some feminists have sounded the alarm about this, a much larger number have remained silent. Why is it that many have misguidedly romanticized terrorists as freedom fighters and condemned both America and Israel as the real terrorists or as the root cause of terrorism? In the name of multicultural correctness (all cultures are equal, formerly colonized cultures are more equal), the feminist academy and media appear to have all but abandoned vulnerable people—Muslims, as well as Christians, Jews, and Hindus—to the forces of reactionary Islamism.

9 Because feminist academics and journalists are now so heavily influenced by left ways of thinking, many now believe that speaking out against head scarves, face veils, the chador, arranged marriages, polygamy, forced pregnancies, or female genital mutilation is either

"imperialist" or "crusade-ist." Postmodernist ways of thinking have also led feminists to believe that confronting narratives on the academic page is as important and world-shattering as confronting jihadists in the flesh and rescuing living beings from captivity.

10 It is as a feminist—not as an anti-feminist—that I have felt the need to write a book to show that something has gone terribly wrong among our thinking classes. The multicultural feminist canon has not led to independent, tolerant, diverse, or objective ways of thinking. On the contrary. It has led to conformity, totalitarian thinking, and political passivity. Although feminists indulge in considerable nostalgia for the activist 60s and 70s, in some ways they are no different from the rest of the left-leaning academy, which also suffers from the disease of politically correct passivity.

11 Is women's studies to blame for all this? Well, yes and no. Had the academy been slightly more hospitable to original, radical, and activist feminist energies and had money been plentiful, there might have been no need to ghettoize the study of gender. But that was not the case. In addition, with some exceptions, the kind of feminist faculty members who could survive in academe were, like their male counterparts, far too dutiful.

12 Today feminists are seen as marginal also because of their obsessive focus on "personal" body rights and sexual issues. This is no crime, but it is simply not good enough. It may shock some to hear me say this, but we have other important things on our agenda.

13 Women can no longer afford to navel gaze—not if they want to play vital roles on the world-historical stage, not if they want to continue to struggle for woman's and humanity's global freedom. And women in America can no longer allow themselves to be rendered inactive, anti-activist, by outdated left and European views of colonial-era racism that are meant to trump and silence concerns about gender.

14 Of course, not all feminists are passive. Many have been helping the female victims of violence in a hands-on way. However, this work is not often taught in women's-studies programs, nor does such hands-on work take place on the campus. Many law schools have domestic-violence clinics; most graduate liberal-arts programs do not. Anti-feminist professors in medical and graduate school do not often teach the pioneering work of feminist mental-health professionals.

15 Some might say that I am being unnecessarily harsh on women who have, indeed, been sounding the alarm about the global rise

in fundamentalist misogyny. Perhaps I am. But I think we can really make a difference. I want more of us to put our shoulder to freedom's wheel.

16 For example, I know that many feminists enjoyed talking about the plight of Afghan women under the Taliban; and why not? This tragedy proved that Feminism 101 was right all along, that men really did oppress women. But few of the televised feminist talking heads wanted to systematically sponsor Afghan women as immigrants or as political refugees. I know because I suggested, privately, that the anti-Taliban American feminists do so. Needless to say, these feminists did not want to launch a military invasion of Afghanistan on behalf of women either. I know. I raised this idea many times. All I got were pitying looks.

17 Some personal disclosures are now in order.

18 First, I am a feminist *and* an American patriot. Yes, one can be both. I am also an internationalist. There is no contradiction here. Finally, I am a religious Jew and am sympathetic to both religious and secular worldviews. Being religious does not compromise my feminism. On the contrary, it gives me the strength and a necessarily humbled perspective to continue the struggle for justice.

19 Second, Afghanistan matters to me; it has touched my life. Once long ago, in 1961, I was held captive there and kept in purdah for five months; some women were exceptionally kind to me. I will never forget them. I was the young bride of a Western-educated Afghan. My American passport was taken away, and I was thrown into (fairly posh) purdah in Kabul. The unexpected curtailment of my freedom was as awful as it was unexpected. I nearly died there—but I finally escaped.

20 I believe that my Western feminism was forged in that most beautiful and tragic of countries. And yes, I also understand that America has not yet done all that is necessary to build up the country, that ethnic warlords and drug lords continue to tyrannize civilians, that women are still imprisoned in chadaris and in brutal arranged marriages, with limited access to medical care, education, and employment.

21 Most academics and activists do not actually do anything; they read, they write, they deliver papers. They may not be able to free slaves or prisoners the way an entering army might, but they can think clearly, and in complex and courageous ways, and they can enunciate a vision of freedom and dignity for women and men. It is crucial, even heroic, that they do so.

22 Both women and religious minorities in non-Western and Muslim countries, and in an increasingly Islamized Europe, are endangered as never before. In 2004 the Dutch filmmaker Theo van Gogh was butchered by a jihadist on the streets of Amsterdam for having made a film, *Submission*, which denounced the abuse of women under Koranic Islam. However, the eerie silence both from feminists and film makers about van Gogh's assassination is deafening and disheartening. The same Hollywood loudmouths so quick to condemn and shame President Bush for having invaded Afghanistan and Iraq have, as of this writing, remained silent about the chilling effect that such an assassination in broad daylight can have on academic and artistic freedom.

23 Perhaps some of the very academics and mainstream feminists whom I am criticizing—but also trying to influence—will devalue what I am saying. Perhaps they will say that I am no longer a feminist—that I have betrayed feminism, not they. It will not change the truth of what I am saying. My hope is that this will resonate with people of all ages; men and women who are quietly doing feminist work within their profession, and there are many; feminists of faith, and there are also many; both Republicans and Democrats; educators both here and abroad; and especially with the so-called ordinary people whose lives and freedom are at stake.

FOR THINKING, DISCUSSING, AND WRITING

1. How does Chesler establish her credentials as a potential critic of feminism? Why do you think she provides this information about herself?
2. What does the writer indicate as some of the accomplishments of feminists? Why then does she call feminists "cowardly herd animals"? What exactly is gender apartheid? Do you believe that "conformity, totalitarian thinking, and political passivity" characterize feminists today? Why or why not? How does the plight of Afghan women serve the writer's argument?
3. What personal disclosures does Chesler make? Why does she include them in her essay?
4. Write an essay in which you argue for or against this statement from the essay: "Nevertheless, feminists are often perceived as marginal and irrelevant; and in some important ways the perception is accurate." Draw upon issues identified in the essay but also on your own reading and personal experience.

MAXINE HONG KINGSTON

No Name Woman

Maxine Hong Kingston (1940–) was born in Stockton, California. She is the author of The Woman Warrior *(1976),* China Men *(1980), and* Tripmaster Monkey *(1989) and the winner both of the National Book Critics Circle Award and the American Book Award. Her most recent publication,* Veterans of War, Veterans of Peace *(2006), is a collection of writings from survivors of five wars, including combatants, war widows, spouses, children, conscientious objectors, and veterans of domestic abuse. In this selection from* The Woman Warrior *Kingston explores the relation between family and cultural history by means of her aunt's experiences in China.*

1 "You must not tell anyone," my mother said, "what I am about to tell you. In China your father had a sister who killed herself. She jumped into the family well. We say that your father has all brothers because it is as if she had never been born."

2 "In 1924 just a few days after our village celebrated seventeen hurry-up weddings—to make sure that every young man who went 'out on the road' would responsibly come home—your father and his brothers and your grandfather and his brothers and your aunt's new husband sailed for America, the Gold Mountain. It was your grandfather's last trip. Those lucky enough to get contracts waved good-bye from the decks. They fed and guarded the stowaways and helped them off in Cuba, New York, Bali, Hawaii. 'We'll meet in California next year,' they said. All of them sent money home."

3 "I remember looking at your aunt one day when she and I were dressing; I had not noticed before that she had such a protruding melon of a stomach. But I did not think, 'She's pregnant' until she began to look like other pregnant women, her shirt pulling and the white tops of her black pants showing. She could not have been pregnant, you see, because her husband had been gone for years. No one said anything. We did not discuss it. In early summer she was ready to have the child, long after the time when it could have been possible."

4 "The village had also been counting. On the night the baby was to be born the villagers raided our house. Some were crying. Like a great saw, teeth strung with lights, files of people walked zigzag across our land, tearing the rice. Their lanterns doubled in the disturbed black

water, which drained away through the broken bunds. As the villagers closed in, we could see that some of them, probably men and women we knew well, wore white masks. The people with long hair hung it over their faces. Women with short hair made it stand up on end. Some had tied white bands around their foreheads, arms, and legs."

5 "At first they threw mud and rocks at the house. Then they threw eggs and began slaughtering our stock. We could hear the animals scream their deaths—the roosters, the pigs, a last great roar from the ox. Familiar wild heads flared in our night windows; the villagers encircled us. Some of the faces stopped to peer at us, their eyes rushing like searchlights. The hands flattened against the panes, framed heads, and left red prints."

6 "The villagers broke in the front and the back doors at the same time, even though we had not locked the doors against them. Their knives dripped with the blood of our animals. They smeared blood on the doors and walls. One woman swung a chicken, whose throat she had slit, splattering blood in red arcs about her. We stood together in the middle of our house, in the family hall with the pictures and tables of the ancestors around us, and looked straight ahead."

7 "At that time the house had only two wings. When the men came back, we would build two more to enclose our courtyard and a third one to begin a second courtyard. The villagers rushed through both wings, even your grandparents' rooms, to find your aunt's, which was also mine until the men returned. From this room a new wing for one of the younger families would grow. They ripped up her clothes and shoes and broke her combs, grinding them underfoot. They tore her work from the loom. They scattered the cooking fire and rolled the new weaving in it. We could hear them in the kitchen breaking our bowls and banging the pots. They overturned the great waist-high earthenware jugs; duck eggs, pickled fruits, vegetables burst out and mixed in acrid torrents. The old woman from the next field swept a broom through the air and loosed the spirits-of-the-broom over our heads. 'Pig.' 'Ghost.' 'Pig,' they sobbed and scolded while they ruined our house."

8 "When they left, they took sugar and oranges to bless themselves. They cut pieces from the dead animals. Some of them took bowls that were not broken and clothes that were not torn. Afterward we swept up the rice and sewed it back up into sacks. But the smells from the spilled preserves lasted. Your aunt gave birth in the pigsty that night. The next

morning when I went for the water, I found her and the baby plugging up the family well."

9 "Don't let your father know that I told you. He denies her. Now that you have started to menstruate, what happened to her could happen to you. Don't humiliate us. You wouldn't like to be forgotten as if you had never been born. The villagers are watchful."

10 Whenever she had to warn us about life, my mother told stories that ran like this one, a story to grow up on. She tested our strength to establish realities. Those in the emigrant generations who could not reassert brute survival died young and far from home. Those of us in the first American generations have had to figure out how the invisible world the emigrants built around our childhoods fit in solid America.

11 The emigrants confused the gods by diverting their curses, misleading them with crooked streets and false names. They must try to confuse their offspring as well, who, I suppose, threaten them in similar ways—always trying to get things straight, always trying to name the unspeakable. The Chinese I know hide their names; sojourners take new names when their lives change and guard their real names with silence.

12 Chinese-Americans, when you try to understand what things in you are Chinese, how do you separate what is peculiar to childhood, to poverty, insanities, one family, your mother who marked your growing with stories, from what is Chinese? What is Chinese tradition and what is the movies?

13 If I want to learn what clothes my aunt wore, whether flashy or ordinary, I would have to begin, "Remember Father's drowned-in-the-well sister?" I cannot ask that. My mother has told me once and for all the useful parts. She will add nothing unless powered by Necessity, a riverbank that guides her life. She plants vegetable gardens rather than lawns; she carries the odd-shaped tomatoes home from the fields and eats food left for the gods.

14 Whenever we did frivolous things, we used up energy; we flew high kites. We children came up off the ground over the melting cones our parents brought home from work and the American movie on New Year's Day—*Oh, You Beautiful Doll* with Betty Grable one year, and *She Wore a Yellow Ribbon* with John Wayne another year. After the one carnival ride each, we paid in guilt; our tired father counted his change on the dark walk home.

15 Adultery is extravagance. Could people who hatch their own chicks and eat the embryos and the heads for delicacies and boil the feet in vinegar for party food, leaving only the gravel, eating even the gizzard lining—could such people engender a prodigal aunt? To be a woman, to have a daughter in starvation time was a waste enough. My aunt could not have been the lone romantic who gave up everything for sex. Women in the old China did not choose. Some man had commanded her to lie with him and be his secret evil. I wonder whether he masked himself when he joined the raid on her family.

16 Perhaps she encountered him in the fields or on the mountain where the daughters-in-law collected fuel. Or perhaps he first noticed her in the market-place. He was not a stranger because the village housed no strangers. She had to have dealings with him other than sex. Perhaps he worked an adjoining field, or he sold her the cloth for the dress she sewed and wore. His demand must have surprised, then terrified her. She obeyed him; she always did as she was told.

17 When the family found a young man in the next village to be her husband, she stood tractably beside the best rooster, his proxy, and promised before they met that she would be his forever. She was lucky that he was her age and she would be the first wife, an advantage secure now. The night she first saw him, he had sex with her. Then he left for America. She had almost forgotten what he looked like. When she tried to envision him, she only saw the black and white face in the group photograph the men had had taken before leaving.

18 The other man was not, after all, much different from her husband. They both gave orders: she followed. "If you tell your family, I'll beat you. I'll kill you. Be here again next week." No one talked sex, ever. And she might have separated the rapes from the rest of living if only she did not have to buy her oil from him or gather wood in the same forest. I want her fear to have lasted just as long as rape lasted so that the fear could have been contained. No drawn-out fear. But women at sex hazarded birth and hence lifetimes. The fear did not stop but permeated everywhere. She told the man, "I think I'm pregnant." He organized the raid against her.

19 On nights when my mother and father talked about their life back home, sometimes they mentioned an "outcast table" whose business they still seemed to be settling, their voices tight. In a commensal tradition, where food is precious, the powerful older people made wrongdoers eat alone. Instead of letting them start separate new lives like the

Japanese, who could become samurais and geishas, the Chinese family, faces averted but eyes glowering sideways, hung on to the offenders and fed them leftovers. My aunt must have lived in the same house as my parents and eaten at an outcast table. My mother spoke about the raid as if she had seen it, when she and my aunt, a daughter-in-law to a different household, should not have been living together at all. Daughters-in-law lived with their husbands' parents, not their own; a synonym for marriage in Chinese is "taking a daughter-in-law." Her husband's parents could have sold her, mortgaged her, stoned her. But they had sent her back to her own mother and father, a mysterious act hinting at disgraces not told me. Perhaps they had thrown her out to deflect the avengers.

20 She was the only daughter; her four brothers went with her father, husband, and uncles "out on the road" and for some years became western men. When the goods were divided among the family, three of the brothers took land, and the youngest, my father, chose an education. After my grandparents gave their daughter away to her husband's family, they had dispensed all the adventure and all the property. They expected her alone to keep the traditional ways, which her brothers, now among the barbarians, could fumble without detection. The heavy, deep-rooted women were to maintain the past against the flood, safe for returning. But the rare urge west had fixed upon our family, and so my aunt crossed boundaries not delineated in space.

21 The work of preservation demands that the feelings playing about in one's guts not be turned into action. Just watch their passing like cherry blossoms. But perhaps my aunt, my forerunner, caught in a slow life, let dreams grow and fade and after some months or years went toward what persisted. Fear at the enormities of the forbidden kept her desires delicate, wire and bone. She looked at a man because she liked the way the hair was tucked behind his ears, or she liked the question-mark line of a long torso curving at the shoulder and straight at the hip. For warm eyes or a soft voice or a slow walk—that's all—a few hairs, a line, a brightness, a sound, a pace, she gave up family. She offered us up for a charm that vanished with triedness, a pigtail that didn't toss when the wind died. Why, the wrong lighting could erase the dearest thing about him.

22 It could very well have been, however, that my aunt did not take subtle enjoyment of her friend, but, a wild woman, kept rollicking company. Imagining her free with sex doesn't fit, though. I don't know any

women like that, or men either. Unless I see her life branching into mine, she gives me no ancestral help.

23 To sustain her being in love, she often worked at herself in the mirror, guessing at the colors and shapes that would interest him, changing them frequently in order to hit on the right combination. She wanted him to look back.

24 On a farm near the sea, a woman who tended her appearance reaped a reputation for eccentricity. All the married women blunt-cut their hair in flaps about their ears or pulled it back in tight buns. No nonsense. Neither style blew easily into heart-catching tangles. And at their weddings they displayed themselves in their long hair for the last time. "It brushed the backs of my knees," my mother tells me. "It was braided, and even So, it brushed the backs of my knees."

25 At the mirror my aunt combed individuality into her bob. A bun could have been contrived to escape into black streamers blowing in the wind or in quiet wisps about her face, but only the older women in our picture album wear buns. She brushed her hair back from her forehead, tucking the flaps behind her ears. She looped a piece of thread, knotted into a circle between her index fingers and thumbs, and ran the double strand across her forehead. When she closed her fingers as if she were making a pair of shadow geese bite, the string twisted together catching the little hairs. Then she pulled the thread away from her skin, ripping the hairs out neatly, her eyes watering from the needles of pain. Opening her fingers, she cleaned the thread, then rolled it along her hairline and the tops of her eyebrows. My mother did the same to me and my sisters and herself. I used to believe that the expression "caught by the short hairs" meant a captive held with a depilatory string. It especially hurt at the temples, but my mother said we were lucky we didn't have to have our feet bound when we were seven. Sisters used to sit on their beds and cry together, she said, as their mothers or their slave removed the bandages for a few minutes each night and let the blood gush back into their veins. I hope that the man my aunt loved appreciated a smooth brow, that he wasn't just a tits-and-ass man.

26 Once my aunt found a freckle on her chin, at a spot that the almanac said predestined her for unhappiness. She dug it out with a hot needle and washed the wound with peroxide.

27 More attention to her looks than these pullings of hairs and pickings at spots would have caused gossip among the villagers. They

owned work clothes and good clothes, and they wore good clothes for feasting the new seasons. But since a woman combing her hair hexes beginnings, my aunt rarely found an occasion to look her best. Women looked like great sea snails—the corded wood, babies, and laundry they carried were the whorls on their backs. The Chinese did not admire a bent back; goddesses and warriors stood straight. Still there must have been a marvelous freeing of beauty when a worker laid down her burden and stretched and arched.

28 Such commonplace loveliness, however, was not enough for my aunt. She dreamed of a lover for the fifteen days of New Year's, the time for families to exchange visits, money, and food. She plied her secret comb. And sure enough she cursed the year, the family, the village, and herself.

29 Even as her hair lured her imminent lover, many other men looked at her. Uncles, cousins, nephews, brothers would have looked, too, had they been home between journeys. Perhaps they had already been restraining their curiosity, and they left, fearful that their glances, like a field of nesting birds, might be startled and caught. Poverty hurt, and that was their first reason for leaving. But another, final reason for leaving the crowded house was the never-said.

30 She may have been unusually beloved, the precious only daughter, spoiled and mirror gazing because of the affection the family lavished on her. When her husband left, they welcomed the chance to take her back from the in-laws; she could live like the little daughter for just a while longer. There are stories that my grandfather was different from other people, "crazy ever since the little Jap bayoneted him in the head." He used to put his naked penis on the dinner table, laughing. And one day he brought home a baby girl, wrapped up inside his brown westernstyle greatcoat. He had traded one of his sons, probably my father, the youngest, for her. My grandmother made him trade back. When he finally got a daughter of his own, he doted on her. They must have all loved her, except perhaps my father, the only brother who never went back to China, having once been traded for a girl.

31 Brothers and sisters, newly men and women, had to efface their sexual color and present plain miens. Disturbing hair and eyes, a smile like no other, threatened the ideal of five generations living under one roof. To focus blurs, people shouted face to face and yelled from room to room. The immigrants I know have loud voices, unmodulated to American tones even after years from the village where they called

their friendships out across the fields. I have not been able to stop my mother's screams in public libraries or over telephones. Walking erect (knees straight, toes pointed forward, not pigeon-toed, which is Chinese-feminine) and speaking in an inaudible voice, I have tried to turn myself American-feminine. Chinese communication was loud, public. Only sick people had to whisper. But at the dinner table, where the family members came nearest one another, no one could talk, not the outcasts nor any eaters. Every word that falls from the mouth is a coin lost. Silently they gave and accepted food with both hands. A preoccupied child who took his bowl with one hand got a sideways glare. A complete moment of total attention is due everyone alike. Children and lovers have no singularity here, but my aunt used a secret voice, a separate attentiveness.

32 She kept the man's name to herself throughout her labor and dying; she did not accuse him that he be punished with her. To save her inseminator's name she gave silent birth.

33 He may have been somebody in her own household, but intercourse with a man outside the family would have been no less abhorrent. All the village were kinsmen, and the titles shouted in loud country voices never let kinship be forgotten. Any man within visiting distance would have been neutralized as a lover—"brother," "younger brother," "older brother"—one hundred and fifteen relationship titles. Parents researched birth charts probably not so much to assure good fortune as to circumvent incest in a population that has but one hundred surnames. Everybody has eight million relatives. How useless then sexual mannerisms, how dangerous.

34 As if it came from an atavism deeper than fear, I used to add "brother" silently to boys' names. It hexed the boys, who would or would not ask me to dance, and made them less scary and as familiar and deserving of benevolence as girls.

35 But, of course, I hexed myself also—no dates. I should have stood up, both arms waving, and shouted out across libraries, "Hey, you! Love me back." I had no idea, though, how to make attraction selective, how to control its direction and magnitude. If I made myself American-pretty so that the five or six Chinese boys in the class fell in love with me, everyone else—the Caucasian, Negro, and Japanese boys—would too. Sisterliness, dignified and honorable, made much more sense.

36 Attraction eludes control so stubbornly that whole societies designed to organize relationships among people cannot keep order,

not even when they bind people to one another from childhood and raise them together. Among the very poor and the wealthy, brothers married their adopted sisters, like doves. Our family allowed some romance, paying adult brides' prices and providing dowries so that their sons and daughters could marry strangers. Marriage promises to turn strangers into friendly relatives—a nation of siblings.

37 In the village structure, spirits shimmered among the live creatures, balanced and held in equilibrium by time and land. But one human being flaring up into violence could open up a black hole, a maelstrom that pulled in the sky. The frightened villagers, who depended on one another to maintain the real, went to my aunt to show her a personal, physical representation of the break she had made in the "roundness." Misallying couples snapped off the future, which was to be embodied in true offspring. The villagers punished her for acting as if she could have a private life, secret and apart from them.

38 If my aunt had betrayed the family at a time of large grain yields and peace, when many boys were born, and wings were being built on many houses, perhaps she might have escaped such severe punishment. But the men—hungry, greedy, tired of planting in dry soil, cuckolded—had had to leave the village in order to send food-money home. There were ghost plagues, bandit plagues, wars with the Japanese, floods. My Chinese brother and sister had died of an unknown sickness. Adultery, perhaps only a mistake during good times, became a crime when the village needed food.

39 The round moon cakes and round doorways, the round tables of graduated size that fit one roundness inside another, round windows and rice bowls—these talismans had lost their power to warn this family of the law: a family must be whole, faithfully keeping the descent line by having sons to feed the old and the dead, who in turn look after the family. The villagers came to show my aunt and her lover-in-hiding a broken house. The villagers were speeding up the circling of events because she was too shortsighted to see that her infidelity had already harmed the village, that waves of consequences would return unpredictably, sometimes in disguise, as now, to hurt her. This roundness had to be made coin-sized so that she would see its circumference: punish her at the birth of her baby. Awaken her to the inexorable. People who refused fatalism because they could invent small resources insisted on culpability. Deny accidents and wrest fault from the stars.

40 After the villagers left, their lanterns now scattering in various directions toward home, the family broke their silence and cursed her.

"Aiaa, we're going to die. Death is coming. Death is coming. Look what you've done. You've killed us. Ghost! Dead ghost! Ghost! You've never been born." She ran out into the fields, far enough from the house so that she could no longer hear their voices, and pressed herself against the earth, her own land no more. When she felt the birth coming, she thought that she had been hurt. Her body seized together. "They've hurt me too much," she thought. "This is gall, and it will kill me." With forehead and knees against the earth, her body convulsed and then relaxed. She turned on her back, lay on the ground. The black well of sky and stars went out and out and out forever; her body and her complexity seemed to disappear, without home, without a companion, in eternal cold and silence. An agoraphobia rose in her, speeding higher and higher, bigger and bigger; she would not be able to contain it; there would be no end to fear.

41 Flayed, unprotected against space, she felt pain return, focusing her body. This pain chilled her—a cold, steady kind of surface pain. Inside, spasmodically, the other pain, the pain of the child, heated her. For hours she lay on the ground, alternately body and space. Sometimes a vision of normal comfort obliterated reality: she saw the family in the evening gambling at the dinner table, the young people massaging their elders' backs. She saw them congratulating one another, high joy on the mornings the rice shoots came up. When these pictures burst, the stars drew yet further apart. Black space opened.

42 She got to her feet to fight better and remembered that old-fashioned women gave birth in their pigsties to fool the jealous, pain-dealing gods, who do not snatch piglets. Before the next spasms could stop her, she ran to the pigsty, each step a rushing out into emptiness. She climbed over the fence and knelt in the dirt. It was good to have a fence enclosing her, a tribal person alone.

43 Laboring, this woman who had carried her child as a foreign growth that sickened her every day, expelled it at last. She reached down to touch the hot, wet, moving mass, surely smaller than anything human, and could feel that it was human after all—fingers, toes, nails, nose. She pulled it up on to her belly, and it lay curled there, butt in the air, feet precisely tucked one under the other. She opened her loose shirt and buttoned the child inside. After resting, it squirmed and thrashed and she pushed it up to her breast. It turned its head this way and that until it found her nipple. There, it made little snuffling noises. She clenched her teeth at its preciousness, lovely as a young calf, a piglet, a little dog.

44 She may have gone to the pigsty as a last act of responsibility: she would protect this child as she had protected its father. It would look after her soul, leaving supplies on her grave. But how would this tiny child without family find her grave when there would be no marker for her anywhere, neither in the earth nor the family hall? No one would give her a family hall name. She had taken the child with her into the wastes. At its birth the two of them had felt the same raw pain of separation, a wound that only the family pressing tight could close. A child with no descent line would not soften her life but only trail after her, ghost-like, begging her to give it purpose. At dawn the villagers on their way to the fields would stand around the fence and look.

45 Full of milk, the little ghost slept. When it awoke, she hardened her breasts against the milk that crying loosens. Toward morning she picked up the baby and walked to the well.

46 Carrying the baby to the well shows loving. Otherwise abandon it. Turn its face into the mud. Mothers who love their children take them along. It was probably a girl; there is some hope of forgiveness for boys.

47 "Don't tell anyone you had an aunt. Your father does not want to hear her name. She has never been born." I have believed that sex was unspeakable and words so strong and fathers so frail that "aunt" would do my father mysterious harm. I have thought that my family, having settled among immigrants who had also been their neighbors in the ancestral land, needed to clean their name, and a wrong word would incite the kinspeople even here. But there is more to this silence: they want me to participate in her punishment. And I have.

48 In the twenty years since I heard this story I have not asked for details nor said my aunt's name; I do not know it. People who can comfort the dead can also chase after them to hurt them further—a reverse ancestor worship. The real punishment was not the raid swiftly inflicted by the villagers, but the family's deliberately forgetting her. Her betrayal so maddened them, they saw to it that she would suffer forever, even after death. Always hungry, always needing, she would have to beg food from other ghosts, snatch and steal it from those whose living descendants give them gifts. She would have to fight the ghosts massed at crossroads for the buns a few thoughtful citizens leave to decoy her away from village and home so that the ancestral spirits could feast unharassed. At peace, they could act like gods, not ghosts, their descent lines providing them with paper suits and dresses, spirit money, paper houses, paper automobiles, chicken, meat, and rice into

eternity—essences delivered up in smoke and flames, steam and incense rising from each rice bowl. In an attempt to make the Chinese care for people outside the family, Chairman Mao encourages us now to give our paper replicas to the spirits of outstanding soldiers and workers, no matter whose ancestors they may be. My aunt remains forever hungry. Goods are not distributed evenly among the dead.

49 My aunt haunts me—her ghost drawn to me because now, after fifty years of neglect, I alone devote pages of paper to her, though not origamied into houses and clothes. I do not think she always means me well. I am telling on her, and she was a spite suicide, drowning herself in the drinking water. The Chinese are always very frightened of the drowned one, whose weeping ghost, wet hair hanging and skin bloated, waits silently by the water to pull down a substitute.

FOR THINKING, DISCUSSING, AND WRITING

1. The selection begins with Kingston's mother telling a story. How does this technique contribute to our understanding of the writer's point? What details in the story provide the reader with an idea of the daughters' lives in old China? What details suggest something about the differing attitudes toward boys and girls?
2. How did Kingston piece together the reasons for her aunt's adultery? Do you find Kingston's conclusions to be reasonable? Why or why not? Why were the villagers so angry at the aunt's behavior? What does the writer mean when she says "Adultery is extravagance" (paragraph 15)?
3. What does Kingston mean by "American-feminine"? Why does she hesitate to call herself "American-pretty"? What does she use as a substitute? Why?
4. Write an essay in which you compare and contrast traditional attitudes toward adultery in China (as presented by Kingston) and what you view as American attitudes today.

DEBORAH TANNEN

Listening to Men, Then and Now

Deborah Tannen (1945–) was born in Brooklyn, New York, earned her PhD in linguistics from the University of California at Berkeley, and has taught at various colleges and universities. She is the author of Conversational Style: Analyzing

Talk among Friends *(1984),* That's Not What I Meant! How Conversational Style Makes or Breaks Your Relations with Others *(1986), and* You're Wearing That?: Understanding Mothers and Daughters in Conversation *(2006). In this piece, written before the turn of the twenty-first century, Tannen evaluates some key elements in the relations between men and women.*

1 A woman and a man meet at the end of the day. He asks how her day was, and she replies with a long report of what she did, whom she met, what they said and what that made her think and feel. Then she eagerly turns to him:

2 She: How was your day?

3 He: Same old rat race.

4 She: Didn't anything happen?

5 He: Nah, nothing much.

6 Her disappointment is deepened when that evening they go out to dinner with friends and suddenly he regales the group with an amusing account of something that happened at work. She is cut to the quick, crestfallen at hearing this story as part of an audience of strangers. "How could he have said nothing happened?" she wonders. "Why didn't he tell me this before? What am I? Chopped liver?"

7 The key to this frustration is that women and men typically have different ideas about what makes people friends. For many women, as for girls, talk is the glue of close relationships; your best friend is the one you tell your secrets to, the one you discuss your troubles with. For many men, as for boys, activities are central; your best friend is the one you do everything with (and the one who will stick up for you if there is a fight).

8 As the millennium approaches and commentators examine how our lives have changed in the last thousand years, I find myself wondering about the change in relations between the sexes. Clearly there has been a transformation. In the past, the woman was deferential, subordinate. Now we are not trying to be partners in a societal arrangement with a clearly defined separation of labor, but rather hoping to be each other's best friends. Yet at least two aspects of women's and men's relations have endured—our differing expectations about the importance of talk in intimacy, and the tendency of women to take the role of listener in conversation with men.

9 In the absence of tape recordings from earlier times, we can look to conversations in literature. For a glimpse of how a 16th-century couple

might have talked to each other, I turned to Shakespeare—and my earliest memory of his plays. When I was at Ditmas Junior High in Brooklyn, my classmates were all atwitter: our teacher had us reading "Julius Caesar" aloud, and, having read ahead, we knew that the next day some poor girl would have to stand and read a passage in which Brutus's wife uses the word "harlot." Susan Ehrlich had the bad luck to be chosen, and I can still see her, tall and brown-haired, reading, "Portia is Brutus's harlot, not his wife."

10 Revisiting those lines today, what strikes me is how similar the sentiment is to what I hear from contemporary women. Portia wants to be Brutus's best friend—and her idea of what this means is very similar to ours. Waking up to discover that her husband has left their bed, she finds him pacing, and implores him to say what is worrying him. Like the modern woman who feels that best friends tell each other secrets, Portia pleads:

11 *Within the bond of marriage, tell me,*
Brutus,
Is it excepted I should know no secrets
That appertain to you?
Am I yourself
But, as it were, in sort or
limitation,
To keep with you at meals,
comfort your bed,
And talk to you
sometimes? Dwell I but
in the suburbs
Of your good pleasure? If
it be no more,
Portia is Brutus's harlot,
not his wife.

12 A similar sentiment emerges in an even more distant conversation—in the Arabian romance of the Bedouin hero Antar, believed to have been written between 1080 and 1400. In one episode, a character named al-Minhal, escaping a king he has wronged, comes upon a ruined castle inhabited by a female demon named Dahiya. She gives him shelter, feeds him, falls in love with him and wins his love by her attentions, which include her conversation. Sounding rather like Portia, Dahiya says:

"I want you to be my companion and to be my lord, and I will be your wife. Disclose to me what is in your heart. Do not believe that I will ever let you go. Open your mind to me for I have need to know your thoughts." They are married on the spot, and, we are told, "Long was their companionship, and they loved each other dearly."

13 I am not suggesting that relationships between women and men were the same then as now. But it's intriguing to think that what women regard as intimacy, talking about what's on your mind, has been a common thread right through the millennium. There's another, related pattern that seems to have endured. It, too, is evident in the case of the husband who can't think of anything to tell his wife but comes up with an amusing story to entertain a dinner gathering. To her, it's a failure of intimacy: if we're truly close, I should hear everything first. To him, I think, the situation of being home with someone he feels close to does not call for a story performance. This creates a paradox. Many women were drawn to the men they fell in love with because the men told captivating stories. After marriage, the women expect that the closer they get, the more the men will open up and tell. Instead, to their deep disappointment, after marriage the men clam up.

14 Once again, looking at how boys and girls are socialized provides a key. Boys' groups are hierarchical; low-status boys are pushed around. One way boys earn and keep status is to hold center stage by verbal performance—boasting, telling jokes or recounting mesmerizing stories. And this seems to work well in winning maidens as well.

15 This aspect of storytelling can be seen as far back as "Beowulf," that Anglo-Saxon saga, usually dated to the eighth century. The hero, a member of a Swedish tribe known as the Geats, wins the attention of Wealhtheow, Queen of Hrothgar, who is serving beer to a gathering of men:

16 *Beowulf spoke, the son of Ecgtheow: "I resolved when I set out to sea, sat down in the sea-boat with my band of men, that I should altogether fulfill the will of your people or else fall in slaughter, fast in the foe's grasp. I shall achieve a deed of manly courage or else have lived to see in the mead-hall my ending day." These words were well-pleasing to the woman, the boast of the Geat. Gold-adorned, the noble folk-queen went to sit by her lord.*

17 Boasting, my colleague Catherine Ball tells me, was a customary male activity in the Anglo-Saxon mead-hall, so it is not surprising that

Wealhtheow was well pleased, even though the exploits Beowulf boasts of have not yet taken place. (In fact, he sounds a little like Cassius Clay predicting what he will do to Sonny Liston.)

18 This scenario—a woman wooed by a man's boasts of exploits in battle—brings us back to Shakespearean icons: Desdemona and Othello. As Othello tells "how I did thrive in this fair lady's love," he explains that she became entranced when she heard him telling "the story of my life":

19 *Wherein I spoke of most*
disastrous chances:
Of moving accidents by
flood and field,
Of hair-breadth scapes
i' th' imminent deadly breach;
Of being taken by
the insolent foe....

And so on, until:

20 *My story being done,*
She gave me for my pains
a world of kisses....
And bade me, if I had a
friend that lov'd her,
I should but teach him
how to tell my story,
And that would woo her.

21 As we know, he wooed her himself with his own story.

22 In our era, the tactic of wooing by verbal performance takes a funny turn. Etiquette books of the' 50s instructed young women to be good listeners if they wanted to win their men, and you need only look around a restaurant to see many women attentively listening to talking men. In place of battle yarns, what I hear, over and over, is that a woman fell in love because "he makes me laugh." That's why Michele Pfeiffer said in 1992 she picked a particular boyfriend, and why Joanne Woodward fell for Paul Newman. I don't hear the same explanation from men as to why they fall in love. What I hear is the corresponding one, as for example when Woody Allen said of his relationship with Soon-Yi Previn: "She's a marvel. And she laughs at all my jokes."

23 We seem to have a situation of *plus ça change*. Even as relationships between men and women have changed, our contrasting expectations about the meaning of closeness still cause confusion and disappointment. And though the performance has shifted from heroic tales to amusing entertainment, more often than not the apportionment of roles has stayed the same: Women are the audience and men are the show.

FOR THINKING, DISCUSSING, AND WRITING

1. What does Tannen believe is the reason that women often feel disappointed in their male partners?
2. How effective is the use of "glue" (paragraph 3) as a metaphor for close relations? What are the connotations of the word "glue"?
3. Do you agree that in male-female relations, men tend to be the talkers and women the listeners, as Tannen suggests? Why? How does this point serve her assertion about the centrality of activities for men?
4. Tannen says that "women and men typically have different ideas about what makes people friends" (paragraph 7). Write an essay in which you either agree or disagree with this statement.

JUDY BRADY

I Want a Wife

Judy Brady (1937–) was born in San Francisco and studied painting at the University of Iowa, earning her bachelor of fine arts degree in 1962. She is a freelance writer who has contributed to several magazines and periodicals. In this now classic essay written for Ms. magazine in 1971, at the height of the feminist movement in America, Brady takes a humorously ironic tone in asking for a wife of her own.

1 I belong to that classification of people known as wives. I am A Wife. And, not altogether incidentally, I am a mother.

2 Not too long ago a male friend of mine appeared on the scene fresh from a recent divorce. He had one child, who is, of course, with his ex-wife. He is looking for another wife. As I thought about him while I was ironing one evening, it suddenly occurred to me that I, too, would like to have a wife. Why do I want a wife?

3 I would like to go back to school so that I can become economically independent, support myself, and, if need be, support those dependent upon me. I want a wife who will work and send me to school. And while I am going to school I want a wife to take care of my children. I want a wife to keep track of the children's doctor and dentist appointments. And to keep track of mine, too. I want a wife to make sure my children eat properly and are kept clean. I want a wife who will wash the children's clothes and keep them mended. I want a wife who is a good nurturing attendant to my children, who arranges for their schooling, makes sure that they have an adequate social life with their peers, takes them to the park, the zoo, etc. I want a wife who takes care of the children when they are sick, a wife who arranges to be around when the children when they are sick, a wife who arranges to be around when the children need special care, because, of course, I cannot miss classes at school. My wife must arrange to lose time at work and not lose the job. It may mean a small cut in my wife's income from time to time, but I guess I can tolerate that. Needless to say, my wife will arrange and pay for the care of the children while my wife is working.

4 I want a wife who will take care of *my* physical needs. I want a wife who will keep my house clean. A wife who will pick up after my children, a wife who will pick up after me. I want a wife who will keep my clothes clean, ironed, mended, replaced when need be, and who will see to it that my personal things are kept in their proper place so that I can find what I need the minute I need it. I want a wife who cooks the meals, a wife who is a *good* cook. I want a wife who will plan the menus, do the necessary grocery shopping, prepare the meals, serve them pleasantly, and then do the cleaning up while I do my studying. I want a wife who will care for me when I am sick and sympathize with my pain and loss of time from school. I want a wife to go along when our family takes a vacation so that someone can continue to care for me and my children when I need a rest and change of scene.

5 I want a wife who will not bother me with rambling complaints about a wife's duties. But I want a wife who will listen to me when I feel the need to explain a rather difficult point I have come across in my course of studies. And I want a wife who will type my papers for me when I have written them.

6 I want a wife who will take care of the details of my social life. When my wife and I are invited out by my friends, I want a wife who will take care of the babysitting arrangements. When I meet people at school

that I like and want to entertain, I want a wife who will have the house clean, will prepare a special meal, serve it to me and my friends, and not interrupt when I talk about things that interest me and my friends. I want a wife who will have arranged that the children are fed and ready for bed before my guests arrive so that the children do not bother us. I want a wife who takes care of the needs of my guests so that they feel comfortable, who makes sure that they have an ashtray, that they are passed the hors d'oeuvres, that they are offered a second helping of the food, that their wine glasses are replenished when necessary, that their coffee is served to them as they like it. And I want a wife who knows that sometimes I need a night out by myself.

7 I want a wife who is sensitive to my sexual needs, a wife who makes love passionately and eagerly when I feel like it, a wife who makes sure that I am satisfied. And, of course, I want a wife who will not demand sexual attention when I am not in the mood for it. I want a wife who assumes the complete responsibility for birth control, because I do not want more children. I want a wife who will remain sexually faithful to me so that I do not have to clutter up my intellectual life with jealousies. And I want a wife who understands that *my* sexual needs may entail more than strict adherence to monogamy. I must, after all, be able to relate to people as fully as possible.

8 If, by chance, I find another person more suitable as a wife than the wife I already have, I want the liberty to replace my present wife with another one. Naturally, I will expect a fresh, new life; my wife will take the children and be solely responsible for them so that I am left free.

9 When I am through with school and have a job, I want my wife to quit working and remain at home so that my wife can more fully and completely take care of a wife's duties.

10 My God, who *wouldn't* want a wife?

FOR THINKING, DISCUSSING, AND WRITING

1. What are some of the sacrifices Brady insists her wife must make in order to take care of her? What does Brady want the freedom to do if she finds a person "more suitable" than her wife? What does she expect her former wife to do? What reason does she offer to justify less than "strict adherence to monogamy" (paragraph 7)?
2. What picture of husbands and wives emerges from this essay? How are these impressions familiar to you? How are they unfamiliar? In what ways do people still regularly identify themselves as "husbands" or

"wives"? What might doing so or not doing so suggest both about their self-image and about how they view their spouses?

3. How is this essay relevant today? How is it not relevant? Does the fact that the essay was written in the seventies affect its impact today? Explain why or why not.
4. Assume that you are the wife Brady wants. Write a letter to her explaining how you feel about your role and responsibilities.

DAVID LEAVITT

The Hate Epidemic

David Leavitt (1961–) is a professor of English at the University of Florida and a short story writer, novelist, and editor. He is the author of Family Dancing *(1985),* The Lost Language of Cranes *(1997),* The Page Turner *(1998), and* The Man Who Knew Too Much: Alan Turing and the Invention of the Computer *(2005). Leavitt is the editor of* Subtropics, *a new literary magazine, and he is coeditor of* The Penguin Book of Gay Short Stories *(1994). In this essay written as an op-ed piece for the* New York Times *on October 19, 1998, Leavitt responds to the death, just a week before, of Matthew Shepard, a twenty-one-year-old student savagely beaten to death in Laramie, Wyoming, because he was gay.*

1 When I read the account of Matthew Shepard's murder, the words that I could not forget were those reportedly used by one of his killers after he and a companion had lured Mr. Shepard out of a Laramie, Wyo., tavern and into the pickup truck in which they would drive him to his place of execution: "Guess what? I'm not gay—and you just got jacked."

2 These words—odors from the abyss, as Forster might have put it—recalled others spoken by the narrator of Eudora Welty's 1963 story "Where Is the Voice Coming From?" which she wrote in a white heat after the assassination of the civil rights leader Medgar Evers. "Now I'm alive and you ain't," Evers's killer tells his dead victim in the story. "We ain't never now, never going to be equals, and you know why? One of us is dead."

3 Certain commonplaces cannot be restated enough: hatred of gay men in this country is an epidemic as pernicious as AIDS, and as unfathomable. Nor is any gay man untouched by this epidemic.

4 It haunts not only the drag queen who takes her life in her hands every time she steps onto the street, not only the middle-aged man who invites a stranger home with whom he has spoken on a phone sex line, not only the isolated college student in Wyoming longing for friendship and trusting in the overtures of moles from the Stasi of hate, but also the forward-thinking, well-adjusted, worldly homosexual man who imagines that in his urban corner of sanity and tolerance, in Greenwich Village or Los Angeles or London, he is somehow immune.

5 He is not immune—either from hatred or from the fear of hatred, which is in many ways even more destructive. Thus even though Mark Mitchell and I have lived together for almost seven years, even though when we stay at the homes of our enlightened parents we are treated by them no differently than, say, my brother and his wife, even though we share a house, a bed, a car and a bank account, when we walk together in any city we never hold hands—and not because we flinch at "public displays of affection" (as might my brother and his wife, for whom such decisions carry little weight) but because we are afraid of being killed.

6 No, gay killings are not everyday occurrences, any more than lynchings were ever a daily event in the South, but the fear colors everything—especially in a year when reported hate crimes against gay people in New York City have increased 81 percent.

7 Certain commonplaces cannot be restated enough. In the brutal con game to which Matthew Shepard fell prey, what was exploited was nothing less than a young man's trust and hope and eager longing, if not for love, then at least for friendship, for camaraderie.

8 In this game, kindness can be held out as bait; sex can be used as a lure. The payoff may be death, as it was for Matthew Shepard, or it may be robbery or gay-bashing or merely unkind, ignorant words. But few of us walk away unscarred, if we are lucky enough to walk away at all.

9 For years AIDS conveniently helped the hate-mongerers do their job, by wiping out gay men in appalling numbers. But now, for the first time in more than a decade, AIDS deaths are down, and it seems as if ignorance is stepping in and pick up the slack.

10 "Shoot a gay or two," a piece of graffito in Laramie announced several years ago. I have seen—and become inured to—a blunter epithet,

one that is found too often on bathroom walls and in university libraries: "Faggots die."

11 Die: That's really what it's all about, if for no other reason than that it is only when faggots die that their systematic persecution ever gets any attention.

12 In part this is our own fault. For instance, when I was robbed a few years ago in Paris by a man who invited me to his apartment building for "coffee," I never reported the incident to the police, or even spoke of it, out of shame. Nor, I suspect, would Matthew Shepard have gone to the police had he merely been beaten to a pulp. And if he had, would it have done any good?

13 *Shoot a gay or two.* Psychiatrists have long speculated that many killers of gay men are themselves repressed homosexuals, which is why, so often, they murder their victims after sex. For these attackers, the mere fact that another man desires them (not to mention the possibility that others might consider them to be gay) is seen as justification for an act of retaliatory violence.

14 This may have been what happened to my friend Lou Inturrisi, a journalist and travel writer, whose body was discovered last August on the floor of his apartment in Rome.

15 His skull had been bashed in; he had not, however, been robbed. His was one of a spate of gay killings in Italy in recent years, only one of which has been solved. In that case, the killer turned out to be a male prostitute.

16 There are many reasons a gay man would go home with a stranger. Perhaps because the thrill of danger excites him. Perhaps because he is naïve. Perhaps because he does not know any better.

17 In the end, however, none of this excuses the person who kills—or those who blame the victim for his own murder, in much the same way that women are often blamed for having encouraged the men who raped them.

18 When I was Matthew Shepard's age, my greatest fear was AIDS, because I had no idea then how the virus was spread. Now, 16 years later, there is still no cure for AIDS, but there is prevention: we can instruct a Matthew Shepard in how to protect himself against infection by H.I.V. But could we instruct him in how to protect himself against hatred?

FOR THINKING, DISCUSSING, AND WRITING

1. What picture of gay men and gay life emerges from this essay?
2. What does the writer suggest about personal responsibility? Under what circumstances do we blame the victim of a crime for his or her fate? Should we do this?
3. In paragraph 11, Leavitt asserts that "it is only when faggots die that their systematic persecution ever gets any attention." What does he mean by "systematic" persecution? What other historical examples of "systematic persecution" can you identify? Do you think Leavitt wants his readers to make these associations? Why or why not?
4. Write an essay about the treatment of gays in colleges in general and on your campus in particular. How does your institution attempt to accommodate gay students if at all? How effective are these accommodations? In what ways do you find them appropriate or inappropriate?

CYNTHIA RUSSETT

All About Eve

Cynthia E. Russett (1937–) has degrees from Trinity College in Washington, D. C., and Yale University. Currently she is Larned Professor of History at Yale. She focuses her research and teaching on American intellectual life in the twentieth century, the history of American women, and the intellectual history of the Gilded Age, among other topics. She is the author of Darwin in America *(1976) and* Sexual Science: The Victorian Construction of Womanhood *(1989). In this essay for the* American Scholar *Russett takes a historical view of what men have thought about women thinking. She wrote the piece in response to comments by the then-president of Harvard University, Lawrence Summers, who asserted that inborn differences between men and women might in part explain why fewer women succeed in science and math careers than men.*

1 Has there ever been a time when people did not speculate about the differences between men and women? Probably not, since men and women are alike in so many obvious ways, and yet different enough to invite endless commentary. When President Lawrence Summers of Harvard recently ventured to suggest that women's lesser success as

scientists might result from lesser innate ability, he placed himself in a long line of philosophers, theologians, scientists, and social and political theorists, stretching back to ancient times, who attempted to differentiate between the sexes by focusing on their mental capacities.

2 The most obvious differences in men and women are of course found in the anatomy and physiology of the human body, and early philosophers needed to concentrate on what could be learned from studying physical characteristics, often extrapolating from bodies to minds. Plato was a notable exception; he was no empiricist, and his ideas about women did not depend on their bodily form. But Plato's ideas are confusing, since they do not cohere, and are fragmentary and sometimes contradictory. His dialogues contain many derogatory comments about women and "womanish" traits. Women are overly emotional; they weep and lack self-control. They are less courageous than men. Plato makes a radical distinction between bodies and souls. The noble individual possesses a soul able to rise above the body to contemplate the Forms. But women are less likely to transcend their bodies, and cowardly men are likely to return in a later incarnation as women. Plato certainly did not see men and women as equals. Women are weaker in body, and perhaps in mind. Men's accomplishments outshine women's.

3 It is worth remembering, though, that Plato lived in a period when equality between men and women was almost inconceivable, and certainly not practiced in the city of Athens. The women he saw around him—uneducated, confined to their homes, unable to participate in philosophical dialogues or in the public life of the polis—were without doubt underdeveloped socially and intellectually. It is remarkable, therefore, that Plato's *Republic* offers a vision of an ideal society very different from that of Athens, one in which both men and women are members of the Guardians, or rulers. In the *Republic*, Plato makes the case for choosing individuals for certain positions on the basis not of their sex but of their abilities. He offers the analogy of two cobblers, one bald and one with abundant hair. You would not suppose that the hairy one had a particular aptitude for cobbling while the bald one did not. So also for the procreative differences between women and men: they are no more significant for channeling the two sexes into different occupations than are variations in hirsuteness. Thus, based on their capacities, women as well as men could be part of a social and political elite. To be sure, women who were educated and trained just like men

would have to put aside a normal home life and the rearing of their children, but the inference is clear that they could be as rational in the service of the state as their male colleagues. What is notable about Plato, compared to Aristotle, is that he was not an essentialist: the male model was the ideal, but at least in utopia women could successfully approximate the male soul.

4 Plato's pupil Aristotle finds no ambiguity whatsoever. In his writings, women are definitely inferior: "We must look upon the female character as being a sort of natural deficiency," Aristotle writes in *Generation of Animals*. Woman's defectiveness lies in her lack of bodily heat and consequent inability to concoct matter—that is, to cause it to develop. Thus, even in reproduction women play a lesser role, since the male provides the form of the fetus, while the female only provides the matter. Men take the active and creative role in conception, women the passive and receptive role. Furthermore, the male child represents the fullness of procreation, while the female child results from a defect in development.

5 Since, unlike Plato, Aristotle was something of an empiricist, he tried to support his views with observations. He suggested, for instance, that women conceive males (or have males conceived on them) when in the prime of life, while only very young or aging women conceive females. He also asserted that the male fetus moves in the womb earlier than the female fetus, indicating greater activity and greater perfection.

6 Thus Aristotle placed much greater emphasis on women's biological inferiority than Plato did. When he turned to the intangible dimension of the soul, however, Aristotle resembles Plato in holding that women's rationality lacks sufficient strength to keep the irrational soul and its desires in check. Unable to control the irrational part of the soul, women let their appetites run away with them, doing as they please rather than as reason ordains. Since women lack internal governance, they require constant governance by men. But unlike Plato, Aristotle made the divide between male and female essentially unbridgeable. There would be no female Guardians in an Aristotelian utopia.

7 In the Middle Ages the theologian Thomas Aquinas continued the Aristotelian paradigm of generation in his *Summa Theologica*, a work that had profound influence on Catholic philosophers and theologians for centuries. Aquinas believed women to be biologically "accidental," that is, unintended in the natural order, though not in God's cosmic

order. For Aquinas, the male seed always intends to create another male, but weakness in the seed or in the female material, or some exterior circumstance such as a south wind that brings greater atmospheric humidity, may result in the creation of a female. More important, Aquinas, like Aristotle, believed women to be intellectually as well as physically inferior to men: "Woman is naturally subject to man because in man the discretion of reason predominates," he wrote. The male is more ordered to "intellectual operation" than the female.

8 Throughout the Middle Ages and the early modern period, disparagement of women's intellect was commonplace in Western civilization. Here and there, however, a voice of dissent arose. Probably the best known of these protests was that of the 15th-century poet Christine de Pisan. Struggling with the sense of inferiority engendered by male misogyny, Christine opens her *Books of the City of Ladies* with a visitation from three allegorical goddesses, Reason, Rectitude, and Justice. These three were carefully chosen to refute men's charges of feminine irrationality, feeble moral sense, and inability to understand abstract concepts of law. Her book inaugurated the "querelle des femmes," a roughly three-century European debate over women"s virtues and vices.

9 Nature continued to explain the differences between the sexes during the Enlightenment of the 18th century. Perhaps the most influential of all the philosophical disquisitions on the nature and role of women was that of Jean-Jacques Rousseau. In his manual of education, *Emile*, Rousseau notes that women have special qualities of mind like "quick wit, taste, [and] grace," but they do not have the ability to be creative or to reason abstractly. They are good at details, bad at the principles underlying them. They do not possess genius. Their education, dictated by their functions as females, should fit them for a domestic life, directed not at drawing out their capacities but at instilling the virtues needed to become loving wives and mothers.

10 For Rousseau there was no question that nature had determined the very different mental and physical characteristics of men and women, but his views did not go unchallenged. Other philosophes, like Helvétius and Baron d'Holbach, argued that environment and schooling shaped the female qualities that Rousseau took to be innate. D'Holbach wrote in *Système Social* (1733): "From the way in which [women] are brought up, it seems that it is only intended to turn them

into beings who retain the frivolity, fickleness, caprices and lack of reason of childhood, throughout their lives."

11 Such was also the central argument of Mary Wollstonecraft's *Vindication of the Rights of Women* (1792), a work that is generally acknowledged to be the founding document of European and American feminism. Outraged at Rousseau's doctrine of women's natural inferiority and his prescription for their education, Wollstonecraft, who otherwise admired him greatly, took it upon herself to write a heated response. Never denying that many women in their current condition lacked true morality and virtue, she insisted that nature had nothing to do with it. Women were what society had made them by encouraging their frivolous pursuits and denying them a serious education. What was needed was to provide little girls with the same education as that of their brothers: "Women must be allowed to found their virtue on knowledge, which is scarcely possible unless they have been educated by the same pursuits as men." The nature/nurture debate on mental endowments was well under way.

12 The discussion of sex differences took a new turn in the early 19th century, when the science of phrenology proposed to present concrete empirical evidence of mental functioning in men and women. Enormously popular in Europe and America in the middle of the century, phrenology asserted that the contours of the skull, its prominences and depressions, revealed the mental qualities and character traits of the individual. The brain had many faculties, each located in a specific place on the brain mass that determined a particular exterior conformation. Careful examination of the head could thus provide information about the person's mind and character.

13 Phrenology did not disturb the conventional wisdom of the time: in men, intellect predominated over feeling; in women, the reverse. "It is almost an axiom that women are guided by feelings, whilst men are superior in intellectual concentration," wrote J. G. Spurzheim in *Phrenology, or the Doctrine of Mental Phenomena* (1833). Yet despite such pronouncements, phrenology on both sides of the Atlantic seems to have been cordial to the aspirations of women, apparently because it managed the considerable feat of positing both that mental endowments were constitutionally determined and that they were malleable. Weak faculties could be strengthened by exercise, overly powerful ones curbed. This reformist optimism gave at least one Scottish feminist grounds for proclaiming that "phrenologists had proved . . . that

women's brains were capable of being improved to a degree which would make them equal and even excel the men in all the better accomplishments of our common nature, and give them power to break the chains of the tyrant and the oppressor, and set them completely free."

14 Always under challenge from the major authorities in psychology and physiology, phrenology saw its claim to scientific status dim even during the years of its greatest popularity. Though phrenology purported to be based on empirical evidence, its pioneering attempt to localize cerebral functions did not, in fact, rest on experimental work. Yet its conception of mental phenomena as biologically based and susceptible to empirical study shaped the future of research in psychology and physical anthropology during the remainder of the 19th century.

15 Physical anthropology, above all, used skull measurement as the sure path to unlocking the secrets of the mind. Its characteristic and crowning achievement was craniology, the study of the skull and brain. Measuring skulls, it was believed, could disclose the size of the brain, with the understanding that bigger was better. "Other things being equal," wrote the eminent French anthropologist Paul Broca in 1861, "there is a remarkable relationship between the development of intelligence and the volume of the brain." In examining the brains of men and women, scientists in Europe and America shared a unanimous conclusion: women's brains were smaller than those of men. In this finding they were correct: women's brains *are* smaller than men's. But it does not follow from this (though many drew the conclusion) that women are less intelligent than men, since their body weight is also less, and less brain mass is required to move it around and maintain motor function. Skull measurement did not, as it happened, prove a reliable indicator of brain weight. Craniologists needed to weigh actual brains. These were in short supply, but enough were found to confirm that women' brains weighed less than men's. To the educated English-speaking public, the gender disparity in brain weights became familiar as "the missing five ounces of female brain," from a phrase in the widely read and reprinted article "Mental Differences Between Men and Women" (1887) by the Darwinian psychologist George John Romanes.

16 Faced with discouraging results from the crude correlation of brain weight with intelligence (in 1894, Havelock Ellis found that the heaviest brain weights yet recorded were those of "a totally undistinguished

individual, an imbecile, the Russia novelist Turgenev, an ordinary workman, a bricklayer, and the French zoologist Cuvier"), physical anthropologists resorted to increasingly sophisticated examinations of brains, analyzing the complexity of their fissures and recesses. Smooth brains indicated low intellect; highly convoluted brains bespoke excellence. Shape mattered too. Despite the collapse of phrenology, scientists still maintained the belief that intelligence was seated in the forefront of the brain. Thus massive foreheads promised intellectual power.

17 By the turn of the 20th century, the correlation of brain measurements, and even of more advanced indices like brain topography, began to be abandoned under the attack of further neuroanatomical research. Scientists interested in the study of the mind had, up until this point, had little recourse but to use somatic analysis; there were, after all, no intelligence tests and indeed no psychological tests of any kind. The endeavor to learn about the mind itself from its physical manifestation, the brain, was reasonable, however much the interpretations drawn from this enterprise were shaped by preconceptions. But now the turn away from somaticism left a void. New analytical instruments would have to be devised. In this country, a graduate student at the University of Chicago, Helen Bradford Thompson, tried to fill the breach with a series of word associations, puzzles, and general-information examinations administered to university undergraduates. Her dissertation, published as *The Mental Traits of Sex*, pioneered what we might consider to be the empirical study of mental differences between the sexes. It was shortly rendered obsolete, however, by the advent of IQ tests and their popularization after World War I.

18 Gradually, in the years after 1918, a consensus grew that IQ tests showed very little difference between the intelligence of men and women. The British psychologist Charles Spearman, referring to the search for such difference, wrote, "The pack of investigators can be called off. . . . They are following a false scent." Yet the idea of sexual difference lingered on. Defeated in one guise, it emerged renewed in another. Probably the most popular new form was the variability hypothesis, the idea that on a bell-shaped curve of intelligence, women cluster around the average, while men are more scattered. At the extremes of genius and idiocy, men predominate.

19 Another new development in the study of intelligence was a more precise understanding that it was not one capacity but many. Thus a person might excel in languages but do poorly in mathematics. The

growing use of Scholastic Aptitude Tests beginning in the 1930s helped to cement this notion and to establish the common wisdom that males do better at mathematics than females. Male variability appeared to be reinforced by the figures for mathematical ability, which show males doing both very badly and very well. At the upper end, male mathematical prodigies have been found to outnumber female prodigies by a large margin. It was on the basis of this kind of information (though these issues are far from conclusively settled) that President Summers made his remarks about the reason for the scarcity of women in scientific careers.

20 Can anything be learned from this lengthy and not always edifying story? One conclusion, at least, seems plausible. Nowhere in the work of these 19th- and 20th-century scientists has mention been made of the influence of the environment on the mental functioning of an individual of either sex. That is because environment was routinely dismissed by them. Nature, not nurture, was what counted. "If a man is gifted with vast intellectual ability, eagerness to work, and power of working," wrote Francis Galton, the father of eugenics, "I cannot comprehend how such a man should be repressed." Hardheaded physician Henry Maudsley sniffed, "Village Hampdens, mute inglorious Miltons, and bloodless Cromwells do *not* sleep in the graves of the rude forefathers of the hamlet." As for gifted women, they "suffered no other hindrance to the exercise and evolution of their brains and their intellect than those that are derived from their constitution and their faculties of development." No obstacles hindered, no customs entrapped them.

21 Not a single psychologist or social theorist alive would hold such a position, when examples of its falsity come daily to mind. Nor does Summers fail to acknowledge the importance of culture in his analysis. He is, however, skeptical about its explanatory power, asserting that "the human mind has a tendency to grab to the socialization hypothesis when you can see it, and it often turns out not to be true." He would prefer to place emphasis on women's comparative unwillingness to accept the long hours and intense commitment demanded by "high-powered" careers like science (without ever asking whether these conditions are desirable). He also prefers to emphasize differences in innate ability. "It does appear," he writes, "that on many, many different human attributes . . . there is relatively clear evidence that whatever the difference means—which can be debated—there is a difference in the standard deviation, and variability of a male and a

female population." At the high end, Summers continues, that means about five males are found for every one female. Fewer females on the rarified heights of scientific intellect results in fewer females in scientific careers.

22 Even if we were to agree that the variability hypothesis was proven, we might suggest that, while science does indeed require a high level of intelligence, most scientific work is not done by geniuses (who do not come along every day). Scientists are no doubt very bright, but an individual does not have to be at the extreme high end of mathematical ability to do well in science. And motivation, of course, counts for much.

23 Lawrence Summers has rekindled a debate that has simmered for centuries, and good will likely come of it, since universities will probably feel the need to work harder at diversifying their science faculties because of the attention the debate has received. It is also likely that research into sex differences in mind and brain will continue. Meanwhile, the wisest statement on this matter might well have been made more than 140 years ago by the British political theorist John Stuart Mill: "I deny that any one knows or can know, the nature of the two sexes, as long as they have only been seen in their present relation to one another. . . . What is now called the nature of women is an eminently artificial thing—the result of forced repression in some directions, unnatural stimulation in others." Any differences that might be found between the sexes, Mill believed, could only be judged natural if they could not possibly be artificial, the effects of education or socialization.

24 We do not live in the Victorian era; the artificialities of women's lives have diminished. Can anyone say that they have been altogether eliminated?

FOR THINKING, DISCUSSING, AND WRITING

1. How does the title of the essay function as an important introduction to the main ideas the writer wishes to express?
2. Why does Russett explore the ideas of Plato and his pupil Aristotle, of Thomas Aquinas and Jean-Jacques Rousseau? How do the men's views on women compare and contrast? What work does Russett see as the "founding document of European and American feminism"? Secure a copy of the tract and read it. Why does Russett place it so centrally in the evolution of thought about women?

3. How did phrenology influence the discussion of sex differences between men and women? What does the writer think is the role of environment on the mental functioning of either sex?
4. Write an essay in which you attempt to address the statement and answer the question that end the essay: "We do not live in the Victorian era; the artificialities of women's lives have diminished. Can anyone say that they have been altogether eliminated?"

JOAN DIDION

Marrying Absurd

Joan Didion (1934–), a graduate of the University of California at Berkeley, published her first novel, Run River, *in 1966 and has written many first-rate works of fiction and nonfiction since then. Her essays particularly have drawn international attention for their keenly observed detail and sharp ironic wit. Her most recent work,* The Year of Magical Thinking, *chronicles her life after the death of her husband in 2003 and her daughter just two years later. In this essay, which first appeared in the* Saturday Evening Post *in 1967 and later in the book* Slouching Toward Bethlehem *(1968), Didion reveals the absurd mores of marriage, Las Vegas style.*

1 To be married in Las Vegas, Clark County, Nevada, a bride must swear that she is eighteen or has parental permission and a bridegroom that he is twenty-one or has parental permission. Someone must put up five dollars for the license. (On Sundays and holidays, fifteen dollars. The Clark County Courthouse issues marriage licenses at any time of the day or night except between noon and one in the afternoon, between eight and nine in the evening, and between four and five in the morning.) Nothing else is required. The State of Nevada, alone among these United States, demands neither a premarital blood test nor a waiting period before or after the issuance of a marriage license. Driving in across the Mojave from Los Angeles, one sees the signs way out on the desert, looming up from that moonscape of rattlesnakes and mesquite, even before the Las Vegas lights appear like a mirage on the horizon: "GETTING MARRIED? Free License Information First Strip Exit." Perhaps the Las Vegas wedding industry achieved its peak operational efficiency between 9:00 p.m. and midnight of August 26, 1965, an

otherwise unremarkable Thursday which happened to be, by Presidential order, the last day on which anyone could improve his draft status merely by getting married. One hundred and seventy-one couples were pronounced man and wife in the name of Clark County and the State of Nevada that night, sixty-seven of them by a single justice of the peace, Mr. James A. Brennan. Mr. Brennan did one wedding at the Dunes and the other sixty-six in his office, and charged each couple eight dollars. One bride lent her veil to six others. "I got it down from five to three minutes," Mr. Brennan said later of his feat. "I could've married them *en masse*, but they're people, not cattle. People expect more when they get married."

2 What people who get married in Las Vegas actually do expect—what, in the largest sense, their "expectations" are—strikes one as a curious and self-contradictory business. Las Vegas is the most extreme and allegorical of American settlements, bizarre and beautiful in its venality and in its devotion to immediate gratification, a place the tone of which is set by mobsters and call girls and ladies' room attendants with amyl nitrite poppers in their uniform pockets. Almost everyone notes that there is no "time" in Las Vegas, no night and no day and no past and no future (no Las Vegas casino, however, has taken the obliteration of the ordinary time sense quite so far as Harold's Club in Reno, which for a while issued, at odd intervals in the day and night, mimeographed "bulletins" carrying news from the world outside); neither is there any logical sense of where one is. One is standing on a highway in the middle of a vast hostile desert looking at an eighty-foot sign which blinks "Stardust" or "Caesar's Palace." Yes, but what does that explain? This geographical implausibility reinforces the sense that what happens there has no connection with "real" life; Nevada cities like Reno and Carson are ranch towns, Western towns, places behind which there is some historical imperative. But Las Vegas seems to exist only in the eye of the beholder. All of which makes it an extraordinarily stimulating and interesting place, but an odd one in which to want to wear a candlelight satin Priscilla of Boston wedding dress with Chantilly lace insets, tapered sleeves and a detachable modified train.

3 And yet the Las Vegas wedding business seems to appeal to precisely that impulse. "Sincere and Dignified Since 1954," one wedding chapel advertises. There are nineteen such wedding chapels in Las

Vegas, intensely competitive, each offering better, faster, and, by implication, more sincere services than the next: Our Photos Best Anywhere, Your Wedding on A Phonograph Record, Candlelight with Your Ceremony, Honeymoon Accommodations, Free Transportation from Your Motel to Courthouse to Chapel and Return to Motel, Religious or Civil Ceremonies, Dressing Rooms, Flowers, Rings, Announcements, Witnesses Available, and Ample Parking. All of these services, like most others in Las Vegas (sauna baths, payroll-check cashing, chinchilla coats for sale or rent), are offered twenty-four hours day, seven days a week, presumably on the premise that marriage, like craps, is a game to be played when the table seems hot.

4 But what strikes one most about the Strip chapels, with their wishing wells and stained-glass paper windows and their artificial bouvardia, is that so much of their business is by no means a matter of simple convenience, of late-night liaisons between show girls and baby Crosbys. Of course there is some of that. (One night about eleven o'clock in Las Vegas I watched a bride in an orange minidress and masses of flame-colored hair stumble from a Strip chapel on the arm of her bridegroom, who looked the part of the expendable nephew in movies like *Miami Syndicate*. "I gotta get the kids," the bride whimpered. "I gotta pick up the sitter, I gotta get to the midnight show." "What you gotta get," the bridegroom said, opening the door of a Cadillac Coupe de Ville and watching her crumple on the seat, "is sober.") But Las Vegas seems to offer something other than "convenience"; it is merchandising "niceness," the facsimile of proper ritual, to children who do not know how else to find it, how to make the arrangements, how to do it "right." All day and evening long on the Strip, one sees actual wedding parties, waiting under the harsh lights at a cross-walk, standing uneasily in the parking lot of the Frontier while the photographer hired by The Little Church of the West ("Wedding Place of the Stars") certifies the occasion, takes the picture: the bride in a veil and white satin pumps, the bridegroom usually in a white dinner jacket, and even an attendant or two, a sister or a best friend in hot-pink *peau de soie*, a flirtation veil, a carnation nosegay. "When I Fall in Love It Will Be Forever," the organist plays, and then a few bars of Lohengrin. The mother cries; the stepfather, awkward in his role, invites the chapel hostess to join them for a drink at the

Sands. The hostess declines with a professional smile; she has already transferred her interest to the group waiting outside. One bride out, another in, and again the sign goes up on the chapel door: "One Moment please—Wedding."

5 I sat next to one such wedding party in a Strip restaurant the last time I was in Las Vegas. The marriage had just taken place; the bride still wore her dress, the mother her corsage. A bored waiter poured out a few swallows of pink champagne ("on the house") for everyone but the bride, who was too young to be served. "You'll need something with more kick than that," the bride's father said with heavy jocularity to his new son-in-law; the ritual jokes about the wedding night had a certain Pangiossian character, since the bride was clearly several months pregnant. Another round of pink champagne, this time not on the house, and the bride began to cry. "It was just as nice," she sobbed, "as I hoped and dreamed it would be."

FOR THINKING, DISCUSSING, AND WRITING

1. In what ways does marriage contribute to gender identification? Why is the ritual of marriage so essential a part of our modern culture? Why does Didion think that marriage in Las Vegas is absurd?
2. What is the significance of the August 26, 1965, date that Didion identifies? In what ways did marriages become something other than a union between two people at that time?
3. What does Didion mean when she writes that Las Vegas is "merchandising 'niceness,' the facsimile of proper ritual, to children who do not know how else to find it, how to make the arrangements, how to do it right"? Why might you agree or disagree with her?
4. Write an essay in which you define the "proper ritual" of marriage. Does it depend on the gender or gender orientation of the two parties, do you think? Why or why not?

CONNECTING IDEAS: Gender Dynamics

1. Traditional definitions of gender originate in biological determinism—you are what your physical body says you are, so to speak. Yet psychological, sociological, and medical dimensions can influence the notion of gender, according to modern thought. Should we redefine the word *gender* so that these other elements have more prominence? Or, should the traditional definition remain constant? Choose one side of the issue and defend your position in an essay.

2. Is sexism still an insidious, hidden force in our culture or have the strides made by women and responses to them by men over the past decades largely eliminated bias based on gender? Consider Kingston's "No Name Woman," Chesler's "The Failure of Feminism," and Russett's "All About Eve," along with other sources of detail from your own reading and experience, as you weigh in on this question.
3. The big question of what is marriage still dominates much social thought in our age, particularly as the question pertains to sanctifying same-sex unions. Should marriage be an option for gay men and women in our country? What would you say about it in a letter to your senator or representative in congress?

7 CHAPTER

Science, Technology, and Health in a Complex World

IN A RENOWNED LETTER TO JOSEPH PRIESTLEY, THE BRITISH scientist who discovered oxygen, Benjamin Franklin, one of eighteenth-century America's foremost statesmen and science enthusiasts, rejoices in "experimental researches into nature" and regrets that he was born too soon to witness "the rapid Progress of *true* Science." He continues: "It is impossible to imagine the height to which may be carried, in a thousand years, the power of man over matter." Franklin believed that science would improve our lives—and he wished also that it could improve human character.

Within a mere hundred years after Franklin, scientific progress in the nineteenth century was astounding: The advances in aerodynamics by Sir George Caley in the early 1800s; the work of Henri Dutrochet (1824), Matthias Schleiden (1838), and Theodor Schwann (1839) in proposing the theory that all living things are made of cells; Charles Darwin's landmark explanation of evolution in *On the Origin of Species by Means of Natural Selection* (1859); and the discovery of radium by Marie Curie in 1898 are just a few. Yet despite such astonishing progress, many thinkers and writers already saw science as posing a frightening threat. Mary Shelley's *Frankenstein*, Robert

Louis Stevenson's *Dr. Jekyll and Mr. Hyde,* the short stories of Nathaniel Hawthorne, various poems by Edgar Allan Poe and Walt Whitman, among others, warn us to beware of the dangers of scientific mastery, and often are suspicious of how science can affect human nature. About evolution, opponents today are especially vocal, seeing it as a godless vision that challenges the Bible's view of creation. David P. Barash in "The Case for Evolution in Real Life" tries to put to rest what he sees as major misconceptions about evolutionary theory.

Two hundred years after Ben Franklin's day—still eight hundred years away from his point of reference—his enthusiasm seems prescient, as if he had viewed the future through a magic crystal ball. In fact, humans have exerted power over matter in countless spheres of activity. We have harnessed the atom and turned it to both useful and horrible ends—lighting cities with more power than any electricity could supply, but also wiping out cities with a single bomb more destructive than innumerable tons of dynamite. (Hiroshima and Nagasaki, Japan, fell to nuclear destruction at the end of World War II.) We have overcome diseases such as smallpox and tuberculosis, yet new and virulent strains of once-eliminated viruses and bacteria are returning, impervious to the once-powerful antibiotics and other drugs we invented. Cancer patients live longer, sophisticated tests indicate debilitating disease before it strikes, vaccinations protect infants and adults from menacing illnesses. (The AIDS virus still defies cure but new treatments give hope and extend lives.)

Yet from good also comes bad: overpopulation, the cost of extended health care for sick people who otherwise might have died, the high cost of drugs and pharmaceutical research, the depletion of the earth's resources and a frightening challenge to the environment. Former Vice President Al Gore shows in "From Pole to Shining Pole" what global warming has produced at the earth's ends. Similarly, in the food production industries, genetic engineering has improved plant stamina and disease resistance and strengthened animals raised for food. Yet outcries here and abroad signal a discomfort, if not downright antipathy, toward scientific tinkering with chromosomes. Many people see that as work for gods, not humans. Certainly the issue is complicated. One might oppose producing sheep with firmer wool and more edible flesh or creating disease-resistant corn and wheat through genetic manipulation in the laboratory. But what if we could save a child's life in utero by modifying or removing the fetus's disease-causing gene? Should we stick to a proscription against human subatomic exploitation or put conscience aside and save a life?

Perhaps no other topic examined in this book raises so many questions as do science, its offspring technology and its often intended focus, health care—all spectacular success stories of our age. So connected are these terms—science, technology, and health—that one more often than not uses them together to talk of the power of the human mind and its creative acts to do good for humanity today. Franklin never saw a laptop or a cell phone or a high-definition television set, yet so ubiquitous today are these fruits of scientific inquiry that it is as hard for us to imagine living without them as it would have been for Franklin to imagine living without a quill pen or a musket. The computer has revolutionized our lives and minds and the way we do business. We surf the Web the way we once (and still) channel-surf our televisions; we enter chat rooms and converse on topics from accountancy to zoos with people halfway around the globe. With a mere click of a technical wonder called a mouse we can furnish a house or purchase groceries, books and music, or even diamonds, without leaving the computer screen. We have become a dot-com generation as we transact more and more business online. In this chapter Brent staples worries about the ubiquitous online experience in "What Adolescents Miss When We Let Them Grow Up in Cyberspace."

Science and technology have their price, certainly: No real people are standing by to take your order; you can skip a visit to the mall, one of America's defining cultural icons; and the time a doctor can spend with you when you're sick depends on efficiencies determined by health-care agents and managers. So in large and small ways we have learned to see science and technology—wonder children of our brains and imaginations—as suspicious, even dangerous tools in the advancement of humanity's goals. Some of the writers in this chapter take a suspicious view of the path of unregulated science. Others find anomalous behavior in the natural world. Whatever one's viewpoint, science will no doubt continue its advance in—or assault on?—our world, producing as yet inconceivable gains as well as suspicious outcomes.

AL GORE

From Pole to Shining Pole

Al Gore (1948–) served as Vice President of the United States under William Jefferson Clinton. Elected to the United States House of Representatives in 1976, he then served two terms in the Senate after elections in 1984 and 1990. His book Earth in the Balance: Ecology and the Human Spirit *(1992) was a best-seller. This selection from* An Inconvenient Truth *(2006) shares Gore's firsthand observations about how global warming is changing dramatically the face of the earth, especially at the North and South Poles.*

1 The story I have tried to tell about global warming is a story that involves a double journey: one metaphorical and one real. The slideshow that I give regularly to audiences around the world is the distillation of my own intellectual journey toward understanding the nature of this crisis and our difficulty in facing up to it. Every part of the slideshow replicates an "Aha!" moment that I have had in the process of my own education. My goal in presenting the slideshow is to recreate that moment of discovery for others.

2 But my own journey toward understanding the crisis has also involved a literal journey to many hard-to-reach places where global warming is in clear evidence, remote pockets of the planet where many of the world's best scientists are frequently hard at work, often under extremely difficult conditions.

3 One can read field studies, talk to scientists, and scrutinize charts, but there's nothing like seeing things for yourself. I have been drawn to these excursions not only because of my hunger to learn as much as I can about the climate crisis, but also in part, I think, because they take me outdoors again and give me a chance to see many truly fascinating places.

4 Exploring hot spots where global warming has left its imprint, I've traveled from the Greenland Ice Dome to the swamps of the Everglades; from the Aral Sea to the Dead Sea; from the North Slope of Alaska to the South Island of New Zealand; from the Serengeti Plains to the Kyzyl Kum Desert; from the Nile to the Congo; from the Skeleton Coast of Namibia to the Galapagos Islands; from Mauna Loa to the Mekong Delta; from the Badlands to the Cape of Good Hope; from Oak Ridge National Laboratory in Tennessee to the Chernobyl Sarcophagus

in Ukraine; from the Amazon Jungle to Glacier National Park; from the highest lake, Titicaca, to the lowest desert, Death Valley. But of all the places I've visited, the North Pole and the South Pole truly stand out.

5 When I went to the South Pole, several things surprised me. First, the ice-and-snow pack there is more than 10,000 feet thick—so I experienced the same altitude sickness that most first-time visitors feel: a slight headache and nausea that soon pass as one acclimates to the height. It didn't occur to me beforehand that the average altitude in Antarctica is far higher than the average altitude on any other continent of the planet; the ice and snow have piled layer upon layer for so many hundreds of thousands of years that they've pushed up the top of the ice cap high into the sky. And geologists tell me that the weight of the ice and snow has pushed down the bedrock underneath it to below sea level.

6 Also, since the precipitation there is so limited, each layer of snow is quite thin, presenting a challenge for scientists seeking data from the layers. The oldest layers near the bottom have been compressed by the weight of the stack, further complicating the task of measuring CO_2 content in the tiny, trapped air bubbles.

7 Third, though I knew it would be cold in Antarctica, I really had no idea how cold. The forecast said "58° below zero," but nothing in my prior experience equipped me to understand what that would mean. And that's when I learned a particularly interesting lesson from one veteran of several seasons at the South Pole Station: "There is no such thing as bad weather," he said, "just bad clothes."

3 Understandably, the scientists who live and work in Antarctica pay a lot of attention to clothes (though very little attention to how the clothes look). The hoods of their specially designed parkas extend far out in front of their faces, because the air is so cold that it must be warmed up—at least a little—before it's breathed in. And most people cannot expose their heads for very long without risking serious frostbite to their ears. As a result, people walk around peering at the outside world through a foot-long tunnel of thick rabbit fur.

9 At the exact location of the South Pole, there is actually a barber pole stuck in the ice. This serves two purposes: it allows visitors to "run all the way around the world," and it is the place where visitors take pictures. The recommended technique for photos, by the way, is to throw off the hood for a few seconds, smile bravely while the picture is snapped, then quickly pull the hood back over the head.

10 Yet another surprise for me was when scientists showed me that near the South Pole, the presence of air pollution in the ice cores visibly declined not long after passage of the U.S. Clean Air Act in 1970; looking back through the annual layers of ice, you can actually see the before and after with your own eyes. One thing both Antarctica and the Arctic have in common is their remoteness from civilization. Yet both of these formerly pristine locations are now marked by industrial pollution. The air above the North Pole contains pollution at levels still rising because of the prevailing wind patterns in the Northern Hemisphere and the higher concentration of industry in that hemisphere.

11 I first visited the Arctic ice cap only two and a half years after visiting Antarctica, and this drove home the startling contrasts. I flew to Deadhorse, Alaska, on the shores of the Arctic Ocean and then traveled by helicopter to a rendezvous with a submarine for the journey due north under the ice cap.

12 On my second trip, I flew to Greenland, where I switched first to a C130 specially equipped with skis, then to a smaller ski-equipped plane. After a three-and-a-half-hour flight due north in the small plane, we landed on an ice floe in the Arctic Ocean and switched to skimobiles.

13 We stopped for a few hours of sleep in tents set up on the ice, then remounted the skimobiles for a two-mile run to the northern edge of the floe. There, Navy corpsmen used brooms to mark a giant X on the spot where a submerged submarine was expected to surface—and we backed away to what we thought was a safe distance.

14 I watched in awe as the giant submarine crashed upward through the ice. But as it rose, a crack shot outward from the break like a lightning bolt, straight toward me. Instantly, I dove to one side of the fissure. As I got to my feet, I noticed the nearby corpsmen smiling; their reaction to the splitting ice had been considerably calmer than mine.

15 After resubmerging, we traveled seven hours due north, all the way to the Pole. When we arrived, the navigational display lined up a row of zeros that made me feel like we had won the jackpot on a high-tech slot machine. We circled around and surfaced exactly at the Pole.

16 I remember climbing out of the conning tower and standing on the ice. What struck me most was the beautiful, almost magical quality of the tiny ice crystals in the air around me, reflecting bright sunlight like airborne jewels.

17 The reason for my two trips under the Arctic ice cap was to learn more about global warming and to convince the U.S. Navy to release

top-secret data to the environmental scientists specializing in the study of global warming's effects on Arctic ice.

18 The reason the Navy has collected data on ice thickness that no one else has is that they've regularly patrolled the Arctic Ocean—under the ice—for almost 50 years in a fleet of specially designed submarines capable of surfacing through the ice. During the Cold War, our strategic military forces were poised to retaliate on a few minutes' notice in the event of an attack by the former Soviet Union. so the submarines in the Arctic had to be capable of surfacing on short notice in the event of a nuclear exchange.

19 But that posed a challenge, because the ice cap is much thicker in some places than in others. Even with their special design, these submarines can surface safely only in spots where the ice is three feet thick or less. So the Navy has long used a special upward-looking radar to measure the thickness of ice above the subs as they make their long journey under the ice cap. And over the past half-century, the Arctic submarines have maintained a careful record of ice thickness for each of the "transects," or trips under the ice.

20 It was that five-decade record of ice thickness, marked "top secret," that I was after. I wanted the Navy and the CIA, which also had authority over the data, to release this one-of-a-kind record to the scientists who desperately needed to answer the crucial questions about global warming: Is the North Polar ice cap melting? And if so, how fast?

21 At first, the Navy strenuously resisted any release of the data, fearing it might be of assistance to enemies of the United States who could use it to figure out the submarine patrol routes. As a member of the Senate Armed Services Committee, I completely understood, and I worked with the Navy to reconcile their legitimate concern with the environmental imperative that was also of critical importance. Bruce DeMars, the four-star admiral who then headed the Navy's Nuclear Propulsion Program and was responsible for all the submarines, actually went with me to the North Pole, listened to me talk about global warming the entire trip, and, despite his initial skepticism, became an invaluable ally. He and President Reagan's CIA director, Bob Gates, were the ones who came up with an innovative solution allowing release of the data under careful safeguards.

22 It was a good thing they did, because the information proved to be even more significant and alarming than the scientists had expected: It showed a dramatic pattern of rapid melting. In recent decades, the

submarine data has been combined with satellite imagery to give an even more comprehensive picture that shows the North Polar ice cap began a fairly rapid retreat in the mid-1970s.

23 While the impact of global warming is most pronounced in the Arctic and the Antarctic. I found dramatic evidence of significant effects at the Equator as well.

24 During two trips to the Amazon rainforests, I found scientists there becoming even more deeply concerned about dramatic shifts in rainfall patterns. In 2005 the Amazon suffered the longest and worst drought in recorded history—with devastating effects.

25 In Kenya, also on the Equator, I heard growing concerns about the increased threat from mosquitoes and the diseases they can transmit in higher altitudes that were formerly too cold for them to inhabit.

26 In all of my journeys, I have searched for a better understanding of the climate crisis—and in all of them I have found not only evidence of the danger we face globally, but an expectation everywhere that the United States will be the nation to lead the world to a safer, brighter future. And as a result, since every journey took me back home, I have returned each time with a deeper conviction that the solution to this crisis that I have traveled so far to understand must begin right here at home.

FOR THINKING, DISCUSSING, AND WRITING

1. What does Gore say surprised him on his visit to the South Pole? Which observation suggests the most serious threat to the South Pole, do you think? What particular threats does Gore observe at the Equator? Why does he use these three global spots as points of reference?
2. What "top secret" information did Gore seek? What problems did he face in getting what he wanted? What ultimately was "even more significant and alarming" than the scientists expected?
3. Gore has taken a narrative approach with carefully observed detail as a way to make his argument. What exactly is his point? Is the narrative approach successful, do you think? Or is the selection too much about Al Gore and not enough about the global warming crisis?
4. Gore writes in the last paragraph that he has found "evidence of the danger we face globally," as well as "an expectation everywhere that the United States will be the nation to lead the world to a safer, brighter future." Write an essay in which you argue about what can be done to address the global warming predicament and whether or not you believe the United States should lead the effort. Provide valid supporting detail to back up your assertions.

DAVID P. BARASH

The Case for Evolution, in Real Life

David P. Barash (1946–) received his PhD from the University of Wisconsin and currently is a professor of psychology at the University of Washington. His most recent book, Madame Bovary's Ovaries: A Darwinian Look at Literature, *written with his daughter Nanelle R. Barash, was published in 2005. In this selection, published in the April 7, 2006, issue of the* Chronicle of Higher Education, *he presents a "catalog of misconceptions" about evolution, one of the volatile political topics of our day.*

1 Noting the role of the Royal Air Force in saving his country during the Battle of Britain, Winston Churchill observed that never had so many owed so much to so few. We owe a great deal—indeed, literally everything—to evolution, and yet never have so many said and written so much about something they understood so poorly. Not that evolution is all that difficult to understand. Rather, so many people have such strong feelings about it, often connected to so many regrettable stock phrases, that clear thought has often been obscured. This is especially unfortunate in today's intellectual—or, more to the point, anti-intellectual—climate, with the Bush administration persistently seeking to trump science with ideology.

2 Notwithstanding recent victories of science over so-called intelligent design in Pennsylvania and Utah, this particular struggle is not likely to end soon. The following catalog of misconceptions, along with responses, is therefore offered for scholars who may well find themselves confronting voices whose amplitude and frequency exceed their wisdom.

3 **It's only a theory."** Biologists often speak of "the theory of evolution," but not because evolution is a guess or mere speculation. My *Random House Dictionary* provides, among its definitions of "theory," the following: "a proposed explanation whose status is still conjectural, in contrast to well-established propositions that are regarded as reporting matters of actual fact." Someone might express a "theory" that Elvis Presley still lives, or that trailer parks attract tornadoes. The same person might also say, "Biologists have a theory that human beings evolved," in which case, knowingly or not, a very different use of the word has been employed. Indeed, my dictionary also gives this

definition of "theory": "a more or less verified established explanation accounting for known facts or phenomena," with examples that include number theory, the theory of relativity, atomic theory, and so forth. In this sense, and this only, evolution is a theory. It is, in fact, as close to truth as any science is ever likely to get. (And, proudly situated in the old-fashioned, pre-postmodernist tradition, I assert that this is very, very close indeed.)

4 **"Evolutionary logic is circular: The fittest are those that survive, and those that survive are the fittest. So it doesn't say anything."** First, natural selection is not about survival, but reproduction: specifically, individuals' and genes' reproducing themselves. Survival is evolutionarily important because—and only because—it contributes to reproduction. Second, "fitness" does not determine natural selection; rather, natural selection is the unavoidable result of how "fit" something is, which is to say, how successful it is in promoting its genes. Fitness leads to the important prediction that natural selection favoring a particular type should result in a larger proportion of that type in future populations. This prediction has been repeatedly tested and confirmed.

5 **"Natural selection is just a negative process; it cannot create anything new."** Natural selection is only "negative" in that certain individuals and their genes fall by the evolutionary wayside in preference to others, which prosper. But evolution is not merely a question of deleting those organisms that are less fit; because of mutation (which provides genetic novelty) and sexual reproduction (which combines DNA in unique ways), new genetic material is constantly being produced. And much depends on this regular generation of genetic diversity, on the world being, as the poet Louis MacNeice put it, "incorrigibly plural." In his poem "Snow," MacNeice went on to feel "the drunkenness of things being various," a variousness that is essential as the building blocks from which evolution constructs those things that we identify as highly adapted organisms, including ourselves.

6 But although the production of diversity is fundamentally random, the power of natural selection is that it is not simply at the mercy of haphazard events, merely eliminating the unfit. It creates novelty because it adds a crucial process: a mechanism for "selective retention."

7 Imagine that instead of those hypothetical monkeys creating all of Shakespeare, we wanted just a single phrase, "to be or not to be." It consists of 18 characters, including spaces. Given the alphabet plus a possible blank space, we have a total of 27 possibilities for each slot. The chance

that one of our monkeys might randomly get the initial "t" is thus 1/27. The chance that it would simultaneously and randomly place an "o" in the second slot is $1/27 \times 1/27 = 1/27$. The chance of getting all 18 characters correct, by chance alone, is thus 1/27 times itself 17 times, which is inconceivably small. (The following analysis, with some modification, was inspired by Richard Dawkins's superb book *The Blind Watchmaker.*)

8 But what if, instead of tossing out every meaningless word and having to start afresh each time, those patterns that were promising—even by a little bit—were retained, and then randomly modified yet again, once more retaining (that is, selecting) those that were more "fit"? I started with 18 random strikes on a computer keyboard and programmed the machine to make a few small changes—introduce some new letters—every "generation." Those changes are equivalent to mutation and sexual recombination, providing regular sources of random variation on an existing theme. Next I added the simple requirement of selectively retaining whatever most closely approximates "to be or not to be," after which the "organism" randomly varies again, with the outcome screened once more for resemblance—however slight—to the target. The result was that after a very small number of generations—usually on the order of 30—the desired outcome was obtained.

9 In one test, for example, I started with "fuwl sazgh ekm fje." Discouraging, perhaps, but after several runs it had become the dimly recognizable "tubl hot nnoq ioby." By run 22, it was "tu bep ok not ts e." And by 29, "to be ok not to bo," which even the most cynical monkey is likely to acknowledge as having just about arrived, and a whole lot more quickly than 1/27 to the 18th power would suggest.

10 Starting with gobbledygook, and using only random variation and selective retention, something new had been created, something so nonrandom, in fact, that it is perhaps the most famous phrase in the English language! One might object, of course, that there is a crucial added factor: Human intelligence was injected into the process. For example, "to pee or not to pee" is also syntactically correct—and an appropriate query on certain occasions—but is unlikely to have echoed down the corridors of literature for 400 years.

11 Shakespeare presumably considered various possible alternatives to Hamlet's renowned dilemma, although he assuredly didn't puzzle through every option. Like a human chess master, as opposed to IBM's chess-playing program, Deep Blue, a creative intellect takes numerous shortcuts. But this, too, is very much what natural selection does. Living

things offer only a very limited subset of what is possible. Instead of a creative human intelligence rejecting certain verbal combinations over others, the environment faced by every living thing rejects certain genetic combinations over others. In arid conditions, it rejects combinations that waste water; in cold conditions, it rejects combinations that waste heat. Among predators it rejects combinations that are clumsy at stalking their prey, while among prey species, it rejects those that are incautious or inept when it comes to avoiding their predators. As Robinson Jeffers put it, in "The Bloody Sire":

What but the wolf's tooth whittled so fine
The fleet limbs of the antelope?
What but fear winged the birds, and hunger
Jeweled with such eyes the great gos hawk's head?

12 The fleet limbs of the antelope, the wings of birds, and the eyes of the goshawk are all marvels of natural design, in no way inferior to the human design of Hamlet's melancholy question. And to understand how these were created, we need only understand how natural selection, based on random building blocks, can nonetheless generate highly nonrandom results.

13 **"Evolution is no longer going on, especially in the case of human beings."** Evolution happens anytime there are changes in a population's genetic makeup. The most powerful mechanism of evolutionary change is natural selection, which operates whenever some individuals leave more genetic representatives than others do. The only way for evolution to cease would be if everyone reproduced equally; more precisely, if genes continued to replace themselves in exactly the same proportion as they currently exist. Just a moment's reflection should convince anyone that evolution is very alive, for human beings as for everything else, so long as "differential reproduction" is going on.

14 That doesn't mean, however, that the conditions of evolution are the same as they have been in the past. The "selective environment" for human beings, for example, has changed dramatically from the Pleistocene. Certain traits that almost certainly were strongly selected against, such as myopia and diabetes, are now neutral or, at worst, only mildly negative. Human ingenuity has come up with eyeglasses and insulin, which only scratch the surface of how modern *Homo sapiens* has modified natural selection, hence its own evolution. Whereas it might have been selectively advantageous to be a good hunter,

gatherer, or mastodon-avoider, now it is selectively advantageous to be able to reproduce despite strontium-90 in our bones or DDT in our fat, and, perhaps, to be positively attracted to ideologies that are unsympathetic to birth control. In any event, we have changed our own evolution, but not ended it.

15 **"Biological evolution no longer matters, having been superseded by cultural evolution."** Cultural evolution is real, and it may in fact be the one sense in which human beings do experience Lamarckian evolution, via a kind of inheritance of acquired characteristics. Cultural evolution, like biological evolution, involves change, but instead of genes, it is based on cultural practice: language; technology; styles of clothing; ways of living; traditions including culinary, religious, military, intellectual, social, sexual; and just about everything else that human beings do outside the anatomy and physiology of their own bodies. Cultural evolution, like biological evolution, requires variation, but instead of genetic mutations, its raw material comes from ideas and concepts, innovations of mind and matter that may ultimately be traceable—however indirectly—to humanity's DNA, but which are not a simple matter of biochemical alterations in genetic material. Cultural evolution, like biological evolution, proceeds by selective retention of whatever works or is favored for any other reason (such as obvious efficiency, the vagaries of fashion, or even the dictates of the powerful). Most important, cultural evolution, because it is Lamarckian and can be "inherited" nongenetically and passed on to others within a single generation, is much faster than biological evolution. To some extent, human beings are like a train traveling on two tracks, but in our case, the wheels on one track (biological evolution) move slowly while those on the other (cultural evolution) move rapidly. No wonder our species feels pulled apart. But this disparity, rather than negating the impact of biological evolution, only italicizes its significance.

16 **"Evolution acts for the good of the species."** All sorts of things evolve: galaxies, stars, a person's thinking, a government's policies. But none of those qualify as evolution as biologists understand the term. People have evolved; a person does not. Evolution involves change, but not the change that takes place in growth, aging, changing one's clothes or even one's mind. To qualify as biological evolution, there must be a change in a population's gene pool over time. This is why only populations evolve, not individuals—because each of us is stuck with our private genetic endowment. And yet individuals are crucial to

evolution, both individual bodies and individual genes. In fact, one of the most important and useful realizations of recent years is that evolution operates most strongly at the lowest possible levels, notably that of individuals and genes, not groups or species.

17 Natural selection works by differential reproduction, with some individuals and their genes more successful than others. A species is the sum total of its individuals and their genes. It has no metaphysical existence of its own, and, as far as can be determined, no one is looking out for the good of the species as a whole, although each component has been selected to look out for itself. Analogously, in a free-market society, individuals and corporations seek to maximize their profits; any larger-order benefit derived by the nation is simply the unintentional summed effects of all those private, enterprising activities going on at a lower level. In the world of living things, there is no one looking out for collective benefit, no equivalent to Medicare, the FBI, or the Department of Education. Indeed, because individuals and genes are selected to maximize their own fitness, with none of them looking out for the interest of the larger group, the overwhelming majority of species that have ever lived are now extinct. Furthermore, when a species is endangered and thus at risk of going under, there is no indication that its constituent individuals are especially inclined to deprive themselves for the good of the threatened whole, and every sign that living things do whatever it takes to promote their own success, not that of the species.

18 The good of the species is purely an artificial construct of human beings, who, identifying an emergent whole (for our own convenience), misguidedly assume that its component parts see things the same way. But, in fact, when species benefit and individual benefit collide, the latter invariably wins.

19 **"We've never found the 'missing link.'"** Mark Twain once said that it was easy to stop smoking; he had done it hundreds of times. Similarly, there is no missing link; there are hundreds of them, or thousands, or millions. Consider two points, representing different species, one of which gave rise to the other. Think of them as connected by a line, representing evolutionary continuity. Now add a third point, more or less midway, and call it "the missing link." Having located this missing link, have you finished your task and bridged the gap between the two points? Not at all. In fact, you have just produced at least two new "missing links." Fill in both of them and you are faced with four. Like the horizon, which

constantly recedes if pursued, the discovery of transitional forms merely adds to the transitional forms not yet identified. Mathematicians say there is an infinite number of points between any two identified points on a line; presumably there are fewer than an infinite number of missing links, but the more we find, the more there are.

20 The foolishness of the concept "missing link" becomes clear when you consider that for there to be some sort of midpoint, one must specify the two ends. Granted that one is modern *Homo sapiens*. But what ancestral form, precisely, holds down the other end of the linked chain: an anthropoid ape, a monkey, a primate, a mammal, a primitive reptile, an early amphibian, a primordial vertebrate, a pre-Cambrian worm? The "missing link" between modern human beings and the Devonian fishes, for example, might be a pre-dinosaurian reptile.

21 Nonetheless, some people are truly bothered by what they see as the paucity of transitional forms in the fossil record. They might just as well, however, be impressed with how many have been found. This applies to forms ancestral to *Homo sapiens* just as it does to other species. Probably the closest to a "missing link" in the human evolutionary lineage is the famous fossil Lucy, a female Australopithecine ("southern ape") of the species *Australopithecus afarensis,* who stood about three feet tall and weighed about 66 pounds. Lucy is as much an intermediate between apes and people as can be imagined. But she isn't alone.

22 There are several other species of *Australopithecus,* some relatively slender and most if not all of them on the line that gave rise to *Homo sapiens*. Others are heavy-bodied and—with the 20/20 vision of hindsight—identifiable as evolutionary dead ends whose descendants eventually went extinct. There is also a growing list of species belonging to the genus *Homo,* including *Homo habilis,* which is pretty much a link between Lucy and us, just as Lucy is a link between ancient apes and modern human beings. Other found links include *Homo erectus,* remains of which are known from Asia as well as Europe. My purpose here is not to provide a detailed list of fossil prehumans, their dates, cranial capacities, or precise relationships—a Sisyphean task, at any rate, because new ones are constantly turning up. Rather it is to note the existence of many links between *Homo sapiens* and earlier, ancestral animals.

23 While it is alive, there is no way to identify a transitional form as such. Maybe its descendants will remain largely unchanged for millions

of years, so that it is not transiting to anything else but is just something that evolved early and persisted late. Or maybe its descendants will go extinct, in which case it is transitional only to a dead end. Or maybe its descendants will be somehow recognizable in the present day, in which case it is transitional in the usual sense of the term. In any event, rather than missing, links are actually quite abundant.

24 **"Disputes among evolutionary biologists show that the foundations of the enterprise are shaky."** Exactly the opposite is true: Creative ferment is the stuff of science. Unlike theology, with which creationists are more familiar, science is founded on ideas, discovery, testing, and refinement rather than on presumably inerrant doctrines of faith. Disputes about the details of evolutionary fine-tuning, far from undermining the validity of evolution, are testimony to the vitality of the whole enterprise, since any worthwhile science raises more questions than it answers. Accordingly there is uncertainty as to whether evolution always proceeds gradually or is punctuated by occasional bursts of change, but no question that it proceeds, and that it does so by the accumulation of genetic modifications.

25 **"Biologists have never actually witnessed natural selection causing an evolutionary change, so the whole enterprise is therefore conjectural."** Wrong again. Evolution is slow, usually taking many thousands of generations. That is not surprising, since it takes time to accumulate an observable effect when, for example, a certain gene may enjoy an advantage of only one in one thousand over its fellows. Given enough time, such a "selection differential" will make a genuine difference—but no biologist has ever lived long enough to detect significant evolutionary change in sequoia trees, for instance, or blue whales, which take many years to produce even a single generation. Hence it is difficult to catch evolution *in flagrante*. But not impossible.

26 Famous cases involve so-called industrial melanism among English peppered moths, the evolution of antibiotic resistance among bacteria, and observations by Peter and Rosemary Grant of adaptive changes in beak shape among Galapagos finches as a result of continuing climate change. Admittedly we have yet to observe one species evolving into another, but that is simply because evolutionary change is slow compared with human life spans. Besides, there is nothing magical about one species' turning into another: Under the influence of artificial selection, people have caused St. Bernards and Chihuahuas, greyhounds and bulldogs to evolve.

27 The key point for our purposes is that once again natural selection has been shown to give rise to evolutionary change during a very short time scale. Of course, peppered moths and finches' beaks may appear to be much ado about nothing, cases of evolution laboring mightily and then bringing forth mere trivialities. Such examples might seem a far cry from horses evolving from terrier-sized *Hyracotherium* to modern Budweiser behemoths, velociraptors arising from the swampy slime, or the human brain expanding from shrew-like insignificance to the crowning, cerebral glory of modern sapient humanity. All these have indeed happened, but to witness such major transitions directly, it is necessary to consult the fossil record. Nonetheless, all evolutionary journeys (including the big ones, so-called macroevolution) begin with small steps (so-called microevolution) and are nothing but their accumulated consequences, over time.

28 Finally, consider this, which I believe undergirds much opposition to evolutionary science, and which I present as distinct from the earlier misconceptions, since it is not a matter of scientific veracity but, rather, opinion: **"Evolution is a put-down, diminishing the special status of human beings."** At the bottom of much opposition to evolution, I suspect, lies a deeper anxiety, that of acknowledging our kinship with "lower" life forms. "In an aversion to animals," wrote the philosopher Walter Benjamin, "the predominant feeling is fear of being recognized by them through contact. The horror that stirs deep in man is an obscure awareness that in him something lives so akin to the animal that it might be recognized." That recognition does not need elaborate scientific backing; it is usually enough to look into a dog's eyes, an act which, interestingly, does not usually evoke horror.

29 In *Civilization and Its Discontents*, Sigmund Freud refers approvingly to a 19th-century German playwright, Christian Garber, who gave this advice to a would-be suicide: "We cannot fall out of this world. We are in it once and for all." That caution applies to us all: We'll eventually die, but aside from that, the world is irretrievably with us. We are stuck in the muck and glory of it all, living creatures among many, biological to the core, created by our biology no less than is a dandelion or a dolphin. We cannot fall out of it, nor is there any reason to do so. For Darwin there was "grandeur in this view of life," in which all living things are linked both by historical continuity—that is, common ancestry—and as the products of the same fundamental process: evolution.

FOR THINKING, DISCUSSING, AND WRITING

1. Which item in Barash's "catalog of misconceptions" about evolution do you find especially convincing? What kind of supporting information has the writer used to convince you of his point?
2. What distinction does the writer make about natural selection? In what ways does it create novelty?
3. In what ways is the last misconception—"Evolution is a put-down, diminishing the special status of human beings"—simply a matter of opinion, not scientific veracity, as Barash points out?
4. The Scopes trial of 1925 resulted in a setback for anti-evolutionists. Only two states of the fifteen in that day with pending anti-evolution legislation passed laws forbidding the teaching of evolution in the schools. And yet today the teaching of evolution seems as controversial in many quarters as it was in the 1920s. Write an essay in which you attempt to explain the current attitudes against teaching evolution in the schools. Draw on Barash's article, your own experiences, and (or) a review of current literature on the topic.

BRENT STAPLES

What Adolescents Miss When We Let Them Grow Up in Cyberspace

Brent Staples (1951–) is an editorial writer for the New York Times *with his own byline. In 1973 he earned a BA with honors from Widener University and in 1977 a PhD in psychology from the University of Chicago, where he held a Danforth Fellowship for graduate study. Staples is an influential observer of American culture and politics. His memoir,* Parallel Time: Growing up in Black and White *(1994), chronicles a difficult childhood in largely black Chester, Pennsylvania. In this 2004 essay he depicts the pitfalls of the online universe available to teenagers.*

1 My 10th-grade heartthrob was the daughter of a fearsome steelworker who struck terror into the hearts of 15-year-old boys. He made it his business to answer the telephone—and so always knew who was calling—and grumbled in the background when the conversation went on too long. Unable to make time by phone, the boy either gave up or appeared at the front door. This meant submitting to the first-degree for which the girl's father was soon to become famous.

2 He greeted me with a crushing handshake, then leaned in close in a transparent attempt to find out whether I was one of those *bad* boys who smoked. He retired to the den during the visit, but cruised by the living room now and then to let me know he was watching. He let up after some weeks, but only after getting across what he expected of a boy who spent time with his daughter and how upset he'd be if I disappointed him.

3 This was my first sustained encounter with an adult outside my family who needed to be convinced of my worth as a person. This, of course, is a crucial part of growing up. Faced with same challenge today, however, I would probably pass on meeting the girl's father—and outflank him on the Internet.

4 Thanks to e-mail, online chat rooms and instant messages—which permit private, realtime conversations—adolescents have succeeded at last in shielding their social lives from adult scrutiny. But this comes at a cost. The paradox is that teenagers nowadays are both more connected to the world at large than ever, and more cut off from the social encounters that have historically prepared young people for the move into adulthood.

5 The Internet was billed as a revolutionary method of enriching our social lives and expanding our civic connections. This seems to have worked well for elderly people and others who were isolated before they got access to the World Wide Web. But a growing body of research is showing that the heavy use of the Net actually isolated younger socially connected people who are unwittingly allowing time online to replace face-to-face interaction with their families and friends.

6 Online shopping, checking e-mail and Web surfing—mainly solitary activities—have turned out to be more isolating than watching television, which friends and family often do in groups. Researchers have found that the time spent in direct contact with family members drops by as much as half for every hour we use the Net at home.

7 This should come as no surprise to two-career couples who have seen their domestic lives taken over by e-mail and wireless tethers that keep people working around the clock. But a startling body of research from the Human–Computer Interaction Institute at Carnegie Mellon has shown that heavy Internet use can have a stunting effect outside the home as well. Studies show that gregarious, well-connected people actually lose friends and experience symptoms of loneliness and depression, after joining discussion groups and other activities. People who communicated with disembodied strangers online found the experience empty

and emotionally frustrating but were nonetheless seduced by the novelty of the new medium. As Prof. Robert Kraut, a Carnegie Mellon researcher, told me recently, such people allowed low-quality relationships developed in virtual reality to replace higher-quality relationships in the real world.

8 No group has embraced this socially impoverishing trade-off more enthusiastically than adolescents, many of whom spend most of their free hours cruising the Net in sunless rooms. This hermetic existence has left many of these teenagers with nonexistent social skills—a point widely noted in stories about the computer geeks who rose to prominence in the early days of Silicon Valley.

9 Adolescents are drawn to cyberspace for different reasons than adults. As the writer Michael Lewis observed in his book *Next: The Future Just Happened*, children see the Net as a transformational device that lets them discard quotidian identities for more glamorous ones. Mr. Lewis illustrated the point with Marcus Arnold, who, as a 15-year-old, adopted a pseudonym a few years ago and posed as a 25-year-old legal expert for an Internet information service. Marcus did not feel the least bit guilty, and was deterred, when real-world lawyers discovered his secret and accused him of being a fraud. When asked whether he had actually read the law, Marcus responded that he found books "boring," leaving us to conclude that he had learned all he needed to know from his family's big-screen TV.

10 Marcus is a child of the Net, where everyone has a pseudonym, telling a story makes it true and adolescents create older, cooler, more socially powerful selves any time they wish. The ability to slip easily into a new, false self is tailor-made for emotionally fragile adolescents, who can consider a bout of acne or a few excess pounds an unbearable tragedy.

11 But teenagers who spend much of their lives hunched over computer screens miss the socializing, the real world experience that would allow them to leave adolescence behind and grow into adulthood. These vital experiences, like much else, are simply not available in a virtual form.

FOR THINKING, DISCUSSING, AND WRITING

1. Why, according to Staples, are adolescents drawn to cyberspace? Do you agree with his analysis? What other reasons could you propose?
2. How does the writer support his point that heavy Internet use "has a stunting effect" outside the home?

3. Staples uses both personal anecdotes and expert testimony to advance his point. Which do you find most effective? Why? Are the cited sources reliable? How can you tell?
4. Write an essay in which you show how cyberspace can have a *positive* influence on adolescents. You might want to acknowledge Staples' thesis and then refute it or show how positive values of the online experience overshadow the negative. Or, if you believe as Staples does, write your own essay on the evils of cyberspace, drawing on evidence that he has not introduced.

NATALIE ANGIER

One Thing They Aren't: Maternal

Natalie Angier (1958–) studied English, physics, and astronomy, and at the age of 22 became a founding staff member for Discover *magazine. Her books include* Natural Obsessions *(1988),* The Beauty of the Beastly *(1995), and* The Canon: A Whirligig Tour of the Beautiful Basics of Science *(2007), in which she draws on conversations with hundreds of the world's top scientists and her own work to create an entertaining guide to scientific literacy. In 1991, she won a Pulitzer Prize for beat reporting and now works for the* New York Times. *In this amusing piece for* Science Times *in 2006, she exposes the not-so-motherly attitudes and actions found in the animal kingdom.*

1 Dear noble, selfless, tender and ferocious defenders of progeny all across nature's phylogeny: How well you deserve our admiration as Mother's Day draws near, and how photogenically you grace the greeting cards that we thrifty offspring will send in lieu of a proper gift.

2 Here is a mother guinea hen, trailed by a dozen cotton-ball chicks. Here a mother panda and a baby panda share a stalk of bamboo, while over there, a great black eagle dam carries food to her waiting young. We love you, Mom, you're our port in the storm. You alone help clip Mother Nature's bloodstained claws.

3 But wait. That guinea hen is walking awfully fast. In fact, her brood cannot quite keep up with her, and by the end of the day, whoops, only two chicks still straggle behind. And the mama panda, did she not give birth to twins? So why did just one little panda emerge from her den? As for the African black eagle, her nest is less a Hallmark poem than an

Edgar Allan Poe. The mother has gathered prey in abundance, and has hyrax carcasses to spare. Yet she feeds only one of her two eaglets, then stands by looking bored as the fattened bird repeatedly pecks its starving sibling to death.

4 What is wrong with these coldhearted mothers, to give life then carelessly toss it away? Are they freaks or diseased or unnatural? Cackling mad like Piper Laurie in *Carrie*?

5 In a word—ha. As much as we may like to believe that mother animals are designed to nurture and protect their young, to fight to the death, if need be, to keep their offspring alive, in fact, nature abounds with mothers that defy the standard maternal script in a raft of macabre ways. There are mothers that zestily eat their young and mothers that drink their young's blood. Mothers that pit one young against the other in a fight to the death and mothers that raise one set of their babies on the flesh of their siblings.

6 Among several mammals, including lions, mice and monkeys, females will either spontaneously abort their fetuses or abandon their newborns when times prove rocky or a new male swaggers into town.

7 Other mothers, like pandas, practice a postnatal form of family planning, giving birth to what may be thought of as an heir and a spare, and then, when the heir fares well, walking away from the spare with nary a fare-thee-well.

8 "Pandas frequently give birth to twins, but they virtually never raise two babies," said Scott Forbes, a professor of biology at the University of Winnipeg. "This is the dark side of pandas, that they have two and throw one away."

9 It is also something that zoos with ever-popular panda displays rarely discuss.

10 "They consider it bad P.R. for the pandas," Dr. Forbes said.

11 Researchers long viewed infanticide and similar acts of maternal skulduggery as pathological, a result of the mother's being under extreme stress. A farmer's child pokes around in a rabbit's nest, for example, and the mother rabbit responds by methodically consuming every one of her eight baby bunnies. By standard reckoning, it made little genetic sense for a mother to destroy her young, and maternal nurturing was assumed to be a hard-wired affair.

12 More recently, scientists have accrued abundant evidence that "bad" mothering is common in nature and that it is often a centerpiece of the reproductive game plan.

13 In the blockbuster movie *The March of the Penguins*, the emperor penguins were portrayed as fairy parents, loving every egg they laid and mourning every egg that cracked before its time. Among the less storied royal penguins, a mother lays two eggs each breeding season, the second 60 percent larger than the first. Just before the second egg is laid, the mother unsentimentally rolls the first egg right out of the nest.

14 In Magellanic penguins, the mother also lays two eggs and allows both to hatch; only then does she begin to discriminate. Of the fish she brings to the nest, she gives 90 percent to the larger chick, even as the smaller one howls for food. In the pitiless cold of Antarctica, the underfed bird invariably dies.

15 Like penguins, many species that habitually jettison a portion of their progeny live in harsh or uncertain environments, where young are easily lost and it pays to have a backup. At the same time, the harshness and uncertainty make it virtually impossible for a mother to raise multiples, so if the primary survives, the backup must go. Sometimes the mother does the dirty work herself. More often, she leaves it to her preferred young to dispatch of its understudy.

16 When Douglas W. Mock of the University of Oklahoma began studying egrets in Texas three decades ago, he knew that the bigger babies in a clutch would peck the smaller ones to death. Still, Dr. Mock was caught off guard by what he saw—or failed to see. He had assumed that the murderous attacks would surely take place while Mom and Dad egret were out fishing.

17 "I figured that, if the parents were around, they'd try to block these things," he said. "I have three older brothers, and I never would have made it if my parents hadn't interceded."

18 Instead, Dr. Mock witnessed utter parental indifference. The mother or father would stand by the side of the nest, doing nothing as one chick battered its sibling bloody. "The parent would yawn or groom itself and look completely blasé," said Dr. Mock, author of "More Than Kin and Less Than Kind: The Evolution of Family Conflict." "In the 3,000 attacks that I witnessed, I never saw a parent try to stop one. It's as though they expect it to happen."

19 Since then, siblicide under parental supervision has been observed in many bird species, including pelicans, cranes and blue-footed boobies.

20 One researcher watched a nest of African black eagles for three days as the larger eaglet alternated between tirelessly stabbing at its sibling and taking food from its solicitous mother's mouth. There was prey to

spare, but the mother did not bother feeding the second, abused baby. When the eaglet's poor, tattered body was finally tossed to the ground, the researcher calculated that it had been pecked 1,569 times.

21 Pigs, too, have their own version of litter culling by sibling rivalry. Piglets are born with little eyeteeth that stick out sideways from their lower jaw, Dr. Mock said, and they use these teeth to slice at the faces of one another as they jockey for the best teats. The runt of the litter is so often sliced and bullied that it cannot get enough milk. It must spend every spare moment fighting to nurse and may get crushed by its mother.

22 In other cases, mothers turn infanticidal because they are born optimists, ever tuned to the sunny expectation that good times lie ahead. Each year they breed for a banquet, producing a maximum of begging bairns as the season starts; and when there is plenty of food, they will provision every young.

23 If the feast does not materialize, however, they cut their losses. Kangaroos have an elaborate method for child rearing through fat and lean years. In a good season, a mother may care for three offspring simultaneously, each at a different stage of development: the eldest, already hopping around on its own but still nursing; the second, a joey, which lives in her pouch and breast-feeds; and the youngest, an embryo stashed internally in a state of suspended animation.

24 During a severe drought, the mother will first refuse her breast to the autonomous juvenile, leaving it to forage as best it can. If the drought continues, her milk dries up and the joey dies and falls from her pouch. At that point, the embryo kept in cold storage begins to develop toward joeyhood. Tomorrow will surely be a better, wetter day.

25 Some mother hawks and owls are practical optimists, not only halving their brood when necessary but also eating them.

26 "Cannibalizing the victim serves the dual function of providing a timely meal and ensuring that there is one less mouth to feed," Dr. Forbes, the University of Winnipeg biologist, writes in his new book, "A Natural History of Families."

27 A hungry mother can be the stuff of nightmares—especially if it is the mother next door.

28 Chimpanzees are exemplary mothers when it comes to caring for their own, said Sarah Blaffer Hrdy, a primatologist and the author of *Mother Nature: A History of Mothers, Infants and Natural Selection.*

29 Unlike humans, Dr. Hrdy said, the apes never abandon or reject their young, no matter how diseased or crippled a baby may be. Yet because female chimpanzees live in troops with other nonrelated females, a ravenous, lactating mother feels little compunction about killing and eating the child of a group mate. "It's a good way to get lipids," Dr. Hrdy said.

30 As meal plans go, cannibalism can be no-muss, no-fuss. A mother nurse shark has two uteri in which her babies develop, safe from the ocean's predators. But the nurse shark is not a mammal, and she has no placenta. How to feed her fetal fish? On the fins and flesh of fellow fetal fish.

31 The mother incubates as many as 20 eggs per womb. The eggs hatch and start to grow, and when their jaws are sufficiently mature, they commence feeding on one another. By gestation's end, just one sharklet emerges from each uterine chamber.

32 Extracting nutrients from one's offspring need not be fatal, though. Among ants of the rare genus *Adetomyrma*, Dr. Forbes writes, "queens chew holes in their larvae and then consume the oozing fluid," a practice that explains why the insects, found in Madagascar, are known as Dracula ants. The sampled larvae recover and mature into ants, but they bear lifelong scars of their early bloodletting.

33 There are voracious mothers and vampiric mothers, and then there are phantom mothers. In the annals of mammaldom, the maximal minimalist of a mother must surely be the rabbit. Only recently have scientists studied rabbit behavior closely enough to appreciate what a marvel of efficiency a breeding rabbit is, said Robyn Hudson of the National University of Mexico.

34 Rabbits live together in complex burrows, where an expecting female will build a little nest and line it with grass and fur that she plucks from her flank. When she is ready to give birth, she enters the chamber and in less than eight minutes plops out 10 pups, "like peas in a pod," Dr. Hudson said.

35 Without bestowing on the litter so much as a single welcoming lick, the mother hops back out, closes up the entrance and leaves the helpless, furless newborns to huddle among themselves in the dark. Over the next 25 days, the mother will return to the nest for a mere two minutes a day, during which she crouches over the pups and they frantically nurse.

36 "Her milk is under high pressure, and it's almost squirted into their mouths," Dr. Hudson said. "You can see them visibly expand, like little grapes."

37 Two minutes are up, and she's out of there. On Day 26, she abandons them completely, and the bunnies must crawl from the nest and make their way in the world on their own.

38 The mother rabbit may seem awfully cold for a warmblood, but her aloofness makes sense. Rabbits are a highly popular prey, and many predators will pursue them into their burrows. To keep the fox from the nursery door, the mother rabbit shuns the room. Her absence may not make her pups' hearts grow fonder, but it may keep those hearts thumping a little longer.

FOR THINKING, DISCUSSING, AND WRITING

1. How does Angier introduce her main point that "nature abounds with mothers that defy the standard maternal script in a raft of macabre ways"? Which examples at the beginning of the essay do you find most forceful in supporting her point? Why?
2. In what ways is "bad mothering" common enough in nature to make it "often a centerpiece of the reproductive game plan"?
3. How do Dr. Douglas W. Mock's studies affect Angier's position? Dr. Scott Forbes's? Dr. Sarah Blaffer Hrdy's? Dr. Robin Hudson's? Which conclusions that they have drawn about animals do you find most surprising? Why?
4. Write an essay in which you consider the behavior of human mothers vis-à-vis the animal kingdom mothers presented in this essay. Can whatever forces move a panda or a penguin or a rabbit or an egret, for example, show up in human motherly conduct? Or are humans basically above such primitive, callous behavior?

HOWARD MARKEL

When Germs Travel

Howard Markel (1960–) is Professor of the History of Medicine and Professor of Pediatrics and Communicable Diseases at the University of Michigan Medical School. He is also Director of the Center for the History of Medicine.

Named as one of the first Fellows at the New York Public Library's Center for Scholars and Writers, he is the author of Quarantine! East European Jewish Immigrants and the New York City Epidemics of 1892 *(1999) and* When Germs Travel: Six Major Epidemics That Have Invaded America and the Fears They Have Unleashed *(2004). In this 1999 essay for the* American Scholar, *Markel explores the link between human migration and the spread of infectious diseases.*

1 History teaches us that society has no shortage of means available to dehumanize "undesirable" groups. The grave risks of this process are magnified when combined with the threat of infectious disease. At such moments, rhetorical scapegoating may be transformed into a mentality of quarantine. Not only does the disease become the "enemy"; so, too, do the human beings (and their contacts) who have encountered the microbe in question. A common symptom of the quarantine mentality is to do everything possible to prevent the spread of an epidemic disease, often neglecting the human or medical needs of those labeled infectious.

2 The annals of human migration have long been intertwined with the history of infectious disease. As humans have roamed and conquered, so have the germs that travel within them. One of the most striking results of the international exploration that began in antiquity and reached its zenith during the Renaissance and Enlightenment eras was the progressive and deadly spread of communicable diseases around the globe. The concept of quarantine—shutting the gates of a town or port to all foreign persons and cargo, and forbidding all residents to leave, in order to stem the tide of an epidemic—was a response to the outbreak of bubonic plague, known as the black death, which killed a fourth of Europe's population in the fourteenth century. In the American experience, one of the most infamous examples of the way germs can travel was the ravaging of Indian populations by the many infections that arrived with explorers from the Old World.

3 In its relatively brief history, the United States has episodically experienced deadly epidemics that sometimes originated from within its borders (diphtheria, measles, typhus fever, poliomyelitis, smallpox) and sometimes came from without (cholera, plague, yellow fever). But regardless of the germ's origin, or even of the scientific understanding of disease transmission, a consistent scapegoat for public health crises in American history has been the newly arrived immigrant. Early nineteenth-century Irish and

German newcomers were supplanted only a few generations later by Jews, East Europeans, Italians, Asians, and Mexicans. Manifestations of immigrant scapegoating, unhappily, have continued to the present.

4 The United States welcomed more than twenty-five million immigrants to its shores between 1880 and 1924. This great wave of American immigration remains one of the most significant pathways of population movement in world history. Not all Americans greeted the newcomers with open arms. The most frequently sounded objection to immigration during this period was an economic one—the perennial fear that immigrants would push Americans out of their jobs, drive down wages, and overuse an already strapped patchwork system of public assistance. A close second objection was tied to racist sentiment, often expressed as apprehension about untoward political beliefs (socialism or anarchism) or the presumed inability of new groups to assimilate into American society. But the most insidious objection that has appeared across our history involves the issue of safeguarding the nation's public health against infections potentially imported by immigrants.

5 Nowhere was the nexus between human migration and infectious disease more clearly drawn than at the immigration reception centers developed by the United States Public Health Service at the turn of the century. And no other American port matched the commerce or passenger flow of New York Harbor. More than 75 percent of all immigrants coming to America during this era had NEW YORK CITY stamped on their steamship tickets. Steerage ships carrying boatloads of newcomers first stopped at the Quarantine Station on Hoffman Island, just off the Narrows in Lower New York Bay, and were inspected for evidence of quarantinable diseases—plague, cholera, yellow fever, smallpox, typhus fever, and leprosy. From there, barges took the immigrants to Ellis Island.

6 The Ellis Island Immigration Center opened in 1892, the same year New York City was struck by immigrant-imported epidemics of typhus fever and cholera. Between that year and 1924, when a series of restrictive laws all but halted immigration for forty-one years, millions of immigrants were scrutinized by uniformed federal officials and physicians using measures of physical, mental, and economic health. To be sure, there were good reasons for developing a careful process of inspection. Protection against infectious disease was just one of a

number of public health, economic, and social concerns. Yet because the process was grounded on the assumption that the immigrants seeking entry were, in the words of Statue of Liberty poet Emma Lazarus, "wretched refuse," cultural insensitivities along "the Line"—the queue of immigrants at Ellis Island—were bound to occur. And occur they did, especially on those busy days when more than five thousand had to be inspected.

7 It is important to note that of the millions seeking entry each year, relatively few were actually rejected for medical reasons. In fact, if one were to compute the average number of immigrants debarred for medical conditions between 1892 and 1924, it would amount to less than one percent of all those who sought entry each year. A far more common reason for exclusion by the Ellis Island inspectors was abject poverty (officially, "Likely to Become a Public Charge"), followed by evidence that the immigrant was a criminal, a contract laborer, or a member of "the immoral classes" (that is, a prostitute).

8 As a brash graduate student, I once cited the statistics on medical rejections to the late historian and social critic Irving Howe. He brusquely waved me away—much as my Yiddish-speaking grandfather would tell me to *Gay aveck!* (Go away!) when I bothered him with an impertinent question. "It doesn't matter. It doesn't matter at all," Howe intoned, "because everyone knew someone—or someone who knew someone—who was quarantined or sent back because of a terrible disease." Of course, he was right. In the diaries and memoirs of immigrants arriving during this period, one repeatedly encounters evidence of the intense fear of the Ellis Island physicians, of the medical examination, and of the deportation that might follow. Matters between the American doctor and the immigrant patient were rarely much better once the immigrant settled into his or her new home.

9 In 1892, for example, a deadly epidemic of typhus fever erupted along New York City's Lower East Side. Almost every case was directly traced to a group of East European Jewish immigrants who had just arrived in a dilapidated steerage steamship. Many Americans were already concerned about the social repercussions of the hundreds of thousands of impoverished Jews fleeing czarist persecutions that year, and the typhus epidemic did nothing to allay their qualms. The epidemiological convenience of the situation is hard to deny: one dreaded infectious disease, one social scapegoat, one neighborhood, even one ship that

brought the "vectors of disease" from the Old World to the New. And while no official expressions of anti-Semitism emanated from the New York City Health Department, its officials' strategies and actions differed decidedly when dealing with people within this particular circle of contagion. In quiet times, the relationship between the municipal public health doctors and the immigrant community—divided by differences in language, class, and social status—was at best ambivalent and at worst contentious and confrontational. In the event of a real public health emergency, like an epidemic, health department doctors often came down on the lives of the immigrants with resounding force. The most common tactics of the sanitary police included forcible evictions from lodging houses, beatings with billy clubs, destruction of pushcarts (the slender support system of many immigrant peddlers), burning of possessions that had been judged by the health inspectors to harbor the seeds of infectious disease, and the harshest restriction of all, quarantine on a distant island, far away from friends, family, and support.

10 In the late fall of 1891, a group of East European Jews living in a tiny shtetl in Russia's Pale of Settlement were evicted by the provincial governor. Although these people and their ancestors had lived in this hamlet for generations, they had little choice but to follow the orders of the armed soldiers who came to announce their eviction. Within a few weeks, the band of tailors, butchers, draymen, laborers, and their families arrived at Odessa on the Black Sea, but they were no more welcome there than they had been in their shtetl. After a narrow escape from czarist soldiers in Odessa and a nomadic trek through Constantinople, Marseilles, and Naples, the exiled Jews finally found passage on the Febre Line steamer *Massilia* and sailed for New York on January 2, 1892. The ship was small and easily tossed about in the rough Atlantic waters. The fastest ships of that era made the crossing in less than seven days; it took the *Massilia* twenty-eight.

11 Accommodations for immigrants on steamships like the *Massilia* can only be described as atrocious. In the words of one long-forgotten Congressional investigation of steerage conditions, conducted in 1911, they were "filthy . . . inadequate . . . almost unendurable." The *Massilia's* steerage compartments consisted of long tiers of berths on either side of the lowest deck of the ship. In the center of this cramped area were benches and tables where the immigrants took their meals, often consisting of rotten potatoes, stale black bread, decaying herring, and a

paltry ration of rancid butter. Alongside the tables were troughs filled with salt water for bathing and personal hygiene. Drinking water was doled from a bucket and often distributed by a communal cup or ladle. The steerage passengers breathed fresh air only on the rare clear days when they went up to the open deck, huddling together to protect themselves from the cold North Atlantic winter. As one U.S. Marine Hospital surgeon observed the day the ship sailed into New York Harbor, "The *Massilia* is one of the best ships afloat for the propagation of typhus fever."

12 Although all the East European Jews from the *Massilia* were examined by doctors at the New York Quarantine Station *and* at Ellis Island on January 30, 1892, not one was detained or excluded for medical reasons. After passing their medical examinations and satisfying the inquiries of immigration officers, the bedraggled immigrants were released under the bond of the United Hebrew Charities, which arranged for temporary lodging on New York's Lower East Side. Only a few weeks later, the *Massilia* Jews were identified in newspapers across the nation as the source of a severe typhus epidemic in New York.

13 Among the many families who had sailed on the *Massilia* were the Mermers: Isaac, aged forty-eight; his wife, Fayer, forty; and their five children, ranging in age from seven to seventeen. During their first two weeks in *Di Goldine Medina* (the Golden Land), the Mermers slept on the floor of a tiny room in a tenement house referred to by the New York press as the "Hotel de Russia." They shared their cramped and dirty space with twelve other immigrants. Early on the morning of February 12, Isaac awoke to the screams of Fayer, who was sweating and dazed. There was a curious purplish-red rash on her body. Fayer's cries were heard by the landlord, who called for a doctor named Leo Dann. Dr. Dann, who spoke Yiddish and lived on the Lower East Side, was a young contract physician hired by the United Hebrew Charities to look after the health of the *grine kuzines* (greenhorns). He was unsure of the exact diagnosis, but the fact that several other boarders had similar symptoms prompted him to notify the health department. A legion of black ambulances soon arrived at the tenement house, and a battery of sanitary police sprang out to search the house for the contagious. In full view of her helpless husband and terrified children, Fayer Mermer was dragged out of the Hotel de Russia kicking and screaming—partially in response to the actions of the armed sanitary police, partially out of a fever-induced delirium.

14 The organism that causes typhus, *Rickettsia prowazekii*, is carried by body lice. The fevers it produces in humans are absolutely incendiary. With a temperature as high as 105 degrees, the typhus patient can become crazed and delirious. Sir Charles Murchison, the leading medical authority on the disease in the late nineteenth century, described the "madness of typhus fever" vividly: "the patient shouts, talks incoherently, and is more or less violent; if not restrained, he will get up and walk around the room, or even throw himself from an open window." Fayer Mermer's worst fears, whether generated by the infection or by previous episodes of persecution, were soon realized. She died six days later, becoming the first victim of the 1892 epidemic. Forty-five more would succumb to typhus over the next few weeks.

15 After the initial public health roundup that morning, Isaac Mermer and his children tried to escape from the Essex Street house to avoid the public health doctors. They were quickly apprehended by the sanitary police and quarantined on North Brother Island in the East River, best known as the long-term home of "Typhoid Mary" Mallon. Even by the standards of 1892, the quarantine island was desolate, inadequate, and, in times of epidemics, dangerously overcrowded. All the surviving Mermers recovered from typhus that winter and were returned to the Lower East Side by late April. But from a public health perspective there is something troubling about their case histories. Isaac and his children *did* develop typhus during their stay on North Brother Island. If the Mermers contracted the disease *before* their arrest and quarantine, their potential flight from the Lower East Side could have carried the infection to other parts of the city.

16 Throughout the epidemic, the health department tacitly assumed that typhus fever had been directly imported from Europe to New york by the *Massilia* Jews, even though outbreaks of typhus were frequent in New York City during the late nineteenth century. Dr. Cyrus Edson, the health department's sanitary inspector who organized the quarantine efforts, may have acted toward the immigrants with what one historian has called a "mixture of sympathy and contempt," but his disease-control methods were effective. By the end of April 1892, all those with typhus had been isolated, and no new cases developed. The epidemic was extinguished in a matter of eight weeks. A glowing tribute to Edson in the *New York Times* congratulated him for "averting a pestilence." More specific was the *New York Tribune's* conclusion that "the isolation of all Jewish suspects and their stringent quarantine . . . was responsible

for the success." In February 1893 city health officials were honored at a testimonial dinner and reception for four hundred people, in recognition of their "brilliant service." Fewer than seventy-five blocks from this feast at Jaeger's Hall on Madison Avenue, Isaac Mermer ate bread and herring with his five children in the tiny flat they now rented on the Lower East Side. The Mermers' views on the practice of public health in New York City would have differed markedly from those of the celebrants who gathered to toast Dr. Edson and his colleagues.

17 Edson, an able writer and frequent contributor to popular magazines and newspapers, informed the citizens of New York that the typhus epidemic and similar public health crises were largely due to the devious and dangerous behaviors of newly arrived East European Jewish and Italian immigrants who "hide in closets, burrow in cellars, run away, do anything to avoid the visit of a physician and lie with the most magnificent elaboration." Many Americans might have agreed with Edson's theory of disease causation, but to an immigrant like Isaac Mermer, who had watched his wife being dragged off to the quarantine island and was doubtless fearful for his own life, fleeing or hiding from the health department made good sense.

18 Even if one agrees with Isaac's motivations for flight, however, the possibility that he was incubating a case of typhus fever and was temporarily successful at eluding the health department doctors may have contributed to the further spread of a serious infectious disease. And Isaac and his children were not alone in hiding from city health officials that winter. The roundup of Jewish "typhus suspects" cost the City of New York weeks of effort and thousands of dollars. The more infected people who fled, of course, the greater the number of new cases. Here is a clear historical example in which hostile attitudes and policies directed at immigrants and enacted by a municipal health department potentially detracted from, rather than protected, the public health. To be sure, the typhus epidemic would have been much more severe if the health department had made no effort at quarantine. On the other hand, there might well have been fewer new cases of typhus after the health department's initial discovery if its methods had not been so intimidating that many immigrants were frightened into noncompliance. Assessing blame may be a common human foible, but when it informs public health policies perceived by those targeted to be punitive or dangerous, that policy is at great risk of failing to protect the health of a community.

19 The Mermers' story is just one of millions that form the intricate mosaic of the American immigration experience, but it puts a human face on some of the problems that may arise when issues of immigration and infectious disease collide. With the passage of the Immigration Act of 1965 and its progeny of laws throughout the 1980s, we have opened our gates to new immigrants from Asia, Africa, Europe, South America, and the Caribbean. Diminishing economic resources and illegal immigration, especially in the "border states" of California, Florida, and Texas, have become concerns that press on our nation's immigration policies. Today, more than a century after the Mermers' ordeal, we also find a return to the perception of immigrants as dangerous vectors of disease, and to social policies that seem focused more on immigrant scapegoating than on sound protection of public health.

20 For example, recently proposed legislation, such as the California Illegal Alien Statute of 1994 (better known as Proposition 187) and the since-revised "Welfare Reform" Act of the 1996 Congress, specifically excluded aliens, both illegal and legal, from most non-emergency medical services. California's statute, which is still being contested in the federal court system, is especially punitive, in that it mandates that all health-care providers report to the authorities for deportation any patient they suspect to be an illegal immigrant. Such a law drives a potentially lethal wedge into the confidential relationship between physician and patient that has been deemed essential since the age of Hippocrates.

21 Now, imagine the potential plight of an illegal immigrant worker in southern California in the late twentieth century. Lured across the Mexican border by significantly higher wages and unscrupulous Americans who knowingly break the law to hire him or her, the illegal immigrant is likely to live in squalid and often unhealthy conditions. Suppose, now, that this same immigrant contracts tuberculosis.

22 The "white plague," incidentally, does not always come to our nation in the bodies of immigrants; there is already plenty of TB in the United States. Tuberculosis is an airborne infection that is spread by an ill person coughing infectious material, the tubercle becilli, into the air. The microbes are then inhaled by a susceptible person. Repeated and extended exposure to someone with tuberculosis spreads the disease. The illegal immigrant, coughing but not obviously ill, does not seek medical attention, knowing that he or she may be refused treatment or

even deported. A number of recent studies of immigrant health behaviors have documented that many legal and illegal immigrants are avoiding health care providers in California because they are afraid of stigmatization, of legal repercussions, of having their children pulled out of school, and of inadequate or harmful medical care. With the growing impression among many immigrants that more punitive regulations are to come, this avoidance behavior is all too likely to spread to the other border states. Thus the illegal immigrant continues his undocumented existence, potentially spreading a deadly infectious disease to others, both foreign and native born.

23 This thought experiment becomes more frightening when one contemplates the appearance of far more rapid killers such as Ebola virus or bubonic plague, both distinct possibilities in a world shrunken by rapid international travel and burgeoning human migration; or the rise of drug-resistant strains of common infectious diseases we once tamed with an arsenal of antibiotics and vaccines. The critical question, again, is whether punitive public health measures that block access to medical care for immigrants can be expected to protect, or to worsen, the state of the nation's public health.

24 One can discern a great deal about late-nineteenth-century American society by the way it treated the immigrants it both sheltered and shunned. No matter how objective and scientific the immigration officials and public health doctors believed their procedures to be, their ideas and theories were forced through an intellectual strainer that assumed a superiority over the immigrants they were charged with inspecting. The mistakes of our predecessors are, of course, much clearer to us than our own can be. And although each time a new epidemic erupts, a different play with different scenes and actors emerges, we can find the past dramas of epidemics and scapegoating culturally embedded in our contemporary responses to these dilemmas. This is not to say that we can reduce all of society's complex problems to Shakespeare's pithy axiom "what's past is prologue." Yet there are powerful lessons to be learned from the past as we struggle with the present. We need to pay close attention to stories like that of the Mermers as we work to develop contemporary immigration and public health policies based on reason and sound data, rather than on such knee-jerk responses as antiimmigrant scapegoating or, for that matter, blind humanitarian support for wide-open immigration.

25 The pathogenic microbe as an agent of illness and death is the ultimate social leveler. It binds all humans who are susceptible to the germ, and, when transmitted through a filter of fear, has the power to divide. The combination of germs and immigrants in American history has commonly resulted in the mounting of a quarantine effort by those charged with protecting the public health. We have, let us hope, learned from these episodes that adequate medical care and facilities—as well as attention to individual rights, economic and recreational needs, cultural and religious differences, and the emotional difficulties that patients may experience in isolation—are elements as essential as the hue and cry for the roundup of victims. These human considerations, unfortunately, can reduce but never cure the many problems arising from the experience of quarantine. Yet they remain important considerations. For those stricken with infectious disease, the burden of illness is wearing enough without added layers of social separation. As we confront new situations in which human migration intertwines with infectious disease, we will do well to learn from both the successes and the failures of the past. How we attempt to handle future conflicts will be as much a measure of our society's perceptions of illness, human rights, and the dignity of the individual as a measure of our medical, scientific, and administrative expertise.

FOR THINKING, DISCUSSING, AND WRITING

1. What are some examples of epidemics caused by migration? What, according to Markel, is "a common symptom of the quarantine mentality"? What exactly is a "quarantine"? When did the practice of "quarantine" originate?
2. Markel begins his essay with the statement, "History teaches us that society has no shortage of means available to dehumanize 'undesirable' groups." Is this a fair statement? Do you agree that social attitudes sometimes influence public health policies? Why or why not? What recent examples can you cite?
3. Markel says that "the critical question, again, is whether punitive public health measures that block access to medical care for immigrants can be expected to protect, or to worsen, the state of the nation's public health." How does Markel answer the question? How would you?
4. Write an argumentative paper in which you support either side of the question of whether undocumented immigrants should be entitled to public health care. Be sure to use Markel's essay to help develop your argument.

MEET JOE BLOG

*Lev Grossman (1969–) grew up in Lexington, Massachusetts, a suburb of Boston, graduated from Harvard College, and took graduate courses in comparative literature at Yale. The author of two novels—*Warp *(1997) and* Codex *(2004)—Grossman worked for numerous dot-coms and wrote freelance pieces on technology and culture. He now works for* Time *as a book critic and, as lead technology writer, covers the consumer electronics industry. He has interviewed luminaries such as Bill Gates, Steve Jobs, Tom Clancy, Salman Rushdie, Al Franken, and Johnny Cash. This piece appeared in the October 28, 2005, issue of* Time.

1 A few years ago, Mathew Gross, 32, was a freelance writer living in tiny Moab, Utah. Rob Malda, 28, was an underperforming undergraduate at a small Christian college in Michigan. Denis Dutton, 60, was a professor of philosophy in faraway Christchurch, New Zealand. Today they are some of the most influential media personalities in the world. You can be one too.

2 Gross, Malda and Dutton aren't rich or famous or even conspicuously good-looking. What they have in common is that they all edit blogs: amateur websites that provide news, information and, above all, opinions to rapidly growing and devoted audiences drawn by nothing more than a shared interest or two and the sheer magnetism of the editor's personality. Over the past five years, blogs have gone from an obscure and, frankly, somewhat nerdy fad to a genuine alternative to mainstream news outlets, a shadow media empire that is rivaling networks and newspapers in power and influence. Which raises the question: Who are these folks anyway? And what exactly are they doing to the established pantheon of American media?

3 Not that long ago, blogs were one of those annoying buzz words that you could safely get away with ignoring. The word blog—it works as both noun and verb—is short for Web log. It was coined in 1997 to describe a website where you could post daily scribblings, journal-style, about whatever you like—mostly critiquing and linking to other articles online that may have sparked your thinking. Unlike a big media outlet, bloggers focus their efforts on narrow topics, often rising to become de facto watchdogs and self-proclaimed experts. Blogs can be about anything: politics, sex, baseball, haiku, car repair. There are blogs about blogs.

4 Big whoop, right? But it turns out some people actually have interesting thoughts on a regular basis, and a few of the better blogs began drawing sizable audiences. Blogs multiplied and evolved, slowly becoming conduits for legitimate news and serious thought. In 1999 a few companies began offering free make-your-own-blog software, which turbocharged the phenomenon. By 2002, Pyra Labs, which makes software for creating blogs, claimed 970,000 users.

5 Most of America couldn't have cared less. Until December 2002, that is, when bloggers staged a dramatic show of force. The occasion was Strom Thurmond's 100th birthday party, during which Trent Lott made what sounded like a nostalgic reference to Thurmond's past segregationist leanings. The mainstream press largely glossed over the incident, but when regular journalists bury the lead, bloggers dig it right back up. "That story got ignored for three, four, five days by big papers and the TV networks while blogs kept it alive," says Joshua Micah Marshall, creator of talkingpointsmemo.com, one of a handful of blogs that stuck with the Lott story.

6 Mainstream America wasn't listening, but Washington insiders and media honchos read blogs. Three days after the party, the story was on Meet the Press. Four days afterward, Lott made an official apology. After two weeks, Lott was out as Senate majority leader, and blogs had drawn their first blood. Web journalists like Matt Drudge (drudgereport.com) had already demonstrated a certain crude effectiveness—witness l'affaire Lewinsky—but this was something different: bloggers were offering reasoned, forceful arguments that carried weight with the powers that be.

7 Blogs act like a lens, focusing attention on an issue until it catches fire, but they can also break stories. On April 21, a 34-year-old blogger and writer from Arizona named Russ Kick posted photographs of coffins containing the bodies of soldiers killed in Iraq and Afghanistan and of Columbia astronauts. The military zealously guards images of service members in coffins, but Kick pried the photos free with a Freedom of Information Act (FOIA) request. "I read the news constantly," says Kick, "and when I see a story about the government refusing to release public documents, I automatically file an FOIA request for them." By April 23 the images had gone from Kick's blog, thememoryhole.org, to the front page of newspapers across the country. Kick was soon getting upwards of 4 million hits a day.

8 What makes blogs so effective? They're free. They catch people at work, at their desks, when they're alert and thinking and making decisions. Blogs are fresh and often seem to be miles ahead of the mainstream news. Bloggers put up new stuff every day, all day, and there are thousands of them. How are you going to keep anything secret from a thousand Russ Kicks? Blogs have voice and personality. They're human. They come to us not from some mediagenic anchorbot on an air-conditioned sound stage, but from an individual. They represent—no, they are—the voice of the little guy.

9 And the little guy is a lot smarter than big media might have you think. Blogs showcase some of the smartest, sharpest writing being published. Bloggers are unconstrained by such journalistic conventions as good taste, accountability and objectivity—and that can be a good thing. Accusations of media bias are thick on the ground these days, and Americans are tired of it. Blogs don't pretend to be neutral: they're gleefully, unabashedly biased, and that makes them a lot more fun. "Because we're not trying to sell magazines or papers, we can afford to assail our readers," says Andrew Sullivan, a contributor to *Time* and the editor of andrewsullivan.com. "I don't have the pressure of an advertising executive telling me to lay off. It's incredibly liberating."

10 Some bloggers earn their bias the hard way—in the trenches. Military bloggers, or milbloggers in Net patois, post vivid accounts of their tours of Baghdad, in prose covered in fresh flop sweat and powder burns, illustrated with digital photos. "Jason," a National Guardsman whose blog is called justanothersoldier.com, wrote about wandering through one of Saddam Hussein's empty palaces. And Iraqis have blogs: a Baghdad blogger who goes by Salam Pax (dear_raed.blogspot.com) has parlayed his blog into a book and a movie deal. Vietnam was the first war to be televised; blogs bring Iraq another scary step closer to our living rooms.

11 But blogs are about much more than war and politics. In 1997 Malda went looking for a "site that mixed the latest word about a new sci-fi movie with news about open-source software. I was looking for a site that didn't exist," Malda says, "so I built it." Malda and a handful of coeditors run *slashdot.org* full time, and he estimates that 300,000 to 500,000 people read the site daily. Six years ago, a philosophy professor in New Zealand named Denis Dutton started the blog Arts & Letters Daily, artsandlettersdaily.com, to create a website "where people could

go daily for a dose of intellectual stimulation." Now the site draws more than 100,000 readers a month. Compare that with, say, the *New York Times Review of Books,* which has a circulation of 115,000. The tail is beginning to wag the blog.

12 Blogs are inverting the cozy media hierarchies of yore. Some bloggers are getting press credentials for this summer's Republican Convention. Three years ago, a 25-year-old Chicagoan named Jessa Crispin started a blog for serious readers called bookslut.com. "We give books a better chance," she says. "The New York Times Book Review is so boring. We take each book at face value. There's no politics behind it." Crispin's apartment is overflowing with free books from publishers desperate for a mention. As for the Times, it's scrutinizing the blogging phenomenon for its own purposes. In January the Gray Lady started up Times on the Trail, a campaign-news website with some decidedly bloglike features; it takes the bold step of linking to articles by competing newspapers, for example. "The Times cannot ignore this. I don't think any big media can ignore this," says Len Apcar, editor in chief of the New York Times on the Web.

13 In a way, blogs represent everything the Web was always supposed to be: a mass medium controlled by the masses, in which getting heard depends solely on having something to say and the moxie to say it.

14 Unfortunately, there's a downside to this populist sentiment—that is, innocent casualties bloodied by a medium that trades in rumor, gossip and speculation without accountability. Case in point: Alexandra Polier, better known as the Kerry intern. Rumors of Polier's alleged affair with presidential candidate Senator John Kerry eventually spilled into the blogosphere earlier this year. After Drudge headlined it in February, the blabbing bloggers soon had the attention of tabloid journalists, radio talk-show hosts and cable news anchors. Trouble is, the case was exceedingly thin, and both Kerry and Polier vehemently deny it. Yet the Internet smolders with it to this day.

15 Some wonder if the backbiting tide won't recede as blogs grow up. The trend now is for more prominent sites to be commercialized. A Manhattan entrepreneur named Nick Denton runs a small stable of bloggers as a business by selling advertising on their sites. So far they aren't showing detectible signs of editorial corruption by their corporate masters—two of Denton's blogs, gawker.com and wonkette.com, are among the most corrosively witty sites on the Web—but they've lost their amateur status forever.

16 We may be in the golden age of blogging, a quirky Camelot moment in Internet history when some guy in his underwear with too much free time can take down a Washington politician. It will be interesting to see what role blogs play in the upcoming election. Blogs can be a great way of communicating, but they can keep people apart too. If I read only those of my choice, precisely tuned to my political biases and you read only yours, we could end up a nation of political solipsists, vacuum sealed in our private feedback loops, never exposed to new arguments, never having to listen to a single word we disagree with.

17 Howard Dean's campaign blog, run by Mathew Gross, may be the perfect example of both the potential and the pitfalls of high-profile blogging. At its peak, blogforamerica.com drew 100,000 visitors a day, yet the candidate was beaten badly in the primaries. Still, the Dean model isn't going away. When another political blogger, who goes by the nom de blog Atrios, set up a fund-raising link on his site for Kerry, he raised $25,000 in five days.

18 You can't blog your way into the White House, at least not yet, but blogs are America thinking out loud, talking to itself, and heaven help the candidate who isn't listening.

FOR THINKING, DISCUSSING, AND WRITING

1. What does the title of this piece tell you about Grossman's intended audience? What other elements in the selection tell you that "Meet Joe Blog" is written for the audience of a popular magazine? (Look especially at the vocabulary and sentence structure.)
2. What in fact are blogs, and how was the word *blog* created? Why, according to Grossman, are blogs so effective? In what ways do they fulfill the promise of computer technology and Web potential? What examples does the writer provide to show the power and impact of blogs and bloggers?
3. The essay contains references to key people and events in recent politics, such as Saddam Hussein, John Kerry, Howard Dean, and Monica Lewinsky. Identify some of these references. In what ways did bloggers influence the conversation surrounding these figures?
4. Visit one of the blogs identified here, or any other blog of your choice, and write an essay about how effective the site is as a form of interactive conversation that attempts to influence thinking on key events. Support your argument with direct references to material on the blogs themselves.

ALEXANDER PETRUNKEVITCH

The Spider and the Wasp

Born in Russia, Alexander Petrunkevitch (1878–1964) taught zoology at Yale University. His major works focus on spiders, which held endless fascination for him: Catalog of Spiders of North, Central, and South America *(1911) and* An Inquiry into the Natural Classification of Spiders *(1936) are definitive works on the subject. He also wrote about philosophy and history and contributed to popular magazines of the day. The now classic piece "The Spider and the Wasp" first appeared in* Scientific American *in 1952. In this essay, Petrunkevitch describes a peculiar phenomenon in nature in which an insect who can easily defend itself against an attacker instead cooperates inadvertently in its own demise.*

1 In the feeding and safeguarding of their progeny, insects and spiders exhibit some interesting analogies to reasoning and some crass examples of blind instinct. The case I propose to describe here is that of the tarantula spiders and their archenemy, the digger wasps of the genus *Pepsis.* It is a classic example of what looks like intelligence pitted against instinct—a strange situation in which the victim, though fully able to defend itself, submits unwittingly to its destruction.

2 Most tarantulas live in the tropics, but several species occur in the temperate zone and a few are common in the southern U.S. Some varieties are large and have powerful fangs with which they can inflict a deep wound. These formidable-looking spiders do not, however, attack man; you can hold one in your hand, if you are gentle, without being bitten. Their bite is dangerous only to insects and small mammals such as mice; for man it is no worse than a hornet's sting.

3 Tarantulas customarily live in deep cylindrical burrows, from which they emerge at dusk and into which they retire at dawn. Mature males wander about after dark in search of females and occasionally stray into houses. After mating, the male dies in a few weeks, but a female lives much longer and can mate several years in succession. In a Paris museum is a tropical specimen which is said to have been living in captivity for 25 years.

4 A fertilized female tarantula lays from 200 to 400 eggs at a time; thus it is possible for a single tarantula to produce several thousand young. She takes no care of them beyond weaving a cocoon of silk to enclose the eggs. After they hatch, the young walk away, find convenient places in which to dig their burrows and spend the rest of their

lives in solitude. The eyesight of tarantulas is poor, being limited to a sensing of change in the intensity of light and to the perception of moving objects. They apparently have little or no sense of hearing, for a hungry tarantula will pay no attention to a loudly chirping cricket placed in its cage unless the insect happens to touch one of its legs.

5 But all spiders, and especially hairy ones, have an extremely delicate sense of touch. Laboratory experiments prove that tarantulas can distinguish three types of touch: pressure against the body wall, stroking of the body hair, and riffling of certain very fine hairs on legs called trichobothria. Pressure against the body, by the finger or the end of a pencil, causes the tarantula to move off slowly for a short distance. The touch excites no defensive response unless the approach is from above where the spider can see the motion, in which case it rises on its hind legs, lifts its front legs, opens its fangs and holds this threatening posture as long as the object continues to move.

6 The entire body of a tarantula, especially its legs, is thickly clothed with hair. Some of it is short and wooly, some long and stiff. Touching this body hair produces one of two distinct reactions. When the spider is hungry, it responds with an immediate and swift attack. At the touch of a cricket's antennae the tarantula seizes the insect so swiftly that a motion picture taken at the rate of 64 frames per second shows only the result and not the process of capture. But when the spider is not hungry, the stimulation of its hairs merely causes it to shake the touched limb. An insect can walk under its hairy belly unharmed.

7 The trichobothria, very fine hairs growing from disklike membranes on the legs, are sensitive only to air movement. A light breeze makes them vibrate slowly, without disturbing the common hair. When one blows gently on the trichobothria, the tarantula reacts with a quick jerk of its four front legs. If the front and hind legs are stimulated at the same time, the spider makes a sudden jump. This reaction is quite independent of the state of its appetite.

8 These three tactile responses—to pressure on the body wall, to moving of the common hair, and to flexing of the trichobothria—are so different from one another that there is no possibility of confusing them. They serve the tarantula adequately for most of its needs and enable it to avoid most annoyances and dangers. But they fail the spider completely when it meets its deadly enemy, the digger wasp *Pepsis*.

9 These solitary wasps are beautiful and formidable creatures. Most species are either a deep shiny blue all over, or deep blue with rusty

wings. The largest have a wingspan of about 4 inches. They live on nectar. When excited, they give off a pungent odor—a warning that they are ready to attack. The sting is much worse than that of a bee or common wasp, and the pain and swelling last longer. In the adult stage the wasp lives only a few months. The female produces but a few eggs, one at a time at intervals of two or three days. For each egg the mother must provide one adult tarantula, alive but paralyzed. The mother wasp attaches the egg to the paralyzed spider's abdomen. Upon hatching from the egg, the larva is many hundreds of times smaller than its living but helpless victim. It eats no other food and drinks no water. By the time it has finished its single Gargantuan meal and become ready for wasphood, nothing remains of the tarantula but its indigestible chitinous skeleton.

10 The mother wasp goes tarantula-hunting when the egg in her ovary is almost ready to be laid. Flying low over the ground late on a sunny afternoon, the wasp looks for its victim or for the mouth of a tarantula burrow, a round hole edged by a bit of silk. The sex of the spider makes no difference, but the mother is highly discriminating as to species. Each species of *Pepsis* requires a certain species of tarantula, and the wasp will not attack the wrong species. In a cage with a tarantula which is not its normal prey, the wasp avoids the spider and is usually killed by it in the night.

11 Yet when a wasp finds the correct species, it is the other way about. To identify the species the wasp apparently must explore the spider with her antennae. The tarantula shows an amazing tolerance to this exploration. The wasp crawls under it and walks over it without evoking any hostile response. The molestation is so great and so persistent that the tarantula often rises on all eight legs, as if it were on stilts. It may stand this way for several minutes. Meanwhile the wasp, having satisfied itself that the victim is of the right species, moves off a few inches to dig the spider's grave. Working vigorously with legs and jaws, it excavates a hole 8 to 10 inches deep with a diameter slightly larger than the spider's girth. Now and again the wasp pops out of the hole to make sure that the spider is still there.

12 When the grave is finished, the wasp returns to the tarantula to complete her ghastly enterprise. First she feels it all over once more with her antennae. Then her behavior becomes more aggressive. She bends her abdomen, protruding her sting, and searches for the soft membrane at the point where the spider's legs join its body—the only spot where she can penetrate the horny skeleton. From time to time, as the exasperated

spider slowly shifts ground, the wasp turns on her back and slides along with the aid of her wings, trying to get under the tarantula for a shot at the vital spot. During all this maneuvering, which can last for several minutes, the tarantula makes no move to save itself. Finally the wasp corners it against some obstruction and grasps one of its legs in her powerful jaws. Now at last the harassed spider tries a desperate but vain defense. The two contestants roll over and over on the ground. It is a terrifying sight and the outcome is always the same. The wasp finally manages to thrust her sting into the soft spot and holds it there for a few seconds while she pumps in the poison. Almost immediately the tarantula falls paralyzed on its back. Its legs stop twitching; its heart stops beating. Yet it is not dead, as is shown by the fact that if taken from the wasp it can be restored to some sensitivity by being kept in a moist chamber for several months.

13 After paralyzing the tarantula, the wasp cleans herself by dragging her body along the ground and rubbing her feet, sucks a drop of blood oozing from the wound in the spider's abdomen, then grabs a leg of the flabby, helpless animal in her jaws and drags it down to the bottom of the grave. She stays there for many minutes, sometimes for several hours, and what she does all that time in the dark we do not know. Eventually she lays her egg and attaches it to the side of the spider's abdomen with a sticky secretion. Then she emerges, fills the grave with soil carried bit by bit in her jaws, and finally tramples the ground all around to hide any trace of the grave from prowlers. Then she flies away, leaving her descendant safely started in life.

14 In all this the behavior of the wasp evidently is qualitatively different from that of the spider. The wasp acts like an intelligent animal. This is not to say that instinct plays no part or that she reasons as man does. But her actions are to the point; they are not automatic and can be modified to fit the situation. We do not know for certain how she identifies the tarantula—probably it is by some olfactory or chemo-tactile sense—but she does it purposefully and does not blindly tackle a wrong species.

15 On the other hand, the tarantula's behavior shows only confusion. Evidently the wasp's pawing gives it no pleasure, for it tries to move away. That the wasp is not simulating sexual stimulation is certain because male and female tarantulas react in the same way to its advances. That the spider is not anesthetized by some odorless secretion is easily shown by blowing lightly at the tarantula and making it jump suddenly. What, then, makes the tarantula behave as stupidly as it does?

16 No clear, simple answer is available. Possibly the stimulation by the wasp's antennae is masked by a heavier pressure on the spider's

body, so that it reacts as when prodded by a pencil. But their explanation may be much more complex. Initiative in attack is not in the nature of tarantulas; most species fight only when cornered so that escape is impossible. Their inherited patterns of behavior apparently prompt them to avoid problems rather than attack them. For example, spiders always weave their webs in three dimensions, and when a spider finds that there is insufficient space to attach certain threads in the third dimension, it leaves the place and seeks another, instead of finishing the web in a single plane. This urge to escape seems to arise under all circumstances, in all phases of life, and to take the place of reasoning. For a spider to change the pattern of its web is as impossible as for an inexperienced man to build a bridge across a chasm obstructing his way.

17 In a way the instinctive urge to escape is not only easier but often more efficient than reasoning. The tarantula does exactly what is most efficient in all cases except in an encounter with a ruthless and determined attacker dependent for the existence of her own species on killing as many tarantulas as she can lay eggs. Perhaps in this case the spider follows its usual pattern of trying to escape, instead of seizing and killing the wasp, because it is not aware of its danger. In any case, the survival of the tarantula species as a whole is protected by the fact that the spider is much more fertile than the wasp.

FOR THINKING, DISCUSSING, AND WRITING

1. Petrunkevitch has taken a topic that many would find unappealing and has turned it into a vivid adventure. How has he achieved the highly visual qualities of the piece? How does his choice of language affect the essay and your response to it?
2. What is the purpose of the background information Petrunkevitch provides in eight paragraphs on the tarntula—its various species, its dwelling place, its mating pattern, and so on? Note that except for its activity related to the tarantula, the wasp does not get so comprehensive a treatment. How do you account for the differences?
3. How does the writer ultimately account for the strange actions of the tarantula?
4. Petrunkevitch suggests that the behavior of the two insects may be analogous to reasoning versus blind instinct. Write an essay in which you distinguish between these two habits of behavior and explain how they operate in humans or other animals. Does intelligence always win out? Why or why not?

Humanities and Science

Lewis Thomas (1913–1993) was a physician who spent most of his career at the Sloan Kettering Cancer Center in New York City. He wrote extensively about science for the general public and in 1974 won the National Book Award for The Lives of a Cell: Notes of a Biology Watcher. *His other works include* More Notes of a Biology Watcher *(1979),* Late Night Thoughts on Listening to Mahler's Ninth *(1984), and* The Fragile Species *(1992). In this essay he considers the worlds of science and the humanities as modes of thought and finds many disappointments in our approach to science teaching.*

1 Lord Kelvin was one of the great British physicists of the late nineteenth century, an extraordinarily influential figure in his time, and in some ways a paradigm of conventional, established scientific leadership. He did a lot of good and useful things, but once or twice he, like Homer, nodded. The instances are worth recalling today, for we have nodders among our scientific eminences still, from time to time, needing to have their elbows shaken.

2 On one occasion, Kelvin made a speech on the overarching importance of numbers. He maintained that no observation of nature was worth paying serious attention to unless it could be stated in precisely quantitative terms. The numbers were the final and only test, not only of truth but about meaning as well. He said, "When you can measure what you are speaking about, and express it in numbers, you know something about it. But when you cannot—your knowledge is of a meagre and unsatisfactory kind."

3 But, as at least one subsequent event showed, Kelvin may have had things exactly the wrong way round. The task of converting observations into numbers is the hardest of all, the last task rather than the first thing to be done, and it can be done only when you have learned, beforehand, a very great deal about the observations themselves. You can, to be sure, achieve a very deep understanding of nature by quantitative measurement, but you must know what you are talking about before you can begin applying the numbers for making predictions. In Kelvin's case, the problem at hand was the age of the earth and solar system. Using what was then known about the sources of energy and the loss of energy from the physics of that day, he calculated that neither the earth nor the

sun were older than several hundred million years. This caused a considerable stir in biological and geological circles, especially among the evolutionists. Darwin himself was distressed by the numbers; the time was much too short for the theory of evolution. Kelvin's figures were described by Darwin as one of his "sorest troubles."

4 T.H. Huxley had long been aware of the risks involved in premature extrapolations from mathematical treatment of biological problems. He said, in an 1869 speech to the Geological Society concerning numbers, "This seems to be one of the many cases in which the admitted accuracy of mathematical processes is allowed to throw a wholly inadmissible appearance of authority over the results obtained by them. . . . As the grandest mill in the world will not extract wheat flour from peascods, so pages of formulas will not get a definite result out of loose data."

5 The trouble was that the world of physics had not moved fast enough to allow for Kelvin's assumptions. Nuclear fusion and fission had not yet been dreamed of, and the true age of the earth could not even be guessed from the data in hand. It was not yet the time for mathematics in this subject.

6 There have been other examples, since those days, of the folly of using numbers and calculations uncritically. Kelvin's own strong conviction that science could not be genuine science without measuring things was catching. People in other fields of endeavor, hankering to turn their disciplines into exact sciences, beset by what has since been called "physics envy," set about converting whatever they knew into numbers and thence into equations with predictive pretensions. We have it with us still, in economics, sociology, psychology, history, even, I fear, in English-literature criticism and linguistics, and it frequently works, when it works at all, with indifferent success. The risks of untoward social consequences in work of this kind are considerable. It is as important—and as hard—to learn *when* to use mathematics as *how* to use it, and this matter should remain high on the agenda of consideration for education in the social and behavioral sciences.

7 Of course, Kelvin's difficulty with the age of the earth was an exceptional, almost isolated instance of failure in quantitative measurement in the nineteenth-century physics. The instruments devised for approaching nature by way of physics became increasingly precise and powerful, carrying the field through electromagnetic theory, triumph after triumph, and setting the stage for the great revolution of twentieth-century physics. There is no doubt about it: measurement works when the

instruments work, and when you have a fairly clear idea of what it is that is being measured, and when you know what to do with the numbers when they tumble out. The system for gaining information and comprehension about nature works so well, indeed, that it carries another hazard: the risk of convincing yourself that you know everything.

8 Kelvin himself fell into this trap toward the end of the century. (I don't mean to keep picking on Kelvin, who was a very great scientist; it is just that he happened to say a couple of things I find useful for this discussion.) He stated, in a summary of the achievements of nineteenth-century physics, that it was an almost completed science; virtually everything that needed knowing about the material universe had been learned; there were still a few anomalies and inconsistencies in electromagnetic theory, a few loose ends to be tied up, but this would be done within the next several years. Physics, in these terms, was not a field any longer likely to attract, as it previously had, the brightest and most imaginative young brains. The most interesting part of the work had already been done. Then, within the next decade, came radiation, Planck, the quantum, Einstein, Rutherford, Bohr, and all the rest—quantum mechanics—and the whole field turned over and became a brand-new sort of human endeavor, still now, in the view of many physicists, almost a full century later, a field only at its beginnings.

9 But even today, despite the amazements that are turning up in physics each year, despite the jumps taken from the smallest parts of nature—particle physics—to the largest of all—the cosmos itself—the impression of science that the public gains is rather like the impression left in the nineteenth-century public mind by Kelvin. Science, in this view, is first of all a matter of simply getting all the numbers together. The numbers are sitting out there in nature, waiting to be found, sorted and totted up. If only they had enough robots and enough computers, the scientists could go off to the beach and wait for their papers to be written for them. Second of all, what we know about nature today is pretty much the whole story: we are very nearly home and dry. From here on, it is largely a problem of tying up loose ends, tidying nature up, getting the files in order. The only real surprise for the future—and it is about those that the public is becoming more concerned and apprehensive—are the technological applications that the scientists may be cooking up from today's knowledge.

10 I suggest that the scientific community is to blame. If there are disagreements between the world of the humanities and the scientific enterprise as to the place and importance of science in a liberal-arts education, the role of science in twentieth-century culture, I believe

that the scientists are themselves responsible for a general misunderstanding of what they are really up to.

11 Over the past half century, we have been teaching the sciences as though they were the same academic collection of cut-and-dried subjects as always, and—here is what has really gone wrong—as though they would always be the same. The teaching of today's biology, for example, is pretty much the same kind of exercise as the teaching of Latin was when I was in high school long ago. First of all, the fundamentals, the underlying laws, the essential grammar, and then the reading of texts. Once mastered, that is that: Latin is Latin and forever after will be Latin. And biology is precisely biology, a vast array of hard facts to be learned as fundamentals, followed by a reading of the texts.

12 Moreover, we have been teaching science as though its facts were somehow superior to the facts in all other scholarly disciplines, more fundamental, more solid, less subject to subjectivism, immutable. English literature is not just one way of thinking, it is all sorts of ways. Poetry is a moving target. The facts that underlie art, architecture, and music are not really hard facts, and you can change them any way you like by arguing about them, but science is treated as an altogether different kind of learning: an unambiguous, unalterable, and endlessly useful display of data needing only to be packaged and installed somewhere in one's temporal lobe in order to achieve a full understanding of the natural world.

13 And it is, of course, not like this at all. In real life, every field of science that I can think of is incomplete, and most of them—whatever the record of accomplishment over the past two hundred years—are still in the earliest stage of their starting point. In the fields I know best, among the life sciences, it is required that the most expert and sophisticated minds be capable of changing those minds, often with a great lurch, every few years. In some branches of biology the mind-changing is occurring with accelerating velocities. The next week's issue of any scientific journal can turn a whole field upside down, shaking out any number of immutable ideas and installing new bodies of dogma, and this is happening all the time. It is an almost everyday event in physics, in chemistry, in materials research, in neurobiology, in genetics, in immunology. The hard facts tend to soften overnight, melt away, and vanish under the pressure of new hard facts, and the interpretations of what appear to be the most solid aspects of nature are subject to change, now more than at any other time in history. The conclusions reached in science are always, when looked at closely, far more provisional and tentative than are most of the assumptions arrived at by our colleagues in the humanities.

14 The running battle now in progress between the sociobiologists and the antisociobiologists is a marvel for students to behold, close up. To observe, in open-mouthed astonishment, the polarized extremes, one group of highly intelligent, beautifully trained, knowledgeable, and imaginative scientists maintaining that all sorts of behavior, animal and human, are governed exclusively by genes, and another group of equally talented scientists saying precisely the opposite and asserting that all behavior is set and determined by the environment, or by culture, and both sides brawling in the pages of periodicals such as *The New York Review of Books*, is an educational experience that no college student should be allowed to miss. The essential lesson to be learned has nothing to do with the relative validity of the facts underlying the argument, it is the argument itself that is the education: we do not yet know enough to settle such questions.

15 It is true that at any given moment there is the appearance of satisfaction, even self-satisfaction, within every scientific discipline. On any Tuesday morning, if asked, a good working scientist will gladly tell you that the affairs of the field are nicely in order, that things are finally looking clear and making sense, and all is well. But come back again, on another Tuesday, and he may let you know that the roof has just fallen in on his life's work, that all the old ideas—last week's ideas in some cases—are no longer good ideas, that something strange has happened.

16 It is the very strangeness of nature that makes science engrossing. That ought to be at the center of science teaching. There are more than seven-times-seven types of ambiguity in science, awaiting analysis. The poetry of Wallace Stevens is crystal-clear alongside the genetic code.

17 I prefer to turn things around in order to make precisely the opposite case. Science, especially twentieth-century science, has provided us with a glimpse of something we never really knew before, the revelation of human ignorance. We have been used to the belief, down one century after another, that we more or less comprehend everything bar one or two mysteries like the mental processes of our gods. Every age, not just the eighteenth century, regarded itself as the Age of Reason, and we have never lacked for explanations of the world and its ways. Now, we are being brought up short, and this has been the work of science. We have a wilderness of mystery to make our way through in the centuries ahead, and we will need science for this but not science alone. Science will, in its own time, produce the data and some of the meaning in the data, but never the full meaning. For getting a full grasp, for

perceiving real significance when significance is at hand, we shall need minds at work from all sorts of brains outside the fields of science, most of all the brains of poets, of course, but also those of artists, musicians, philosophers, historians, writers in general.

18 It is primarily because of this need that I would press for changes in the way science is taught. There is a need to teach the young people who will be doing the science themselves, but this will always be a small minority among us. There is a deeper need to teach science to those who will be needed for thinking about it, and this means pretty nearly everyone else, in hopes that a few of these people—a much smaller minority than the scientific community and probably a lot harder to find—will, in the thinking, be able to imagine new levels of meaning that are likely to be lost on the rest of us.

19 In addition, it is time to develop a new group of professional thinkers, perhaps a somewhat larger group than the working scientists, who can create a discipline of scientific criticism. We have had good luck so far in the emergence of a few people ranking as philosophers of science and historians and journalists of science, and I hope more of these will be coming along, but we have not yet seen a Ruskin or a Leavis or an Edmund Wilson. Science needs critics of this sort, but the public at large needs them more urgently.

20 I suggest that the introductory courses in science, at all levels from grade school through college, be radically revised. Leave the fundamentals, the so-called basics, aside for a while, and concentrate the attention of all students on the things that are *not* known. You cannot possibly teach quantum mechanics without mathematics, to be sure, but you can describe the strangeness of the world opened up by quantum theory. Let it be known, early on, that there are deep mysteries, and profound paradoxes, revealed in their distant outlines, by the quantum. Let it be known that these can be approached more closely, and puzzled over, once the language of mathematics has been sufficiently mastered.

21 Teach at the outset, before any of the fundamentals, the still imponderable puzzles of cosmology. Let it be known, as clearly as possible, by the youngest minds, that there are some things going on in the universe that lie beyond comprehension, and make it plain how little is known.

22 Do not teach that biology is a useful and perhaps profitable science; that can come later. Teach instead that there are structures squirming inside all our cells, providing all the energy for living, that are essentially foreign creatures, brought in for symbiotic living a billion or so

years ago, the lineal descendants of bacteria. Teach that we do not have the ghost of an idea how they got there, where they came from, or how they evolved to their present structure and function. The details of oxidative phosphorylation and photosynthesis can come later.

23 Teach ecology early on. Let it be understood that the earth's life is a system of interliving, interdependent creatures, and that we do not understand at all how it works. The earth's environment, from the range of atmospheric gases to the chemical constituents of the sea, has been held in an almost unbelievably improbable state of regulated balance since life began, and the regulation of stability and balance is accomplished solely by the life itself, like the internal environment of an immense organism, and we do not know how *that* one works, even less what it means. Teach that.

24 Go easy, I suggest, on the promises sometimes freely offered by science. Technology relies and depends on science these days, more than ever before, but technology is nothing like the first justification for doing research, nor is it necessarily an essential product to be expected from science. Public decisions about what to have in the way of technology are totally different problems from decisions about science, and the two enterprises should not be tangled together. The central task of science is to arrive, stage by stage, at a clearer comprehension of nature, but this does not mean, as it is sometimes claimed to mean, a search for mastery over nature. Science may provide us, one day, with a better understanding of ourselves, but never, I hope, with a set of technologies for doing something or other to improve ourselves. I am made nervous by assertions that human consciousness will someday be unraveled by research, laid out for close scrutiny like the workings of a computer, and then, *and then!* I hope with some fervor that we can learn a lot more than we now know about the human mind, and I see no reason why this strange puzzle should remain forever and entirely beyond us. But I would be deeply disturbed by any prospect that we might use the new knowledge in order to begin doing something about it, to improve it, say. This is a different matter from searching for information to use against schizophrenia or dementia, where we are badly in need of technologies, indeed likely one day to be sunk without them. But the ordinary, everyday, more or less normal human mind is too marvelous an instrument ever to be tampered with by anyone, science or no science.

25 The education of humanists cannot be regarded as complete, or even adequate, without exposure in some depth to where things stand in the various branches of science, and particularly, as I have said, in the areas of

our ignorance. This does not mean that I know how to go about doing it, nor am I unaware of the difficulties involved. Physics professors, most of them, look with revulsion on assignments to teach their subject to poets. Biologists, caught up by the enchantment of their new power, armed with flawless instruments to tell the nucleotide sequences of the entire human genome, nearly matching the physicists in the precision of their measurements of living processes, will resist the prospect of broad survey courses; each biology professor will demand that any student in his path must master every fine detail within that professor's research program. The liberal-arts faculties, for their part, will continue to view the scientists with suspicion and apprehension. "What do the scientists want?" asked a Cambridge professor in Francis Cornford's wonderful *Microcosmographia Academica*. "Everything that's going," was the quick answer. That was back in 1912, and universities haven't much changed.

26 The worst thing that has happened to science education is that the great fun has gone out of it. A very large number of good students look at it as slogging work to be got through on the way to medical school. Others look closely at the premedical students themselves, embattled and bleeding for grades and class standing, and are turned off. Very few see science as the high adventure it really is, the wildest of all explorations ever undertaken by human beings, the chance to catch close views of things never seen before, the shrewdest maneuver for discovering how the world works. Instead, they become baffled early on, and they are misled into thinking that bafflement is simply the result of not having learned all the facts. They are not told, as they should be told, that everyone else—from the professor in his endowed chair down to the platoons of postdoctoral students in the laboratory all night—is baffled as well. Every important scientific advance that has come in looking like an answer has turned, sooner or later—usually sooner—into a question. And the game is just beginning.

27 An appreciation of what is happening in science today, and of how great a distance lies ahead for exploring, ought to be one of the rewards of a liberal-arts education. It ought to be a good in itself, not something to be acquired on the way to a professional career but part of the cast of thought needed for getting into the kind of century that is now just down the road. Part of the intellectual equipment of an educated person, however his or her time is to be spent, ought to be a feel for the queernesses of nature, the inexplicable things.

28 And maybe, just maybe, a new set of courses dealing systematically with ignorance in science might take hold. The scientists might discover in it a new and subversive technique for catching the attention

of students driven by curiosity, delighted and surprised to learn that science is exactly as Bush described it: an "endless frontier." The humanists, for their part, might take considerable satisfaction watching their scientific colleagues confess openly to not knowing everything about everything. And the poets, on whose shoulders the future rests, might, late nights, thinking things over, begin to see some meanings that elude the rest of us. It is worth a try.

FOR THINKING, WRITING, AND DISCUSSING

1. What does Thomas say are the two most serious impressions that most people hold about scientific knowledge even today? Whom does he accuse of being guilty of misleading the public about what science is and what scientists do?
2. Why does Thomas refer to a great nineteenth-century scientist at the beginning of the piece and to "poets" at the end? How do these references help frame the essay and establish the parameters of his argument?
3. How would you define "scientific truth"? "Poetic truth"? How, if at all, can these truths complement each other? Give an example.
4. Write an essay in which you argue for the importance of humanists over scientists *or* scientists over humanists. Which do you think makes the more important contribution to society? Why?

CONNECTING IDEAS: Science, Technology, and Health in a Complex World

1. In what ways do science and technology continue to hold promise for creating a better future? In what ways do they seem to impede it? Choose one side or the other of this potential argument and write an essay addressing the issue with valid supporting details. Draw on writers in this chapter whom you feel touch on the issue, one side or the other.
2. Science and technology education in America has drawn considerable criticism over the last decades. What is your view of how we do and should teach science and technology? How do your own experiences reflect your beliefs? In what ways are Lewis Thomas and David Barash dealing with scientific education? How are their arguments related, if at all?
3. Markel, Staples, Angier, and Gore sound alarms about the problems and aberrations in science, technology, and the natural world. What common elements can you identify in their arguments? Is there an alarmist cast to their positions? Or, do you think the writers have made logical points that we need to acknowledge?

CHAPTER 8

Language and Word Power

LANGUAGE DEFINES THE HUMAN SPECIES. ONLY WE humans have language at the center of our lives to communicate with each other.

For this key element in human identity, we note intense and important debate. From the earliest days of the American republic, patriots linked language and liberty, viewing speech, the oral manifestation of language, as essential to democracy's growth. But whose language are we talking about? The value of bilingual education, the use of Ebonics (Black English), the reduced formality and hyper-abbreviations of Web talk, racial and gender slurs on campus and in the workplace—across the nation controversy about the language issue rages. In Quebec, the subtle (and sometimes incendiary) battle between French and English as partners or antagonists in expression surfaces regularly, with English championed one day, French the next. In our country proposals in many states for English-only laws spawn debate and conflict. Many immigrant groups in the United States object to these laws, which, some argue, challenge a foreign culture to its core and take away the voice of a people. But others say, live here, speak our language. A Spanish version of "The Star Spangled Banner" caused quite a furor in many segments of the country a while ago. Unimaginable, the critics said: our national anthem in a foreign tongue.

Over recent years research into language use and language production has often focused on members of other species thought to display and use intelligence. Taking gorillas and chimpanzees as objects of study, some researchers have argued that nonhumans can exercise language too. By placing objects with different shapes on a magnetic board, for example, Sarah, a chimpanzee used in scientific studies, could communicate, as could Lana, another chimpanzee, by using the keyboard of a special computer. In yet another study the famous chimp Washoe learned to use American Sign Language (ASL) to communicate with hand gestures.

Yet despite what some consider powerful evidence that these animals could combine words to express wishes with an impressive syntactic sensitivity (also reported in dolphins), many psychologists and linguists challenge the assumption that nonhuman primates are actually producing language. The intricate rules of grammar seem to distinguish human language from the communicative grunts and gestures of animals. Yes, monkeys might show a rough grammar in their vocal interactions, but their "sentences" lack the spontaneity, creativity—and complexity—of human expression. Sentences from chimpanzees, research shows, are always very short. More important, perhaps, chimps do not naturally connect objects they see with words they hear in the way that, say, human toddlers can. Most researchers now believe that animal communication is much more primitive than the language of humans and that the use of language by nonhuman primates does not really reflect their intelligence and potential. So, one of the key features of the human animal, and only the human animal, is the elaborate, conceptual, inventive communication reflected through language.

Yet we cannot help asking what exactly *is* language. The research into chimpanzees and dolphins has merely exacerbated the debate. But there probably never was a time when people did not attempt to explain language. It is a gift of the supernatural, societies with a strong belief in magic assert. In the Judeo-Christian world, the idea has lingered: In the beginning was the word, the Bible teaches; the word is divine. Divine, perhaps, but not without controversy and divergent use. In the Old Testament, the building of the Tower of Babel, a marvelous structure supposedly reaching to the heavens, was suspended because of the confusion of tongues. (And hence the verb *to babble* was born.)

In the advancement of human thought, philosophers soon distinguished between God's word and human words, and in the early twentieth century, scholars developed the idea that our language determines our thought. The particular habits and contents of language are socially constructed, that is, built and influenced by societies and the interactions of their peoples. In short, in every intellectual arena today—neurobiology, philosophy, linguistics, cultural studies, computer science—scholars are seeking to determine the nature of language, its origins, its purposes, its effects, and its relation to other activities, from thinking and feeling to politics.

In everyday life, too, questions about language abound. Why do we as adults have more difficulty than children learning a new language? Why do we have formal languages and street languages, home languages, and languages for love? Why do we talk one way to children and another way to elders? Why do we need to be careful of what we say and how we say it? Is it true that we can suffer stones and sticks but "names will never harm"? In "Body in Trouble" Nancy Mairs explores the language we use to identify physical impairment and how it reflects our views on human disabilities.

Several of the writers in this chapter deal with the perceived differences between languages. Walter Benn Michaels questions the notion of one language's superiority to another. Richard Rodriguez shows the impact of learning English on his Spanish-speaking social environment at home and in school. Throughout, the selections will challenge your notions of language use and reaffirm its importance in our lives.

TONY EARLEY

The Quare Gene

The Samuel Milton Fleming Chair in English at Vanderbilt University, Tony Earley (1961–) grew up in Texas but considers himself a native North Carolinian. He has contributed many short stories and articles to magazines such as Harper's *and* Tri-Quarterly. *He is the author of* Here We Are in Paradise *(1994), a collection of short stories, and a novel,* Jim the Boy *(2000). Earley considers the relation between language and personal identity in this piece from the* New Yorker.

1 I do not like, I have never liked, nor do I expect to like watermelon. For the record, I consider this a private, dietary preference, not a political choice, neither a sign of failing character nor a renunciation of Southern citizenship. I simply do not like watermelon. Nor, for that matter, do I like grits, blackberries, cantaloupe, buttermilk, okra, baked sweet potatoes, rhubarb, or collard greens. Particularly collard greens. I don't even like to look at collard greens. But, because I am a Southerner—a North Carolinian, of Appalachian, Scots-Irish descent, the offspring of farming families on both sides—my family finds my refusal to like the foods they like somehow distressing. When I eat at my grandmother's red-roofed, high-ceilinged Victorian barn of a house, in Polk County, North Carolina, my relatives earnestly strive to persuade me that I am making a big mistake by not sampling this or that, that I should just *try* the greens, have just a little *slice* of watermelon, a small *bite* of cantaloupe. They tell me that I will get used to the seeds in blackberries, the meatiness of grits, the swampy odor of greens boiled too long in a big pot. And when I passionately and steadfastly refuse, as I have done for the last thirty-seven years, they stare at me for a few seconds as if they didn't know me, their mouths set sadly, before looking down at their plates as if preparing to offer up a second grace. Then my grandmother pronounces, "Tony Earley, you're just quare."

2 According to my edition of the Shorter Oxford English Dictionary, "quare" is an Anglo-Irish adjective from the early nineteenth century meaning "queer, strange, eccentric." Most other dictionaries, if they list the word at all, will tell you that it is dialectical, archaic, or obsolete, an anachronism, a muted, aging participant in the clamoring riot of the English language. But when spoken around my grandmother's table, by my parents and aunts and uncles and cousins, "quare" is as current as the breath that produces it, as pointed as a sharpened stick. In my family's lexicon, "quare" packs a specificity of meaning which "queer," "strange," "eccentric," "odd," "unusual," "unconventional," and "suspicious" do not. The only adjective of synonymous texture would be "squirrelly," but we are a close bunch and would find the act of calling one another squirrely impolite. So, in my grandmother's dining room, when "quare" is the word we need, "quare" is the word we use.

3 Nor is "quare" the only word still hiding out in my grandmother's house which dictionaries assure us lost currency years ago. If I brought a quare person to Sunday dinner at Granny's and he ate something that

disagreed with him, we might say that he looked a little peaked. Of course, we might decide that he was peaked not because he had eaten something that disagreed with him but because he had eaten a bait of something he liked. We would say, Why, he was just too trifling to leave the table. He ate almost the whole mess by himself. And now we have this quare, peaked, trifling person on our hands. How do we get him to leave? Do we job him in the stomach? Do we hit him with a stob? No, we are kinder than that. We tell him, "Brother, you liked to have stayed too long." We put his dessert in a poke and send him on his way.

4 When I was a child, I took these words for granted. They were part of the language I heard around me, and I breathed them in like air. Only when I began to venture away from the universe that revolved around my grandmother's table did I come to realize that the language of my family was not the language of the greater world. I was embarrassed and ashamed when my town-bred classmates at Rutherfordton Elementary School corrected my speech, but by the time I entered college and signed up for an Appalachian-studies class I wasn't surprised to learn that my family spoke a dialect. I had begun to suspect as much, and was, by that time, bilingual: I spoke in the Appalachian vernacular when I was with my family and spoke standard English when I wasn't. This tailoring of speech to audience, which still feels a shade ignoble to me, is not uncommon among young people from my part of the world. In less generous regions of the greater American culture, the sound of Appalachian dialect has come to signify ignorance, backwardness, intransigence, and, in the most extreme examples, toothlessness, rank stupidity, and an alarming propensity for planting flowers in painted tractor tires.

5 This is not some sort of misguided, Caucasian appeal for ethnicity, nor is it a battle cry from the radical left against the patriarchal oppression of grammar, but the fact is that for me standard English has always been something of a second language. I have intuitively written it correctly from the time I started school, but speaking it still feels slightly unnatural, demands just enough conscious thought on my part to make me question my fluency. When I am introduced to a stranger, when I meet a more showily educated colleague in the English department at Vanderbilt, when I go to parties at which I feel unsure of my place in the evening's social pecking order, I catch myself proofreading sentences before I speak them—adding "g"s to the ends of participles, scanning clauses to make sure they ain't got no double negatives,

clipping long vowels to affectless, Midwestern dimensions, and making sure I use "lay" and "lie" in a manner that would not embarrass my father-in-law, who is a schoolteacher from California. Occasionally, even my wife, whose Southern accent is significantly more patrician than my own, will smile and ask, "What did you just say?" And I'll realize that I have unwittingly slipped into the language of my people, that I have inadvertently become "colorful." I'll rewind my sentence in my head so that I can save it as an example of how not to speak to strangers. Only in the sanctity of Granny's house can I speak my mother tongue with anything resembling peace of mind.

6 In 1904, a librarian and writer named Horace Kephart, having recently left his wife and children and suffered a nervous breakdown, moved to the mountains around Bryson City, North Carolina. Although he traveled there initially to distance himself from human contact, he soon recovered enough to take an active interest in the world in which he found himself. An avid gatherer of information and a compulsive listmaker, Kephart spent the rest of his life compiling exhaustive journals and records detailing the geography, history, culture, and language of the southern Appalachians—a pursuit that resulted in countless magazine articles, a celebrated handbook, *Camping and Woodcraft*, and two editions of a book entitled *Our Southern Highlanders*.

7 Although Kephart had chosen the Appalachians over the deserts of the Southwest somewhat randomly, he arrived in western North Carolina at a particularly fortuitous time for a man of his particular talents. In the roadless hollows of the Blue Ridge and the Smokies, Kephart found a people isolated by their hostile, vertical geography and living largely as their ancestors had, in the later half of the eighteenth century, when the great Scots-Irish migration out of Pennsylvania first filled the region with people of European descent.

8 "No one can understand the attitude of our highlanders toward the rest of the earth," Kephart wrote,

> *until he realizes their amazing isolation from all that lies beyond the blue, hazy skyline of their mountains. Conceive a shipload of emigrants cast away on some unknown island, far from the regular track of vessels, and left there for five or six generations, unaided and untroubled by the growth of civilization. Among the descendants of such a company we*

would expect to find customs and ideas unaltered from the time of their forefathers. . . . The mountain folk still live in the eighteenth century. The progress of mankind from that age to this is no heritage of theirs.

9 Because the Scots-Irish settlers had spoken to and been influenced by so few outsiders, the language they brought with them from Scotland and Ireland, by way of Pennsylvania, had been preserved remarkably intact. And the English dialect that Kephart encountered in North Carolina was in many ways closer to the Elizabethan English of Shakespeare or the Middle English of Chaucer than to anything that had been spoken in England for centuries. Coincidentally, had Kephart come to these mountains a generation later, his research would have been less definitive. Within a few years after his death, in 1931, road-building initiatives, radio, and the Sears, Roebuck catalogue had begun to open even the darkest hollows of the Appalachians to twentieth-century America. In a very short time, the resulting cultural homogenization had turned the southern highlands into a vastly different world from the one that Kephart had originally discovered.

10 When I first read "Our Southern Highlanders," late last year, it held for me the power of revelation. It told me who I was—or at least where I came from—in a way that I had never fully understood before. All the words I had thought specific to my family had entries in a dictionary compiled from Kephart's research. And all of them—with the exception of "quare," which is a mere two hundred years old—were words of Middle English origin, which is to say anywhere from five hundred to eight hundred years old. Although most of the people I meet today wouldn't have any idea what it's like to eat a bait, Chaucer would have.

11 Of course, words of Middle English origin are mere babes compared with the words of Latin, Greek, and Hebrew etymology that constitute much of our language. The Latin and Greek roots of the words "agriculture" and "barbarian" were old long before the primitive tribes of the British Isles painted their faces blue and grunted in a dialect resembling English. So I am less taken by the age of the words of the Appalachian vernacular which found their way into my grandmother's house than I am by the specific history they hold.

12 The word "quare," for me, contains sea voyages and migrations. It speaks of families stopping after long journeys and saying, for any one of a thousand reasons, "This is far enough." It speaks to me of generations of farmers watching red dirt turn below plow blades, of young men

stepping into furrows when old men step out. It speaks to me of girls fresh from their mothers' houses crawling into marriage beds and becoming mothers themselves. It bears witness to the line of history, most of it now unmappable, that led to my human waking beneath these particular mountains. If language is the mechanism through which we inherit history and culture, then each individual word functions as a type of gene, bearing with it a small piece of the specific information that makes us who we are, and tells us where we have been. My first cousin Greg and I came down with the same obscure bone disease in the same knee at the same age. For us, the word "quare" is no less a genetic signifier of the past than the odd, bone-eating chromosome carried down through history by one wonders how many limping Scots-Irish.

13 The last time I remember talking to my great-grandfather Womack, he was well into his nineties, and our whole family had gathered on the porch of the house he built as a young man, along Walnut Creek, in the Sunny View community of Polk County. When I tell this story, I choose to remember it as a spring day—though it may not have been—simply because I like to think that the daffodils in his yard were blooming. (My grandmother, who is eighty-three now, helped him plant them when she was a little girl.) At some point, everyone else got up and went inside, leaving Paw Womack and me alone on the porch. I was in high school, a freshman or sophomore, and was made self-conscious by his legendary age. He had been born in another century. His father had been wounded at Gettysburg. A preacher's son, he had never uttered a swear word or tasted alcohol. He had farmed with a mule until he was well into his eighties, and he had never got another car after one that he bought in 1926 wore out. He voted for Woodrow Wilson. He was *historical.* I felt that the family had somehow chosen me to sit with him; I felt that I needed to say something. I got out of my chair and approached him as one would a sacred relic. I sat down on the porch rail facing him. I remember his immense, knotted farmer's hands spread out on the arms of his rocker. We stared at each other for what seemed like a long time. Eventually, I blushed. I smiled at him and nodded. He smiled back and said, "Who are you?"

14 I said, "I'm Reba's boy. Clara Mae's grandson."

15 "Oh," he said. "Reba's boy."

16 If we ever spoke again, I don't remember it.

17 It seems significant to me now that when I told Paw Womack who I was I didn't give him my name. My position as an individual was secondary to my place in the lineage that had led to my sitting on his porch. I identified myself as a small part of a greater whole. *Who are you?* I'm Reba's boy, Clara Mae's grandson, Tom Womack's great-grandson. *Where are you from?* Over yonder. *Why don't you like watermelon?* I don't know. I guess I'm just quare.

18 Ironically, just as I have learned I to appreciate the history contained in the word "quare," I have also had to accept the fact that it is passing out of my family with my generation. Neither I nor my cousins use it outside Granny's house unless we temper it first with irony—a sure sign of a word's practical death within a changing language. Of course, no language is a static property: the life cycles of words mirror the life cycles of the individuals who speak them. Every language, given enough time, will replace each of its words, just as the human body replaces each of its cells every seven years. The self-appointed guardians of English who protest that the word "celibate" means "unmarried," and not "abstaining from sexual intercourse," are wasting their time. "Sounds are too volatile and subtle for legal restraints," Samuel Johnson wrote in the 1755 Preface to his "Dictionary of the English Language"; "to enchain syllables, and to lash the wind, are equally the undertakings of pride."

19 I tell myself that the passing of Appalachian vernacular from my family's vocabulary is not a tragedy, or a sign of our being assimilated into a dominant culture, but simply the arrival of an inevitable end. "Tongues, like governments," Dr. Johnson wrote, "have a natural tendency to degeneration." I tell myself that it is a natural progression for my children to speak a language significantly different from that of my ancestors, but the fact that it has happened so suddenly, within the span of a single generation—my generation—makes me wonder if I have done something wrong, if I have failed the people who passed those words down. Sometimes the truest answer to the question "Who are you?" is "I don't know."

20 Words and blood are the double helix that connect us to our past. As a member of a transitional generation, I am losing those words and the connection they make. I am losing the small comfort of shared history. I compensate, in the stories I write, by sending people up mountains to look, as Horace Kephart did, for the answers to their questions, to look

down from a high place and see what they can see. My characters, at least, can still say the words that bind them to the past without sounding queer, strange, eccentric, odd, unusual, unconventional, or suspicious. "Stories," says the writer Tim O'Brien, "can save us." I have put my faith in the idea that words, even new ones, possess that kind of redemptive power. Writers write about a place not because they belong there, but because they want to belong. It's a quare feeling.

FOR THINKING, DISCUSSING, AND WRITING

1. Earley frames the essay with contradictory perspectives: the first few paragraphs insist on the writer's separation, the final paragraph expresses the longing to belong. How does this seeming paradox help you to understand Earley's point?
2. Why does Earley use lists in his essay, especially in the first and fifth paragraphs? How are these lists similar? How do they differ? What effect do you think he intends them to have? How are they successful? What other lists can you locate? What purposes do they serve?
3. What exactly is a dialect? How is it distinguished from a language? How useful are these distinctions? Earley says in paragraph 5 that when he speaks in dialect he has "inadvertently become 'colorful.'" What does he mean? What might this observation suggest about the relation between language and social class?
4. Earley says that "the life cycles of words mirror the life cycles of the individuals who speak them." Write a paper in which you analyze this statement. Be sure to provide enough illustrations and examples to support your point as powerfully as possible. Include relevant personal experience or other sources of detail.

SANDRA CISNEROS

An Offering to the Power of Language

Sandra Cisneros (1954–), a novelist and poet, is a frequent contributor to numerous magazines and other periodicals. She is the author of two collections of poems, Bad Boys *(1980) and* Loose Women *(1994), and the novels* The House on Mango Street *(1984) and* Caramelo *(2002). In this piece for the October 26, 1997, issue of the* Los Angeles Times, *Cisneros explores the impact of language on personal identity.*

1 "*Mi'ja*, it's me. Call me when you wake up." It was a message left on my phone machine from a friend. But when I heard that word "*mi'ja*," a pain squeezed my heart. My father was the only one who ever called me this. Because his death is so recent, the word overwhelmed me and filled me with grief.

2 With my father's death, the thread that links me to my other self, to my other language, was severed. Spanish binds me to my ancestors, but especially to my father, a Mexican national by birth who became a U.S. citizen by serving in World War II. My mother, who is Mexican American, learned her Spanish through this man, as I did. Forever after, every word spoken in that language is linked indelibly to him.

3 I continue to analyze and reflect on the power a word has to produce such an effect on me. As always, I am fascinated by how those of us caught between worlds are held under the spell of words spoken in the language of our childhood. After a loved one dies, your senses become oversensitized. Maybe that's why I sometimes smell my father's cologne in a room when no one else does. And why words once taken for granted suddenly take on new meanings.

4 "*Mi'ja*" (MEE-ha) from "*mi hija*" (me EE-ha). The words translate as "my daughter." Daughter, my daughter, daughter of mine, they're all stiff and clumsy, and have nothing of the intimacy and warmth of the word "*mi'ja*." "Daughter of my heart," maybe. Perhaps a more accurate translation of "*mi'ja*" is, I love you.

5 When I wish to address a child, lover or one of my many small pets, I use Spanish, a language filled with affection and familiarity. I can only liken it to the fried-tortilla smell of my mother's house or the way my brothers' hair smells like Alberto VO5 when I hug them. It just about makes me want to cry.

6 The language of our *antepasados*, those who came before us, connects us to our center, to who we are and directs us to our life work. Some of us have been lost, cut off from the essential wisdom and power. Sometimes, our parents or grandparents were so harmed by a society that treated them ill for speaking their native language that they thought they could save us from that hate by teaching us to speak only English. Those of us, then, live like captives, lost from our culture, ungrounded, forever wandering like ghosts with a thorn in the heart.

7 When my father was sick, I watched him dissolve before my eyes. Each day the cancer that was eating him changed his face, as if he was

crumbling from within and turning into a sugar skull, the kind placed on altars for Day of the Dead. Because I'm a light sleeper, my job was to sleep on the couch and be the night watch. Father always woke several times in the night choking on his own bile. I would rush to hold a kidney-shaped bowl under his lips, wait for him to finish throwing up, the body exhausted beyond belief. When he was through, I rinsed a towel with cold water and washed his face.—*Ya estoy cansado de vivir*, my father would gasp.—*Si, yo se,* I know. But the body takes its time dying. I have reasoned, since then, that the purpose of illness is to let go. For the living to let the dying go, and for the dying to let go of this life and travel to where they must.

8 Whenever anyone discusses death, they talk about the inevitable loss, but no one ever mentions the inevitable gain. How when you lose a loved one, you suddenly have a spirit ally, an energy on the other side that is with you always, that is with you just by calling their name. I know my father watches over me in a much more thorough way than he ever could when he was alive. When he was living, I had to telephone long distance to check up on him and, if he wasn't watching one of his endless *telenovelas*, he'd talk to me. Now I simply summon him in my thoughts. *Papa*. Instantly, I feel his presence surround and calm me.

9 I know this sounds like a lot of hokey new-age stuff, but really it's old age, so ancient and wonderful and filled with such wisdom that we have had to relearn it because our miseducation has taught us to name it "superstition." I have had to rediscover the spirituality of my ancestors, because my own mother was a cynic. So it came back to me a generation later, learned but not forgotten in some memory in my cells, in my DNA, in the palm of my hand that is made up of the same blood of my ancestors, in the transcripts I read from the great Mazatec visionary Maria Sabina Garcia of Oaxaca.

10 Sometimes a word can be translated into more than a meaning. In it is the translation of a world view, a way of looking at things and, yes, even a way of accepting what others might not perceive as beautiful. "*Urraca*," for example, instead of "grackle." Two ways of looking at a black bird. One sings, the other cackles. Or, "*tocayola*," your name-twin, and, therefore, your friend. Or, the beautiful "*estrenar*," which means to wear something for the first time. There is no word in English for the thrill and pride of wearing something new.

11 Spanish gives me a way of looking at myself and at the world in a new way. For those of us living between worlds, our job in the universe is to help others see with more than their eyes during this period of chaotic transition. Our work as bicultural citizens is to help others become visionary, to help us all examine our dilemmas in multiple ways and arrive at creative solutions; otherwise, we all will perish.

12 What does a skeleton mean to you? Satan worship? Heavy-metal music? Halloween? Or maybe it means—Death, you are a part of my life, and I recognize you, include you in mine, I even thumb my nose at you. Next Saturday, on the Day of the Dead, I honor and remember my *antepasados*, those who have died and gone on before me.

13 I think of those two brave women in Amarillo who lost their jobs for speaking Spanish, and I wonder at the fear in their employer. Did he think they were talking about him? What an egocentric! Doesn't he understand that speaking another language is another way of seeing, a way of being at home with one another, of saying to your listener, I know you, I honor you, you are my sister, my brother, my mother, my father, my family. If he learns Spanish, or any other language, he would be admitting I love and respect you, and I love to address you in the language of those you love.

14 This Day of the Dead I will make an offering, *una ofrenda*, to honor my father's life and to honor all immigrants everywhere who come to a new country filled with great hope and fear, dragging their beloved homeland with them in their language. My father appears to me now in the things that are most alive, that speak to me or attempt to speak to me through their beauty, tenderness and love. A bowl of oranges on my kitchen table. The sharp scent of a can filled with *campaxiuchil*, marigold flowers for Day of the Dead. The opening notes of an Agustin Lara bolero named "Farolito." The night sky filled with moist stars. *Mi'ja*, they call out to me, and my heart floods with joy.

FOR THINKING, DISCUSSING, AND WRITING

1. How did Cisneros's father die? What role did the writer play in caring for him? Why did she have this particular job?
2. Why do you think that Cisneros chose "*mi'ja*" as the first word of her essay? How does the placement help her establish her theme? What, according to the writer, is "a more accurate translation" of the word? At the beginning of the selection she says that the word *mi'ja* "overwhelmed me and filled me with grief." What words in English or

some other language have the same impact on you? What does this suggest to you about "the power of language"?

3. In paragraph 5, Cisneros says that she uses Spanish because it is "a language filled with affection and familiarity." How do languages have their own "character"? What, if any, is the character of English, do you think?
4. The writer says that "speaking another language is another way of seeing, a way of being home with one another." Write an argumentative paper in which you either agree or disagree with this statement. Be sure to provide illustrations and examples to support your argument.

BARBARA CARTON

Why Does "Everybody" Now Put "Everything" in Quotation Marks?

Barbara Carton (1950–) is a national news staff reporter for the Wall Street Journal, *in which this selection was first published in 1999. She received a special award for education reporting from the Education Writers Association in 2002. In this selection she weighs in on what she sees as an "'epidemic' of runaway 'quotation marks.'"*

Our "goal" is to help our customers conserve energy.

—*Letter from Atlas Oil Co., Westwood, Massachusetts*

Thank you for . . . keeping your "health" club as clean as possible.

—*Locker-room sign, World Trade Center, New York*

1 Call it overzealous marketing. Or pretentiousness. Maybe it's the work of those who might charitably be called "challenged, punctuationwise."

2 Whatever the reason, an "epidemic" of runaway "quotation marks" is raging in the world of words.

3 "I've seen it in letters I get from my brother," says Michael Pemberton, an assistant professor of English at the University of Illinois. "Quotation marks around words that seem so amazingly commonplace I can't understand why he's doing it."

4 "I've seen it a lot in Yellow Pages advertising," adds Richard Dowis, president of the Society for the Preservation of English Language and Literature, in Waleska, Ga. He has also noticed signs such as the ones in

diners that say, "Please pay the 'cashier.'" They will have *cashier* in quotation marks as if to suggest the person behind the counter isn't really up to snuff.

5 The "Doonesbury" cartoon that ran Friday in the *New York Daily News*, among other newspapers, contained this bit of conversation:

6 "You think he'll be 'impressed' by quotation marks?"

7 "Sure—he's a college boy."

8 Tom McArthur, who edits the Oxford Companion to the English Language in Cambridge, England, sees errant quotes popping up throughout Britain. "I have a colleague on a committee here who is a structural engineer," he says. "His writing is peppered with this kind of quotation."

9 As any of our academic experts could explain, the rightful job of quotation marks is to denote words first uttered elsewhere, or titles of books and other works. They are also used to enclose nicknames or unfamiliar terms.

10 In its proper place, the quotation mark keeps company with timeless and noble utterances. Misplaced, as it is with growing frequency, it surrounds commonly understood words. But why?

11 Modern-day stress is one reason.

12 A lot of these quotation marks are stress-related. Marvin Owen, general manager of Automated Church Systems Inc. of Florence, S.C., says his six staff writers employ quotes for added punch. "If something's really important," Mr. Owen says, "you've got to do whatever you can to get it in front of them." Really important, following this precept, is the Sunday-offerings tally that the software firm compiles for churches across the country. Parishioners at these churches receive their "Record of Contributions" in quotes.

13 At the Fitness Co., New York-area manager Bonnie Patrick had irony as well as stress in mind when she wrote the World Trade Center sign thanking members for keeping the health club clean. "Our point was, if you leave your sneakers out, as everybody does, on top of the lockers, they smell and it's an unhealthy situation and we belong to a *health* club," says Ms. Patrick. "We were trying to do a play on words and, at the same time, get the point across."

14 For some reason, stores (among other users of English) find quotation marks irresistible when the word "all" comes up. According to a sign at the Souper Salad deli in downtown Boston, "One hot lid fits 'all' size coffee cups." Super Stop & Shop grocery stores in the same city advertise" 'All Natural' Jumbo Sea Scallops." Similarly, the Appalachian Mountain Club lists various services in a letter to members, noting that membership entitles them to discounts on"'all of the above.'"

15 Mary N. Bruder of Pittsburgh, a former English teacher who operates the "Grammar Lady" Web site, has noticed people using the apostrophe to form plurals, "tomato's," for example, and figures it's part of the same trend affecting quotation marks.

16 It would seem to be. Indeed, the "trend" appears to have had its "origins" long ago. Witness this bit from a 1985 Dave Barry column:

17 "Dear Mr. Language Person: What is the purpose of the apostrophe?

18 "The apostrophe is used mainly in hand-lettered small-business signs to alert the reader that an 'S' is coming up at the end of a word, as in: WE DO NOT EXCEPT PERSONAL CHECK'S. Another important grammar concept to bear in mind when creating hand-lettered small-business signs is that you should put quotation marks around random words for decoration, as in 'TRY' OUR HOT DOG'S, or even TRY 'OUR' HOT DOG'S."

19 John Broderick, author of "The Able Writer: A Rhetoric and Handbook," suspects that many people have a "vague feeling" about quotation marks, but "are not literate enough—literally, widely and well-read enough—fully to have grasped the subtleties involved."

20 Consider this sign placed on three stores in the Boston area: "Join Our Team. Economy Hardware. 'Hiring.'"

21 "The writer seems to try to disassociate himself or herself from taking full responsibility for the word," says Prof. Broderick, who teaches English at Old Dominion University in Norfolk, Va. "Maybe they're only 'hiring' until the job is filled." Similarly, in the case of the Atlas letter about conservation. "Maybe the oil company doesn't want to be forced actually to achieve their 'goal.'"

22 Dr. Broderick adds: "I'm trying to be kind in finding interpretations."

23 Rob Renaud, general manager of the hardware stores that are "hiring," blames the sign company. "It wasn't our idea to put the quotation marks there." he says. "We just wanted to stress hiring, and maybe that's their style of stressing something. We wanted a sign that stood out, not a regular old help-wanted sign."

24 Sign painter Rick Hammar, of Pelham, N.H., installed the quotation marks for Mr. Renaud, but he usually prefers stars. "Like, we did some bumper stickers and on the very top line we had a star, then it said, 'Think Women' and then another star, and then in big bold letters, it said, 'Think Republican.'"

25 In any case, Mr. Hammar says, sign painters don't call these kinds of punctuation "quotation marks"—they call them "slashes." Besides, he says, "We have a license in art to do what we want."

FOR THINKING, DISCUSSING, AND WRITING

1. To what does Carton attribute the overuse of quotation marks? What, according to Carton, are the "proper" uses of the quotation mark? What reason does she give for people surrounding common words with quotation marks?
2. Where does Carton herself use quotation marks unnecessarily in the essay? Why do you think she does this? Where in the essay does she use quotation marks she approves of? What do the quotation marks convey?
3. Carton refers to many authorities in this short essay. What does this suggest about the relation between language usage and authority? How might we determine the appropriate uses of devices like quotation marks?
4. Think about some other linguistic or grammatical practices that have become commonplace but which may still concern people, such as the phrase *between you and I* or the pronunciation of the word *nuclear* as *nuc-u-lar*, or the use of a heart sign to indicate love or a "smiley face" to indicate happiness. Write a paper in which you analyze such practices.

NANCY MAIRS

Body in Trouble

Nancy Mairs (1943–) has taught at the University of California and the University of Arizona and has written a number of works, including collections of poems, such as In All the Rooms of the Yellow House *(1984), and essays,* Remembering the Bone House *(1989) and* A Troubled Guest *(2001). Currently Mairs is a Research Associate with the Southwest Institute for Research on Women. In this essay from* Waist-High in the World *(1996), she describes how physical disability affects one's perspective on life.*

1 In biblical times, physical and mental disorders were thought to signify possession by demons. In fact, Jesus's proficiency at casting these out accounted for much of his popularity among the common folk (though probably not among swine). People who were stooped or blind or subject to seizures were clearly not okay as they were but required fixing, and divine intervention was the only remedy powerful enough to cleanse them of their baleful residents.

2 Theologically as well as medically, this interpretation of the body in trouble now seems primitive, and yet we perpetuate the association underlying it. A brief examination of "dead" metaphors (those which have been so thoroughly integrated into language that we generally overlook their analogical origins) demonstrates the extent to which physical vigor equates with positive moral qualities. "Keep your chin up," we say (signifying courage), "and your eyes open" (alertness); "stand on your own two feet" (independence) "and tall" (pride); "look straight in the eye" (honesty) or "see eye to eye" (accord); "run rings around" (superiority). By contrast, physical debility connotes vice, as in "sit on your ass" (laziness), "take it lying down" (weakness), "listen with half an ear" (inattention), and get left "without a leg to stand on" (unsound argument). The way in which the body occupies space and the quality of the space it occupies correlate with the condition of the soul: it is better to be admired as "high-minded" than "looked down on" for one's "low morals," to be "in the know" than "out of it," to be "up front" than "back-handed," to be "free as a bird" than "confined to a wheelchair."

3 Now, the truth is that, unless you are squatting or six years old, I can never look you straight in the eye, and I spend all my time sitting on my ass except when I'm taking it lying down. These are the realities of life in a wheelchair (though in view of the alternatives—bed, chair, or floor—"confinement" is the very opposite of my condition). And the fact that the soundness of the body so often serves as a metaphor for its moral health, its deterioration thus implying moral degeneracy, puts me and my kind in a quandary. How can I possibly be "good"? Let's face it, wicked witches are not just ugly (as sin); they're also bent and misshapen (crooked). I am bent and misshapen, therefore ugly, therefore wicked. And I have no way to atone.

4 It is a bind many women, not just the ones with disabilities, have historically found themselves in by virtue of their incarnation in a sociolinguistic system over which they have had relatively little power. (Notice how virile the virtues encoded in the examples above.) Female bodies, even handsome and wholesome ones, have tended to give moralists fits of one sort or another (lust, disgust, but seldom trust). As everyone who has read the *Malleus Maleficarum* knows, "All witchcraft comes from carnal Lust which is in Women insatiable." If a good man is hard to find, a good woman is harder, unless she's (1) prepubescent, (2) senile, or (3) dead; and even then, some will have their doubts about her. It is tricky enough, then, trying to be a good woman at all, but a crippled woman

experiences a kind of double jeopardy. How can she construct a world that will accommodate her realities, including her experience of her own goodness, while it remains comprehensible to those whose world-views are founded on premises alien or even inimical to her sense of self?

5 Disability is at once a metaphorical and a material state, evocative of other conditions in time and space—childhood and imprisonment come to mind—yet "like" nothing but itself. I can't live it or write about it except by conflating the figurative and the substantial, the "as if" with the relentlessly "what is." Let me illustrate with an experience from a couple of years ago, when George and I went to a luncheon honoring the Dalai Lama, held at a large resort northwest of Tucson. Although we were not enrolled in the five-day workshop he had come here to lead, we found ourselves in the hallway when the meeting room disgorged the workshop participants—all fourteen hundred of them—into a narrow area further constricted by tables laden with bells, beads, and brochures. And let me tell you, no matter how persuaded they were of the beauty and sacredness of all life, not one of them seemed to think that any life was going on below the level of her or his own gaze. "Down here!" I kept whimpering at the hips and buttocks and bellies pressing my wheelchair on all sides. "Down here! There's a person down here!" My only recourse was to roll to one side and hug a wall.

6 Postmodern criticism, feminist and otherwise, makes a good deal of the concept of wall-hugging, or marginality, which is meant to suggest that some segment of the population—black, brown, yellow, or red, poor, female, lesbian, what have you—is shouldered to the side, heedlessly or not, by some perhaps more numerous and certainly more powerful segment, most frequently wealthy, well-educated Euro-American males. Regardless of the way marginality is conceived, it is never taken to mean that those on the margin occupy a physical space literally outside the field of vision of those in the center, so that the latter trip unawares and fall into the laps of those they have banished from consciousness unless these scoot safely out of the way. "Marginality" thus means something altogether different to me from what it means to social theorists. It is no metaphor for the power relations between one group of human beings and another but a literal description of where I stand (figuratively speaking): over here, on the edge, out of bounds, beneath your notice. I embody the metaphors. Only whether or not I like doing so is immaterial.

7 It may be this radical materiality of my circumstances, together with the sense I mentioned earlier that defect and deformity bar me from the

ranks of "good" women, which have spurred me in the past, as they no doubt will go on doing, to put the body at the center of all my meditations, my "corpus," if you will. Not that I always write *about* the body, though I often do, but that I always write, consciously, *as* a body. (This quality more than any other, I think, exiles my work from conventional academic discourse. The guys may be writing with the pen/penis, but they pretend at all times to keep it in their pants.) And it is this—my—crippled female body that my work struggles to redeem through that most figurative of human tools: language. Because language substitutes a no-thing for a thing, whereas a body is pure thing through and through, this task must fail. But inevitable disappointment does not deprive labor of its authenticity.

8 And so I use inscription to insert my embodied self into a world with which, over time, I have less and less in common. Part of my effort entails reshaping both that self and that world in order to reconcile the two. We bear certain responsibilities toward each other, the world and I, and I must neither remove myself from it nor permit it to exclude me if we are to carry these out. I can't become a "hopeless cripple" without risking moral paralysis; nor can the world, except to its own diminishment, refuse my moral participation.

9 But is a woman for whom any action at all is nearly impossible capable of right action, or am I just being morally cocky here? After all, if I claim to be a good woman, I leave myself open to the question: Good for what? The most straightforward answer is the most tempting: Good for nothing. I mean really. I can stand with assistance but I can't take a step; I can't even spread my own legs for sex anymore. My left arm doesn't work at all, and my right one grows weaker almost by the day. I am having more and more trouble raising a fork or a cup to my lips. (It is possible, I've discovered, though decidedly odd, to drink even coffee and beer through a straw.) I can no longer drive. I lack the stamina to go out to work. If I live to see them, I will never hold my own grandchildren. These incapacities constitute a stigma that, according to social scientist Erving Goffman, removes me from normal life into a "discredited" position in relation to society.

10 From the point of view of the Catholic Church, to which I belong, however, mine must be just about the ideal state: too helpless even for the sins other flesh is heir to. After all, parties aren't much fun now that I meet the other revelers eye to navel, and getting drunk is risky since I can hardly see straight cold sober. No matter how insatiable my carnal Lust, nobody's likely to succumb to my charms and sully my reputation.

But I am, by sympathy at least, a Catholic *Worker*, part of a community that wastes precious little time fretting about the seven deadlies, assuming instead that the moral core of being in the world lies in the care of others, in *doing* rather than *being* good. How can a woman identify herself as a Catholic Worker if she can't even cut up carrots for the soup or ladle it out for the hungry people queued up outside the kitchen door? Physical incapacity certainly appears to rob such a woman of moral efficacy.

11 Well, maybe moral demands should no longer be placed on her. Perhaps she ought simply to be "excused" from the moral life on the most generous of grounds: that she suffers enough already, that she has plenty to do just to take care of herself. This dismissive attitude tends to be reinforced when the woman lives at the height of your waist. Because she "stands" no higher than a six-year-old, you may unconsciously ascribe to her the moral development of a child (which, in view of Robert Coles's findings, you will probably underestimate) and demand little of her beyond obedience and enough self-restraint so that she doesn't filch candy bars at the checkout counter while you're busy writing a check. (God, I can't tell you how tempting those brightly wrapped chunks are when they're smack up against your nose.) "Stature" is an intrinsic attribute of moral life, and the woman who lacks the one may be judged incapable of the other.

12 I am exaggerating here, of course, but only a little. Beyond cheerfulness and patience, people don't generally expect much of a cripple's character. And certainly they presume that care, which I have placed at the heart of moral experience, flows in one direction, "downward": as from adult to child, so from well to ill, from whole to maimed. This condescension contributes to what Goffman calls "spoiled identity," though he does not deal satisfactorily with the damage it inflicts: without reciprocity, the foundation of any mature moral relationship, the person with a defect cannot grow "up" and move "out" into the world but remains constricted in ways that make being "confined to a wheelchair" look trivial. And so I would say that while it is all right to excuse me from making the soup (for the sake of the soup, probably more than "all right"), you must never—even with the best intentions, even with my own complicity—either enable or require me to withdraw from moral life altogether.

13 So much for carrot-cutting, then, or any other act involving sharp instruments. But wait! One sharp instrument is left me: my tongue. (Here's where metaphor comes in handy.) And my computer keyboard is . . . just waist high. With these I ought to be able to concoct another

order of soup altogether (in which I'll no doubt find myself up to my ears). In other words, what I can still *do*—so far—is write books. Catholic Workers being extraordinarily tolerant of multiplicity, on the theory that it takes all kinds of parts to form a body, this activity will probably be counted good enough.

14 The world to which I am a material witness is a difficult one to love. But I am not alone in it now; and as the population ages, more and more people—a significant majority of them women—may join me in it, learning to negotiate a chill and rubble-strewn landscape with impaired eyesight and hearing and mobility, searching out some kind of home there. Maps render foreign territory, however dark and wide, fathomable. I mean to make a map. My infinitely harder task, then, is to conceptualize not merely a habitable body but a habitable world: a world that wants me in it.

FOR THINKING, DISCUSSING, AND WRITING

1. The writer refers to a "sociolinguistic system" (paragraph 4) that seems to be controlled by some and to exert power over others. What is she referring to? What examples does she note? Can you think of any more?
2. How does Mairs first try to make it clear that language is tricky or difficult, something that we all should think about more carefully?
3. Mairs says that "the soundness of the body so often serves as a metaphor for its moral health" (paragraph 4). What does she mean? Why might you agree or disagree with her? What values does she imply about language?
4. Write an essay about how society should accommodate people with disabilities. Does our current society do an effective job, do you think? Why or why not?

ELIZABETH AUSTIN

A Small Plea to Delete a Ubiquitous Expletive

Elizabeth Austin, a Girl Scout leader and frequent commentator on Chicago Public Radio, has written for Washington Monthly, Time, Self, *and* U.S. News and World Report, *where this piece first appeared on April 6, 1998. In this essay she questions the use of the "F" word in civil discourse.*

1 Oh, f—.

2 The "F" word, as it's called in more polite circles (including magazines such as this one), is increasingly hard to escape. Those who rarely use it themselves nonetheless hear it frequently—on the street, on the job, at the health club, at the movies—anywhere two or three disgruntled citizens might gather. Most people have uttered the word; everyone can define it. But even those who aren't particularly shocked by it don't want to hear it all the time. The toughest of tough guys cringes inwardly when somebody says it in front of his mother. Becoming a parent induces instant hypersensitivity to the word's ubiquitous presence in movies, on cable TV, in music, and in the loose talk of childless friends.

3 In its simplest and oldest usage, the "F" word refers to copulation. This usage has a long, frequently jolly, occasionally distinguished history. Shakespeare made glancing puns about it, and Scottish poet Robert Burns included it in his racier verses. More commonly today, though, the "F" word is used to express not desire but derision, not heat but hostility. Even when used as a kind of verbal space holder, a rougher, hipper equivalent of "you know" (as in "I f—ing love that f—ing movie," or in the Army patois that has been common for decades), it carries a rude message. It is both a gauge and an engine of our ever plummeting standards of civility. Yet enough people are fed up with it that it's possible to erase the "F" word from public parlance and civil discourse.

4 **Last word.** A couple of generations back, calling for a public elimination of the "F" word would have been preposterous, since the word was never uttered in polite company (loosely defined as anywhere middle-class women were likely to hear it). In the late '60s, however, the loud, open use of the "F" word became a true shibboleth, dividing the student radicals from the Establishment "pigs" they delighted in tweaking. In Jerry Rubin's words, the "F" word was "the last word left in the English language. Amerika cannot destroy it because she dare not use it."

5 But America took that dare. From the early '70s on, the "F" word started turning up with increasing regularity in movies, literature, and real life, according to Jesse Sheidlower's exhaustive volume, *The F-Word*. Many linguists and social critics celebrated the "F" word's coming out as a healthy abandonment of prudishness; a few still do. But civic virtuecrats today make a stronger case that public use of the word is a prime example of the "broken window" theory of social decay. When

we put private frustrations and the right to be foulmouthed ahead of public order and civility, we coarsen society and risk an avalanche of rage and violence. Despite its near universality, the "F" word remains a fighting word.

6 So let's get rid of it. Scholars of social norms say all that's necessary to remove offensive language from public speech is a critical mass of people willing to take up cudgels against it. University of Chicago law Prof. Randal Picker describes such sudden overthrows of social standards as "norms cascades." If society is ripe for change, he contends, a single, powerful catalyst can engineer swift, widespread transformation. Picker cites Jesse Jackson, whose call for a switch from "black" to "African-American" changed the nation's nomenclature almost overnight. A more subtle but equally effective norms cascade was engineered by a handful of feminist writers in the early 1970s. Author-activist Robin Morgan remembers furiously listing words then commonly used to describe women, both in conversation and in print. "Produce and animals is what we were," she recalls. "We were 'chicks' and 'lambs' and 'birds' and 'bitches,' and there was always the infamous 'cherry.'" When Morgan and other feminist leaders publicly insisted on being called women, they started a norms cascade that eventually erased not only chick and bitch but girl and lady as well.

7 The "F" word seems like a particularly ripe target for a new generation of linguistic activists from both sides of the ideological divide. Erasing the word from civil discourse is one goal that Phyllis Schlafly could share with Andrea Dworkin. Here are a few modest proposals to help make that happen:

8 ■ Police should start ticketing drivers who use the "F" word (or the correlating hand gesture), thereby boosting civility and calming road rage simultaneously. Although this could raise some First Amendment hackles, keep in mind that "fighting words" are not protected speech. One simple test of the fighting words concept is whether a fight actually ensues. Slapping a $100 ticket on a driver whose uplifted finger sparked a collision should pass any constitutional test.

9 ■ The Motion Picture Association of America movie rating system should be overhauled to give an automatic NC-17 rating to any film that uses the "F" word even once. An NC-17 rating all but guarantees diminished viewership. Writers and directors who considered the

word necessary to their artistic expression could still get their movies made; they'd just have to make the decision to trade lucrative ticket sales to teenagers for their artistic license.

10 ▪ Authors who salt their books with gratuitous "F" words should get the same critical treatment as those who sprinkle their prose with casual racial epithets. Certainly, there are times when the "F" word expresses precisely what a writer means to convey. But we need literary critics who understand the distinction between necessary frankness and the adolescent desire to shock.

11 ▪ Most important, we must delete the "F" word from our own lives. The most lasting shifts in social standards are those that begin at cocktail parties and around water coolers. We can wipe out the "F" word simply by refusing to use it ourselves and quietly but firmly objecting when others use it within earshot. The next time someone uses the "F" word in casual conversation, Judith Martin, better known as Miss Manners, suggests responding: "I'm not used to that sort of language." (If you can't say that line with a straight face, try: "We don't use that word anymore.")

12 Objecting to the "F" word isn't censorship. You can still use it as a punch line, if you like. You'll just risk the freezing silence and icy glares now reserved for white people who use the "N" word in public. Similarly, you're free to use it among your intimates, as a term of (in Sheidlower's words) "endearment, admiration, [or] derision." The rules of public civility have always included the naked-and-sweaty exemption. How you talk in the locker room or bedroom is up to you.

13 Ultimately, a social norm is nothing more, and nothing less, than the sum of individual decisions. In reconsidering the "F" word, you may prize your right to say it above your neighbor's right not to hear it. But personally, I'm swearing off.

FOR THINKING, DISCUSSING, AND WRITING

1. What does Austin believe to be the most effective way to rid our society of the overuse of the "F" word? How realistic do you think the writer's suggestions are for erasing the "F" word from civil discourse? Give your reasons.
2. What is Austin's tone in this selection? Who is her intended audience? How do you know? Does her tone change any place in the essay? Where? How do you know?

3. Austin asserts in paragraph 3 that use of the "F" word is "both a gauge and an engine of our ever plummeting standards of civility." What does she mean by this? Do you agree with her? Why or why not?
4. If a word has come into common use over time, is it possible then to argue that it is generally offensive? Write a paper in which you address this issue. Be sure to use Austin's essay to help illustrate your points.

CHANG-RAE LEE

Mute in an English-Only World

Author of the book Native Speaker *(1995) and the novel* Aloft *(2007), Change-rae Lee (1965–) attended Yale University and received an MFA from the University of Oregon, where he teaches creative writing. Born in Korea, he immigrated to the United States with his family when he was three years old. In this 1996 essay he shows the effects of the English language on his Korean-born mother in America.*

1 When I read of the troubles in Palisades Park, New Jersey, over the proliferation of Korean-language signs along its main commercial strip, I unexpectedly sympathized with the frustrations, resentments and fears of the longtime residents. They clearly felt alienated and even unwelcome in a vital part of their community. The town, like seven others in New Jersey, has passed laws requiring that half of any commercial sign in a foreign language be in English.

2 Now I certainly would never tolerate any exclusionary ideas about who could rightfully settle and belong in the town. But having been raised in a Korean immigrant family, I saw every day the exacting price and power of language, especially with my mother, who was an outsider in an English-only world.

3 In the first years we lived in America, my mother could speak only the most basic English, and she often encountered great difficulty whenever she went out.

4 We lived in New Rochelle, New York, in the early 1970s, and most of the local businesses were run by the descendants of immigrants who, generations ago, had come to the suburbs from New York City. Proudly dotting Main Street and North Avenue were Italian pastry and cheese shops, Jewish tailors and cleaners, and Polish and German butchers and bakers. If my mother's marketing couldn't wait until the weekend,

when my father had free time, she would often hold off until I came home from school to buy the groceries.

5 Though I was only 6 or 7 years old, she insisted that I go out shopping with her and my younger sister. I mostly loathed the task, partly because it meant I couldn't spend the afternoon playing catch with my friends but also because I knew our errands would inevitably lead to an awkward scene, and that I would have to speak up to help my mother.

6 I was just learning the language myself, but I was a quick study, as children are with new tongues. I had spent kindergarten in almost complete silence, hearing only the high nasality of my teacher and comprehending little but the cranky wails and cries of my classmates. But soon, seemingly mere months later, I had already become a terrible ham and mimic, and I would crack up my father with impressions of teachers, his friends and even himself. My mother scolded me for aping his speech, and the one time I attempted to make light of hers I rated a roundhouse smack on my bottom.

7 For her, the English language was not very funny. It usually meant trouble and a good dose of shame, and sometimes real hurt. Although she had a good reading knowledge of the language from university classes in South Korea, she had never practiced actual conversation. So in America, she used English flashcards and phrase books and watched television with us kids. And she faithfully carried a pocket workbook illustrated with stick-figure people and compound sentences to be filled in.

8 But none of it seemed to do her much good. Staying mostly at home to care for us, she didn't have many chances to try out sundry words and phrases. When she did, say, at the window of the post office, her readied speech would stall, freeze, sometimes altogether collapse.

9 One day was unusually harrowing. We ventured downtown in the new Ford Country Squire my father had bought her, an enormous station wagon that seemed as long—and deft—as an ocean liner. We were shopping for a special meal for guests visiting that weekend, and my mother had heard that a particular butcher carried fresh oxtails, which she needed for a traditional soup.

10 We'd never been inside the shop, but my mother would pause before its window, which was always lined with whole hams, crown roasts and ropes of plump handmade sausages. She greatly esteemed

the bounty with her eyes, and my sister and I did also, but despite our desirous cries she'd turn us away and instead buy the packaged links at the Finast supermarket, where she felt comfortable looking them over and could easily spot the price. And, of course, not have to talk.

11 But that day she was resolved. The butcher store was crowded, and as we stepped inside the door jingled a welcome. No one seemed to notice. We waited for some time, and people who entered after us were now being served. Finally, an old woman nudged my mother and waved a little ticket, which we hadn't taken. We patiently waited again, until one of the beefy men behind the glass display hollered our number.

12 My mother pulled us forward and began searching the cases, but the oxtails were nowhere to be found. The man, his big arms crossed, sharply said, "Come on, lady, whaddya want?" This unnerved her, and she somehow blurted the Korean word for oxtail, soggori.

13 The butcher looked as if my mother had put something sour in his mouth, and he glanced back at the lighted board and called the next number.

14 Before I knew it, she had rushed us outside and back in the wagon, which she had double-parked because of the crowd. She was furious, almost vibrating with fear and grief, and I could see she was about to cry.

15 She wanted to go back inside, but now the driver of the car we were blocking wanted to pull out. She was shooing us away. My mother, who had just earned her driver's license, started furiously working the pedals. But in her haste she must have flooded the engine, for it wouldn't turn over. The driver started honking and then another car began honking as well, and soon it seemed the entire street was shrieking at us.

16 In the following years, my mother grew steadily more comfortable with English. In Korean, she could be fiery, stern, deeply funny and ironic; in English, just slightly less so. If she was never quite fluent, she gained enough confidence to make herself clearly known to anyone, and particularly to me.

17 Five years ago, she died of cancer, and some months after we buried her I found myself in the driveway of my father's house, washing her sedan. I liked taking care of her things; it made me feel close to her. While I was cleaning out the glove compartment, I found her pocket English workbook, the one with the silly illustrations. I hadn't seen it in nearly 20 years. The yellowed pages were brittle and dog-earned. She had fashioned a plain-paper wrapping for it, and I wondered whether she meant to protect the book or hide it.

18 I don't doubt that she would have appreciated doing the family shopping on the new Broad Avenue of Palisades Park. But I like to think, too, that she would have understood those who now complain about the Korean-only signs.

19 I wonder what these same people would have done if they had seen my mother studying her English workbook—or lost in a store. Would they have nodded gently at her? Would they have lent a kind word?

FOR THINKING, DISCUSSING, AND WRITING

1. The writer's mother had problems with the English language. Why, then, does the writer say that he sympathizes with English speakers who object to Korean language signs in a New Jersey commercial strip? Is he sincere, do you think? Ironic? Using reverse psychology? How effective is his approach and why?
2. The essay chronicles the kinds of problems speakers of other languages have when they come up against American language and culture. What ways can you suggest for easing the language burden on nonnative speakers? Or do you think that the issue of language in this case is insurmountable? Explain why you hold the ideas that you do.
3. The writer refers to mimicking his own father and the resulting laughter. However, when the writer mimics his mother, a reprimand follows. How do you explain such different reactions to the same kind of situation?
4. Write an essay on whether—and how—American society should ease the burden of speakers of other languages who come to live and work here.

RICHARD RODRIGUEZ

Public and Private Language

Richard Rodriguez (1944–) grew up in San Francisco, the son of Mexican-American parents. With degrees from Stanford, Columbia, and the University of California at Berkeley, Rodriguez has written widely for popular periodicals like Harper's, Time, *and* U.S. News and World Report. *He is the author of* Days of Obligation: An Argument with My Mexican Father *(1992) and* Brown: The Last Discovery of America *(2002). This selection appears in the autobiographical* Hunger of Memory *(1986), reissued in paperback in 2004. Rodriguez writes here about speaking Spanish and English and the degrees of public and private discourse that their use implies.*

1 Supporters of bilingual education today imply that students like me miss a great deal by not being taught in their family's language. What they seem not to recognize is that, as a socially disadvantaged child, I considered Spanish to be a private language. What I needed to learn in school was that I had the right—and the obligation—to speak the public language of *los gringos*. The odd truth is that my first-grade classmates could have become bilingual, in the conventional sense of that word, more easily than I. Had they been taught (as upper-middle-class children are often taught early) a second language like Spanish or French, they could have regarded it simply as that: another public language. In my case such bilingualism could not have been so quickly achieved. What I did not believe was that I could speak a single public language.

2 Without question, it would have pleased me to hear my teachers address me in Spanish when I entered the classroom. I would have felt much less afraid. I would have trusted them and responded with ease. But I would have delayed—for how long postponed?—having to learn the language of public society. I would have evaded—and for how long could I have afforded to delay?—learning the great lesson of school, that I had a public identity.

3 Fortunately, my teachers were unsentimental about their responsibility. What they understood was that I needed to speak a public language. So their voices would search me out, asking me questions. Each time I'd hear them, I'd look up in surprise to see a nun's face frowning at me. I'd mumble, not really meaning to answer. The nun would persist, "Richard, stand up. Don't look at the floor. Speak up. Speak to the entire class, not just to me!" but I couldn't believe that the English language was mine to use. (In part, I did not want to believe it.) I continued to mumble. I resisted the teacher's demands. (Did I somehow suspect that once I learned public language my pleasing family life would be changed?) Silent, waiting for the bell to sound, I remained dazed, diffident, afraid.

4 Because I wrongly imagined that English was intrinsically a public language and Spanish an intrinsically private one, I easily noticed the difference between classroom language and the language of home. At school, words were directed to a general audience of listeners ("Boys and girls.") Words were meaningfully ordered. And the point was not self-expression alone but to make oneself understood by many others. The teacher quizzed: "Boys and girls, why do we use that word in this

sentence? Could we think of a better word to use there? Would the sentence change its meaning if the words were differently arranged? And wasn't there a better way of saying much the same thing?" (I couldn't say. I wouldn't try to say.)

5 Three months. Five. Half a year passed. Unsmiling, ever watchful, my teachers noted my silence. They began to connect my behavior with the difficult progress my older sister and brother were making. Until one Saturday morning three nuns arrived at the house to talk to our parents. Stiffly, they sat on the blue living room sofa. From the doorway of another room, spying the visitors, I noted the incongruity—the clash of two worlds, the faces and voices of school intruding upon the familiar setting of home. I over-heard one voice gently wondering, "Do your children speak only Spanish at home, Mrs. Rodriguez?" While another voice added, "That Richard especially seems so timid and shy."

6 *That Rich-heard!*

7 With great tact the visitors continued, "Is it possible for you and your husband to encourage your children to practice their English when they are home?" Of course, my parents complied. What would they not do for their children's well-being? And how could they have questioned the Church's authority which those women represented? In an instant, they agreed to give up the language (the sounds) that had revealed and accentuated our family's closeness. The moment after the visitors left, the change was observed "*Ahora*, speak to us *en inglés*," my father and mother united to tell us.

8 At first, it seemed a kind of game. After dinner each night, the family gathered to practice "our" English. (It was still then *inglés*, a language foreign to us, so we felt drawn as strangers to it.) Laughing, we would try to define words we could not pronounce. We played with strange English sounds often overanglicizing our pronunciations. And we filled the smiling gaps of our sentences with familiar Spanish sounds. But that was cheating, somebody shouted. Everyone laughed. In school, meanwhile, like my brother and sister, I was required to attend a daily tutoring session. I needed a full year of special attention. I also needed my teachers to keep my attention from straying in class by calling out, *Rich-heard*—their English voices slowly prying loose my ties to my other name, its three notes, *Ri-car-do*. Most of all I needed to hear my mother and father speak to me in a moment of seriousness in broken—suddenly heartbreaking—English. The scene was inevitable: One Saturday morning I entered the kitchen where my parents were

talking in Spanish. I did not realize that they were talking in Spanish however until, at the moment they saw me, I heard their voices change to speak English. Those *gringo* sounds they uttered startled me. Pushed me away. In that moment of trivial misunderstanding and profound insight, I felt my throat twisted by unsounded grief. I turned quickly and left the room. But I had no place to escape to with Spanish. (The spell was broken.) My brother and sisters were speaking English in another part of the house.

9 Again and again in the days following, increasingly angry, I was obliged to hear my mother and father: "Speak to us *en inglés.*" *(Speak.)* Only then did I determine to learn classroom English. Weeks after, it happened: One day in school I had my hand raised to volunteer an answer. I spoke out in a loud voice. And I did not think it remarkable when the entire class understood. That day, I moved very far from the disadvantaged child I had been only days earlier. The belief, that calming assurance that I belonged in public, had at last taken hold.

10 Shortly after, I stopped hearing the high and loud sounds of *los gringos.* A more and more confident speaker of English, I didn't trouble to listen to *how* strangers sounded, speaking to me. And there simply were too many English-speaking people in my day for me to hear American accents anymore. Conversations quickened. Listening to persons whose voices sounded eccentrically pitched, I usually noted their sounds for an initial few seconds before I concentrated on *what* they were saying. Conversations became content-full. Transparent. Hearing someone's *tone* of voice—angry or questioning or sarcastic or happy or sad—I didn't distinguish it from the words it expressed. Sound and word were thus tightly wedded. At the end of a day, I was often bemused, always relieved, to realize how "silent," though crowded with words, my day in public had been. (This public silence measured and quickened the change in my life.)

11 At last, seven years old, I came to believe what had been technically true since my birth: I was an American citizen.

12 But the special feeling of closeness at home was diminished by then. Gone was the desperate, urgent, intense feeling of being a home; rare was the experience of feeling myself individualized by family intimates. We remained a loving family, but one greatly changed. No longer so close; no longer bound tight by the pleasing and troubling knowledge of our public separateness. Neither my older brother nor sister rushed home after school anymore. Nor did I. When I arrived

home there would often be neighborhood kids in the house. Or the house would be empty of sounds.

13 Following the dramatic Americanization of their children, even my parents grew more publicly confident. Especially my mother. She learned the names of all the people on our block. And she decided we needed to have a telephone installed in the house. My father continued to use the word *gringo.* But it was no longer charged with the old bitterness or distrust. (Stripped of any emotional content, the word simply became a name for those Americans not of Hispanic descent.) Hearing him, sometimes, I wasn't sure if he was pronouncing the Spanish word *gringo* or saying gringo in English.

14 Matching the silence I started hearing in public was a new quiet at home. The family's quiet was partly due to the fact that, as we children learned more and more English, we shared fewer and fewer words with our parents. Sentences needed to be spoken slowly when a child addressed his mother or father. (Often the parent wouldn't understand.) The child would need to repeat himself. (Still the parent misunderstood.) The young voice frustrated, would end up saying, "Never mind"—the subject was closed. Dinners would be noisy with the clinking of knives and forks against dishes. My mother would smile softly between her remarks; my father at the other end of the table would chew and chew at his food, while he stared over the heads of his children.

15 My *mother!* My *father!* After English became my primary language, I no longer knew what words to use in addressing my parents. The old Spanish words (those tender accents of sound) I had used earlier—*mamá* and *papá*—I couldn't use anymore. They would have been too painful reminders of how much had changed in my life. On the other hand, the words I heard neighborhood kids call *their* parents seemed equally unsatisfactory. *Mother* and *Father; Ma, Papa, Pa, Dad, Pop* (how I hated the all-American sound of that last word especially)—all these terms I felt were unsuitable, not really terms of address for *my* parents. As a result, I never used them at home. Whenever I'd speak to my parents, I would try to get their attention with eye contact alone. In public conversations, I'd refer to "my parents" or "my mother and father."

16 My mother and father, for their part, responded differently, as their children spoke to them less and less. She grew restless, seemed troubled and anxious at the scarcity of words exchanged in the house. It was she who would question me about my day when I came home from school. She smiled at the small talk. She pried at the edges of my sentences to

get me to say something more. (What?) She'd join conversations she overheard, but her intrusions often stopped her children's talking. By contrast, my father seemed reconciled to the new quiet. Though his English improved some what, he retired into silence. At dinner he spoke very little. One night his children and even his wife helplessly giggled at his garbled English pronunciation of the Catholic Grace before Meals. Thereafter he made his wife recite the prayer at the start of each meal, even on formal occasions, when there were guests in the house. Hers became the public voice of the family. On official business, it was she, not my father, one would usually hear on the phone or in stores, talking to strangers. His children grew so accustomed to his silence that, years later, they would speak routinely of his shyness. (My mother would often try to explain: Both his parents died when he was eight. He was raised by an uncle who treated him like little more than a menial servant. He was never encouraged to speak. He grew up alone. A man of few words.) But my father was not shy, I realized, when I'd watch him speaking Spanish with relatives. Using Spanish, he was quickly effusive. Especially when talking with other men, his voice would spark, flicker, flare alive with sounds. In Spanish, he expressed ideas and feelings he rarely revealed in English. With firm Spanish sounds, he conveyed confidence and authority English would never allow him.

17 The silence at home, however, was finally more than a literal silence. Fewer words passed between parent and child, but more profound was the silence that resulted from my inattention to sounds. At about the time I no longer bothered to listen with care to the sounds of English in public, I grew careless about listening to the sounds family members made when they spoke. Most of the time I heard someone speaking at home and didn't distinguish his sounds from the words people uttered in public. I didn't even pay much attention to my parents' accented and ungrammatical speech. At least not at home. Only when I was with them in public would I grow alert to their accents. Though, even then, their sounds caused me less and less concern. For I was increasingly confident of my own public identity.

18 Today I hear bilingual educators say that children lose a degree of "individuality" by becoming assimilated into public society. (Bilingual schooling was popularized in the seventies, that decade when middle-class ethnics began to resist the process of assimilation—the American melting pot.) But the bilingualists simplistically scorn the value and

necessity of assimilation. They do not seem to realize that there are *two* ways a person is individualized. So they do not realize that while one suffers a diminished sense of *private* individuality by becoming assimilated into public society, such assimilation makes possible the achievement of *public* individuality.

FOR THINKING, DISCUSSING, AND WRITING

1. Rodriguez uses the words *public* and *private* to indicate different concepts of language. What do the words mean generally? How do they serve to particularize the idea of language and identity?
2. How does Rodriguez use dialogue to good advantage? What does it contribute to the essay?
3. How did Rodriguez learn to speak English confidently? Would this method work for all speakers of other languages who wanted to learn English, do you think? Why or why not?
4. Write an essay in which you consider Rodriguez's point in the final paragraph where he distinguishes between bilingualism and assimilation.

WALTER BENN MICHAELS

Last Words

Walter Benn Michaels (1948–) has a PhD from the University of California, Santa Barbara, and has taught at Johns Hopkins University and the University of California at Berkeley. Currently professor of American literature and literary theory at the University of Illinois at Chicago, he is the author of Our America: Nativism, Modernism, and Pluralism *(1995),* The Shape of the Signifier *(2005), and, more recently,* The Trouble with Diversity: How We Learned to Love Identity and Ignore Inequality *(2006). In this essay for the October 1, 2006, issue of the* New York Times Magazine, *he considers the phenomenon of vanishing languages.*

1 The subject of disappearing languages has been in the news for some time—the standard prediction is that roughly half of the 6,000 languages currently spoken are, as Unesco puts it, "doomed"—but it has recently been given new impetus in the United States by the fear expressed by some conservative commentators that English is being

added to the list. Will American English survive "the immigrant flood" of Spanish-speaking migrants, recent columns in the weekly Human Events have asked. Their answer is, "tragically," no. But would it really be a tragedy if English vanished?

2 Of course, the idea that English is a vanishing language seems a little implausible (it's the second-most-spoken language in the world), but then it was only a few years ago that the U.S. dominated world basketball, and look what has happened there. Furthermore, there's a long history on this continent of immigrant languages killing off the indigenous ones. Scholars believe that there used to be as many as 300 Native American languages. Now there are fewer than 200. What happened? Well, one thing that happened was that missionaries and the federal government did their best to get the Indians to stop talking in what J.D.C. Atkins, a 19th-century commissioner of Indian affairs, called their "barbarous dialect" and to start talking in "civilized" languages like English. And another was that even when they couldn't kill off the language, they were often quite effective at killing off the people who spoke it. Hence English flourished, and languages like Tlingit, for example, didn't.

3 Things are obviously better today. Not only are almost no English speakers being murdered by linguistically evangelizing Mexicans; no Spanish speakers are complaining about how barbarous English is. In fact, few people today think that any languages are either barbarous or civilized. "No language," as the linguist John Edwards has written, "can be described as better or worse than another on purely linguistic grounds"; all "languages are always sufficient for the needs of their speakers." Which is why the effort to get people to stop speaking in their own tongues (taking them away to special boarding schools, punishing them when they didn't speak English) and to start speaking in yours looked then, and still looks now, like an essentially arbitrary use of power. Theirs is just as good as yours: why should they give it up?

4 So the good news is that progress has been made; no one any longer thinks that one language is better than another. But the bad news is that many languages are dying anyway. In fact, for various social and economic reasons, they are dying faster than ever. Many of the Native American languages that still exist are spoken by a very few old people, and while no one is trying to force them to stop speaking whatever it is they speak, no one is having much success in persuading their children and grandchildren to continue speaking it. So where the

tragic figure of 19th-century language loss was a child discouraged from speaking her own language and made to speak English instead, the tragic figure of 21st-century language loss is an elder allowed, and even encouraged, to speak her own language but with no one around to speak it to. The 19th-century problem was about people who couldn't use their languages; the problem now is about the languages themselves—"tragically," they're disappearing.

5 But why would it be a tragedy if English disappeared? Why is it a tragedy if Tlingit disappears? Although we can all agree it's a bad thing to try to get people to stop using their language, it's hard to see why it's a bad thing if their language disappears. Why? Because the very thing that made it a mistake for the missionaries to try to stop people from speaking Native American languages (it's not as if English was better) makes it a mistake to care whether people continue to speak Native American languages (it's not as if English is worse).

6 We can see the point clearly by pretending for a second that English really is starting to vanish. Suppose our children start speaking a little Spanish, our grandchildren become bilingual and our great-grandchildren speak only Spanish. Since we can't speak Spanish, we can't talk to them. But if that's a problem, it won't last for long, and once it is solved, there will be no problem left. Just as the language we speak does everything we need it to do, the language they speak will do everything they need it to do. No doubt it's unfortunate that our descendants won't be able to read Shakespeare in the original. But, truth to tell, we're not doing much of that ourselves anyway. It's not as if we're native speakers of Elizabethan English. That's why there's a market for "No Fear Shakespeare": the Bard on one page; a "translation into modern English—the kind of English people actually speak today" on the other. And, of course, instead of Shakespeare and Joyce, our descendants will be able to read Cervantes and Borges—the classics of their literature if not of ours.

7 Which is the whole point. Our language is the one we speak, not the one our ancestors spoke. My great-grandparents could read only Yiddish. Am I supposed to feel a stronger connection to Abramovich's "Kliatche" ("Mare"), a book I never heard of until I looked up Yiddish classics on the Web two minutes ago, than, say, to "Vanity Fair," a book my ancestors wouldn't have understood one word of? And are my descendants supposed to feel they are losing their cultural heritage just because the old books they are reading are not the same as the old books I read?

8 Obviously not. Their cultural heritage will be the books they read; their language will be the one they speak. A language will have been lost, but like the old joke about the great train robbery (no loss of train), no one will have lost his language. And no one will have lost his literature or his cultural heritage or what our English supremacists say they most want to retain, their American identity. You can read "No Fear Cervantes" in Spanish; you can sing "The Star-Spangled Banner" in Spanish; you can invade Iraq in Spanish; you can even lose the finals of the World Basketball Championship in Spanish. Although this year (Spain 70, Greece 47), it didn't happen.

FOR THINKING, DISCUSSING, AND WRITING

1. Michaels recognizes that the possibility of the English language's vanishing is implausible, but how does he counter the notion of implausibility? How effective are his points, do you think? What reasons does he give for the disappearance of more than a hundred Native-American languages?
2. The writer quotes linguist John Edwards as saying that no language is "better or worse than another on purely linguistic grounds." Why might you agree or disagree with the statement? How would the proponents of the "English-only" movement respond?
3. Why does Michaels believe that it's no tragedy if English disappeared?
4. Write an essay called "If English Disappeared" and state your views on a future in this country and worldwide without the English language.

CONNECTING IDEAS: Language and Word Power

1. Writers like Sandra Cisneros, Chang-rae Lee, and Richard Rodriguez in this chapter examine part of the immigrant experience through the use of language. Write an essay in which you compare and contrast their views of language in regard to non-native speakers of English.
2. What is your view on the use of the "F" word in everyday discourse and in written work? Note how the writer of "A Small Plea to Delete a Ubiquitous Expletive," Elizabeth Austin, puts part of the phrase in quotation marks. What do you think Barbara Carton would say about that?
3. What is your view of the power of language? Does language have power in fact? How does it stand up to actions or deeds? How has language helped shape the world as we know it? What do we mean when we say that a picture is worth a thousand words—does the statement diminish language in any way, do you think?

CHAPTER 9

Beliefs, Values, and the Human Condition

THE ISSUE OF VALUES AND ETHICS HAS OCCUPIED human consciousness for centuries as we human beings attempt to define appropriate moral choices in our relations with others in the world around us.

Many people do try to lead morally unambiguous lives. The manner in which we meet the ordinary demands on us as husbands, wives, parents, children, caregivers, and citizens, for instance, grows from profound personal beliefs and values that help define our character. But in extraordinary ways, too, ordinary people follow deep-seated moral principles to commit acts of ethical valor and courage. Risking dismissal, an accountant for a large corporation notes fiscally dishonest practices and reports her findings to the Internal Revenue Service. In a local hospital a nurse finds several thousand dollars in the bed sheets of a discharged patient and without a second thought returns the money promptly. A worker returning from a hard day rushes into a burning building against great odds to rescue a trapped and helpless old woman. A passerby breaks a car window with his elbow to save a child from a crash that killed all other passengers.

Ethical people will not cheat or steal or harm others to forward their own interests; they are faithful to a system of values that suffuses their existence. Whether learned at home, at school, in church or synagogue or mosque, or at the feet of a respected relative, community member, or friend, or a dynamic combination of these elements, the beliefs that guide us shape the way we respond to the world and its problems. We read every day how American citizens contribute time and money to worthy causes, from hurricane relief to starving African children, from the urban homeless to animals in distress, from disease-ridden seniors to the sight- and hearing-impaired. High school and college students undertake charitable causes that require great effort and long hours. Corporations donate money and equipment to further relief efforts. Neighborhoods galvanize to keep their streets safe and clean.

In the fourth century B.C.E., Aristotle developed a theory of morality rooted in a sense that people had some distinctive end to accomplish or purpose to achieve. Every pursuit, he says in the *Nichomachean Ethics*, aims at some good, although he did puzzle over just what good human behavior aimed toward. The great philosophers including Plato, Aquinas, Hegel, Hume, Kant, and Spinoza all turned their eyes to ethics at some point in their investigation of knowledge: what system of moral principles or values, of right or good conduct, should guide our actions? In other words, how do we live a life of good?

Asking how to lead a life of good, however, is not the same as asking how to live the good life, a question that occupies much of society today, and takes root in a kind of materialism and self-absorption that critics cite in condemning what they see as our society's unethical behavior. These critics believe that in our time Aristotle's idea of "good" has completely escaped our attention. They habitually refer to society's deteriorating morality, nowhere perhaps as loudly as in the arena of honesty. Truth and falsehood mingle in the public consciousness, one often indistinguishable from the other. In this chapter, Stephanie Ericsson in "The Ways We Lie" has classified our deceptions; so diverse are they that she gives us pause about our commitment to truthfulness as an important human value. And Langston Hughes in "Salvation," another selection here, explores the painful consequences of a lie that grows in significance to an entire community.

The attacks on contemporary morality are legion. Critics complain about violence at the hands of young people and about parents who abandon their children, about pornography on the printed page and on celluloid, about improper conduct among elected officials perceived as paragons of correct behavior, and about celebrity crimes that bring endless media attention into our living rooms. Our behavioral models are glamorous superheroes who influence our notions of right action. Superman, Batman, Spider-Man, and Charlie's Angels evoke in us "a sharp mixture of projection, longing, admiration, and aspiration" in the words of Virginia Postrel in another chapter selection, "Superhero Worship."

Parents, politicians, teachers, and business leaders decry the loss of values and morality across society. School districts have banned books deemed immoral and have instituted values-clarification programs; religious leaders have demanded a return to prayer in the schools. On college campuses the values debate is vociferous as critics question the ethical fiber of today's students. Too much drinking: moral disintegration. Ubiquitous, loveless sex more an athletic exercise than a deep human commitment: deplorable. Indifference to politics: another black mark. Obsessive attention to jobs and money: yet another ill. Of course, the self-righteous easily could isolate almost any subgroup of our culture and lodge against it various complaints of ethical lapses: lawyers, doctors, ethnic groups, and geographical groups, members of different economic classes or social strata.

Despite all the negative clamor, to view our society as essentially corrupt is to deny the efforts of millions focused on doing the right thing—whatever their philosophy, religion, and (or) intellectual acuity lead them to believe the right thing is. The environment, gun-control, euthanasia, animal rights, the torture of prisoners—these are only a few of the innumerable contemporary issues that draw men and women into debate and action over personal beliefs and values. True, many people address these issues along partisan lines, and often do not show a proclivity toward clear thinking, but usually, one can identify a system of moral principles and values that underlie commitment to a particular position or action. One person's ethical guidelines can be another's loathing, of course, with many gradations between polar positions, and so it is often impossible, and probably not even desirable, to determine the absolute correct way to address an issue. Yet to assume that all positions are relativistic—that is, anyone's opinion goes—is to belie the struggle to identify the principles of good conduct that should guide individual lives and produce a society based on ethical standards. To have even a measure of validity, any moral position must take root in identifiable beliefs subject to discussion and review.

The selections in this chapter (and, to be sure, in many other chapters of this book) address important issues in the values conversation, and they share a common goal of trying to distinguish right from wrong. As you know, personal beliefs and values underlie our daily thoughts and actions in both subtle and overt ways. We must see in the human condition the possibilities of great advances in establishing criteria for just behavior.

As you read, be sure to consider your own beliefs in light of the ideas and assertions here.

MARTIN LUTHER KING JR.

I Have a Dream

Martin Luther King Jr. (1929–1968), a central twentieth-century figure, was a clergyman and civil rights leader noted for his belief in nonviolence. He was propelled onto the national stage with the famous Montgomery boycott of 1954. King founded the Southern Christian Leadership Conference, and was awarded the Nobel Peace Prize in 1964. He was assassinated in 1968. King delivered the moving "I Have a Dream Speech" during the 1963 March on Washington. The extraordinary rhythms and poetic language have helped make the speech unforgettable in the history of human rights in America.

1 Five score years ago, a great American, in *whose symbolic shadow we stand*, signed the Emancipation Proclamation. This momentous decree came as a great beacon light of hope to millions of Negro slaves who had been seared in the flames of withering injustice. It came as a joyous daybreak to end the long night of captivity.

2 But one hundred years later, we must face the tragic fact that the Negro is still not free. One hundred years later, the life of the Negro is still sadly crippled by the manacles of segregation and the chains of discrimination. One hundred years later, the Negro lives on a lonely island of poverty in the midst of a vast ocean of material prosperity. One hundred years later, the Negro is still languishing in the corners of American society and finds himself an exile in his own land. So we have come here today to dramatize an appalling condition.

3 In a sense we have come to our nation's capital to cash a check. When the architects of our republic wrote the magnificent words of the Constitution and the Declaration of Independence, they were signing a promissory note to which every American was to fall heir. This note was

a promise that all men would be guaranteed the unalienable rights of life, liberty, and the pursuit of happiness.

4 It is obvious today that America has defaulted on this promissory note insofar as her citizens of color are concerned. Instead of honoring this sacred obligation, America has given the Negro people a bad check; a check which has come back marked "insufficient funds." But we refuse to believe that the bank of justice is bankrupt. We refuse to believe that there are insufficient funds in the great vaults of opportunity of this nation. So we have come to cash this check—a check that will give us upon demand the riches of freedom and the security of justice. We have also come to this hallowed spot to remind America of the fierce urgency of *now*. This is no time to engage in the luxury of cooling off or to take the tranquilizing drugs of gradualism. *Now* is the time to make real the promises of Democracy. *Now* is the time to rise from the dark and desolate valley of segregation to the sunlit path of racial justice. *Now* is the time to open the doors of opportunity to all of God's children. *Now* is the time to lift our nation from the quicksands of racial injustice to the solid rock of brotherhood.

5 It would be fatal for the nation to overlook the urgency of the moment and to underestimate the determination of the Negro. This sweltering summer of the Negro's legitimate discontent will not pass until there is an invigorating autumn of freedom and equality. 1963 is not an end, but a beginning. Those who hope that the Negro needed to blow off steam and will now be content will have a rude awakening if the nation returns to business as usual. There will be neither rest nor tranquility in America until the Negro is granted his citizenship rights. The whirlwinds of revolt will continue to shake the foundations of our nation until the bright day of justice emerges.

6 But there is something that I must say to my people who stand on the warm threshold which leads into the palace of justice. In the process of gaining our rightful place we must not be guilty of wrongful deeds. Let us not seek to satisfy our thirst for freedom by drinking from the cup of bitterness and hatred. We must forever conduct our struggle on the high plane of dignity and discipline. We must not allow our creative protest to degenerate into physical violence. Again and again we must rise to the majestic heights of meeting physical force with soul force. The marvelous new militancy which has engulfed the Negro community must not lead us to a distrust of all white people, for many of our white brothers, as evidenced by their presence here today, have

come to realize that their destiny is tied up with our destiny and their freedom is inextricably bound to our freedom. We cannot walk alone.

7 And as we walk, we must make the pledge that we shall march ahead. We cannot turn back. There are those who are asking the devotees of civil rights, "When will you be satisfied?" We can never be satisfied as long as the Negro is the victim of the unspeakable horrors of police brutality. We can never be satisfied as long as our bodies, heavy with the fatigue of travel, cannot gain lodging in the motels of the highways and the hotels of the cities. We cannot be satisfied as long as the Negro's basic mobility is from a smaller ghetto to a larger one. We can never be satisfied as long as a Negro in Mississippi cannot vote and a Negro in New York believes he has nothing for which to vote. No, no, we are not satisfied, and we will not be satisfied until justice rolls down like waters and righteousness like a mighty stream.

8 I am not unmindful that some of you have come here out of great trials and tribulations. Some of you have come fresh from narrow jail cells. Some of you have come from areas where your quest for freedom left you battered by the storms of persecution and staggered by the winds of police brutality. You have been the veterans of creative suffering. Continue to work with the faith that unearned suffering is redemptive.

9 Go back to Mississippi, go back to Alabama, go back to South Carolina, go back to Georgia, go back to Louisiana, go back to the slums and ghettos of our northern cities, knowing that somehow this situation can and will be changed. Let us not wallow in the valley of despair.

10 I say to you today, my friends, that in spite of the difficulties and frustrations of the moment I still have a dream. It is a dream deeply rooted in the American dream.

11 I have a dream that one day this nation will rise up and live out the true meaning of its creed: "We hold these truths to be self-evident; that all men are created equal."

12 I have a dream that one day on the red hills of Georgia the sons of former slaves and the sons of former slaveowners will be able to sit down together at the table of brotherhood.

13 I have a dream that one day even the state of Mississippi, a desert state sweltering with the heat of injustice and oppression, will be transformed into an oasis of freedom and justice.

14 I have a dream that my four little children will one day live in a nation where they will not be judged by the color of their skin but by the content of their character.

15 I have a dream today.

16 I have a dream that one day the state of Alabama, whose governor's lips are presently dripping with the words of interposition and nullification, will be transformed into a situation where little black boys and black girls will be able to join hands with little white boys and white girls and walk together as sisters and brothers.

17 I have a dream today.

18 I have a dream that one day every valley shall be exalted, every hill and mountain shall be made low, the rough places will be made plain, and the crooked places will be made straight, and the glory of the Lord shall be revealed, and all flesh shall see it together.

19 This is our hope. This is the faith with which I return to the South. With this faith we will be able to hew out of the mountain of despair a stone of hope. With this faith we will be able to transform the jangling discords of our nation into a beautiful symphony of brotherhood. With this faith we will be able to work together, to pray together, to struggle together, to go to jail together, to stand up for freedom together, knowing that we will be free one day.

20 This will be the day when all of God's children will be able to sing with new meaning

My country, 'tis of thee,
Sweet land of liberty,
Of thee I sing:
Land where my fathers died,
Land of the pilgrims' pride,
From every mountain-side
Let freedom ring.

21 And if America is to be a great nation this must become true. So let freedom ring from the prodigious hilltops of New Hampshire. Let freedom ring from the mighty mountains of New York. Let freedom ring from the heightening Alleghenies of Pennsylvania!

22 Let freedom ring from the snowcapped Rockies of Colorado!

23 Let freedom ring from the curvaceous peaks of California!

24 But not only that; let freedom ring from Stone Mountain of Georgia!

25 Let freedom ring from Lookout Mountain of Tennessee!

26 Let freedom ring from every hill and molehill of Mississippi. From every mountainside, let freedom ring.

27 When we let freedom ring, when we let it ring from every village and every hamlet, from every state and every city, we will be able to speed up that day when all of God's children, black men and white

men, Jews and Gentiles, Protestants and Catholics, will be able to join hands and sing in the words of the old Negro spiritual, "Free at last! free at last! Thank God almighty, we are free at last!"

FOR THINKING, DISCUSSING, AND WRITING

1. What course of action does King advise his listeners to take in spite of their frustrations? What personal beliefs underlie his recommendation?
2. Why does King begin his address with the words "five score years ago"? Why in the second paragraph does he then repeat "one hundred years later" four times? What other repetitions do you find in the speech? What effect does he gain, for example, by repeating, "Let freedom ring," in paragraphs 21 through 27? Why has he used them?
3. What philosophy does King advocate in paragraph 6, particularly with the statement "we must rise to the majestic heights of meeting physical force with soul force"? How has this philosophy influenced American values? How has it influenced world values? How could you apply the philosophy in your own life?
4. Choose another ethnic or racial group and compose an "I Have a Dream" speech that might reflect their status and aspirations in contemporary American society.

STEPHANIE ERICSSON

The Ways We Lie

Stephanie Ericsson (1953–) is a writer and screenwriter who was born in San Francisco and began writing at the age of fifteen. Her works include Shamefaced *(1985),* Women of AA: Recovering Together *(1985), and* Companion Through the Darkness: Inner Dialogues on Grief *(1993). Ericsson reveals in this selection the many faces of the lies people tell.*

1 The bank called today and I told them my deposit was in the mail, even though I hadn't written a check yet. It'd been a rough day. The baby I'm pregnant with decided to do aerobics on my lungs for two hours, our three-year-old daughter painted the living-room couch with lipstick, the IRS put me on hold for an hour, and I was late to a business meeting because I was tired.

2 I told my client that traffic had been bad. When my partner came home, his haggard face told me his day hadn't gone any better than mine, so when he asked, "How was your day?" I said, "Oh, fine," knowing that one more straw might break his back. A friend called and wanted to take me to lunch. I said I was busy. Four lies in the course of a day, none of which I felt the least bit guilty about.

3 We lie. We all do. We exaggerate, we minimize, we avoid confrontation, we spare people's feelings, we conveniently forget, we keep secrets, we justify lying to the big-guy institutions. Like most people, I indulge in small falsehoods and still think of myself as an honest person. Sure I lie, but it doesn't hurt anything. Or does it?

4 I once tried going a whole week without telling a lie, and it was paralyzing. I discovered that telling the truth all the time is nearly impossible. It means living with some serious consequences: The bank charges me $60 in overdraft fees, my partner keels over when I tell him about my travails, my client fires me for telling her I didn't feel like being on time, and my friend takes it personally when I say I'm not hungry. There must be some merit to lying.

5 But if I justify lying, what makes me any different from slick politicians or the corporate robbers who raided the S&L industry? Saying it's okay to lie one way and not another is hedging. I cannot seem to escape the voice deep inside me that tells me: When someone lies, someone loses.

6 What far-reaching consequences will I, or others, pay as a result of my lie? Will someone's trust be destroyed? Will someone else pay *my* penance because I ducked out? We must consider the *meaning of our actions*. Deception, lies, capital crimes, and misdemeanors all carry meanings. *Webster's* definition of *lie* is specific:

1. *a false statement or action especially made with the intent to deceive;*
2. *anything that gives or is meant to give a false impression.*

7 A definition like this implies that there are many, many ways to tell a lie. Here are just a few.

The White Lie

> *A man who won't lie to a woman has very little consideration for her feelings.*
>
> —*Bergen Evans*

8 The white lie assumes that the truth will cause more damage than a simple, harmless untruth. Telling a friend he looks great when he looks like hell can be based on a decision that the friend needs a compliment more than a frank opinion. But, in effect, it is the liar deciding what is best for the lied to. Ultimately, it is a vote of no confidence. It is an act of subtle arrogance for anyone to decide what is best for someone else.

9 Yet not all circumstances are quite so cut-and-dried. Take, for instance, the sergeant in Vietnam who knew one of his men was killed in action but listed him as missing so that the man's family would receive indefinite compensation instead of the lump-sum pittance the military gives widows and children. His intent was honorable. Yet for twenty years this family kept their hopes alive, unable to move on to a new life.

Façades

Et tu, Brute?

—*Caesar*

10 We all put up façades to one degree or another. When I put on a suit to go to see a client, I feel as though I am putting on another face, obeying the expectation that serious businesspeople wear suits rather than sweatpants. But I'm a writer. Normally, I get up, get the kid off to school, and sit at my computer in my pajamas until four in the afternoon. When I answer the phone, the caller thinks I'm wearing a suit (though the UPS man knows better).

11 But façades can be destructive because they are used to seduce others into an illusion. For instance, I recently realized that a former friend was a liar. He presented himself with all the right looks and the right words and offered lots of new consciousness theories, fabulous books to read, and fascinating insights. Then I did some business with him, and the time came for him to pay me. He turned out to be all talk and no walk. I heard a plethora of reasonable excuses, including in-depth descriptions of the big break around the corner. In six months of work, I saw less than a hundred bucks. When I confronted him, he raised both eyebrows and tried to convince me that I'd heard him wrong, that he'd made no commitment to me. A simple investigation into his past revealed a crowded graveyard of disenchanted former friends.

Ignoring the Plain Facts

Well, you must understand that Father Porter is only human . . . .

— *A Massachusetts priest*

12 In the '60s, the Catholic Church in Massachusetts began hearing complaints that Father James Porter was sexually molesting children. Rather than relieving him of his duties, the ecclesiastical authorities simply moved him from one parish to another between 1960 and 1967, actually providing him with a fresh supply of unsuspecting families and innocent children to abuse. After treatment in 1967 for pedophilia, he went back to work, this time in Minnesota. The new diocese was aware of Father Porter's obsession with children, but they needed priests and recklessly believed treatment had cured him. More children were abused until he was relieved of his duties a year later. By his own admission, Porter may have abused as many as a hundred children.

13 Ignoring the facts may not in and of itself be a form of lying, but consider the context of this situation. If a lie is *a false action done with the intent to deceive*, then the Catholic Church's conscious covering for Porter created irreparable consequences. The church became a coperpetrator with Porter.

Deflecting

When you have no basis for an argument, abuse the plaintiff.

— *Cicero*

14 I've discovered that I can keep anyone from seeing the true me by being selectively blatant. I set a precedent of being up-front about intimate issues, but I never bring up the things I truly want to hide; I just let people assume I'm revealing everything. It's an effective way of hiding.

15 Any good liar knows that the way to perpetuate an untruth is to deflect attention from it. When Clarence Thomas exploded with accusations that the Senate hearings were a "high-tech lynching," he simply switched the focus from a highly charged subject to a radioactive subject.[1] Rather than defending himself, he took the offensive and accused the country of racism. It was a brilliant maneuver. Racism is

[1] Ericsson refers to the 1991 Supreme Court hearings to confirm Thomas. Anita Hill had accused Thomas of sexual harassment.

now politically incorrect in official circles—unlike sexual harassment, which still rewards those who can get away with it.

16 Some of the most skilled deflectors are passive-aggressive people who, when accused of inappropriate behavior, refuse to respond to the accusations. This you-don't-exist stance infuriates the accuser, who, understandably, screams something obscene out of frustration. The trap is sprung and the act of deflection successful, because now the passive-aggressive person can indignantly say, "Who can talk to someone as unreasonable as you?" The real issue is forgotten and the sins of the original victim become the focus. Feeling guilty of name-calling, the victim is fully tamed and crawls into a hole, ashamed. I have watched this fighting technique work thousands of times in disputes between men and women, and what I've learned is that the real culprit is not necessarily the one who swears the loudest.

Omission

The cruelest lies are often told in silence.

—R. L. Stevenson

17 Omission involves telling most of the truth minus one or two key facts whose absence changes the story completely. You break a pair of glasses that are guaranteed under normal use and get a new pair, without mentioning that the first pair broke during a rowdy game of basketball. Who hasn't tried something like that? But what about omission of information that could make a difference in how a person lives his or her life?

18 For instance, one day I found out that rabbinical legends tell of another woman in the Garden of Eden before Eve. I was stunned. The omission of the Sumerian goddess Lilith from Genesis—as well as her demonization by ancient misogynists as an embodiment of female evil—felt like spiritual robbery. I felt like I'd just found out my mother was really my stepmother. To take seriously the tradition that Adam was created out of the same mud as his equal counterpart, Lilith, redefines all of Judeo-Christian history.

19 Some renegade Catholic feminists introduced me to a view of Lilith that had been suppressed during the many centuries when this strong goddess was seen only as a spirit of evil. Lilith was a proud goddess who defied Adam's need to control her, attempted negotiations, and when this failed, said adios and left the Garden of Eden.

20 This omission of Lilith from the Bible was a patriarchal strategy to keep women weak. Omitting the strong-woman archetype of Lilith from Western religions and starting the story with Eve the Rib has helped keep Christian and Jewish women believing they were the lesser sex for thousands of years.

Stereotypes and Clichés

> *Where opinion does not exist, the status quo becomes stereotyped and all originality is discouraged.*
>
> —*Bertrand Russell*

21 Sterotype and cliché serve a purpose as a form of shorthand. Our need for vast amounts of information in nanoseconds has made the stereotype vital to modern communication. Unfortunately, it often shuts down original thinking, giving those hungry for the truth a candy bar of misinformation instead of a balanced meal. The stereotype explains a situation with just enough truth to seem unquestionable.

22 All the "isms"—racism, sexism, ageism, et al.—are founded on and fueled by the stereotype and the cliché, which are lies of exaggeration, omission, and ignorance. They are always dangerous. They take a single tree and make it a landscape. They destroy curiosity. They close minds and separate people. The single mother on welfare is assumed to be cheating. Any black male could tell you how much of his identity is obliterated daily by stereotypes. Fat people, ugly people, beautiful people, old people, large-breasted women, short men, the mentally ill, and the homeless all could tell you how much more they are like us than we want to think. I once admitted to a group of people that I had a mouth like a truck driver. Much to my surprise, a man stood up and said, "I'm a truck driver, and I never cuss." Needless to say, I was humbled.

Groupthink

> *Who is more foolish, the child afraid of the dark, or the man afraid of the light?*
>
> —*Maurice Freehill*

23 Irving Janis, in *Victims of Group Think*, defines this sort of lie as a psychological phenomenon within decision-making groups in which loyalty to the group has become more important than any other value, with the result that dissent and the appraisal of alternatives are suppressed. If you've ever worked on a committee or in a corporation, you've encountered groupthink. It requires a combination of other forms of lying—ignoring facts, selective memory, omission, and denial, to name a few.

24 The textbook example of groupthink came on December 7, 1941. From as early as the fall of 1941, the warnings came in, one after another, that Japan was preparing for a massive military operation. The Navy command in Hawaii assumed Pearl Harbor was invulnerable—the Japanese weren't stupid enough to attack the United States' most important base. On the other hand, racist stereotypes said the Japanese weren't smart enough to invent a torpedo effective in less than 60 feet of water (the fleet was docked in 30 feet); after all, U.S. technology hadn't been able to do it.

25 On Friday, December 5, normal weekend leave was granted to all the commanders at Pearl Harbor, even though the Japanese consulate in Hawaii was busy burning papers. Within the tight, good-ole-boy cohesiveness of the U.S. command in Hawaii, the myth of invulnerability stayed well entrenched. No one in the group considered the alternatives. The rest is history.

Out-and-Out Lies

The only form of lying that is beyond reproach is lying for its own sake.

—*Oscar Wilde*

26 Of all the ways to lie, I like this one the best, probably because I get tired of trying to figure out the real meanings behind things. At least I can trust the bald-faced lie. I once asked my five-year-old nephew, "Who broke the fence?" (I had seen him do it.) He answered, "The murderers." Who could argue?

27 At least when this sort of lie is told it can be easily confronted. As the person who is lied to, I know where I stand. The bald-faced lie doesn't toy with my perceptions—it argues with them. It doesn't try to refashion reality, it tries to refute it. *Read my lips . . .* No sleight of hand.

No guessing. If this were the only form of lying, there would be no such things as floating anxiety or the adult-children-of-alcoholics movement.

Dismissal

Pay no attention to that man behind the curtain! I am the Great Oz!

—*The Wizard of Oz*

28 Dismissal is perhaps the slipperiest of all lies. Dismissing feelings, perceptions, or even the raw facts of a situation ranks as a kind of lie that can do as much damage to a person as any other kind of lie.

29 The roots of many mental disorders can be traced back to the dismissal of reality. Imagine that a person is told from the time she is a tot that her perceptions are inaccurate. "*Mommy, I'm scared.*" "No you're not, darling." "*I don't like that man next door, he makes me feet icky.*" "Johnny, that's a terrible thing to say, of course you like him. You go over there right now and be nice to him."

30 I've often mused over the idea that madness is actually a sane reaction to an insane world. Psychologist R.D. Laing supports this hypothesis in *Sanity, Madness and the Family,* an account of his investigation into the families of schizophrenics. The common thread that ran through all of the families he studied was a deliberate, staunch dismissal of the patient's perceptions from a very early age. Each of the patients started out with an accurate grasp of reality, which, through meticulous and methodical dismissal, was demolished until the only reality the patient could trust was catatonia.

31 Dismissal runs the gamut. Mild dismissal can be quite handy for forgiving the foibles of others in our day-to-day lives. Toddlers who have just learned to manipulate their parents' attention sometimes are dismissed out of necessity. Absolute attention from the parents would require so much energy that no one would get to eat dinner. But we must be careful and attentive about how far we take our "necessary" dismissals. Dismissal is a dangerous tool, because it's nothing less than a lie.

Delusion

We lie loudest when we lie to ourselves.

—*Eric Hoffer*

32 I could write the book on this one. Delusion, a cousin of dismissal, is the tendency to see excuses as facts. It's a powerful lying tool because it filters out information that contradicts what we want to believe. Alcoholics who believe that the problems in their lives are legitimate reasons for drinking rather than results of the drinking offer the classic example of deluded thinking. Delusion uses the mind's ability to see things in myriad ways to support what it wants to be the truth.

33 But delusion is also a survival mechanism we all use. If we were to fully contemplate the consequences of our stockpiles of nuclear weapons or global warming, we could hardly function on a day-to-day level. We don't want to incorporate that much reality into our lives because to do so would be paralyzing.

34 Delusion acts as an adhesive to keep the status quo intact. It shamelessly employs dismissal, omission, and amnesia, among other sorts of lies. Its most cunning defense is that it cannot see itself.

The liar's punishment . . . is that he cannot believe anyone else.

—George Bernard Shaw

35 These are only a few of the ways we lie. Or are lied to. As I said earlier, it's not easy to entirely eliminate lies from our lives. No matter how pious we may try to be, we will still embellish, hedge, and omit to lubricate the daily machinery of living. But there is a world of difference between telling functional lies and living a lie. Martin Buber once said, "The lie is the spirit committing treason against itself." Our acceptance of lies becomes a cultural cancer that eventually shrouds and reorders reality until moral garbage becomes as invisible to us as water is to a fish.

36 How much do we tolerate before we become sick and tired of being sick and tired? When will we stand up and declare our *right* to trust? When do we stop accepting that the real truth is in the fine print? Whose lips do we read this year when we vote for president? When will we stop being so reticent about making judgments? When do we stop turning over our personal power and responsibility to liars?

37 Maybe if I don't tell the bank the check's in the mail I'll be less tolerant of the lies told me every day. A country song I once heard said it all for me: "You've got to stand for something or you'll fall for anything."

FOR THINKING, DISCUSSING, AND WRITING

1. What are some of the "serious consequences" of telling the truth? Is it ever better to tell a lie rather than the truth? Why or why not? What does Ericsson think about this notion?
2. If, as Ericsson insists, we all lie, is it then possible that lying, rather than an aberration, is simply part of the normal psychological arsenal that people use to navigate the world? If so, then how can it be wrong? Explain your responses.
3. What is your reaction to Ericsson's assertion that "madness is actually a sane reaction to an insane world"? Why might you agree or disagree with this assertion?
4. What do you see as the relation between lying and values? For example, what are the values of someone who lies? Write an essay in which you explore responses to the question.

LANGSTON HUGHES

Salvation

Born in Joplin, Missouri, Langston Hughes (1902–1967) was reared by his maternal grandmother, Mary Langston. Her first husband died in the raid on Harpers Ferry as a follower of John Brown, and she was an abiding influence on Hughes. He studied for a year at Columbia University and later completed his college education at the historically black Lincoln University in Pennsylvania. Hughes's poetry collections include The Weary Blues *(1926) and* Montage of a Dream Deferred *(1951). This selection, from Hughes's autobiography,* The Big Sea *(1940), tells the story of his "conversion" to Christ. Salvation was a key event in the life of his community, but Hughes tells comically, and poignantly, of how he bowed to pressure by permitting himself to be "saved from sin."*

1 I was saved from sin when I was going on thirteen. But not really saved. It happened like this. There was a big revival at my Auntie Reed's church. Every night for weeks there had been much preaching, singing, praying, and shouting, and some very hardened sinners had been brought to Christ, and the membership of the church had grown by leaps and bounds. Then just before the revival ended, they held a special meeting for children, "to bring the young lambs to the fold." My aunt spoke of it for days ahead. That night I was escorted to the front

row and placed on the mourners' bench with all the other young sinners, who had not yet been brought to Jesus.

2 My aunt told me that when you were saved you saw a light, and something happened to you inside! And Jesus came into your life! And God was with you from then on! She said you could see and hear and feel Jesus in your soul. I believed her. I had heard a great many old people say the same thing and it seemed to me they ought to know. So I sat there calmly in the hot, crowded church, waiting for Jesus to come to me.

3 The preacher preached a wonderful rhythmical sermon, all moans and shouts and lonely cries and dire pictures of hell, and then he sang a song about the ninety and nine safe in the fold, but one little lamb was left out in the cold. Then he said: "Won't you come? Won't you come to Jesus? Young lambs, won't you come?" And he held out his arms to all us young sinners there on the mourners' bench. And the little girls cried. And some of them jumped up and went to Jesus right away. But most of us just sat there.

4 A great many old people came and knelt around us and prayed, old women with jet-black faces and braided hair, old men with work-gnarled hands. And the church sang a song about the lower lights are burning, some poor sinners to be saved. And the whole building rocked with prayer and song.

5 Still I kept waiting to *see* Jesus.

6 Finally all the young people had gone to the altar and were saved, but one boy and me. He was a rounder's son named Westley. Westley and I were surrounded by sisters and deacons praying. It was very hot in the church, and getting late now. Finally Westley said to me in a whisper: "God damn! I'm tired o' sitting here. Let's get up and be saved." So he got up and was saved.

7 Then I was left all alone on the mourners' bench. My aunt came and knelt at my knees and cried, while prayers and songs swirled all around me in the little church. The whole congregation prayed for me alone, in a mighty wail of moans and voices. And I kept waiting serenely for Jesus, waiting, waiting—but he didn't come. I wanted to see him, but nothing happened to me. Nothing! I wanted something to happen to me, but nothing happened.

8 I heard the songs and the minister saying: "Why don't you come? My dear child, why don't you come to Jesus? Jesus is waiting for you. He wants you. Why don't you come? Sister Reed, what is this child's name?"

9 "Langston," my aunt sobbed.

10 "Langston, why don't you come? Why don't you come and be saved? Oh, Lamb of God! Why don't you come?"

11 Now it was really getting late. I began to be ashamed of myself, holding everything up so long. I began to wonder what God thought about Westley, who certainly hadn't seen Jesus either, but who was now sitting proudly on the platform, swinging his knickerbockered legs and grinning down at me, surrounded by deacons and old women on their knees praying. God had not struck Westley dead for taking his name in vain or for lying in the temple. So I decided that maybe to save further trouble, I'd better lie, too, and say that Jesus had come, and get up and be saved.

12 So I got up.

13 Suddenly the whole room broke into a sea of shouting, as they saw me rise. Waves of rejoicing swept the place. Women leaped in the air. My aunt threw her arms around me. The minister took me by the hand and led me to the platform.

14 When things quieted down, in a hushed silence, punctuated by a few ecstatic "Amens," all the new young lambs were blessed in the name of God. Then joyous singing filled the room.

15 That night, for the last time in my life but one—for I was a big boy twelve years old—I cried. I cried, in bed alone, and couldn't stop. I buried my head under the quilts, but my aunt heard me. She woke up and told my uncle I was crying because the Holy Ghost had come into my life, and because I had seen Jesus. But I was really crying because I couldn't bear to tell her that I had lied, that I had deceived everybody in the church, that I hadn't seen Jesus, and that now I didn't believe there was a Jesus any more, since he didn't come to help me.

FOR THINKING, DISCUSSING, AND WRITING

1. According to Hughes, what is a revival meeting like? How do "preaching, singing, praying, and shouting" affect the "sinners" and "young lambs"?
2. How does Hughes feel after his salvation? Why? What ethical principle did he violate? Does he finally believe in Christ after this experience? How do you know?
3. What exactly is a *conversion* in the religious sense that Hughes has used the word here? What conversion really takes place in this piece?

4. Write an essay in which you consider the circumstances under which a person might—or even should—lie in order to satisfy others. Do you believe that lying is ever justifiable?

TOM REGAN

Who Are You Animal Rights Activists Anyway?

Tom Regan (1938–) was born in Pittsburgh and attended Theil College in Western Pennsylvania. He received a doctorate from the University of Virginia and now is Professor Emeritus of Philosophy at North Carolina State University. Recognized as a key intellectual leader of the animal rights movement, he has produced a number of important books on the subject, including All That Dwell Therein: Essays on Animal Rights and Environmental Ethics *(1982),* Animal Sacrifices: Religious Perspectives on the Use of Animals in Science *(1986),* The Case for Animal Rights *(1983), and* Empty Cages: Facing the Challenge of Animal Rights *(2004). This selection from* Empty Cages *examines the animal rights issue in light of its advocates and opponents.*

1 Do animals have rights? Different people give different answers. Sometimes people give different answers because of a disagreement about the facts. For example, some people believe cats and dogs, chickens and hogs do not feel anything; others believe they do. Sometimes different answers are given because of a disagreement over values. For example, some people believe animals have no value apart from human interests; others believe the opposite. Disagreements of both kinds are important certainly, and both will be explored along the way. As important as these kinds of disagreements are, neither touches a more basic source of division, this one concerning the idea of animal rights itself.

2 Some people think this idea is synonymous with being kind to animals. Since we should be kind to animals, the inference is obvious: animals have rights. Or they think animal rights means avoiding cruelty. Since we should not be cruel to animals, the same conclusion follows: animals have rights. Given either of these two ways of understanding animal rights, it is hard to explain why the idea is so controversial, with animal rights advocates on one side and animal rights opponents on the other.

3 The heated, often acrimonious controversy that pits advocates against opponents tells us that these familiar ways of thinking (we should be kind to animals; we should not be cruel to them) fail to capture the real meaning of animal rights. Its real meaning, as it turns out, is both simple and profound.

4 Animal rights is a simple idea because, at the most basic level, it means only that animals have a right to be treated with respect. It is a profound idea because its implications are far-reaching. How far-reaching? Here are a few examples of how the world will have to change once we learn to treat animals with respect.

We will have to stop raising them for their flesh.
We will have to stop killing them for their fur.
We will have to stop training them to entertain us.
We will have to stop using them in scientific research.

5 Each example illustrates the same moral logic. When it comes to how humans exploit animals, recognition of their rights requires abolition, not reform. Being kind to animals is not enough. Avoiding cruelty is not enough. Whether we exploit animals to eat, to wear, to entertain us, or to learn, the truth of animal rights requires empty cages, not larger cages.

Untruth in Labeling

6 Opponents think animal rights is an extreme idea, and it is not unusual for them to pin the label "extremists" on animal rights advocates. It is important to understand how this label is used as a rhetorical tool to prevent informed, fair discussion; otherwise, chances are we won't have an informed, fair discussion.

7 "Extremists" and "extremism" are ambiguous words. In one sense, extremists are people who will do anything to further their objectives. The terrorists who destroyed the twin towers of the World Trade Center were extremists in this sense; they were willing to go to any lengths, even if it meant killing thousands of innocent human beings, to further their ends.

8 Animal rights advocates (ARAs) are not extremists in this sense. Let me repeat this: ARAs are not extremists in this sense. Even the most militant advocates of animal rights (the members of the Animal Liberation Front, say) believe there are absolute moral limits to what can be done in the name of animal liberation, acts that should never be

performed, they are so bad. For example, the ALF opposes hurting let alone killing human beings.

9 In another sense, the word *extremist* refers to the unqualified nature of what people believe. In this sense, ARAs are extremists. Again, let me repeat this: ARAs really are extremists, in this sense. ARAs really do believe that it is always wrong to train wild animals to perform tricks for human amusement, for example. But in *this* sense, *everyone* is an extremist. Why? Because there are some things all of us (one hopes) oppose unqualifiedly.

10 For example, everyone reading these words is an extremist when it comes to rape; we are against rape all the time. Each of us is an extremist when it comes to child abuse; we are against child abuse all the time. Indeed, all of us are extremists when it comes to cruelty to animals; we never favor that.

11 The plain fact is, extreme views sometimes are correct views. That being so, the fact that ARAs are extremists, in the sense that we have unqualified beliefs about right and wrong, by itself provides no reason for thinking that we must be mistaken. So the question to be examined is not, "Are ARAs extremists?" It is, "Are we right?" As we shall see, this question is hardly ever fairly asked, let alone fairly answered. Collusion between the media and powerful special interests sees to that.

The Media

12 One barrier to fair discussion of animal rights is the media. As so often happens today, our perception of the "real world" is based on what we see on television or read in the newspaper. This should raise a red flag immediately. Perhaps Paul Watson exaggerates when he states that "[T]he media is only concerned with four elements: sex, scandal, violence and celebrities, and if you don't have one of those elements in your story then you don't have a story."[1] Still, there's a lot of truth in what Watson says. Safe landings? Hard to get those covered. The media loves a plane crash. Add some sex, scandal, and a few celebrities, mix and stir and you're vying for front page coverage. Any doubts about this, just watch the news tonight or read the paper tomorrow.

13 Because the media looks for what is sensational, they can be counted on to cover animal rights when something unlawful or

[1] Watson's quote appeared in an article in the *Collegian*, published by California State University in 2003.

outlandish occurs. Members of the Animal Liberation Front firebomb a lab. An antifur activist throws a pie in Calvin Klein's face. These are the sorts of stories we get to watch or read. As for the peaceful protest that took place outside a fur store yesterday, or the lecture on animal rights given at the law school last night? Hardly ever covered. Nonsensational animal rights news doesn't "bleed" enough for the media's tastes. No wonder the general public views ARAs as a band of merry pranksters and social misfits. All too often, this is the only message that works its way through the media's filters.

Special Interest Politics

14 That the general public tends to have a negative picture of ARAs is not the result only of the media's appetite for the sensational; it is also due to what the media is fed by the public relations arms of major animal user industries. By "major animal user industries" I mean the meat industry, the fur industry, the animal entertainment industry, and the biomedical research industry, for example. The people who work in these industries speak with one voice, tell the same story, even use the same words to denigrate their common enemy: animal rights extremists.

15 The origin of the most recent chapter in this story here in the United States is not hard to find. It begins in 1989 with the publication of the American Medical Association's white paper "Use of Animals in Biomedical Research: The Challenge and the Response." Among the AMA's recommendations: People who believe in animal rights "must be shown to be not only anti-science but also (a) responsible for violent and illegal acts that endanger life and property, and (b) a threat to the public's freedom of choice." ARAs must be seen as people who are "radicals," "militants," and "terrorists," who are "opposed to human well being." By contrast, sane, sensible, decent people must be shown to favor animal welfare, understood as humane, responsible use of animals, by humans, for humans.

16 The AMA's strategy was both simple and inspired. If the public's perception of using animals in research could be structured as a contest between know-nothing animal rights extremists who hate humans and have an insatiable appetite for violence, on the one hand, and wise scientific animal welfare moderates, true friends of humanity, on the other, ARAs would be repudiated and the ideology of humane, responsible use would prevail.

17 Since 1989, a steady stream of press releases, memos, e-mail messages, press conferences, and website miscellany, denouncing ARA extremists and lauding reasonable animal welfarists, has flowed from the AMA's and other biomedical research industry's public relations offices straight into the hands of reporters, news directors, and editors. How does this work? Here is one example.

18 The Foundation for Biomedical Research describes itself as "the nation's oldest and largest organization dedicated to improving human and animal health by promoting public understanding and support for the humane and responsible use of animals in medical and scientific research." FBR's website includes a page entitled "Journalist Resources," featuring three links. One is "Expert Opinion," which is described in this way: "FBR works to bring scientists and journalists together to inspire exceptional, outstanding and ongoing news coverage that contributes to public understanding and appreciation for the humane and responsible use of animals in medical and scientific research. When you need to quote an expert from the American research community, contact us first."

19 "To inspire exceptional, outstanding . . . coverage." That's positive and appealing. Who could be against that?

20 A second link is "FBR News Tips," described as "a monthly tip sheet for journalists that promotes story ideas that will strengthen public understanding and respect for the humane and responsible use of animals in medical research. It provides a summary of the latest medical discoveries, as well as reliable contact information. In every case, the research described demonstrates the essential need for lab animals in medical research."

21 "Humane and responsible use of animals in medical research" that is "essential." Hard to be against this, either.

22 And the third link? This one is "Animal activism," where FBR presents "a record of all known criminal activities committed in the name of 'animal rights' since 1981."

23 Let's see, now. "Animal activism" equals "criminal activities committed in the name of 'animal rights'," which equals "illegal and violent acts." If *that's* what "animal rights" involves, who (except those who support criminal, illegal, and violent acts) could possibly be for it?

24 There we have the basic story: Animal welfare moderates versus animal rights extremists. Wise scientists who treat animals humanely versus know-nothing, emotionally overloaded ARAs bent on destruction.

This is the message special interest groups like FBR spoon-feed the media. Does it work? Does the media slant its coverage because of efforts like FBR's? Before we answer, let's do some imagining. Here we have an earnest forty-something reporter, lucky to have a permanent job; his salary, together with his wife's, falls far short of being enough to cover all the bills, now that both their children are attending prestigious colleges. His beat includes biomedical research. On a monthly basis, he receives FBR's tip sheets. On a daily basis, he receives the latest installment of authoritative quotes from "experts" who support research using animals. And on a timely basis, he receives an up-to-date inventory of "criminal activities committed in the name of 'animal rights.'"

25 So let us ask ourselves: what are the odds of this reporter's giving an impartial, fair story about the "latest medical break-through using animals"? Might the odds be just a tiny bit skewed in one direction rather than another? Should we mention that among the newspaper's biggest advertisers are major animal user industries, including economically powerful interests (major pharmaceutical companies, for example) represented by FBR? Or that the reporter's 401 (k) is heavily invested in these same industries, as are those of the newspaper's publisher and editorial staff? Can we really think, when we think about it objectively, that the odds of an impartial, fair story about the "latest medical breakthrough using animals" are even-steven?

26 There may be some people who will answer yes, but my experience tells me they would be in the minority. Most people, once they understand how the cards are stacked, understand why the news is dealt the way it is. Remember the old adage He who pays the piper calls the tune? Its truth did not pass away when paid pipers became an extinct species. The plain fact is, many people have a negative image of animal rights because much of the media presents ARAs in a negative light. And much of the media presents ARAs in a negative light because the media is relentlessly fed a negative image by the spokespersons for the financially powerful and influential major animal user industries. It's not all that surprising, once we stop to think about it.

All Aboard!

27 With so prestigious a group as the AMA having raised the sails, it did not take long for other major animal user industries to come on board. The meat industry. The animal entertainment industry. Sport hunters

and rodeo enthusiasts. The story is everywhere the same. Animal welfare moderates versus animal rights extremists. Law-abiding citizens versus law-breaking terrorists. By way of example, consider the following discussion of animal welfare and animal rights from the Fur Information Council of America. First, we have a description of the sane, sensible position of those who favor animal welfare:

> *Animals enrich our lives in many ways. They provide food, clothing and companionship. Animals used for medical research have given us important advances in medicine that have saved millions of lives. Most people today recognize that the use of animals under humane circumstances is important.*
>
> *Animal welfare organizations also support the wise use of animals under humane conditions. The animal welfare ethic has been promoted over the past century by many groups, including the fur industry. Working with the government and the veterinary community, industries that involve animal use have adopted high standards for the treatment of animals. For instance, today there are strict regulations governing livestock; guidelines have been implemented for the care of animals used in medical research; and humane care standards have been implemented by the fur industry.*

28 Next, we have a description of the "out-of-touch-with-reality" extremists who favor animal rights:

> *In the past few years, however, an extreme movement called "animal rights" has emerged. The basic philosophy of these groups dictates that humans have no right to use animals for any purpose whatsoever. These groups oppose the use of animals for food, clothing, medical research, and in zoos and circuses . . . .*
>
> *The majority of Americans support animal welfare groups, but do NOT support [any] out-of-touch-with-reality, publicity-hungry animal rights groups . . . . Animal welfare groups support humane treatment and responsible care of animals while the animal rights philosophy not only condemns the use of all animals for any purpose but it also is known for its increasingly terroristic tactics. The current mindset of the animal rights movement is, "Believe what I believe . . . or else."*

29 True to the spirit of the AMA's white paper, the debate over fur is framed here as a contest between animal welfare moderates, who favor "humane treatment and responsible care of animals," and animal

rights extremists who, like the criminals who blew up the twin towers of the World Trade Center, resort to "terroristic tactics."

30 But (you might well ask) is this true of all ARAs? Do we all favor terrorism and intimidation? This is what the Fur Information Council is saying. They presume to tell us what "[t]he current mindset of the animal rights movement" is, not what a small handful of ARAs think. *The mindset of the movement* is, "Believe what I believe . . . or else," where the "or else" carries with it the threat of one "terroristic tactic" or another. ARAs must really be terrible people.

"They Would Never Do That, Would They?"

31 Having adopted a proactive strategy, one pillar of which is the depiction of ARAs as lawless terrorists, the major animal user industries face a daunting challenge. For their strategy to work, there *has to be* illegal, terroristic activity attributed to ARAs. And not just a little. What is needed is a lot. It did not take long before anti-ARA forces decided that they would need to do a little freelance terrorist work of their own.

32 Consider this possible scenario. Why not hire someone to infiltrate the animal rights movement, as an agent provocateur, with one main purpose: to find a malleable person in the movement who could be "encouraged" (shall we say) to try to do something that would really discredit ARAs. Like, maybe this person could be "encouraged" to try to murder someone. And not just anyone. No, the "someone" should be a pillar of the community, someone who (what an odd coincidence) just happened to be a leader in a major animal user industry, someone who just happened to have been famously outspoken in his criticisms of ARAs. An attempt on his life would be perfect. It would show the public that ARAs really are extremists who will stop at nothing to further their ends. It is not hard to visualize the headline: "Animal Rights Terrorist Attempts to Murder Pillar of Community."

33 A few problems would have to be solved. It takes time to find the right person for the job. It takes money to pay all the players. Who is going to come up with the necessary cash? Well, suppose the pillar himself could pay for the attempt on his life. Suppose the pillar himself (such is his influence) could arrange to have the local police on hand to arrest the would-be murderer. "Nah," you might say, "This is too fanciful, too conspiratorial. I don't think anyone in a major animal user industry would ever do anything like this." Think again.

34 Leon Hirsch, past president of the Norwalk, Connecticut-based U.S. Surgical Corporation, played the role of the pillar of the community. Hirsch's former company manufactures staples used in place of ordinary sutures in many operations. During Hirsch's tenure, physicians received training by practicing on live dogs, who were vivisected, then killed. ARAs (led by Friends of Animals, also located in Norwalk) mounted an in-your-face campaign against Hirsch and his company back in the late 1980s. His ingenious way of getting even was to put up the necessary money to arrange for an ARA to try to murder him.

35 On November 11, 1989, a man on the payroll of a firm Hirsch had hired drove a young woman named Fran Trutt, a self-professed ARA, along with her two recently purchased pipe bombs, from New York City to Norwalk. When she placed the bombs adjacent to Hirsch's parking space, Hirsch's friends in the Norwalk police department just happened to be on hand to arrest her.

36 The resulting story (not the bombs, which never exploded) was the real bombshell. There it was: "Animal Rights Terrorist Attempts to Murder Pillar of Community." As John C. Stauber and Sheldon Rampton observe, "Normally, of course, company presidents do not arrange their own murder, but Hirsch was neither crazy nor suicidal. He was trying to engineer an embarrassing scandal that would discredit the animal rights movement."

37 Hirsch would have succeeded, too, except for one thing: the ensuing trial brought to light extensive tape transcripts that implicated everyone, from Hirsch on down, who had hatched the plot to discredit ARAs. Friends of Animals sued Hirsch, who sold U.S. Surgical in 1998, but their suit was unsuccessful, and he never faced any criminal charges. Perhaps not surprisingly, Fran Trutt was the only person to serve time (a year in prison, followed by a year on probation). She seems to have left the movement.

It Only Gets Worse

38 This is not the only case where people in major animal user industries have taken on the job of trying to make sure there is enough "ARA terrorism" to go around. Books, not just people, can be deceiving. The infamous Ku Klux Klan leader, David Duke, knows this. One of his books, *African Atto*, is a manual written for violent black street

gangs, supposedly authored by an "insider" (that is, a gang member). Another of his books (like the first, this one was not published under Duke's name, for obvious reasons), is a sex manual written by and for the "liberated" woman. You know the type: mindless of "family values," lusting after sexual adventures with the next guy to turn the corner.

39 In both cases, Duke's books were written to reinforce prejudicial stereotypes of the sort Duke wants his constituency to fear: the predatory black male, in the one case, the liberated woman (whatever her race), in the other. Given the familiar stereotype of ARAs as misanthropic violent lawbreakers who are antiscience, antireason, anti-American, anti-everything any decent human being values, one might expect to find a fraudulent animal rights exposé written by someone posing as an ARA insider.

40 This expectation was fulfilled with the publication of *A Declaration of War: Killing People to Save Animals and the Environment*, written anonymously by an author identified only as "Screaming Wolf." A real charmer, Screaming Wolf makes it clear that there is no limit to the violence real ARAs ("liberators") are prepared to carry out. It is not just the university researcher who uses animals in harmful studies, not just the furrier, not just the hunter, whose lives are at risk; it is the researcher's children, the furrier's rabbi or minister, the hunter's friends or business associates. In short, *anyone* can be chosen as a legitimate, justifiable victim by the army of "liberators" who have decided the time has come to kill people in order to save animals and the environment.

41 Haven't the major animal user industries been saying as much? Screaming Wolf (a liberator "insider") is only confirming what these industries have been saying about ARAs all along. The industries could not have done a better job of discrediting ARAs if they had hired some fictitious Screaming Wolf to write this book for them.

42 And that is precisely what happened. At least this is the judgment I reached when I reviewed the book, more than a decade ago, a judgment that, to date, no one has successfully refuted. *A Declaration of War* is nothing more than a work of fraudulent provocation, a work of fiction disguised as fact. And a clever work of fiction it is. For liberators, you see, will rarely take credit for their actions. In general, they prefer to remain anonymous.

43 Consider the illogic of this logic. Suppose a researcher's car is blown up. Or she dies or disappears mysteriously. Or strangers rape her daughter. Then liberators will either take credit for this or they will not. If they do, then they did it. If they don't, then they probably did it anyhow. Here, most assuredly, is a strategy that *cannot fail* to create the appearance that animal rights terrorism is on the rise.

44 And the moral of the story is? The moral of the story is simple. The next time the media shows or tells a story about "animal rights terrorism," we should all think twice before buying into its veracity. We do not know how often the violent, unlawful acts the media attributes to ARAs actually were paid for by someone trying to do what Leon Hirsch tried to do: discredit the animal rights movement by encouraging impressionable ARAs to break the law. And we do not know how often the violent acts the media attributes to ARAs actually are carried out by people who, paid or unpaid, have nothing to do with the movement. What we do know is, all this happens some of the time, which should be reason enough to make us raise a skeptical eyebrow when we open tomorrow morning's paper and read "Animal Rights Terrorists" do one bad thing or another.

FOR THINKING, DISCUSSING, AND WRITING

1. What, according to Regan, is the real meaning of animal rights? Why does he call the meaning both simple and profound? What is your reaction to his list of "how the world will have to change once we learn how to treat animals with respect"? What "moral logic" does each example illustrate, do you think?
2. Regan's argument is an all-or-nothing affair. Why might you agree or disagree with his approach? Would it be possible to accept some positions of the ARAs and reject others and still be viewed as a supporter of animal rights?
3. Conspiratorial elements lie at the heart of Regan's position. That is, people intent on discrediting ARAs, he says, bring deliberate harm to the effort. Why might you agree or disagree with his belief, based on the argument presented here? Which examples do you find most forceful in convincing you of his position?
4. Write an essay in which you present your own arguments for or against animal rights. Draw on elements of Regan's essay, where appropriate. Be sure to support your position with convincing examples and details.

MOLLY IVINS

Get a Knife, Get a Dog, but Get Rid of Guns

Molly Ivins (1944–2007), a nationally syndicated political writer whose column for the Fort Worth Star Telegram *appeared in 113 newspapers, was born in Monterey, California, and grew up in Houston, Texas. She graduated from Smith College in 1966 and attended the Columbia University School of Journalism. Author of the best-selling* Molly Ivins Can't Say That Can She? *(1990) and the amusingly titled* Who Let the Dogs In? Incredible Political Animals I Have Known *(2004), she boasted as one of her highest honors that the Minneapolis police force named its mascot pig after her. In this piece from her* Nothin' But Good Times Ahead *(1993), she attacks "gun nuts" in her usual spirited, and often harsh, style.*

1 Guns. Everywhere guns.

2 Let me start this discussion by pointing out that I am not antigun. I'm pro-knife. Consider the merits of the knife.

3 In the first place, you have to catch up with someone in order to stab him. A general substitution of knives for guns would promote physical fitness. We'd turn into a whole nation of great runners. Plus, knives don't ricochet. And people are seldom killed while cleaning their knives.

4 As a civil libertarian, I, of course, support the Second Amendment. And I believe it means exactly what it says:

5 *As well-regulated militia being necessary to the security of a free state, the right of the people to keep and bear arms shall not be infringed.* Fourteen-year-old boys are not part of a well-regulated militia. Members of wacky religious cults are not part of a well-regulated militia. Permitting unregulated citizens to have guns is destroying the security of this free state.

6 I am intrigued by the arguments of those who claim to follow the judicial doctrine of original intent. How do they know it was the dearest wish of Thomas Jefferson's heart that teenage drug dealers should cruise the cities of this nation perforating their fellow citizens with assault rifles? Channeling?

7 There is more hooey spread about the Second Amendment. It says quite clearly that guns are for those who form part of a well-regulated militia, that is, the armed forces, including the National

Guard. Their reasons for keeping them away from everyone else get clearer by the day.

8 The comparison most often used is that of the automobile, another lethal object that is regularly used to wreak great carnage. Obviously, this society is full of people who haven't enough common sense to use an automobile properly. But we haven't outlawed cars yet.

9 We do, however, license them and their owners, restrict their use to presumably sane and sober adults, and keep track of who sells them to whom. At a minimum, we should do the same with guns.

10 In truth, there is no rational argument for guns in this society. This is no longer a frontier nation in which people hunt their own food. It is a crowded, overwhelmingly urban country in which letting people have access to guns is a continuing disaster. Those who want guns—whether for target shooting, hunting, or potting rattlesnakes (get a hoe)—should be subject to the same restrictions placed on gun owners in England, a nation in which liberty has survived nicely without an armed populace.

11 The argument that "guns don't kill people" is patent nonsense. Anyone who has ever worked in a cop shop knows how many family arguments end in murder because there was a gun in the house. Did the gun kill someone? No. But if there had been no gun, no one would have died. At least not without a good foot race first. Guns do kill. Unlike cars, that is all they do.

12 Michael Crichton makes an interesting argument about technology in his thriller *Jurassic Park*. He points out that power without discipline is making this society into a wreckage. By the time someone who studies the martial arts becomes a master—literally able to kill with bare hands—that person has also undergone years of training and discipline. But any fool can pick up a gun and kill with it.

13 "A well-regulated militia" surely implies both long training and long discipline. That is the least, the very least, that should be required of those who are permitted to have guns, because a gun is literally the power to kill. For years I used to enjoy taunting my gun-nut friends about their psychosexual hang-ups—always in a spirit of good cheer, you understand. But letting the noisy minority in the NRA force us to allow this carnage to continue is just plain insane.

14 I do think gun nuts have a power hang-up. I don't know what is missing in their psyches that they need to feel they have the power to kill. But no sane society would allow this to continue.

15 Ban the damn things. Ban them all.

16 You want protection? Get a dog.

FOR THINKING, DISCUSSING, AND WRITING

1. What is Ivins's interpretation of the Second Amendment? Why might you agree or disagree with her analysis? What other readings of the amendment are possible, do you think? How valid are they?
2. What is Ivins's purpose in comparing cars and guns?
3. How does Ivins's style suit her topic here? Do you find her too argumentative? Why or why not? What does she accomplish by mocking those who oppose gun control?
4. Write an essay in which you explore your own views on the right to bear arms in our society. Should we allow people a wide berth in interpreting the Bill of Rights guarantee? Or, given the record of violence in our age—car bombs, Columbine, the massacre at Virginia Tech, to name a deadly few—should we bring to bear any limitations on this right in the name of moral principles for good conduct?

MICHAEL IGNATIEFF

If Torture Works . . . .

Michael Ignatieff (1947–) is a member of Parliament in the Canadian government. Born in Toronto, from 2000 to 2005 he lived in the United States, where he was director of Harvard University's Carr Center for Human Rights Policy. He is an author, a journalist, a documentary filmmaker, and an international scholar who has held positions at Cambridge, Oxford, and Harvard. His books include The Lesser Evil: Political Ethics in an Age of Terror *(2004) and a collection of essays for which he served as editor,* American Exceptionalism and Human Rights *(2005). In this piece for the April 2006, issue of* Prospect Magazine, *he points to the problems facing those, like him, who oppose torture under any circumstances.*

1 It is difficult to think about torture honestly. In a recent article on the interrogation techniques employed by the US, the writer Mark Bowden observed that few "moral imperatives make such sense on a large scale, but break down so dramatically in the particular." The moral imperative—do not torture, any time, anywhere, in any circumstances—is mandated by the UN convention against torture and other cruel, inhuman or

degrading treatment or punishment. "No exceptional circumstances whatsoever, whether a state of war or a threat of war, internal political instability or any other public emergency," says the convention, can "be invoked as a justification of torture." That terrorists themselves torture does not change these imperatives. Our compliance does not depend on reciprocity.

2 As long as we stay on this high ground of unconditional prohibition, we seem to know where we are. Problems begin when we descend into the particular, when we ask what exactly counts as torture.

3 Since no state wants to be seen as torturing suspects but all states want to be able to extract information to protect their citizens, the key question is whether states can use methods of "coercive interrogation" that do not qualify as torture. When the torture convention was ratified by the US Senate in 1994, maintaining a meaningful distinction between coercive but lawful interrogation and outright torture was a central concern. The Senate ratified the convention on the understanding that torture should be reserved for "severe physical or mental pain or suffering" resulting in "prolonged mental harm." Once the war on terror began, the parsing of the convention went still further. In the now notorious memos submitted by the office of legal counsel to the White House in 2002, these definitions were stretched to the point that the threshold for torture "must be equivalent in intensity to the pain accompanying serious physical injury, such as organ failure, impairment of bodily function or even death." Any physical abuse below that standard counted as "coercive interrogation." Some forms of coercive interrogation, the lawyers admitted, might not be torture, but they would still be defined as "inhuman and degrading treatment."

4 When in 1978 the European court of human rights investigated British interrogation practices in Northern Ireland during the early 1970s, it concluded that a range of painful practices constituted inhuman and degrading practice even if they did not qualify as torture. When the Israeli supreme court ruled against Israeli interrogation techniques in 1999—techniques that included holding suspects in painful positions with hoods, and vigorously shaking the head and shoulders—it also ruled against them as inhuman and degrading, but not as torture.

5 There is thus a conceptual and practical distinction between torture and coercive interrogation. There is a further distinction—at least in theory—between methods of coercive interrogation that are lawful and

permissible and those that may be inhuman and degrading. While this distinction exists in theory, most human rights activists would deny that such a distinction can be observed in practice.

6 Human rights activists accept that reliable information is essential for combating terrorists and that interrogation is a central feature of any counterterrorist strategy. Kenneth Roth, of Human Rights Watch, argues that "respect for the Geneva conventions does not preclude vigorously interrogating detainees about a limitless range of topics." What work is the word "vigorously" doing in this sentence? It is intended to make it clear that a human rights defender takes seriously the necessity of getting from detainees real information that may prevent future terrorist attacks. But what, in specific terms, might "vigorous" interrogation actually entail? Clearly, Roth and anyone else who cares about human rights wants to exclude any form of abuse. But what exactly counts as abuse in a "vigorous" interrogation?

7 In order to prevent vigorous interrogation from slipping down any slope, human rights activists want to collapse the distinction between "coercive interrogation" and "torture," and to ban any physical or psychological coercion. But there is a significant distinction between the two. As legal theorist and federal judge Richard Posner has argued, "almost all official interrogation is coercive, yet not all coercive interrogation would be called 'torture' by any competent user of the English language." As the political philosopher Jean Bethke Elshtain writes, "when human rights groups label 'unpleasant or disadvantageous treatment of any kind' torture . . . they fail to discriminate between cases," for example, between "sleep deprivation and amputation or burning or some other horror."

8 Clear thinking about torture is not served by collapsing the distinction between coercive interrogation and torture. Both may be repugnant, but repugnance does not make them into the same thing. If coercion and torture are on a moral continuum, at what point on the continuum, to use Posner's words, does queasiness turn to revulsion? Vigorous interrogation might mean lengthy, exhausting, harassing exchanges with interrogators. Provided that there was no physical contact between interrogator and subject, no deprivation of food or water harmful to health, this might qualify as lawful interrogation. But at every ratchet of coercion, moral problems arise. Sleep deprivation will not leave physical or permanent psychological scars, but as Menachem Begin, who was interrogated in Soviet Russia, remembered, "anyone

who has experienced this desire [for sleep] knows that not even hunger or thirst are comparable with it."

9 It might be lawful to deceive a subject under interrogation, by stating that all of his associates are already in detention when they are still at large. But other forms of deception can inflict excruciating psychological anguish. Threatening a subject with the imminent death or torture of those dearest to him may not leave any physical marks, but it rightly can constitute torture, not just coercion, in even the US Senate's definition. Both Elshtain and Posner have argued against the moral perfectionism that elides the distinction between coercion and torture, and have stressed the cruel, if regrettable, necessity of using coercive methods on a small category of terrorists who may have information vital to saving the lives of innocent people. Posner justifies coercive interrogation on utilitarian grounds: saving the lives of many counts more, in moral terms, than abusing the body and dignity of a single individual. Elshtain justifies coercive interrogation using a complex moral calculus of "dirty hands": good consequences cannot justify bad acts, but bad acts are sometimes tragically necessary. The acts remain bad, and the person must accept the moral opprobrium and not seek to excuse the inexcusable with the justifications of necessity.

10 My own work on "lesser evils" brings me close to the Elshtain position. I agree with her that necessity may require the commission of bad acts, which necessity, nevertheless, cannot absolve of their morally problematic character—but I still have a problem. If one enumerates the forms of coercive interrogation that have been judged to be inhuman and degrading by the Israeli and the European courts—hooding, holding subjects in painful positions, exposing them to cold or heat or ear-splitting noise—these techniques also seem unacceptable, though at a lower threshold of awfulness, than torture. Like Elshtain, I am willing to get my hands dirty, but unlike her, I have practical difficulty enumerating a list of coercive techniques that I would be willing to have a democratic society inflict in my name. I accept, for example, that a slap is not the same thing as a beating, but I still don't want interrogators to slap detainees because I cannot see how to prevent the occasional slap deteriorating into a regular practice of beating. The issue is not, as Elshtain implies, that I care overmuch about my own moral purity but rather that I cannot see any clear way to manage coercive interrogation institutionally so that it does not degenerate into torture.

11 On the issue of regulation, there are those—Alan Dershowitz, for example—who believe that banning torture and coercion outright is unrealistic. Instead, the practice should be regulated by court warrants. But judicialisation of torture, and of coercive interrogation techniques involving stress and duress, physical abuse, sleep deprivation and so on, could lead to torture and coercion becoming routine rather than an exception. A position in favour of outright prohibition of both torture and coercive interrogation has gained strength from the abuses at Abu Ghraib, and from the memos of the office of legal counsel and the White House parsing the torture convention into permission for coercive interrogation. It seems clear from the dire experience of Abu Ghraib that outright prohibition of both torture and coercive interrogation is the only way to proceed. Rules for interrogations, with penalties in the uniform code of military justice, should be mandatory.

12 Absolute prohibition, however, is easy. Enforcement is hard, and even rules and punishment for infraction are not enough. The crucial element for enforcement of rules and procedures against abuse of detainees is habeas corpus, the legal requirement of any detaining power in a democracy to produce detainees before a court of law and justify detention to a duly appointed legal authority. As long as the US—or any state, for that matter—has the power to detain at pleasure and in secret, abuse of detainees is inevitable. International pressure, domestic mobilisation and, finally, congressional legislation are all necessary to stop the practice of "ghost detainees," whose identities remain concealed and who may be held outside the US, inside the US, or in third countries. It should be mandatory that every single detainee held by the US, whether a citizen or not, be publicly known. If operational necessity—keeping the enemy from knowing who is in custody—requires secrecy, disclosure of their names to congress and the courts can be undertaken in camera. It should also be mandatory that every detainee of the US, whether citizen or not, whether held onshore or offshore, should have habeas corpus access to a federal court, together with the legal capacity to make representations to that court about treatment and detention.

13 I am not so naive as to suppose that federal court review of detention will always provide effective remedies for detainees. But evidence of the impact of recent supreme and federal court rulings on the tribunal review process at Guantánamo, and on ordinary treatment of the

detainees, does suggest that court review and access, however imperfect, is the only reliable way to keep detention under the rule of law.

14 So I end up supporting an absolute and unconditional ban on both torture and those forms of coercive interrogation that involve stress and duress, and I believe that enforcement of such a ban should be up to the military justice system plus the federal courts. I also believe that the training of interrogators can be improved by executive order and that the training must rigorously exclude stress and duress methods.

15 Two significant problems remain. First of all, there is the problem of the exceptional case, one where lives can be saved by the application of physical methods that amount to torture. "Ticking bomb cases" cannot be wished away. They might arise especially where an American or European city faced the threat of WMD. An outright ban on torture and coercive interrogation leave a conscientious security officer with little choice but to disobey the ban. In this event, as the Israeli supreme court has said, even a conscientious agent acting in good faith to save lives should be charged with a criminal offence and be required to stand trial. At trial, a defence of necessity could be entered in mitigation of sentence, but not to absolve or acquit. This is the only solution I can see that remains consistent with an absolute ban on torture and coercive interrogation. Let us not pretend that the enforcement of this rule would be easy. Where the threat could be shown to be genuine, it seems evident that few legal systems would punish such a conscientious offender. So an outright ban on torture creates the problem of the conscientious offender. This is a small price to pay for a ban on torture.

16 Does an outright ban on torture and coercive interrogation meet the test of realism? Would an absolute ban on torture and coercive interrogation using stress and duress so diminish the effectiveness of our intelligence-gathering that it would diminish public safety? It is often said—and I argued so myself—that neither coercive interrogation nor torture is necessary, since entirely lawful interrogation can secure just as effective results. There must be some truth to this. Israeli interrogators have given interviews assuring the Israeli public that physical duress is unnecessary. But we are grasping at straws if we think this is the entire truth. As Posner and others have tartly pointed out, if torture and coercion are both as useless as critics pretend, why are they used so much? While some abuse and outright torture can be attributed to individual sadism, poor supervision and so on, it must be the case that other acts of torture occur because interrogators believe,

in good faith, that torture is the only way to extract information in a timely fashion. It must also be the case that if experienced interrogators come to this conclusion, they do so on the basis of experience. The argument that torture and coercion do not work is contradicted by the dire frequency with which both practices occur. I submit that we would not be "waterboarding" Khalid Sheikh Mohammed—immersing him in water until he experiences the torment of nearly drowning—if our intelligence operatives did not believe it was necessary to crack open the al Qaeda network that he commanded. Indeed, Mark Bowden points to a Time report in March 2003 that Sheikh Mohammed had "given US interrogators the names and descriptions of about a dozen key al Qaeda operatives believed to be plotting terrorist attacks." We must at least entertain the possibility that the operatives working on Sheikh Mohammed in our name are engaging not in gratuitous sadism but in the genuine belief that this form of torture—and it does qualify as such—makes all the difference.

17 If they are right, then those who support an absolute ban on torture had better be honest enough to admit that moral prohibition comes at a price. It is possible, at least in theory; that subjecting interrogators to rules that outlaw torture and coercive interrogation, backed up by punishment if they go too far, will create an interrogation regime that allows some interrogation subjects to resist divulging information and prevents our intelligence services from timely access to information that may save lives.

18 If there is a significant cost to an outright ban on coercive interrogation and torture, what can possibly justify it? Many of the arguments that human rights activists make in justification amount to the claim that torture shames their moral identity as human beings and as citizens, and that they do not wish such acts to be committed in their names. Other citizens in a democracy may not value their own moral scruple over the collective interest in having accurate security information, even if collected by dubious means. It may be obvious to human rights activists how to adjudicate these claims, but it is not obvious to me. That is, I do not see any trumping argument on behalf of the rights and dignity of security detainees that makes their claims prevail over the security interests (and human right to life) of the majority. The best I can do is to relate the ban on torture to the political identity of the democracies we are trying to defend—by claiming that democracies limit the powers that governments can justly exercise over the human

beings under their power, and that these limits include an absolute ban on subjecting individuals to forms of pain that strip them of their dignity, identity and even sanity.

19 We cannot torture, in other words, because of who we are. This is the best I can do, but those of us who believe this had better admit that many of our fellow citizens are bound to disagree. It is in the nature of democracy itself that fellow citizens will define their identity in ways that privilege security over liberty and thus reluctantly endorse torture in their name. If we are against torture, we are committed to arguing with our fellow citizens, not treating those who defend torture as moral monsters. Those of us who oppose torture should also be honest enough to admit that we may have to pay a price for our own convictions. Ex ante, of course, I cannot tell how high this price might be. Ex post—following another terrorist attack that might have been prevented through the exercise of coercive interrogation—the price of my scruple might simply seem too high. This is a risk I am prepared to take, but frankly, a majority of fellow citizens is unlikely to concur.

FOR THINKING, DISCUSSING, AND WRITING

1. What does Ignatieff mean by "coercive interrogation"? How does it differ from torture? Do you agree that there is a "conceptual and practical distinction between torture and coercive interrogation"? Why or why not? How does the concept of "inhuman and degrading treatment" affect the two notions?
2. The writer names a number of policy makers and scholars who participate in the debate about the use of torture, among them Mark Bowden, Richard Posner, Jean Bethke Elshtain, and Alan Dershowitz. Find out some information about these people—who are they, what have they written, why should we pay attention to them?
3. Why might you agree or disagree with the idea that "necessity may require the commission of bad acts, which necessity, nevertheless, cannot absolve of their morally problematic character"? What are the ethical issues underlying an anti-torture position? What does Ignatieff mean when he says, "We cannot torture, in other words, because of who we are"? And why does he believe that many people will disagree with him?
4. Write an essay in which you support or refute this comment from the essay: "neither coercive interrogation nor torture is necessary, since entirely lawful interrogation can secure just as effective results."

JAN HOFFMAN

The Last Word on the Last Breath

Jan Hoffman is a reporter for the New York Times. *This piece appeared on October 10, 2006. Hoffman writes here about a major ethical issue facing us today: who has the right to determine when a gravely ill patient can die?*

1 The patient, only 35, had been in a persistent vegetative state for 15 years. Recently, he had developed septic bedsores and pneumonia. His kidneys were failing, and despite the feeding tube, he was losing weight. Now he was in cardiac arrest. He was dying.

2 But the young staff doctor had no choice. The patient's relatives, convinced that the man could communicate, had insisted that all revival efforts be made. So the doctor gave the patient a few mouth-to-mouth breaths, climbed on the bed and began vigorous chest compressions, trying cardiopulmonary resuscitation.

3 The patient was intubated, shocked with electric paddles and injected with epinephrine. Blood spurted as a central line was inserted into the large vein in his groin to administer medicine and fluids. EKG electrodes were placed on his arms and legs: streams of paper spilled over the floor, as the hospital room filled with people and shouted orders.

4 After 15 minutes, the doctors called the time of death.

5 "Kneeling on that bed, doing CPR, felt not only pointless, but like I was administering final blows to someone who had already had a hard enough life," said the doctor, Daniel Sulmasy, now a New York internist, medical ethicist and Franciscan friar, recalling this experience from his internship. "Why was I forced to crack this person's ribs? Why couldn't we have let the patient die in peace?"

6 Extreme cases like this one are rare. But the question of who has final say over whether CPR should be attempted on a gravely ill patient—the doctor, the patient or the patient's representative—is live and unsettled in law and medicine.

7 Many doctors believe that their medical judgment about whether CPR will be effective in a given patient's case, and their knowledge of the havoc it can wreak on a dying body, should prevail. But a patient's representative, who is often a relative, may believe that every medical option should be exercised and that a miracle could be just a chest

compression away. And patients' families, spurred on by TV medical dramas, often mistakenly believe that CPR is almost always effective—a notion emphatically disproved by studies.

8 The debate over who makes the decision raises fundamental challenges to medical integrity as well as patients' rights and can rub feelings raw for all concerned. Hospitals around the country and some state legislatures have wrestled with how to balance these competing values, reaching different conclusions.

9 New York is one of the few states with a law that directly addresses resuscitation orders. In New York, even when a doctor believes that CPR would be medically futile, if the patient is incapable of indicating a preference for or against it and the patient's designated representative insists it be performed, the physician must ultimately go to court to prevail. Texas, which has a complex advance directive law that includes checks and balances, ultimately sides with physicians, immunizing them from litigation.

10 Hawaii passed legislation this year giving great weight to a patient's "comfort care" document, which specifies the patient's preferences in dire medical situations. Nonetheless, if the patient has indicated no resuscitation but "the provider's own conscience" dictates otherwise, a medical professional may override the document.

11 "The black and white of the law has significant limitations in the emotional gray area of decision making around serious illness and dying," said William H. Colby, a lawyer who represented the family of Nancy Cruzan, a patient in a vegetative state whose parents won the right to refuse medical treatment for her. Mr. Colby is the author of "Unplugged: Reclaiming Our Right to Die in America."

12 One side effect of state legislation has been confusion. A 2004 survey of Oklahoma judges found that many felt uncomfortable and undereducated about their state's laws about resuscitation.

13 In recent years, many hospitals have quietly developed policies underscoring that doctors, not family members, should have the final authority to make these medical decisions.

14 But to pre-empt such clashes and elicit the patient's wishes, a simple document developed in Oregon about treatments like CPR is being increasingly used in at least 14 states. When elderly invalids are rushed to the hospital, usually in no condition to discuss resuscitation, the bright pink form called Physician Orders for Life-Sustaining Treatment, or Polst, travels with them and can stand in as a doctor's order.

15 Many physicians and patient advocates say that casting these end-of-life conversations as adversarial needlessly provokes tensions. Instead, they say, the focus should be on achieving a goal of end-stage care that both sides can agree on.

16 Typically, an order on a chart is a doctor's green light to staff: give this medicine, do this therapy. A do not resuscitate, or D.N.R., order is a red light, an order not to do something. Such an order is needed because it is counterintuitive: the assumption in health care is that everyone who goes into cardiac arrest would want to be revived. Even though the success rate of CPR is poor and the likelihood great that its impact will be more burdensome than beneficial, health care providers need explicit permission not to try it.

17 Unlike other life-sustaining measures, like feeding and breathing tubes, which afford families and physicians a bigger window of time to make decisions, CPR is an emergency procedure. That is one reason hospitals want a D.N.R. order in place if a patient suffers a cardiac arrest.

18 Patients can choose not to be resuscitated, and their informed consent to a D.N.R. order is generally inviolate. But friction arises when a patient is near death and has not been interviewed about resuscitation and the doctors need to obtain that consent from the patient's representative, usually a family member. Doctors initiate these painful conversations when they believe a resuscitation effort would be "medically futile," a term whose definition is debated widely in medical and bioethics journals.

19 Doctors can fumble this most delicate of conversations. "With gravely ill patients, doctors sometimes foster these D.N.R. disputes by saying that a patient is getting better," said Dr. Joseph J. Fins, author of "A Palliative Ethic of Care: Clinical Wisdom at Life's End." "We focus on the minutiae of one organ system at a time, fostering hope when there is nothing but the grim reality that the patient will die. Then all of a sudden we tell the family it's futile and we're surprised that they're surprised."

20 Jane Greenlaw, an ethicist at the University of Rochester Medical Center, said that in New York, if neither a patient nor a representative has consented to a D.N.R. order, medical personnel have to try to resuscitate patients "because you don't have permission not to."

21 But she said: "It's the medical person's decision about when it's time to stop. That person can say after 15 minutes, 'This is over, we've tried.' And to some families, that means everything."

22 Families often believe that consenting to a D.N.R. order implies they are giving up on their loved one, signing a death warrant, turning their backs on hope. They can be haunted by guilt and a fear that they have betrayed their religious faith.

23 One woman, who did not want to be identified out of concern for family privacy, felt trapped between her medical knowledge and her family's wishes. Last year, she was the health care agent for her father, who was treated for end-stage cancer of the larynx in the intensive care unit at New York-Presbyterian Hospital/Columbia. He developed acute respiratory disease. The cancer had metastasized: tumors were punching bulges in his forehead. He was too sick to endure more chemotherapy or radiation. After he languished for nearly two months in the intensive care unit, the doctors approached the woman with a D.N.R. consent form.

24 The woman, a nurse in the hospital's coronary care unit, understood the implications fully. But she also had to face her grieving mother.

25 "My mom thought that if you'd sign the D.N.R., we would be abandoning him," she said. "My mom kept saying, 'There will be a miracle, there will be a miracle.' I felt caught in between. I am a nurse, but I am also a daughter."

26 She had seen chest compressions done many times. "I knew it would break my dad's bones and that he wouldn't make it," she said. "The decision was so hard for me."

27 After five and a half months in intensive care, her father slipped into a coma and his organs began to shut down. As doctors rushed to his bedside, the family stopped them, saying, "Enough," and then, "Thank you for all you've done." He died without a D.N.R. order in place.

28 The widespread misunderstanding about CPR itself can make a family's agony worse. The technique, which has been an accepted medical procedure for about 40 years, can be successful in patients who have a sudden, unexpected heart attack or severe respiratory distress. But it was not intended to be used routinely for very sick patients, for whom cardiac arrest is expected. Some studies show that the long-term survival for hospitalized patients given CPR is about 15 percent; some find even smaller percentages. But according to a 1996 article in The New England Journal of Medicine, the long-term survival rate on TV medical dramas for patients given CPR was 67 percent.

29 The need for policies dealing with D.N.R. orders began to be felt in the late 1980's. CPR-related techniques had become increasingly sophisticated. Running a code, as the process is called, became more protracted. End-of-life conundrums, ethical and legal, proliferated. At the same time, with the rise of the patients' rights movement and its concomitant distrust of paternalistic doctors, patients and their families wanted a greater voice in decision-making.

30 In New York, doctors at one hospital had a casual way of indicating to staff, without informing families, which patients should not be resuscitated: purple stickers were affixed to their charts. Occasionally, stickers were placed on the wrong charts or fell off. After these and other stories came to light, New York passed a law in 1987 that addressed the conditions under which a physician could write a D.N.R. order. Patient consent was essential.

31 The statute did say that if resuscitation was "medically futile" and no representative could be found to consent to the D.N.R. order, a doctor could write one, if another doctor also signed it. Under these narrow circumstances, a doctor's judgment that CPR would be useless was sufficient. But what if a "medically futile" patient's decision-maker insisted that CPR be performed anyway? Could a doctor's judgment prevail?

31 In 2003, an upstate New York hospital, seeking policy guidance, put the question to Attorney General Eliot Spitzer.[1] Mr. Spitzer interpreted the state law to mean that even in these cases, a doctor could not enter a D.N.R. order over the objections of a family. A doctor's only recourse was to proceed to mediation, and then, if necessary, to court.

32 "We have gone from one extreme to the other," said Dr. Kenneth Prager, chief of medical ethics at New York-Presbyterian/Columbia, "from physicians making unilateral decisions to the situation where the family and the patient have all control."

33 At the same time the New York statute was being enacted, stories around the country emerged of doctors going through the motions of a code for the benefit of a family. Hospital slang like "slow code" (to suggest a leisurely walk to the bedside), "Hollywood code" (in deference to TV hospital programs) or "light blue code" (an allusion to code blue, the term for a cardiac arrest resuscitation) became public.

[1] Spitzer was elected governor of New York State in 2006.

34 In reaction, states passed advanced-care directive laws and hospitals drafted new ethics policies.

35 Certainly the goal of the legislation was to create dignity and transparency in end-of-life decisions. And in a litigation-rich era, the policies and laws were also intended to help insulate doctors from lawsuits.

36 Dr. Robert V. Brody, chairman of the ethics committee at San Francisco General Hospital, where the policy ultimately favors the doctor's decision, says the task of performing CPR usually falls to the younger resident staff at a hospital rather than to an attending physician. The burden is mostly felt, he said, at smaller community hospitals, that may not have the deep pockets to withstand a lawsuit. "Nurses and doctors hate it," Dr. Brody said. "It's a mess."

37 George Annas, a health law expert at Boston University Law School, said that in such cases, doctors wound up doing what they considered to be forced bad practice.

38 "We're back to the days of light blue, slow code, Hollywood codes," Professor Annas said.

39 He added that a doctor could not be successfully sued for refusing to administer CPR if the procedure would have violated good medical practice.

40 Dr. Sulmasy, chief ethicist at St. Vincent's Manhattan Hospital and New York Medical College, studied a half-dozen cases in which the decision makers for a dying patient refused to consent to a D.N.R. order.

41 "We measured the stress of making a D.N.R. decision for someone else and found it was like someone surviving a house fire," he said. "Before the attorney general's opinion, we could say to some families, 'This is it, your loved one is dying.' And they would say, 'All right, it's your decision. As long as it's not on me.' And they could get on with the task of mourning."

42 Dr. Fins thinks that the focus on D.N.R. orders is in itself misguided.

43 "D.N.R. is a game plan for the last 15 minutes of your life," he said. "By planning for those last 15 minutes, we're distorting priorities. Instead of talking about futility, we should be discussing what has utility, like pain management, comfort, closure. Recasting the discussion has led to turning irresolvable dilemmas into problems that can be addressed."

FOR THINKING, DISCUSSING, AND WRITING

1. How do you account for the fact that the question of who has final say about keeping a gravely ill patient alive, "the doctor, the patient, or the patient's representative," is still "unsettled in law and medicine"? In what way is the question about medicine? About the law? In what way is it about ethics?
2. How do people misperceive the use of CPR? What causes the misperception? What, in fact, is the success rate of CPR? How has the technique been misapplied? How do many families feel about consenting to a D.N.R. order?
3. How does New York law address resuscitation orders? Texas? Hawaii? How has Oregon's *Polst* contributed to the situation? Why might you agree or disagree with Dr. Kenneth Prager's assertion that, "We have gone from one extreme to the other"?
4. Write an essay in which you lay out your views on how to "create dignity and transparency in end-of-life decisions." Of course, you have the option to write about why you oppose all end-of-life decisions if you believe that it is always correct to keep a patient alive.

VIRGINIA POSTREL

Superhero Worship

A Phi Beta Kappa graduate of Princeton University, Virginia Postrel (1960–) writes the monthly "Commerce and Culture" column for the Atlantic *and is an influential writer on economics and politics. She is the author of* The Future and Its Enemies *(1998) and* The Substance of Style *(2003). Postrel was editor of* Reason *for eleven years, and editor-at-large in 2000 and 2001. Prior to that, she was a reporter for* Inc. *and the* Wall Street Journal. *The essay below appeared in the October 2006 issue of the* Atlantic. *In it, she explores the concept of the glamorous superhero defined by the media and how the American public, "the real-world audience," identifies with the character.*

1 When *Superman* debuted in 1978, it invented a whole new movie genre—and a new kind of cinematic magic. Today, hundreds of millions of dollars depend on the heroic box-office performances of costumed crusaders whom Hollywood once thought worthy only of kiddie serials or campy parodies. The two *Spider-Man* movies rank among the top ten of all time for gross domestic receipts, and

X-Men: The Last Stand and *Superman Returns* are among this year's biggest hits.

2 Superhero comics have been around since Irving Thalberg and Louis B. Mayer ruled the back lot, but only recently has Hollywood realized the natural connection between superhero comics and movies. It's not just that both are simultaneously visual and verbal media; that formal connection would apply equally to the "serious" graphic novels and sequential art that want nothing to do with crime fighters in form-fitting outfits. Cinema isn't just a good medium for translating graphic novels. It's specifically a good medium for *superheroes.* On a fundamental, emotional level, superheroes, whether in print or on film, serve the same function for their audience as Golden Age movie stars did for theirs: they create glamour.

3 If that sounds crazy, it's because we tend to forget what glamour is really about. Glamour isn't beauty or luxury; those are only specific manifestations for specific audiences. Glamour is an imaginative process that creates a specific, emotional response: a sharp mixture of projection, longing, admiration, and aspiration. It evokes an audience's hopes and dreams and makes them seem attainable, all the while maintaining enough distance to sustain the fantasy. The elements that create glamour are not specific styles—bias-cut gowns or lacquered furniture—but more general qualities: grace, mystery, transcendence. To the right audience, Halle Berry is more glamorous commanding the elements as Storm in the *X-Men* movies than she is walking the red carpet in a designer gown.

4 "You'll believe a man can fly," promised *Superman's* trailers. Brian Chase, a forty-year-old Los Angeles lawyer and comic-book enthusiast, recalls, "They *did* make you believe it." He says that after seeing the movie for the first time, when he was thirteen, he "ran back from the theater jumping over things. I was embarrassingly convinced. I projected myself into it, and I was not going to let it go for the world." That is the emotional effect of glamour, and it's something superhero comics have delivered since Superman hit print in 1938. The *Superman* movie's marketing slogan was thus more than a promise of convincing special effects. It was a pledge to engage the audience's dreams without ridicule. In *Superman*, only the villains were silly. A decade later, Tim Burton's operatic *Batman* made even the clown-faced Joker seem genuinely scary. Influenced by Frank Miller's reinvention of Batman as the Dark Knight, Burton's *Batman* movies portrayed a dangerous world in

desperate need of a masked hero. Instead of the campy straight man of the 1960s television series or the tame Mister Rogers of the 1950s comic books, Batman was again a glamorous creature of the night, powerful and mysterious.

5 The superhero movies that have followed, like the comics from which they were derived, have engaged their subjects without emotional reservation. They may have humor (Marvel comics like *Spider-Man* and *The Fantastic Four* are famous for it), but they lack the kind of irony that punctures glamour and makes the audience feel foolish for its suspension of disbelief, the sort of campy mockery exemplified by the *Batman* television show or Joel Schumacher's disastrous *Batman & Robin*, featuring a smirking George Clooney in the lead.

6 The superhero fans who wear costumes to comics conventions, buy miniatures of their favorite characters, or line up for artists' autographs aren't themselves glamorous. But neither were the Depression-era housewives who bought knockoffs of Joan Crawford's gowns or wrote fan letters to Gary Cooper. And neither are the *InStyle* readers who copy Natalie Portman's latest haircut or wear a version of Halle Berry's Oscar dress to the prom. But all are acting on glamour's promise. Glamour is, to quote a fashion blurb, "all about transcending the everyday." The whole point of movie glamour was—and is—escape. "What the adult American female chiefly asks of the movies is the opportunity to escape by reverie from an existence which she finds insufficiently interesting," wrote Margaret Farrand Thorp in *America at the Movies* (1939). Movies are "the quickest release from a drab, monotonous, unsatisfying environment in dreaming of an existence which is rich, romantic, glamorous."

7 Superheroes appeal to a different sort of romanticism. Brian Chase draws a distinction between himself and other members of a hip e-mail list called Glamour: "Their idea of glamour would be to get invited to the right party. To me growing up, the idea of glamour was to be the guy who could save the right party from a meteor." Says Richard Neal, owner of Zeus Comics, an upscale comics store in Dallas, "It's not just superpowers but dashing good looks, villains you can fight, getting aggression out." (Buff and business-savvy, Neal bears no resemblance to the classic comics-store proprietor, represented so memorably on *The Simpsons*.)

8 Superheroes are masters of their bodies and their physical environment. They often work in teams, providing an ideal of friendship based

on competence, shared goals, and complementary talents. They're special, and they know it. "Their *true* identities, the men in colorful tights, were so elemental, so universal, so transcendent of the worlds that made them wear masks that they carried with them an unprecedented optimism about the value of one's inner reality," writes Gerard Jones in *Men of Tomorrow: Geeks, Gangsters and the Birth of the Comic Book.* "We all knew that Clark Kent was just a game played by Superman and that the only guy who mattered was that alien who showed up in Metropolis with no history and no parents."

9 Comic-book heroes, like all glamorous icons, cater to "dreams of flight and transformation and escape." Those words are from one of the best books ever written on glamour: Michael Chabon's 2000 novel, *The Amazing Adventures of Kavalier and Clay.* Like many a Hollywood story, *Kavalier and Clay* is wise to the perils of trying to live out glamorous dreams in the real world, again and again showing the tragicomic effects of such attempts. Early on, for instance, young Joe Kavalier almost drowns while attempting a Houdini-like escape designed to gain entrance to what he imagines is a glamorous private club for magicians. (It is, in fact, a rather run-down place whose dining room "smelled of liver and onions.") On the eve of World War II, Joe and his cousin Sammy create a successful comicbook hero called the Escapist, whose villainous foes include Hitler himself. Their glamorous illusion is that such fights are easy to win.

10 Chabon explicitly defends the escapism of comics. After the war, his Kavalier reflects:

> *Having lost his mother, father, brother, and grandfather, the friends and foes of his youth, his beloved teacher Bernard Kornblum, his city, his history—his home—the usual charge leveled against comic books, that they offered* merely an easy escape from reality, *seemed to Joe actually to be a powerful argument on their behalf . . . . It was a mark of how fucked-up and broken was the world—the reality—that had swallowed his home and his family that such a feat of escape, by no means easy to pull off, should remain so universally despised.*

11 Still, glamour is always vulnerable to those who love it. The more we're drawn to a glamorous person, place, or thing, the more we scrutinize it, seeking to fill in the details—which ultimately destroys the mystery and grace. Someone will always look for the hidden flaws, the seamy side of the story. Hence the demand for gossip about Princess

Diana's bulimia or Jennifer Lopez's romantic problems. These *Behind the Music*-style revelations replace the transcendence of glamour with the mundane problems of mere celebrity. Beyond these grubby details is a more mythic kind of debunking: the artistic revisionism that warns of glamour's dangers and disappointments. The power of such revisionism, however, depends on the emotional pull of the original. Someone who knows little and cares even less about Hollywood dreams will miss the pity and terror of *Sunset Boulevard.* Someone who scorns superheroes as infantile won't understand the scary wonder of *Watchmen*, the brilliant 1987 graphic novel in which Alan Moore and Dave Gibbons deconstruct superheroes. To the wrong audience, glamour, even revisionist glamour, will seem like camp.

12 One way to balance the real and ideal while preserving glamour is to give the audience an insider's view. So superhero comics now tend to situate their stories in a world like our own, with ubiquitous, sensationalist media and inescapable trade-offs between personal and professional life. To their audience inside the comics, the superheroes are powerful and mysterious celebrities subject to public adulation and tabloid attacks. The real-world audience, by contrast, gets a glimpse behind the mask, a chance to identify with the character and to experience glamour once removed—to imagine *what it would be like to be glamorous*, and how much hard work, sacrifice, and attention to detail that seemingly effortless power requires. This double vision acknowledges the art behind the illusion. Glamour may look easy, but it never is.

FOR THINKING, DISCUSSING, AND WRITING

1. What is the key connection between superhero comics and movies? Why does Postrel emphasize the notion of glamour throughout her piece?
2. How does the writer define *glamour* and its effect on audiences? Do you agree with her definition? Why or why not? Why does she reject some of our conventional definitions, like *beauty* or *luxury*? Would you agree with the blog quote that glamour is "all about transcending the everyday"?
3. Other than their intrinsic glamour, what qualities identify the superheroes?
4. Write an essay in which you explore the relation between glamorous superheroes and American values. What does the infatuation with

"costumed crusaders" say about the culture's values and principles, do you think? In what way is the relation positive? Negative?

CONNECTING IDEAS: Beliefs, Values, and the Human Condition

1. Although only Tom Regan in "Who Are You Animal Rights Activists Anyway?" addresses the issue of activism head on, in a sense, all the writers who take up the important causes in this chapter are activists. In an essay explain what you see as the connection between ethical behavior and activism. You may choose one of the issues addressed by the writers here and explore the activist dimension of their work, or select another aspect of the ongoing values conversation—abortion, saving the environment, the drug crisis, or prayer in schools, for example.
2. In what ways have the writers in this chapter dealt with ethical issues that you respond to deeply? Choose any two selections and show how they presented important values that either resonate with or challenge your own views. Provide supporting detail from the selections themselves, as well as from your own readings and experiences, where relevant.
3. Select a key issue in today's world and explain how your own ethics bring you to a particular conclusion about how to behave in regard to the issue. Be sure to explore your moral framework—that is, the principles that lead you to choose one mode of behavior over another, or several others.

credits

Charlotte Allen, "The Return of the Happy Housewife"by Charlotte Allen from *The Los Angeles Times*, Sunday, March 5, 2006. Copyright 2006. Reprinted by permission of the author.

Natalie Angier, "One Thing They Aren't: Maternal" by Natalie Angier from the *New York* Times, May 9, 2006. Copyright 2006 by The New York Times Co. Reprinted with permission.

James Atlas, "Making the Grade" by James Atlas. First published in *The New Yorker*, April 14, 1997. Copyright 1997 by James Atlas, permission of The Wylie Agency.

Elizabeth Austin, "A Small Plea to Delete a Ubiquitous Expletive" by Elizabeth Austin from *U.S. News & World Report*, April 6, 1998. Copyright 1998 *U.S. News & World Report*, L.P. Reprinted with permission.

David P. Barash, "The Case for Evolution, in Real Life" by David P. Barash from *Chronicle of Higher Education*, April 7, 2006. Volume 52, Issue 31 p. B10. Copyright 2006. Reprinted by permission of the author.

David Blankenhorn, "The Deadbeat Dad" by David Blankenhorn from *Fatherless America: Confronting Our Most Urgent Social Problem*. Copyright 1995 Institute for American Values. Reprinted by permission of BASIC BOOK, a member of Perseus Books Group.

Leon Botstein, "Curtailing High School: a Radical Proposal" by Leon Botstein. Reprinted with permission from the *Presidency*, Winter 2002. The American Council on Education, 2002.

Judy Brady, "I Want a Wife" by Judy Brady from *Ms.* Magazine, Premier issue, 1971. Copyright 1970 by Judy Brady. Reprinted by permission of the author.

William Branigin, "Sweatshops Are Back" by William Branigin from *The Washington Post*, February 24, 1997. Copyright 1997, *The Washington Post*, reprinted with permission.

Mary Cantwell, "The Burden of a Happy Childhood" by Mary Cantwell. Copyright 1998 by Mary Cantwell. Originally published in the *New York Times Magazine*. Reprinted by permission of the author.

Barbara Carton, "Why Does "Everybody" Now Put "Everything" in Quotation Marks?" by Barbara Carton from *The Wall Street Journal*, March 15, 1999. Copyright 1999. Reprinted by permission.

Phyllis Chesler, From "The Death of Feminism: What's Next in the Struggle for Women's Freedom" by Phyllis Chesler. Copyright 2005. Reprinted by permission of Palgrave Macmillan.

Sandra Cisneros, "An Offering to the Power of Language" by Sandra Cisneros. Copyright 1997 by Sandra Cisneros. First published in *The Los Angeles Times*, October 26, 1997, Section M. Reprinted by permission of Susan Bergholz Literary Services, New York. All rights reserved.

Judith Ortiz Cofer, "The Paterson Public Library" by Judith Ortiz Cofer from *The Latin Deli*. Copyright 1993 University of Georgia Press. Reprinted by permission.

William Deresiewicz, "The Dispossessed" by William Deresiewicz. Reprinted from *The American Scholar*, Volume 75, No. 1, Winter 2006. Copyright 2006 by William Deresiewicz.

Joan Didion, "Marrying Absurd" from *Slouching Towards Bethlehem* by Joan Didion. Copyright 1966, 1968, renewed by 1996 by Joan Didion. Reprinted by permission of Farrar, Straus and Giroux, LLC.

Joan Didion, "On Going Home" from *Slouching Towards Bethlehem* by Joan Didion. Copyright 1966, 1968, renewed by 1996 by Joan Didion. Reprinted by permission of Farrar, Straus and Giroux, LLC.

Will Durst, "Happy National Apathy Day" by Will Durst from the *New York Times*, November 2, 1998. Copyright 1998 by

The New York Times Co. Reprinted with permission.

Tony Earley, "The Quare Gene" from *Somehow Form A Family* by Tony Earley, 2001 by Tony Earley. Reprinted by permission of Algonquin Books of Chapel Hill.

Stephanie Ericson, "The Ways We Lie" by Stephanie Ericsson. Copyright 1992 by Stephanie Ericsson. Reprinted by permission of Dunham Literary, Inc. as agents for the author. Originally published by *The Utne Reader.*

Mark Essig, "Continuing the Search for Kinder Executions" by Mark Essig from the *New York Times,* October 21, 2003. Copyright 2003 by The New York Times Co. Reprinted with permission.

Molly Evans, From *Nothin' But Good Times Ahead* by Molly Ivins, copyright 1993 by Molly Ivins. Used by permission of Random House, Inc.

Richard Florida, "Where the Brains Are" by Richard Florida. First published in the *Atlantic Monthly* October 2006 and used with the permission of Richard Florida and Susan Schulman Literary Agency New York. All rights reserved.

Henry Louis Gates Jr., "In the Kitchen", from *Colored People: A Memoir* by Henry Louis Gates Jr., copyright 1994 by Henry Louis Gates Jr. used by permission of Alfred A. Knopf, a division of Random House, Inc.

Al Gore, Reprinted from: An *Inconvenient Truth* by Al Gore. Copyright 2006 by Al Gore. Permission granted by Rodale, Inc., Emmaus, PA 18098.

Lev Grossman and Anita Hamilton, "Meet Joe Blog" by Lev Grossman, Anita Hamilton from *Time Magazine,* October 28, 2005. Copyright 2005, Time, Inc. All rights reserved. Reprinted by permission.

Lani Guinier, Reprinted with permission of The Free Press, a Division of Simon & Schuster Adult Publishing Group, from *Tyranny of The Majority: Fundamental Fairness in Representative Democracy* by Lani Guinier. Copyright 1994 by Lani Guinier. All rights reserved.

Quentin Hardy, "Showing Off" by Quentin Hardy from *The Wall Street Journal,* January 11, 1999. Copyright 1999. Reprinted with permission.

Shelby Harper, "Indoctrination Isn't Teaching" by Shelby Steele from the *New York Times,* January 10, 1997. Copyright 1997 by The New York Times Co. Reprinted with permission.

Timothy Harper, "They Treat Girls Differently, Don't They?" By Timothy Harper from *Sky Magazine,* December 1996. Copyright 1996 by Timothy Harper. Reprinted by permission of the author.

Jan Hoffman, "The Last Word on the Last Breath" by Jan Hoffman from the *New York Times,* October 10, 2006. Copyright 2006 by The New York Times Co. Reprinted with permission.

Linda Hogan, "Waking Up the Rake" from *Dwellings: A Spiritual History of The Living World* by Linda Hogan. Copyright 1995 by Linda Hogan. Used by permission of W. W. Norton & Company, Inc.

Langston Hughes, "Salvation" from *The Big Sea* by Langston Hughes. Copyright 1940 by Langston Hughes. Copyright renewed 1968 by Arna Bontemps and George Houston Bass. Reprinted by permission of Hill and Wang, a division of Farrar, Straus and Giroux, LLC.

Michael Ignatieff, 2005 by Michael Ignatieff. This piece originally appears in *Torture: Does It Make Us Safer? Is It Ever OK?* Edited by Kenneth Roth and Minky Worden, Amy D. Bernstein, Contributing Editor. Reprinted with the permission of The New Press. www.thenew press.com

Martin Luther King Jr., "I Have a Dream" by Martin Luther King Jr. Copyright 1963 Martin Luther King Jr., copyright renewed 1991 Coretta Scott King. Reprinted by arrangement with The Heirs to the Estate of Martin Luther King Jr., c/o Writers House as agent for the proprietor New York, NY.

Martin Luther King Jr., "Letter from the Birmingham Jail" by Martin Luther King Jr. Copyright 1963 Martin Luther King, Jr., copyright renewed 1991 Coretta Scott King. Reprinted by arrangement with The Heirs to the Estate of Martin Luther King Jr., c/o Writers House as agent for the proprietor New York, NY.

Barbara Kingsolver, "Stone Soup" from *High Tide in Tucson: Essays from Now or Never* by Barbara Kingsolver. Copyright 1995 by Barbara Kingsolver. Reprinted by permission of HarperCollins Publishers.

Maxine Hong Kingston, "No Name Woman", from *The Woman Warrior* By Maxine Hong Kingston, Copyright 1975, 1976 by Maxine Hong Kingston. Used by permission of Alfred A. Knopf, a division of Random House, Inc.

Edward I. Koch, "Death and Justice: How Capital Punishment Affirms Life" by Edward I. Koch, from *The New Republic,* Volume 192, April 15, 1985. Copyright 1985. Reprinted by permission of the author.

Jonathan Kozol, From Amazing Grace by Jonathan Kozol, copyright 1995 by Jonathan Kozol. Used by permission of Crown Publishers, a division of Random House, Inc.

David Leavitt, "The Hate Epidemic" by David Leavitt from the *New York Times,* October 19, 1998. Copyright 1998 by The New York Times Co. Reprinted with permission.

Chang-rae Lee, "Mute in an English-Only World" by Chang-rae Lee from the *New York Times,* April 18, 1996. Copyright 1996 by The New York Times Co. Reprinted with permission.

Nancy Mairs, *"Waist-High in the World"* by Nancy Mairs Copyright 1996 by Nancy Mairs Reprinted by permission of Beacon Press, Boston.

Howard Markel, "When Germs Travel" by Howard Markel. Reprinted from *The American Scholar,* Volume 68, No. 2, Spring 1999. Copyright 1999 by Howard Markel.

Walter Benn Michaels, "Last Words" by Walter Benn Michaels. Copyright 2006. Originally published in the *New York Times Magazine,* October 1, 2006. Reprinted with permission.

Stephen Mihm, "Does Eating Salmon Lower The Murder Rate?" by Stephen Mihm from the *New York Times,* April 16, 2006. Copyright 2006 by The New York Times Co. Reprinted with permission.

George Orwell, "A Hanging" from *Shooting an Elephant and Other Essays* by George Orwell, Copyright 1950 by Sonia Brownell Orwell and renewed by 1978 by Sonia Pitt-Rivers, reprinted by permission of Harcourt, Inc.

Karen S. Peterson, "Looking Straight at Gay Parents" by Karen S. Peterson. *USA Today.* March 10, 2004. Reprinted with permission.

Alexander Petrunkevitch, "The Spider and the Wasp" by Alexander Petrunkevitch. August 1952. Reprinted with permission. Copyright 1952 by Scientific American, Inc. All rights reserved.

Virginia Postrel, "Superhero Worship" by Virginia Postrel from *The Atlantic Monthly,* October 2006. Vol. 298, No. 3. Reprinted by permission of the author.

Tom Regan, "Who Are You Animal rights Activists Anyway?" by Tom Regan from *Empty Cages: Facing the Challenge of Animal Rights.* Copyright 2005. Reprinted by permission of Rowman & Littlefield Publishing Group.

Matt Ridley, *U.S. News & World Report,* "Why Should Males Exist?" by Matt Ridley August 18, 1997, page 52. Copyright 1997 U.S. News & World Report, L.P. Reprinted with permission.

Richard Rodriguez , From *Hunger of Memory* by Richard Rodriguez. Reprinted by permission of David R. Godine, Publisher, Inc. Copyright 1982 by Richard Rodriguez.

Katie Roiphe, "Campus Climate Control" by Katie Roiphe from the *New York Times,* March 5, 1999. Copyright 1999 by The New York Times Co. Reprinted with permission.

Cynthia Russett, "All About Eve" by Cynthia Russett. Reprinted from *The American Scholar* Volume 74, No. 2 , Spring 2005. Copyright 2005 by Cynthia Russett.

Gary Soto, "Black Hair" from *Living Up the Street* (Dell, 1985) 1985 by Gary Soto. Used by permission of the author.

Brent Staples, "What Adolescents Miss When We Let Them Grow Up in Cyberspace" by Brent Staples from the *New York Times,* May 29, 2004. Copyright 2004 by The New York Times Co. Reprinted with permission.

Deborah Tannen, "Listening to Men, Then and Now," by Deborah Tannen, the *New York Times Magazine,* May 16, 1999, copyright Deborah Tannen. Reprinted by permission.

Lewis Thomas, "Humanities and Science," copyright 1983 by Lewis Thomas, from *Late Night Thoughts on Listening to Mahler's Ninth* by Lewis Thomas. Used by permission of Viking Penguin, a division of Penguin Group (USA) Inc.

James Thurber, "University Days" from the book *My Life and Hard Times* Copyright 1933, 1961 by James Thurber. Reprinted by arrangement with Rosemary A. Thurber and The Barbara Hogenson Agency. All rights reserved.

John Updike, "A Sense of Change" by John Updike from *The New Yorker,* 4/26/99 and 5/3/99. Reprinted by permission: John Updike. Originally published in *The New Yorker.* All rights reserved.

J. Wallerstein and S. Blakeslee, "The Children of Divorce," from *Second Chances: Men, Women and Children a Decade After Divorce.* Copyright 1989 by Judith S. Wallerstein and Sandra Blakeslee. Reprinted by permission of Houghton Mifflin Company.

Judith Warner, "The Parent Trap" by Judith Warner from the *New York Times*, February 8, 2006. Copyright 2006 by The New York Times Co. Reprinted with permission.

E. B. White, "Once More to the Lake" from *One Man's Meat*, text copyright 1941 by E. B. White. Copyright renewed. Reprinted by permission of Tilbury House, Publishers, Gardiner, Maine.

Malcolm X, From *The Autobiography of Malcolm X* by Malcolm X and Alex Haley, copyright 1964 by Alex Haley and Malcolm X. Copyright 1965 by Alex Haley and Betty Shabazz. Used by permission of Random House.

William Zinsser, Excerpt from "Simplicity" from *On Writing Well*, 6th ed. by William Zinsser. Copyright 1976, 1980, 1985, 1988, 1990, 1994, 1998, 2001 by William K. Zinsser. Reprinted by permission of the author.

index

Additional Titles of Interest

Note to Instructors: Any of these Penguin-Putnam, Inc., titles can be packaged with this book at a special discount. Contact your local Allyn & Bacon/Longman sales representative for details on how to create a Penguin-Putnam, Inc., Value Package.

Allison, *Bastard Out of Carolina*
Alvarez, *How the Garcia Girls Lost Their Accents*
Augustine, *The Confessions of St. Augustine*
Austen, *Persuasion*
Austen, *Pride and Prejudice*
Austen, *Sense and Sensibility*
Bloom, *Shakespeare: The Invention of the Human*
C. Brontë, *Jane Eyre*
E. Brontë, *Wuthering Heights*
Burke, *Reflections on the Revolution in France*
Cather, *My Ántonia*
Cather, *O Pioneers!*
Cellini, *The Autobiography of Benvenuto Cellini*
Chapman, *Black Voices*
Chesnutt, *The Marrow of Tradition*
Chopin, *The Awakening and Selected Stories*
Conrad, *Heart of Darkness*
Conrad, *Nostromo*
Coraghessan-Boyle, *The Tortilla Curtain*
Defoe, *Robinson Crusoe*
Descartes, *Discourse on Method and The Meditations*
Descartes, *Meditations and Other Metaphysical Writings*
de Tocqueville, *Democracy in America*
Dickens, *Hard Times*
Douglass, *Narrative of the Life of Frederick Douglass*
Dubois, *The Souls of Black Folk*
Equiano, *The Interesting Narrative and Other Writings*
Gore, *Earth in the Balance*
Grossman, *Electronic Republic*
Hawthorne, *The Scarlet Letter*
Hutner, *Immigrant Voices*
Jacobs, *Incidents in the Life of a Slave Girl*
Jen, *Typical American*
M. L. King Jr., *Why We Can't Wait*
Lewis, *Babbitt*
Machiavelli, *The Prince*
Marx, *The Communist Manifesto*
Mill, *On Liberty*
More, *Utopia and Other Essential Writings*
Orwell, *1984*
Paine, *Common Sense*
Plato, *The Republic*
Postman, *Amusing Ourselves to Death*
Rose, *Lives on the Boundary*
Rossiter, *The Federalist Papers*
Rousseau, *The Social Contract*
Shelley, *Frankenstein*
Sinclair, *The Jungle*
Steinbeck, *Of Mice and Men*
Stevenson, *The Strange Case of Dr. Jekyll and Mr. Hyde*
Stoker, *Dracula*
Stowe, *Uncle Tom's Cabin*
Swift, *Gulliver's Travels*
Taulbert, *Once Upon a Time When We Were Colored*
Thoreau, *Walden*
Truth, *The Narrative of Sojourner Truth*
Woolf, *Jacob's Room*
Zola, *Germinal*

viii Good intro to what may be "transferable." ; 4 SLOs